JEFFERSON DAVIS
AND HIS GENERALS

Modern War Studies

Theodore A. Wilson
General Editor

Raymond A. Callahan
J. Garry Clifford
Jacob W. Kipp
Jay Luvaas
Series Editors

JEFFERSON DAVIS AND HIS GENERALS

The Failure of Confederate Command in the West

Steven E. Woodworth

University Press of Kansas

Maps reproduced from *Ordeal by Fire: The Civil War and Reconstruction,*
by James M. McPherson. Copyright © 1982 by Alfred A. Knopf, Inc.
Reprinted by permission of Alfred A. Knopf, Inc.

Published by the University Press of Kansas (Lawrence, Kansas
66045), which was organized by the Kansas Board of Regents and is
operated and funded by Emporia State University, Fort Hays State
University, Kansas State University, Pittsburg State University,
the University of Kansas, and Wichita State University

Library of Congress Cataloging-in-Publication Data

Woodworth, Steven E.
    Jefferson Davis and his generals : the failure of Confederate
command in the West / Steven E. Woodworth
        p.   cm. – (Modern war studies)
    Includes bibliographical references (p. 371).
    ISBN 0-7006-0461-8 (alk. paper)
    1. Davis, Jefferson, 1808–1889–Military leadership.
2. Mississippi River Valley–History–Civil War, 1861–1865–
Campaigns. 3. United States–History–Civil War, 1861–1865–
Campaigns. 4. Generals–Confederate States of America.
5. Confederate States of America. Army–History. I. Title.
II. Series
E467.1.D26W82   1990   89–28668
973.7'462–dc20   CIP

British Library Cataloguing in Publication Data is available.

Printed in the United States of America

For My Mother and Father

CONTENTS

ILLUSTRATIONS AND MAPS

Illustrations

Maps

PREFACE

As civil war approached in the spring of 1861, comparisons of the rival presidents, Abraham Lincoln of the United States and Jefferson Davis of the would-be Confederate States, seemed encouraging to good southerners. Both men had been born in Kentucky, separated from each other by barely a hundred miles in distance and eight months in time. There the similarity ended. Davis's family had gone south and eventually–in the person of Jefferson's older brother–made its fortune in cotton. Lincoln's had gone to the Midwest but never risen much above the level of subsistence farming. Davis had had every advantage in life–most notably, the advantage of a West Point education. Lincoln was a self-taught frontier lawyer who had had to work his way up from the bottom rung of the social ladder.

As the two men looked to the tasks that lay before them in 1861, Davis had reason to be confident. There had been West Point, then extensive military experience–including combat–as well as political and administrative experience as congressman, senator, and secretary of war. The prairie lawyer from Illinois could not boast such a successful political career, and the sum of his military experience consisted of a few weeks of haphazard soldiering during the Black Hawk War as captain of a company of Illinois militia that never saw action.

Yet Lincoln became a great commander in chief. Demonstrating tremendous analytic ability, decisiveness, and a rare knack for getting along with people coupled with the ability to stand up to almost any amount of pressure, Lincoln learned quickly and became a good strategist and an excellent director of the North's war effort.

What then of Jefferson Davis? What sort of commander in chief was he? Did he possess those qualities that made Lincoln successful? And what use did he make of his superior preparation for the role he was to play–in particular, how did he use his knowledge of and acquaintance with the country's top military men in his selection of generals? To answer these questions we must turn to the Civil War's western theater.

The Virginia front was by far the more prestigious theater. There Robert E. Lee and Stonewall Jackson directed their brilliant campaigns. There the largest and most celebrated armies of the war, the northern Army of the Potomac and the southern Army of Northern Virginia, fought the war's bloodiest and most famous battles. Yet the war's outcome was decided not there but in the vast expanse that stretched west from the Appalachian Mountains to the Mississippi and beyond. Here, in the West, the truly decisive battles were fought. Here, too, Jefferson Davis's abilities were put to the greatest test. A study of Davis's handling of the eastern front might have much value and might very well reveal the Confederate president as a success within that area. By contrast in the West vast distances, unfavorable topography, complicated political problems, and difficult generals would try Davis to the utmost and take the full measure of the man. If he were to fall short anywhere, it would be here.

Opinion on Jefferson Davis ranges from the very positive to the very negative. Certainly Davis now is widely admired and venerated in the South. Yet his detractors seem to have set the tone for the assessment of Davis as a war leader. His enemies, then and later, claimed that he had too much confidence in his own military genius and that he interfered with his generals. His defenders, on the other hand, have tended to argue that his confidence in his own genius was well founded and that the interference with the generals was warranted. Indeed, they have sometimes gone to embarrassing lengths to portray him as a hero. This argument about whether Jefferson Davis was a hero or a villain, a genius or an incompetent, seems unprofitable. It would be much more productive to consider Davis for what he really was: a man of great ability and great dedication who nevertheless had certain shortcomings that prevented his achieving his goal. This is not to say, as T. Harry Williams did in *Lincoln and His Generals* (New York: Vintage Books, 1952), that Davis was mediocre. The magnitude of the task he undertook and the narrowness of the margin by which he fell short place him well above the level of mediocrity. Nor is it to say that it was somehow Davis's fault that the South lost, that the Confederacy would have gained its independence if not for Davis. Plenty of others contributed far more to the Confederate defeat than Jefferson Davis. But had he possessed certain other qualities, Davis might perhaps have achieved southern independence despite the failures of other southerners. In pointing out the areas in which he fell short, my intention is not to belittle Davis or to dismiss his many strengths. Rather, since in the end he did fail, we need to answer the question of how a man of his obvious qualifications could fall short of the goal he seemed so well prepared to attain.

Needless to say, this is not the first book to touch on Davis, his conduct of the war, or his relations with the generals who served in the western theater. There have been numerous biographies of the Confederate president,[1] but on the whole they are a disappointing lot. It is doubtful that any other historical figure has been the subject of so much poor scholarship and poor writing. With few exceptions the Davis biographies are as unsatisfactory as they are laudatory to Davis. They are especially weak in the treatment of the war and Davis's dealings with his generals.

Among the many biographies of the generals themselves,[2] there are some useful and objective discussions of Davis's relations with individual generals. There are also accounts that tend to follow the line taken by Davis's enemies during the war. This is particularly true of studies of those generals whose relations with Davis were more critical and more problematic, such as Joseph E. Johnston.

There have also been studies of individual armies[3] and of Confederate strategy.[4] Particularly noteworthy here are Thomas L. Connelly's *Army of the Heartland* and *Autumn of Glory* and Connelly's and Archer Jones's *Politics of Command*. In the first two books Connelly deals with the Army of Tennessee and, along the way, gives extensive attention to Davis's relations with that army and its generals. The books are heavily researched, highly critical, and much acclaimed, but some of their criticisms of Davis and some of the generals seem unduly harsh. In any case they deal only with the Army of Tennessee. *The Politics of Command* treats the influence of various networks of relationships among high-ranking military and civilian Confederates, especially among those who attempted to influence Confederate strategy in favor of a major concentration of forces in the West.

While all of these works have some bearing on the present study and have, to a greater or lesser extent, been useful in its preparation (see the Bibliographic Essay), there has not yet been a broad, in-depth study on the interaction of the unique personality of Jefferson Davis with the equally unique personalities of his generals within the crucible of war. Something on the order of what T. Harry Williams did for Lincoln has been lacking in the scholarship on Jefferson Davis.

That in itself may be a large part of the reason that certain false notions of Davis's conduct as commander in chief have proved so persistent. It is here that Davis's enemies have been especially successful in defining the terms of the debate. Their assertions that Davis thought himself a military genius and interfered much with his generals have been taken for the most part as givens. Woodrow Wilson, in his *History of the American People* (New York: Harper & Bros., 1903), stated that Davis "too much loved to rule, had too overweening a confidence in himself, and took leave to act as if he understood much better than those did who were in actual command what should be done in the field." Nor has this assessment changed much in the last century. Grady Mc-Whiney, in an essay entitled "Jefferson Davis and His Generals" in his 1973 book *Southerners and Other Americans* (New York: Basic Books, 1973), summed up what continues to be the consensus view of Jefferson Davis when he stated, "Davis seems to have had no doubts about his ability to direct a war." Thus what Davis's enemies confidently asserted during the war—that Davis believed himself all but infallible and therefore exercised an overbearing authority on his military subordinates from secretary of war on down—has been accepted with almost equal confidence by most historians ever since. One of the most recent scholarly works on Jefferson Davis, Michael Ballard's *A Long Shadow: Jefferson Davis and the Final Days of the Confederacy* (Jackson: University Press of Mississippi, 1986), a treatment not of how the war was lost but of how

Davis's reputation rose out of the ashes of southern defeat, demonstrates the persistence of this view in the statement that Jefferson Davis was "a strong believer in his military prowess." Even Davis's defenders, such as Frank Vandiver, have accepted that much. In *The Making of a President: Jefferson Davis, 1861* (Richmond: Virginia Civil War Commission, 1962), Vandiver asserted that "in handling military matters . . . Davis showed no uncertainty. He discharged the role of Commander-in-Chief with a deft and sure touch." That this view did not quite fit the facts has been suggested by several historians over the years. Hamilton J. Eckenrode hinted at it in his biography of Davis over fifty years ago. Connelly and Jones touch on it briefly in passing in *The Politics of Command*. The present study goes farther in revealing a Jefferson Davis much different from the man described by either his defenders or his detractors.

ACKNOWLEDGMENTS

One of the most pleasant things about completing a work is the opportunity it provides of giving a well-deserved word of thanks to some of the many people without whose help it would have been impossible. I would first like to mention Professor Ira D. Gruber, my thesis director at Rice University, who suggested this topic to me and with whom I worked closely. His comments have helped me to avoid a number of pitfalls and to clarify my thinking on a unifying theme. Professors Harold M. Hyman and Gilbert Cuthbertson, the other members of my thesis committee, also made a number of helpful comments. I am also indebted to Herman Hattaway for his useful and positive suggestions for improving the manuscript. In addition, I am grateful to Lynda Crist, Mary Dix, and S. W. Higginbotham of the Jefferson Davis Association, Rice University, for their good advice and cordial assistance to me in finding my way through the voluminous primary source material on Jefferson Davis as well as for calling my attention to a number of secondary sources I might otherwise have missed. Wendell Thompson and Amelia Thompson, the librarians at Bartlesville Wesleyan College, were helpful and patient with what must surely have been a record number of interlibrary-loan requests. Finally, I am thankful that God has blessed me with a wonderful family, several members of which have been of special assistance to me in this undertaking. Ralph L. Woodworth and Erma Woodworth read the manuscript and offered a number of useful suggestions. A special note of thanks is due to my wife, Leah, who did nearly all the typing, corrected my spelling, and gave me plenty of encouragement and moral support.

1

THE MAN AND THE HOUR

The train station was not large. Indeed, had anyone cared to compare the train stations of the capital cities of the world in this second month of the year 1861, this one, in proportion to the size of the republic whose seat of government it was, would have bid fair to be the smallest of them all. Not that the citizens of Montgomery, Alabama, could be faulted for this seeming failure to provide a more worthy facility – their city was as new to the role of capital as their far-flung country was to that of independent nation among the powers of the earth, and a bit less than two weeks was hardly time enough to erect such structures as befitted the governing city of "King Cotton's" empire.

It was, however, time enough to erect a government of sorts; and that was the cause of the huge crowd that packed the diminutive railroad station – its smallness making the crowd seem even larger – and spilled out into the street beyond, a phenomenon not seen every day in one-horse cities of the rural South, particularly at this extremely late hour of the night.[1] The excitement on this night was not to be wondered at, for the train that was now pulling into the station bore as its chief cargo no ordinary passenger. On board was the president-elect of the Confederate States of America, the first president of his country, the unanimous choice of the delegates of the sovereign states; in two days, on February 18, 1861, he was to be inaugurated. Good reason, then, for the citizens of Montgomery, as well as the vast flocks of office seekers, office holders, political aspirants, and representatives of one thing or another, the ambitious and the just plain curious who had for days been overloading the town's rather limited lodging facilities, to turn out and shout, middle of the night or not.

The train stopped, and the president-elect stepped down amid a continuous roar of cheering punctuated by the measured booming of an artillery salute. Those close enough to see might have noticed that he wore a look of great weariness, as well he might, since this scene, on a somewhat smaller scale, had been repeated at every one of two dozen or so stations where the train had stopped between Montgomery and his home in Mississippi. It had been a long trip. Because of the South's incomplete rail network, he had had to go by way of Chattanooga and Atlanta, and the journey had lasted over a week. At each stop on this circuitous route, as he related in a letter to his wife several days later, he had been met by "bonfires at night, firing by day; shouts and salutation in both." The pattern was always the same, night or day. The crowds roared until the president-to-be, the gaunt, proud man who personified so

1

well the character of the society whose chosen leader he was, appeared at the rear platform of the train and addressed them on the rightness and necessity of secession and the glorious future that awaited them as an Independent Confederacy.[2]

It was therefore a profoundly weary president-elect who stepped down off the train in Montgomery that night and whose carriage was escorted by a mass of yelling, cheering humanity to the finer of Montgomery's two hotels, the Exchange. There, he got a thunderous ovation, continuing for some thirty minutes, from the crowd now gathered outside the hotel. Yielding to the inevitable, he stepped out onto a balcony.

On hand to give a welcoming speech was one of the South's greatest orators and foremost fire-eaters, William Lowndes Yancey. Long an ardent secessionist, Yancey was seeing in the events of this turbulent winter his fondest dreams coming true, and he could proudly say that he had done as much as any man to make it all happen. Yancey was a brilliant stump speaker, with a genius for putting into words the unspoken feelings of an entire society. He was doing it now, and it made his welcoming speech more memorable than the few words the tired president-elect would say upon its conclusion before retiring for the night. Yancey articulated the confidence of southerners in their new leader, their assurance that he was the ideal man to lead them through whatever might lie ahead, and the enthusiasm that had thronged railroad stations in this man's progress across the South and raised this exultant multitude in the midnight streets of a town normally drowsy enough by day. As Yancey came to the conclusion of his speech he summed up in a single sentence the South's confidence in its choice for commander-in-chief. "The man and the hour," he proclaimed, "have met."[3]

President-elect Jefferson Davis, a graduate of West Point, a hero of the Mexican War, one of the United States' most highly acclaimed secretaries of war, United States senator, and lately major general of the Mississippi militia, did seem to be uniquely fitted to provide the military and political leadership the Confederacy would need in the armed conflict that perceptive observers, including Davis himself, saw in the offing. If training and experience could prepare and courage and determination sustain an effective wartime president, then Jefferson Davis was, by all accounts, the man for the job. He was, it seemed, the man for the hour. It remained now for him to show himself, as his countrymen so confidently believed him to be, equal to the task at hand.

Jefferson Davis was born of Welsh and Scots-Irish stock on June 3, 1808, in southwestern Kentucky, not far from the Tennessee line.[4] The large family to which he was the final addition inhabited a double log cabin considerably more commodious than that in which, eight months later and less than a hundred miles away, Abraham Lincoln was born.[5] Jefferson's father, Samuel Davis, was a tobacco farmer and horse breeder of middling fortune. A native of Georgia, the elder Davis had served that state during the Revolutionary War, first with mounted troops and later as a captain of infantry during the siege of Savannah. Samuel Davis tended to be restless, and Kentucky could hold him no more than Georgia had. When Jefferson was two years old, the family left his native state and moved to Louisiana. It too proved unsatisfactory and was soon abandoned in favor of Mississippi, where the Davises settled near Woodville, in the southwestern corner of the state.[6]

Mississippi was still a raw frontier society, and educational opportunities were few. Samuel Davis set great store by education, and so after young Jefferson had attended a year at what he later described as "the usual log-cabin schoolhouse" and had nearly reached the mature age of eight years, his father sent him off to the College of St. Thomas, a Catholic boarding school in Kentucky. The boy made the journey up the Natchez Trace in the company of Maj. Thomas Hinds, who had commanded a battalion of dragoons at the battle of New Orleans.[7] Along the way the party made a stopover of several weeks near Nashville, Tennessee, at the home of Hinds's old commander, Andrew Jackson. Hermitage, as Jackson's home was called, was a roomy log house surrounded by stately oak trees, beyond which were broad fields of cotton and grain.[8] It was an impressive setting, but eight-year-old Jefferson Davis seemed to be most impressed by the formidable old general himself.[9]

Jefferson was not only the sole Protestant but also the smallest boy at the school. Still, he seemed content enough. His mother, however, was considerably less satisfied with the arrangement. She had never been party to the idea of sending her youngest son off to boarding school, and it was apparently at her urging that he was summoned home after two years. Thereafter it was decided that the educational climate of southwestern Mississippi had improved enough to allow the young scholar to pursue his studies closer to home, and for the next three years he attended the "country academy," still meeting in a log cabin.[10]

The educational deficiencies there also remained, at least to some extent. By the time Jefferson was thirteen, it was decided that he should return to Kentucky, this time to sophisticated Lexington and prestigious Transylvania University, the oldest institution of higher learning west of the Appalachians, which boasted a student body larger than that of Harvard.[11] A number of well-known scholars were on the Transylvania faculty at this time, and though Davis apparently had to struggle to make up for the gaps in his previous education, he profited from his time spent there.[12] Nor were academic benefits the only ones offered by the university. In Lexington Davis made the acquaintance of the upper layer of Kentucky society, including that of the great political leader Henry Clay, developing attitudes and friendships that were to stay with him for life.[13] One friend, five years his senior, was at once his fellow student and his idol: a young Kentuckian by the name of Albert Sidney Johnston.[14]

A little over a year after coming to Transylvania, in the summer of 1824, Davis received word that his father had died back on the farm in Mississippi.[15] After this, Jefferson's oldest brother, thirty-nine-year-old Joseph Davis, became almost like a father to him. Whereas their father had never been more than a moderately successful farmer, owning a handful of slaves, Joseph Davis was already a successful lawyer and rich planter with numerous slaves and a vast tract of fertile bottomland in a bend of the Mississippi River a few miles south of Vicksburg.[16] Joseph had also gained a degree of political influence, of which Jefferson quickly became the beneficiary. Even before his father's death, Jefferson had received an appointment to the United States Military Academy at West Point.[17] Normally a much-sought-after political boon, the West Point berth was not entirely welcome to sixteen-year-old Jefferson, who had in mind finishing up at Transylvania and then attending law school at the University of Virginia and pursuing a legal career of his own. In any case, military life did not appeal to him. His brother was finally able to prevail upon him to accept the appointment by promising that if he was still dissatisfied after a year at the academy he could withdraw and pursue his other plans.[18]

Though apparently satisfied enough with West Point to remain there the entire four years, graduating in 1828, young Davis was anything but a model cadet. He managed to keep his slate clean for one month, but after that it was mostly downhill.[19] Though he laughed off his brother's fears that he would get himself thrown in the guardhouse and insisted that he had "enough prudence to keep from being confined," there was not much about his behavior that could have been characterized as prudent.[20] By the end of his first year at West Point, Davis was rated as one of the fifteen worst-behaved cadets in the academy's 250-cadet enrollment at that time.[21] He capped it off that summer by managing to get himself court-martialed for being caught–visibly intoxicated, it might be added–inside Benny Haven's tavern, a notorious local dive that was strictly off limits to cadets. The court did not believe his rather lame excuse that he entered the establishment to get out of the rain, which, he claimed, made it impossible for him to remain in his tent. Nor did they seem impressed by his argument that malt liquor, hard cider, and porter were not "spiritous liquors." Davis was sentenced to be dismissed from the academy but was granted clemency and allowed to stay.[22] Not that his behavior thereafter was unobjectionable–Cadet Davis racked up demerits at an appalling rate for an assortment of offenses that included skipping class, skipping chapel, leaving dirty clothes strewn around his room, wearing his hair too long, attending a rather spirited Christmas Eve eggnog party that degenerated into a riot after he left (that one got him arrested and confined to quarters again), spitting on the floor, making noise during study hours, and firing his musket out the window of his room.[23]

On one occasion his errant behavior nearly cost him his career and his life as well. He was at Benny Haven's again late one night when someone brought word that an officer was coming. Davis and another cadet dashed off into the darkness. They knew they had to get back to the academy quickly, and they also knew that it would not do to meet the officer heading toward them. Accordingly, they chose to avoid the main road and take a shortcut that led along the bluffs of the Hudson. It was dark, and the way was uncertain. The cadets were hurrying, and their recreation at Benny Haven's may have rendered them not quite steady on their feet. Whatever the reason, Davis slipped and fell down a rocky cliff, landing on the riverbank sixty feet below. He was badly hurt and might have been killed had it not been for some tree branches that broke his fall. His life was despaired of for a time, and he was laid up during a long period of recovery.[24]

Not all of Davis's West Point escapades revolved around misbehavior, and one actually reflected rather well on him. A certain professor had taken an intense dislike to Davis. He missed no chance to belittle the cadet from Mississippi and on one occasion suggested in class that Davis would be unable to handle himself in an emergency due to the "mediocre nature" of his mind. One day the class met in the building that contained the magazine. There, surrounded by large amounts of gunpowder, they were to learn how to make "experimental fireballs," apparently a primitive sort of incendiary hand grenade. One of the fireballs somehow ignited. Davis called this fact to the attention of the professor. "What shall I do, sir?" he asked calmly. "This fire-ball is ignited."

"Run for your lives!" shrieked the professor, who promptly took his own advice. Contemptuously, Davis picked up the bomb and tossed it out the window before it exploded.[25]

Cool he may have been, but his academic performance left a great deal to be desired. He had narrowly passed the entrance exam, and after four years at the academy, his academic performance was still mediocre at best—though this may have been partly the result of his being a voracious reader of whatever he could lay his hands on regarding every imaginable subject but the one he was supposed to be studying at the time.[26] Davis graduated twenty-third in a class of thirty-two.

Yet despite his thoroughly undistinguished career as a cadet, Davis was still deeply influenced by West Point. The academy left its mark on him in his ramrod-straight posture, his increased reserve and formality, and his respect for military professionalism—attributes that lasted through the rest of his life. His West Point days were also significant for the friendships formed there.[27] Although Davis was a classmate of Robert E. Lee and Joseph E. Johnston, he was never close to either of these men.[28] Instead his circle centered on his old university hero Albert Sidney Johnston. Their common Transylvania experience formed a link between them that became the basis of a lasting friendship. Another member of Davis's "set" of West Point cronies was a smooth-talking cadet by the name of Leonidas Polk.[29] Not a man to make close friends easily, Davis developed a rapport with Johnston and Polk during his West Point days that stayed with him throughout his life—so much so, that sixty-one years after his graduation from West Point, as he lay bedridden with his final illness in November 1889, he told his wife, "I have not told what I wish to say of my classmates Sidney Johnston and Polk. I have much more to say of them. I shall tell a great deal of West Point, and I seem to remember more every day."[30] Davis's loyalty to the military academy as an institution and, most important, his unshakable loyalty to the friends he made there would be traits he would carry with him to the grave.[31]

All this did not, however, prevent Davis from harboring a certain degree of dissatisfaction with army life after graduation. Stationed first at Fort Crawford, near Prairie du Chien, Wisconsin, at the confluence of the Mississippi and Wisconsin rivers, and later at Fort Winnebago, near the portage of the Wisconsin and Fox rivers, the new second lieutenant of infantry found the environment anything but stimulating.[32] Davis continued to contemplate a law career or other civilian employment.[33] Even after a year or two had allowed time for adjustment, his brother still had to talk him out of applying for a position as a civil engineer with a Mississippi railroad company.[34]

Aside from the inconveniences of army life at an isolated post in the midst of a wilderness, there were also dangers. On one occasion, while leading a wood-cutting party in northern Wisconsin, Davis became separated from his men during an attack by hostile Indians. He managed to save his scalp by hiding in dense underbrush.[35] Nor was the Wisconsin weather congenial to Davis's Mississippi-bred constitution. During one winter of unusually heavy snow and ice, he suffered such a severe case of pneumonia that he nearly died. Even after his recovery, he remained throughout his life highly susceptible to colds, which would in turn develop into bronchitis and trigger attacks of acute neuralgia that incapacitated him for days or weeks at a time.[36] Chronic ill health was a factor in the sometimes rather irritable disposition that complicated most of Davis's dealings with other people, including his Civil War generals.

Despite the hardships and dangers and the often boring nature of his work, Davis's speculation about other careers went no farther than that. He stayed in the army for seven years, influenced in part by the strong military tradition in his family. Not only had his father fought in the Revolutionary War, but three of his brothers had fought at New Orleans in the War of 1812.[37] Besides, as Jefferson explained in a letter to his sister, a military career was the only life for which his West Point training had prepared him.[38]

When he resigned in the summer of 1835, he was a first lieutenant of dragoons. He had gained a reputation as a spirited and efficient officer who also tended to be somewhat impudent and insubordinate if he thought his rights were being infringed in any way.[39] He had also learned a great deal about day-to-day procedures in a peacetime army. Davis's reason for resigning was Sarah Knox Taylor, the daughter of his commander, Col. Zachary Taylor. The romance had proceeded much against the wishes of Colonel Taylor, but he apparently relented at length, and the couple was married in June 1835.[40] Their happiness was to be of very short duration. Less than three months after the wedding, both of the newlyweds contracted malaria while on a visit to Davis's sister in Louisiana. The young bride succumbed, and for some time it appeared that her husband would soon follow her to the grave. However, Davis did recover and, deeply saddened, went to live with his brother Joseph on his huge plantation, Hurricane.[41] So large was Joseph's estate that he was able to detach a fraction of it to form a very substantial plantation for Jefferson, who named it Brierfield and spent most of the next several years there in relative seclusion, devoting his time to improving the plantation and studying and discussing political philosophy with his brother.

In 1842 Davis entered the world of practical politics, running unsuccessfully for the state legislature. Two years later he was a presidential elector on the Democratic ticket and campaigned actively for James K. Polk (no immediate relation to his friend Leonidas) and the annexation of Texas. In 1845 he was elected to Congress. During that campaign he married his second wife, Varina Howell, member of a wealthy Natchez family.[42] Davis had been in Congress but a short time when war broke out with Mexico. Eager for military glory, he immediately wrote to a friend back in Mississippi, observing that his (Davis's) military training and experience ought to make him very valuable to the country at a time like this and expressing his hope that he might be elected colonel of a regiment of volunteers.[43] He soon got his wish, receiving the command of the First Mississippi Rifles.

Davis resigned his seat in Congress and, in July 1846, joined his regiment at New Orleans. At his insistence the Mississippi troops had been equipped with the recently designed Whitney percussion rifle, the most modern then available, rather than with the proven but soon-to-be-obsolete flintlock smoothbore muskets that had been recommended by army general in chief Winfield Scott.[44] Davis was a strict disciplinarian, so much so as to occasion a few complaints, though on the whole the regiment was devoted to him and well behaved.[45] (In later years the ability to keep order and good discipline among volunteer troops while still maintaining their respect and affection was one that the Confederate president would greatly admire.)

Davis and his Mississippians got their first chance to distinguish themselves at the battle of Monterrey and did so with relish. The battle was characterized more by reckless courage than skillful maneuver, but that did nothing to decrease the glory for the victors. Jefferson Davis and his Mississippi Rifles, together with other units, stormed several enemy redoubts including the key fort of the Mexican defenses. The Mississippians, who had the added inspiration of seeing their colonel always out in front in the hottest of the fighting, stood to the bloody task manfully and made an important contribution to the American victory.

The Mexican forces at Monterrey, cut off by American troops from any re-

treat or reinforcement, sought terms of surrender, and Davis was among those
appointed by Gen. Zachary Taylor, now reconciled to his former son-in-law,
to negotiate with the Mexicans. In negotiating, the Americans proved no match
for the cunning of their opponents, and the surrender agreement that resulted
seemed so favorable to the soundly whipped Mexican garrison that it was finally repudiated by the United States government.[46]

The affair did, however, provide Davis with an adventure. When the negotiations were completed, all that was needed was the signature of the Mexican
commander on the surrender document. For this purpose the document was
left with the Mexican representatives. The next day Davis was to ride into the
fortified city and pick up the signed document at the commanding general's
headquarters.

As Davis was about to set off on this errand, he encountered his old friend
of Transylvania and West Point days, Albert Sidney Johnston, who was serving
as a staff officer to General Taylor. Johnston offered to ride along, and Davis
gladly accepted. As the two riders approached the Mexican lines, they began
to note with increasing apprehension the hostility of the Mexican soldiers and
civilians. Infantrymen appeared on rooftops and at other vantage points, and
Davis and his companion found themselves looking down a number of gun-
barrels. Hiding their growing concern, they continued steadily on what was
suddenly beginning to seem an incredibly long ride.

The whole matter was made worse by what otherwise would have been a
rather comic occurrence several weeks earlier. When the army had been set
down on the coast at Port Isabel, Texas, at the beginning of the campaign,
Johnston's only uniform had accidentally gotten soaked with sea water. When
it dried it was found to have shrunk considerably so as to be no longer usable.
The result was that on this ride Johnston was wearing a red flannel shirt, blue
jeans, and a low-crowned felt hat. This was the typical garb of Johnston's
adopted state of Texas, and the Mexicans recognized it as such. From a doorway a gnarled old woman pointed at Johnston and hissed under her breath,
"Tejano!" The Mexicans hated Texans, a sentiment which was warmly recipro-
cated, and Johnston's attire did nothing to ease the tension as the two Americans rode slowly onward under the malevolent gaze, and perhaps the gunsights,
of hundreds of Mexicans.

Davis and Johnston entered the city and put themselves beyond any hope
of help from their comrades should either mob or military decide to vent its
frustrations on them. A Mexican officer appeared, which opened the possibility of safe conduct through the potentially violent soldiers and civilians to
the headquarters of the commanding general. The officer, however, who turned
out to be a member of the Mexican commander's staff, wheeled his horse and
started to ride off without helping the Americans. Johnston, reacting instantly,
suggested they detain the officer briefly. Spurring their horses across his path,
the two men blocked his escape. The Mexican officer, suddenly realizing that

any violence that broke out now would result in at least three deaths, starting with his own, became quite cooperative and conducted Davis and Johnston to the general's headquarters. They were received with much show of graciousness, and having obtained the signed document that was the object of their excursion, they rode back to the American lines without further difficulty, although Davis discovered later that his pistol had been stolen.

The incident made a great impression on Davis. For the remainder of his days, he firmly believed that it was only that quick thinking of Albert Sidney Johnston in deciding, in effect, to take the Mexican officer hostage that had saved them both from probable death. Davis's already high opinion of Johnston was confirmed and strengthened. Years later he was to remark that in this affair Johnston "exhibited that quick perception and decision which characterize the military genius."[47] Though Jefferson Davis certainly could not have suspected it as he rode back through the dusty streets of Monterrey carrying the signed instrument of surrender, he was going to have need of more than one military genius.

After the battle of Monterrey, Davis visited Mississippi on a brief furlough. When he returned to Taylor's army in Mexico, a change of strategy had reduced its numbers and put it on the defensive while the main force under Gen. Winfield Scott advanced on Mexico City from Vera Cruz on the Gulf Coast. Mexico's general-president, the infamous Antonio López de Santa Anna, decided to strike Taylor's weakened army. In the battle of Buena Vista, February 22 and 23, 1847, the outnumbered Americans were hard-pressed, and for a time the issue was in doubt. At the climax of the battle a regiment of poorly disciplined volunteers in a key position gave way before a Mexican cavalry charge. The Mississippians were sent into the breach, where their colonel deployed them so that in conjunction with a nearby Indiana regiment they made an unorthodox V-formation with the open end toward the charging Mexican cavalry. Davis had his men hold their fire until the Mexicans were almost inside the mouth of the V. Then at his order the Mississippians and Hoosiers loosed a terrific crossfire that cut the Mexican unit to pieces. The survivors streamed back in disorder, and the American position was once more secure.[48]

Davis, though he had received an extremely painful wound in the foot, had remained in the saddle directing his men.[49] Upon the regiment's return to Mississippi that summer, he became an instant hero.[50] The fact that he was wounded and had to get around on crutches added to his fame. Later, his V-formation would be criticized as alternately accidental or stupid, and it would be pointed out that such a formation was largely a factor of the terrain that prevailed on the Buena Vista battlefield.[51] Still, he had stopped the charge of the Mexican cavalry. His discipline had paid off, and his men had fought like regulars while other volunteer regiments broke for the rear. His performance and that of his regiment were impressive enough to draw the observation from another American officer who had participated in the battle with considerable distinction, Capt. Braxton Bragg, that the Mississippi Rifles had been the only volunteer unit to really fight well in that battle.[52]

Davis tended to take his martial accomplishments rather seriously and did not bear criticism well when it concerned the performance of his Mississippi Rifles. The casting of aspersions on his regiment's wartime service, even the suggestion that its exploits might not have been quite as glorious as popular rumor and purple oratory would have them, was likely to elicit from him a ferocious reply and even a challenge to mortal combat. By 1850 he had come near fighting two duels.

One altercation involved a senator from Mississippi, Henry S. Foote. On Christmas Day, 1847, the two were eating breakfast at the Washington boarding house where they both resided. Words were exchanged and then blows, and then the affair degenerated into a brawl. Davis, whose Buena Vista wound kept him on crutches for some two years afterward, was not too hobbled to use his crutch as a weapon. The pugilists waded into each other, Foote swinging his fists and Davis wielding his crutch. Though they failed to do any significant damage to each other, Davis did succeed in knocking off his adversary's wig. An enraged Foote demanded satisfaction, and Davis would have liked nothing better than to give it to him, but they were dissuaded by their friends.[53]

Thereafter in speeches before the state legislature and in the Senate Davis continued to maintain every iota of his and his regiment's reputation for greatness.[54] He was not really a quarrelsome man by nature, but he had very well-defined ideas about what was due him, and he was prepared to insist upon it—violently if need be. In view of the almost superhuman task to which Davis would one day be called, it was an unfortunate personality trait.

No sooner had Davis returned from Mexico than honors began to be showered on him. In May 1847 President Polk offered him an appointment to a vacancy in the rank of brigadier general. Although Polk would have preferred someone else, he had "become satisfied that the public opinion of the country is so strong in favor of Col. Jefferson Davis of Mississippi . . . that to appoint any other . . . would give great dissatisfaction."[55] To the president's astonishment, the hero of Buena Vista rejected the appointment on the grounds that he commanded volunteers, which were really militia, and the appointment of militia officers of whatever rank lay with the states and not with the president. The colonel of Mississippi militia instructed the commander in chief that his action had therefore been unconstitutional.[56] The incident is revealing in two ways. First, Jefferson Davis was firmly devoted to duty; and though he might entertain the most bizarre conceptions of where his duty lay, once he conceived a thing to be his duty, he would follow it, even contrary to his inclinations or apparent self-interest. Second, he had an unfortunate tendency to engage in legalistic quibbling. It was one of his weaknesses that he could rarely resist the temptation of besting another person by pointing out in some technicality how he was right and the other person wrong.

Another honor that fell into the conquering hero's lap, and one he was not disposed to reject, was election to fill a vacant seat in the United States Senate in 1848. Two years later he was reelected. Shortly thereafter the leadership of the state Democratic party approached him in hopes that he could bail them out of a predicament. The Democratic candidate had dropped out of the race for governor when it had become obvious he could not win.[57] Would Jefferson Davis, the ever-popular war hero, be willing to resign his Senate seat and become the standard-bearer of the Democratic party in the gubernatorial election? The race was a forlorn hope, even with Davis's war record, and he knew it. Not only would he get a late start, but the whole battle would have been an uphill fight in any case because of the ruckus kicked up in connection with the Compromise of 1850. The problem was that the southern Democrats in general, and especially Jefferson Davis and others like him, were against the compromise, while the majority of the South, including Mississippi, was for it. This led to Davis and others of like opinion being branded, with some reason, disunionists. Not that he would have looked at it that way—quite the contrary, he was really a strong nationalist at heart, but he sincerely believed the nation was based on a proslavery reading of the Constitution and felt that if the North did not respect such an interpretation, the South should seek its rights outside the Union.

So it was a dubious honor that the state Democratic party sought to bestow on the war hero. Despite the hopeless nature of the campaign he was asked to undertake, Davis believed it his duty to step into the breach. Accordingly, he resigned his Senate seat and gamely entered the race for governor. Predictably, he lost, though in a surprisingly close election.[58] Thereafter he returned to Brierfield, and for a time it appeared that his public life was over.

Then in early 1853 newly elected president Franklin Pierce requested him to join his cabinet as secretary of war. Davis accepted the position and gained a reputation as one of the country's most able and innovative secretaries of war. He introduced camels to the United States Army for cavalry service on the western plains (though nothing much ever came of this) and set out on a concerted program of improvements for West Point aimed at making it as good as any military academy in the world. He also worked hard to secure increases in the numbers and pay of the regular army. When the Crimean War broke out, it was Davis who decided a United States Army commission should be sent to observe the effects of recent advances in military technology. During Davis's tenure the army adopted the new rifle musket that was to do such execution in the Civil War, and an officer by the name of William J. Hardee was assigned to write a tactics manual to go with it. Though these latter improvements, along with other innovations adopted by the army during these years, may have been more the work of War Department experts than of the secretary himself, Davis at least put no obstacle in the way of such advances and in some cases actively supported their introduction.[59]

As secretary of war, Davis also dabbled in some less obviously military projects. He supervised additional construction on the Capitol and administered other public works projects. He also pushed for his favorite project, the construction by the government of a transcontinental railroad on a southern route.[60] To facilitate this last scheme, he arranged for the Gadsden Purchase, securing for the United States the important Gila Valley route and completing the territory that was to become the forty-eight contiguous states.[61] When Pierce and his cabinet left office in 1857, Davis was once again elected to the United States Senate from Mississippi. In the Senate he naturally served on the military affairs committee. He advocated continued United States expansion, particularly in regions that could yield new slave states. Finally, his position in the Senate gave him an ideal platform from which to play a key role in the crisis that culminated in secession.

The national Democratic party had serious problems as it looked to the election of 1860. Having embraced popular sovereignty when it seemed vague enough to satisfy all parties, the Democrats found themselves in an embarrassing situation when actual practice demonstrated that the doctrine could not, after all, make slavery and freedom mean the same thing. When Sen. Stephen A. Douglas of Illinois insisted on an honest interpretation of the theory he had championed, he became pariah to the southern members of the party. This was where Davis came in.

In February 1860 Davis offered for the approval of the Senate a set of seven resolutions stating his position (the orthodox southern one) on the issues that were dividing the party and the country. There was not the slightest chance that the resolutions would pass and indeed they were quickly buried. Their purpose, however, was to bring to center stage certain principles (with the strong suggestion that they represented Democratic orthodoxy) on which the party's only electable candidate, Douglas, could never run.[62] Such was Davis's contribution to secession. Though he was never counted a fire-eater and honestly hoped that the Union could be preserved, he believed that it must be on southern terms, and that meant, as Davis's Senate resolutions spelled out, complete protection for slavery in every territory of the United States. Douglas had rejected that position, and Davis had become his determined foe.

The Democratic convention, under the influence of Davis's resolutions, deadlocked and split; the sundered halves nominated competing tickets. Southerners threatened to secede should a Republican be elected, but with the Democratic party split, little else was likely. Lincoln was elected, and one by one the states of the South declared themselves out of the Union. Though serving on a congressional committee that vainly sought compromise, Davis recommended to those who asked him that the southern states form a government of their own before Lincoln, the "Black Republican," was inaugurated on March 4.[63] Whether on his instigation or not, that was what the southern states were in the process of doing on the noisy night in February 1861 when Davis arrived in Montgomery.

After the secession of Mississippi, Davis resigned from the Senate and returned home. He was not interested in the job of president of the new government but rather desired to be its chief general in the war he believed must necessarily follow disunion.[64] His first boost in that direction came when the governor of Mississippi appointed him major general commanding all of the state's militia. Davis was happy with this assignment and had begun to make preparations for the coming struggle when he received word that the Confederate convention meeting in Montgomery, Alabama, had unanimously chosen him as president. On the day when the telegram arrived, Davis was engaging in one of his favorite hobbies, working in his rose garden. His wife was with him and saw him receive and read the telegram. His face, she later related, might have been that of a man reading his death sentence. "Oh God, spare me this responsibility," he groaned. Then he added wistfully, "I would love to head the army."[65] But such was not the choice of the people's representatives. Duty had called once again, and Jefferson Davis would never shirk his duty as he saw it. Requested to repair to Montgomery at once, he left his home on February 11, arriving in the new capital five days later—after a grueling journey replete with whistle-stop speeches—and was inaugurated on the eighteenth.

In taking charge of the embryonic Confederate government, Davis faced a number of problems, chief of which was Fort Sumter, the large brick structure in the middle of the harbor of Charleston, South Carolina, whose Federal garrison represented to both sides the symbol of continuing federal authority in the South. As such the garrison had to go, as far as Davis was concerned, and it was on his direction that the general whom he had sent to command the Confederate forces at Charleston, P. G. T. Beauregard, opened fire on April 12, 1861.[66]

The bombardment of Fort Sumter had the effect Davis had desired in the upper South. Four more states, including all-important Virginia, seceded from the Union and joined the Confederacy. Three others—Maryland, Missouri, and Davis's native state of Kentucky—were in turmoil and seemed about to tip into the Confederate column. The existence of the Confederacy was an established fact now, and no one need imagine any longer that negotiations might end its reality. Only overwhelming defeat in war could put a stop now to what had been started in Montgomery. Thus the second result of the attack on Sumter was the actuality of war. The North was galvanized by this southern aggression and settled down in earnest to the task of suppressing the rebellion by military force.

Jefferson Davis (National Archives)

Few men in the United States in 1861 seemed better prepared by training and experience to undertake the leadership of a nation at war than Jefferson Davis, certainly not the prairie lawyer from Illinois who had recently taken the helm in Washington. Davis had graduated from West Point, managed a large plantation, commanded an entire regiment in battle (something neither Lee nor Grant could boast at this time), and been an unusually active secretary of war and an effective senator. He was honest, courageous, determined, and completely devoted to his duty as he understood it.

At the same time, no man is without his shortcomings, and there were some less auspicious aspects of Davis's character–though few seemed disposed to notice them in the euphoria surrounding the formation of the Confederacy. Davis could be proud, and his firmness might impress some as being akin to stubbornness. Perhaps more than is normal in the human creature, he found it difficult to admit he had been wrong. This betrayed him quite naturally into attempts to force others to admit that they had been wrong. He was not a man to overlook a slight or to handle a difficult personality gently, and he had a tendency to become mired in bureaucratic and legalistic technicalities. These were problems he would have to overcome if he was to be effective in leading his new country through the extraordinary times that lay ahead.

Davis's military preparation, viewed closely, could prove good or bad for the Confederacy depending on how he applied it. He took great pride in his West Point education and his military experience, especially as colonel of the Mississippi Rifles. This pride, and the high opinion of his own ability that went with it, could be helpful if it enabled him to make difficult decisions and issue orders confidently, but it could be very dangerous if it convinced him that he need never learn and improve as a commander. Similarly, if he used the solid military training he had received at West Point as a basis for well-thought-out innovations and creative solutions to new situations, his education could be a great advantage. On the other hand, it could be very detrimental should he allow it to lock him into sterile conventionality, vintage 1828.

There was another factor to consider as well, and that was the new president's physical condition. At first glance this might seem to be excellent. Davis was tall, nearly six feet, and seemed taller because of his erect posture.[67] He was slender and his fair hair was turning to a dignified gray.[68] Yet Davis was not a healthy man. A British journalist who saw Davis in Montgomery described him as having "eyes deep set, large and full–one seems nearly blind, and is partly covered with a film, owing to excruciating attacks of neuralgia."[69] In fact, sometime before 1850 Davis had lost the sight in his left eye, possibly the result of a corneal ulcer or even glaucoma. Although the blindness was not, as Davis and his contemporaries believed, caused by neuralgia, the Confederate president also suffered from this affliction and had for a number of years. It affected the nerves in the face, ears, throat, and related areas and, though it did not damage the nerves, caused stabbing pains that could at times be almost unbearable. Periodic attacks of neuralgia could prostrate Davis for as long as they lasted. At times a seizure seemed to be triggered by bronchitis, to which Davis's life-threatening bout with pneumonia seems to have left him susceptible. However, Davis's neuralgia may have been in large part psychosomatic, perhaps the result of extreme stress and Davis's taut, tense personality. Davis also suffered from what his contemporaries referred to as dyspepsia, a chronic sour stomach that not surprisingly tended to lead to a sour disposition. It now seems probable that Davis's dyspepsia was actually a peptic ulcer, a serious medical condition of the stomach often resulting from a failure to cope with emotional stress.[70] Taken together, these health problems boded ill for Jefferson Davis's future performance as Confederate president.

Though a careful observer in the spring of 1861 might have had some reason to wonder what sort of wartime president Davis would make, it had to be conceded that no one in the South—or the North, for that matter—could boast of more impressive credentials for the task Jefferson Davis was assuming. If he had shortcomings, others did as well, and it could not be denied that he had tremendous strengths. Whether he would capitalize on his strengths and overcome his weaknesses to the degree necessary to be an effective commander in chief and whether he would be a good strategist and judge of men remained to be seen.

2

ORGANIZING THE WESTERN THEATER

Overwhelming tasks faced the new president. An entire government had to be created from scratch.[1] Every office had to be filled, and there was no shortage of applicants for the positions in the new bureaucracy. First in Montgomery and then, after the secession of Virginia and relocation of the Confederacy's capital, in Richmond the new president was deluged with office seekers.[2] Completing the initial round of appointments brought little respite from the plethora of trivial concerns that plagued the chief executive throughout the war. There were resignations to be considered, replacements to be appointed, promotions to be approved, disputes to be settled, and requests to be dealt with. Applicants craved for themselves, their sons, nephews, brothers, or husbands all manner of commissions, promotions, exemptions, or positions. Deserters appealed to the president to save them from the firing squad; draftees, from the enrollment officer. In a society that had not yet learned to think of government as a bureaucratic machine, everyone turned with his request directly to the president, by letter if necessary, but preferably in person. From the mother who begged for the discharge of her "baby boy" (a veritable infant of some eighteen years) to the correspondent who gravely informed the president that he was determined one day to command the armies of the Confederacy and would therefore enlist as soon as he was old enough, Davis faced the full gamut of the trivial distractions that a modern-day White House staff would have weeded out.

A certain amount of Davis's time and energy were dissipated in such mundane matters, yet there were major political problems to be dealt with. The Confederacy was a new "nation" and would require skillful political handling to avoid fragmentation. Congress had to be kept happy and the various governors placated. Neither task was easy, and Davis did not have great success in either one, though perhaps he did as well as could have been expected. Problems with all representatives of local interests within the Confederacy, whether governors, senators, or justices of the peace, were complicated by the fact that, though the Confederacy was founded on an extreme view of states' rights, its states would have to forego some of their rights for the time being in order to wage a successful war.

Foreign policy also competed for Davis's attention. Emissaries to the various countries of the world had to be selected and their instructions formulated. Decisions had to be made on such issues as how best to induce the intervention of France and Britain and how to gain international recognition. These too were difficult, well-nigh impossible undertakings for the fledgling Confederacy. Davis thew himself into the many tasks he faced with great determination, but he had never administered anything near this size before. As secretary of war during the 1850s, he had handled seven clerks and an army of ten to fifteen thousand men. Now he presided over some seventy thousand civilian employees and an army that would soon number in the hundreds of thousands. It was a monumental job, and Davis made it no easier by immersing himself in details that could and should have been left to cabinet secretaries or even clerks. The president habitually overworked himself, a practice that led to fatigue and aggravated his already poor health.[3] Despite his constant exhaustion the British newspaperman who had previously noticed Davis's blind eye interviewed Davis at the outset of the war and wrote that the new president spoke with "the utmost confidence and greatest decision."[4]

Much would depend on Davis's being able to maintain his confidence and decisiveness under the tremendous stress to which he would be subjected as wartime president, for diplomacy and politics and all the other day-to-day concerns of being president all put together were dwarfed by the importance of the one crucial need that faced the Confederacy and demanded its president's attention: The would-be nation was locked in a battle for its very existence. As commander in chief, Jefferson Davis, more than any other man, was responsible for bringing victory. If he failed in that, nothing else that he did would count for much.

The task of defending the Confederacy was one of staggering proportions, involving a military frontier that stretched from the Virginia tidewater westward across the Appalachians, the hills and rivers of Tennessee and Kentucky, and the Mississippi River to the Great Plains beyond. Besides this there was a coastline of several thousand miles to guard against an enemy whose naval superiority gave him the potential of descending in force on any point on the coast at any time.

Davis made the decision early on that the Confederacy would follow a policy of attempting to hold as much of its territory as possible rather than maintaining a more flexible defense such as the Americans had used in the War of Independence or even resorting to guerrilla tactics. There were a number of reasons for this, some of them fairly good; others less so. For one thing, the Civil War was going to involve vastly larger armies than the relative handful of men who had followed George Washington. These armies were going to consume great amounts of supplies. The more territory the Confederacy lost, the less it would have to provide supplies for its armies. Another reason for a rigid defense was slavery. The South was fighting primarily to maintain a "peculiar institution" that was far too fragile to survive the passage of an invading army. To save slavery, it was necessary to keep Federal armies off southern soil as much as possible. Then, too, the Confederacy was anxious to prove its legitimacy among the nations of the world, and it was generally assumed that legitimate nations did not suffer their territory to be overrun wholesale by invading armies. Finally, a rigid defense designed to stop the enemy at the frontiers or on the beaches appealed to Jefferson Davis's personality as well as to the desires of local politicians from every one-horse town and backwoods crossroads on the fringes of the Confederacy who insisted that the defense of their particular bailiwicks be the special concern of the Confederate government.[5]

Accordingly, Davis distributed the available forces of the Confederacy around the rim of its territory. On the coast this meant parceling out a fairly substantial number of soldiers to port cities and at forts guarding the entrances to rivers or sheltered sounds and waterways. It was not a wise disposition of forces. With its naval superiority the attacker could always bring overwhelming forces to bear on whatever point it chose to assault, while the Confederate garrisons along the rest of the coast remained idle. The North did gain a number of successes along the coast, but with a few exceptions, the decisive battles of the war were not fought there, largely because the North failed to realize the potential of amphibious operations.[6] As the war went on and the pressure of necessity mounted, Davis came to realize, to a certain extent, that garrisoning the coast was an uneconomical use of manpower, and some of the troops stationed there were transferred to active armies.

Within the sometimes questionable framework of defending every inch of Confederate soil, Davis selected a strategy well suited to the military, economic, and industrial realities facing the South. It was called the "offensive-defensive" in the military terminology of the day, and it could be likened to a boxer who, knowing himself to be physically outmatched, hangs back on the ropes, allows his opponent to wear himself out throwing punches, and looks for an opening for a counterpunch that while not equal to the prodigious blows of the stronger opponent, might still through good timing and crisp execution succeed in putting the adversary on the canvas.[7] It was a strategy fitted to defense of a land frontier, where the enemy's supply lines and rear areas would be vulnerable to the feints and full-scale counterpunches Davis had in mind.

This strategy was also a good choice since the majority of the Civil War's fighting took place on the land front that ran, at the war's outset, from Chesapeake Bay on the east to the Great Plains on the west. This front, in turn, was divided into two unequal sections by the rugged Appalachian Mountains. To the east of this divide, between the mountains and the coast, lay the smaller but more prestigious theater of the war. Here in Virginia, the rival capitals Richmond and Washington were separated by a scant one hundred miles. The naive but widely held belief that to capture the enemy's capital was to win the war tended to focus attention on this small corner of the country. In addition, Virginia was located on the more densely populated east coast, and this added to the disproportionate attention it received; each side had its largest single army in Virginia.

At first it appeared that the Virginia front would be the Confederacy's problem area. It was probably this, along with pressure from Confederate congressmen tired of living in a backward Alabama town, that influenced Davis, somewhat against his better judgment, to approve the removal of the capital from Montgomery to Richmond, where he could keep a close eye on operations in Virginia. The proximity of Washington, D.C., to the South's border meant that the Federals would have made a major effort in Virginia even had the Confederate capital not been located there. After the move to Richmond, cries of "On to Richmond" in the northern press and public left no doubt as to the inevitability of a Virginia campaign.

In Virginia, Davis had two highly renowned but very hard to handle generals: Pierre G. T. Beauregard (the "Hero of Fort Sumter") and Joseph E. Johnston. On July 21, 1861, Beauregard and Johnston teamed up to defeat the ill-prepared Union drive on Richmond at the first battle of Manassas (Bull Run). There followed a long period of quiet on the eastern front while the northern army in this theater, now called the Army of the Potomac, licked its wounds and built up its strength. By the time another northern offensive was launched in April of 1862, Beauregard had been transferred to the West, leaving Johnston, already in top command in Virginia, as the defender of Richmond.

The Union general who led the new offensive, George B. McClellan, had recognized one of the two factors that made the Virginia theater extremely difficult for the Federals. The rivers in eastern Virginia flow from west to east so that a northern army advancing from Washington to Richmond would have to make successive crossings. Each river was thus a natural barrier which a resourceful defender could use. McClellan decided to avoid this problem by landing his army on the eastern coast of Virginia and advancing up the peninsula between the James and York rivers straight to Richmond. He was within a few miles of his goal when a great misfortune befell him. His opposite number, Joseph E. Johnston, was wounded and was replaced by the man who for several months had held the title of commanding general of all Confederate armies in the field but had actually been functioning as the president's chief of staff and top military advisor—Robert E. Lee.

McClellan thereupon discovered the second factor that made Virginia so difficult for northern generals. Washington was too close and its officials too skittish. By playing on this sensitivity, Lee, with the aid of the brilliant Thomas J. "Stonewall" Jackson, was able to prevent McClellan's receiving large numbers of reinforcements. Then, demonstrating the combination of audacity and tactical skill that both sides soon came to recognize as genius, Lee drove McClellan back down the peninsula. But for the Union general's own considerable skills, Lee might have destroyed the Army of the Potomac altogether.

Thereafter, throughout the rest of 1862 and 1863, the war in the East followed a fairly set pattern. A Union general would advance on Richmond, taking care to keep Washington covered at all times, and hope through some means or other to defeat the dreaded Lee. Lee, outnumbered at times by two-to-one or more, would do something audacious and utterly unexpected and soundly thrash the Army of the Potomac. The Federals would retreat; the unfortunate commander would be relieved; and another hopeful general would advance to be disgraced. In 1864 and 1865 the different genius of U.S. Grant drove Lee back into the Richmond defenses, whereupon Grant besieged and finally captured the Confederate capital. By that time, however, the war had already been lost elsewhere – in the West.

The western theater turned out to be far more of a problem area for the Confederacy than the East. The front was larger and vastly more complicated, and Davis was never able to find a winning team of generals for it. In the West, Davis's abilities as a strategist, a commander, and a judge of men were put to their greatest test. There many of the crucial decisions were made and a fair proportion of the decisive battles fought.

The area in which the war in the West was played out was bordered on the east by the Appalachian Mountains. Rugged, relatively infertile, and sparsely settled, this region was, for military purposes, a wasteland. Lack of railroads, poor wagon roads, and rough country made it next to impossible for an army in this region to haul in its supplies, and an absence of farms meant there could be no living off the land. On the west, the theater of operations drifted off into the sheer emptiness of the arid plains. There was no natural barrier here comparable to the Appalachians in the East, but there was the equally effective constraint that beyond a certain point, an army was simply too far from anything of military significance to be of use.

The terrain in between these two boundaries was as well adapted to military operations as any in the South. There were railroads, though not many. Since wagon roads were of uncertain quality and likely to be unusable in bad weather – and since wagons were in any case an inefficient means of bringing up supplies over long distances – what railroads there were became strategic items of the first magnitude. With few exceptions the land was relatively well populated and dotted with farms or plantations, so there were excellent prospects for drawing supplies from the countryside. The land itself was mostly flat or rolling with some substantial hills here and there, occasional bluffs along the rivers, and foothills along the fringe of the Appalachians. Woods and swamps were strewn about liberally enough to present numerous headaches to any general who was poorly served by his staff.

The most important features in this vast area were three large rivers. The westernmost was the Mississippi, flowing due south from Cairo at the southern tip of Illinois to the Gulf of Mexico just beyond New Orleans; next, the Tennessee, whose navigable portion ran due north from Florence, Alabama, to Paducah, Kentucky; and still further east, the Cumberland, which rose in eastern Kentucky and flowed south into Tennessee and past Nashville before curving north again to join the Ohio above Paducah. The fact that these rivers, unlike the rivers of Virginia, ran due north or south was ominous for the Confederacy. They could not be used as bulwarks of defense but instead could provide an invading army with something no railroad or wagon road could give: a virtually unbreakable supply line.

A fourth river, less important than the first three but significant in its own way, was the Red. Flowing along the northern boundary of Texas and then across Louisiana in a southeasterly direction to join the Mississippi below Vicksburg, its connections to Louisiana's tangled maze of bayous and to Texas beyond made it a conduit for the supplies and produce of the trans-Mississippi West on their way to the rest of the Confederacy—the more important for the lack of railroads west of the Mississippi.

Expecting the North to fight rather than submit to the dismemberment of the country, Jefferson Davis had, even before the bombardment of Fort Sumter, turned to the military preparation of the South. Being a westerner who was born in Kentucky and called Mississippi home, he did not neglect that region. In setting up the Confederacy's western defenses he had the help, such as it was, of two other men. One was Secretary of War Leroy Pope Walker. An Alabama lawyer and politician of no military training or experience other than a nominal commission as a brigadier general of the state militia, Walker owed his appointment more to political factors than anything else. He had been a secessionist fire-eater, and that group needed some recognition in a cabinet for the most part composed of men who had been less hasty in advocating such a drastic step. Then, too, he was from Alabama, and that state ought to be represented in the cabinet. Walker and his friends had applied political pressure, and Davis made the appointment.[8]

The Confederacy's first secretary of war was a hard worker but dissipated much of his effort in laborious attention to detail. Though competent to handle the business side of the department, he was no help at all when it came to matters of strategy. When he did try to take a hand in ordering even a minor troop movement, the result was confusion.[9] Davis saw the role of the secretary of war as that of "constitutional advisor" to the president. His system for working with his secretaries of war—and indeed with anyone who served in high strategic position at the Confederate capital—was "free conference": frequent and extensive discussions that Davis saw as times of give and take in which joint decisions were forged.[10] The final responsibility, of course, remained with the president, and in practice, so did all of the decision-making power. The significance of a particular secretary of war was therefore dependent on his persuasiveness and on the extent to which his military ability commanded the respect of the president. Walker was so deficient in the latter respect that by the end of his tenure at the War Department he had Davis convinced (in view of Davis's appreciation for West Point training, admittedly not a difficult task) that no civilian was competent to handle that post.[11] This was not to say Davis intended to appoint military men to that position; that came later. Instead, he had resolved, not altogether reluctantly, to run military affairs himself while some politician handled the routine business. Later, more able secretaries of war would play more significant roles, and Davis would bristle at the suggestion that every act of the secretary of war was made at his direction. Yet he never allowed much room for independent decision and frankly admitted that "the President is responsible for every order of the War Department."[12] In any case, when it came to military decisions, Walker was a nonentity.

The second man who could have been of some assistance to Davis in setting up the South's defenses west of the Appalachians was Gen. Samuel Cooper. An aged and colorless cipher, Cooper had been born in New York (a fact which galled many a southerner, though it never seemed to bother Davis) and graduated from West Point while Jefferson Davis was a boy of six attending a log cabin school in Mississippi. An uneventful career brought him by 1852 to the post of adjutant general of the United States Army.[13] As such he had worked closely with Secretary of War Jefferson Davis, and apparently Davis had found him a very amenable subordinate. When secession came, Cooper cast his lot with the South—under the influence possibly of southern ideas but more likely of his wife, a granddaughter of the famous Virginia statesman George Mason.[14]

Davis showed great confidence in Cooper by giving him the combined roles of adjutant and inspector general. Furthermore, Davis intended that the position should be more than the sum of the two that had been merged to create it. "The Adjt. & Ins. Genl. in our service," Davis wrote later in the war, "is not a Bureau officer, but holds the commission of *General* in the C.S. Army. He is by assignment the Chief of Staff of the whole army." His rank, Davis believed, should preclude any idea that he was a mere "organ for the transmission of instructions" from the president or the secretary of war.[15] Indeed, Cooper was the highest ranking general in the Confederate army, and Davis expected for him a role similar to that played by Lee during the first half of 1862 and by Bragg during 1864. Thus, the position of adjutant and inspector general was intended and had the potential to be the basis of a modern command system, the like of which the North did not develop until much later in the war. Even then the Confederate system was superior in giving the commanding general more control over the various War Department bureaus. A lack of such control drove commanding generals in the United States to distraction for decades after the war.

The creation of such a position showed Davis's excellent understanding of the workings of army high command and of the kind of system needed to get the most out of the South's limited resources. The appointment of Samuel Cooper to fill that crucial position showed that Davis dismally misjudged the man's character and ability. A partial reason for this mistake was that Davis's previous association with Cooper had been in the day-to-day administration of a peacetime army less than one-tenth the size of the one the Confederacy was now attempting to sustain. The pressure of war demonstrated that Cooper had been fit for nothing more rigorous than the peacetime routine.

Another factor was Davis's unwillingness to see the faults of his friends. It was at once one of his most admirable traits and yet, when carried to excess, one of his most unfortunate weaknesses that he was almost unshakably loyal to anyone whom he considered his friend. He would believe no evil of these comrades, and criticism of them he tended to take as if it were aimed personally. One of the most difficult things that Davis as commander in chief had to face was accepting the fact that a man whom he liked and respected was simply not a competent general. In some cases the president was never able to bring himself to that point.

To his credit, though, Davis was not long in recognizing that Cooper neither would nor could be the kind of army chief of staff he had envisioned. His use of Robert E. Lee in what amounted to the job of chief of staff in 1862 was a tacit admission that Cooper would never be equal to the task. While maintaining Cooper in the position of adjutant and inspector general and persevering in the theory that the post was not one of a mere errand-boy to the president, Davis in practice allowed it to become just that. As the war progressed, the correspondence of the Adjutant and Inspector General's Office became more and more mundane, finally reaching a level of almost unrelieved triviality. Davis, realizing Cooper's inadequacy but liking him as a person, chose not to hurt the old soldier by removing him but rather to allow the position to sink into decrepitude along with him. Yet in doing so, Davis made it difficult if not impossible to give the South, in practice as opposed to theory, the modern command system it so desperately needed.

From neither Walker nor Cooper, then, could Davis expect much help in developing a defensive scheme for the West or in making any other strategic decision—a fact which did not seem to deter him from moving ahead. The first order of business was the securing of New Orleans and the mouth of the Mississippi River. For this task Davis chose his old Mexican War division commander, David Emmanuel Twiggs. A native of Georgia, son of a Revolutionary War general, and veteran of the War of 1812, Twiggs was tall and florid with a white mane of hair and beard and a booming parade-ground voice.[16] He had served as a general in the Mexican War, although the extent to which he had distinguished himself in that conflict was a matter of some controversy. He saw no action at all on the first day of the battle of Monterrey, being incapacitated by a prodigious dose of castor oil he had taken shortly before in the belief that it would allow a bullet to pass through his intestines without harm. Yet his performance during the remainder of that and other battles had been enough to impress the colonel of the Mississippi Rifles.[17] After the war Davis helped sponsor a testimonial dinner for Twiggs (who, however, declined the honor) and successfully agitated in Congress to see that Twiggs got a brevet promotion to major general and a ceremonial sword with golden scabbard and jeweled hilt.[18] If admiration of Twiggs's Mexican War exploits was far from unanimous, a substantial number of people, including a majority in Congress, apparently shared Davis's high opinion of the venerable general.

In early 1861 Twiggs had been a brigadier general in the army of the United States, charged with the command of the Department of Texas. There the federal government was maintaining large numbers of troops to protect the Texans from marauding Indians. When in February of that year these same Texans had declared themselves out of the Union and demanded the immediate surrender of their erstwhile defenders, Twiggs, who had recently stated that "if an old woman with a broomstick should come with full authority from the state of Texas" he would surrender to her, promptly complied.[19] The Texas secession convention was so impressed with Twiggs's cooperativeness that it gave him a vote of thanks, commending "his patriotism, moral courage and loyalty to the Constitution of the United States, embracing the rights and liberty of his native" South. The people in Washington, where Buchanan, who had recently discovered a reasonable facsimile of a backbone, was still president, did not look at the matter quite that way. An order was issued at President Buchanan's behest, dismissing Twiggs from the army in disgrace, "for his treachery to the flag of his country." Infuriated at this suggestion of treason on his part, Twiggs wrote to Buchanan, threatening to come to his home in Lancaster, Pennsylvania, for the express purpose of defying him to mortal combat. Fortunately, that was something Twiggs never got around to.[20] Instead, the last day of May 1861 found Twiggs arriving not in Lancaster but in New Orleans, armed with a commission signed by Jefferson Davis and making Twiggs a brigadier general, the highest rank then authorized in the Confederate army.[21]

Davis's appointment had been prompted by his own respect for his former division commander and encouraged by leading citizens of New Orleans who shared that opinion.[22] It was not one of his wiser choices. The governor of Louisiana, at first quite satisfied with Twiggs, was by autumn complaining that the general, a septuagenarian, was decrepit and senile.[23] Davis, who was never very good at owning up to his mistakes, irritably complained that it was all the fault of those citizens of New Orleans who had recommended Twiggs: "They should sooner have informed me of the mistake they had made."[24] Upon being removed, Twiggs charged that the local displeasure with him resulted from his failure to allow public funds to flow in the direction of certain influential cliques, an accusation which might not have been completely without foundation.[25] Twiggs was replaced by Mansfield Lovell, former deputy commissioner of streets for New York City (the New York street department seems to have been a hotbed of secessionist sympathy; the commissioner himself was by this time in Confederate uniform).[26] Lovell was an intelligent, able, and energetic West Pointer who had been wounded and won a brevet for gallantry in the Mexican War. Eventually he would be ill-used by a South that could never forget his northern antecedents and attributed his every misfortune to treachery. For now, though, the governor and people of Louisiana at last seemed satisfied.

The Twiggs appointment, although a mistake, caused no serious mishap and was corrected before things got out of hand. Still, it was an example of Davis's tendency to make errors in judgment regarding those for whom he had preexisting feelings of friendship or admiration. With Twiggs, as with Cooper, his sentiment did not run so deep as to prevent him from recognizing that a mistake had been made and correcting it—even if he refused to accept any blame. The Leonidas Polk appointment presented an altogether different situation.

Polk was the man Davis chose to head up the Confederate defenses at the other end of the all-important Mississippi Valley. Born in Raleigh, North Carolina, in 1806 to a family that had acquired large landed estates, Leonidas Polk attended the University of North Carolina for one year before being appointed to West Point. There he met Davis and was a roommate and close friend of Albert Sidney Johnston. Polk loved military life and also savored the pleasures of fashionable society, even going so far as to attend a dancing school. Still, he was able to keep his grades up and ranked high in his graduating class of 1827.[27]

In his junior year Polk acquired, for the first time in his life, an interest in religion. Religion at West Point meant Episcopalianism, a denomination deemed to be sufficiently dignified and patrician for an officer and a gentleman. Its chief practitioner at West Point, Chaplain (later Bishop) Charles McIlvaine, was an impressive figure and certainly knew how to make the most of the academy's favorable setting. Possessing a powerful and expressive voice that would have equipped him for the stage, he somehow seemed peculiarly suited to a pulpit. Although he wrote out his sermons in advance, he had the ability to extemporize brilliantly. Jefferson Davis described one occasion when, as McIlvaine preached during chapel, the window directly behind him displayed a view of great dark thunderheads piling up in the summer sky over the beautiful Hudson River valley. McIlvaine managed to weave the sights and sounds of the gathering storm into his sermon, Davis recalled, "so that the crash of one fitted into a great outburst of the other. They seemed to belong to one another—the sermon and the storm."[28] Nevertheless, it was not considered fashionable among the West Point cadets to be actively religious, and through three years at the academy, Leonidas Polk was in this as in every other aspect the height of fashion.[29]

Then in the spring of his junior year Polk was involved in an infraction of the academy's rules. He and a number of other cadets were found to have been tracing their drawing assignments from the originals rather than sketching them freehand as the instructor had intended. The resulting punishment substantially lowered Polk's class standing and badly wounded his pride. It did not, however, bring any immediate repentance. Polk argued extensively that the prac-

Leonidas Polk (National Archives)

tice of tracing originals, though forbidden by the rules, had been widespread and generally winked at. Therefore, he insisted, the crackdown that had caught him was unfair.[30] This blow to his self-confidence was compounded a few days later when he was further shaken by having a dream concerning the Last Judgment. In this frame of mind he went to see the chaplain. After meeting several times with McIlvaine and carefully reading a book the chaplain had recommended to him, Polk became a convert.

The new convert was often made painfully aware of the fact that religious devotion was still not popular among his fellow cadets. Yet Polk's popularity, persuasiveness, and apparent sincerity gradually helped to change that attitude, and by the time he graduated there were several other cadets openly professing religious affiliation. Immediately after graduation Polk horrified his father, a Revolutionary War veteran, by resigning his commission and entering an Episcopal theological seminary. In 1830 he was ordained, and eight years later, at the age of thirty-two, he was appointed missionary bishop of the Southwest.

His territory—the rough frontier states of Alabama, Mississippi, Louisiana, Arkansas, the Indian Territory (present-day Oklahoma), and the Republic of Texas—was not exactly a stronghold of Episcopalianism, but Polk ambitiously went at the task of carving out a diocese and enjoyed moderate success. In 1841 he was elected bishop of Louisiana and established himself very comfortably there on a large sugar plantation with some four hundred slaves inherited by his wife. Mrs. Polk could have chosen instead a sum of money for her inheritance but took the slaves at her husband's behest. Naturally, the bishop required his slaves to be good Episcopalians. All did not go well, however, on the Polk plantation. In 1849 a cholera epidemic killed 106 slaves. The next year a tornado devastated some of his property, including a $75,000 sugar house, and an early frost ruined a third of his sugar crop.[31] In addition, Polk left much to be desired as a manager.[32] In the end his creditors took the plantation, and Polk and his family moved to New Orleans.[33]

Long before this time, Polk's attitudes on the issues that were eventually to divide the country had undergone considerable change. As a young convert he had considered slavery an evil that ought to be slowly phased out. But by the 1850s he had come to approve of slavery and was avidly pursuing his scheme of creating a "University of the South," free from all taint of northern thought, where southern young men of breeding could receive a proper aristocratic education. Polk believed this was a job for the Episcopalians. "Baptists and Methodists," he opined, "have not the bearing or the social position or prestige, required to command the public confidence."[34] Polk pushed the idea energetically, and in the summer of 1857 an organizational meeting was held at a scenic southern location with the descriptive name of Lookout Mountain. Making use of the commanding view from the mountaintop, the bishop surveyed the surrounding country for a good location for the school.[35]

As it turned out, the land that Polk had contemplated from the top of

Lookout Mountain became not a campus but a battlefield. Before the university could be opened, secession interrupted the bishop's ambitious plans. Polk was an ardent secessionist. Presiding over the Louisiana diocese at that time, he greeted that state's announced departure from the Union with enthusiasm and added his own contribution to the schism by having the Louisiana diocese secede from the Protestant Episcopal Church of the United States.[36] Despite all this zeal for disunion, Polk was by no means eager for war, nor did he think it was inevitable. It was the responsibility of the North to refrain from starting a war. To a friend Polk wrote, "I cannot but think and hope that the good sense and Christian feeling of the North will prevail over passion and pride, and that we shall be saved from such a disaster and be permitted to go in peace."[37]

Nor was he content merely to "hope" the North would acquiesce in the South's secession. Polk had a habit of pressing people with unsolicited advice. On this occasion the beneficiary of his words of wisdom was the harassed lame-duck president James Buchanan. In a letter Polk expressed confidence in the president's patriotism and integrity but feared he lacked adequate knowledge of southern sentiment. The South, he informed the chief executive, was determined on its course, and any effort on the part of the federal government to enforce the laws would result in "ruthless carnage." Then he reasoned with the president: "Doubtless you are required to enforce the laws; but assuredly no sane man will say 'without regard to consequences.' That would be madness. A right to exercise a sound discretion [comes with the job]. . . . And to assume the responsibility of exercising that right . . . involves the highest exercise of courageous independence and the most discriminating and considerate regard to the duties of your own position and the best interests of those whose destinies are in your hands."[38]

In the end the North proved to be deficient in Polk's brand of "good sense and Christian feeling," and the bishop's efforts to secure peaceable disunion came to nothing. His letter to Buchanan, though, revealed an aspect of his character that did not augur well for the South. "The right to exercise a sound discretion" in the face of orders from a superior—and generally to do whatever seemed best in his own eyes regardless of what superiors might desire or command—was a thing that Polk valued very highly indeed.

When war came, Polk quickly decided on a military role for himself in the conflict. He had had no military experience of any sort since leaving the academy some thirty-four years before, and there is no reason to believe that in all those years he read so much as a single book dealing with martial matters.[39] He was, in any case, not an especially learned man. He was unfamiliar with the classics and, as a close friend admitted, knew little of theology and had sketchy knowledge at best of canon law. The chief talent that most observers noted in him was his tremendous persuasiveness and charisma. He had a way with people, and he could, it was said, be "extremely charming" in conversation.[40] But by any standard, Bishop Leonidas Polk's military credentials were not impressive. He was barely qualified to serve as a second lieutenant, yet in the emergency facing the South, there might have been justification for making him a major or even a lieutenant colonel. Jefferson Davis made him a major general.

Unfortunate as this was, there could be no disputing that quick action had been necessary in arranging for the defense of the Confederacy's northwestern frontier. This area was critical for several reasons, including the presence of the crucial Mississippi and the nearby Tennessee rivers and the proximity of the two key border states of Missouri and Kentucky. Both were teetering on a fine edge between Union and Confederacy, Kentucky in a dreamlike state of neutrality and Missouri in a state of bare-knuckle frontier mayhem. The Confederacy needed a good man on watch there with clear instructions and a clear head.

In the spring of 1861 such was not the case on the Mississippi Valley front. When Tennessee had seceded from the Union, it had, like all the other states choosing that course, raised a provisional army of its own and appointed a major general as commander of it. The man Tennessee selected for that job was Gideon J. Pillow.[41] Pillow was a veteran of the Mexican War, but to an even larger extent than was true in the case of Twiggs, Pillow's merit was a matter of opinion. He was the product of the most snobbish level of Tennessee's antebellum high society, having been raised in the rich plantation district around Columbia.[42] He owed his Mexican War appointment as a brigadier general and subsequent promotion to major general to the fact that he was a former law partner of then-president James K. Polk rather than to any military qualifications.[43] So unpopular was the appointment that Polk thought to use a clever maneuver to avoid the necessity of submitting it for confirmation. When political pressure forced a showdown, the Senate, in a wholly symbolic vote that took place after the war was over and Pillow was back in civilian life, confirmed the nomination along strict party lines, with the Democrats supporting their president and his man Pillow and the Whigs opposing him.[44] Nor was he especially popular with his fellow officers or with his commander Winfield Scott, who considered him insubordinate.[45] During the 1850s Pillow had run unsuccessfully for United States senator and had hoped in vain for the vice-presidential spot on the 1856 Democratic ticket. Despite his somewhat checkered past, Pillow was a man of great personal magnetism. He was handsome in a way that allowed him to seem both distinguished and dashing at the same time, and he looked very much the part of the great general he fancied himself to be. He only lacked sound judgment to direct his seemingly boundless energy.[46]

By the spring of 1861 Pillow had his strong admirers and equally strong detractors. After Tennessee officially joined the Confederacy and the Tennessee army that Pillow commanded became part of the Confederate army, both admirers and detractors bombarded Davis with demands that Pillow be given either an important position in the Confederate army or no position at all, depending on the writer's point of view.[47] Though it is not clear just how Davis himself felt about Pillow, it seems that he entertained some wise doubts as to the lawyer-general's capability. Davis had voted to confirm Pillow's nomination back in 1848, but that was a highly partisan vote and Davis was a loyal Democrat.[48] Joseph Davis, Jefferson's brother, detested Pillow as a general, and it seems likely that Jefferson shared this opinion at least to some extent.[49]

Davis found it impossible, though, to ignore political pressure entirely. He could not insult Tennessee, by no means the most solidly prosouthern of the Confederate States, by refusing to accept its chief general into Confederate service. Nor was Davis insensitive to practical politics in the appointment of generals. Later in the war he wrote, "The attempt to place officers not identified with the people and of unrecorded services has been frequently rejected by me."[50] Pillow's services were certainly undistinguished if not necessarily "unrecorded," but the controversial Tennessee general did seem to be "identified with the people"; Davis accordingly made the appointment. Pillow was to be a brigadier general and have charge of the defense of Tennessee, since that was what he was doing already. The president, however, had no intention of leaving Pillow to muddle along indefinitely in that vital command. Instead, he had in mind to place over Pillow a higher-ranking general who could supervise him and keep him from doing something foolish, such as undertaking any one of the innumerable half-baked offensives he had been clamoring to launch since taking command. This higher-ranking general would, of necessity, be a major general in order to have clear superiority over Pillow, and he would naturally be someone whom Davis could trust—someone, it turned out, like Leonidas Polk.

It is doubtful that Davis had had Polk in mind from the outset. The two had not kept in touch since leaving the military academy, and it is more likely Davis would have preferred to give the position to his other friend of West Point days, Albert Sidney Johnston. However, Johnston, now a brigadier general in the United States Army, was stationed in California, two or three months away in those days before the transcontinental railroad. Although Davis was not among those who thought the war might not last that long, there were certainly limits to the amount of time he was inclined to leave a man like Pillow unattended in one of the Confederacy's most sensitive commands. Polk was probably aware that Johnston was temporarily out of the picture when he wrote to Davis in mid-May, expressing concern over the vulnerability of the Mississippi Valley. "It seems to me that a man of the highest military character should be charged with our defenses. . . . In a word, what is wanted in the Valley is a head." He went on to suggest that the ideal man for this job would be "our old friend Gen'l Johnston." Finally, he concluded by offering his own services for whatever assignment Davis thought him qualified.[51] With all that Polk said, Davis was in complete agreement. But Johnston was in California, and Davis needed someone now. So it was that he turned to Leonidas Polk.

He wrote back to Polk, assuring him that for the time being there was no cause for alarm since the northerners would undoubtedly be deterred from advancing for several months by the heat of the southern summer. He concluded by saying, "It would gratify me very much to see you." Davis's motive behind this remark is not clear. He may have merely wanted to talk to a man he felt he could trust about the general attitude and morale of the people of the Mississippi Valley, or it may have occurred to him, as Polk had likely intended, to use the bishop in a military capacity.[52] Polk took no chances and hastened to Richmond with all due speed. His form—tall and of large build, with white hair and luxuriant white side whiskers framing a ruddy face that one observer characterized as "intellectual"—soon became a familiar sight, as he conferred with the president and popped in and out of the War Department, in keeping with his penchant for giving unsolicited advice on any and all subjects.[53] Polk dined with Davis and the members of the Confederate cabinet and also held several interviews with General Lee. He had at least two "long & full conversations" with the president and was very pleased with Davis's receptiveness and favorable reaction. "The interview," he confided in a letter to his wife, "will not be otherwise than productive of good results."[54] Those "good results," from Polk's point of view, became apparent on June 25, when he was issued official orders appointing him major general and assigning him to command a region comprising the Mississippi Valley from the northern border of Tennessee to the mouth of the Red River, opposite the point where the southern boundary of the state of Mississippi touched its namesake river, and the valley of the Tennessee River from the Tennessee-Kentucky line southward to a point well above the head of navigation at Florence, Alabama. His command also included West Tennessee, or that portion of the state between the Mississippi and the navigable portion of the Tennessee.[55]

The choice of what territory to include within the new command was a wise one. The Mississippi and Tennessee rivers were obvious avenues of invasion, veritable highways leading into the heart of the South, and it made sense to create a unified defense on both banks of each river. It also made sense to include West Tennessee in the department, since the rivers were close enough that a successful northern advance on either of them would outflank the defenses on the other.

Even the choice of Polk as commander had something to commend it. Davis believed, not entirely without foundation, that Polk's extensive travels as missionary bishop of the Southwest as well as his long residence in Louisiana had given him a broad familiarity with the Mississippi Valley region and a popularity there that would inspire the confidence and enthusiasm of the people of the region.[56] For temporary service in that special area, he might indeed have been useful. Though Davis was gambling on a man nearly devoid of military experience, perhaps, as Lincoln once remarked of another general, Polk would "fight well on his own dung hill."[57]

As the summer of 1861 faded and the South—its preliminary defensive dispositions in the West complete—awaited the northern onslaught, the overall performance of Jefferson Davis as commander in chief could be favorably assessed. The real test was yet to come, but the president had handled the preparations reasonably well. In the office of adjutant and inspector general as he envisioned it, he had endowed the Confederate army with a better system of high command than the United States Army had ever had before or would have until nearly the end of the century. He had recognized the need to take immediate steps for the defense of the crucial Mississippi River and the slightly less important but still vital Tennessee River. He had handled the division of territory into regional defensive departments wisely, keeping the defenses centered on the rivers and, in Tennessee where the defense of each river was dependent on the other, placing the two under a unified command.

In choosing generals to command these defenses, the president's performance had been considerably less impressive, though no irremediable mistakes had yet been made. Davis could be a good judge of military men, but he had one critical blind spot: The closer his personal association with the officer in question, the less reliable was his judgment. It was not that all his close associates were military incompetents. It was just that he was unwilling to admit that any of them could be. This failing in part led him to choose Cooper and Twiggs for positions neither was fit to fill. In these cases, however, the personal connection between Davis and the generals was superficial enough to allow Davis to recognize—if not accept blame for—his mistakes and correct them. This he did in the latter case by removing the unfit individual and in the former by quietly relegating Cooper and the innovative position of adjutant and inspector general to trivial duty—a solution that was of great detriment to the Confederate system of high command. Pillow's appointment was largely a political move, and Davis intended to limit the amount of damage that general could do by sending a responsible person to look after him. In Polk's appointment, though, the personal factor surfaced with a vengeance. Polk's qualifications were at best questionable, and if, like Cooper and Twiggs, he turned out to be incompetent, it was going to be much more difficult for the commander in chief to take the hard measures the Confederacy would need.

3

KENTUCKY

Leaving Richmond during the first week of July, Polk headed west to assume his command.[1] Having taken time out in Nashville to fire off a letter to Davis telling him how he ought to handle things in another section of Tennessee, Polk continued on to his own jurisdiction, arriving in mid-July and setting up his headquarters in Memphis.[2] News of his appointment had preceded him, and predictably, reaction in the Mississippi Valley had been mixed. Some of the letters coming into the War Department inquired when he would be there and intimated that there was not a moment to spare.[3] Others were less enthusiastic about the new commander, and their number included particularly the many admirers of Tennessee's homegrown hero, General Pillow. However, none was more disturbed at the supersession than Gideon J. Pillow himself.[4] In fact, he was outraged. Was he not a major general of the Tennessee forces commanding the entire army of the state of Tennessee? How then could Richmond presume to send someone to command him? Patiently, Secretary of War Walker explained that Polk was being sent to command the Confederate troops, not the Tennessee army.[5] This was true, but virtually all the troops in this area were part of the Tennessee army and had not yet been officially inducted into Confederate service. That being the case, it looked as if Polk would be without a command and Pillow would remain in charge of the Mississippi Valley defenses. The matter was presently cleared up when Tennessee's governor Isham G. Harris issued an order placing the Tennessee troops under Polk's command.[6]

Pillow, then, held the Confederate rank of brigadier, and Polk was his commanding officer. It was a situation that Pillow did not like at all, and he responded to it by harboring a smoldering resentment that flared into open feuding as the summer wore on.[7] The occasion was another of Pillow's ill-conceived schemes for the invasion of Missouri. Polk saw the folly of the idea belatedly, Pillow not at all, and the tension between them increased.[8] Within a few weeks Pillow had countermanded one of Polk's orders to a subordinate unit. When Polk had demanded an explanation, the Tennesseean had protested rather disingenuously that he "had no motive to gratify but to serve the country" and complained that he was "tied down and allowed no discretion." Polk replied that he would allow Pillow plenty of discretion so long as that officer did not "exceed [his] lawful authority."[9] The reply failed to satisfy Pillow and, in view of the course Polk was soon to take respecting his own superiors, was extremely ironic. In any case, the two generals would continue to bicker until

34

Pillow resigned in a huff that winter, only to change his mind and be given his commission back a few months later.[10]

In the meantime, Polk had to deal not only with an unwilling subordinate but also a political and military situation that was anomalous, to say the least. Between the states that styled themselves part of the southern confederacy and the solidly loyal free states of the North lay a band of slave states whose status was in dispute and whose populations were divided. Polk's sector fronted on two of these, Missouri and Kentucky. Both states were in the midst of internal struggles over which way they would cast their lots, but they were going about it in two radically different ways.

Shortly after Fort Sumter, Missouri secessionists had made plans to use the largely prosouthern state militia to seize the Federal arsenal in St. Louis and distribute the arms there to other secession-minded Missourians. With the southern faction in control militarily, the political formalities of secession could have been easily arranged. The plan was afoot and the militia assembled, but the Unionist Missourians and Federal authorities in the state got wind of the plot and, with help from Washington, raised a loyal home guard. In a surprise raid this outfit bagged most of the secessionist militia and chased the rest off toward the southwestern part of the state. Prosouthern Missourians, taking exception to the fact that men who had been scheming to storm a government arsenal, steal government arms, and shoot government soldiers had been treated as if they were committing treason against their government, began to retaliate with everything from bushwhacking to going off and joining the pro-Confederate Missouri forces under one of the state's most prominent citizens, Sterling Price. The fight for Missouri was on, wide open and very ugly, and the only certainties were that Missouri was up for grabs and some momentous things were going to be decided there in the next few months.[11]

Kentucky's fate was also in doubt, and its strategic importance was even greater than Missouri's. The state's government, like its people, was divided on the issue of secession, the governor favoring it while the legislature by and large opposed it. The result of this split was Kentucky's unprecedented course of declaring itself neutral between the Federal government and the rebellious states. Neither side, the state's government solemnly warned, would be allowed to send its troops onto Kentucky soil.

It was an entirely unrealistic decision; fighting was bound to spill over into Kentucky sooner or later. When it did, the state would have to choose one side or the other at least officially. Neutrality simply could not last, but while it lasted it was an incredible boon to the Confederacy. A neutral Kentucky, closed to invading Federal armies and stretching from the Appalachians in the East to the Mississippi in the West, would provide an impenetrable shield for the heartland of the South. The longer Kentucky stayed neutral, the greater its protective value would be, as northern armies built up and northern offensive ability grew. Furthermore, if Kentucky could be persuaded to come down solidly in the Confederate camp—if, say, some Federal commander would do the South the incalculable favor of marching his troops into the state, violating its neutrality and turning public opinion against the North—the South's independence would be a good deal closer. Lincoln believed the Union had to have Kentucky and remarked that "to lose Kentucky is nearly the same as to lose the whole game."[12] Davis too knew the importance of his native state, and both presidents strove to treat Kentucky with the utmost sensitivity.[13] Much was riding on which side made the first blunder.

This, then, was the situation that faced Davis's newly created major general Leonidas Polk. The new commander's attention was first drawn to Missouri, which had already been the scene of action and where it seemed a Confederate army with a resourceful leader could achieve the most. This was all the more true because any Confederate army intervention at all in Kentucky would be about as beneficial as a bull in a china shop.

By the end of July, Polk's troops had moved upstream and occupied the river town of New Madrid, Missouri.[14] Believing his forces were too weak to move into the interior of the state, he began inundating Richmond with requests for reinforcements, warning that Federal strength at Cairo at the southern tip of Illinois was increasing and that Missouri was about to be overrun.[15] Davis favored a campaign into Missouri, that being one of his main reasons for including the state in Polk's department, but he was taken aback by the general's requests for more troops. He had Cooper write Polk asking how many troops he had, what he was doing with them, and what he planned to do with all the troops he was asking for now.[16] By the time this correspondence had taken place, it was nearly the end of August, and Polk's attention had been attracted elsewhere.

New Madrid was a good place to erect fortifications to prevent Union gunboats, presently under construction near St. Louis, from descending the Mississippi River, and that was precisely what Polk had planned to do there since first occupying it back in July.[17] Now, though, his eyes were fixed on another Mississippi River town some sixty miles upstream via the serpentine meanderings of the river, which he considered an even better location for the batteries of heavy guns that would be needed to stop the Union gunboats. If he could only seize this town and fortify it before Union troops arrived, he thought he could defy all the gunboats and armies the North could muster to dislodge him. The town was Columbus, Kentucky.

The idea was not original with Polk. The state of Tennessee contained a considerable number of people who were extremely sensitive to the possibility of a Federal descent of the Mississippi. This group was centered on Memphis but had enough pull in Nashville to persuade the legislature to take some positive steps very early in the conflict. In April 1861, two weeks after the fall of Sumter, the Tennessee legislature voted to authorize Governor Harris, who was supervising the raising and organizing of a provisional state army prior to the state's official incorporation into the Confederacy, to send whatever aid he thought would be advisable for the purpose of holding Columbus against any possible Federal advance. As it turned out, Governor Harris did not think any aid was appropriate just then, since he had a healthy respect for the political consequences such an incursion would have on Kentucky neutrality and since all his plans for the defense of Tennessee would collapse without that neutrality.[18]

But while Harris might hesitate, Pillow would not. A politician by profession and inclination, he was quick to recognize and seize on a popular idea. Nor did it take him long to come up with a military reason for putting the idea into action. The country south of the Tennessee-Kentucky line was too hard to defend, he claimed; he had to have Columbus. In May he had dispatched a special messenger to the governor of Kentucky asking permission to occupy Columbus, permission which, under the circumstances, the governor did not dare grant. Pillow, anticipating this, had written to Davis explaining the situation as he saw it and warning that if the governor should withhold his consent, Pillow was just going to have to go ahead and "take the responsibility of acting on [his] own judgment."[19] Somehow Pillow was dissuaded from carrying out his rash plan, and Governor Harris, learning of the general's dangerous intent, cautioned him not to send troops into Kentucky or do anything else that would disturb that state's neutrality.[20] The danger was avoided, but this close call no doubt helped confirm Davis in his opinion that someone was going to have to be sent to supervise Pillow, an understandable precaution in view of the fact that any chief of state might well have had nightmares at the prospect of his country's policy being determined on the considered judgment of the likes of Gideon J. Pillow. Now, however, three months later, the man whom Davis had sent to rein in Pillow was about to revive one of Pillow's most nightmarish ideas.

After being rebuffed in his earlier designs on Kentucky in general and Columbus in particular, Pillow had directed his glory-hunting efforts toward Missouri and had hatched several foolhardy plans for exploits in that state. Squelched by Polk in that direction as well, Pillow had stewed for a time and contemplated what avenues showed the most promise of winning distinction for him. The result of these contemplations was a renewed interest in Columbus. Curiously—in view of the animosity between Pillow and Polk, as well as the fact that one of Polk's chief duties was to prevent Pillow from getting into exactly this sort of trouble—the Kentucky town was a temptation to which Polk also proved susceptible. Around the end of August, Pillow began pressuring Polk to allow the seizure of Columbus by Pillow's forces.[21] Little persuading was necessary, and Polk soon made the idea his own.

It is uncertain whether Davis would have approved Polk's idea of seizing Columbus, Kentucky, had he been notified in advance. Polk held Davis's confidence to an infinitely greater degree than Pillow, and it was a confidence no amount of bungling could shake. On August 28 Davis had responded to a letter from Kentucky's governor asking for a pledge of continued Confederate respect for Kentucky neutrality by assuring the governor that "the Government of the Confederate States of America neither intends nor desires to disturb the neutrality of Kentucky." However, there had been rumors that Kentucky was allowing its Unionist citizens to organize and drill themselves as home-guard units and to receive arms from north of the Ohio River—although actually both factions were playing at this game.[22] Davis had heard the rumors and considered such activity to be a breach of neutrality. In his letter to the governor he had sternly warned that "neutrality, to be entitled to respect, must be strictly observed between both parties."[23] Perhaps Davis would have looked at the matter of occupying Columbus somewhat differently at the end of August than he had in the middle of May. In any case he was not going to be given a chance to express himself on the issue until the occupation was an accomplished fact.

Things in Kentucky seemed to be heading for a crisis; and one way or the other, neutrality did not appear to have long to last. At the moment, that appeared to be good news for the Confederacy. On August 30 the Federal commander for the western region, former pathfinder and presidential candidate John Charles Fremont, had made an ill-advised proclamation in which he had essentially declared an end to slavery in the area of his command and had threatened to hang rebels taken in arms.[24] It was not an announcement calculated to win the hearts of undecided Kentuckians, of which there were still a great number. As if that were not enough, Fremont ordered one of his subordinates, an unprepossessing brigadier general by the name of U. S. Grant, to take some troops and seize Columbus.[25] Had Fremont sat down and contrived a scheme to drive Kentucky into the arms of the Confederacy, he could hardly have done better.

Once word of Fremont's actions spread around, Kentucky might very well have declared for the South and invited Confederate armies into the state to protect it from the northern intruders and their bloodthirsty abolitionist leader. There might have been some Unionists in the Kentucky legislature, but there were certainly no abolitionists. In the political maelstrom that would have followed a Federal "invasion" of the state, those still ambivalent would very likely have stampeded to join the prosouthern faction, and even the strongest Unionists might have wavered in their determination. With Kentucky in the Confederate fold, the South's position would have been enormously strengthened. Invited by Kentucky's government, Polk could have marched into the state at the head of an army of liberation, to be welcomed and joined by the populace. With this in mind, Tennessee governor Harris, who was deeply involved in the political maneuvering to bring Kentucky into the Confederacy, fired off a telegram to Polk on September 2, recommending he not send any of his troops into the interior of Missouri just now but maintain them all in readiness pending the outcome of events in Kentucky.[26] If Polk could leave well enough alone for a few more days, Confederate victory might be much closer without a battle being fought.

Polk could not. He had no doubt been casting lustful eyes on Columbus for some time when, around the end of August, Grant's force had appeared at the little town of Belmont, Missouri, directly across the river from Columbus. Polk became alarmed, believing correctly that the Federals intended to occupy Columbus in the near future.[27] On September 1, duplicating Pillow's method, he sent a note to the governor of Kentucky. It was "of the greatest consequence to the Southern cause in Kentucky or elsewhere," he explained, "that I should be ahead of the enemy in occupying Columbus and Paducah."[28] Paducah was another Kentucky town even farther north than Columbus, located on the Ohio River at the mouth of the Tennessee. Its position gave it great strategic importance, since whoever controlled it could block access to the Tennessee River. Unless the Confederates could find some way of preventing Union forces from ascending the Tennessee, Columbus would be worthless, since Union forces on the Tennessee could easily outflank it. Polk made his plans to take both towns, Columbus first, then Paducah.

On September 3 his plan was put into action. Confederate troops under General Pillow boarded steamers at New Madrid and proceeded up the Mississippi as far as Hickman, Kentucky. There, in order to avoid Grant's batteries on the west bank of the river at Belmont, they landed and marched the remaining twenty miles or so to Columbus.[29] They found the town unoccupied by any other military force, set up camp, and began to dig in.

The operation had been a complete success. At the same time it was one of the most decisive catastrophes the Confederacy ever suffered. Kentucky's neutrality had been resoundingly flaunted. A Confederate army had not only entered Kentucky territory, it had possessed itself of a Kentucky town and was busily setting up fortifications there as if it intended to remain on a permanent basis—which indeed it did. With the demise of Kentucky neutrality went whatever profit the Confederacy might have reaped from the blunders of Fremont. As if all that were not enough, Polk, having occupied Columbus, was slow in seizing Paducah, and U. S. Grant, a man who understood the importance of rapid movements, beat him there and seized the town, making Columbus a worthless position that had to fall whenever the North got around to pushing on its exposed flank.[30]

Polk felt some regret at having missed Paducah, but none at the havoc he had wreaked with the Confederacy's interests in Kentucky by his high-handed seizure of Columbus. In fact, writing from that town on September 14, he told Davis, "I believe, if we could have found a respectable pretext, it would have been better to have seized this place some months ago." Kentucky, Polk explained, "was fast melting away under the influence of the Lincoln government," and only Polk's bold advance into the state had halted this alarming process.[31]

Throughout the planning and execution of the Columbus movement, Polk had kept the Richmond authorities completely in the dark, probably because he was afraid Davis would have vetoed the scheme had he known about it. Indeed, as Polk was preparing his movement, Davis was writing the general a letter taking him to task about some rumors that had reached Richmond regarding the direction of affairs in Missouri and admonishing him to "keep me better advised of your forces and purposes."[32]

When news of Polk's movement finally reached Richmond, the response of the Confederate high command was hesitant and confused. The incident did not come at a favorable moment for Davis, who had been sick for most of the summer. In May he was reported to be sick with "a chill."[33] In July it was noted that he was "in wretched health," overworked, overanxious and apparently suffering from neuralgia.[34] In August he was described as having an "attack of ague," and for a time his health was a matter of "some apprehension" around Richmond.[35] Although he was thought to be on the mend by late August, he confided as late as September, the day before Polk's move, that for some time he had been too sick even to write a letter.[36] In essence the Confederacy had been virtually without a commander in chief during much of the summer of 1861.

Still, none of this could account fully for the tentative, wavering manner in which Davis ultimately handled Polk's adventure. News of the movement first reached Richmond on September 5, two days after the event, in a telegram sent to the president the previous day by Tennessee governor Isham G. Harris. Harris was aghast at what Polk had done, rightly seeing in it the doom of all his efforts to woo the Kentuckians into the Confederacy. The presence of Confederate troops in Kentucky would "injure our cause in the State," he wrote. "Would it not be well to order their immediate withdrawal?"[37] Davis realized at once that the governor was right. On his copy of the telegram he wrote a quick note to Secretary of War Walker: "Telegraph promptly to Genl Polk to withdraw troops from K[entuck]y & explain movement." In answer to Harris, Walker was to "inform him of [Davis's] action [in ordering the withdrawal of Polk's troops] & that the movement was unauthorized." Finally, Davis instructed Walker to "ask Gov. Harris to communicate to [Kentucky] Gov. [Beriah] Magoffin," to assure him that Polk's movement did not represent a deliberate Confederate violation of his state's proclaimed neutrality.[38] The secretary of war did as he had been ordered and quickly got off telegrams to Polk and Harris.[39]

Meanwhile, on September 4, the same day of his telegram to Davis, Governor Harris had sent a similar one to Polk himself. Hinting that perhaps the whole thing had been Pillow's doing and thus no fault of Polk's, Harris said it was "unfortunate," since "the President and myself are pledged to respect the neutrality of Kentucky." Could not the troops be removed?[40] Polk responded the same day. Pillow had acted on his orders, he wrote, and he himself had been acting "under the plenary powers delegated to me by the President." Just when or whether Davis might have granted Polk "plenary powers" remains unclear, but if he did at all it would have been strangely out of character for a president so jealous of his prerogatives and so punctilious about delegating any authority he believed the constitution required him to exercise himself. Polk went on to state that the troops would not be withdrawn. In a final gratuitous flourish he added that he had never "received official information" that the Confederacy was pledged to respect Kentucky's neutrality.[41] If this was not an outright lie it was certainly a first cousin to one. Whether or not he had ever received an "official" notice of it, there can be no disputing that Polk knew what Davis's policy was regarding Kentucky.

Probably realizing that Harris would also contact Davis, Polk decided to send the president a telegram of his own to justify his actions. Sent on September 4, it arrived in Richmond on the fifth, although apparently later in the day than Harris's dispatch. In content it was much the same as the one Polk had sent the Tennessee governor, mentioning "plenary power" and military necessity and proclaiming, "It is my intention now to continue to occupy and keep this position."[42] Reading this telegram, Davis seemingly began to lose his resolve. The good judgment and decisiveness with which he had at first responded gave way to hesitance and uncertainty. Harris was right: Polk's presence in Kentucky was a political disaster. But what if Polk was also right and his presence was at the same time a military necessity? It was for the president to decide which should take precedence. But he did not. Instead, he left the decision to Polk. "The necessity must justify the action," he telegraphed in reply.[43] The move was acceptable, that is, but only if it was really necessary. With Polk deciding on the necessity of the matter, there could be little doubt as to the outcome. The president's irresolute course, along with some of the confusion it spawned, was inadvertently summed up by an addled War Department clerk who wrote in his diary a week later, "Gen. Pillow had advanced, and occupied Columbus, Ky. He was ordered, by telegraph, to abandon the town and return to his former position. Then the order was countermanded, but he remains."[44]

The War Department itself was in a state of flux. For some time Davis had been working on easing Secretary Walker out of his cabinet. By September 16, the Confederacy had a new secretary of war, Judah P. Benjamin of Louisiana, lately attorney general of the Confederacy. Benjamin knew no more of military matters than did Walker, but he was highly efficient and intelligent. He also seemed to have a talent for ruffling the feathers of generals, and within a few months he would nearly drive "Stonewall" Jackson out of the army.[45] Yet he could be most charming—his enemies said ingratiating—and he had been making a point of cultivating the favor of Jefferson Davis. The same clerk who had commented on the government's handling of the Columbus affair had also noted Benjamin as a frequent and sociable visitor around the department's offices and observed in his diary that should Benjamin actually become secretary of war he would "have a great influence with the President, for he had studied his character most carefully."[46]

Benjamin would be a better secretary of war than Walker, though by no means the Confederacy's best. He would run his department in a businesslike and efficient manner and have a modest input in strategic decision making.[47] Yet even had he taken office a fortnight earlier and thus been secretary at the time of Polk's advance into Kentucky, he could hardly have handled the matter any differently than Walker. The secretary of war had carried out Davis's orders promptly and to the letter. None of the mistakes could be laid to his charge, nor had he created confusion by attempting to impose his will against that of his superior.

It was September 8, five days after the occupation of Columbus, before Polk finally got around to writing Kentucky's governor, who by this time must have also been somewhat bewildered. Admitting that he should have written earlier, Polk lamely professed that he had not had time. He gave his stock justification for the affair and concluded by promising that his Confederate troops would leave Kentucky if the Federals did so simultaneously. If this occurred, Polk promised that they would not be back unless the Federals came back first—an offer which, all things considered, could not have impressed the governor very much.[48]

To add to the chaos, Adjutant and Inspector General Cooper, probably acting at Davis's behest, telegraphed Brig. Gen. Felix K. Zollicoffer, who commanded a small Confederate force that was maintaining the rebel government's authority in the strongly Unionist area of East Tennessee. Cooper instructed that the Federal occupation of Paducah (in response to Polk's move on Columbus) had violated Kentucky neutrality and that it was now permissible for Zollicoffer to move his troops into that state.[49] Zollicoffer promptly made preparations to do so, to the utter distraction of those Tennesseeans and prosouthern Kentuckians who were still angling to get Kentucky to secede.

One such Kentuckian was Simon Bolivar Buckner. Buckner, the son of a War of 1812 veteran, was born in a Kentucky log cabin in 1823 and entered West Point a little over seventeen years later. As a cadet he studied hard, behaved himself, and excelled in fencing. Ranking eleventh of the twenty-five graduates of 1844, the young Kentuckian went on to serve in the Mexican War, where he was slightly wounded and won two brevets. After the war Buckner taught infantry tactics for several years at West Point before resigning his commission in 1855. He went into private business, first in Chicago—where his northern wife had inherited valuable real estate and where Buckner rose to the rank of major in the Illinois militia—and later in Louisville, Kentucky.[50] In the summer of 1861 Buckner's "business" became preparing for war. He was at present brigadier general and commander of the Kentucky State Guard, a force of four thousand solidly pro-Confederate militia currently drilling and organizing inside Kentucky and ready to go into Confederate service as soon as the cloak of their state's neutrality was thrown off.[51]

Simon Bolivar Buckner (National Archives)

Buckner himself was a self-consciously chivalrous man, brave, generous, intelligent, and loyal to what he considered to be his duty. He judged others
by the same knightly standards he prided himself on maintaining, and if in
his eyes they fell short, his attitude toward them might turn less than courteous. This mindset led him to place an inordinate amount of value on style,
so that a smooth and polished person could expect Buckner's favorable opinion
much sooner than a rough and tactless one, regardless of which one had the
truth of the matter on his side. This was to become significant later in the war.

During the weeks preceding the Columbus affair, while both North and
South maneuvered to win the favor of Kentuckians, Buckner had received two
offers of commissions in the United States Army. The first came from general
in chief Winfield Scott. The second, on August 17, came from Secretary of
War Cameron by order of Lincoln himself and was an offer of a commission
as brigadier general. Buckner turned both down. Though all his property lay
in Kentucky or in the North, he was firmly committed to the South.[52] It was
a stand that had cost him much already and that would cost him a great deal
more if Kentucky went the wrong way.

Consequently, Buckner was appalled when he learned what Polk had done.
In late August Buckner had been to Richmond to discuss the Kentucky situation with the Confederate authorities. It is not clear whether he had a face-to-
face meeting with Jefferson Davis during this time, but on September 3 he
did hand in a memorandum for Davis requesting various forms of Confederate
aid, particularly arms, for his Kentucky State Guard. A reply was sent to Buckner in Richmond by Adjutant and Inspector General Cooper, no doubt on
orders from Davis, suggesting that Polk and Zollicoffer might be of some help,
although not with arms since the Confederacy had none to spare. Apparently
Buckner was also assured that a high-ranking commission would be waiting
for him as soon as political circumstances would allow. Barely a week later
Buckner was back in Kentucky amid drastically altered conditions. The fat was
in the fire now; and Buckner hastened to write to Richmond, hinting broadly
that "no political necessity now exists for withholding a commission, if one
is intended for me."[53] He was also concerned about the way Kentucky neutrality
had been ended and feared that Polk's clumsiness would cause this soon-to-be-
divided state to divide on terms highly favorable to the North. In a letter to
the Richmond authorities written September 13, he pleaded for a withdrawal
of Confederate forces, saying it would make possible the rallying of thousands
of Kentuckians to the Confederate standard. Without Paducah, he astutely
pointed out, Columbus was worthless. Why not abandon it, stop Zollicoffer's
movement, and point to the Federals as the disturbers of Kentucky's peace?
Whatever military advantage was given up, Buckner argued, would be more
than offset by political factors.[54] To Buckner's entreaty, as well as to Governor
Harris's renewed pleas, Davis could reply only that the move had been presented to him as a military necessity and that if the troops could be safely

withdrawn now, he would approve it.[55] He doubted that this could be done and, in a letter to Polk, confided, "We cannot permit indeterminant quantities, the political elements, to control our action in cases of military necessity." Military factors must take priority over political ones. Besides, he believed, Polk's offer to match a Union withdrawal ought to be enough to satisfy neutrality-minded Kentuckians.[56] In any case by this time, more than a week after Polk's occupation of Columbus, it was too late to salvage Kentucky, and Davis probably knew it.

Although the chief blame must rest on Polk, Davis's indirect role in the debacle that may have cost the Confederacy Kentucky and its best chance of final victory was nonetheless decisive. Forced by political pressure to appoint an incompetent general—Pillow—he had allowed himself to be so blinded by past friendship as to appoint an equally incompetent and even more headstrong general—Polk—to keep the first out of trouble. He had failed, partially because of his ill health, to monitor adequately the actions and intentions of these generals. When the fateful advance into Kentucky was made, he had let slip whatever fleeting chance he may have had to salvage the situation there by disclaiming the movement and ordering an immediate withdrawal. He had allowed a lame argument of tactical military necessity to govern a strategic political decision of vital importance, even though he was the only man in the country whose position enabled—and required—him to weigh military against political considerations. He had permitted his course to be plotted by the decision of a general who, even had he been competent, was in such a position that he could see only a narrow and incomplete view of the total situation. Worst of all, despite the disaster in Kentucky, he retained Leonidas Polk in his command and maintained his confidence in him.

It was a dismal performance, and the South would suffer for it. Yet all was not lost, and as the autumn of 1861 approached, Davis and many other southerners suddenly found reason to hope that Confederate fortunes would soon improve. During the hot months of summer a rider had crossed the deserts of the Southwest, traversing the continent from Los Angeles to Richmond. On September 5, 1861, the second day after Polk's men had seized Columbus, he called at the Confederate White House, where the president, still very sick, lay in bed in an upstairs room.[57] The sunburned caller was informed of the president's indisposition and asked to return at another time, but Jefferson Davis, recognizing the firm voice and steady tread in the hallway below, bounded out of his sickbed and raced down the stairs to greet his old friend. Albert Sidney Johnston had arrived.[58]

4

THE COMING OF ALBERT SIDNEY JOHNSTON

Like Davis, Albert Sidney Johnston was a native of Kentucky. Though Johnston was five years older than Davis, the two became good friends when both were attending Transylvania University. They were again comrades at West Point, where Johnston was two classes ahead of Davis. Johnston was a very impressive cadet. For most of his time at the academy, he ranked second in his class, and since the first-ranked cadet was bookish and disliked responsibility, Johnston received the coveted position of adjutant of the corps of cadets. Though a senior math final, which unfortunately consisted of the only two problems in the course he could not solve, dropped him in the class standings from second to eighth, he was nevertheless held in high esteem by both his instructors and his classmates, all of whom considered him likely to go far in the military profession.[1] An inch over six feet in height, of powerful build and striking appearance, he looked to be the very model of a dashing officer. His commanding presence, added to his intelligence and decisiveness, made him one to whom others naturally turned for leadership.

After graduation Johnston served with competence in the Black Hawk War. Then in 1834, after eight years in the army, he resigned his commission in order to spend more time with his ailing wife. Two years later, after his wife had finally succumbed to tuberculosis and the "expert" medical treatment of that day, the thirty-three-year-old widower set off for Texas to help the newborn republic sustain the freedom it had recently won at San Jacinto. Enlisting as a private, Johnston rose rapidly through the ranks and within a year became commanding general of the Texas army. Thereafter he served a two-year stint as the Lone Star Republic's secretary of war. In this capacity he gained valuable experience in directing fractious volunteer armies as well as in defending a vast frontier with woefully inadequate resources.[2]

By the time Texas was annexed to the United States, Johnston had come to consider the Lone Star State his home. Annexation made a Texas army superfluous, so Johnston sought help from his old friend Jefferson Davis, now a United States congressman from Mississippi, in obtaining the post of colonel of a regiment of the regular United States Army[3] Davis would have been glad to help, but events made his aid unnecessary. Within months of Johnston's writing to Davis, war broke out with Mexico. Soon Johnston was colonel of a regiment of Texas volunteers. Unfortunately, the Texans had been allowed to enlist for a very short period, and before they had seen any action, their term of enlistment expired. Not even Johnston's rare skill in handling volunteer

Albert Sidney Johnston (Library of Congress)

troops was of any avail: The men could be persuaded neither to reenlist nor to extend ther terms. They wanted to go home; and go home they did, leaving their erstwhile colonel without a command.[4] Johnston was too valuable an officer to remain unemployed in time of war. Gen. Zachary Taylor, commanding the American army advancing across the Rio Grande into Mexico, was so impressed with Johnston that on several occasions in later years he expressed the opinion that Albert Sidney Johnston was "the best soldier he had ever commanded."[5] Taylor promptly found employment for Johnston as inspector general of all the volunteer troops in the army. Once again Johnston's role required him to deal extensively with the temperamental American citizen-soldier.

At Monterrey, where Col. Jefferson Davis led his Mississippi Rifles in storming Mexican forts, Johnston too was in the thick of the fighting. When the commander of the volunteer division fell, Johnston supplied the needed leadership, at one point rallying troops who had panicked in the face of charging Mexican lancers and by his conspicuous courage and commanding presence inspiring them to turn and beat off the Mexican attack.[6] Several times during the battle, Davis and Johnston worked together, and the Mississippian was greatly impressed by Johnston's bravery and presence of mind. It was also at Monterrey, after the battle, that the two men made their tension-filled ride into town to pick up the signed instrument of surrender.

After his service in the Mexican War, Johnston tried his hand at planting and for three years worked hard to carve a paying plantation from the Texas prairie. Financial difficulties ultimately forced him to sell the farm and, though he had hoped for an appointment to an army command, accept the post of paymaster for the forts on the Texas frontier. The new job involved traveling thousands of miles every year, transporting tens of thousands of dollars in gold along an outlaw- and Indian-infested frontier. It was an arduous and unrewarding task, and by 1855, Johnston was more than ready to accept the commission offered him by Secretary of War Jefferson Davis as colonel of the newly formed Second Cavalry. Among Johnston's subordinates in the regiment were Lt. Col. Robert E. Lee, Maj. William J. Hardee, captains Earl Van Dorn and Edmund Kirby Smith, and Lt. John Bell Hood.[7]

For two years Johnston's task was once again to defend the far-flung Texas frontier from the depredations of the Comanches. This task he considered could best be accomplished by taking the initiative. It would be folly, he knew, to scatter his troopers along the frontier at every point the Indians might strike or to have them wait in their forts until the damage was done and then go dashing off to wear out their horses in pursuit of raiders who were already long gone by the time word of their depredations reached the army posts. Instead, he would take the war to the Indians, relentlessly tracking down marauding bands of Kiowas and Comanches.[8] It was an effective strategy, and Johnston's reputation continued to grow. In 1857 he was detached from the regiment and ordered to lead an army expedition to assert national authority over the rebellious Mormons in Utah. This assignment brought him a brevet promotion to the rank of brigadier general as well as a great deal of difficult and frustrating service. Johnston met the demanding task with intelligence and energy, and by 1860, when he gave up the Utah command for a brief rest before assuming direction of the Pacific Coast department, his renown had soared to even greater heights. Many considered him the army's best general and a likely heir to the aging general in chief Winfield Scott.

He had exercised his new command but a few months when the secession of his adopted state, Texas, prompted him to resign his commission.[9] This he did despite a telegram from Washington offering him chief command of the entire United States Army second only to Scott. The offer had first been made to Robert E. Lee, who had declined it.[10] Johnston too declined the offer, for though he regretted secession, he felt he could never bear arms against his own state and people. His thoughts at first were of remaining in California and retiring to civilian life, but news of Sumter and the subsequent calls to arms touched his southern sympathies and roused his fighting spirit. He determined to go east and cast his lot with the Confederacy. Perhaps his old friend Jefferson Davis could find a place for him as a colonel or brigadier general in the new Confederate army.[11]

The normal way of traveling from the west coast to the east would have been by ship from San Francisco or Los Angeles, sailing either around Cape Horn at the southern tip of South America or to the Isthmus of Panama, crossing that narrow strip of land by any one of several methods and then reembarking in another ship on the Atlantic side. Either way one would eventually land at a port city on the East Coast. For Johnston, though, as an officer on his way to join those already in arms against the United States, this route was out of the question. He would almost certainly have fallen into the hands of a government that was not at all amused at being so used by the officers whose training it had provided. There remained, then, only the arduous and dangerous overland route.

On June 16, 1861, Johnston rode out of Los Angeles headed east. On the other side of the continent, in Richmond, an ambitious Anglican bishop named Polk was beginning to be in evidence around the War Department offices and the Confederate White House. In New Orleans the decrepit Twiggs had had two weeks to settle into his new assignment and still possessed at least a fair amount of the confidence of the governor and people of Louisiana. At the other end of the Confederacy's long segment of the Mississippi, Tennessee's very own Gideon J. Pillow had for a full month been ruminating on what to do about a Kentucky town named Columbus, which stood on some high bluffs along the Mississippi. And while all this was going on, Albert Sidney Johnston, former general-in-chief of the Army of the Republic of Texas and lately brevet brigadier general of the regular United States Army, rode steadily across the scorching Mojave Desert.

Before leaving California, Johnston had been joined by a small group of southern men also on their way to stand by their states in the struggle now beginning. Although at fifty-eight he was by far the oldest of their number, he had no trouble handling the demanding pace they kept up over all kinds of terrain. His years of riding up and down the Texas frontier as army pay-master stood him in good stead on that score. Their route took them through Apache country, and twice they stumbled upon the gruesome remains of stagecoach massacres. There was another reason they dared not allow their vigilance to lapse for a moment; United States troops at several forts along the trail had been alerted that the former high-ranking general on his way to join the rebels would be passing through the country, and patrols were out scour-ing the desert for any sign of Johnston and his friends. The nature of the land they had to cross provided obstacles of its own. In the desert there were dry crossings of as much as seventy miles between water holes.[12]

Back east news of Johnston's approach had preceded him. In the North bets were being placed as to whether he would get through, and in the South, he was anxiously awaited. Just eight days after Johnston had ridden out of Los Angeles, Robert E. Lee, his former lieutenant colonel in the Second Cavalry and now a full general of the Confederate army, wrote to his wife: "I hear that my old colonel, A. S. Johnston, is crossing the plains from California."[13] By August 11 South Carolina's governor Pickens had heard that Johnston and his party had crossed the Colorado River at Yuma, Arizona, on July 1, and he thought the news important enough to pass on to Davis, along with the estimate that Johnston would reach San Antonio by September 1.[14] Actually, Johnston and his men were traveling much faster than Pickens imagined. They entered Confederate territory at El Paso, Texas, and Johnston continued across the state and through Louisiana to New Orleans, then finally on to Richmond. He arrived there on September 5, just as the neutrality and possible coopera-tion of his native state of Kentucky were being fumbled away, the Confederate high command was in shambles, and the president ill.[15] His arrival was most welcome.

Davis, of course, was ecstatic. He believed, with good reason, that the com-ing of Albert Sidney Johnston was the best possible thing that could have hap-pened to the Confederacy. Years later Davis expressed his feelings in regard to Johnston's arrival: "He came and by his accession I felt strengthened, knowing a great support had thereby been added to the Confederate cause. . . . I hoped and expected that I had others who would prove generals; but I knew I had one, and that was Sidney Johnston."[16] Davis was not alone in his favorable opinion of Johnston. As Johnston had made his way through the South to Richmond, he had been met everywhere by cheering crowds. Newspapers were filled with his praises.[17]

Just as there was a consensus on his virtue, there was agreement on where he could best serve the cause. On August 28 Polk, always ready with an opinion, had written a letter to Davis stating: "I have now had ample opportunity to judge of the field you have assigned me, as well as of the fields around me, which had been assigned to other officers." He observed that what was really needed was an overall commander for the entire western theater and that the only man for the job was their mutual friend Albert Sidney Johnston.[18] On September 9 a Memphis citizens' committee had petitioned that Johnston be given the western command.[19] On the thirteenth Buckner had suggested the same, and on the fifteenth, Sen. G. A. Henry of Tennessee added his recommendation.[20] Davis needed none of this advice. Johnston, he felt, was especially well suited for command in the West.[21] He was a native of Kentucky and longtime resident of Texas. He had extensive experience with the rugged individualists who would be molded into western armies, and he showed every indication of possessing the genius and resolution that would enable him to hold his own though outnumbered. After his arrival in Richmond, Johnston met with Davis several times during the following days to discuss his new assignment. For the first time Johnston learned that he was to be a full general in the Confederate army. When told he was to serve in the West, Johnston seemed as pleased at the prospect as everyone else in the Confederacy.[22]

On September 10 official orders were issued assigning Johnston to the command of a huge area that would include the Confederate states of Tennessee and Arkansas, the western part of Mississippi, and the border states of Kentucky, Missouri, and Kansas. For good measure the Indian Territory was thrown in too. In essence, Johnston was being given everything in the West except for the coastal defense. The orders suggested that he set up his headquarters at Memphis but gave him leave to move it at will. He was authorized to call on the governors of Arkansas, Tennessee, and Mississippi for new levies of troops and to accept whatever volunteers might come in from Kentucky and Missouri.[23] The arrangement was a good one. The West needed a single commander to coordinate defensive efforts from the Appalachians to the Great Plains, and Davis's new structure provided just that for all of the northward-facing defenses. Very likely Davis had had this arrangement in mind for some time, perhaps since first considering the problem of the Confederacy's western defenses. He had delayed implementing the system of unified command for the excellent reason that until the arrival of Johnston, he had no one qualified to exercise such command.

As Davis prepared to put his system into operation, the full import of the situation in Kentucky had not yet become apparent in far-off Richmond. Davis was still thinking in terms of a neutral Kentucky sheltering the Deep South from the Appalachians to the Mississippi. Military action in the West meant Missouri, and it was there that Davis expected Johnston to direct most of his attention.[24] However, no sooner had Johnston left Richmond than it became apparent he was entering a vastly altered situation. On September 13 Davis received a telegram from Polk notifying him that on the previous day the Kentucky legislature had passed a resolution ordering the Confederate troops out of the state.[25] The resolution also requested northern troops to move in and help drive the Confederates out.[26]

Davis realized that some final decision would have to be made regarding Confederate policy toward Kentucky, and he believed Johnston was the man to make it. On September 13, after the general had left Richmond, Davis sent him a supplementary order, directing him to travel to his new headquarters by way of Nashville, where he would "confer with Governor Harris, and after learning the facts, political and military," determine whether to send more troops into Kentucky or withdraw the ones already there.[27] It was also understood that he would stop in East Tennessee and confer with General Zollicoffer regarding the best course for that officer to take.[28]

Davis's dispatch caught up with Johnston at Chattanooga, and characteristically, he wasted no time coming to a decision. He had already conferred with Zollicoffer at Knoxville and had ordered him to occupy Cumberland Gap, Kentucky, the northern gateway to East Tennessee. Continuing on to Nashville, Johnston met with Governor Harris and quickly and sensibly decided that all the political aspects had been settled by the action of Kentucky's legislature. Neutrality being a thing of the past, military considerations might as well prevail. Militarily, the pressing need on the Nashville front was to occupy the strategic south-central Kentucky town of Bowling Green. Johnston had heard (erroneously, it turned out) that Polk was about to seize Paducah.[29] If that occurred, the western end of Johnston's three-hundred mile line east of the Mississippi would be secure. With Zollicoffer holding Cumberland Gap, the only feasible path of invasion for a northern army would be down the railroad that connected Louisville and Nashville. The best place to stop such a drive was Bowling Green.

Having arrived at this decision, Johnston acted on it immediately. Gathering what troops he could find around Nashville, he placed them under the command of Kentuckian Simon B. Buckner and sent them hurrying up the railroad to Bowling Green. Buckner still did not have a Confederate commission, being officially nothing more than brigadier general of the Kentucky State Guard, and Johnston had to commit the irregularity of appointing him a brigadier general of Confederate troops pending the president's approval.[30] Johnston need not have worried; Buckner's presidential appointment was already on the way.[31] By September 18 Buckner, irregular commission and all, had established his force of 4,000 men at Bowling Green.[32]

After staying a few days in Nashville, Johnston hastened to Columbus, inspecting the defensive arrangements Polk had made there and finding that far from advancing on Paducah, the bishop-general was fearful of an enemy force that was supposed to be advancing on Columbus from Paducah and was calling on Richmond for reinforcements.[33] Although Polk was wrong in believing that blue-coated hordes were about to descend on Columbus, he was right about one thing: He needed more men. In fact, every commander along Johnston's extended line needed more men. The weakness of the Confederate defenses, suddenly exposed by Kentucky's entrance into the war, was almost overwhelming, or would have been to a lesser man than Johnston.

Under his command were Zollicoffer and his 4,000 men at Cumberland Gap, Buckner with another 4,000 at Bowling Green, and Polk with 11,000 at Columbus.[34] There were also a few men garrisoning two new forts, Henry on the Tennessee River and Donelson on the Cumberland, just south of the Tennessee-Kentucky line. Then there were the Missourian Sterling Price and his 10,000 men, now in Confederate service, in the southwestern part of that state, and Brig. Gen. William J. Hardee with a small force in northeastern Arkansas. Altogether Johnston had less than 40,000 men to cover his vast front.[35] The enemy had more than 90,000 and was receiving new troops at a faster rate than he was.[36]

Johnston was painfully aware of his vulnerable situation and took what steps he could to remedy it. While still in Nashville, he had made a speech to a large crowd and addressed his listeners as "soldiers," explaining that he did so because they were all soldiers of the reserve corps—a strong hint that greater demands would have to be made on the manpower resources of the South.[37] In a more direct step, Johnston, writing from Nashville, had warned Davis that he had "not over half" the troops that would be necessary.[38] For the time being, though, Richmond considered it had no troops to spare.

By the time he had reached Columbus and conferred with Polk, Johnston was even more convinced that something needed to be done about his lack of troops. He decided to use the authority granted to him in his original orders and called on the governors of Arkansas, Tennessee, and Mississippi for troops, but the results were not encouraging. The recruits were slow to arrive and much fewer than requested. To top it off, the ever-helpful Secretary of War Benjamin rebuked Johnston for requesting troops from Mississippi, there being some trivial political reason against it. Johnston ordered Hardee and his small force from northeastern Arkansas to join Buckner at Bowling Green, but otherwise there seemed little he could do in the short run to strengthen his front in Kentucky.[39]

Yet the shortage of manpower paled in comparison to the shortage of weapons. The problem afflicted all parts of the Confederacy, and neither Johnston nor Davis nor anyone else could do very much to alleviate it. Confederate agents in Europe frantically tried to buy up all the arms they could to be slipped through the blockade if possible. An arms factory in Richmond turned out 1,000 rifles per month.[40] In Tennessee, Governor Harris appealed to the populace to bring in their private weapons to be bought by the state and issued to soldiers, and the legislature passed laws for the impressment of private arms and compensation of the owners.[41] Ordnance works, a factory making percussion caps, various other arms-related workshops, and a powder mill turning out four hundred pounds of gunpowder per day were established at Nashville. However, all this proved inadequate to arm the enormous numbers of troops the Confederacy needed, and throughout the fall months of 1861 large portions of Johnston's troops remained unarmed or armed with obsolete and inadequate flintlock smooth-bore muskets.[42]

The situation might have been better had Davis fully realized the extent of the need in the western theater of the war. Certain organizational peculiarities in the way the "Provisional Army" of the state of Tennessee had been set up before Tennessee had officially joined the Confederacy and while Governor Harris was still supervising its military preparations led to a gross overestimation in the number of troops available. Johnston had straightened out the inconsistencies and knew how many men he had, but apparently some misconceptions still prevailed in Richmond.[43] Besides that, Governor Harris's entire design for the defense of Tennessee, as well as his calculations as to how many regiments Tennessee could spare for service in Virginia, had been based on the assumption of Kentucky neutrality. The defenses had been concentrated in the Mississippi Valley, while the rest of Tennessee's long northern border had been neglected.[44] Johnston had been quick to recognize and react to the situation created by Polk's self-willed blundering, but covering that much extra ground meant stretching his line a good deal thinner than anyone in Richmond could conceive just then. In fairness to Davis, he was faced with pressures and distractions sufficient to explain his slighting of occurrences several hundred miles from the capital. His attention and concern were becoming more and more caught up in military affairs in Virginia, where Gen. George B. McClellan was preparing a huge Union advance on Richmond. Though the president never forgot the western theater and never totally neglected it, he failed to accord it the top priority it deserved and required. His proximity to the Virginia front caused him to lose his perspective on the war as a whole.

Another reason for Davis's lack of attention to the West, ironically, was his tremendous confidence in Albert Sidney Johnston. Referring to Johnston years later, Davis wrote, "So great was my confidence in his capacity for organization and administration, that I felt, when he was assigned to the Department of the West, that the undeveloped power of that region would be made sufficient not only for its own safety, but to contribute support if need be to the more seriously threatened East."[45] Johnston was a great man, a great leader of men, and potentially an excellent general, but he could not work such miracles as Davis seemed to expect. That elevation of Johnston to the status of demigod, along with an overemphasis on eastern affairs, kept Davis from bestirring himself as energetically as he might have in order to provide the men and material necessary to defend the West.

Johnston continued to point out the unpleasant fact that with no men and no guns there was not much he could do, and Davis, who apparently preferred not to be reminded of this dearth, became increasingly irritable in his response to his old friend's requests. Late in September Johnston heard that a blockade runner full of British-made rifles had docked at Savannah, Georgia, and he telegraphed Davis to see if he could get some. Since he was 30,000 rifles short, Johnston explained, could he not have some or all of this shipment?[46] Davis's telegram came back the next day. The president informed him rather testily that the shipment was much smaller than Johnston imagined and that most of it was already promised to units in the East. Johnston would be sent what could be spared (he eventually got 1,000 rifles from this shipment). Davis concluded by admonishing the general, "Rely not on rumors."[47]

As the months dragged by and the Federal armies massing in northern Kentucky and southern Illinois grew while Confederate arms and reinforcements dribbled in, Johnston became more desperate. Finally in January 1862 he sent a staff officer to Richmond to confer personally with Davis and explain to him the necessity of strengthening the defenses of Tennessee. The officer did not find the president in a receptive mood. "My God!" Davis exploded. "Why did General Johnston send you to me for arms and reinforcements when he must know I have neither? He has plenty of men in Tennessee, and they *must* have arms of some kind—shotguns, rifles, even pikes could be used. . . . Where am I to get arms or men?" Patiently the staff officer explained that both could be gotten by removing defenders from less important or less hard-pressed places such as Pensacola, Savannah, Charleston, New Orleans, or even Virginia. Davis would not hear of it. These places could not, he felt, be stripped of their defenses or even slightly weakened. The conference ended with the president urging the staff officer: "Tell my friend, General Johnston, that I can do nothing for him, that he must rely on his own resources."[48]

His resources not being such that he could rely on them, Johnston was left with only one alternative besides abandoning Kentucky and Tennessee: He bluffed.[49] If he could convince the Federal commanders that they were not strong enough to attack and if he could maintain the ruse for several months, perhaps then Richmond could spare him the troops required to set up a real defensive line. As a strategy it was a forlorn hope that should not have worked even for a week. It only needed a Federal commander with nerve enough to give the Confederate front a good shove at just about any point he chose, and the whole elaborate contrivance would come crashing down; before the dust cleared, the Confederacy would have grown smaller by several states. Yet it was all Albert Sidney Johnston had against the growing Union armies, and for over four months the trick worked.

Johnston pushed his available forces as far forward as possible and did his best to make them look as numerous as possible. Small units were ordered to make raids and to "create the impression in the country that this force is only an advance guard."[50] Every conceivable step was taken to convince the Federal general—the gruff, red-headed and very able William Tecumseh Sherman—that he was about to be attacked by an overwhelming force of Rebels. Sherman, a resolute and ingenious man, had as yet very little firsthand experience at conducting a major war and was completely taken in by the ruse. Convinced that he was badly outnumbered by the Confederates when in fact the reverse was the case, he began to wonder how he was going to protect Louisville or even keep the Rebels south of the Ohio River at all. He also began sending reports on his "dilemma" to his superiors, along with frantic appeals for more troops. His superiors had the distinct advantage of not having Albert Sidney Johnston's audacious bluff played out under their very noses and of knowing that the bold Confederate could not possibly have anywhere near the number of troops that Sherman thought he had. Union leaders pondered whether Sherman was not beginning to lose his grip, and soon the northern newspapers were carrying stories that Sherman was insane. Indeed, so successful was Johnston's psychological warfare that Sherman did seem to undergo something of a nervous breakdown. The Federal authorities decided he needed a rest, and on November 15, he was replaced by the slow-moving and lackluster Don Carlos Buell as commander of the Union forces in most of Kentucky.[51]

While keeping up his ploy, Johnston himself traveled from one part of his command to another, going wherever enemy attack seemed most imminent.[52] One portion of his front that concerned him greatly was the area where the Tennessee and Cumberland rivers passed from Tennessee into Kentucky. Polk's failure to secure Paducah at the same time he took Columbus had left the mouths of these rivers in Union hands. Johnston was acutely aware of what would happen should the Federals move up those rivers in force and warned Polk that in that case his position at Columbus would be quickly and easily outflanked.[53] So far the Federals, taken up with the imaginary host with which they presumed Johnston was about to sweep down on Louisville, did not seem to have noticed the prospects offered by the two rivers. Before they did, something was going to have to be done to keep them off the rivers, or else Johnston's overstretched defensive line would be shattered beyond hope of repair.

When Johnston had assumed command in the West, initial steps had already been taken for the defense of the Tennessee and the Cumberland. Two forts had been started, and since this had been done before Polk had scuttled Kentucky neutrality, it had been necessary to build them in Tennessee as close to the Kentucky line as possible. Because of this, neither fort was located on the most advantageous terrain. By far the worse of the two was Fort Henry on the east bank of the Tennessee River. So unfavorable was its situation that it could be commanded by fire from bluffs on the other side of the river, which was at this point a part of Kentucky due to a kink in the boundary line, and at high water the fort was virtually inundated. About ten miles to the east the other fort, Donelson, stood on the west bank of the Cumberland River. Though somewhat better sited than Fort Henry, it too left much to be desired. Both forts were stout earthworks, but neither had enough heavy guns.[54]

Leonidas Polk, during the period of his command in the area, had taken no interest whatsoever in this part of the front, and he was not inclined to do so now. Egged on by the powerful Mississippi Valley lobby, he concentrated on Columbus as if it were the entire theater of the war. While he was right in seeing the Mississippi as a strategic feature of the utmost importance, his mistake was in failing to recognize that unless the Tennessee and Cumberland were also held, the Mississippi, at least as far south as Vicksburg, Mississippi, would become untenable for the Confederacy. So, blissfully ignorant, Polk continued transforming Columbus into one enormous fortification. In Johnston's entire department, there were only three Confederate engineer officers, and somehow Polk had managed to grab all three of them and set them to work on his Mississippi River fortifications while Forts Henry and Donelson languished.

Shortly after taking command in the West, Johnston had ordered one of the officers, Lt. Joseph K. Dixon, to proceed to Fort Donelson and see what was to be done for the situation there. Polk, loath to give up one of his engineers, first delayed Dixon's departure and then informed Johnston that he could not spare anyone at the moment. Johnston had to send two more stern orders before the engineer was released.[55] Dixon surveyed the sites and reported to Johnston that both forts, though incomplete and not in the best of positions, had some value; it would not be advisable to give up all the work that had already gone into them by abandoning them and starting over someplace else. Instead, he recommended various improvements to strengthen the forts. One of these was the construction of another fort on the heights overlooking Fort Henry, Kentucky neutrality being of no further consequence.[56]

Johnston took Dixon's advice and determined to strengthen Forts Henry and Donelson. The general area of the river defenses he added to Polk's command.[57] For actual commander of the forts, however, Johnston wanted Maj. A. P. Stewart appointed brigadier general.[58] Benjamin, probably acting for Davis who in turn probably acted on Polk's advice, instead appointed a Kentuckian named Lloyd Tilghman.[59] Tilghman, a West Point graduate, Mexican War veteran, experienced engineer, and, for the last ten years, resident of Paducah, Kentucky, was dedicated and courageous but unfortunately tended to be extremely deliberate. Though he was concerned enough about Confederate weakness at Henry and Donelson to take the unusual step of writing directly to the president, his concern somehow failed to carry over into a sense of urgency in completing the work.[60] To make matters worse, Polk allowed the construction of the forts to proceed in a highly disorganized fashion. Tilghman, Dixon, and the department's chief engineer bickered and got in one another's way. Pillow got into the act, countermanding orders, shuffling engineer officers around, and generally adding to the confusion. The result was that the work went forward by fits and starts and was never actually finished.[61]

While work on the forts, such as it was, went on, Johnston continued to worry about this seam in his defenses and to work at finding more troops to send to the exposed area. This was, under the circumstances, no easy task; and it must therefore have come as a considerable shock to him to learn that now that the fortifications at Columbus were complete, Polk was about to detach some of his men to join a partisan group. Partisans professed to practice guerrilla warfare against the Federals, but somehow most of them never seemed to accomplish much, and before the war was over many a man in the ranks of the regular Confederate army would more than suspect that the partisans were in fact nothing but glorified draft-dodgers. The Confederate forces in Kentucky had not one man to spare for such a dubious assignment, and Johnston so informed Polk. If Polk had more men than he felt he needed for the defense of Columbus, Johnston instructed, he should send some over to beef up the force guarding the Tennesee and Cumberland rivers.[62]

Polk did not take the hint, and so a few days later Johnston sent him an order: Take 5,000 men, including some cavalry and artillery, put them under General Pillow, send them over to the Cumberland River, and be quick about it.[63] There were few things that Leonidas Polk liked less than sending away some of his troops and this occasion was no exception. Polk wrote back at once that he had better not; he was about to be attacked by an overwhelming force.[64] Johnston replied that after the transfer Polk might not have as many men as would be desirable, but he would have as many as Johnston could afford, and therefore he had better get on with sending the troops.[65] Polk thereupon sent his resignation to Davis.[66] Davis begged him to stay on, assuring him that the "present condition of the service imperiously demands your continuance in the army."[67] It may have been the president's plea that persuaded Polk to stay, or it may have been the turn events took while the letters were passing between Richmond and Columbus, for on November 6, a Federal force really did appear in the vicinity of Columbus.

To be sure, it was not an overwhelming force. It was, however, Brig. Gen. U. S. Grant and about 3,100 Union troops, coming down the Mississippi River on steamboats and looking for a fight. They found one at Belmont, Missouri, the same place where the presence of Union troops had so upset Polk some two months before. The Federal forces had since abandoned the town and it had been occupied by a few regiments of Polk's men. Grant's men disembarked just above Belmont and pitched into the Rebel encampment in a straightforward and uncomplicated manner. At first the Federals drove the Confederates. Then, when reinforcements came across the river from Columbus, the Confederates drove the Federals. The bluecoats got back in their steamboats and went back up the river. The little fight had decided absolutely nothing, but Polk was quite pleased with himself. He promptly reported a great victory won and Grant himself killed—a report that was, on both counts, greatly exaggerated.[68] Davis, impressed by Polk's glowing account, was quick to send his congratulations. "Accept for yourself and the officers and men under your command," he telegraphed the bishop-general a few days later, "my sincere thanks for the glorious contribution you have made to our common cause."[69]

Johnston saw in the "battle" of Belmont no reason for Polk to retain troops needed for the weak area around the Tennessee and Cumberland, and he continued to send orders that the movement be made at once.[70] Polk responded by sending Johnston a copy of his resignation and informing his former roommate that he would stay on "if my services were essential to the success of the army."[71]

While waiting to see what effect this would have on his superior, Polk had another adventure of sorts, this one somewhat less enjoyable than the affair at Belmont. At the camp at Columbus was a large cannon that was the pride of Polk's army and so had been nicknamed by the troops "Lady Polk" in honor of the bishop's wife.[72] It had done good service during the Belmont affair, thundering away at the Union steamboats and the troops they had landed across the river. When the battle had ended, the big gun had remained loaded, though no one could remember with what. The captain in charge of the piece requested permission from the chief of artillery to unload the cannon by firing it. The chief of artillery thought it would be better to draw out the load, and so permission was denied. A few minutes later Polk happened along, and the eager captain approached him for permission.[73] Polk readily agreed and stayed to watch the show. The show, as it turned out, was much more spectacular than anyone had bargained for. As soon as the lanyard was pulled, the monstrous cannon burst, touching off a nearby powder magazine in a really first-class display of pyrotechnics—but one with tragic consequences. Two officers and seven men were killed, several others were wounded, and two were blown into the river. Polk and his staff were blown backward several feet.[74] The general was stunned, and his clothes were blown off, but otherwise he seemed to be unhurt.[75] The next day he was discovered to be somewhat more seriously injured, so General Pillow had to take over the command. Polk went through a convalescence of several weeks.[76] In early December he wrote Davis to withdraw his resignation.[77]

The bishop-general's stubbornness was well represented by his interim replacement. Pillow continued to insist that Columbus was threatened by hordes of bluecoats, at the same time hatching a plan to capture the main Federal base at Cairo.[78] Finally, Johnston gave up in disgust and decided to try to find the necessary troops elsewhere.[79] By this time Johnston had been holding the Federals back for some two months with nothing more than a bluff and had, much to Davis's irritation, been keeping Richmond informed of the Confederacy's weakness in the West. Despite this, very few reinforcements had been forthcoming, and the South's defenses west of the Appalachians remained dangerously weak. Albert Sidney Johnston would have to continue the thankless task of trying to handle his difficult subordinates so as to use his tiny forces to best advantage.

It had been a wise move to set up a unified command for all of the South's northward-facing defenses from the Appalachians to the Great Plains. Davis believed his own presence was necessary in Virginia but wanted someone to provide the same sort of supervision and coordination west of the Appalachians. Unfortunately, he tended to suspect that with Kentucky in the war, the job might be too big for one man. For now, though, he was willing to leave the unified command system intact.[80]

It had been an even wiser move to appoint Albert Sidney Johnston to that command. Johnston was strong-minded, decisive, and tough. He knew how to handle the westerner in the role of volunteer soldier, and he knew how to get by on a shoestring when it came to maintaining a long frontier with a fraction of the force he should have had. Thus Jefferson Davis deserves credit for both the establishment of the unified command and the appointment of Johnston.[81]

Davis's performance after appointing Johnston was less impressive. The president had allowed his nearness to the eastern front to ruin his perspective for the defense of the nation as a whole. He had also allowed his confidence in Johnston to run to such extremes as to expect that unhappy general virtually to work miracles. This attitude caused Davis to neglect his duty of seeing that adequate arms and reinforcements were sent to the western front, for though the shortages there could not have been completely remedied, the situation could have been improved had Davis exerted himself as he should. When Johnston had told the truth about the Confederacy's weakness in the West, Davis had become irritated. He had replied to the general that no more arms could be sent, but Johnston, realizing the president did not fully appreciate the critical state of affairs in the West, had continued his attempts to explain. Davis's anger at Johnston's persistence had been aggravated partially by his constant state of overwork and ill health and partially from his frustration at not being able to meet the demands of every fighting front. It was ominous, though, in that it showed a man not quite confident in his role as commander in chief and not at his best when the situation was most difficult.

The president had also handicapped his chief western general by providing him with a number of incompetent subordinates. There were various reasons for this: in Polk's case, previous friendship; in others, political pressure; in still others, the need to get an unfit man out of a sensitive area and the hope that he might make good someplace else, say, in the West. After wisely appointing Albert Sidney Johnston, Jefferson Davis had shown an unfortunate neglect of the Confederacy's western front. It was a dangerous business. All that was necessary for disaster was a northern push against some weak spot in Johnston's line, or a foolish move by any one of Johnston's foolish underlings. Should these two events occur at the same time and place, the result could be a catastrophe. No one knew this better than Albert Sidney Johnston. If reinforcements did not come, sooner or later his thin line must give way and disintegrate. It was simply a question of when and where.

5

THE GATEWAY TO EAST TENNESSEE

When the break finally came, it was at the eastern end of Johnston's line and involved not one but two of Davis's unfortunate appointments: Felix Zollicoffer and George Crittenden. Felix Kirk Zollicoffer was a Tennessee politician and newspaperman, one of the state's leading citizens. His career included service in Congress as well as the editorship of the influential Nashville *Banner*.[1] He had seen some military service as a lieutenant of volunteers during the Seminole War. His military credentials were thus not exceptionally impressive. His fellow Tennesseeans, however, considered him brave, talented, and fully qualified to command a brigade.

One especially important Tennesseean who held this curious opinion was Gov. Isham G. Harris. For Harris it was a congenial belief since it meshed nicely with the course of political expediency in his state. Zollicoffer was a Whig, and like other southern Whigs he had not been among the first wave of pro-secession hotheads—a crowd composed mainly of Democrats. Now that war had come, it was important to prevent prewar party bickering from resurfacing. It was therefore with some regret that Harris, surveying the list of Tennesseeans appointed to the rank of brigadier general in the Confederate forces by mid-July 1861, found that all were Democrats and original secessionists. This was not calculated to bring about political harmony, and harmony was a goal that seemed doubly important in Tennessee, where moderates had been strong and in which a sizable minority, mainly in the eastern part of the state, not only continued to doubt the wisdom of secession but rejected it outright. To help remedy the grievous error of having too many generals of one political party, Harris wrote up a list of worthy Whigs and submitted it to Davis with the recommendation that he make them brigadier generals. At the top of the list was the name of Felix K. Zollicoffer, politician, newspaperman, and for a brief period many years before, lieutenant of some volunteer troops.[2] A few days earlier, Polk, passing through Tennessee on the way to take over his command at Memphis, had written to Davis about the danger presented by Tennessee Unionists in the eastern part of the state and had suggested that Zollicoffer be put in command of a force to suppress them.[3] The idea must have been appealing to Davis. After all, Zollicoffer was popular, especially in Tennessee, and he knew how to influence people. He might be just the man to persuade the Unionists to see things the Confederate way. Regardless, the Unionists were unable to conduct any organized large-scale warfare; thus, even a general with Zollicoffer's minimal experience ought to be able to handle a few riots and

61

desultory guerrilla raids. The neutrality of Kentucky guaranteed that that was all Zollicoffer would face.

Zollicoffer himself was very anxious to have the position and made sure the president was aware of him by sending several updates on military affairs in Tennessee, including at least one extensive analysis of the situation there.[4] About the time Zollicoffer was writing these dispatches, Davis's attention was absorbed by the first Manassas campaign in Virginia; once that was over, he was impressed enough with Zollicoffer and his special political qualifications to appoint him brigadier general and, taking Polk's advice, to place him over a small force in East Tennessee to put down the Unionists.[5] By the end of July, Zollicoffer had set up his headquarters in Knoxville.[6]

Up until the beginning of September, when the entry of Kentucky into the war added a new dimension to Zollicoffer's duties, things had gone relatively smoothly. Then in the Kentucky crisis Zollicoffer helped nail the coffin shut on the dream of a Confederate Kentucky by his quick move into the state to seize strategic Cumberland Gap after being informed by Cooper that the Federals had violated Kentucky neutrality by occupying Paducah at the other end of the state. Before completing his movement on Cumberland Gap, Zollicoffer conferred with Johnston, who was on his way to Memphis to assume overall command in the West, and got his approval for the move.

The opening weeks of operations in Kentucky found Zollicoffer encamped at Cumberland Gap with a small force facing the possibility of direct Union attack. This prospect sprang largely from Lincoln's intense interest in East Tennessee. Lincoln had hoped that there would be enough Unionists throughout the South to prevent the secessionists from waging a long or successful war for disunion. In most states he was disappointed on this score, but in Tennessee there were plenty of Unionists. Unfortunately, they were concentrated in the eastern part of the state, a mountainous area almost impossible for an army to reach from the north—or so Lincoln's generals said. Lincoln wanted them to try, so that communication and cooperation could be established with the East Tennessee Unionists, who were in the meantime being exposed to considerable hardships at the hands of the Confederates, who, perversely, considered them traitors. The northern gateway to East Tennessee was Cumberland Gap, exactly where Zollicoffer and his men were camped.

Zollicoffer was in over his head, confused by intelligence reports from his front, nervous because he could not ascertain what was going on, and worried that the Federals might use railroads to converge quickly against either his force or the one at Bowling Green. It seemed to him that the best plan would be to fortify Cumberland Gap so that it could be held with a small portion of his force. With the rest of his men he would edge over to the west so as to get within supporting distance of Bowling Green. Besides, that would cut down the chance of an enemy force slipping between him and the rest of Johnston's army.[7] So far it was an excellent idea, but then Zollicoffer added that with the two forces in supporting distance of each other they "would be able to advance more safely and effectively."[8] That was fine too—within certain limits. Johnston, when he replied to Zollicoffer's dispatch setting forth these ideas, thought Zollicoffer knew the limits. Passing over the part about advancing, he simply advised Zollicoffer to go ahead and move to his left and to act on his own discretion since Johnston was too far away to give specific orders.[9]

Meanwhile, Davis, though he still liked Zollicoffer, began to suspect that it might be a good idea to have a more experienced and trustworthy general on the scene to exercise some immediate supervision over Zollicoffer. So, just as he had appointed Polk to look after Pillow, Davis chose another man in whom he had great confidence to have top command under Johnston of the Confederate forces advancing into eastern Kentucky. That man was George B. Crittenden.[10]

Like Davis and many others who played key roles in the Civil War, George Bibb Crittenden was a native of Kentucky. He was born there in 1812, the son of Kentucky statesman and senator J. J. Crittenden and the grandson of a Revolutionary War major. He attended West Point and graduated in 1832 but resigned within a year to practice law.[11] During the early 1840s he served in the army of the Republic of Texas. On one occasion he was captured and forced by the Mexicans to draw lots with the other prisoners to see which man in every ten would be executed. Crittenden got one of the long straws and lived to fight another day.[12] During the Mexican War he rejoined the United States Army, but although he won a brevet for gallantry at Churubusco, he was court-martialed in August 1848 and cashiered on charges of drunkenness.[13]

At that time Davis had been a friend of J. J. Crittenden for over a decade, and during the Mexican War he had become a close friend of Thomas L. Crittenden, brother to George. Jefferson Davis and Thomas Crittenden had traveled to Mexico together, where Thomas had served as an aide on the staff of Davis's father-in-law, Zachary Taylor.[14] While Davis was recovering from his Buena Vista wound, Thomas had been very helpful, even writing out letters that Davis dictated to him.[15] After returning from the war, Davis referred to Thomas as "*our* noble boy" in a letter to Senator Crittenden.[16]

It may therefore have had something to do with Davis's close association with the Crittenden family that when George Crittenden got himself court-martialed and kicked out of the army for drunkenness, Davis immediately took up his cause. As senator from Mississippi, he met first with President Polk; when Polk proved hesitant to reverse the decision of the court-martial, Davis led a campaign that culminated in the Senate Military Affairs Committee's condemnation of the court-martial on various technicalities and eventually in the reinstatement of George Crittenden.[17] Davis had sincerely believed in Crittenden's innocence. So in late 1861, as he looked for an able military commander whose name would be popular in Kentucky and who would be able to guide the well-meaning but befuddled Zollicoffer away from pitfalls, it was not surprising that his first choice was George B. Crittenden.

It occurred to Davis, however, that certain "personal considerations" might make service in Kentucky a painful matter for Crittenden. For one thing, his father, who had striven mightily to work out a compromise that would head off secession and civil war, was still a United States senator from Kentucky and completely loyal to the Union. For another, George's brother Thomas had also remained with the Union and was a general in the Union army in Kentucky. With these facts in mind, Davis wrote to George Crittenden unofficially, asking whether he would like to have the command of an army marching into eastern Kentucky. "I have thought of you," Davis assured the Kentuckian, "as my first choice" for this command.[18] Crittenden, pleased and doubtless flattered, saw no problem with the arrangement Davis proposed and was soon in Richmond conferring with the president on the details of his assignment. Davis explained that Crittenden would be given ten regiments and with these he would be expected to advance from Cumberland Gap toward the heart of Kentucky.[19] The Kentuckian was pleased with this and set out at once for his new command.[20]

Unfortunately, there were some drawbacks to this plan. First, there were not ten armed Confederate regiments to be had in East Tennessee. Second, Crittenden, even had he been a first-rate military man, would have been handicapped by unfamiliarity with the current strategic situation there.[21] Arriving in East Tennessee, Crittenden quickly began to demonstrate that he was anything but first-rate. The exact territorial limits of his command had been left up to General Johnston, and Johnston specified that it should include the eastern half of Tennessee and as much of Kentucky as Crittenden could take.[22] Crittenden thereupon proceeded to set up his headquarters at Knoxville.[23] This was not exactly what Davis had had in mind. As he saw it, Crittenden was no more the man to handle the unrest in East Tennessee than Zollicoffer was the one to handle an advance into eastern Kentucky.[24] Crittenden had hardly set up shop in Knoxville—and informed Richmond that as soon as he got his ten regiments he would be off for Kentucky—before he received a telegram from Secretary of War Benjamin ordering him back to Richmond for further consultation with Davis.[25]

The situation was extremely sensitive in East Tennessee at that time. Some prominent and popular citizens had come out for the Union, and if they were not handled just right, the political damage could be made a great deal worse than it already was. Crittenden had plunged into the intricacies of the East Tennessee Unionist issue immediately upon arriving in that region, and Davis may have considered his proceedings somewhat clumsy and heavy-handed.[26] In addition, the president simply may not have wanted the Kentuckian Crittenden taking the unpleasant measures in East Tennessee that could be handled better by the popular Tennesseean Zollicoffer. In any case Crittenden left Richmond again about the middle of December armed with new orders: He was to command all of Zollicoffer's troops, but "unless otherwise ordered by General

Johnston" (a hint to that general as to what Davis's wishes were in the matter), his territory should not include East Tennessee. In case he did, after all, become involved with East Tennessee Unionists, his orders spelled out exactly what policy Richmond wanted him to follow.[27]

In the meantime Zollicoffer, who had been informed that Crittenden was to take command in that district, was wondering where his new commander was. In Crittenden's absence Zollicoffer decided to take some action of his own. Believing that Cumberland Gap was now adequately fortified to allow him to move his main force elsewhere, he advanced most of his troops to the northwest—a little closer to Bowling Green but closer to the enemy too—and began looking for a good place to go into winter quarters. One place that looked like an especially good prospect to him was Mill Springs.[28]

Mill Springs was situated on the southern bank of the upper Cumberland River in Kentucky about fifty miles west-northwest of Cumberland Gap and ninety miles due east of Bowling Green. It was not a bad spot for Zollicoffer's army. The position was strong, for at this point the south bank of the river was a bluff while the north bank was low and flat.[29] The surrounding countryside yielded plentiful supplies, and the location of Mill Springs allowed Zollicoffer to cover Cumberland Gap while still being close enough to the Confederate force at Bowling Green that given ample warning of a Federal advance, the two forces might possibly support each other.[30] Zollicoffer would have had a better chance of help from Bowling Green had he continued farther west as he had originally planned to do, but Mill Springs' obvious advantages were not to be passed up.[31] Besides if the Federals threatened both forces at once, there would be no support anyway.

So far Zollicoffer had done well.[32] Johnston was pleased with the steps taken and wrote Zollicoffer that "every move is entirely approved."[33] Had Zollicoffer stopped where he was and settled back to wait for spring, it would be almost impossible to find fault with his handling of the eastern Kentucky command. Unfortunately for the Confederacy, and, most especially, for himself, that is not what Zollicoffer did. Just when the idea came to him is not clear, but the day after his men moved into Mill Springs, Zollicoffer was writing to inform Johnston that as soon as possible he intended to cross the larger part of his force to the north bank of the river. In fact, his men were out looking for boats at that very moment.[34] Johnston had barely finished writing his letter of commendation on Zollicoffer's previous moves when he received word of that officer's latest idea. Immediately recognizing the error of Zollicoffer's intention, Johnston at once got off a dispatch to him warning against crossing the river, but it arrived too late.

There were several reasons for Zollicoffer's ill-advised movement. For one thing, he was naturally aggressive and enthusiastic. For another, he had heard there was a force of some eight hundred or so Union troops just north of the river, and he had hopes of catching them and bagging the lot. Then, too, there was Zollicoffer's poor understanding of topography and its effect on military operations. With a perverse sort of reasoning he imagined that the position on the low, flat north bank was much stronger than that on the high bluff on the south bank. This, he thought, was because on the north bank he could locate himself in a bend of the river and thus have his rear and both flanks protected.[35] To a trained military man the position on the north bank looked more like what it really was: a potential trap. To make matters worse, the Cumberland was not fordable at Mill Springs, though it was at several other places both above and below the town. There was always the chance, therefore, that the enemy might slip across and get in Zollicoffer's rear. To guard against this contingency, the general left a small portion of his command on the south side to cover his wagon train and supplies—not that it mattered really; if the Federals ever got on those bluffs on the south side, there would be nothing left for Zollicoffer but the formalities of surrender.[36]

Finally, to add the conclusive element lacking for disaster, Zollicoffer found that having crossed the river, he could not get back over. He had had very few boats in the first place, and it had taken some time to get his men across. Even if he could cross back, the enemy forces in his front, now closer, more numerous, and more alert than before, would almost certainly, he thought, attack and catch his army—in the analogy Lincoln used on another occasion "entangled upon the river, like an ox jumped half over a fence and liable to be torn by dogs front and rear without a fair chance to gore one away or kick the other."[37] This was precisely the sort of impossible situation Jefferson Davis had hoped to avoid by placing Crittenden over Zollicoffer. That Crittenden had failed to prevent the mistake was partially the fault of his being recalled to Richmond for further conference with the president. Crittenden knew nothing of Zollicoffer's crossing of the Cumberland until his return, and by that time Zollicoffer had already informed Johnston that it was too late for him to pull back to the south bank. Yet this in itself is a severe indictment of Crittenden's generalship: He ought to have known of the movement in advance and prevented it. On November 30 Zollicoffer had expressed his intentions in a letter to Johnston. This letter Johnston received on December 4, the day the first of Zollicoffer's troops crossed the river. The operation was not completed until the eighth, the day Crittenden was ordered to return to Richmond. Crittenden had arrived in East Tennessee on December 1 and, like the rear-echelon commander he was, set up his headquarters in Knoxville.[38] Communications between Knoxville and Zollicoffer's army northwest of Cumberland Gap were slow, and Zollicoffer did not even know Crittenden had arrived and taken command until December 10, by which time it was too late to withdraw and Crittenden had already gone back to Richmond to see Davis.[39]

Crittenden was gone for about a week, and when he returned and heard what Zollicoffer had done, he at least had the sense to order him back across the river. This Zollicoffer had already decided was impossible. In any case, the order could have little impact since Crittenden continued to make his headquarters in Knoxville and communications with Zollicoffer remained wretched. Each general complained to Richmond that he was not receiving dispatches from the other, and Zollicoffer added that he was not receiving supplies either. Crittenden was back in Knoxville for a week before Zollicoffer discovered that his commander had visited Richmond. Then he thought Crittenden was still there.[40]

Meanwhile, Zollicoffer was not at all displeased with his precarious situation and cheerfully informed Richmond that he was in "almost undisputed possession of both banks of the Cumberland" from the Tennessee line upward and that the right flank of Johnston's line was thus secure.[41] Under the circumstances there was little for Davis to do. Johnston and Crittenden were his men on the spot, and he trusted them. Zollicoffer's reports were favorable, and there seemed no reason for the president to intervene and little to be accomplished if he did. Johnston and Crittenden knew all was not well, but Johnston could not be spared from other sectors long enough to visit Zollicoffer and decide whether it was practical to pull the troops back across the river. Crittenden could and should have gone in person but for some reason remained in Knoxville throughout the month of December. Both generals therefore had to rely on Zollicoffer's judgment that withdrawal was too dangerous to be attempted, and Zollicoffer's judgment was colored by the fact that he saw no special reason to withdraw in the first place.

Finally, early in January, Crittenden arrived at Zollicoffer's camp and found the situation every bit as bad as he had feared. By this time Federal forces under the command of Gen. George H. Thomas had approached so close that it actually was too dangerous to attempt a withdrawal across the river. By January 18, Thomas's troops were within six miles of Zollicoffer's camp, and it was obvious that the Federals were planning an attack.[42] Faced with a desperate situation, Crittenden decided on a desperate expedient. The Confederates were badly outnumbered, partly the result of Davis's failure to send adequate forces to the West, but Crittenden thought he saw a way to even the odds somewhat. The Federal force was in two sections. One, under Thomas, was located at Logan's Crossroads; the other, at Somerset, was some miles away and separated by Fishing Creek. It had been raining lately, and the creek was running full to the banks. This, Crittenden hoped, would prevent the two Federal forces from supporting each other and allow the Confederates to concentrate on one part and destroy it. It was therefore decided to attack the camp at Logan's Crossroads at dawn on the nineteenth.[43]

The rain continued through the night of the eighteenth and morning of the nineteenth, and the night march from Mill Springs to Logan's Crossroads became a misery of darkness, rain, and mud. The Confederate troops that went into battle that morning were tired, cold, wet, and disorganized. The slowness of the march had cost them the advantage of surprise; and to make matters worse, the flintlock muskets with which a number of them were armed had been rendered all but useless by the dampness. Nevertheless, they pitched into the Union forces and, for a time, drove them back. Then things started going wrong.

Whatever shortcomings Zollicoffer may have had as a general, he was no coward. He did not send his men into battle, he led them, and he led from the front. His men knew it and loved him for it. At the height of the battle, which has gone by a number of names but is generally known as the battle of Mill Springs, Zollicoffer was far ahead of his men, conspicuous in a white raincoat. The rain and smoke of battle had reduced visibility, and Zollicoffer's eyesight was not very good anyway. Besides, Civil War battlefields were places of general confusion, and this was Zollicoffer's first full-scale battle. However it may have been, Zollicoffer saw a regiment of troops that appeared to be firing into Confederate lines. Riding up to the colonel of the regiment, he cautioned him against firing on "our own" troops. At some point the two realized that they were not on the same side. The colonel was faster on the draw, and Zollicoffer became the first Confederate general to die in battle.[44]

Zollicoffer was a brave man who had waded into waters a little over his head. Despite his inexperience he might have made a good colonel. With close supervision he might even have grown into the job of brigadier general, but he never should have had an independent command in an active theater of the war. Davis had correctly perceived this but had been horribly mistaken in the man he had chosen to oversee Zollicoffer. Crittenden was not equal to the task. Irresponsible, lazy, alcoholic, Crittenden might have had more military training than his unfortunate subordinate, but he had not half the character of Zollicoffer.

The Confederates would almost certainly have lost the battle of Mill Springs even had Zollicoffer not fallen at its height. The Union troops were well armed and well trained and fought every bit as hard as the Confederates. The loss of the popular Zollicoffer simply made matters worse. The Union line stiffened and held; the Confederate advance ground to a halt. Then the Federals countered with a bayonet charge, and the southern army went to pieces. The troops streamed back toward Mill Springs in a wild stampede, and nothing that could be done by the highly uninspiring Crittenden could stop them.[45] Indeed, Crittenden may well have been intoxicated during the battle. The remnant of the army crossed to the south side of the Cumberland, abandoning its artillery, wagons, and supplies, as well as all of its dead and wounded.[46] The retreat did not stop until the troops reached Chestnut Mound, Tennessee, about fifty miles due east of Nashville.[47]

The troops were thoroughly demoralized, and the army was quickly melting away through desertion. Rumors were afoot regarding Crittenden's alleged "constant inebriation" and even accusing him of treachery. Davis was bombarded with requests for the removal of Crittenden.[48] Though doubting the authenticity of the reports of Crittenden's drunkenness and possible treason, Davis authorized Albert Sidney Johnston to institute an investigation and to take what action he thought the results justified, even going so far as to relieve Crittenden of command if necessary.[49] Several days later, still believing Crittenden innocent but concerned about his army's low morale and its lack of confidence in Crittenden, Davis had Secretary of War Benjamin issue orders that disbanded Crittenden's army and distributed its forces among other units. Crittenden was to be given a corps command in Johnston's army at Bowling Green.[50]

Crittenden himself was not ignorant of the charges leveled against him, and to clear his name, he demanded a court of inquiry to look into the causes of the defeat at Mill Springs.[51] Orders for a court of inquiry were duly issued by the War Department, but the court never had a chance to submit any findings.[52] A little over two months after the battle of Mill Springs, Crittenden was relieved of his command and placed under arrest for drunkenness.[53] Ten days later he submitted his resignation. He would still have a chance to vindicate himself, but it would be at a court-martial rather than a court of inquiry, and he would have more than the Mill Springs debacle for which to answer. His resignation was to be held pending the verdict of the court-martial. When the opportunity to clear his name finally arrived, Crittenden sidestepped the whole issue by claiming that a technical error in the orders authorizing the court-martial made the whole proceeding illegal. It was not a tactic that inspired confidence in his innocence, and Adjutant General Cooper accordingly informed Crittenden that since he had not availed himself of this chance to plead his case, his resignation was accepted. Crittenden protested and appealed to the family friend Jefferson Davis. If Cooper's order were allowed to stand, it would appear that Crittenden had not taken every opportunity to establish his innocence and so was admitting his guilt. That, of course, was exactly how it did appear, but Davis specified that the offending words be dropped from Crittenden's official file and that his resignation be accepted without comment.[54] Considering Jefferson Davis's blind devotion to his friends, it was quite an accomplishment for him to accept the resignation at all, especially since he did not believe Crittenden was guilty of drunkenness at Mill Springs or elsewhere and found no fault with any of his actions. Two decades later Davis was still maintaining Crittenden's innocence.[55]

Crittenden had been Davis's main mistake in the handling of the eastern Kentucky front. Though possessing military training, he was unfit to hold any rank. Characteristically, Davis was insensible to this because of his long and close friendship with Crittenden and his family. In selecting Crittenden, Davis duplicated the error he had made in appointing Polk to oversee Pillow. He had based his choice on friendship rather than military ability. The appointments of Twiggs and Cooper had been similarly imprudent. When it came to his friends at least, the president was an atrocious judge of generals.

Zollicoffer had been more or less equal to the strictly limited task for which he was originally appointed; that is, maintaining Confederate authority over the East Tennessee Unionists. In any case his appointment was a virtual political necessity. Even when the opening of the Kentucky front and the nonappearance of Crittenden had cast him adrift in waters too deep for him, he had given a creditable performance up until his one strategic mistake. Davis cannot be blamed for choosing Zollicoffer. He can be, however, for choosing Crittenden. Had he instead selected someone like Simon B. Buckner, the story might have ended much differently.

Some blame may also be assigned to Davis for the failure to give the western theater its proper allotment of the Confederacy's men and material. Crittenden's and Zollicoffer's position at Mill Springs would not have been as desperate—and their chances for victory would have been much greater—had they not been so severely outnumbered. Davis could not have supplied all that was needed, but he could have sent more than he did. Johnston had informed him of the need, and large numbers of troops were committed to guarding places of little strategic importance—mainly along the coasts—merely to keep the local governments from complaining. Some two weeks before the battle of Mill Springs, Davis had written the governor of Mississippi, "I shall much regret if any successful raid be made against the villages of our coast."[56] Two months after the battle Davis would write, "I acknowledge the error of my attempt to defend all the frontier, seaboard and inland," but by that time the policy of dispersion had contributed to further southern disasters.[57]

The weakness of the Confederacy's western defenses meant there could be no margin for error. Every blunder by an inept general would have disastrous effects on Johnston's thin-stretched line. Such were the potential consequences of the battle of Mill Springs. With Crittenden's army gone, the gateway to East Tennessee stood wide open to the Federals. Worse still, the whole of Johnston's line in Kentucky had come unhinged. An enterprising Federal commander, pushing the advantage gained at Mill Springs, could probably have flanked Johnston right out of Nashville and most of the rest of Tennessee. Johnston knew it, and it worried him. Yet with large Federal forces menacing the rest of his line, there was little he could do except make provisions for a last ditch stand by the Tennessee militia around Nashville if it came to that.[58]

The Federals did have an enterprising commander in George H. Thomas. Thomas, as the Confederates would one day discover, was a man who knew how to use a victory. He would have been glad to exploit his success at Mill Springs for all it was worth, but he was not allowed to. One reason was the difficulty of attempting to supply an army advancing from eastern Kentucky. Another was the fact that Thomas's superior, Don Carlos Buell, who commanded all the Federal forces between the Cumberland and the Appalachians, had his mind set on a more direct attack on Nashville. The most important reason, however, was that within a few weeks of Mill Springs another enterprising Federal commander had knocked an even bigger hole in Johnston's sparse line.

6

COLLAPSE

The point along Johnston's line that gave way this time was the area that had
been causing him so much worry for several months: the Tennessee and Cumberland river defenses.[1] While the events leading up to the battle of Mill Springs
had been taking place in eastern Kentucky, Polk had been becoming increasingly convinced that a large Federal advance was impending against Columbus. Johnston, who did not share Polk's single-minded obsession with Columbus and the Mississippi River defenses in general, looked for the blow to
fall there, at Forts Henry and Donelson, or at Bowling Green. On January
14, 1862, intelligence reports indicated a major Federal force moving up the
Tennessee River to attack Fort Henry.[2] Though this movement turned out
to be only a small scouting force that lobbed a few shells at the fort from outside effective range and then turned and went back down the river, it was a
further clue as to the Federals' intentions.[3]

Polk thought it was only a feint to draw attention away from Columbus,
but Johnston knew better.[4] The retirement of the scouting force was only a
reprieve. Sooner or later the Federals would recognize his weakness and make
a concerted push, but with his meager resources of men and arms, there was
very little he could do about it.[5] It was too late to begin fortifying more advantageous positions from which to defend the rivers. Johnston sent what men
he could to Fort Henry and warned Tilghman to be alert.[6] At about the same
time Johnston discovered that Tilghman was still trying to make up his mind
whether to fortify the high ground just across the river from Fort Henry. "It
is most extraordinary," exclaimed the profoundly shocked Johnston. "I ordered
General Polk four months ago to at once construct those works. And now,
with the enemy upon us, nothing of importance has been done. It is most
extraordinary." Hoping still to make up for Polk's negligence, Johnston immediately wired Tilghman: "Occupy and intrench the heights opposite Fort
Henry. Do not lose a moment. Work all night."[7] Such haste, however, simply
did not seem to be part of Tilghman's character. The works were never built.

Meanwhile, Johnston also sent a detachment to Clarksville, on the Cumberland River between Fort Donelson and Nashville, to see if the Union forces
could be stopped there and kept out of Nashville in the event of the fall of
Fort Donelson; the answer was no.[8] Beyond that, Johnston could only continue hoping Richmond would find more troops to send him. Richmond did
find a few—a brigade from western Virginia, a few others—but not nearly
enough.

Ironically, it was one of Richmond's efforts to bolster Johnston's strength that triggered the Federal attack. Since Davis felt there were so few troops to be spared from the Virginia front or from coastal defense, he decided to help Johnston by sending him someone who could perhaps help him do more with what he had. The man he sent was the "hero" of Fort Sumter and Manassas, Pierre Gustave Toutant Beauregard.

When Beauregard was born on May 28, 1818, the third of seven children of a southern Louisiana sugar planter, his last name was not merely Beauregard but Toutant-Beauregard. The Toutant-Beauregards, like the other families that inhabited that region of Louisiana, were fiercely French, and young Pierre apparently spoke little or no English until he was twelve years old. The occasion for his learning this new language was his going off to boarding school in New York. Yet even there he remained in an atmosphere at least partially French, attending a school kept by two brothers who had served under Napoleon Bonaparte. It was here that he developed his lifelong fascination with the Corsican general and here that he made his decision to follow a military career himself.

His request that his father arrange for him an appointment to West Point brought strenuous protests from his family, who felt this would require far too much association with Americans for any good Louisiana Creole. Pierre, however, remained adamant. His father relented, pulled some political strings, and the matter was arranged. It was at West Point that Pierre became painfully aware that he did not have a typical American name. In order to remedy this embarrassing problem at least in part, he decided to drop the hyphen from his last name, retaining "Toutant" as an extra middle name. As he became increasingly Americanized, he began to sign himself simply "G. T. Beauregard." Pierre was considered by his fellow cadets to be grave and reserved, a far cry from his later, more colorful self. In any case, he was a good student, ranking second out of forty-five in his 1838 graduating class and thus meriting assignment to the army's elite corps of engineers.

Assignments followed in various parts of the country. In 1841, while stationed in southern Louisiana, he met and married the beautiful Marie Laure Villere, also a Creole and the daughter of a wealthy Louisiana planter. Later, while he was stationed at Fort McHenry near Baltimore, a fancied slight by a fellow officer drew from Beauregard a challenge to a duel—shotguns at thirty paces—which would have come off had not both parties been arrested. Throughout his adult life he would be quick to take offense at real or imagined insults.

With the coming of the Mexican War, Beauregard clamored for a combat assignment and fretted lest peace break out before he had a chance to distinguish himself. He was not to be disappointed. Winfield Scott, commanding the army that was to march from Vera Cruz to Mexico City, made him part

Pierre Gustave Toutant Beauregard (National Archives)

of the select group of engineer officers that functioned as the general's staff. Though serving with distinction and receiving plenty of recognition in Scott's reports, Beauregard fumed that he was not singled out for special praise above the other engineer officers, particularly Robert E. Lee.

At the storming of Chapultepec, Beauregard outdid himself. Accompanying a regiment of light infantry commanded by Col. Joseph E. Johnston, he engaged in extensive theatrics for the particular benefit and inspiration of the troops. Reaching the parapet, he rushed to be the first to take down the Mexican flag but, getting lost in the maze of corridors inside the fortress, arrived too late. Hopping from unit to unit—now aiming a cannon, now directing a political general where to take his troops—Beauregard managed to be satisfyingly conspicuous and to be among the first to enter Mexico City. Though receiving two brevet promotions and high praise from General Scott, Beauregard, true to form, remained bitter that he was given no more recognition than Lee. In private he also manifested a condescending attitude toward the brilliant Winfield Scott, who after all had not done things the way Napoleon (or Beauregard) would have done them.

After the war Beauregard went on sick leave for several months. His health was not good and had not been for much of his time in Mexico. When he returned to duty, his post was again in Louisiana, supervising the construction of forts on the Mississippi River. He also worked on problems of river navigation and even developed a patented dredging machine. His enthusiasm for this invention, as well as for certain other of his schemes (his "cure" for the bite of a mad dog consisted of some Mexican seeds dissolved in a glass of the best sherry, three times a day), gained for him in some circles the reputation of a crackpot. Realism and common sense were never among Beauregard's strengths, just as lack of imagination was never one of his weaknesses.

In 1850 Beauregard's wife died in childbirth. Although grief-stricken, Beauregard remarried in a few years. The new bride was also a Creole, and depending on whom one chooses to believe, Caroline Deslonde was either beautiful or "plain and plump." The marriage gave Beauregard a powerful brother-in-law in Louisiana politician John Slidell.

Throughout the 1850s Beauregard remained embittered at the thought that the army had not given him his due.[9] His persistent demands that the army reimburse him for certain farfetched medical expenses led one War Department bureaucrat to quip that "a bad claim never dies."[10] By 1856 Beauregard was so dissatisfied with the army that he considered joining the filibusterer William Walker in his mad adventures at turning Nicaragua into a slave empire. Having been talked out of this folly, Beauregard two years later ran for mayor of New Orleans but was defeated.

In 1860 he became interested in the question of who would be the next superintendent of West Point. Traditionally this prestigious job had gone to an engineer officer, and engineer officer Beauregard had a candidate in mind. To his outrage, however, he learned that Sen. Jefferson Davis was trying to have the job thrown open to members of other branches. Beauregard enlisted his brother-in-law Senator Slidell, and started some heavy-handed political wire pulling. It worked, and in December of 1860, Beauregard set off for New York.

By the time he officially assumed command at West Point on January 23, 1861, several states had already declared themselves out of the Union. Louisiana's convention had already met and was just three days from voting for that state's secession. Beauregard was not unaware of the secession crisis and had even told the army's chief of engineers that if Louisiana seceded and war broke out between North and South, he would resign and go with his state. In view of this, Beauregard's acceptance of the West Point command fails to make much sense unless he merely wanted the prestige of having held the position; he may have hoped that it would give him a better angle on promotion in the new confederacy the South was obviously about to set up. Shortly after Beauregard's arrival at the military academy, a Louisiana cadet sought him out and asked him if he should resign. The superintendent's advice was: "Watch me; when I jump, you jump. What's the use of jumping too soon?"

Beauregard was not to enjoy a long tenure at West Point, nor was he to have the privilege of "jumping." The folly of appointing him to such a position soon suggested itself to his superiors, and five days after taking up the command, he was ordered to relinquish it. This he considered grossly unfair, and he demanded that the federal government pay his travel expenses back to Louisiana. Since he was now taking up arms against that same government, its liability for the expense was spurious, but Beauregard continued to press his claim even after he became a Confederate general.

Beauregard resigned his commission in the United States Army effective February 20, 1861, and offered his services to Louisiana. To his disgust the post of commanding general of Louisiana's forces went not to him but to Braxton Bragg. Bragg did his best to smooth Beauregard's ruffled feathers, but while assuring Bragg that it was nothing personal, Beauregard maintained that he could not submit to the "injustice" that was being done him. Scorning the governor's proffered commission as a colonel, he enlisted as a private in a company of aristocratic Creoles styling themselves the "Orleans Guards."

This, of course, was not how the would-be Napoleon planned to spend the war. Once again he got Slidell and his political friends to go to bat for him. Once again the tactic was successful, and soon Beauregard was summoned to Montgomery. There, after a long conference with Davis on February 26, he was sent to take command of the various militia and volunteer organizations gathering in Charleston, South Carolina, to menace the Federal garrison in Fort Sumter. This command brought with it the rank of brigadier general, the Confederacy's first.[11] At Charleston Beauregard had his hour of glory when Fort Sumter surrendered under his bombardment. Then, three months later at Manassas he was again victorious. Both affairs could easily have turned out differently, but things had gone Beauregard's way, and he became a national hero.[12]

Until this point the relationship between Beauregard and Davis had not been marked by any lasting animosity. Beauregard had recovered from his outrage at Davis's uncooperativeness in Beauregard's quest for the West Point superintendency; in February he had written Davis a letter congratulating him on his being elected president and, incidentally, offering his services to the Confederate army.[13] Davis, for his part, had probably never felt any resentment toward Beauregard. In a letter he wrote several weeks later, the president described the Creole general as "full of talent and of much military experience" and praised him for his "zeal and gallantry."[14] Davis had made Beauregard the Confederacy's first brigadier general, and when the Confederacy's expansion and the impending war had indicated the need for higher ranks, he had appointed him one of the first five full generals, junior only to men who had been his superiors in the old army. For all this there was no closeness between the two.[15] Davis had been unfamiliar enough with Beauregard to anglicize the general's first name to "Peter" when sending his nomination as brigadier general to Congress for confirmation.[16] The association between Beauregard and his commander in chief could, therefore, be whatever they made of it. There was no reason to suspect that it would be unfriendly except that the two men shared a certain touchiness in their personalities that made them very unlikely to overlook an offense.

The trouble started shortly after Manassas. Beauregard began to complain about Commissary Gen. Lucius B. Northrop, whom many considered to be inadequate and who was a good friend of Jefferson Davis.[17] The Creole's remarks must have rankled the president, but believing it was his duty to try to get along with such a potentially valuable general, Davis rose above his feelings and wrote Beauregard a mild and conciliatory letter. He did the same with other complaints that Beauregard began producing regularly.[18]

Davis was less patient when in October 1861 Beauregard submitted his report on the battle of Manassas. In the report he claimed that before the battle he had had a plan that would have brought the capture of Washington and Baltimore but that he had been prevented by the president from carrying it out.[19] In truth the plan had never been put in writing but had been communicated verbally to Davis by one of Beauregard's aides.[20] It was a typical piece of Beauregard planning: grandiose, overelaborate, and totally unrealistic. Davis had rightly dismissed it, but in Beauregard's report, the president's course of action was made to look very bad indeed. To make matters worse, a synopsis of the report found its way into the Richmond newspapers, where Davis first learned of it and correctly suspected Beauregard of planting it as a self-promotional stunt.[21]

The whole controversy arose from the southern people's disappointment in the failure of the Manassas victory to achieve the capture of Washington and an end to the war. In reality it never could have, but each of the chief participants in Confederate strategy making in Virginia—Beauregard, Joseph E. Johnston, and Davis—was very concerned to show that whatever had happened (or failed to happen) was not his fault. Thus Beauregard's ambush in the newspapers was especially irksome. Davis took him to task in a letter accusing the general of trying "to exalt yourself at my expense."[22] That, of course, was exactly what Beauregard had been trying to do; but he did not appreciate Davis's observation to that effect. He therefore chose to reply by writing not to Davis but to the editor of a Richmond newspaper—for publication. His letter was melodramatically headed "Centreville, Virginia—within hearing of the enemy's guns" and was full of thinly veiled abuse of the president.[23]

As if this were not enough to turn Davis against him, Beauregard insisted on questioning the right of the secretary of war to give orders to him and had to be put in his place by the president.[24] Then, too, the Creole's lifestyle and manner were not such as to impress favorably the austere Mississippian. Beauregard entertained lavishly at his Centreville headquarters, dining on roast duck and sipping cognac juleps with the likes of Prince Jerome Bonaparte of France and the three beautiful Cary sisters of Baltimore. Valley Forge it was not. Beuregard had the Cary sisters make Confederate battle flags out of their petticoats, and he promised to plant one of the flags on the Washington Monument. That was not the worst of it either, at least as far as Davis was concerned. Beauregard simply could not restrain himself from engaging in political machinations. He would send letters to various congressmen and senators, setting forth in dramatic terms the most outlandish of strategic plans, which these same congressmen and senators then proceeded—with straight faces, one presumes—to advance on the floor of Congress in debates that could have been little short of ludicrous.[25]

At some point Davis probably began to reason that Beauregard could be of greater service to the Confederacy elsewhere than in northern Virginia. Perhaps the proximity of the national capital provided too much of a temptation for Beauregard's politically scheming nature, while at the same time making political authority a little too close by and hard for him to stomach. Perhaps the fact that the Virginia front was foremost in the public eye gave too much play to Beauregard's tendency to show off. Perhaps Beauregard would do better in the West. The possibility had been discussed before, and after Fort Sumter he had very nearly been sent there. He had expressed a great concern for the safety of the West, especially the Mississippi Valley.[26] In any case Johnston needed some sort of help, and Davis felt he could spare no troops. If nothing else Beauregard's name would encourage enlistment and raise the spirits of those in the ranks. And so the decision was made to send Beauregard west. Davis had high hopes, and in writing to Polk with news of Beauregard's transfer, he described the Creole as "an able engineer and full of resources" who was "courteous and energetic."[27]

All that remained was to convince him to go. Although Beauregard may have been as anxious to get away from Richmond and its authority as Davis was to have him away, he was reserved when approached by a congressman, one of his political allies, who had been sent to sound him out on the issue. Beauregard stipulated he would not agree unless he was guaranteed that the western forces would be reinforced enough to take the offensive and that he could return to Virginia after he had settled affairs in the West. The congressman promised to consult with Davis on the matter and later telegraphed Beauregard that he was sure the president would consent. He was sure of nothing of the sort and to avoid unpleasantness had neglected to mention Beauregard's stipulations to Davis.[28] Beauregard, however, knew nothing of that and unsuspectingly prepared to go west and find new worlds to conquer.

He arrived at Bowling Green on February 4, 1862, and met with Johnston, who was heartily glad to see him.[29] Beauregard was of medium height and build with olive complexion, high cheekbones, and a neat mustache. His hair had been jet black when the war started but was now almost white; his imported hair dyes were not making it through the Federal blockade.[30] Nevertheless, he looked every inch a soldier. His formidable reputation had preceded him, and his arrival somewhat raised the drooping morale of the western troops.

One western Confederate who did not cheer at the Creole's approach was Leonidas Polk. Polk was distressed to learn that Beauregard was to be made his immediate superior in command of the western end of Johnston's line. Offended, Polk again sent in his resignation, observing that his services apparently were no longer needed. Once more Davis urged him to reconsider. He spoke of the positive moral effect of Polk's presence in the army and the value of the special knowledge the bishop had gained of the Mississippi Valley.[31] Again Polk allowed himself to be talked into staying, though he was no more happy at taking a subordinate role where he had formerly commanded than Pillow had been under similar circumstances a few months before.[32]

Unfortunately for the South, Beauregard's reputation and the fact that he was coming west were also known to others, among them the Union generals Halleck and Grant. Moreover, they had heard false reports that Beauregard was bringing with him fifteen regiments of Virginia troops, and they decided that they had better act before he arrived. Grant had for some time been wanting to take troops up the Tennessee and have a go at Fort Henry. Halleck, his superior, had been dragging his feet. Now he told Grant to go ahead and see what he could do.[33]

So on February 6 the moment Johnston had dreaded arrived. Grant reached Fort Henry with 15,000 men on transports. Accompanying his flotilla were four vessels representing the United States Navy: squat, black, ugly creatures known as ironclad gunboats. The South had nothing like them and would never be able to build anything comparable to them except in negligible numbers. They were a technological innovation of this war, and they would play an enormously significant role, especially in the West where rivers were so important. They were, it seemed, impervious to enemy cannon fire. In their presence any conventional warship was obsolete. It would presently be seen how forts would do against them.

Grant landed his force, and his troops began slogging through the swampy ground near the fort on their way to surround the place. Meanwhile, the commander of the Federal gunboats moved in to begin his bombardment. The Confederates were in no position to offer a stiff resistance. Fort Henry, poorly designed and located in the first place, was nearly flooded by the high water in the river. On top of this, it was incomplete and had far too few heavy guns. Its commander, General Tilghman, wisely sent the bulk of the garrison over to Fort Donelson before Grant's troops had had time to take up their positions. Then with a handful of men he stayed to hold out as long as possible—which did not prove to be very long. The gunboats wasted no time shooting the place to pieces. Tilghman took off his coat and joined one of the depleted gun crews in serving a cannon for a time, but it was no use. Grant still not having arrived on the scene, Tilghman surrendered to the navy. So low was the fort's location and so high was the river that when a naval officer came over to accept the surrender, his boat crew rowed right through the gate and into the fort.[34]

The fall of Fort Henry opened the Tennessee River to the Federals as far south as Florence, the highest point a steamboat could ascend. Within days Federal gunboats were ranging that far, destroying bridges, putting ashore raiding parties, and generally spreading consternation. Fear of the black-hulled monsters grew out of proportion to their actual strength. Davis, however, maintained a level head; in reply to a dispatch from a panic-stricken local official regarding a possible raid by the gunboats he wrote, "The number of men who can have been transported by four gunboats should never be allowed to tread upon our soil and return. I hope you may also capture the gunboats."[35]

The real damage, though, in the loss of the river was that it virtually destroyed communication—and especially transportation—between the parts of Tennessee on either side of the river. Johnston's army was thus split in two. The day after Fort Henry fell, Johnston and Beauregard met with other generals at Bowling Green to determine what was to be done next. It was decided that if the gunboats were that powerful, Fort Donelson would not last either. At its fall, Federal gunboats would soon be at Nashville, and if Johnston's army was still at Bowling Green, it would be trapped north of the Cumberland. To avoid this, the army was to be brought down from Bowling Green to Nashville and fortifications were to be started on the Cumberland just below Nashville, in hopes that if Fort Donelson held out long enough the new defense works would be sufficiently complete to keep the gunboats out of the city.[36]

Johnston knew this was a forlorn hope.[37] He also knew it was vital to hold Nashville, which besides being the capital of Tennessee was also one of the Confederacy's two main supply depots and an important industrial center. The Nashville gunpowder plant alone had delivered 100,000 pounds of powder by February 1862. The area was also a major food-producing region, with over half the hogs slaughtered in the Confederacy during that winter originating around Nashville.[38] Tennessee's capital city had to be held, and Johnston decided to make his main fight for the city at Fort Donelson. For that purpose he threw some 12,000 reinforcements into the fort.[39] It is not quite clear what his thinking was in making this decision. He believed the Federals would take Fort Donelson with gunboats alone, without the need for land forces. If this were so, the infantry he was sending would be of no use. Perhaps he intended them to ensure that the garrison's retreat was not cut off. Perhaps he was not quite sure what they would do but thought they might be of some assistance. In any case, almost everyone had gotten out of Fort Henry before it sur- rendered, and Johnston gave strict orders that when Fort Donelson could not be held any longer the troops should be evacuated.[40] Though it was impractical for him to take his whole army to Fort Donelson, he had determined to do something.[41] What he did was a mistake, but it need not have been a disaster. The disaster was the work of the men he sent to command the reinforced garrison.[42]

There were three brigadier generals at Fort Donelson. The junior of them was Buckner, usually not a bad general. Next in seniority was Pillow, definitely a bad general. In command was John B. Floyd, arguably the worst general the Confederacy would ever have. Floyd and his brigade had been sent to Johnston around the end of December as part of the meager reinforcements the govern- ment felt it could spare at that time.[43] Floyd's availability probably had some- thing to do with the fact that he was not especially useful where he was. He and his brigade were fresh from the disastrous West Virginia campaign, in which not even the genius of Robert E. Lee had been able to transcend Floyd's poor judgment and uncooperativeness.[44]

Floyd was a political general clear through. A popular Virginia politician and former governor, he had been secretary of war in the Buchanan administra- tion. In that capacity he had not hesitated to let his southern sympathies guide his actions—or so many northerners believed. Specifically, it was suggested he had been rather free in transferring federal ordnance supplies to southern states. On one occasion he had given an order to ship 121 heavy cannon from Pitts- burg, Pennsylvania, to the Gulf Coast for the arming of forts that would not be built for several years. The order aroused protest and was never carried out since by the time the matter got back to the war office, Floyd was no longer secretary, having been forced to resign over some highly irregular financial deal- ings with a War Department contractor.[45] Floyd's prosouthern scheming while secretary of war had aroused quite a bit of anger in the North, and in certain quarters there were harsh mutterings about treason and what ought to be done with this particular type of traitor.

With the coming of war Jefferson Davis had felt compelled to appoint Floyd a brigadier general to gratify the onetime governor's many supporters in Vir- ginia and elsewhere. Davis did not have a very high opinion of Floyd and did not intend him to have chief command of one of the most vital points in the Confederacy, but it seemed to be the way of things in the West that Davis's third-rate appointees somehow managed to find their way into the positions where they could do the most damage. Floyd, Pillow, and Buckner, then, would command at Fort Donelson. Johnston had not really intended it that way either, but their troops were available and their relative seniority determined the chain of command.[46]

As these arrangements proceeded, it was also decided that–communication being all but severed with the western part of Johnston's line–Beauregard would go there and take over the immediate command. It was also agreed that Columbus would have to be abandoned, just as Buckner had foreseen six months before. Delaying actions were to be fought along the Mississippi at Columbus, New Madrid, Island No. 10, Fort Pillow (in Tennessee north of Memphis), and at Memphis itself, in hopes that some more permanent defense would eventually be developed.[47]

In Richmond there was great concern over the state of affairs in the West. At last the realization dawned that that theater had been neglected too long. Davis took steps personally to see that troops were started on their way to Johnston from Virginia, New Orleans, Pensacola, and whatever places could spare a few. Within days nearly 10,000 men were on the march.[48] Before they arrived, however, Fort Donelson's fate would already be decided.

On February 13 U. S. Grant and company arrived at Fort Donelson, but there was little fighting that day.[49] Grant placed his lines around the fort in preparation for the attack by the gunboats the next day. Then, if all went as it had at Fort Henry, the gunboats would batter the fort into submission; but this time there would be no escape–Grant's men were already in place. Within the fort the Confederates were thinking along the same lines. The infantry they could handle, but the prospect of facing the dreaded gunboats was extremely disquieting.[50]

On the afternoon of the fourteenth the gunboats moved in. They came four abreast, guns blazing, and the redoubtable Floyd promptly dissolved into jelly. In panic he sent off a dispatch to Johnston stating, "The fort cannot hold out twenty minutes."[51] Then to Floyd's amazement–and very likely that of everyone else on either side–the fort did hold out. The gun duel between the fort and the boats thundered on for two hours, and the boats got the worst of it. It was discovered that even iron plates were not proof against heavy guns at close range. The flagship was hit fifty-nine times, its pilot house wrecked, the pilot killed, and the commander of the flotilla wounded. Finally, the steering gear was shot away, and the riddled gunboat drifted back downstream. One by one the other gunboats were knocked out until none was left to renew the attack.[52] Fort Donelson had proved a general rule that would hold true throughout the war: No reasonably well-built fort could be battered into submission by warships, even ironclads. When the Confederates recovered from their astonishment, they were exultant. Both Floyd and Pillow got off messages to Johnston informing him of the day's victory. Pillow called it "the fiercest fight on record" and claimed that not a single Confederate had been killed. Johnston happily passed the good news along to Richmond.[53]

The Confederates had won the first round, but while the troops rejoiced that evening, the generals were having a gloomy conference. They were surrounded, the enemy was receiving constant reinforcement, and no one knew when the gunboats might be back or whether the fort could fight them off again. The three generals recognized what should have been obvious in the first place: Once they allowed the enemy to surround it, Fort Donelson was a trap. They then addressed the problem of how to get out of the trap and decided to make an all-out attack at dawn the next morning. If everything went as planned, the army would break out of Grant's encircling lines and head for Nashville to join Johnston.[54]

The Confederates struck hard the next day and, taking Grant's troops by surprise, drove them back and opened an escape route.[55] "On the honor of a soldier," Pillow melodramatically telegraphed Johnston, "the day is ours!" Floyd too got off a dispatch claiming another great victory. Johnston in turn reported to Richmond that a "brilliant victory" had been won at Fort Donelson.[56] So it stood, as far as Johnston knew, when he turned in around midnight.

As the day-long battle had come to a close, the way out of the trap had stood wide open before the Confederates. Buckner moved to take advantage of it, but at that point, for some strange reason, Pillow had ordered him to pull his troops back inside the fort.[57] Buckner had protested, and while they discussed the matter, Floyd rode up. Buckner explained the situation, and Floyd ordered him to continue with the original plan: The army would evacuate the fort.[58] Pillow then told Floyd his side of the story—that the men were tired and hungry and needed to retrieve their blankets and knapsacks. This was no time to start a long march. Thereupon Floyd flip-flopped and, agreeing with Pillow, sent everyone back to the fort.[59] It was a move of sublime stupidity that probably could have been achieved only through the combined efforts of a Floyd and a Pillow.

Thus as Albert Sidney Johnston slept in truly blissful ignorance in Nashville, the three generals in Fort Donelson met in the wee hours of the morning of February 16 for yet another conference on what they ought to do next. Their situation was much as it had been the night before—except that their men were exhausted and demoralized (except those who were dead), and during the retreat back to the fort the Federals had been able to seize some very advantageous positions for an assault of their own that would probably come the next morning. As Floyd and Pillow waited for Buckner to arrive at the place designated for the meeting, Pillow entertained his superior by roundly criticizing Buckner's performance in that day's fighting.[60] Buckner himself, when he did show up, was in a dismal frame of mind. He announced that his men would not be able to hold their positions for thirty minutes once the enemy attacked, and he expected that would come first thing in the morning.[61]

Pillow remonstrated. Of course Buckner could hold out. The fort was good for a few more days, and by that time they ought to be able to find another way out. Maybe they could use some steamboats that were supposed to show up that morning and ferry all the troops to the other side of the river.[62] Buckner was not interested in any more of Pillow's ideas. The two had been on bad terms ever since the Mexican War, and the preceding day's events had done nothing to improve matters.[63] Buckner, who was beginning to display an irrational and almost perverse pessimism, insisted his lines would collapse and the fort would fall. Perhaps the blundering of Floyd and Pillow had discouraged Buckner to the point of complete despair. Undoubtedly the Kentucky general was tired, possibly even exhausted into a state of irrationality. Or it may be that Buckner, like many another general North and South, had simply lost his nerve. In any case he seemed determined that the fort should surrender at once and would hear of nothing else. Any further attempt to cut their way out, he declared morosely, would result in 75 percent casualties and would be an immoral squandering of human life. Floyd agreed with Buckner on the potential casualty rate of another escape attempt. He also agreed that no general had the right to order his men to such a slaughter. That left just one alternative. "We will have to capitulate," Floyd finally admitted, "but, gentlemen, I cannot surrender; you know my position with the Federals; it wouldn't do; it wouldn't do!"[64] What Floyd had in mind was the northern reaction to his pro-Confederate conniving as secretary of war. There had been talk of hanging, and Floyd did not want to hang. He admitted his reasons for not surrendering were personal, whereupon Buckner pointed out that that should not influence him in deciding whether or not to send his men to certain death.[65] Pillow spoke up and said he would never let the Yankees take him alive. Surrendering had not been his idea, and if that was what they meant to do, he was leaving. Floyd turned to Buckner with a proposition. If he turned the command over to Buckner, would Buckner let him take his brigade and leave before the surrender went into effect? Buckner agreed. Thereupon Floyd said to Pillow, "I turn the command over, sir!" Pillow at once said, "I pass it"; and Buckner, who had insisted on surrendering, was left to carry out that unpleasant duty himself.[66]

One of the steamboats did show up that morning, and Floyd pulled rank to commandeer it for the evacuation of his brigade. The brigade consisted of five regiments, four from Floyd's home state of Virginia and one from Mississippi. Floyd detailed the Mississippi regiment to guard the landing and keep other would-be escapees from mobbing the boat. Then, standing on the deck of the steamboat and flourishing his saber he yelled, "Come on, my brave Virginia boys!" The Virginia boys were happy to comply, and Floyd had them ferried across two regiments at a time. By the time that was finished, it was too late to go back for the Mississippians, and they were left to their fate. Pillow, meanwhile, had not found anything as commodious as a steamboat, but he and his chief of staff did manage to find, tied up somewhere along the river-bank, an old abandoned scow, barely big enough for the two of them. Hastily clambering into this undignified conveyance, they paddled themselves to the other shore.[67] A few others managed to escape. Here and there an individual slipped through Union lines, and a promising Mississippi cavalry colonel named Nathan Bedford Forrest led his men out through an area of flooded backwaters the scouts had labeled impassable. For the majority of the garrison, though, there was no alternative to surrender. Nearly half of Johnston's troops east of the Tennessee went into captivity.

Buckner worked out the details of the surrender with Grant, his old army friend turned opponent. As the two talked, Buckner mentioned that things would have been different had he been in command. Grant allowed that had that been the case he would have used different tactics. When informed of Pillow's efforts to escape, Grant remarked that the cowardly general might have saved himself the trouble: "If I had captured him," he quipped, "I would have turned him loose. I would rather have him in command of you fellows than a prisoner."[68]

Jefferson Davis's role in the disastrous events that led to the fall of Forts Henry and Donelson and the surrender of almost half of Johnston's army was, in many respects, similar to the one he played in the Mill Springs debacle. Forced by political pressure to make a general of a man as unfit as Gideon Pillow, Davis had been appalled to discover that this general had somehow managed to lodge in the place where he could to the most damage. The same had been true of Floyd. Davis could hardly have avoided these appointments without stirring political hostility even faster than he actually did. The bickering of Congress and the obstructionism of governors was already a serious problem. Pillow and Floyd had outranked Buckner—a man who at least had professional military training—not because that was the way Davis wanted it, but because Kentucky's late entry into the war had prevented Buckner from being appointed as early as Pillow and Floyd were.

The western front was still desperately weak, but Davis had begun to realize the danger there and had done his best to send what troops he felt could be spared. Ironically, his attempt to give Johnston another good general, Beauregard, had triggered the northern attack, and his decision to transfer a brigade from western Virginia had brought the wretched Floyd as well. Johnston would have been better off had Davis taken away one of his brigades. In any case, it would take the shock of major disaster—the fall of Forts Henry and Donelson—to give Davis a clear perspective on where the Confederacy's defensive resources should be allocated.

Johnston, who had been awakened before dawn on the sixteenth with news that Fort Donelson was surrendering, generously refused to find fault with Floyd and Pillow and shouldered all the blame himself.[69] The press was filled with howls for his removal, and the uproar was all the worse because Johnston's civilian countrymen, like his military opponents, had been completely deceived by his bluff and imagined he had a huge army.[70] Clearing up this misconception would fully expose the South's weakness to the still-partially-ignorant enemy. So Johnston bore the abuse in silence.[71]

Despite Johnston's generosity Floyd and Pillow were finished.[72] Davis's wrath was thoroughly kindled, and the specter of Floyd's Mississippi regiment waiting forlornly at Fort Donelson's boat landing did nothing to assuage it. Pillow undertook a long campaign to persuade the War Department to remove the official censure against him. His letters at least indicated he had probably not been involved in treachery; his stupidity alone was adequate to explain the most improbable of actions. He was finally returned to active duty but never held a significant position. Commanding generals tended to be as anxious to pass him off as he had been to pass the command and responsibility that morning at Fort Donelson.

The fall of Fort Donelson completed the collapse of the Confederate defensive front in the West. The stalemate Albert Sidney Johnston had succeeded in maintaining against all probability in the face of overwhelming forces was over. Southern troops were reeling backward along the whole line, from the Appalachians to the Mississippi, and within three weeks, the defeat at Pea Ridge (Elkhorn Tavern), Arkansas, would put the trans-Mississippi forces into retreat as well.[73] Kentucky was gone, so was Missouri. So, for that matter, was the western two-thirds of Tennessee, including Nashville and, within a few weeks, Memphis. Control of the major rivers gave the Federals immediate access to Louisiana, Mississippi, and Alabama. The heart of the South was exposed, and all that stood between it and the Union forces were Johnston's ragtag troops, poorly clothed, poorly fed, very poorly armed, and in pitifully scant numbers. They were clustered in units of varying size scattered across the South from the Appalachians to the Ozarks, and they were all desperately marching southward to avoid being cut off and destroyed. They were discouraged as they had never been before.

This, it seemed, was the Confederacy's darkest hour. Things could not get much worse if the dream of a southern nation was ever to become reality. If it was, Albert Sidney Johnston was going to have to pull off a first-class military upset. It would be the ultimate test of his ability as a leader; if he failed, the springtime that was just now beginning to warm the bloodstained fields around Fort Donelson and the as yet untouched hillsides above an obscure Tennessee River steamboat stop called Pittsburg Landing might well be the Confederacy's last.

7

SHILOH

Johnston brought the remnants of his forces across the Cumberland at Nashville by February 23, 1862, and continued south. The Tennessee River still separated the troops under his immediate command from those farther west under Beauregard, and the Federal gunboats could ascend the Tennessee as far as Florence, just south of the Alabama-Tennessee line. Johnston knew he had to unite his forces, and he knew that because the Mississippi Valley was more important than Middle Tennessee, the assembly point should be west of the Tennessee River. That meant he would have to march his troops south into Alabama and then west into Mississippi. Middle Tennessee, for the time being, would be abandoned.

Just when Johnston hit upon his plan of campaign is not clear, nor is it certain when he chose Corinth, Mississippi, as the place to concentrate his forces. Before the fall of Fort Donelson, Mansfield Lovell, the commander at New Orleans, had written to Johnston advising that the reinforcements coming from New Orleans be sent to Corinth first because it was strategically located in regard to railroads and rivers.[1] Four days later another correspondent mentioned the strategic importance of Corinth.[2] Since Corinth's key position was readily apparent to most trained military men, Johnston probably needed no one's advice to see that it was the ideal place for him to consolidate his scattered forces. With his troops united at Corinth, he could wait and see what opportunities the enemy would offer him.[3]

Until his troops were united, however, he was extremely vulnerable. The march on Corinth, therefore, was of the greatest urgency. In order to confuse the enemy and throw off any possible pursuit, Johnston cleverly arranged to give the impression that his army was falling back on Chattanooga to the southeast rather than on Decatur and then Corinth to the southwest.[4] Once again his ruse was successful, and the Federals remained confused as to just what his army was up to.[5] Grant was sure Johnston was headed away from the other Confederate forces in the West instead of toward them. "The rebels have fallen back to Chattanooga instead of Murfreesboro," he reported on February 25.[6]

The force under Johnston's immediate command reached the town of Murfreesboro, Tennessee, some thirty-five miles south of Nashville, on February 23. However, delays occurred because of heavy rains that washed out the bridge over Stones River there.[7] As a result, the army did not get under way again until the last day of February.[8] Bad weather and muddy roads continued to slow the army's progress, and by March 4, it was only twenty-five miles south

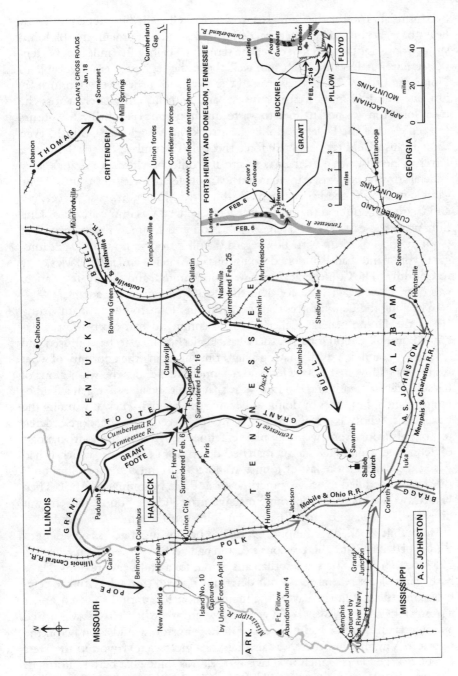

Map 7.1 Kentucky and Tennessee, Winter and Spring 1862

of Murfreesboro near the Tennessee town of Shelbyville.[9] Burdened down by heavy baggage, including much-needed supplies and equipment, it took Johnston's troops another week to cover the remaining eighty-five miles to the Tennessee River at Decatur, Alabama, well above the highest point accessible to Union gunboats.[10] There they crossed the river and turned west. Corinth lay just one hundred miles west-northwest, and with his army safely across the river, Johnston was not inclined to waste any more time on southward detours to keep clear of the Federals. Boldly he struck out straight for Corinth, even though this would take his small force through Tuscumbia, on the Tennessee River in northwestern Alabama, where it would be closer to Grant's large Federal army just downstream than to the Confederate forces in Corinth.[11] The gamble paid off as the Federals remained inactive. Johnston's ruse succeeded, and Grant still doubted that the Confederate general was in the area, thinking him far to the east.[12] On March 24 Johnston and his men finally arrived at Corinth and linked up with Beauregard.[13] Polk's troops, now under Beauregard's command, had abandoned Columbus on March 2 and fallen back slowly to Corinth.[14] The Confederate forces were now united, and the greatest danger was over. Once again Johnston had successfully deceived his enemy.

In keeping the Union forces confused and idle, Johnston had the unwitting aid of the Union general Halleck, whose command had recently been extended over all Union forces in the West. Halleck tended to be confused and idle anyway, and he was still having a hard time digesting the enormity of what his troops had won at Forts Henry and Donelson. Besides, he was jealous of his subordinate Grant and did not want that quiet, businesslike general grabbing any more headlines by doing something spectacular—such as winning the war. Grant, who was anxious to follow up his success, was therefore ordered to hold his troops somewhere along the Tennessee River in the southern part of Tennessee while Buell's army marched down from Nashville (which it had seized the day after the last of Johnston's forces had pulled out) to join him. Buell was scheduled to arrive sometime around the beginning of April. Then Halleck would take over the whole massive army and, he hoped, win the war himself. The delay he caused had given Johnston the time he needed.

Meanwhile, back in Richmond, Davis had been inaugurated as president of the Confederate States (his previous election had been provisional) on February 22, 1862. The occasion was less than auspicious for a number of reasons. Davis had been sick for several weeks but determined to go through with the ceremony regardless. On the day of the inauguration Richmond shivered under a steady rain driven by a raw, cold wind. News from the battlefronts was mixed and uncertain. Rumor had it that Joseph E. Johnston would soon be on the retreat in Virginia, but there was also talk of a great victory won in the West at a place called Fort Donelson. Davis himself was somewhat better informed. He knew the Virginia army would be falling back, and the day before he had been in possession of what he described as "very imperfect intelligence" regarding some sort of "disaster at Fort Donelson." "I cannot believe," he wrote his brother Joseph in Mississippi, "that our army surrendered without an effort to cut the investing lines and retreat to the main body of the army."[15] Shortly before leaving for the capitol to give his inaugural address, the president had learned the worst.[16] As the procession made its way through the streets of Richmond, Varina, the president's wife, had her curiosity aroused by the fact that the carriage was moving at a snail's pace and black footmen in dark suits were walking solemnly along beside it. She asked the coachman why. "This ma'am," he replied innocently, "is the way we always does in Richmond at funerals and sichlike."[17] Under the circumstances the president's speech was about as upbeat as could be expected. There had been hardship and suffering, he admitted, and there was going to be more, but though "the tide for the moment is against us, the final result in our favor is not doubtful."[18]

Davis certainly believed this, but he also knew very well that for victory to be achieved the state of affairs in Tennessee would have to be remedied. The sudden collapse of Johnston's front after the fall of Fort Donelson had thrown the populace of the region into near panic. A stream of letters began to pour into Richmond, complaining that the army was demoralized and its leaders incompetent and begging, as the only relief for their plight, that the president "take the field in person" and, at the head of the Confederacy's western army, lead them to victory. Prominent citizens of several states, soldiers, and even a high-ranking general (Hardee) shared the view that only Davis's presence could save them.[19] It was an assessment toward which Davis himself could easily have been inclined. His greatest glory had been won on the battlefields of Monterrey and Buena Vista, and while, deep down, he might entertain a degree of uncertainty about his abilities as a grand strategist, he seemed much more confident of his ability to lead an army in battle. A military career had been his top choice when secession had come. Upon first being chosen Confederate president, he had truthfully written in his letter of resignation as commanding general of the Mississippi militia, "Proud of the station to which the too kind estimate of the people's representatives elevates me, I retire from it with sincere regret."[20] Later in the war he would confide to his wife, "If I could take one wing and Lee the other, I think we could between us wrest a victory from those people."[21]

The temptation, therefore, must have been great, as one letter writer after another urged him to come out and take command of the army. That Davis did not succumb was the result of his appreciation for the other responsibilities that rested on him and his trust in Albert Sidney Johnston. The exaggerated confidence that had assumed Johnston could work miracles with neither troops nor guns had given way to a more realistic yet more solid appreciation of Johnston's qualities as a general. "My confidence in you has never wavered," the president wrote his western commander in late March, "and I hope the public will soon give me credit for judgement rather than arraign me for obstinancy." Johnston, he was convinced, had "done wonderfully well," and he went on to express the hope that the general would be able to unite his forces and fall on one of the separate Union armies. Failing this, Davis believed the only hope was that the people of the Confederacy's heartland would "rally *en masse* with their private arms, and thus enable you to oppose the vast army which will threaten the destruction of our country." For this purpose and this purpose only Davis contemplated repairing in person to the western army. "I have hoped to be able to leave here for a short time and would be much gratified to confer with you and share your responsibilities. I might aid you in obtaining troops; no one could hope to do more unless he underestimated your military capacity."[22]

Davis was determined now to do his best to help Johnston, whether that meant going west to rouse the people or staying in the capital to push reinforcements along from other fronts. In the end he wisely chose the latter course. From Richmond the president took an active role in the campaign. In dispatches he urged Johnston to "send to me frequently information of your condition and purposes" and encouraged the general in his plans to beat the Federals in detail.[23] "I hope you will be able to close with the enemy before his two columns unite." Davis telegraphed. "I anticipate victory."[24]

Besides advice and encouragement, the president strove to provide material help as well. "I am making every effort," he wrote his brother, "to assemble a sufficient force to beat the enemy in Tennessee, and retrieve our waning fortunes in the West."[25] He was not exaggerating. For the first time in the war the Confederate president directed an almost ruthless concentration of forces. Troops were taken from the defenses of such important coastal cities as Charleston and New Orleans.[26] The entire Florida coast was stripped—except for a garrison guarding the mouth of the Apalachicola River and the route it commanded into central Georgia—and the troops thus freed were hurried northward to join Johnston.[27] Among these there came from the Gulf Coast cities of Mobile and Pensacola during the first week of March 10,000 well-trained troops, along with the general who had been commanding the Confederate forces in that sector, Braxton Bragg.

Bragg was born in 1817 in Warrenton, North Carolina. His father was an ambitious man who would eventually own some twenty slaves but who was nevertheless snubbed as plebian by some of the more aristocratic elements in that prosperous tobacco-growing region. Bragg's father decided early that studious young Braxton should pursue his education at the United States Military Academy and, with the help of an older son already established in the state legislature, had obtained the necessary appointment. Braxton, described as a "tall, ungainly" young man, entered West Point in 1833. Despite occasional demerits for such offenses as keeping a jug of whiskey and throwing bread in the mess hall, he graduated in 1837, ranking fifth in a class of fifty.

As a young officer, Bragg established a reputation for efficiency and intelli-

Braxton Bragg (Library of Congress)

gence but also for contentiousness—so much so that the story (obviously apocry-
phal) had circulated that while serving in the dual role of company commander
and post quartermaster at a small fort, Bragg, in his capacity as commander,
had made a requisition for supplies, which, in his capacity as quartermaster,
he had refused. He then carried on an exchange of nasty letters with himself
and finally, unable to resolve the dispute, referred the whole matter to the post
commander, who is supposed to have exclaimed, "You have quarreled with
every officer in the army, and now you are quarreling with yourself."

Bragg had indeed quarreled with a fair number of his fellow officers, notably
with general in chief Winfield Scott. Bragg even allowed some of his scathing
criticisms to appear in print—anonymously. Testifying at congressional hear-
ings dominated by Democrats and generally hostile to Scott (who was a Whig)
and writing certain indiscreet letters to superior officers finally got Bragg court-
martialed and reprimanded for disrespect. Still, he was highly esteemed by
many in the army as a first-class young officer who showed great promise for
the future. In spite of his prickly exterior he had won many friends among
his fellow officers, the closest of which was another young lieutenant by the
name of William Tecumseh Sherman.

In the Mexican War Bragg commanded a battery of light artillery under
Zachary Taylor and distinguished himself at Monterrey and Buena Vista, where
he fought alongside Jefferson Davis and his Mississippi Rifles in the hottest
part of the battle. Bragg's exploits brought him national fame and three brevet
promotions, as many as any officer in the conflict. Upon returning home from
the war, Bragg was feted and toasted from one end of the country to the other,
even being presented with a sword by the citizens of Warrenton, North Carolina, who had previously scorned his family's humble origins. In 1849 the
celebrated Colonel Bragg married a rich and beautiful heiress from the sugar-
planting country of Louisiana.[28]

Despite the dangers and privations they had shared in Mexico and the fact
that each admired the other's conduct on the field of battle, there was little
kind feeling between Braxton Bragg and Jefferson Davis.[29] Bragg, as an artillery
officer, bitterly opposed the reforms that Davis, as secretary of war, proposed
introducing for the artillery. He objected even more strenuously to Davis's insistence on stationing artillery on the frontier, considering it a waste of men
and horses "to chase Indians with six-pounders." Bragg also thought it was
dreadfully inconvenient to have to live at an isolated frontier post, and it did
not take him long to weary of such a life. In December 1855 Bragg went to
Washington to discuss the matter with Davis personally and, failing to get any
satisfaction from the secretary of war, turned in his resignation. Davis promptly
accepted it. Bragg hated Davis for that and expressed the utmost satisfaction
that Davis had not become president at the end of Pierce's term. "He could
drive me out of the Army," Bragg observed grimly, "but not from my party."
Thus matters stood, on the eve of the Civil War, between Jefferson Davis and

the man who would become one of his chief western generals, as their political enemies would have it, by reason of favoritism.

When war came Bragg's adopted state of Louisiana was not slow in finding a position for him. He was appointed the state's general in chief, much to the disgust of the ambitious Beauregard. In March 1861 Bragg received a commission as brigadier general in the Confederate army and was assigned to the command at Pensacola. The South needed the services of every good officer it had, and in any case, the animosity between Davis and Bragg was probably less strong on Davis's side. (Davis had a way of making people extremely angry with him and then wondering what it was that had upset them.) While at Pensacola Bragg began to attract the favorable notice of the president for his energy and efficiency in organizing and training troops as well as for his unselfish offer to send four of his best regiments to Virginia in exchange for four newly raised regiments. In September he was promoted to major general and given charge of all of Alabama and West Florida.

Despite these promotions he was incensed when the command at New Orleans went to Mansfield Lovell. He felt that as a Louisianan it was rightly his, and he continued to believe that Davis was "not overwell inclined towards" him. In reality Davis was shrewdly assessing Bragg and discovering that the Confederacy had in him an officer of great potential value. Davis had remarked that Bragg was "the only General in command of an Army who has shown himself equal to the management of volunteers and at the same time commanded their love and respect."[30]

By December 1861 Davis's estimation of Bragg had risen so high that he was anxious to detach the trans-Mississippi region from Johnston's command and put it under Bragg. Davis believed Johnston had his hands full in Kentucky, an opinion that was probably strengthened by Johnston's annoying habit of pointing out the obvious but unpleasant truth that with no guns and no men he was not going to stop any kind of Federal attack. The trans-Mississippi was in complete disarray, with the Missouri general Sterling Price and the Confederate general Ben McCulloch apparently unwilling to cooperate. Training was poor; organization almost nonexistent. Davis determined that Bragg was the only man to bring order out of the chaos.[31]

Had Bragg accepted the challenge, it would have been a mistake. The Mississippi River was the most obvious invasion route in the entire Confederacy. Federal strategy could not possibly fail to aim a thrust down the length of that river. Given this certainty, to divide defensive zones along the river would be to invite the enemy to split the seams of the defense. In order to stop a Mississippi Valley offensive, Confederate forces on both sides of the river would have to work together. Unless both were under a single general, the job of making them collaborate would rest squarely on the commander in chief Jefferson Davis; and Davis, in locating himself so close to the active Virginia fighting front, was too removed to enforce cooperation across the Mississippi. At this juncture at least, the mistake was averted. Bragg was given a choice and decided that under the circumstances the trans-Mississippi command was "not enticing."[32] With Bragg uneager to go, the area was kept under Johnston's supervision, and its immediate command was given to Earl Van Dorn.[33] Still, it was significant— and ominous—that Davis had shown a tendency to view the Mississippi River as a dividing line in a neat system of geographical departments rather than as a potential highway of enemy invasion.

For the time being, then, Bragg remained in Pensacola, where he became increasingly alarmed at the disasters the Confederacy was suffering in Kentucky and Tennessee. He came to realize Davis's error in trying to hold every last inch of the southern coastline as well as every other bit of real estate in the Confederacy, when the wiser course would be to abandon nonstrategic points and concentrate Confederate strength where it was most needed.[34] This opinion Bragg expressed in his letters to Richmond, which may have further impressed Davis since he was also beginning to see the advisability of greater concentration.[35]

In keeping with this new insight and in order to reinforce the hard-pressed Johnston, Davis ordered Bragg to take most of his troops and move north. Specifically, Bragg was to join Beauregard's forces until the two halves of Johnston's army could link up. Bragg left Mobile on February 27 and arrived at Beauregard's headquarters in Jackson, Tennessee, five days later.[36] Beauregard was glad to see him. At this time Bragg was one of the highest-rated generals in the Confederacy. Almost everyone seemed to have a good opinion of him, and even Jefferson Davis was coming to rank him nearly equal to Albert Sidney Johnston.[37]

Braxton Bragg was a complicated personality. He was himself highly self-disciplined and valued self-discipline in others. When a person fell short in that trait, as was often the case, Bragg could be a very strict disciplinarian. This had made the troops he commanded some of the best drilled and trained in the Confederate army. Even so, he exercised a paternal care for his men, seeing to their welfare and even visiting hospitals and making attempts (however clumsy) at joking with them.

Pushing himself and his subordinates hard, Bragg sometimes drove himself to the point where he impaired his health, which was in any case rather fragile. Ill health in turn tended to aggravate his rather grouchy disposition. When he did not like someone, he generally said so in plain terms. Tact and the ability to get along with those he disliked were qualities that did not come easy for him. Still, the Civil War was to demonstrate that he had improved tremendously since his days as a controversial young officer. He made a real effort to accommodate others, even when it was completely contrary to his nature. Perhaps he had matured with age. Perhaps he was impressed that Jefferson Davis had overcome their prewar hostility to make him a general and was inspired to emulation. Whatever the reason, Bragg would do much better at getting along with people than his previous record gave cause to expect.

The situation Bragg found at Beauregard's headquarters was not encouraging. Upon coming west Beauregard had been shocked to discover how weak the forces really were. He had been looking for a place to win glory, and this was certainly not it. He felt betrayed after the assurances he had received before leaving Virginia and became depressed and agitated. That in turn made him sick. He had had throat surgery before leaving Virginia, but apparently the problem was caused or at least exacerbated by nervousness, as Beauregard himself had admitted in a telegram to Richmond several days earlier.[38] In the same telegram he had begged that Bragg be sent to join him and said that, if necessary, he would serve under Bragg, who held a lower rank.[39] To make such a statement, the proud and ambitious Beauregard must have been well nigh hysterical. The fact was he simply could not handle the responsibility that rested on him, and for over a week, claiming he was too sick, he had refused to take official command of the troops Johnston had placed under him.[40] Sick he may have been, but the cause was his failure of nerve.

Bragg's arrival helped somewhat, and shortly thereafter Beauregard recovered enough to assume official command.[41] Still, Bragg hardly dared leave him alone lest he relapse into his state of near panic. To compound matters, Polk, who was now serving under Beauregard, was almost as frantic as his commander. The two fed the fires of each other's worry whenever they were together, prompting Bragg to confide in a letter to his wife that "every interview with Genl. Polk turns [Beauregard's recovery] . . . back a week."[42] Bragg worked to bring a semblance of order to Beauregard's sector, while Beauregard sent one dispatch after another urging Johnston to hurry and join him.[43]

Beauregard's nerves were somewhat relieved when Johnston finally arrived on March 24.[44] During the long trek south from Bowling Green, Johnston had managed to restore his men's morale, and the 17,000 or so he brought with him were confident he had a plan that would reverse their misfortunes. Altogether, Johnston now had under his immediate command about 40,000 men.[45] They were as yet poorly organized and lacked uniforms and, for the most part, proper weapons. Many of the troops were still armed with old flintlocks, and others had nothing better than shotguns. There was no cure for the lack of proper weapons; better ones were simply not available. The organizational system could be improved, but even for that there was little time. Albert Sidney Johnston was going to have to lead his ragged army into battle within a matter of days.

From the time the Confederate defenses in Kentucky had collapsed, it had been clear what Johnston needed to do. Beyond escaping destruction in the immediate aftermath of the disasters at Forts Henry and Donelson, he would have to unite all of his scattered forces before the enemy could unite theirs. Then he could assault a portion of the enemy's forces with all of his own. Having defeated that part, he could then—in theory at least—proceed to gobble up the others bit by bit and retake all the territory he had lost. It was simple enough, but as a famous philosopher of war once wrote, "Everything is very simple in war, but the simplest thing is difficult."[46] So it was in this case, yet by the beginning of April things were starting to fall into place. The enemy had moved slowly and Johnston's forces had escaped destruction. He had succeeded in uniting his forces before the enemy; and now, within striking distance of his base at Corinth, there was a sizable Federal encampment. Grant's troops had for some time been camped on the west bank of the Tennessee River at Pittsburg Landing, about thirty miles from Corinth. Grant had about 40,000 men, and Buell's 35,000 were on the way to join him and would arrive in a few days. If Johnston struck quickly, his numbers would be at least equal to Grant's, maybe a little better. He would have to take the offensive, and that would be costly; but if he waited for Grant—or Halleck or whoever—to come and attack him in his prepared positions, he could be sure that when they did come it would be in overwhelming strength. His only chance was to attack at once. On the night of April 2, 1862, he gave the order to advance.[47]

The army that marched out of Corinth the next morning was as green and ill prepared as any army that ever went out to battle. It was not the fault of Johnston or his generals. Bragg was indisputably one of the best generals of the war when it came to training soldiers, and Hardee had written the United States Army's official manual of infantry tactics. There was simply not enough time. Many of the regiments were brand new—enough of them, when added to bad roads, bad planning, and bad or nonexistent staff work, to turn what should have been a day's march into a three-day fiasco.

Like Robert E. Lee, Albert Sidney Johnston tended to place too much confidence in his subordinates. Johnston, who in any case did not like to get bogged down by excessive attention to details, had graciously, if unwisely, been letting the proud and opinionated Beauregard have a substantial part in drawing up the detailed plans for the army's operations. The specifics of the marching orders were Beauregard's, and as was typical with Beauregard's planning, they had the least possible connection with reality. They would have made most railroad timetables look simple and flexible by comparison. Such a scheme should never have been tried with a hodgepodge army that had been together less than a week and contained many units that had never made a day's march before, but Beauregard could never resist the urge to get fancy. The units were to march on different roads, converging and passing between each other at various intersections according to a rigid schedule, in a scheme that was something like the convolutions of a modern-day marching band on a monstrous scale.

The result was a monstrous 40,000-man traffic snarl. The time set for the attack had to be changed from dawn on the fourth to the same time on the fifth, then to the sixth. Johnston did his best to keep everyone moving and to be as patient as he could. He knew all about volunteer soldiers and ragtag armies; such things could happen. Still, with every day bringing Buell's thousands that much closer, even Albert Sidney Johnston's patience could wear thin. By late afternoon of the third day, it had worn away. When it was reported that an entire division of Bragg's corps, several thousand men, was missing, Johnston exploded. "This is perfectly puerile!" he fumed. "This is not war! Let us have our horses." With that he mounted up and, staff officers hastily mounting and clattering along behind, galloped off to find the lost division. He found it standing in the road, blocked by Polk's wagon train; unceremoniously ordering the wagons out of the way, Johnston got the troops moving again.[48]

Similar incidents occurred again and again as the army's handful of trained and experienced officers struggled to maintain control and keep the column moving. It was a depressing spectacle, and to complete the dismal picture, it rained for most of the three days that the army was on the road.[49] By the evening of April 5 the army was finally drawn up within a mile or two of the enemy, ready to attack the next morning. However, the Confederate generals meeting together that night were anything but elated. Beauregard was the most discouraged. The attack, he believed, ought to be called off. It had depended upon surprise, and surprise was now impossible since the approach had taken three days instead of one. Besides, many Confederate soldiers had begun to wonder if their rifles would still fire after the damp weather. They had decided to find out—and the resulting rattle of small-arms fire should have been enough to alert every Yankee for miles around. If it did not, there were other things that should have. Wherever Albert Sidney Johnston rode throughout the army, the soldiers (who, if one were to believe most of the newspaper editors and politicians in the country, had totally lost faith in him) would greet him with intense and vociferous cheers, in spite of all that could be done to quiet them.[50] The soldiers' lack of discipline had manifested itself in other ways, too, and it now developed that the men had managed to dispose of five day's rations in just three days. The enemy, Beauregard lamented, would be "entrenched to the eyes." The men were without rations. It was time to call the whole thing off and go back to Corinth. Even the usually more resolute Bragg saw no use in going on.[51]

The fact was that Beauregard and Bragg had lost their nerve. Things had gone wrong, as things will in war, and it had been too much for them. Returning to Corinth would only demoralize the troops and allow the Federals to attack in overwhelming force in their own good time. No matter how unfavorable things might seem now, it was still the best chance the Confederates would have in the West for a long time to come, and unless they did something with it, maybe their last chance. That very day a telegram had arrived from Davis for Johnston, expressing the president's hope that they would succeed in catching Grant's army and destroying it before Buell could come up.[52] It was Davis's final contribution to the campaign. He had worked hard to scrape together all the troops he could and get them concentrated in northeastern Mississippi. He had conferred with Johnston about strategy and had supported him faithfully when nearly everyone else in public office was clamoring for his removal.[53] Now Davis added one final bit of encouragement to press the attack to a decisive conclusion. Yet as the army's senior generals stared glumly at one another and contemplated Beauregard's and Bragg's litany of reasons why the attack could not possibly succeed, few of them spoke up in favor of pushing ahead. The awesome weight of responsibility, the entire burden of deciding the fate of a 40,000-man army and perhaps of a nation rested squarely on the shoulders of Albert Sidney Johnston. He was as tired and frustrated as any of the others, and in the event of failure, he had the most to lose. Yet, dismissing the arguments for turning back, he insisted that they must and would attack the next day and crush Grant's army. No doomsayers could shake his determination. "I would fight them if they were a million," he grimly declared.[54] Later, before retiring for the night, he told his staff, "Tomorrow . . . we will water our horses in the Tennessee River."[55]

Grant's forces were camped on the rolling hills behind Pittsburg Landing on the Tennessee River. Their encampment was about three miles wide and was bounded on the north by Owl Creek and on the south by Lick Creek. The ground around both creeks was swampy and presented a fairly effective barrier to military movements. Near the center of the Union encampment was a little white country church named Shiloh.

Johnston's plan of attack was to assault the Federals along their entire front but to hit hardest against their left flank, tear it loose from Lick Creek, and then roll up the whole Union line into the pocket formed by Owl Creek and the Tennessee River. This would put Pittsburg Landing in Confederate hands and cut off Grant from his boats, leaving him with the alternative of surrender or annihilation. To carry out this plan, Johnston intended that Polk should command the Confederate left, Hardee the center, and Bragg, with a special oversized corps, the crucial right. A force would be held in reserve under John C. Breckinridge, a Kentucky politician and former United States vice-president turned general.[56]

Unfortunately, though explaining these dispositions in a letter to Davis, Johnston merely went over them verbally with Beauregard and once again allowed that general to draw up the detailed orders for the army.[57] The resulting arrangement was drastically different from what Johnston had envisioned. The army's three corps were to be strung out in three parallel lines stretching from one end of the front to the other; then they were to attack one behind the other.[58] It would prove to be a disastrous plan, but by the time Johnston discovered what Beauregard had done, it was too late to rearrange the troops.[59]

One factor, at least, was working in the Confederates' favor as they prepared for battle: The Union generals had no idea whatsoever of the impending assault. This may have been in part because the Union army was making its own fair share of noise those days. Confederate soldiers were not the only ones to whom the idea of test-firing their rifles had occurred, and Federals added their own contribution to the intermittent pop-popping of rifle fire that reverberated through the woods. Down on the river one of the Union transports had a steam calliope and blasted out one patriotic air after another as entertainment for the troops.[60] Besides that, the immediate commander of the camp around Shiloh Church was William Tecumseh Sherman, recently returned to active duty after suffering a kind of nervous breakdown in the face of Johnston's effective bluffing. Sherman was not about to let the wily Confederate deceive him this time. Like everyone else, he could hear the crackle of rifle fire from the picket lines, but he surmised that it was nothing more than some errant Confederate cavalry or perhaps a regiment or two of infantry—nothing to worry about. Confidently he telegraphed Grant, who was a few miles down the river, that he did "not apprehend anything like an attack" on his position.[61] Grant, probably glad that his friend Sherman was no longer imagining Confederate armies where there were only skirmishers, complacently telegraphed Halleck, stating, "I have scarcely the faintest idea of an attack . . . being made upon us."[62] Johnston, then, would have the advantage of surprise after all.

Could Beauregard have known this it might have eased his mind somewhat, for even as the troops were forming up to go into battle on the morning of Sunday, April 6, he approached Johnston to make one more try at talking him out of the attack.[63] Other officers of like mind joined in to apply more pressure. Johnston remained steadfast, and as they talked, they heard gunfire break out in earnest at the front. This was no practice firing but unmistakably the sound of a real battle getting under way. Johnston concluded the discussion, stating, "The battle has opened, gentlemen; it is too late to change our dispositions," and rode off to the front.[64]

In later years critics would say Johnston should have stayed in the rear to direct the army from there, but with the deployment Beauregard had created, there was little for an army commander to do but keep the attack going and feed in troops. Johnston left Beauregard in the rear to handle this, and both were happy with the arrangement. Johnston knew that an army of raw volunteers would have to be led from the front, and that is what he intended to do.

At first the attacking Confederate lines swept all before them, and the shocked Federals reeled back toward the river. Gradually resistance stiffened, and the battle became a disorganized collection of vicious little fights between regiments or brigades. One result of Beauregard's wretched planning was that none of the corps commanders could control his units. The three lines compacted together; units became mixed. Men in battle for the first time found themselves being led by officers they did not know. There could be little maneuvering or massing of troops against key points. All that the generals could do was try to keep the men moving forward.

All things considered, Johnston did a remarkable job of it. For a few fiery hours there in the fields and thickets rolling back from the Tennessee River, Albert Sidney Johnston and his loose-jointed army of half-trained, poorly armed, and largely inexperienced Confederates came as close as anyone ever would to dealing U. S. Grant a decisive defeat. Johnston's army had not even been an army two weeks before but a mere assemblage of widely separated units. The history of such troops in this and other wars indicated they would soon panic and run away. They did not. Instead they stayed and fought on in the fiercest battle the country had yet seen. General Johnston knew how to lead volunteer troops.

He was at the front all day. At one point he rebuked a junior officer whom he found looting a captured Federal camp. "None of that, sir," he said sternly. "We are not here for plunder." Then, softening at the crestfallen expression of the young man who had apparently thought he was only collecting rightful spoils of war, Johnston picked up a tin cup and said, "Let this be my share of the spoils today."[65] Later, he found a large number of wounded bluecoats and ordered his staff physician to care for them. The doctor remonstrated; Johnston might need him. The general promised he would let him know before leaving the area, but in the confusion of battle the promise was forgotten, as Johnston galloped off to attend to another part of his line.[66]

Johnston did his best to salvage the attack plan Beauregard had so miserably botched. Early in the fight he pulled a brigade out of Polk's third wave and led it around to the right flank where he had originally intended the main effort to be made. Later, with the crucial right wing stalled, he shifted two front-line brigades in that direction and ordered Breckinridge's entire reserve corps to go in on the right.[67] Doggedly the Confederates battered their way forward against increasingly tough Federal resistance.

Early in the afternoon, at the height of the battle, a serious problem developed. Though the Federal line had, as intended, been torn loose from Lick Creek and a battalion of Mississippi cavalry actually had, as Johnston had predicted, watered its horses in the Tennessee River, the rolling up of Grant's army was not proceeding according to schedule.[68] A stubborn division of Federals had lodged in one of the patches of woodland that dotted the landscape, and it seemed that no amount of Confederate persuasion could dislodge them. The position, which came to be called the "Hornets' Nest," was vital, as it stood directly in the way of the Confederate advance. Bragg was on the scene and desperately trying to hammer the Federals loose, but the confusion engendered by Beauregard's poor tactics meant that Bragg could not mass troops to throw against the Hornets' Nest but could make only piecemeal attacks. Johnston rode over to see if he could help. The attack had faltered, and a Tennessee regiment, pushed a little beyond the limits of endurance for men in battle for the first time, had refused an order to charge yet again. Riding along the front of the regiment's line, Johnston shouted encouragement to the men. Reaching out as he rode down the line, he tapped their bayonets with his tin cup. "These will do the work," he assured them. "Men, they are stubborn; we must use the bayonet." Then riding to the center of the regiment's line, he wheeled his horse and called out, "I will lead you!" The Tennesseeans charged one more time, and this time they carried the section of the enemy's line in front of them.[69]

Most of the Hornets' Nest, however, remained intact, and the fight raged on. Johnston's horse was slightly wounded in two places. A bullet ripped the sole of Johnston's boot, and he joked to an aide, "They almost tripped me up that time." Soon after, though, a stray bullet struck him in the right calf, a few inches below the knee. A major blood vessel was cut. At first unaware that he had been hit, Johnston soon reeled in the saddle from loss of blood.[70] The only man near him at the time was Tennessee's governor Isham G. Harris, who had raised all the Tennessee troops he could, brought them to the army, and stayed on as a volunteer aide.[71] Harris asked Johnston if he was wounded. "Yes," he replied calmly, "and I fear seriously." Seeing that the general was about to pass out, Harris brought his horse alongside and, holding the wounded man in the saddle, guided their horses into a draw sheltered from enemy fire. He lifted Johnston to the ground. Harris did not know what to do; the staff doctor was not back yet. Soon it was too late. Albert Sidney Johnston was dead.[72]

History can never reveal what would have happened had Johnston not been killed. In Grant, who had in the meantime arrived on the battlefield, he had the toughest and most resourceful opponent the North had to offer. The delay at the Hornets' Nest had already cost precious time—time that Grant was putting to good use to establish a last-ditch defensive line around Pittsburg Landing. Buell's troops were very close now, and his lead division would be across the river and in Grant's lines before sundown. In view of these facts, many have concluded that by the time Johnston fell, it would already have been impossible for him to win the battle.[73] Yet Johnston had been doing the "impossible" for months. He had done the "impossible" to get to Shiloh with a sizable army. Perhaps with him in command, his men could have found the "something extra" that was needed for victory. Even had he lost the battle yet lived, Johnston might still have changed the course of the war. He would probably not have been guilty of the failures of resolve by which his successors repeatedly snatched defeat out of the jaws of victory. Moreover, while he might not have developed the reputation for tactical wizardry of a Robert E. Lee, his might have been the genius of a George Washington, holding a battered and tattered army together and keeping its morale up by sheer force of character, suffering defeats at times but always coming back, and somehow persevering to final victory. Whatever he might have been, by 2:30 P.M., April 6, 1862, the question was moot.

The loss of Johnston's leadership took some of the impetus out of the Confederate attack.[74] Bragg continued to pound at the Hornets' Nest, and around five o'clock it finally fell.[75] He and the other generals then began marshaling their troops for the final advance on Grant's last line of defense. Whether they could have broken this line and destroyed Grant's army is uncertain. There was not much daylight left, but there was enough to try, and it was the last chance the Confederates had to make a victory out of Shiloh. However, as the troops started to move forward, an order arrived from Beauregard directing that the action be broken off and the troops pulled back out of range of the enemy's guns.[76] Beauregard, as the second-ranking general present, had succeeded to the command upon the death of Johnston. He had been at the rear of the battle all day and stayed there even after taking command. He was also "greatly prostrated" from the nervous ailment with which he had been suffering for two months and was not physically equal to the requirements of army command.[77] He had been impressed when, as the battle lines drew closer to the river, the Union gunboats had begun to lob their huge shells landward. What he did not know because he was so far from the fighting was that the height of the riverbanks (about one hundred feet at this point) forced the Union gun crews to elevate their pieces so much that most of the shells sailed harmlessly over the heads of the attacking Confederate troops. The closer they got to the Union lines, the safer they were from the fire of the gunboats.[78] Physically exhausted, and fearing that his troops were being slaughtered by the heavy guns of the boats in the river, Beauregard ordered the withdrawal.[79]

The generals at the front could hardly believe the order. One general, seeing a body of troops retreating, ordered their officers arrested and the movement reversed before he learned of Beauregard's order. Upon receiving Beauregard's message, which contained the words, "the victory is sufficiently complete," Bragg burst out, "My God, was a victory ever sufficiently complete?" He quickly inquired whether the messenger had given the order to anyone else, hoping such a mistake could yet be averted. That it was already too late was soon proved when Bragg saw other units pulling back.[80] Bragg, Hardee, and Polk were unanimous afterward in stating that the withdrawal order had cost them their last chance for victory.[81]

After effecting the withdrawal on the evening of the sixth, Beauregard should have ordered the army to retreat to Corinth.[82] If success was not attainable that day, it would certainly be no closer on the next. Instead, Beauregard kept the army at Shiloh in the captured Federal camps, in the absurd hope that they could take up in the morning where they had left off the night before. Grant had other ideas. Given the night to get his army in hand and the 35,000 fresh troops of Buell's army as reinforcements, he struck back ferociously at dawn. The Confederates were driven back relentlessly, taking even more punishment and losing all the ground they had gained at such great price the previous day. Finally, by midafternoon, it became apparent to Beauregard and other officers that the army could take no more and was about to go to pieces. Beauregard ordered a retreat, and the battered army dragged itself back to Corinth.[83]

At the close of the first day's fighting Beauregard had telegraphed Richmond, claiming a "complete victory" and reporting the death of Johnston.[84] Davis was shaken by the news of his friend's death. "The report that Genl. A. S. Johnston was killed sadly distressed me," the president wrote that evening. "Victory however great cannot cheer me in the face of such a loss. God grant it may not be true and that he yet lives to sustain the cause for which he was willing to die." Only as further reports confirmed the sad news could Davis bring himself to accept Johnston's loss as certain.[85] In a message to Congress the next day, he admitted the death of Johnston but exulted "that it has pleased Almighty God to crown the Confederate arms with a glorious victory over our invaders." After sketching briefly how the battle had come about, Davis stated that "at last accounts" the enemy was "endeavoring to effect his retreat."[86] Upon reflection Davis could probably take some comfort in thinking that his friend had not died in vain but had won a "complete victory" that would open up the reconquest of Tennessee, Kentucky, and maybe even Missouri.[87] It must, therefore, have been a considerable shock to learn that instead of advancing to reap the easy fruits of a "complete victory," Beauregard had fallen back to Corinth and was calling for reinforcements. Certainly it did not improve his opinion of Beauregard.

Meanwhile, Beauregard was in a tight spot. Corinth was a key rail junction; the Confederacy's only real east-west railroad, the Memphis and Charleston, ran through the town. Dubbed the "vertebrae of the Confederacy," this railroad was so important that after the fall of Fort Donelson the possibility had been broached in Confederate cabinet meetings of abandoning Richmond in order to defend it.[88] Also, if Corinth was lost, Fort Pillow, the last Confederate stronghold on the Mississippi above Memphis, would be outflanked and would have to be relinquished. In fact, Beauregard himself said of Corinth, "If defeated here we lose the whole Mississippi Valley and probably our cause."[89] These were high stakes, yet it was difficult to imagine how the Confederates could hold Corinth. The army had lost some 10,000 men at Shiloh, one man in four; though it had been reinforced by Van Dorn's 20,000 men from the trans-Mississippi and was now even stronger than when it had marched off for Shiloh, it was still vastly outnumbered by the gigantic Union army it faced.

Halleck had come down to Pittsburg Landing and taken command in person. Besides the armies of Grant and Buell, he brought in some 25,000 troops who had been operating on the Mississippi, creating a combined army of well over 100,000 men. With this host he began to advance on Corinth, and just to be on the safe side (Halleck always liked to be on the safe side) and in case the Rebels were contemplating any more surprise attacks, he traveled at a crawl and had his men entrench thoroughly at the end of each day's march. He was not coming very fast, but he was coming, and there seemed to be nothing Beauregard, with his army of less than half the size of Halleck's, could do to stop him.

Attacking such a force in its entrenchments was out of the question. Even without the fortifications an assault would probably be suicidal unless it were possible to isolate some exposed portion of the Union army, and Halleck was taking great pains to see that such opportunities did not arise. On a couple of occasions the recklessness of one of Halleck's subordinates nearly presented Beauregard with the chance he was looking for. Yet each time his plans were a little too elaborate and his expectations a little too unrealistic; the strikes were never carried out.[90] Prospects looked equally bleak for Beauregard should he simply keep the army in its entrenchments around Corinth and await Halleck's arrival. Halleck had enough men to employ the slow but sure method that military men of that day referred to as "regular approaches." If Halleck used it—and no one doubted for a minute that he would—the destruction or capture of Beauregard's army was virtually assured should it be trapped and surrounded in Corinth.

Beauregard could have tried to take the initiative away from the plodding Halleck by some bold slash at his communications. It would have been dangerous, and there is no way of knowing whether it would have worked. Robert E. Lee would successfully defend Virginia against overwhelming forces for more than two years with such daring maneuvers, but Beauregard was not Lee and did not feel up to taking the risks involved. By May 25 Halleck had approached so close that Beauregard had no choice but to retreat.[91] Elaborate preparations were undertaken to keep Halleck confused while the Confederate army slipped away unmolested. These measures were successful, and by May 30 the evacuation of Corinth was complete.[92] Beauregard fell back to Tupelo, about fifty miles to the south.

Meanwhile, in Richmond, a careworn and very unhappy Jefferson Davis waited impatiently for Beauregard's explanation of why the vital rail junction of Corinth had been abandoned without a fight. It had not been an encouraging spring for the Confederate president. Besides the reverses in Kentucky and Tennessee, disaster had struck on the lower Mississippi, and in Virginia, McClellan's Army of the Potomac was within sight of the spires of Richmond. Davis's wife and children had already been evacuated from the threatened city. Within the southern capital the most bizarre rumors were afoot. One of them had it that Beauregard and Bragg had "notified the authorities that they will obey no further orders from Jeff Davis."[93] Such talk was another indication of the despair that pervaded in the apparently doomed city. The president was therefore in no mood to hear that in the one area where a costly but "complete" victory had been won, the Confederate retreat continued unchecked and without battle being given.

After Shiloh, Davis had redoubled his efforts to reinforce Beauregard's army. The governors of the southern states had been called on for still more men and arms.[94] Troops were transferred from hypersensitive Charleston and seriously threatened New Orleans.[95] So desperate was the president to send whatever help he could to the western army that he told the governor of Georgia "pikes and knives will be acceptable" if rifles or muskets could not be obtained.[96] Everything possible had been tried. To make matters worse, just about the time Beauregard decided to pull out of Corinth, a letter from him had arrived in Richmond emphasizing the importance of Corinth and stating his determination to hold it "to the last extremity."[97] In reply Davis had had his military advisor, Lee, write a letter to Beauregard hinting that things were bad all over and that Beauregard was going to have to try something desperate pretty soon rather than keep on retreating.[98] Now Beauregard had abandoned Corinth considerably before "the last extremity." Whatever excuses the general had to offer the beleaguered president were going to have to be very good.

At first Beauregard handled this by simply offering no excuses at all. When prodded by Davis to make some kind of explanation for the movement, Beauregard telegraphed that he had not had time to explain earlier but would presently send a letter explaining the retreat, which, he assured the president, had been "most brilliant and successful."[99] Curiously, the busy Beauregard had found time to write a long article for publication in a Mobile, Alabama, newspaper, defending his actions and modestly stating, "The retreat must be looked upon, in every respect, by the country as equivalent to a brilliant victory."[100] Jefferson Davis, for one, did not look at it that way, and he was not inclined to wait any longer for an explanation. He dispatched his aide with a list of questions for Beauregard to answer regarding the retreat from Corinth.[101] By this time Davis was beginning to doubt the wisdom of sending Beauregard to the West in the first place. He began to think that the Creole general might do better back in Charleston, where he had been so popular at the beginning of the war and where the present commander, John C. Pemberton, was tremendously unpopular and becoming more so every day. Bragg had been considered as a replacement and would have been acceptable to the Charlestonians, but Beauregard, pleading his own ill health, had insisted that Bragg could not be spared from the administrative duties of the western army. Knowing that the proud Beauregard would not easily give up the command of the Confederacy's second largest army, Davis slyly suggested to the governor of South Carolina that Beauregard might be the man for Charleston. Suppose the governor convinced Beauregard to put in for a transfer?[102] The governor thought it was a first-rate idea and undertook to get in touch with Beauregard at once.[103] Charleston was a backwater of the war, without major strategic importance, and putting Beauregard there would amount to putting him on the shelf. In a way it would be a demotion, since his responsibilities would be drastically reduced—yet those reduced responsibilities were about the extent of Beauregard's capacity. As Davis wrote to his wife in as succinct and accurate an analysis of Beauregard as anyone has ever made, "There are those who can only walk a log when it is near to the ground, and I fear [Beauregard] has been placed too high for his mental strength, as he does not exhibit the ability manifested on smaller fields."[104]

Before Beauregard's letter of explanation could arrive and before the general had had a chance to respond to the invitation to Charleston, he opened a way for Jefferson Davis to remove him sooner than expected from a position of major responsibility. In mid-June, without requesting permission and almost without warning, Beauregard decided his chronic ill health entitled him to a week or two of vacation at the popular resort area of Bladon Springs, north of Mobile. Accordingly, he turned over the command temporarily to Bragg and left, writing to Richmond to assure the authorities that he would be at Bladon Springs only "long enough to restore my shattered health." Then he would return to take over the army—which Bragg by that time should have sufficiently organized—and launch an offensive.[105] Apparently, Beauregard expected the war to wait while he took his ease at a spa.

This unprecedented action made Davis's next move simple.[106] If Beauregard's health was so bad he needed an indefinite period of rest, that was reason enough to remove him. If more reason were needed, there was the fact that Beauregard had essentially deserted his post in the face of the enemy and very much without permission, leaving his second in command to manage as best he could. In doing so, he had hamstrung Davis's efforts to provide a new commander for the troubled lower Mississippi sector. Just before Beauregard had announced his intention of taking a vacation, Davis had sent an order for Bragg to assume the lower Mississippi command. Now, however, with chief command of the Confederacy's main western army suddenly dumped in his lap, Bragg was unable to comply. "I am disappointed at the failure to execute my order," Davis wrote Bragg on learning of Beauregard's departure, "and fear the loss of time which has occurred may produce irreparable injury." The injury Davis feared was to the safety of the vital Mississippi Valley. The situation there was critical at the moment, and Confederate forces in that sector could not afford to be hamstrung by drawn-out confusion over who was to take command. "Send Genl Van Dorn with all possible dispatch," Davis ordered Bragg.[107] As for Beauregard, he had done enough to get himself removed from command two or three times. Davis, therefore, did not hesitate to inform Bragg that his temporary command of what had been Beauregard's army was now permanent.[108]

Beauregard, of course, never forgave Davis for this action. He made a habit thereafter of referring to the president as "that living specimen of gall and hatred," or simply "that Individual." To a friend he wrote, "If the country be satisfied to have me laid on the shelf by a man who is either demented or a traitor to his high trust, well, let it be so."[109] The Creole's enormous conceit assured him that the country would not be satisfied, and in part he was right. A few months later both of Louisiana's senators presented Davis with a petition signed by fifty-nine members of Congress protesting Beauregard's removal and calling for his reinstatement.[110] A portion of the press added its voice in much more raucous terms. Some disgruntled editors had already lashed out at the president, and with each difficult decision new enemies were made and old ones challenged to new heights of vituperation. "Cold, haughty, peevish, narrow minded, pig-headed, *malignant*," snarled the *Southern Literary Messenger,* "he is the cause [of our misfortunes]. While he lives, there is no hope."[111] Davis could take that, not with the wry humor of a Lincoln, but with a stoic determination to suffer anything for the cause. What mattered was that the country that had entrusted its leadership to him succeed in the struggle in which it was now engaged, and if that were to be achieved, Beauregard had to go. With Bragg in command in Mississippi and with adequate reinforcements from elsewhere in the Confederacy, Davis hoped it might be possible through a "desperate effort to regain what Beauregard has abandoned in the West."[112]

Jefferson Davis participated actively in the Shiloh campaign, working hard to procure the necessary troops and get them concentrated on northeastern Mississippi and giving Johnston frequent advice and encouragement. At the same time the president wisely resisted the panic cries that he resort personally to Tennessee and take over the active command of Johnston's army. Such a move would, in effect, have deprived the Confederacy of its commander in chief (that is, Davis could not have exercised that function effectively while trying to be a field commander at the same time). Davis's resistance to this temptation is the more impressive in view of the fact that he had originally desired to be not president but commanding general of the Confederacy. Later, during Beauregard's retreat from Corinth and thereafter, Davis played a less active though still important role in western affairs because his attention was partially diverted by the peninsula campaign in Virginia—a bad effect of locating the capital at Richmond.

Despite the distracting proximity of the Virginia front, Davis was able, during the spring of 1862, to do some clear thinking about the needs of the western theater and the importance of concentrating the Confederacy's limited forces. To a large extent this clarity came in response to harsh necessity. If the succession of Confederate disasters in the West had not been checked, the war could well have ended in 1862. Davis had wisely removed substantial numbers of troops from coastal defenses and sent them to reinforce Johnston. Notable among the units thus transferred was Bragg's Pensacola force. These troops had been on the Florida coast since the outbreak of the war and had seen almost no action at all. They were well trained, and their commander was a good general of whom the South needed to make better use. Without this force there could hardly have been a battle of Shiloh.

Davis's dealings with his generals in the West had been enormously complicated by the events of the Shiloh campaign—most important, by the death of Albert Sidney Johnston. Davis had had almost unlimited faith in Johnston, and Johnston had come as close as humanly possible to warranting that confidence. Once the military disasters of January and February 1862 had relieved Davis of most of his unrealistic expectations as to what Johnston could do with such scant resources, the president and his chief western general had made an excellent team. This teamwork could probably never be equaled by Davis in combination with any other general, except perhaps Lee. From now on Davis would face an infinitely more difficult problem in finding and using good generals in the West.

This was immediately illustrated in Davis's attempts to cope with Beauregard. The flamboyant general and the austere president had not had a good relationship while Beauregard was in Virginia, and events in the West had done nothing to draw them closer. Davis rightly suspected Beauregard of botching the battle of Shiloh but may have been slightly unfair to the general over his failure to halt the advance of Halleck's enormous army on Corinth. Still, Davis's assessment of Beauregard as basically unequal to the responsibility of commanding a major field army was entirely correct. In view of Davis's realization of Beauregard's inadequacy, it seems strange, not that Davis eventually made Beauregard's vacation from the army permanent, but that he waited so long, allowing a general whom he believed to be incompetent to continue in command of the Confederacy's most important western army. This failure to take quick and decisive action to remedy a bad situation was to be repeated in the future, as Davis addressed the formidable task of handling his western generals.

The battle of Shiloh itself must be considered a Confederate defeat. Johnston's goal of crushing the Union forces in Tennessee piece by piece and then regaining lost ground was not achieved. The South had thrown its best punch and failed to put its opponent on the canvas. More important, the losses of Shiloh, particularly the loss of Albert Sidney Johnston, could never be made good. Yet the battle had held some value for the South. The blow had staggered the northern forces in the West and shocked the northern generals. It gave the likes of Halleck and Buell an excuse to move with such ponderous slowness that the Confederacy had time to lick its wounds and try again to break the tightening stranglehold of the North.

8

THE GIBRALTAR OF THE WEST

While first Johnston and then Beauregard had struggled to turn back the Union advance through Kentucky and Tennessee and into Mississippi, Confederate arms had met with no greater success in stopping a Union drive up the valley of the Mississippi from its mouth below New Orleans. By mid-June 1862 virtually the entire Mississippi Valley was in northern hands. The last remaining Confederate stronghold along the whole length of the river was the town of Vicksburg, Mississippi. Perched on its bluffs high above the river and bidding defiance to Federal warships and soldiers, Vicksburg earned, during the year-long struggle that followed, a reputation that led Jefferson Davis to call it "the Gibraltar of the West."[1]

The disintegration of the Mississippi Valley defenses had started back in February 1862 with the fall of Forts Henry and Donelson. That double catastrophe had necessitated giving up Columbus, which Polk had taken at such great political cost and which was now outflanked by the Federal advance up the Tennessee River. The next Confederate stand was made at New Madrid, Missouri, where Polk had originally planned to set up his fortifications, and at the adjacent Island No. 10. A pitifully ineffective defense was made here by troops under Gen. John P. McCown, ending on April 7, the second day of Shiloh, with the surrender of 7,000 men.

This left the river open to the Federals as far south as Fort Pillow in Tennessee. That bastion had proved a much tougher nut to crack, especially since the Federal naval force facing it was seriously handicapped by the lack of a cooperating land force. Halleck had drawn off the troops that had been operating along the river to join his massive army creeping toward Corinth. Without army cooperation the navy was unable to take Fort Pillow, which held out until Beauregard's retreat from Corinth left its flank exposed. Then, like Columbus, it too had to be abandoned. On June 1, the day after the last of Beauregard's troops left Corinth, the Confederate garrison began pulling out of Fort Pillow, leaving no Confederate defenses on the Mississippi between the Federal fleet and the city of Memphis.[2] Less than a week later, on June 6, the Federal gunboats arrived at Memphis. There were bluffs at Memphis, and given time to prepare, the Confederates might have presented a respectable defense there. They were not given time, and the only resistance was offered by a makeshift fleet of armed riverboats that had been brought up the river from New Orleans.[3] It lasted about ninety minutes, and then Memphis too was lost.[4]

South of Memphis the land along the Mississippi is dismally flat. No high ground rises to break the monotony—or to provide a place for defenders to make a stand—until the river reaches Vicksburg, nearly two hundred miles to the south as the crow flies. By the time the Union forces coming down the river from Memphis reached Vicksburg around the end of June, they were greeted by a Union force already there—the Union naval squadron, with its accompanying land force, that had captured New Orleans.

Rumors of a Federal attack on New Orleans had been rampant since the late summer of 1861.[5] In fact, around the beginning of February 1862 a report circulated in Richmond that New Orleans had already fallen.[6] Though the rumor was false, no one could fail to see that sooner or later the North was bound to take aim at the South's largest city and most important seaport. The uneasiness about New Orleans had hastened the removal of the decrepit Twiggs and his replacement by the younger and more active Lovell. A northerner who had come south after the battle of Manassas, Mansfield Lovell was as committed a Confederate as any in the South, and he did all he could for the defense of New Orleans. As it turned out, nothing he did made very much difference.

The chief river defenses of New Orleans against a force advancing from the Gulf of Mexico were two forts, St. Philip on the east side of the river and Jackson on the west. By April 15, 1862, a force of seagoing warships under Flag Officer David Farragut had made its way through the difficult channels at the mouth of the Mississippi and arrived just below the forts. After a five-day mortar bombardment failed to reduce the forts to submission, Farragut determined to take his ships up the river anyway.[7] Accordingly, in one thunderous night, his fleet ran past the forts despite the blazing guns of their batteries and the efforts of another makeshift Confederate riverboat fleet.[8] Farragut had demonstrated another rule of Civil War naval combat: Even the best of forts could rarely stop ships, even wooden ones, from running past them. In order to destroy the ships, it was necessary somehow to detain them under the guns of the forts.[9] Lovell had attempted this, having various booms of logs and chains rigged across the river, but the current had been too strong and had washed the obstructions away. When that had occurred, Lovell had known that the game was pretty well up and that whenever the Union fleet came upriver, at least part of it would get through. On the night of April 24 every ship passed but one.[10] The running of the forts was especially disastrous because the surrounding terrain was so swampy and impassable that the only way to get to the forts was by river. With Federal warships on the river between the forts and New Orleans, the Confederate garrisons would be cut off from supplies and communication and would have no choice but to surrender. Worse still, there remained no means to defend New Orleans. As soon as Federal warships arrived off the levee, the city would have to capitulate, and so it did on April 29.

It might have helped had the armed Confederate steamers that were sent up the river to Memphis been kept at New Orleans, but the advance down the river from the north had seemed more of a threat than any possible action by the blue-water Federal navy. Regardless, Davis had been confident that the forts could stop the wooden vessels.[11] He had informed Lovell in no uncertain terms that "the fleet maintained at the port of New Orleans and its vicinity is not a part of your command."[12] Then he had ordered the flotilla to move upriver despite the protests of its own commander. According to one source at least, the naval commander, who was in Richmond at the time New Orleans fell, upon hearing of the disaster burst into the president's office and blurted out, "I believe if I had been there in my proper place this might not have happened." Jefferson Davis is then said to have "buried his face in his hands."[13] Whether true or not, this story illustrates the anguish and confusion the president must have felt at trying–unsuccessfully–to shuffle forces to meet two serious threats at once. It was a feeling he would experience frequently before the war was over.

Two Confederate ironclads had been under construction at New Orleans, which, had they been completed, might have played havoc with the Federal fleet. One of them, the *Louisiana,* was nearly finished. Curiously, its design had been selected by Leonidas Polk, and he had even tried to get Davis to name a colonel on Polk's staff as captain of the vessel. That, however, was a decision Davis never had to make. Nor did he have to decide whether to keep the boat at New Orleans, as many were urging him, or send it up the river, as he seemed inclined to do.[14] The *Louisiana* remained unfinished when the city fell and had to be scuttled to prevent its falling into Union hands. Meanwhile, Lovell successfully removed the government's supplies from New Orleans and evacuated his troops before the enemy arrived. He also ordered the heavy guns that were on the way to strengthen New Orleans' defenses to be diverted to Vicksburg, and he made provisions to use his troops to cover that city.[15]

Lovell's forces reached Vicksburg on May 12. They had been preceded by a couple of engineer officers and some men whom Beauregard had sent to begin building fortifications there.[16] Several days after the arrival of Lovell's men, a brigadier general appeared under orders from Beauregard to take command of the place. This created considerable confusion since Lovell believed Vicksburg to be in his department and not subject to Beauregard or his appointees.[17] In fact, no clearly defined line had ever been drawn between the departments. The northward-facing and southward-facing Confederate defenders had retreated until they had, in a sense, backed into each other. The dispute was ironed out, and Lovell was left with the supervision of Vicksburg's defenses, at least for the present.[18] It was fortunate that a decision was made quickly, for Farragut allowed little time for preparation. On May 18 his advance squadron showed up, and within a few days the rest of his seagoing fleet was assembled. Eight days later the fleet began a month-long intermittent bombardment that culminated when Farragut ran his ships past the batteries on June 28 and made contact with the Union fleet of ironclad river gunboats that had come all the way down the river past Island No. 10, Fort Pillow, and Memphis.[19]

Also on June 28 Maj. Gen. Earl Van Dorn assumed personal command of the Vicksburg defenses.[20] Ever since the fall of New Orleans the public outcry against Lovell had been growing. Though a court of inquiry would eventually find that Lovell had erred only in failing to notify the government that the river obstructions had been swept away, that he had in other respects performed as well as anyone could have, and that under the circumstances nothing could have prevented the fall of New Orleans, public opinion would have it otherwise.[21] Lovell's unpardonable sin of being born in the North made him an ideal scapegoat, and generally the nicest things he was being ac-cused of were "imbecility and incompetency."[22] Less generous-minded south-erners were thinking more in terms of cowardice and, of course, treachery, and Louisiana's governor was hinting broadly that certain "officers" ought to be "cashiered or shot."[23] The governor of Mississippi was in no better humor, and even the president's brother Joseph, who had recently had to flee his plan-tation just south of Vicksburg, disliked Lovell and thought he "had become so obnoxious that he could do no good."[24] Although Jefferson Davis did not hold Lovell guilty for what had happened, he tended to agree with his brother insofar as he considered Lovell too unpopular to be able to do much good.[25] Troops would not fight well if they believed their commander to be a fool or a traitor. Davis therefore planned to have Bragg take over the top command in Lovell's department. This idea was foiled when Beauregard went on vaca-tion and left Bragg in charge of the Confederacy's main army in the West. Since Bragg, who had been promoted to full general after Shiloh, was the only man whom Davis could trust with that important command, someone else would have to be found for the southern Mississippi River defenses—in short, Earl Van Dorn.

Van Dorn had been born just twenty-five miles downriver from Vicksburg near the town of Port Gibson, Mississippi, in 1820, son of a local judge and great-nephew of Andrew Jackson. Admitted to West Point in 1838, the cadet from Mississippi stayed near the bottom of the class rankings and wavered on the fine edge of washing out of the academy altogether for unsatisfactory con-duct. During his third year he lacked just seven of the two hundred annual demerits that would have mandated expulsion. Somehow he made it through, finishing a dismal fifty-second out of the fifty-six graduates in the class of 1842. In the years that followed, Van Dorn earned a reputation as a daring young officer.[26] He was wounded three times in Indian wars and once in the Mexican War.[27] In that conflict his conspicuous gallantry had won him a brevet promo-tion to the rank of captain.[28] It also won him the attention of Jefferson Davis, who would later remark that Van Dorn had been noticed more often for bravery than any other officer in that war.[29]

In his career as an Indian fighter on the plains, Van Dorn was equally fear-

Earl Van Dorn (Courtesy Mississippi Department of Archives and History)

less. As a major in the Second Cavalry Van Dorn led an expedition of six companies of cavalry and one of infantry, along with a handful of Indian scouts, in search of a Comanche and Kiowa camp that was reported to contain 10,000 individuals. Undeterred by this numerical disparity Van Dorn searched relentlessly until the expedition finally discovered the abandoned village. A count of campfires and lodge sites led to an estimate of only 2,000 Indians, but Van Dorn had demonstrated his imperviousness to fear in a way that must have given some of his subordinates more than a few uneasy moments.[30]

Van Dorn, whose friends called him "Buck," was strikingly handsome with blue eyes, dark skin, and wavy blonde hair, and if at five feet five inches his height was not striking, it at least made him the epitome of the ideal small, compact cavalryman. Women often found him extremely attractive. While stationed in Alabama, he went through a whirlwind courtship and soon married sixteen-year-old Caroline Godbold, overcoming the reluctance of her parents.

The approach of the Civil War found Van Dorn stationed on the Texas frontier, where he enjoyed friendly relations with the aged departmental commander Brig. Gen. David E. Twiggs. After Lincoln's election Van Dorn asked Twiggs what he should do; apparently taking his commander's advice, he then resigned his commission and offered his services to his home state of Mississippi. Mississippi was glad to have him and soon made him senior brigadier general of the state forces, second only to Maj. Gen. Jefferson Davis. The two worked closely together in creating an army for the state of Mississippi and became good friends. Davis even had the younger officer to his house for dinner to meet Mrs. Davis and the children.[31] When Davis was elected president of the Confederacy, Van Dorn succeeded him as commander of the Mississippi forces. Inducted into the Confederate army, Van Dorn served first in Texas, then in Virginia, and then, after Bragg had declined the job, in command of the trans-Mississippi region.[32]

Van Dorn had found the trans-Mississippi department in disarray. Indeed, the disarray had been Davis's chief reason for assigning an eastern general to take over the western command. The confusion involved primarily two Confederate forces. One, under former Missouri governor Sterling Price, was composed chiefly of Missourians and was operating in the southwestern part of that state. The other was located in northwestern Arkansas and was under the command of Texas general Ben McCulloch. For some time Price and McCulloch had steadfastly refused to cooperate with each other. Price, who was very popular in the West but whom Davis rightly distrusted as an amateur, was a major general of the Missouri militia and thought that fact entitled him to command over McCulloch, who had only a Confederate brigadier's commission. McCulloch, a colorful figure who had distinguished himself at the battle of San Jacinto where Texas independence had been won and then served as a Texas Ranger, a United States marshal, an Indian fighter, and an officer in the Mexican War, saw it otherwise, referring to Price as an "old militia general" leading "a half-armed mob."[33] The collection of troops, both Price's and McCulloch's, of which Van Dorn assumed command was indeed anything but a well-disciplined army. It was rather an unconventional assortment of individuals—Missourians, Texans, Arkansans, and even a few regiments of Confederate Cherokees and Choctaws from the Indian Territory.

Despite this Van Dorn began at once to dream big. "I must have St. Louis," he wrote his wife, "then huzza!"[34] Reality, however, proved to be far less enchanting. On March 7, 1862, Van Dorn met the enemy in his first battle as an army commander, not at the gates of St. Louis but in front of a little Arkansas crossroads called Elkhorn Tavern in the shadow of an Ozark range prosaically named Pea Ridge. Van Dorn hoped to catch the enemy unawares by circling around to attack from the rear, but his poor planning and management of the operation led to confusion and delays. The element of surprise was lost, and when the battle finally was joined, the Confederates went into action in two widely separated segments, unable to support each other.[35] On the right the segment under McCulloch met disaster almost at once. The Indians made one good charge and then settled down to celebrate their momentary success by scalping the prisoners and dancing around the captured cannon. The remainder of McCulloch's troops became disheartened and soon gave up the fight when McCulloch himself was killed. On Van Dorn's front the situation was better at first, but after exhausting his men in a day of costly and to a large extent fruitless assaults, Van Dorn missed his chance to make a respectable withdrawal and had his army routed when the Federals took the offensive the next morning.[36]

"I was not defeated," Van Dorn wrote in his report to Johnston, "but only failed in my intentions." The Mississippian was at some pains to place the events of the recently concluded campaign in the best possible light, at least as it pertained to himself. He attributed the nondefeat to "a series of accidents, entirely unforeseen and not under my control and a badly disciplined army." After this inadvertent self-indictment he went on to opine that the enemy must be "somewhat paralyzed" as a result of the battle and to propose making the most of this supposed state of paralysis by marching forthwith on St. Louis or, perhaps, New Madrid and thus relieving the pressure on the Confederate forces east of the Mississippi.[37] Johnston remained unconvinced and shortly before Shiloh ordered Van Dorn and his men to cross the river and join the Confederate army assembling at Corinth. Van Dorn arrived too late for the battle and since that time had served under Beauregard and Bragg.

The veterans of Shiloh, like Van Dorn's western troops, did not entirely approve of the dapper Mississippian. Confederate soldiers tended to be a fairly tough lot, and they liked their generals to appear especially manly. In this aspect Van Dorn did not always measure up. "He looked to me more like a dandy than a general of an army," wrote one disgusted veteran. "He was small, curely or kinky headed, exquisitely dressed, [and] was riding a beautiful bay horse, evidently groomed with as much care as his rider, who was small looking and frenchy."[38]

Whatever the common Confederate soldier might think of Van Dorn, Jefferson Davis retained faith in his Mississippi protégé. Now, with the southern Mississippi River defenses in need of a commander and with Bragg, the president's first choice, unavailable, Davis again turned to Van Dorn.[39] Concur-

rently, Davis carried out a thoroughgoing rearrangement of command assignments in the West. Such an action had been needed for some time because of
changes in personnel and in the military situation. Beauregard had suggested
one alteration that would have put all of Mississippi and Alabama under the
main general in the West.[40] Although it was a good idea in itself, it would have
increased Beauregard's responsibility, and that was the last thing Davis wanted
to do.

At the end of June, with Beauregard safely out of the way at his health spa,
Davis was free to make the necessary changes. Bragg's command, formerly held
by Johnston and then Beauregard, was now enlarged as Beauregard had suggested to include Louisiana east of the Mississippi River plus all of Mississippi
and Alabama and the western part of Georgia as far east as Atlanta. On the
other hand, Bragg's department was to be shorn of its trans-Mississippi portion—Davis had always considered such a region too big for one man, even
Albert Sidney Johnston—and this was to form another independent department.[41] Making the Mississippi River a dividing line would prove to be a costly
mistake, but otherwise Davis's new dispositions were prudent, as far as they
went. He should also have included the entire state of Tennessee in Bragg's
department; as it was, East Tennessee constituted a separate department.

All of this had very little immediate effect on affairs at Vicksburg. Van Dorn,
rankled to be now subordinate where he had previously been independent,
nevertheless graciously accepted Davis's assurance that the move reflected no
lack of confidence in him.[42] He would remain in charge of the Vicksburg
defenses, but now, at least theoretically, he would answer to Bragg rather than
directly to Richmond. In reality, Jefferson Davis's interest in the defense of
a town just fifteen miles from his own plantation was so intense that he and
Van Dorn kept up a steady correspondence, Van Dorn reporting the day-to-
day progress of the siege and Davis pledging that everything possible was being
done to support him and asking if there was anything else he needed.[43]

Actually, there was not a great deal for Van Dorn to do. He arrived at Vicksburg at about the same time the fleet of northern river gunboats joined up
with Farragut's deep-water squadron. The combined fleets continued the bombardment of Vicksburg for another two weeks, while Van Dorn waited ex-
pectantly for the enemy to make an infantry landing that would lead to a "foot
by foot" fight for the city.[44] The landing was never made; the Union commanders simply considered they did not have enough men to risk an assault.

Instead, it was the Confederates who initiated the next action. In the swamps
along the Yazoo River (a tributary that emptied into the Mississippi near
Vicksburg) they had been working on a secret weapon: an ironclad gunboat
of their own. Named the *Arkansas,* it was another makeshift job, and its engines were faulty and left much to be desired. Even so, it was fairly well protected against enemy shot, and it was the only ironclad the Confederates had.
Davis had been anxiously keeping track of its preparation and, having learned

his lesson from the debacle at New Orleans, placed it under Van Dorn's direction.[45] Van Dorn ordered it to pitch into the Federal fleet as soon as it was ready, and on July 14 it did so.[46] The result was a wild free-for-all in which a number of Union vessels got more or less shot up and the *Arkansas* came wheezing through on its junkyard engines and tied up at the Vicksburg wharf, somewhat worse for the wear but basically intact, prompting a jubilant exchange of telegrams between Van Dorn and Davis.[47]

The next few days were occupied with the Union fleet's attempts to destroy the *Arkansas*. These operations climaxed in another spectacular run by Farragut's squadron past the batteries.[48] A desultory bombardment was kept up for several days. Then, believing that it was useless to try any longer to sink the *Arkansas* or reduce the city by gunfire alone and fearing that the falling level of the Mississippi would trap his deep-water ships, Farragut took his squadron back down the river on July 24.[49] Three days later the river squadron pulled back to the north. Vicksburg had successfully weathered its first siege, an affair of some sixty-seven days.[50]

Van Dorn, however, was not satisfied with this victory. His attention was drawn down the river to the area around Baton Rouge, the capital of Louisiana, now occupied by Federal troops. The enemy was said to be making great inroads on the land adjacent to the river above Baton Rouge and to be committing such depredations as confiscating cotton and "stealing" slaves. The Confederates had available for use on this front one heavy gun, and a junior officer suggested it be placed at a town called Port Hudson, Louisiana, about ten or fifteen miles above Baton Rouge. This, he hoped, would contain the Federal forays out of that city.[51] In April Mansfield Lovell, at Beauregard's suggestion, had started constructing earthworks there as a backup position in case New Orleans should fall. In fact, New Orleans fell before the works could be completed, and they had to be abandoned in the general retreat to Vicksburg.[52] The location was a promising one, but Van Dorn thought he had a better idea. Why not capture Baton Rouge? The Federals did not have many men there or available in New Orleans, and Van Dorn had already considered having the *Arkansas* run down the river and clear it of Federal shipping all the way to New Orleans.[53] If they succeeded at Baton Rouge, perhaps even New Orleans could be retaken. Even before the Federal fleets had withdrawn from Vicksburg, Van Dorn began checking to see how many men the Federals were keeping at Baton Rouge.[54] As soon as the pressure on Vicksburg eased, he dispatched a force of four thousand men to the vicinity of Baton Rouge under Maj. Gen. John C. Breckinridge.[55]

A cousin of Mary Todd Lincoln, John Cabell Breckinridge was born near Lexington, Kentucky, in 1821, of the best Kentucky blue-blood stock. His grandfather had fought in the War of Independence and later helped Thomas Jefferson draft the famous Kentucky Resolutions of 1798. His uncle had attended Transylvania University as a classmate of Jefferson Davis.[56] Young John

John Cabell Breckinridge (National Archives)

C. Breckinridge had also attended Transylvania, where he studied law. When the Mexican War came, Breckinridge, like any bright young man with political ambitions, had gone off to fight in it. Using what political pull he already had, he managed to have himself appointed a major in the Third Kentucky. The regiment arrived with Scott's army too late for any fighting and spent several months with the occupation forces in Mexico City. During this time Breckinridge's chief duties were legal and included defending Gideon J. Pillow, who was brought before a court of inquiry for having been part of a conspiracy to thwart Scott's political aspirations and perhaps have him removed as commanding general by depriving him of credit for the victories at Churubusco and Contreras. This credit Pillow had decided to take for himself. To buttress this absurdity, bogus letters were produced, at least one of which Pillow wrote but persuaded a subordinate to sign. In the machinations that followed, Pres. James K. Polk, Pillow's old law partner, came to the rescue. The court of inquiry was packed with officers sympathetic to Pillow, and obligingly let the conniving politician-general off the hook.

With this legal "victory" under his belt, John C. Breckinridge returned to civilian life and continued his upward climb in the fields of law and politics. In 1849 he was elected to the state legislature, and two years later, to Congress.[57] In his youth Breckinridge had been one of the rare southerners who thought the institution of slavery was a necessary evil, but during the turbulent decade of the 1850s, his relatively moderate views on the issue gave way to a rabid sectionalism. He might consider slavery an evil, but no northern "fanatics" were going to prevent that evil from spreading wherever a southerner cared to take it. By 1854 his views had progressed so far in this direction that he played an active and crucial role in seeing that an explicit repeal of the Missouri Compromise was tacked onto Douglas's Kansas-Nebraska bill. In this endeavor he worked closely with Secretary of War Jefferson Davis, whose goals were the same.[58] In 1856 Breckinridge was elected vice-president on the ticket with James Buchanan. Four years later, when the Democratic party split into northern and southern wings, he became the presidential candidate of the rabid proslavery faction and, losing to Lincoln, was subsequently elected to the Senate from Kentucky.

Though he did not announce for the South immediately after Fort Sumter, he clearly intended to convince Kentucky to secede. It occurred to the Union authorities in that state that his frequent and heated secessionist pronouncements were beginning to sound very much like giving aid and comfort to the enemy. Accordingly, orders were issued for his arrest, and Breckinridge, getting wind of the matter, headed as quickly as a fast horse would carry him for the nearest outpost of the Confederate army. That happened to be the force under Buckner that Albert Sidney Johnston had dispatched to Bowling Green immediately after taking charge in the West. Buckner received his fellow Kentuckian cordially and sent him on his way to Richmond and his old political ally Jefferson Davis, along with a recommendation that he be appointed a brigadier general. Davis was also glad to see Breckinridge; so glad, in fact, that he apparently considered making him secretary of war in place of Walker, who had recently been eased out of office and for whom Benjamin was filling in. In the end Benjamin received the permanent appointment as secretary of war, and Davis gave Breckinridge a brigadier general's commission and sent him back to Johnston, who placed him in command of the army's Kentucky brigade.[59]

By the time Breckinridge and his division, including the old Kentucky brigade, marched for Baton Rouge in late July 1862, Breckinridge had been promoted to major general, one of only two politicians to be assigned that rank by Jefferson Davis.[60] The promotion had been purely political, too, for though he had served at Shiloh and thereafter under Beauregard and Van Dorn, Breckinridge had not demonstrated any dazzling military ability.[61] Still, Kentucky was a vital border state that the Confederacy was trying hard and against increasing odds to win, and for that purpose the popular Kentuckian Breckinridge in the uniform of a Confederate general was a valuable symbol. He was considered by some to be "the handsomest man in the Confederate army," yet he was also known as a hard-drinking, tobacco-chewing, rough-and-ready sort of general. Like so many southern generals he was proud, self-willed, and stubborn. Like most political generals he was no disciplinarian. On one occasion a captain in Breckinridge's division ordered a private to sweep the captain's tent. The private refused in profane terms and was thrown in the guardhouse. When Breckinridge heard of it, he dashed out of his headquarters, jumped on his horse, and, whipping the animal to a gallop with his slouch hat, rode off to find and chew out the hapless captain. He then forced the officer to apologize to the private and release him.[62] Clearly, Breckinridge could be appallingly irresponsible at times, yet when sober and in good form, he could usually be a fairly passable general.

He approached Baton Rouge cautiously and finally determined on a plan. His men would attack from the land side while the *Arkansas* came down and blasted the waterfront. By the time he was ready to begin, about half his men were out of action because of various sicknesses endemic to the fetid Louisiana climate.[63] It was decided to proceed anyway, and right on schedule, the *Arkansas* steamed down the river. Then, at the worst of all possible times, the jerry-built ironclad's rickety engines completely gave out, and it drifted forlornly toward the Union fleet. The captain had no alternative but to scuttle the craft. With the *Arkansas* out of the picture, Breckinridge's task was made even more difficult; but he still drove the Federals back under the cover of their naval guns before himself withdrawing and setting up camp about ten miles away. Without naval support, the complete conquest of Baton Rouge was beyond the means of this small, disease-ridden force. Van Dorn dispatched reinforcements to Breckinridge in hopes of cleaning out Baton Rouge once and for all and sent Davis a message informing him of the situation. The president was deeply sorry to hear of the loss of the *Arkansas* but heartily approved of Van Dorn's and Breckinridge's actions and expressed the hope that the success would "be made complete."[64]

While preparing for another attack on Baton Rouge, which he hoped Breckinridge could carry out by August 14, Van Dorn decided to go ahead and fortify Port Hudson.[65] If he could create a Confederate fortress there that Union warships dared not pass and if the Union gunboats could be prevented from descending past Vicksburg, it would give the Confederacy control of that stretch of the river. The ability of most ships to run past batteries was not widely understood, and regardless, few naval commanders were as resolute as David Farragut. All in all there was a fair prospect of success. Unless the Confederacy succeeded in holding some section of the river, the trans-Mississippi was virtually cut off, as no large bodies of troops and very little in the way of supplies could traverse a river patrolled by enemy gunboats. Also, the Red River, conduit for the products of the trans-Mississippi that were already desperately needed in the East, emptied into the Mississippi between Vicksburg and Port Hudson. If the Confederacy controlled both these points, it controlled the mouth of the Red and had relatively easy access to the beef and grain of the trans-Mississippi. If either Vicksburg or Port Hudson were lost, the Confederacy was cut in half, and though it had survived such a situation for a few months, it was unlikely that it could thus survive permanently.

Accordingly, Van Dorn put his lone heavy gun at Port Hudson and immediately began trying to scrape up more guns so as to create a respectable battery.[66] When vital operations in other sectors prevented him from strengthening Breckinridge for another essay at Baton Rouge, Van Dorn ordered that general to take his whole force to Port Hudson to secure the place.[67] By the end of August he had a fairly heavy battery in place but was still looking for more guns.[68]

Jefferson Davis recognized at once the importance of what Van Dorn was doing but was unable to send the reinforcements that were needed because a major new campaign had opened up in Tennessee. He sent what he could, including some trained artillerists and another heavy cannon—captured in Virginia that summer—for Port Hudson. He also informed Van Dorn that a new commander had been appointed for the trans-Mississippi department and suggested Van Dorn consult with him about possible cooperation.[69]

The new man was Theophilus H. Holmes, and he was not a good choice. A starchy relic of the prewar United States Army, Holmes was a native of North Carolina and a good friend of Jefferson Davis. He had ranked forty-fourth among the forty-six graduates of his West Point class of 1829. Despite this poor academic performance he had gone on to win a brevet in the Seminole War of the 1830s and another at Monterrey in 1846.[70] Though about the same age as Davis, Robert E. Lee, Joseph E. Johnston, and other prominent Confederates, Holmes seemed to be well past his prime by the time of the Civil War. In fact, he may have been suffering from arteriosclerosis.[71]

Though present at Manassas he had seen no action.[72] He later held the command of the North Carolina district before being called back to Virginia to take part in the peninsula campaign. There he had not exactly distinguished himself. At one point his division of green troops had been about to disintegrate in panic, and only he had remained calm—primarily because he was nearly deaf. In the midst of the thunderous battle he had emerged from the house he was using as a headquarters and remarked, "I thought I heard firing."[73] Nor was Holmes an easy man to work with. He could be brusque—some would say downright discourteous.[74] He also had a disturbing tendency to get caught up in the affairs of his own department to the point of forgetting the rest of the war.

Holmes's appointment was the more unfortunate since the man Van Dorn had left in charge of the trans-Mississippi, Maj. Gen. T. C. Hindman, was doing a remarkable job and showed promise of being the sort of commander who could cooperate well with forces east of the river.[75] Thomas Carmichael Hindman was a thirty-four-year-old native of Knoxville, Tennessee. As a young man he had moved to Mississippi, served with conspicuous gallantry in the Second Mississippi during the Mexican War, become a lawyer, and been elected to the legislature. Still not content he moved to Helena, Arkansas, during the 1850s, where his strident politics and his imperious nature brought conflict, enemies, and near death at the hands of a political assassin. It also brought him prominence and election to Congress. Somewhere along the line he also got himself a wife by the direct expedient of climbing over a convent wall. Hindman was active in pushing Arkansas into secession, and in the war that followed, his political prominence had brought rapid advancement in rank.[76] Unlike most political generals, though, he could be fairly efficient. When he had taken over in Arkansas, he had had just 9,000 men, including 3,000 unreliable Indians.[77] By an application of the conscript act that was so rigorous it bordered on the use of out-and-out press-gangs, he created in six months, out of an area that had supposedly been stripped of all military potential, an army of 20,000.[78] This army he was now planning to lead against the Union force that had dealt Van Dorn his nondefeat at Pea Ridge. T. C. Hindman was a colorful character. He was scarcely over five feet tall and wore his hair in long, curling locks. A dandy in dress, he affected patent leather boots, pink kid gloves, and frilled shirt fronts. The whole thing was completed by a rattan cane that he never seemed to be without. His manner was jaunty, but he was often tyrannical toward subordinates. His character was not without its flaws, some of which were yet to surface.[79]

Confident in Hindman, Van Dorn begged Davis not to appoint anyone to the trans-Mississippi command just now, warning that it would only create trouble.[80] Davis replied that the trans-Mississippi department was large and important and hinted that it might be too much for the relatively young and inexperienced Hindman.[81] Besides, though Davis left it unsaid, he was no doubt mindful that Hindman was a political general while Holmes was a West Point-trained, regular army man. That was important to Davis, who valued his own West Point education highly, but even more important was Davis's personal friendship with Holmes. Though the North Carolinian had been a failure in the East, Davis was anxious to give him another chance, and the West seemed to be the place for second chances. So west Holmes would go, despite Hindman's efficiency, Van Dorn's protests, and his own decrepitude. Davis had again allowed personal ties to blind him to the shortcomings of a general. This time, at least, there was the mitigating factor that he had also chosen a military professional over a political general, but in this case his preference for professionals did not serve him well.

Holmes, who would soon be known among his troops as "Granny Holmes," proved to be useless to Van Dorn in his operations against Baton Rouge and in his fortification of Port Hudson, but fortunately for the Confederacy the Union commander at New Orleans that summer was a political general who never seemed quite equal to whatever military situation he faced. He allowed the work at Port Hudson to proceed unmolested until that point was fairly secure.[82]

Jefferson Davis had, with a couple of exceptions, performed his duties as commander in chief very creditably during the summer of 1862. He was distracted by the at times alarming proximity of the Virginia fighting front and, after Robert E. Lee had had to replace the wounded Joseph E. Johnston at the head of the Army of Northern Virginia, deprived of what was in effect his chief of staff. Nevertheless, he took an active interest in the crucial defense of the Mississippi River. Having learned from the mistakes of the previous fall and winter, he showed a good grasp of the priorities necessary to make the most of the Confederacy's scant resources, and he evaded the pitfalls of dispersing the southern forces to defend every piece of southern territory.

He had, however, made two serious mistakes. One was the appointment of the inadequate Holmes to the trans-Mississippi command. It was a mistake typical of Jefferson Davis, a man who usually assessed his enemies much more accurately than he did his friends. Like the earlier blunders in appointing Polk and Crittenden, it would eventually prove costly. Holmes's uncooperativeness would make it that much harder to get the Confederate forces to work together across the Mississippi.

A more fundamental mistake—perhaps Davis's principal conceptual error of the war in the West—was the separation of the trans-Mississippi from the rest of the western area. Even a better general than Holmes would still feel a primary responsibility to his own department, and cooperation across departmental lines would not happen consistently unless a higher authority made it happen. Cooperation across the Mississippi River, the most obvious invasion route in the South, was vital; by making the Mississippi a departmental dividing line and creating on either side of it departments that were independent of each other and reported directly to Richmond, Jefferson Davis had placed the task of ensuring interaction squarely on his own shoulders. As long as he stayed in Richmond, it was a task he would have difficulty performing.[83]

It was a curious mistake, because it revealed a decline in the quality of Davis's strategic thinking. In setting up first Polk's and then Johnston's commands, Davis had avoided the pitfall of separating the trans-Mississippi. While on such issues as concentration of forces and subordination of inland naval forces to army command he was learning his lessons well, he actually seemed to be going backward on the more fundamental questions of strategy. Apparently the pressure, the confusion, "the fog of war" were all blurring Davis's strategic insights—a discouraging development, since Davis was a man who rarely admitted mistakes and who, having made a bad decision and been put on the defensive about it, might never change.

9

BRAGG MOVES NORTH

After taking Corinth Halleck had been content to consolidate his gains and spread his massive army out in relatively small garrisons to hold what had been won. The next spark of aggressiveness he showed was to send Buell with over 40,000 men marching east from Corinth to seize Chattanooga.[1] Chattanooga is located in the southeastern part of Tennessee near the Georgia line. It was a vital transportation center and the chief city of that part of the state. If it fell, the Confederate presence in Tennessee would be just about extinguished. Furthermore, a Federal-occupied Chattanooga would make a good jumping-off place for an advance on Atlanta, and at that point the Confederacy had very little with which to oppose such an advance. The unpleasant fact was that it also had very little with which to oppose an advance on Chattanooga.

East Tennessee had very nearly been lost to the Confederacy after Crittenden's and Zollicoffer's defeat at Mill Springs. The January 1862 battle had resulted in the virtual elimination of Crittenden's army—the right flank of Albert Sidney Johnston's long, thin line in Kentucky—as an effective fighting force. The victorious Union commander George H. Thomas had wanted to follow up his success by pushing into East Tennessee, and the Confederates could scarcely have stopped him. However, he was restrained by his superior Buell because of logistical considerations and because Buell had in mind the conquest of Nashville. Four weeks after Mill Springs, Grant's victory at Fort Donelson had made Buell's advance on Nashville as simple as marching down and occupying the city. Accordingly, the Union troops that would have been used to exploit the Mill Springs victory with an advance into East Tennessee were instead used to exploit the Federal success at Fort Donelson by an advance into Middle Tennessee. Buell's forces, including Thomas and his men, had marched down through Nashville and then joined Halleck's huge army for its push to Corinth. With the latter place securely in his hands, Halleck dispatched Buell to take East Tennessee.

The Confederate defensive dispositions in that sector had changed since the panic and confusion following Mill Springs. With Zollicoffer dead and Crittenden disgraced, distrusted by the army, and charged with drunkenness, Davis had had to find a new commander for East Tennessee. His preference for the post was Simon B. Buckner.[2] Buckner would have been a fairly good choice and indeed later in the war did some of his best work in that region.[3] However, by the time Davis tapped him for the position in the spring of 1862, he was already bottled up in Fort Donelson and soon thereafter became a prisoner of war. Johnston, still commanding at that time, could spare no other generals from his department and suggested that Davis send someone from the East.[4] Accordingly, the president detached Brig. Gen. E. Kirby Smith from the Army of Northern Virginia and ordered him to East Tennessee.[5]

A Floridian, Edmund Kirby Smith had ranked about the middle of his West Point class of 1845. Though his family had decided upon a military career for him when he was still quite young, he twice came very close to seeing that career end before it had begun: first, when he was almost expelled from West Point for lapses in behavior, and then, when his poor eyesight nearly led to his being denied a commission upon graduation. He did get the commission though, and served first with the infantry and later, after distinguishing himself in battle during the Mexican War, in Albert Sidney Johnston's elite Second Cavalry, resigning as a major when Florida seceded. Before reporting to Jefferson Davis at Montgomery, Smith had taken time to visit his mother at home. It had been Davis's intention to give Smith command of Forts Jackson and St. Philip below New Orleans, but the matter could not wait, so Twiggs received the command and Smith, as a lieutenant colonel, was sent to Virginia instead.[6] He served in the Shenandoah Valley, rising rapidly to the rank of brigadier general, which he attained a few days before the first battle of Manassas.[7]

During that battle he and his brigade fortuitously arrived on the field at precisely the right moment to help turn the tide.[8] As the brigade was being deployed into line, Smith had gone down with a bullet in the chest, and his capable second in command had taken over and led the brigade through the rest of the fight.[9] Nevertheless, once Smith had been taken back to Richmond to recuperate and word got around that he was not, as had originally been reported, dead, he became an instant celebrity, hailed as a military genius and likened to the great Prussian general Gebhard von Blücher, whose timely arrival on another field had brought allied victory at Waterloo.[10] This was heady stuff for a man who six months before had never commanded anything bigger than a company of cavalry, and the problem with Kirby Smith was that he started believing it. Hereafter he developed unfortunate symptoms of a badly overinflated ego, with little inclination to cooperate or to take orders.[11]

By early September he had recovered from his wound, but before returning to duty he proposed to the beautiful Cassie Selden. The sprightly young daughter of a prominent Lynchburg family, Cassie had waged a summer-long campaign to capture the bachelor general from Florida, culminating in decisive victory when the two were married on September 24. Davis extended Smith's sick leave so the couple could have a honeymoon. On return from his leave Smith was promoted to major general and ordered to take command of the Department of East Tennessee.[12]

As commander in East Tennessee Kirby Smith faced an unusual task. His fighting front faced northwest rather than north, running from Chattanooga on his left flank to Cumberland Gap on his right. While Halleck's juggernaut

Edmund Kirby Smith (Library of Congress)

of an army was creeping down on Beauregard and then occupying Corinth, two relatively small Union forces were moving against East Tennessee, one threatening Cumberland Gap and the other, Chattanooga.[13] Small as these forces were compared to the major armies facing each other in Mississippi, they were bigger than Kirby Smith's meager force, depleted as it was from sending reinforcements to Beauregard. Unable to meet the two dangers at opposite ends of his department, Smith sought help wherever he could: from John C. Pemberton, commander of the Atlantic coastal defenses; from Gov. Joe Brown of Georgia; and directly from Richmond.[14] Pemberton replied that he could spare no more men.[15] Brown said the same and began complaining to Davis that the defense of his state was being neglected.[16] Davis explained to Brown that there were simply no more troops to be had unless the governor could raise new levies or spare some of the forces assigned to coastal defense, a subject about which Brown was touchy.[17] Smith was assured that great confidence was placed in his "judgment and vigor" and told he was going to have to rely on his own resources.[18] Under the circumstances this was a confidence that Smith did not entirely share, and he was soon inquiring of the Richmond authorities which way he ought to retreat when he was forced out of East Tennessee, southward into Georgia or northeastward into Virginia.[19] Davis correctly instructed him that if it came to that, he should fall back into Georgia.[20] This was especially good advice since Smith had been contemplating a retreat into western Virginia, a disastrous move that would have allowed the Federals to seize not only Chattanooga but also Atlanta and much of the rest of Georgia.[21]

The president was not, however, willing to see East Tennessee abandoned. More strenuous efforts were made to find reinforcements. Beauregard was asked about the possibility of returning some of the troops he had borrowed from East Tennessee.[22] Faced as he was with Halleck's enormous army, he felt he could not afford to part with any, but from various other places, the president and Secretary of War George W. Randolph, who had replaced Benjamin that spring, managed to find enough troops to secure East Tennessee, at least against the present threat.[23]

Soon after, Beauregard left on his rest cure, and Bragg succeeded to command of the army. At about this time (mid-June 1862) the Confederates became aware that Halleck had divided his forces and was sending Buell east with a major contingent to take Chattanooga. Though the city might be held against the force it now confronted, it was doomed if Buell arrived before the Confederates made some drastic adjustments. Kirby Smith abandoned Cumberland Gap—which was of less importance than Chattanooga and had in any case already been outflanked by Federal troops moving through nearby mountain passes—and concentrated most of his forces at Chattanooga, keeping only enough troops around Knoxville to guard the vital east-west rail link. This deployment, however, still did not give him enough troops to meet Buell.

Somehow more troops were going to have to be found, or Chattanooga would be lost.

Davis could provide no futher reinforcements. The threat in Virginia was genuine; nothing could be spared from that front. The trans-Mississippi was less important but too far away to render timely assistance to East Tennessee. Theoretically at least, the president could have pulled even more men out of the already-reduced coastal garrisons at such places as Charleston and Savannah. Politically, though, this might have been difficult. Complaints had already started to come in from these quarters to the effect that they were being abandoned to the mercy of the Federals.[24] The crux of it all was that the Confederacy had fewer men than the North, and its generals were going to have to fight and win on this basis or else it did not have much of a future. Davis could only hope that the generals he had selected could make do with the troops he had given them. In reply to expressions of concern from East Tennessee politicians, Davis assured them that everything possible had been done to reinforce Kirby Smith and that, though Bragg would send help to Smith if he could, Davis feared there was "little hope of that."[25]

Bragg certainly would have agreed with that assessment. Upon assuming command of the army, Bragg's plan was to take advantage of the divison of Halleck's forces by striking straight ahead at the portion of the Federal forces that had stayed put while Buell had moved east. There were some problems with this plan. First, Bragg's army was in no condition to move then because it lacked wagons to haul supplies. Second, the host that remained to face Bragg in northern Mississippi still outnumbered his army three-to-two even without Buell's troops. Nevertheless, Bragg determined to move north as soon as he could get adequate wagons for the army's supplies. He suggested to both Kirby Smith and the Richmond authorities that whatever reinforcements were needed in East Tennessee be taken from Georgia or from coastal defense.[26] In reply, Secretary of War Randolph explained to Bragg that troops were already being sent to Smith from Georgia and that this was still insufficient. He pointed out that Beauregard had borrowed six regiments from Smith and never returned them and urged Bragg to help Smith if he could.[27] Still Bragg felt he could not release any men. If he sent reinforcements to Smith, Bragg explained, he would be completely on the defensive in Mississippi.[28]

The fact was that Bragg had not had enough time to consider the strategic situation and decide what he ought to do. After being immersed in the day-to-day details of running the army for Beauregard, he had suddenly found himself in command and had found that the job took some getting used to.[29] Having been in charge less than two weeks when he was called upon to decide whether or not he should send troops to Kirby Smith, his thinking on the issue was unclear. Thus, within two days of insisting that he could spare no men for East Tennessee, he abruptly changed his mind and dispatched a small divison from his army, sending it by rail in a roundabout route that took it through Mobile but was still faster than walking.[30]

The division Bragg sent was under the command of Maj. Gen. John P. McCown. By no means one of Bragg's favorite officers, McCown, a member of the West Point class of 1840, had bungled the defense of New Madrid and, as far as Bragg was concerned, was not fit to command a division. Bragg may have been using the movement as a test: If someone like McCown could handle the logistics of getting from Tupelo to Chattanooga, the rest of the army could not possibly find the matter difficult.[31] Whatever his motives for sending McCown, Bragg considered it his duty to warn Kirby Smith that McCown was not to be trusted in any position of major responsibility. Upon McCown's arrival Smith promptly demonstrated his opinion of Bragg's advice by placing McCown in overall command of the forces on the vital Chattanooga front.[32] It was not an auspicious beginning for the working relationship between Bragg and Kirby Smith. At the same time that he informed Smith of McCown's approach, Bragg promised that as soon as possible he would take the rest of his force and hit the rear of Buell's column, then still west of the lower Tennessee River.[33] With McCown's men in Chattanooga, Bragg hoped Kirby Smith would be able to hold that strategic town.[34]

Within about a week the reinforcements began arriving, but Smith remained convinced that he could hold Chattanooga only if Bragg could distract Buell (who, fortunately for the Confederates, was moving slowly enough to allow them plenty of time for deliberation). In order to facilitate Bragg's catching Buell from behind, Smith sent out two far-ranging cavalry raids to create confusion and hopefully induce Buell to stop or detach some of his troops. One of the raids was aimed at Middle Tennessee and was commanded by Nathan Bedford Forrest. The other, under John Hunt Morgan, headed for Kentucky. Bragg, meanwhile, was still unable to move for want of wagon transportation.[35] Nor was Bragg entirely convinced that such a move was the best available to him—especially after he inferred from certain intelligence reports that Buell's army was not marching on Chattanooga at all but actually pulling back in order to be transferred to the East.[36]

By this time Davis had become concerned enough about the situation to try to learn more specifically what was happening and what was planned. For this purpose he dispatched one of his aides to visit Bragg's headquarters at Tupelo and report back as soon as possible. The aide found the army healthy, well trained, and in good spirits, evidence of Bragg's great skills as a trainer and organizer. He found, however, that Bragg was still undecided as to whether he ought to strike the rear of Buell's column or advance straight ahead as he had originally intended. Davis wanted to know if Bragg was considering taking his whole army over to Chattanooga and joining Kirby Smith for a combined campaign, but as far as the aide could tell, he was not.[37]

Several days later Bragg wrote to Kirby Smith, insisting that Smith had enough troops to handle Buell without any further help from Bragg, who had at last come to the realization that the forces in front of him were too strong to allow him to take the offensive in Mississippi.[38] By the next day he had had another change of mind and decided to shift his army to Chattanooga and join Smith.[39] There were several reasons for his decision. Bragg was anxious to go on the offensive. He knew that Davis hoped the ground that Beauregard had lost would be won back. He also knew the southern people had not reconciled themselves to the loss of Kentucky and Tennessee. Besides, southerners simply expected offensive action from their generals, and Bragg was eager to prove himself. Upon taking command he had issued a statement to the troops promising that before long they would be on the attack again.[40] It was therefore with great chagrin that he had found himself unable to advance, first because of lack of transportation, then because of a drought that became so severe that an army on the march would have been unable to find adequate drinking water. Finally, he realized that the Federal forces remaining in northern Mississippi were too numerous and too well entrenched to allow a direct attack with what force he had. In a letter to Richmond he had lamented that could he have foreseen this "barrier to operations . . . a considerable portion of this force would have been thrown into East Tennessee, where successful operations might have been carried on."[41] It may have been this reference that caused Davis to inquire whether that was in fact Bragg's intent. Although it was not, Davis's query on this point may have spurred Bragg to actually do it.

Bragg was also influenced by the successful exploits of the cavalry raiders Smith had sent out. Bragg had high praise for Forrest's Middle Tennessee foray and joined Smith in recommending Forrest for promotion to brigadier general.[42] Unknown to Smith and Bragg, Davis had recently promoted Forrest to that rank. Nathan Bedford Forrest was one of the most colorful and controversial characters of the war. Born in Tennessee in 1821, he had barely six months' formal schooling there and in northern Mississippi, where his family moved when he was thirteen. Three years later his father, a blacksmith, died, and young Bedford Forrest was left to make his own way in the world. In 1841 rumors reached northern Mississippi that the Mexicans were about to invade Texas again. Forrest was among the volunteers who made their way to Texas only to discover that no invasion threatened and that there was no need for their services. Forrest found himself stuck in Houston, Texas, without money for his return trip and had to work splitting rails at fifty cents a hundred till he had saved enough for his fare. Back in Mississippi he partnered with his uncle in the livestock and livery-stable business. All went well until a long-standing feud between his uncle and the Matlock family finally came to a head. One day in the public square of Hernando, Mississippi, Forrest and his uncle were ambushed by three Matlocks and one of their friends. The uncle was shot and killed almost immediately, but in the gunfight that followed Bedford Forrest killed one of the bushwackers and wounded the other three.

Several years later he moved to Memphis and discovered a business in which there was a great deal of money to be made: slave trading. Even southerners, who saw slavery as the chief pillar of their culture, were often averse to the seamy business of the slave trade and sometimes felt contempt for those who practiced it. Forrest, with his unusual personality, seemed to be popular enough in Memphis, but to those who did not know him, that part of his past may have been a mark against him.

At the onset of the Civil War Forrest enlisted as a private in a Tennessee regiment, but Governor Harris, who knew and liked him, got him a discharge so that Forrest could recruit his own battalion of cavalry. This he did, recruiting men who could furnish their own arms, "shotguns and pistols preferable," and partially equipping the battalion at his own expense. He had served at Fort Donelson, where he had insisted there was a way out and had actually exited with his command and anyone else that wanted to come, wading the horses through a hundred yards of flooded backwater that was "about to the saddle skirts." He had also fought at Shiloh, distinguishing himself especially in covering the Confederate retreat, in which he was severely wounded. He had fully recovered, though, in time to lead the raid into Middle Tennessee that summer.

Nathan Bedford Forrest was six feet two inches tall, with a swarthy complexion, blue-gray eyes, steel-gray hair, and a black chin beard. His men were said to fear him more than they feared the enemy, and though at times it was probably true, they practically idolized him as well. He had had no military education whatsoever, yet he seemed to be a natural military genius with an intuitive grasp not only of tactics, but also of logistics (although the word probably was not in his vocabulary). His ferocity in battle was to become proverbial. By the time the war ended he had been wounded four times, had twenty-nine horses shot out from under him, and killed thirty enemy soldiers in personal combat. A man of many paradoxes, Forrest neither smoked, drank, nor chewed tobacco, but he had a terrible temper and could be extremely profane.[43]

His raid, which had so impressed Bragg, had created utter havoc in Middle Tennessee, destroying railroad bridges and convincing the Federals he was actually going to capture Nashville. In one particularly memorable affair he seized an entire Federal brigade, general and all, along with several hundred thousand dollars' worth of supplies.[44] When questioned later as to how he had managed this, he replied simply, "I just took the short cut and got there first with the most men." His famous success formula was thus born.[45]

In some aspects, Morgan's raid had been even more impressive than Forrest's. John Hunt Morgan was an Alabama native who had spent most of his adult life in Kentucky. In the Mexican War he had served as a first lieutenant in the First Kentucky Mounted Volunteers and after the war had tried unsuccessfully to obtain a commission in the regular army. Failing in that endeavor, he had made his fortune in various businesses, including slave trading. He had

Nathan Bedford Forrest (National Archives)

numerous vices, chief of which was gambling. His wife had died in 1861, and shortly afterward he had raised a company of Kentuckians to fight for the Confederacy and been commissioned a captain. Though he had fought at Shiloh, that was his only conventional battle. Unlike the multifaceted Forrest, Morgan's talents and tastes ran exclusively to guerrilla warfare. Hit-and-run fighting was, in a way, the ultimate form of gambling, and Morgan pursued it with the same sort of compulsive drive.[46]

Certainly, as his raid into Kentucky that summer was to demonstrate, he was good at it. Like Forrest he rampaged around the countryside destroying railroads and Federal supply depots and beating any Union force he came up against. On one occasion he captured a Federal telegraph station, had his own operator take over, and countermanded all the orders that had been issued for his pursuit. The panic he created among the Union rear-echelon types was a source of even more confusion; one Federal general reported the raider's 900-man force as 5,000, prompting a disgusted Lincoln to telegraph Halleck: "They are having a stampede in Kentucky. Please look to it."[47] Halleck promptly telegraphed Buell, "Do all in your power to put down the Morgan raid even if the Chattanooga expedition should be delayed." This, of course, was exactly what the Confederates had wanted in the first place, but Morgan was not finished yet. He tied Buell's logistics in knots by demolishing a railroad tunnel on the main Federal supply line. This he did with his usual flair by pushing flaming boxcars into the tunnel until the structural timbers burned through and the tunnel collapsed, putting the railroad out of business. Buell, who was never one to advance without abundant supplies, now ground to a halt.[48] Yet as far as Bragg was concerned, what was most impressive about Morgan's raid was his reception from the people of Kentucky. He had set out with 900 men in his ranks and returned with 1,200. Many more recruits were available, he assured his superiors. The people of Kentucky had apparently learned their lesson about despotic northern rule and were now ready to welcome Confederate troops as liberators.[49] If this was true, perhaps the reconquest of Tennessee and Kentucky might not be as hard as it appeared.[50]

Finally, Bragg was influenced to join Smith's campaign because McCown had shown that large bodies of troops could be shifted quickly from Tupelo to Chattanooga. Bragg had seen how the incompetent McCown had moved his few thousand men in a week; surely the whole army could get through.[51] Convinced, then, that Chattanooga was threatened and that a great opportunity beckoned to him if he went there, Bragg gave the orders on July 21, 1862, for the main portion of his troops to be transferred to Chattanooga. In Mississippi, he would leave Maj. Gen. Sterling Price with 16,000 men to guard the northern frontier of the state and make sure that the Federal troops were not pulled off that front to join Buell against Bragg. Also remaining in Mississippi would be Earl Van Dorn, commanding the defenses of Vicksburg and Port Hudson and also having about 16,000 men. Once affairs were put in order there, Bragg expected Van Dorn to join Price in an advance into Tennessee that would complement his own movement at the other end of the state.[52] Unfortunately, he left the command system somewhat muddled. Van Dorn outranked Price and so would command once their forces were joined. Until then, however, the two were independent, having different responsibilities and reporting directly to Bragg. Since Bragg would be out of touch for some time while moving into enemy territory, this meant that in essence Price and Van Dorn were responsible to no one at all. This was a recipe for failure, but somehow Bragg missed it.[53]

Another important mistake made at the outset of the campaign was the fault of Davis rather than Bragg. Whatever Bragg's faults may have been, he was a good judge of generals. He correctly perceived that the army under his command contained a number of inadequate generals, including the president's old crony Leonidas Polk. On the other hand, the army contained a number of promising young brigadier generals. Bragg explained this in a letter to Davis without specifically naming Polk and asked that the otherwise rigid rules of promotion by seniority be set aside so that some of the good young generals could be advanced and some of the useless "dead weight" of higher-ranking but less-qualified men be purged.[54]

Davis assured Bragg, "I wish to aid and sustain you in every practicable manner," but he refused this request, citing various legal technicalities that, he maintained, did not allow him to comply.[55] Davis could be legalistic, and he was often accused of rigidity. Yet less than a decade earlier, as secretary of war, he himself had attempted to circumvent the rules of seniority in order to promote able younger men. Perhaps the passage of time and the growth of wartime pressures were robbing Davis of some of his previous flexibility. More likely, it was the suggestion, clearly implied if not stated in Bragg's letter, that Leonidas Polk constituted part of the army's "dead weight" that turned Davis against the whole idea. Certainly the president had no intention of removing Polk. In Jefferson Davis's eyes his friends could do no wrong, and this fact was already apparent enough that even an outspoken man like Braxton Bragg was not going to press the issue. In his letter Bragg had hinted broadly at Polk's incompetence, but when Davis asked pointedly who it was that Bragg was calling unfit, he had replied by naming only several minor division commanders.[56] Polk would stay.

Despite its sprinkling of incompetent generals, the army, or at least the largest part of it, made it from Tupelo to Chattanooga in less than three weeks, arriving there and taking position before the incurably slow Buell, who had in the meantime entered the vicinity, could get around to starting his attack.[57] Bragg's move was bold and impressive, securing Chattanooga and depriving Buell of the initiative.

Unfortunately, it also put him in another confused command situation. When Davis had rearranged the command structure in the West after the departure of Beauregard, he had made the mistake of constituting East Tennessee, Kirby Smith's command, a separate department, independent of Bragg and answering directly to Richmond.⁵⁸ Bragg had never learned of this clumsy arrangement until several days after arriving with his army in Smith's department. Bragg was embarrassed, and the whole situation could have become ugly except that Smith was painfully aware of the need for Bragg's presence and for the moment was doing his best to be cooperative.⁵⁹ Before news of Bragg's movement had reached East Tennessee, Kirby Smith had written to Bragg suggesting that he do exactly what he was presently undertaking and, in desperation, stating his willingness to serve under Bragg in that case.⁶⁰ When he received word of the operation, Smith left his headquarters in Knoxville to meet Bragg at Chattanooga.⁶¹ There the two generals assured each other of their willingness to cooperate and agreed that since their only goal was "the success of our cause," no serious misunderstanding could develop.⁶²

Jefferson Davis was of the same mind and wrote to Bragg describing Smith as "one of our ablest and purest officers," so that Davis could "confidently rely" on Bragg and Smith being able to work together.⁶³ To Kirby Smith the president wrote that he hoped the junction of Smith's forces with Bragg's would "enable the two armies to crush Buell's column and advance to the recovery of Tennessee and the occupation of Kentucky." He also confided, "For weeks past it has been my purpose to visit your line, but it has not been possible thus far, and the approaching meeting of Congress may not permit me to do so hereafter."⁶⁴ Perhaps if Davis had been able to visit the western forces, he would have recognized and remedied a serious flaw in the command structure there. When Bragg's and Smith's armies were united, Bragg's superior rank would give him overall command. Otherwise, he would be able to issue no orders but would have to rely on Smith's concurrence. This was the same arrangement that prevailed in Mississippi between Van Dorn and Price, and in the end it would prove even more detrimental here. Whether in Richmond or at the front Davis should have seen the potential problem and dealt with it. He did not, and there the matter stood. However, at this juncture no conflict was evident since Smith promised to follow Bragg's directions and undertake no movement without his approval.⁶⁵

At their meeting in Chattanooga, Bragg and Smith worked out a basic plan for the coming campaign. One of the first items the generals had to take into consideration was the fact that Bragg's army was not ready to take offensive action. Only the infantry of the army had been shipped to Chattanooga by railroad; the cavalry, artillery, and wagon trains were making the journey on hoof, and they were not expected to arrive for another two weeks.⁶⁶ The infantry was all Bragg needed to stop Buell from taking Chattanooga, but the infantry alone could not undertake an extended campaign. Therefore, it was decided that while Bragg and his troops waited in Chattanooga, Kirby Smith, relieved now of the necessity of covering two widely separated points, would unite his entire force and, along with a couple of brigades from Bragg's army, go up to Cumberland Gap to deal once and for all with the small Federal force that had been causing so much trouble there. Having disposed of that threat, Smith was to return to assist Bragg. Bragg would maneuver into Buell's rear and force him to fight under conditions favorable to the Confederates in order to maintain his supply lines. With Kirby Smith's force present to help out, the Confederates would be able to dispose of Buell.[67]

With Buell's army out of the way, Smith and Bragg would then march north and occupy Kentucky, to be received there, they assumed, by a grateful populace and thousands of recruits. The late-summer drought would have lowered the water level in the Tennessee and Cumberland rivers enough to keep the Union gunboats out, and that would allow the Confederates to build some forts—strong, well-sited forts this time—that would keep the gunboats out for good. The Federal armies remaining in West Tennessee and northern Mississippi would have their supply lines cut and would have to retreat—theoretically with Price and Van Dorn in hot pursuit. When they reached Kentucky, there would be a grand battle, and these Federals too would be taken care of. The Confederate frontier would be established on the Ohio, and all of the year's lost territory would be recovered. If, on the other hand, this strategy should be wrecked by Buell's receiving large reinforcements from West Tennessee and northern Mississippi, Bragg expected Price and Van Dorn to dispose of the remaining Federal forces in those areas and then threaten Buell's rear.[68] Either way, it seemed the Confederates were bound to win.

Smith immediately readied his troops to undertake the first part of the plan, the movement on Cumberland Gap. Even before he left Knoxville, though, he began to have doubts about the plan he and Bragg had just designed. He had reports that the Federals at Cumberland Gap were well entrenched and had a month's supply of food on hand. Even if he succeeded in taking a page from the Federals' own book and positioning his force at the rear of the gap by using other mountain passes, Kirby Smith would be faced with the prospect of a month-long siege. Since he did not find this prospect pleasant, he suggested an alternative to Bragg: Bypassing the Federals at Cumberland Gap, he would leave them cut off behind him with a small force to watch them and with the rest of his force strike out for Lexington and the heart of the Kentucky bluegrass region.[69]

This would have been a fine plan, except that Kirby Smith was forgetting about Buell's army, which, with the new levies it was now receiving from the North, would be too big for Bragg to handle alone. Eliminating Buell's army was the key to the campaign, and Smith would not be contributing to it at all by wandering up into Kentucky when the decisive battle was supposed to be fought in Middle Tennessee.[70] Perhaps Smith was losing his nerve. He wrote to Davis at this time, confessing, "I feel the great responsibility of my position," and suggesting that another general be sent to take over his command, under whom he would then serve as a subordinate.[71] Davis did not respond to this curious request. On the other hand, it may be that Smith was still suffering from an overinflated ego and that his desire to take off on his own hook and invade Kentucky without Bragg was a symptom of an unhealthy ambition. Certainly Smith would have been quick to disclaim any such motive. In a letter to his wife about this time Smith mentioned the subject of ambition. After comparing himself to Napoleon, Cortez, and Moses, he added, "I care not what the world may say, I am not ambitious."[72] Though this might have an exceedingly hollow ring to it, the workings of Kirby Smith's mind during this period often seemed to be erratic and illogical, and the most likely explanation is that both motives, hunger for glory and fear of responsibility, were working on him simultaneously. That tended to make him an unstable commander and a difficult man with whom to cooperate, as Bragg would learn to his sorrow.

Bragg was skeptical of Smith's plan to bypass Cumberland Gap and head for Lexington, pointing out that Smith must not go too far away until Buell had been defeated.[73] Grudgingly Smith agreed and promised not to advance on Lexington until Bragg thought the time was right. He argued, however, that every day's delay would decrease their advantages in Kentucky.[74] He also wrote to Davis, explaining his plan, urging the necessity of it, and insinuating that Bragg had concurred.[75] Apparently, Kirby Smith never abandoned the idea of heading straight for the bluegrass region as soon as he skirted Cumberland Gap, for he continued making preparations for such a move.[76] Bragg had warned him that if he started north before Bragg could support him, Buell might quickly move his troops to Kentucky by rail and annihilate Smith's force. Smith was not impressed. Send some cavalry to tear up the railroads, he advised Bragg before setting off for the mountain passes.[77]

Upon reaching the rear of Cumberland Gap, Smith decided the Federal fortifications there were impregnable and the garrison could hold out twenty or thirty days. He also decided that, mountain roads being what they were, he could not draw his supplies from Tennessee. Since the locality in which he then found himself did not have adequate provisions for his army, he had only one choice as he saw it: He would march on Lexington. Gleefully he sent off a dispatch informing Bragg of this.[78]

Under the circumstances, Bragg had little choice but to approve of Smith's action. It did, however, put him in a difficult position.[79] He was still unable to move his army out, because his wagons and artillery were taking longer than expected to reach Chattanooga. Bragg blamed "inefficient officers," and he was probably right.[80] At least some of the army's artillery were traveling very leisurely indeed. One artillerist reported getting his watch fixed, going swimming at least five times, eating very well, and attending five dances, all on the way from Tupelo to Chattanooga. Some members of his battery were regularly drunk and disorderly. Another soldier, somewhat more genteel, had dinner with a local family and sat for three or four hours, talking, reading poetry, and listening to the piano. On several occasions the officers had unlimbered a cannon and staged a firing demonstration for the entertainment of the ladies who had come out to see the troops.[81]

Meanwhile Bragg was languishing in Chattanooga, wondering what was delaying the rest of his army and preventing him from getting on with the war. Also, Kirby Smith's premature move had now changed the nature of the operation. What would have been a campaign to cut off and destroy Buell's army in Middle Tennessee became a raid to penetrate deep into Kentucky. The problem with this was that Bragg and Smith would be far from their supply sources and would therefore have to live off the land and keep moving most of the time. They would not be able to wait for the ideal opportunity but would have to strike quickly. Still, the plan had great potential. If the Confederates could disrupt Union communications and supplies, and if the people of Kentucky would rise en masse against the Federals, Buell might yet be beaten. The crucial factor was what the Kentuckians did. As Smith expressed it in letters to Bragg and Davis, "Our presence will give the true men of Kentucky the opportunity for rallying to our standard"; and "should they [the Kentuckians] reinforce me and strike for our cause all will be well; on the contrary, should they fail to do so it cannot be concealed that my position will be a very precarious one."[82]

On August 27, 1862, Bragg was finally able to begin his movement northward.[83] By this time Buell knew what was going on and was himself moving in that direction.[84] For a time the two armies, Bragg's and Buell's, traveled on parallel courses up through the state of Tennessee, each striving to outrun the other.[85] If Buell's army could get ahead of Bragg's, its own supply lines would be secure, Smith's army would be cut off and all but doomed, and the people of Kentucky would never have a chance to throw their weight one way or the other. On the other hand, if Bragg's men won the race, Buell's communications would be severed, and that general would (in theory) have to force a battle under unfavorable circumstances and—what was particularly important to the Confederates—quickly. Bragg still hoped that in that case Smith would join him for the showdown with Buell.[86] As a further bonus for beating Buell to Kentucky, Bragg would be able to threaten Louisville and even Cincinnati. The cities were very lightly defended at the time and in an advanced state of panic from the mere appearance of Kirby Smith in central Kentucky. In Cincinnati business had come to a standstill as every able-bodied man was employed in digging trenches to be manned by assorted home-guard units and a motley collection of rustic "squirrel hunters" who had emerged from the woods at the governor's frantic pleas for volunteers.[87]

Buell had a head start. Kirby Smith's movement had alerted him, and he had abandoned his position in front of Chattanooga before Bragg was ready to march.[88] By the time Bragg's army left Chattanooga, Buell's troops were already in the neighborhood of Nashville, eighty miles farther north.[89] After several days on the march Bragg's men were still toiling through the mountainous region just north of Chattanooga.[90] However, Buell made the mistake of pausing at Nashville to throw up fortifications there.[91] Perhaps he thought Nashville was Bragg's immediate objective. In any case, his hesitation gave Bragg a desperately needed edge of several days marching. By September 7 Buell realized where Bragg was headed and got his men across the Cumberland at Nashville and moving north again.[92] Bragg was in high spirits, and he was pushing his men hard. The troops' morale was also high, and though footsore they were covering a great deal of territory.[93] On September 9, just two days behind Buell, Bragg crossed the Cumberland at a point about fifty miles east of Nashville.[94] By September 11 Buell's army was approaching Bowling Green, the Kentucky town whose occupation by Confederate troops Albert Sidney Johnston had ordered a year earlier. Bragg's army was several miles east of Buell's and about even with it. Advanced elements of Bragg's troops were nearing Cave City, squarely between Buell and his base at Louisville.[95] Bragg had won the race.

Kirby Smith, meanwhile, had been enjoying successes in some ways even more exhilarating. After giving his troops a week's rest at Barbourville, just north of Cumberland Gap, he headed them northwest toward Lexington and bluegrass country on August 25, two days before Bragg got under way from Chattanooga. The first few days of the march brought little encouragement, as the army struggled through a region of sparse population and sparser supplies and where such inhabitants as there were did not tend to be well disposed to the tattered and dusty troops who trudged past their homesteads. The fifth day of the march, however, presented a starkly different prospect. As the head of the column reached the top of an eminence known as Big Hill, the soldiers got their first glimpse of the bluegrass and were "astonished and enchanted," as Kirby Smith would write in later years, by the sight of this "long rolling landscape, mellowing under the early autumn rays."[96] The Confederates were not to have undisputed possession of the promised land they saw spread out before them. The tail of the column had hardly swung down the north slope of Big Hill before the head made contact with the enemy a few miles short of Richmond, Kentucky.

Smith's advance guard consisted of two brigades on loan from Bragg, and the general commanding it was one of the most remarkable and able men in this or any other army. Brig. Gen. Patrick Ronayne Cleburne, whom Jefferson Davis would later call "the Stonewall Jackson of the West," had been born in County Cork, Ireland, on St. Patrick's Day, 1828, the son of a prominent doctor. Eighteen years later, humiliated when insufficient knowledge of Greek and Latin caused his failure at an examination for entrance into the apothecary's trade, young Cleburne ran off and enlisted in the British army. After three years he had risen to the rank of corporal; despite assurances from his captain that he would soon be commissioned if he stayed, he bought his discharge and took ship for America.

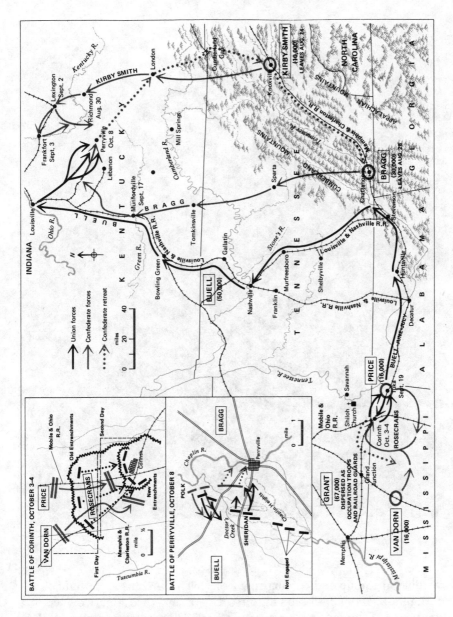

Map 9.1 The Western Theater, Summer–Fall 1862

Patrick Ronayne Cleburne (National Archives)

Settling in the up-and-coming town of Helena, Arkansas, he fulfilled his youthful aspirations by becoming first a clerk and then a part owner of a drugstore. The United States, though, offered far broader opportunities than Cleburne's native Ireland, and a fast-growing town like Helena was an ideal place to catch the scent of such new possibilities. The young Irishman decided to move on to greater things, and selling his interest in the drugstore, he took up the study of law and soon hung out his shingle.[97] He was prominent and well liked in Helena and took an active role in civic affairs. He was a vestryman at St. John's Episcopal Church and a member of the Sons of Temperance, an organization advocating prohibition of "spiritous liquors" and requiring its members to take a pledge of total abstinence except for medicinal purposes.[98]

Cleburne became friends with another young Helena lawyer and future Confederate general, Thomas C. Hindman. Hindman was the same age as Cleburne and had come to Helena in 1854 from Tennessee. Over the next two years Cleburne, with the aid of Hindman's Tennessee acquaintance Gideon Pillow, kept the hotheaded young Hindman out of at least one duel. In 1856 Hindman involved his friend in deeper trouble. Hindman and Cleburne were allies that year in a political battle against the Know-Nothing party over a seat in the state senate. Hindman, revealing a bent toward tactlessness, had had published in a Helena newspaper an unsigned letter referring to the Know-Nothing candidate as "the mulatto would-be Senator." A few days later Hindman learned that his enemies were planning to ambush him that afternoon as he walked from his law office to the Commerce Hotel for dinner. Hindman was no coward, but he hoped to improve the odds as much as possible; since Cleburne was said to be a good shot and since his law office was next door to Hindman's, Hindman asked him to come along and back him up if shooting started.

The Irishman was willing and prepared himself by pocketing two derringers he kept in his office. Shortly after one o'clock Hindman and Cleburne stepped out onto Porter Street and began their walk. A block and a half on Porter Street, a left turn on Front Street, and then another half block would bring them to the Commerce. They passed beyond the block of offices where they had started and crossed River Alley—so far, so good. The next block was taken up completely by the long side of Myrtle & Moore's Drygood Store. The young lawyers strode steadily along the side of the building, and reaching Front Street, they turned to pass across the front of the store. Just ahead was the Commerce. Suddenly the midday stillness was shattered by a blast of gunfire from the doorway of the store, where two of Hindman's enemies had been hiding. Hindman went down with a bullet in the side, and as Cleburne whirled to face the assailants he was shot in the back by a third gunman who was concealed in another entranceway farther up the street. Keeping his feet, Cleburne returned the fire. In the shoot-out that followed, Cleburne stood in the open street with four gunmen firing at him from doorways and windows. When it was over, one of the attackers was dying and the other three were hiding in the back of the store while Cleburne remained where he was, a pistol in each hand, bellowing his defiance and daring them to come out if any of them was man enough. None of them was, and presently Cleburne collapsed. For a time his life was in danger, but eventually both he and Hindman recovered.[99]

Pat Cleburne was not born in the South, and he never owned a slave. Yet as the Civil War approached, he had no doubts as to what his course would be. A few weeks after Sumter he expressed his feelings in a letter to his brother. "I am with the South in life or death, in victory or defeat," he wrote. "I never owned a negro and care nothing for them, but these people have been my friends and have stood by me on all occasions." Now he was going to stand by them. He had enlisted as a private in a local volunteer company in 1860. In the spring of 1861, as the troops were being organized into larger units, he was chosen in rapid succession captain of his company and then colonel of his regiment, the Fifteenth Arkansas. The regiment was sent to join the forces of Gen. William J. Hardee in northeastern Arkansas, and Cleburne and Hardee soon became close friends.[100] Hardee's skill as a military instructor may have helped Cleburne master his new trade as an officer even more quickly than he otherwise would have. Yet Cleburne, with all the dogged loyalty of his nature, would be pulled along by Hardee's penchant for army intrigues into positions that would not only do serious injustice to the man at whom they were aimed but also harm Cleburne's career and the Confederacy's hopes for independence.

Cleburne and his men were transferred east of the Mississippi along with Hardee to join the forces of Albert Sidney Johnston in Kentucky. By early March 1862 Cleburne's merit as an officer was already making him conspicuous, and he was promoted to brigadier general.[101] Barely a month later Cleburne and his brigade formed part of the first assault wave at Shiloh. He had done well there, and by the time Bragg and Smith had begun preparing for their present northward movement, Bragg had come to think very highly of the young Irish general. (Undoubtedly he was one of the promising young brigadiers Bragg had in mind for rapid promotion when he urged Davis to clear some of the incompetent generals out of the army.) As Bragg waited in Chattanooga for his wagons and artillery to arrive, he dispatched Cleburne with his own and one other brigade—essentially a small division—to beef up the force with which Kirby Smith would march against Cumberland Gap.[102]

Cleburne—or "Old Pat" as his soldiers affectionately called the thirty-four-year-old general—was just under six feet tall, slender and wiry with broad shoulders and the habit, learned in the British army and never forgotten, of carrying himself ramrod straight. He had gray eyes, high cheekbones, and a high forehead framed with black hair. Despite his good posture, his movements could not be described as graceful. Indeed, the impression he made was more of stiffness and awkwardness, perhaps the result of his shy, quiet personality.[103] He was a disciplined man who instilled discipline in the men he commanded. He abstained from liquor and tobacco because, as a member of his staff later explained, "he felt responsible for the lives of his men, and feared the possible effects of intoxicants for proper discharge of his duties." Besides, "a single glass of wine," the staff officer continued, "would disturb the steadiness of his hand in use of the pistol, and effect his calculations in playing chess."[104] Whatever his calculations on the chessboard may have been, those he made on the battlefield were seldom in error.

Near Richmond, Kentucky, Cleburne was about to give a demonstration of those calculations. The men of his two brigades tramped down the long slope of Big Hill and fanned out on either side of the road to make contact with the Union soldiers who were waiting to dispute their advance into the sleepy Kentucky town of Richmond and the "long rolling landscape" of the bluegrass beyond. The clash that followed was brief, being brought to a close prematurely by fall of night, but Cleburne had no thought of stopping there. With Smith's permission he made preparations to strike the enemy a crushing blow as soon as daylight returned. At first light the troops went forward. The sides were evenly matched numerically, but the Federals were green and untrained while Cleburne's men were veterans of Shiloh and of Cleburne's own rigorous training. The result was never in doubt, though Cleburne was unable to stay and savor the victory he had orchestrated. Early in the attack one of Cleburne's colonels was wounded. Stopping to speak with him, Cleburne himself was hit in the cheek by a bullet that knocked out some teeth and then emerged from his mouth, which was open at the moment. Spitting blood and unable to talk, Cleburne was forced to retire from the field, but the maneuvers he had ordered before being wounded carried his troops to a smashing victory. More than three-fourths of the Federal force was killed, wounded, or captured, and the Confederates also seized nine cannon, ten thousand rifles, and the entire Federal supply train.[105] No organized Federal forces now stood between Kirby Smith and Lexington. After a day of rest (it was Sunday), thanksgiving, and burying the dead, Smith's army continued its advance.

Bragg, meanwhile, was intent on reaping the fruits of his successful race against Buell. He decided to concentrate his forces as soon as possible at Glasgow, Kentucky.[106] This would put him between Buell and Kirby Smith and at the same time keep him in position to cut Buell off from Louisville. By the fourteenth, when Buell's troops began arriving in Bowling Green, Bragg had his army together near Glasgow. On that day one of Bragg's brigadiers made an unauthorized small-scale attack on a small Federal stronghold at Munfordville, Kentucky, and was soundly repulsed. The next day, Bragg, unwilling to let the defeat go unavenged, ordered his entire force to converge on the little fort and its hapless 4,000-man garrison.[107] Munfordville was on the Green River about twenty miles northwest of Glasgow and in many ways was an even more advantageous position. With Bragg in Munfordville, Buell could not threaten Smith in Lexington or draw supplies from his base at Louisville. As long as Bragg remained there and resolute, Buell was not likely to reach Louisville without a fight.

The Federal force at Munfordville never had a chance, and on September 17—the same day on which two other armies were meeting several hundred miles to the east to dispute the crossing of Antietam Creek—the Federal commander at Munfordville, an Indiana businessman with no experience at all in war, gave up without a shot being fired. The surrender was formally received by Simon B. Buckner, recently exchanged and promoted to major general after having surrendered Fort Donelson seven months earlier.[108]

This left Bragg in a commanding position. He had won the race to Kentucky. He had cut Buell's supply lines. Now, according to all the rules of warfare, Buell was going to have to do something about it. In this case that probably meant attacking Bragg at once in order to reopen a line of supply. In such a battle Bragg would have all the advantages, even without Kirby Smith. Buell's alternative was to slip around Bragg and reach Louisville by roads other than those Bragg blocked.[109] This was possible, but with any luck Bragg ought to be able to take the plodding northern general in flank if he tried such a move. Bragg, therefore, settled down at Munfordville and confidently waited for Buell to get on with it. To Bragg's increasing annoyance, however, Buell did nothing.

Buell was an extraordinarily methodical, deliberate general. In fact he was dead slow. The movement from near Chattanooga to Bowling Green had been about the fastest thing anyone under Buell's command had ever done, and Bragg had beaten him to his destination despite spotting him several days' march and traversing rougher country. Part of what made Buell so slow was the enormous supply train he insisted his army drag with it wherever it went. Now, however, his huge supply train was coming in handy. His army could last for some time without receiving anything from Louisville, and he could actually afford to wait longer than Bragg, who was depending for supplies on what his men could gather from the surrounding countryside. Eventually, there would be no supplies left within range of Bragg's foraging parties, and then it would be Bragg who would be in a tight spot. All that was required of Buell was to do nothing, and that was something Buell did very well.[110]

Up to this point Bragg had conducted a brilliant campaign. He had improvised well in the face of Smith's uncooperativeness. Davis, deeply absorbed in Lee's invasion of Maryland, had nevertheless taken time to write and say that he fully approved of Bragg's handling of the situation.[111] Now, however, he began running into difficulties. Supplies were running low around Munfordville. He got some supplies from Smith, but they were not nearly enough. He could not attack Buell, since the Federal army outnumbered his and was strongly entrenched. Things might have been different had Smith been on hand, but Smith was not interested. He had spread his troops throughout the bluegrass region to gather supplies, and then when the few thousand Union troops cut off at Cumberland Gap had tried to escape to the north, he had sent his whole available force chasing them all over eastern Kentucky.[112] Bragg could not order Smith to join him since he did not command him until they were actually united. To Bragg's urging that Smith join him, Smith replied that he could not leave the bluegrass area "exposed."[113] All the while, Smith was urging Bragg to hurry up and defeat Buell. This, he explained, was a political as well as a military necessity, since "Buell's army had always been the great bugbear to these people [the Kentuckians], and until [it is] defeated we cannot hope for much addition to our ranks in Kentucky."[114]

Lack of a proper reception in Kentucky was the second major problem Bragg faced, and it was a much more fundamental one than his awkward situation at Munfordville. The whole campaign had been based on the assumption that Kentucky would rise as soon as Confederate armies appeared within its borders. Indeed, the reception in central Kentucky was much better than what Smith and his men had received in the mountainous eastern portion of the state.[115] As Smith's men marched into Lexington, the town went wild. Confederate flags appeared, cheering crowds lined the streets, baskets of food and buckets of cold water were brought out for the weary soldiers. Smith dashed off a jubilant dispatch to Bragg assuring him they would soon have 25,000 Kentucky recruits.[116] Somehow, though, the recruits had failed to materialize. Enthusiasm was high, but volunteers were few. Two weeks after his exultant message to Bragg, Smith commented bitterly, "The Kentuckians are slow and backward in rallying to our standard. Their hearts are evidently with us, but their blue-grass and fat [cattle] are against us."[117] In a letter to his wife he was at once more explicit and more sympathetic. "I see their magnificent estates, their fat cattle & fine stock," he wrote, "[and] I can understand their fears & hesitancy—they have so much to lose."[118] Several regiments were formed, but that was all. Bragg had no better results and tended to agree with Kirby Smith as to the reason. He had 15,000 extra rifles and no one to use them. "Unless a change occurs soon," he warned in a letter to Richmond, "we must abandon the garden spot of Kentucky to its cupidity. The love of ease and fear of pecuniary loss are the fruitful sources of evil."[119]

Kirby Smith was probably right about one thing: The Kentuckians, even those of Confederate sympathies, were not going to flock to the southern standard until Bragg and Smith demonstrated they were not just raiding but had come to stay. That meant defeating Buell. Bragg's problem was that after his hard marching and brilliant maneuvering had come to nothing, he believed he could not defeat Buell until his army was strengthened either by larger numbers of Kentucky recruits or by Smith's force. When he could no longer maintain the army at Munfordville, Bragg had reluctantly moved it to Bardstown, forty-five miles to the northeast. This put him closer to Lexington and possible cooperation with Kirby Smith, but unfortunately it also left a clear path for Buell to reestablish his supply lines and secure Louisville. When Smith still insisted on keeping his troops around Lexington, Bragg hit upon another idea. Since late 1861, when the faction of prosouthern Kentuckians claiming to be the state's legitimate government (as opposed to the actual Unionist government) had petitioned for admission, the Confederacy had counted Kentucky as one of its states. Recently the Confederate Congress had passed a conscription act, making, with few exceptions, all men of military age subject to the draft. If adequate numbers of Kentuckians could not summon the courage to volunteer, Bragg reasoned, why not draft them instead? In order to do this, some sort of state government would have to be installed. Fortunately, the Confederate governor of Kentucky had accompanied the army into the state in order to combine his "moral, political, and civil influence with that of the Confederate army."[120] This was his chance. Bragg would proceed with the governor to Frankfort, the state capital, and there have him officially inaugurated. At the same time, since Frankfort was less than twenty-five miles from Lexington, Bragg might finally be able to make contact with Kirby Smith. Inaugurating a Confederate governor for Kentucky might also encourage volunteering by demonstrating that the Confederates had come for good. Then if that failed, there was always the draft.

In the meantime, in Mississippi Van Dorn and Price were conducting a dismal campaign. It would be hard to conceive of two more drastically different generals than Sterling Price and Earl Van Dorn—even in their appearance and manner. Van Dorn was a short, slender military professional with the tendency to be somewhat of a dandy, while Price was a big, hulking amateur whose propensities were less refined.

Born in Virginia in 1809, Price was only a few months younger than Jefferson Davis. The son of a moderately wealthy planter of an old Virginia family, Price studied law before migrating to Missouri and becoming a successful merchant and tobacco planter. He was an imposing figure, tall and massive, yet appearing at the same time distinguished, so that his reticence was viewed as a sign of dignity rather than an indication of slow mental processes. He entered politics and was elected to the state legislature and then to Congress, where he was when the Mexican War broke out. With the aid of his political ally President Polk, he received authority to raise and command a regiment of Missouri volunteers, despite the fact that the sum of his military knowledge consisted of a few militia musters and service in the campaign that drove the Mormons out of the northwestern part of Missouri. Although his department commander had stated that infantry was needed and cavalry was not wanted, Price had insisted on raising cavalry. He soon found himself in charge of occupying already-conquered New Mexico. Price's sloppy administration and lax discipline helped create an unfortunate revolt among the inhabitants, which he was at least able to put down. Then, having been promoted to brigadier general, he proceeded to lead an expedition into the Mexican province of Chihuahua, contrary to the explicit orders of the War Department. Though he was successful here as well, his penchant for disobeying orders and generally following his own lights in disregard of his superiors did not bode well for his usefulness to the future Confederacy.

Upon returning from the Mexican War, Price was hailed as a great military hero. In 1853 he was elected governor of Missouri as the candidate of the pro-slavery wing of the state's Democratic party. As governor he did nothing to stop the Missouri border ruffians who were terrorizing Kansas; he also endorsed a resolution calling for secession unless Kansas was admitted as a slave state. Returning to private life in 1857, he again took up tobacco farming. In 1861 he was among the prosouthern Missourians who were outraged by the

Sterling Price (Chicago Historical Society)

unceremonious way in which that state's incipient secession movement was put down by Federal forces. Joining the rebels, Price became head of the pro-southern Missouri forces and, along with his troops, was eventually inducted into Confederate service.[121] He won several minor victories in Missouri. Despite his involvement, along with Van Dorn, in the miserable affair at Pea Ridge, Price gained considerable fame throughout the South, being compared to George Washington and otherwise lionized as a man who owed his military success to "native good sense" rather than attendance at some elitist military school. Needless to say, this was a line of thinking not at all attractive to Jefferson Davis, with his respect for professional military training, but very attractive to increasing numbers of his political enemies, who were already beginning to condemn the president for what they saw as his overreliance on West Point graduates. Such adulation did not endear Price to the president, and in any case, the two men's personalities seemed destined to clash.

In April 1862 Price and his men were brought east of the Mississippi, along with Van Dorn and the rest of the trans-Mississippi forces, to join Beauregard's army at Corinth. By June, discontented at not being permitted to fight in his own state and, probably, at not finding himself on the fast track to promotion, Price decided to cut to the heart of the problem. Securing a leave, he took his aide and set off for Richmond to see the president. It was the worst of all possible times for the Missouri general to appear in the Confederate capital. McClellan's Union army was within sight of the city, within which the political climate had heated to a fever pitch. Certain malcontent anti-Davis politicians had begun talking of deposing Davis and installing Price in his place as a sort of generalissimo. The affair never progressed to the point of becoming a full-fledged plot, but with a Federal army at the gates, loose talk was at a peak. Price knew nothing of the matter, and Davis never took it very seriously, but the Missouri general's arrival at such a time could only have aroused suspicions.[122]

The disgruntled Missourian met briefly with the president on Monday, June 16, and urged that he (Price) be transferred to Arkansas with all the Missouri troops under his command. Davis asked him to submit his proposal to the secretary of war in writing. Three days later Price gave his written proposal to Randolph. It called for the creation of an independent trans-Mississippi department, answerable directly to Richmond and under the command of an officer who could be trusted to use his discretion broadly. For this job Price modestly nominated himself, and he suggested that he and his Missouri troops should then launch a major effort to wrest their home state from Union control. After waiting nearly another week, Price requested another meeting with the president to find out what action would be taken.

The second meeting, with Price's aide and Secretary of War Randolph present, was considerably stormier than the first, though it began on a conciliatory note. The president explained that he regretted the transfer of Price's Missourians to Mississippi and that it had been effected by the department commander without his knowledge. Still, the troops were needed there and could not be sent back. As for creating a separate trans-Mississippi department, that had already been done, but so had the choosing of a general to command it: Gen. John B. Magruder, presently serving with Lee's army in Virginia, had received orders to take over the new department. Enraged at finding his considerable ambitions thus thwarted, Price exploded spectacularly. "Well, Mr. President," he thundered, "if you will not let me serve *you,* I will nevertheless serve my *country.* You cannot prevent me from doing that. I will send you my resignation, and go back to Missouri and raise another army there without your assistance, and fight under the flag of Missouri, and win new victories for the South in spite of the Government."

Unimpressed by the Missourian's bombast, Davis replied coldly. "Your resignation," he informed Price in a voice that dripped with contempt, "will be promptly accepted, General; and if you do go back to Missouri and raise another army, and win victories for the South, or do any service at all, no one will be more pleased than myself, or—more surprised."

"Then I will surprise you, sir!" roared Price, slamming a huge fist on the table, so that the ink bottles jumped. This concluded the interview. Back at his hotel Price wrote out his resignation while his young aide, a newspaperman in civilian life, harangued the crowd that had gathered out front, denouncing Davis and proclaiming Price's intention to quit the Confederate army. To emphasize the point, the young officer tore the Confederate insignia off his own uniform. Later he was joined by the general himself, who added a few "turbulent remarks" of his own before the crowd dispersed.

Meanwhile, Davis had cooled down. Though he had no use for Price personally, considering him "the vainest man he had ever met," he had to face the fact that the Confederacy needed Price, if not as a general then at least as a political symbol in uniform. Price was enormously popular throughout the South and especially in the trans-Mississippi. Moreover, his Missouri troops worshipped him and were not, in any case, overly enthused about service east of the Mississippi. Should Price be allowed to quit the army and go home, the result among the western army's Missouri contingent might be mass desertion or even mutiny. At the same time there would be the devil to pay among the trans-Mississippi elements in Congress as well as political complications of other sorts. All in all, Jefferson Davis had to conclude, Price would be more trouble outside the army than in. The next day, subordinating his pride to his sense of duty, he returned Price's letter of resignation along with a note that Bragg would be instructed to return Price and his Missourians to the west bank of the Mississippi as soon as the situation east of the river permitted. To pacify the Missouri general still more, Davis had Randolph send him a letter promising that when Price finally did return to the west bank, he would be second in command to Magruder, who would have orders for an immediate full-scale campaign to "liberate" Missouri. Placated but resentful, Price withdrew his resignation and headed back for Mississippi.[123]

Now, with the fall campaign in full swing, Price was half of the two-headed command system Bragg had left behind in Mississippi, and the only common ground this burly politician-general shared with the other half of the system, the diminutive and foppish West Pointer Van Dorn, was a burning ambition to win glory and promotion. No sooner had Bragg left for Chattanooga to begin his march into Kentucky than Price was chafing to advance into West Tennessee.[124] He wrote to Van Dorn seeking his cooperation, but Van Dorn was still occupied with the business of trying to take Baton Rouge and fortify Port Hudson.[125] And so the month of August passed, with Price hounding Van Dorn to finish up and Bragg urging both of them to advance posthaste lest the Federals in West Tennessee detach reinforcements for Buell.[126]

By the end of the month Van Dorn was finally ready to move, and recognizing the fortified Union position at Corinth, Mississippi, as the key to the campaign, he suggested to Price that they combine their forces and outflank Corinth—cutting it off from the rest of Grant's army—by moving into Tennessee to the west of it.[127] This was not very different from what Price had proposed a few weeks before, but now the Missouri general had other ideas.[128] He remonstrated with Van Dorn, that if he moved west from his present position directly south of Corinth, it would leave undefended the railroad running south from Corinth and expose various machine shops and supply depots to possible Federal forays. Besides, Bragg had recently telegraphed him that the Federal force at Corinth—20,000 men under Grant's subordinate William S. Rosecrans—was supposed to be crossing the Tennessee River at Eastport in the northeastern corner of Mississippi and heading for Nashville to reinforce Buell. This Price was expected to prevent, if possible, by pouncing on Rosecrans while that general's army was straddling the river, or failing that, to follow close on his heels so as to help Bragg deal with the combined forces of Rosecrans and Buell. Why not, Price suggested to Van Dorn, come along and help dispose of Rosecrans?[129]

Now it was Van Dorn's turn to demur. With a curious logic he argued that Rosecrans's force was not going to Nashville, or if it was, it had already left and Price could do nothing about it. Why miss the action in West Tennessee by chasing Rosecrans all the way to Nashville, only to miss the battle there, too? Let Bragg and Kirby Smith worry about Rosecrans, Van Dorn urged, while he and Price combined their forces and made short shrift of whatever Federals were left in West Tennessee.[130]

Price saw matters otherwise. He felt himself bound by orders from Bragg to move toward Nashville and try to catch Rosecrans and defeat him. The real problem with Price and Van Dorn was that while their correspondence was excruciatingly polite and chivalrous, each viewed the other with little respect and considerable condescension.[131] Unwilling to share glory with Van Dorn and loath to entrust his army to Van Dorn's direction, Price used Bragg's orders, which were not really very specific, as an excuse to undertake independent operations. Hearing that Rosecrans had evacuated Corinth and that part of his force was at Iuka covering the embarkation of the rest ten miles away at Eastport, Price determined to attack.[132] Arriving at Iuka on September 11, Price met only slight Federal resistance and captured a fair amount of supplies.[133] That was fine in itself, but it raised a disturbing question: If Rosecrans was not here, where was he? Price was soon to be enlightened on this subject.

Halleck, who had been promoted to overall commander of the Union armies, had ordered Grant to relieve some of the pressure on Buell by initiating his own attack. Always ready to take the offensive, Grant had seen his chance when Price had moved to Iuka. Grant utilized Rosecrans's force—which, contrary to Confederate intelligence, had never left Corinth—and made plans to trap Price's army against the river and destroy it. Rosecrans's men worked their way around to the rear of Price's army, and on September 19, two days after Bragg's bloodless victory at Munfordville, the trap was sprung. Only an acoustical fluke, which prevented half of Grant's force from hearing and thus joining in the battle in which the other half was engaged, saved Price from destruction. The Missouri general faced the situation with his characteristic aggressiveness.[134] Learning that there were Federal troops in the area, he had attacked, and his assault had just sufficed to pry open one jaw of the snare while the other, kept ignorant by the strange acoustical conditions, remained motionless. The Confederate force escaped after suffering casualties of one tenth of its total number.[135] Even then, however, Price's officers were barely able to talk him out of renewing the battle—and facing what everyone but Price could see would be certain destruction—on the morrow.[136]

Within a few days, though, a reaction seemed to set in, as the Missourian realized how close he had come to disaster at Iuka. It was therefore a much-chastened Price who informed Van Dorn that he was ready to cooperate in an attack on Corinth.[137] Van Dorn, who had spent the last several weeks complaining to Richmond and making what he hoped were threatening movements with his army along the Tennessee line west of Corinth, was overjoyed to hear that Price had finally seen the light.[138] He was less happy to learn that, far from being in Nashville causing problems for Bragg, Rosecrans was still somewhere around Corinth. That meant that Van Dorn's latest maneuver had put him in the embarrassing situation of being exactly between two Federal armies, each of which was larger than his own. If the Federals should notice this, Van Dorn sheepishly explained in a dispatch to Price, "I would be in a bad way just at this time."[139]

Thus both southern generals had plenty of motivation to quit their antics and unite their forces as quickly as possible. The prospect of imminent annihilation having focused their thoughts, they were at once able to agree on a time and place of rendezvous and finally brought their armies together south-west of Corinth on September 28.[140]

By this time, however, Jefferson Davis had become thoroughly alarmed at what was occurring in his home state of Mississippi. Van Dorn had been telegraphing the president and secretary of war that he needed reinforcements, that Price should be put under his orders, and that Bragg was out of reach and therefore could not deal with these matters.[141] Other sources were report-ing the disharmony between the two Confederate commanders in Mississippi, and some were suggesting that in concentrating on an offensive into West Ten-nessee Van Dorn was leaving Vicksburg and Port Hudson dangerously ex-posed.[142] Davis was in a delicate position. He could not believe that Bragg had departed for Kentucky leaving no more complete instructions than Van Dorn seemed to have. For all Davis knew, if he attempted to straighten things out, he might inadvertently create an even bigger mess by working at cross-purposes with whatever Bragg might have intended. Davis sent a dispatch to Bragg, in-forming him of the dilemma in Mississippi and stating, "I am at a loss to know how to remedy [these] evils without damaging your plans." It was serious business too, since as the president pointed out, "if Van Dorn, Price, and Breckinridge each act for himself, disaster to all must be the probable result."[143] However, Davis's deference to Bragg was of no use: It simply took too long for messages to get to and from Bragg's position in what was essentially still enemy territory. Whatever order was to be brought to the situation would have to be imposed by Davis.

At first he had replied to Van Dorn's complaints by saying the general could have certain troops that were available in the area as reinforcements, but only if this did not conflict with any instructions Bragg might have given. He had also pointed out that once the two armies were combined Van Dorn would command by virtue of his higher rank.[144] This was obvious but ineffectual, since Price would not take his army to where Van Dorn was. When the confu-sion had persisted, Davis in frustration had telegraphed Van Dorn that coopera-tion was absolutely necessary, that Van Dorn's rank made him the com-mander, and that that must have been what Bragg intended.[145] Finally, after all else had failed, Davis simply instructed the secretary of war to issue an order to Van Dorn immediately to assume command of all troops in Mississippi, concentrate them, make provision for the defense of Vicksburg, and, with the rest of the troops, move into West Tennessee.[146]

By this time, however, it was September 29, and Van Dorn and Price had already united and were considering their next step—which, as it turned out, was to attack Corinth. They reasoned that the campaign into West Tennessee could not proceed until this Federal stronghold was taken. Accordingly, Van Dorn made elaborate plans and began to carry them out; yet the whole thing began to look depressingly like Pea Ridge all over again. First, he feinted with the combined army in the direction of West Tennessee, hoping to convince

Grant and Rosecrans not to reinforce Corinth. Instead his move had the opposite effect. Rosecrans, who commanded at Corinth, was unsure of exactly
what Van Dorn intended, but in order to be ready for anything, he pulled all
his scattered forces together at Corinth, whence he could move in whatever
direction Van Dorn threatened. As it developed, he had no need to move at
all, since Van Dorn came right to him. Van Dorn approached Corinth from
the north. Although this side of town was more heavily fortified, he hoped
that by thus approaching from the rear he would catch the Federals off guard.
Unfortunately, as at Pea Ridge, Van Dorn managed the approach march poorly, and it took so long that the enemy had plenty of time to prepare. In addition, Van Dorn had a female spy inside the town who proved to be a dubious
asset. Though she did her best, most of the information she provided was inaccurate. As a result, Van Dorn seriously underestimated the number of Federal
troops he was facing.[147]

On October 3 Van Dorn hurled his forces against the strongly entrenched
Federals in a series of headlong frontal attacks. He had hoped for a quick victory, but when the bloody, day-long battle had failed to win the town, he
kept his army in place for another day of hammering with fruitless, at times
almost suicidal, assaults on the Federal earthworks. When Van Dorn finally
called off the slaughter and pulled his battered and much-depleted army away
from the fields around Corinth, he was still unconvinced that the campaign
was a total loss. Retreating only a short distance, he camped for the night and
made plans to attack and take a smaller Federal stronghold as a prelude to having another go at Corinth. Fortunately, his officers were able to talk him out
of such rashness, and the retreat continued the next day.[148] By this time, however, Van Dorn found his escape blocked by another Federal force moving up
to support Corinth. Although he maneuvered his way out of this trap, his
army reached the relative safety of Holly Springs, Mississippi, with a tally of
nearly 5,000 lost from its original 25,000 men. Of these, some 2,000 were
captured or missing on the retreat from Corinth.[149] The campaign had been
an unrelieved failure and had done nothing to further Bragg's effort in Kentucky.

By the time the battle of Corinth was fought, it may have been too late to
help Bragg anyway. The people of Kentucky had not risen to throw out the
"abolitionist hordes," and Buell's ponderous imperturbability had prevented
Bragg from winning a military victory when, by most of the established laws
of warfare, he had probably earned one. As Buell reached Louisville, the outlook was very grim for Confederate control of Kentucky, but there was always
the chance that Bragg might contrive another upset of the sort that had shifted
the war to Kentucky in the first place. Bragg, in any case, was going to try.

On October 2, the day before Van Dorn began his unsuccessful attack on
Corinth, Bragg attended the inauguration of Kentucky's Confederate governor
and learned simultaneously that Buell's army was advancing from Louisville.[150]
Buell had been under considerable pressure from Washington to find the Con-

federate army and fight it and had at last sent his army, reinforced by thousands of new levies rushed down by the midwestern governors, heading along several roads in the general direction of Frankfort and Lexington.

In this movement Bragg saw his opportunity. He had left most of his force at Bardstown. Kirby Smith's force was near Frankfort. While Smith struck the Federals in front, Bragg planned to have the Bardstown contingent swing over and hit them in the flank.[151] Although this plan was partially based on faulty information, it nevertheless stood a good chance of success. In fact, it might have led to a brilliant victory that would have destroyed a portion of Buell's army.[152] But the plan was never put into action.

The man in charge at Bardstown was Leonidas Polk. That was not Bragg's design, but Polk's rank made him second only to Bragg within the army. When Bragg went to Frankfort for the inauguration, Polk automatically took command of the troops at Bardstown. Still, Bragg had sent Polk an order to attack, and that should have been straightforward enough. Apparently, it was not.

Besides being a basically incompetent general, Polk had the added fault of hating to take orders. When he received Bragg's instructions to attack Buell in front of Frankfort, he decided that the order was unwise and that he would not obey it. So as to shift some of the responsibility for this defiance, he decided to call a council of war to deliberate the question of whether or not to obey Bragg's order. That evening all of the general officers in Polk's command met to discuss the matter. Polk was a very persuasive man, and he used all of his powers in presenting his case: Bragg did not understand the situation; to obey the order would be suicidal; once enlightened on the true state of affairs, even Bragg would agree that the order should have been disregarded. Polk's charm was effective, and the generals, from the plodding Hardee, who was next in command in Bragg's absence, all the way down to the second-lowest-ranking brigadier, were thoroughly under his spell. There was one exception, however. The junior-ranking brigadier general hesitantly spoke up, suggesting that since Bragg had given an order and they were soldiers, perhaps they had better obey. Besides, if they failed to make the attack as ordered, Kirby Smith's forces would be left to make an unsupported frontal assault that would result in horrendous casualties. Polk applied more pressure to the recalcitrant brigadier. Suppose Bragg had not ordered such a movement—would it then be a wise one? Having just heard Polk's forcefully delivered assessment of the situation and with all of his superiors glaring at him in apparent agreement with the bishop-general, the officer was forced to concede that perhaps it would not. In that case, Polk rationalized, they ought not to comply even though Bragg had ordered it. With this he put the confused and embarrassed brigadier to silence and then sent a dispatch to Bragg explaining that he had disobeyed the order because all of his generals had advised him to do so.[153] Instead of making the move Bragg was counting on, Polk retreated to Danville, Kentucky.

Polk's disobedience probably cost the army a victory and might have been much more costly had Bragg not learned of it in time to call off Kirby Smith's attack. One disaster, however, Bragg could do nothing to avert. Polk's retreat had rendered it impossible for Bragg to keep Smith's forces in Frankfort. The capital of Kentucky would have to be evacuated and at a most inopportune time. The new governor was interrupted during his inaugural address by Federal shells falling in the city. He cut his speech short and left with Bragg and his staff. The crowd that was present for the occasion at first assumed that they were riding off to lead the troops in an attack on the enemy, but when it was clear that they were instead reteating and that Frankfort would be abandoned, the day's high spirits were replaced with gloom and widespread denunciation of Bragg, who was generally held to be responsible for this latest disaster.

Meanwhile, Polk, the actual culprit, was sending off a dispatch to Bragg admonishing his commander for allowing the army to become too scattered, even though it was Polk's obstinacy that had kept the army from being united and had added to the dispersion.[154] Nor was Polk through disobeying orders. After retreating from Frankfort, Bragg decided to concentrate his forces at Harrodsburg and then see what could be done about Buell. Polk persisted in taking his troops to Danville even after being ordered to move on Harrodsburg, and Bragg had to repeat the command in no uncertain terms before Polk saw fit to obey it.[155] In the midst of this, with Buell's army only a few miles away and its position not definitely known at Confederate headquarters, Bragg had to endure a lengthy and didactic dispatch from Hardee, who was by now completely in the thrall of Polk, lecturing him as if he were a dull first-year cadet at West Point. "Do not scatter your forces. There is one rule in our profession which should never be forgotten; it is to throw the masses of your troops on the fractions of the enemy. . . . Strike with your whole force first to the right then to the left."[156] Braxton Bragg had much more patience than he ever got credit for.

The collision with Buell's army, when it finally occurred, was anticlimactic. Kirby Smith commanded the right wing of Bragg's newly combined forces, and Polk, the left. Buell was making a feint against Smith while planning to strike Polk with his main force. Bragg's subordinates were confused as to just what Buell was up to and kept Bragg confused as well by feeding him inaccurate information. Kirby Smith insisted he was facing Buell's main force, and at first Polk was inclined to agree but then changed his mind.[157] To make matters worse, Polk's stubbornness and defiance of Bragg's orders had placed half the army's cavalry so badly out of position that Bragg was sorely lacking in the kind of cavalry reconnaissance that might have told him where the enemy was and what he was doing.[158]

Bragg finally agreed with Kirby Smith and ordered Polk to attack quickly, dispose of the force he was facing, and then assist Kirby Smith.[159] The force under Polk's supervision, under the immediate command of Hardee, was ranged near the small Kentucky town of Perryville. As was the case in many a Civil War battle, neither Confederates nor Federals had come there looking for a fight; in this instance, they had come looking for water, a scarce commodity in this summer of severe drought. Just west of Perryville flowed a small stream known locally as Doctor's Fork. It flowed, that is, at other times of the year. At present it merely lent its bed to a series of small and stagnant pools. These normally unattractive bodies of water had, under the circumstances, seemed desirable enough to induce Hardee to stop there for the night before continuing his march to Harrodsburg the next day. The creek bed had also attracted a portion of Buell's command, looking to replenish its water supply before continuing east to find and destroy the Confederate army. Though some skirmishing occurred that evening, Hardee remained unaware that he faced a major Federal force as he penned his dispatch lecturing his commander on tactics.[160]

Bragg's orders called for Polk to use Hardee's troops to destroy whatever enemy force they confronted early the next morning, but as usual Polk was slow to obey. Though Bragg's order had used the word "immediately," Polk would later excuse his disobedience on the ground that it was not really clear what was meant by the term.[161] Bragg had to go to the scene in person to get the fight under way.[162] Strangely, since without knowing it Bragg was attacking the main Federal force, the battle turned out to be a tactical success for the Confederates, mainly because the Union generals were even more inept than the Confederate and failed to get more than a fraction of their troops into the fight.[163] At one point during the disjointed battle, a Federal brigadier, obviously mistaking Polk for someone else, rode up to the bishop-general announcing, "I have come to your assistance with my brigade," and asking where he should put it. "There is some mistake about this," Polk replied blandly. "You are my prisoner."[164]

Later, Polk himself narrowly avoided a similar fate. As the struggle continued into the dusk, Polk saw what he thought was a Confederate brigade firing on other Confederate troops. "Dear me," he thought, "this is very sad and must be stopped." Riding up to the offending brigade commander, he began to berate the officer for his supposed mistake. When the Union officer, who was equally deceived as to Polk's identity, protested that he was sure the troops he had been firing on were the enemy, Polk exploded. "Enemy! Why I have just left them myself. Cease firing, sir; what is your name, sir?" The officer identified himself and even gave his regiment, an Indiana outfit. "And pray, sir, who are you?" he asked. It occurred to Polk that he had made a mistake. Fortunately (for himself at any rate) the good bishop was never at a loss for subterfuge. Rising in the stirrups and shaking his fist in the Union officer's face, he thundered, "I'll soon show you who I am, sir. Cease firing, sir, at once!" Riding along the Federal line, he ordered the troops to cease firing, then galloped to the nearest Confederate brigade and directed it to open fire on the distressed Federals.[165]

The hard-fought and bloody battle actually decided very little. After it was over, Bragg concluded that there was no use in trying to continue the occupation of Kentucky and determined to fall back into Tennessee. Though Buell did not press the Confederates closely during their retreat, one incident yet remained in this campaign that would have an important bearing on Jefferson Davis's relations with his generals.

Kirby Smith's force brought up the rear during the retreat and had charge of the army's wagon trains; in front of him was Polk's section of Bragg's original army. The Union pursuit was not energetic, yet Smith's imagination conjured up Yankee hordes that followed hot on his heels.[166] Polk's nerves must have been none too steady either, for unencumbered by wagons, he had his men traveling at a pace that threatened to leave the distraught Smith behind. Bragg finally had to admonish Polk: "If we pass on so rapidly Smith's front will be open to the enemy and he will be surrounded. In saving our army we must help him, having imposed our trains on him, by which he is retarded; besides, I have no doubt we can whip the force behind us."[167] Polk slowed enough to maintain contact with Smith, and then the two began to commiserate on their trials in having such an incompetent commanding general. Within days Smith was writing long letters to an apparently sympathetic Polk, castigating Bragg thoroughly, especially for nearly abandoning him on the retreat.[168] It was probably this affair, on top of the frustration of the whole failed campaign—much of the blame for which devolved on him—which prompted Smith to write to Davis requesting that he never be forced to serve with Braxton Bragg again.[169]

The events of Bragg's Perryville campaign and all that went with it are integral to the story of Jefferson Davis and his generals—not so much because of what Davis did in regard to the campaign, but rather because of what he failed to do and what effects the results of this failure would have on his future attempts to find winning generals for the western theater. Davis had supported Bragg and Kirby Smith with what reinforcements he could and encouraged Bragg to carry out his bold plan. These actions were good, as far as they went, and had helped to shift the scene of conflict in the West from northern Mississippi to central Kentucky. Once again, as at Shiloh, the president's offensive-defensive strategy had proved its value. An attempted Federal advance, this time against Chattanooga, had been met with a surprising counterblow. If neither Shiloh nor Bragg's Kentucky campaign had delivered the hoped-for knockout punch, each had at least rocked the enemy back on his heels for a time. The credit for the overall strategy, much of the credit for encouraging and supporting the campaign, and possibly even the credit for the idea that sparked it belong to Jefferson Davis. Davis had also attempted to bring some order out of the chaos Van Dorn and Price, under Bragg's flawed arrangement, were making in Mississippi. Of course, he could have moved more decisively in this, but there was always the chance that such intervention might ruin some master plan Bragg had intended. The accusations of his critics notwithstanding, Davis was usually very hesitant to interfere with his generals' plans and dispositions.

Unfortunately, what Davis had left undone—aggravated by the dubious contributions of Polk, Kirby Smith, Price, and Van Dorn—had cancelled out many of the potential benefits from his wise decisions. When Bragg had pointed out that some good young brigadiers in his army were overshadowed by incompetent superiors and hinted that Polk was one of the latter, the president had refused to rise above bureaucratic habit and myopic personal devotion to rid the army of this "dead weight." Polk's presence in such a high rank had hurt the Confederacy badly before and would continue to do so increasingly unless Davis overcame his prejudice and judged the man on his merits. Later in the war, referring to an unrelated case, Davis would write, "No officer has a right to stop troops moving under the orders of superior authority—if he assumes such power he does it at his hazard and must be justified by subsequent events rather than by good intentions."[170] This was precisely what Polk had done in disobeying Bragg's orders during the Perryville campaign. That disobedience may have cost the South an important victory, yet Davis failed even to rebuke Polk, let alone remove him from his responsible position.

Yet the failure to remove "dead weight" and advance promising young officers more rapidly was to bulk even larger as the war went on. In the latter stages of the conflict, Jefferson Davis would more and more find himself in the predicament of having no available general who was experienced in high command but not a proven failure or at least discredited. The promising young generals such as Cleburne, whom Bragg had wished to promote, remained just that—promising, but inexperienced and untested in the upper echelons of command. While these men should have been gaining valuable experience in division and corps command, less competent senior generals continued to make costly mistakes.

Besides neglecting to remove bad generals and promote good ones, Davis had failed to ensure cooperation among his generals. When Bragg had departed Mississippi for Chattanooga, Davis, his immediate superior, had failed to see that he left a workable arrangement in that state. So ignorant was he of Bragg's dispositions there that when problems arose he was unable to set them straight without fear of unwittingly sabotaging Bragg's plans. When Bragg and his army had arrived in Kirby Smith's department to begin that campaign, Davis had failed to place both Smith and the department unequivocally under Bragg's command. Rather, he had relied on the two generals cooperating with each other, and the resulting lack of harmony and collaboration, due primarily to Smith's headstrong glory-seeking, had handicapped if not wrecked the campaign.[171]

One reason for Davis's deficiency in this area was his exaggerated view of the possibilities of voluntary cooperation. He presumed that if two generals had the best interests of the Confederacy at heart, they could not possibly disagree on major questions regarding the conduct of operations. That this was not true he had to learn the hard way, partially through the Kentucky campaign. A further reason for Davis's unrealistic confidence in his generals' cooperation was his own iron self-discipline and total dedication to the cause. He was a man with a great capacity for harboring animosity, but he almost never allowed his animosity to prevent him from doing what he thought was best for the South. He tended to expect this same self-discipline and dedication from his generals.

A more important reason for Davis's failure to play the more active part that was needed in the Kentucky campaign was his absorption with Lee's Antietam campaign. Lee had accomplished much in the summer of 1862, and with Bragg and Smith in Kentucky and Price and Van Dorn preparing to advance into West Tennessee, it appeared that the tide of the war had turned and that final Confederate victory might await Lee's army just north of the Potomac. Davis even considered joining Lee in Maryland to negotiate a peace that would secure Confederate independence. Things were happening on the diplomatic front as well. It looked as if the Confederacy might finally gain recognition from Britain and France. It was right for the president to concern himself with these things, but it was impossible for him at the same time to act as general in chief of the western theater.

The outcome of the Kentucky campaign complicated enormously Davis's problems in dealing with his generals. The failure to defeat Buell and hold Kentucky was not primarily Bragg's fault, but, as usual, the commanding general got the blame. Bragg's popularity, which had been phenomenal both inside and outside the army at the start of the campaign, began a long and steady decline. This problem was made worse by the suave and charming Polk, who managed to persuade a fair number of the army's generals, including Hardee and Kirby Smith, that Bragg's folly would have brought their destruction had not he, Leonidas Polk, intervened to prevent disaster. Further hostility to Bragg came from Buckner and other Kentuckians who, besides being under the influence of Polk, could not forgive Bragg for telling the truth about Kentucky's failure to fight for the Confederacy.[172]

Jefferson Davis would now be faced with some thorny problems: Should he keep Bragg in his present position? If so, should he remove Polk? or certain other officers? If he kept them, he would have to find a way to get them to work harmoniously together, and whatever he did, he would have to try to resolve the lack of cooperation that had contributed to the defeats at Corinth and Perryville. The fall and winter of 1862 and 1863 would be spent in attempting to find solutions to all of these problems.

10

UNIFIED COMMAND

A storm of criticism broke around Braxton Bragg on his return from Kentucky. Politicians, editors, and generals howled for his removal.[1] Part of this criticism issued from political enemies of the Davis administration, for whom nothing Davis did was satisfactory and no general he sustained could be competent. Bragg, as commanding general of a bold but unsuccessful campaign, was a prime target of their vitriol. This was especially so since, for some reason, Bragg was now perceived as a special friend of Davis. Their prewar relations had never been close or very cordial. Yet by the summer of 1862 Davis was being accused of keeping Bragg in command of the army for personal rather than military reasons. Davis's political enemies, whose numbers were growing almost daily, sensed that the issue of Braxton Bragg could damage the administration and so attacked Bragg as a way of getting at Davis.[2] Even before the Perryville campaign, Davis had written Bragg explaining, "You have the misfortune of being regarded as my personal friend, and are pursued therefore with malignant censure by men regardless of truth and whose want of principle to guide their conduct renders them incapable of conceiving that you are trusted because of your known fitness for command, and not because of friendly regard."[3] After Perryville the outcry only worsened.

Additional censure came from a group of high-ranking generals centering on Leonidas Polk. Polk, Hardee, and Smith openly and bitterly denounced Bragg. Smith told another general "that General Bragg had lost his mind."[4] He had also written to Davis that he would rather have a lower position anywhere else in the Confederacy than to keep the rank he had and continue serving under Bragg.[5] Both Hardee and Smith had been greatly influenced by Polk, and that general seems to have mounted a behind-the-scenes campaign to have Bragg removed from command.[6] Polk ranked second only to Bragg within the western army and may have believed that if Bragg were removed he would succeed to the job. In any case, he passed false information against Bragg to members of Congress and approached other generals to urge them to join in calling for Bragg's removal. He spoke contemptuously of Bragg to his friends and boasted that if he "had been in chief command," the outcome of the Perryville campaign would have been much different. Beating Buell and conquering Kentucky, he insisted, "could have been easily done."[7]

The chief pillar of Polk's anti-Bragg strategy within the army was the next-ranking officer, Lt. Gen. William Joseph Hardee. Hardee, born in Georgia in 1815, was the grandson of a Revolutionary War officer and the son of an of-

William J. Hardee (Courtesy Georgia Department of Archives and History)

ficer of the War of 1812. Though his father had become a comfortably successful cotton planter and a moderately prominent local politician, young William desired to carry on the family's military tradition, and after four years of insistent application, he was finally appointed to West Point in 1834. His performance there was mediocre, and he graduated twenty-sixth among the forty-five members of the class of 1838.

His army career was also without note until 1840, when as a lieutenant in the Second Dragoons he was sent to France to study cavalry tactics at the French Royal Cavalry School at Saumur. This was more the result of his political connections than of any distinction he had achieved in military service. After a year's instruction he returned to his regiment and began teaching the troops the fancy French maneuvers he had learned while he was away. For the first time the War Department seemed to notice his existence (at least for reasons other than political), and he was promoted to captain.

Hardee's Gallic expertise stood him in less good stead when the Mexican War broke out. No sooner had Zachary Taylor's army, of which Hardee was a part, taken up its position along the Rio Grande than Hardee managed to get himself captured, along with his entire company. There was later much squabbling about where the blame should lie for this debacle, and none of it was ever officially attached to Hardee. In any case, he was soon exchanged and transferred to Scott's command, where he did considerably better, winning two brevets and being conspicuous enough to prompt the Georgia legislature to award him a ceremonial sword.

After the war Hardee's military career continued much as it had before. His most important service was creating a new manual of tactics, made necessary by the introduction of the rifled musket with its vastly increased range and accuracy.[8] Adopted by the army with the approval of Secretary of War Jefferson Davis, the manual Hardee produced became the standard text by which officers both North and South learned their trade through the early years of the Civil War, but it hardly solved the problem of what to do on a battlefield dominated by the rifled musket. By the later years of the war the common soldier, following his own healthy instinct for self-preservation, generally ignored Hardee's unrealistic instructions. U. S. Grant, at the other end of the chain of command, admitted that he had never really given Hardee's book a careful reading.[9] The fault was not that the book had become obsolete but that it was to a large extent obsolete when Hardee wrote it. Military technology was going through a revolution during those years, and Hardee lacked the mind to grasp it. Instead, he drew heavily on a manual used in the French army. The French were considered to have the world's finest army, and though the Prussians were to give drastic refutation of this in less than two decades, it seemed natural during the 1850s to ape the French in all things military. Indeed, so heavily did Hardee rely on his French manual that he was accused of making little more than a translation; in parts, at least, the charge was true.

Nevertheless, the manual as Hardee wrote it brought him tremendous prestige within the army and was probably largely responsible for his attaining high rank in the Confederate army—that and his acquaintance with Jefferson Davis. While Davis served on the Senate Military Affairs Committee during the late 1850s, the two men worked closely together on reform of West Point, where Hardee was commandant of cadets. Hardee was never as personally close to Davis as Polk was, but he had the future Confederate president's deep respect.

At secession Hardee resigned and was commissioned first in the Georgia forces and then in the Confederate army, serving at Mobile and later in northern Arkansas. There, in his first wartime semi-independent command, his performance was lackluster at best. He joined with enthusiasm in the confusion and bickering to which Price, McCulloch, Pillow, and Polk were all contributing. Transferred along with his force to Bowling Green, Hardee became part of Albert Sydney Johnston's main army. During the months that followed he displayed two of his most striking traits as a general. The first was an utter dread of responsibility. He wrote, "I am glad the responsibility does not rest with me, it is weighty and I would not bear it if I could."[10] Yet this awareness of the burden that weighed on his superiors was not enough to prevent his indulgence in his second characteristic as a general: a propensity toward gossiping, backbiting, and criticizing his seniors. This activity was all the more dangerous for its covertness. While press and politicians were clamoring for Johnston's removal after the fall of Fort Donelson, Hardee was confiding in letters to various friends that Johnston had lost the confidence of the army, had indeed failed, and ought to be removed.

Hardee had served at Shiloh, and later it was at least partly on his advice that Beauregard had evacuated Corinth.[11] Bragg, upon taking over command of the western army, seems to have entertained the same high opinion of Hardee that many held before coming to know him well. When he had asked Davis to remove the "dead weight" from the army before the Kentucky campaign, he had referred to Hardee as his only "suitable major-general."[12]

Hardee's performance during the Kentucky campaign had not been outstanding, but Bragg retained his confidence in him. What Bragg did not know was that Hardee was rapidly becoming perhaps his most dangerous enemy within the army. Partially through the influence of Polk, who seems to have gained considerable sway over Hardee, and partially through his own proclivity to find fault with his superiors, Hardee became a bitter critic of Bragg. He also became the mainstay of Polk's anti-Bragg campaign, at least within the army. As former commandant of cadets at West Point and, more important, author of the tactics manual every young officer was frantically trying to memorize, Hardee had much more influence within the army than the bishop-turned-soldier could ever hope to, even with his insinuating manners. The two generals therefore worked out a plan. While Polk wrote letters to Jefferson Davis and otherwise used his connections with the influential men of the country, Hardee would endeavor to turn the army's officer corps against Bragg. At this he proved to be highly efficient, especially with the corps he had now come to command. He had the perfect vehicle for his purpose in the classes of instruction he had already instituted for his officers. Though the format he followed was similar to that of a West Point classroom, Hardee mixed lessons with innuendo against and outright criticism of Bragg.[13] Hardee soon had his subordinates, some of whom were abler men than he, believing that their army commander was a blundering incompetent whose judgments could never be trusted. This was especially tragic for the Confederacy in the case of Pat Cleburne, whose loyalty to Hardee's anti-Bragg teachings stunted his career and prevented the Confederacy from utilizing his talents as it should have.

Meanwhile Davis, at least for the time being, was not taken in by the anti-Bragg campaign. He took a more reasonable attitude toward Bragg. Before news of the retreat out of Kentucky had reached Richmond, the president had written Bragg praising his "brilliant achievements" in the campaign and admitting that "without the aid of the Kentuckians, we could not long occupy the state and should have no sufficient motive for doing so."[14] After learning of the failure of the operation, Davis had directed Bragg to "send an intelligent officer" from his army to brief him on what had happened and what was planned.[15] Bragg at once complied, sending off a staff officer with a written explanation of his plans for the army.[16] Davis, however, was anxious to hear the Perryville campaign explained by Bragg personally and, on the same day that Bragg dispatched his staff officer, had Cooper telegraph Bragg to visit Richmond, if he could, for a few days' conference.[17] Again Bragg lost no time in obeying; leaving the army temporarily under Polk's command, the next day he was on the train for Richmond.[18]

Bragg remained in Richmond for a week, conferring with Davis and Secretary of War Randolph every day from 10:00 A.M. to 4:00 P.M.[19] Bragg was not a fancy talker, but he explained what had happened "in a direct and frank manner," and Davis was impressed with his "self-denying temper in relation to his future position."[20] The talks satisfied Davis that the opinion he had already formed was substantially correct: Withdrawing from Kentucky had been the only possible move considering that the state's population had not rallied as expected to the Confederate standard. Though Davis realized that Bragg was not without his faults and though he admitted that "another Genl. might excite more enthusiasm," he believed that Bragg was the best general he had available for the western theater.[21]

Having decided to keep Bragg, Davis was rightfully concerned that the hostility to Bragg among certain generals might spread to the point that it sapped Bragg's effectiveness. To prevent this, Davis attempted to persuade Smith and Polk, the most vocal critics, to take a more responsible course. To Smith he wrote a long and friendly letter, admitting that the results of the Kentucky campaign had been "a bitter disappointment" but pointing out that Bragg was the best general to be had and urging Smith to continue in his current position and cooperate with Bragg in future operations. Bragg, Davis informed Smith, "uniformly spoke of you in the most complimentary terms, and does not seem to imagine your dissatisfaction."[22] The president also invited Smith to come to Richmond for a few days to talk things over.[23] Accordingly, a few days after Bragg's departure Smith arrived in the Confederate capital.[24] Smith hoped to see Bragg replaced by Joseph E. Johnston, the superior under whom he had won so much glory in Virginia.[25] He tried but failed to win the president over to his viewpoint. Davis, on the other hand, succeeded in persuading Smith at least to stay at his present post and refrain from criticizing Bragg publicly.[26]

Returning from Richmond, Smith happened to meet Bragg on the train. It was a tense moment for those present, all of whom, including Smith, whose conscience may have been bothering him, expected a "stormy meeting." Smith felt compelled to tell Bragg what he had told Davis, but as the Floridian himself related in a letter to his wife a few days later, Bragg "spoke kindly to me & in the highest terms of praise and admiration of my 'personal character and soldierly qualities'—I was astonished."[27] Smith was neither the first nor the last person to have Braxton Bragg figured all wrong.

With Leonidas Polk, Davis was less successful in effecting a reconciliation with Bragg. After returning to his department, Bragg, who evidently was unaware of the extent of Polk's hostility, ordered the bishop to proceed to Richmond "as bearer of important dispatches and for the purpose of conferring personally in regard to the state of military affairs" in Bragg's sector, particularly in relation to problems which Bragg had noticed after his return.[28] Bragg's trust in Polk as an envoy to Richmond was greatly misplaced, for no sooner did he arrive than he tried to talk Davis into relieving Bragg of his command. The president attempted to persuade Polk, as he had Kirby Smith, to take a more reasonable view, but to no avail. After returning to the army, Polk continued his vendetta against his commanding officer.

The controversy placed Davis in a difficult position. He knew Bragg was a fairly good general, and he respected him for his selfless devotion to the cause. On the other hand, Polk was his old friend whose faults he steadfastly overlooked. Davis never should have appointed Polk and, having appointed him, should have relieved him after the Kentucky campaign. In extenuation of Davis it can be said that he was apparently unaware of Polk's disobedience of orders during the campaign; Bragg did not make an issue of that incident until driven to it by the incessant claims of Polk and his friends that Polk had saved the army from Bragg's folly. Nevertheless, Polk's open and unrestrained denunciation of his commander should have been enough to warn Davis that the bishop would be a detriment to the army. Davis simply could not be objective about Leonidas Polk. He would keep both Polk and Bragg if he could, but he would keep Polk in any event. His repeated failure to remove Polk was one of his most serious personnel-related mistakes and would eventually have grave consequences.

At this point, however, Bragg's detractors, though vocal, were in the minority; the majority of the army's generals still supported their commander (Hardee's efforts not yet having borne fruit).[29] Bragg himself did his utmost to be conciliatory, which did not come easy to a man of his temperament. This approach served to placate Smith somewhat, though all kindness seemed lost on Polk.[30]

The matter that Bragg had wanted Polk to discuss in Richmond was a proposed movement by his army into Middle Tennessee in hopes of taking Nashville. Throughout the Perryville campaign, while Confederate troops had been operating in Kentucky and Nashville had been held by only a small Union force, Tennessee's governor and congressional delegation had been clamoring loudly for someone – Bragg, Price, anyone – to retake the city.[31] While the question was still undecided in Kentucky, Davis and Bragg had wisely turned down these requests. However, once it became apparent that, for now at least, the Confederacy was not going to prevail in Kentucky, it seemed reasonable to try to profit from the campaign by taking Middle Tennessee. Therefore, some of the reinforcements on their way to Bragg were diverted to the Nashville area once news of Bragg's retreat reached Richmond.[32] This small force had established itself at Murfreesboro, thirty-five miles southeast of Nashville, but could do little to take the state capital because the Federal army formerly commanded by Buell had come directly to Nashville after Bragg pulled back from Perryville and now held the city in force.[33] Buell had been replaced by Rosecrans, the victor of Corinth and a much more formidable opponent.

Bragg planned to take his army down through Chattanooga and then up to Murfreesboro. The same old problem would apply here, though, that had plagued him in Kentucky. Without help from Kirby Smith's troops, his army was too small to handle the Federal army it faced. Bragg had discussed this with Davis while in Richmond and left a memorandum on the subject with the president. After returning to Tennessee, Bragg had become even more impressed with the need for cooperation and had written to Richmond pointing out that "movements involving so much should [not] be left to the uncertainty of two officers agreeing in their views, however much the Government may confide in them or they in each other." It was this situation that he had intended Polk to pursue more fully with the president.[34]

Fortunately, even before Bragg had dispatched Polk, Davis had recognized the importance of having a clear-cut system to bring about cooperation between the Confederacy's two armies in Tennessee. Bragg had no sooner left Richmond than orders had been drawn up specifying that Bragg was authorized to call on Smith for as many troops "as the exigency of the operation may demand."[35] While Bragg was cautioned not to strip East Tennessee of all troops, this new order substantially gave him the authority he would have needed for success in Kentucky and was an excellent start for his campaign on Nashville.[36]

Thus strengthened, Bragg took his army up to Murfreesboro. Even with rein-forcements from Kirby Smith, Bragg's force was not so large as to allow him to hurl it at the Federal entrenchments around Nashville in a repeat of Van Dorn's ill-advised assault on the same Federal commander at Corinth. Instead, Bragg would have to devise some way to lure the Federals into a fight on open ground. His plan was relatively simple. He would threaten Nashville by keep-ing his main force at Murfreesboro. Meanwhile, his cavalry, under such leaders as the fearsome Nathan Bedford Forrest, would range all around the city, cut-ting off highway, railroad, and telegraph communications and gobbling up any Union foraging parties they might find. Rosecrans would be unable to receive supplies from his base in the North and unable to draw provisions from the surrounding countryside. Before long he would have to come out in force to drive off the threatening Confederates; when he did, Bragg would have his chance to beat him in the open field.[37]

Bragg put the plan into action and immediately began seeing results. By mid-November Rosecrans and his troops were completely confined within their fortified lines at Nashville and virtually under siege. Bragg and his Confederates, on the other hand, were obtaining enough supplies from the surrounding area to provide for the entire army at Murfreesboro and send out a surplus for use by Confederate armies elsewhere.[38] Though the cavalry could not cut off the supplies that came by way of the Cumberland River and Rosecrans was thus able to prepare at leisure for the coming fight, the situation was favorable for the Confederates. Essentially, they controlled all of Middle Tennessee out-side of Nashville and could benefit from the region's abundance. Hence Bragg could afford to wait as long as Rosecrans might choose to delay.

Davis had also taken matters in hand with regard to the defenses of Missis-sippi, and here his reorganization had begun even before the Perryville and Corinth campaigns had reached their climax. As Van Dorn and Price had argued about their differing plans of campaign and then finally united and moved on Corinth, reports had reached the capital that all was not well in Mississippi.[39] To remedy this situation, Davis ordered Maj. Gen. John C. Pemberton, who had been commanding the defenses of Charleston, South Carolina, to proceed to Mississippi and take command of that state and the portion of Louisiana east of the Mississippi River.[40] Theoretically at least, this was the area that Van Dorn had left behind in taking the offensive. Van Dorn would then, it was assumed, carve out a new department for himself in West Tennessee.

Sending Pemberton to Mississippi settled a couple of problems besides pro-viding what Davis hoped would be a competent commander who could devote his full attention to the defense of the state and allay the fears of its frantic politicians. The move was well received by the South Carolinians, who heartily detested Pemberton; and it made a place for the troublesome Beauregard, who would soon be finishing his rest cure at Bladon Springs.

Born in Philadelphia in 1814, the second of thirteen children, John C. Pemberton enjoyed the best education available in that city before entering West Point in 1833.[41] Like Davis, Pemberton had had an unimpressive career at the academy, being arrested his freshman year for throwing bread in the mess hall and his senior year for possessing a jug of whiskey.[42] He ranked twenty-seventh out of fifty graduates in the class of 1837, twenty-two places behind his classmate Braxton Bragg.[43]

After serving in the Seminole War, Pemberton was assigned to a number of frontier posts from Kansas to Minnesota, but it was while stationed at Fort Monroe, Virginia, in 1846 that he met and married Martha Thompson, daughter of a wealthy Virginia shipowner. In the Mexican War Pemberton served with distinction, being twice wounded and receiving two brevet promotions as well as a vote of commendation from the Pennsylvania legislature and a sword from the citizens of Philadelphia.[44] He also gained the respect of a fellow officer, Capt. U. S. Grant. Grant later recalled that

an order was issued that none of the junior officers should be allowed horses during the marches. Mexico is not an easy country to march in. Young officers not accustomed to it got footsore. This was quickly discovered, as they were soon found lagging behind. But the order was not revoked, yet a verbal permit was accepted, and nearly all of them remounted. Pemberton alone said, No, he would walk, as the order was still extant not to ride, and he did walk, though suffering intensely the while. . . . He was scrupulously particular in matters of honor and integrity.[45]

The remaining years before the Civil War brought more service at frontier outposts. When secession became reality and war loomed on the horizon, Pemberton found himself in a dilemma. He had strong states'-rights views, and apparently he honestly believed the South was right. Even more important, he had a southern wife. His mother and his brothers, two of whom had already enlisted for the North, begged him to remain loyal, but his wife's entreaties prevailed over those of his northern family. In April 1861, despite the urgings of General Scott, he resigned his commission and went south, where, his wife assured him, "Jeff Davis has a post ready for you."

As it turned out, the post he received had little to do with Davis. Pemberton became a lieutenant colonel in the army of Virginia, his adopted state. After the absorption of Virginia's army into that of the Confederacy, Pemberton, in November 1861, was promoted to brigadier general and was ordered to Charleston, South Carolina, to serve under Robert E. Lee in defending the Confederacy's southern Atlantic coastline. When Lee departed to retrieve sagging Confederate fortunes in western Virginia, Pemberton rose to major general and department commander.

Though he had been stationed in South Carolina for a time as a young of-

John C. Pemberton (National Archives)

ficer and had been influenced by the state's ideas, Pemberton, the Pennsylvania Confederate, had apparently never learned the knack of getting along with the South Carolinians. This, in all fairness, was by no means an easy task. Even the genteel Lee, whose father had defended South Carolina in the Revolutionary War, found it difficult to obtain the approval and cooperation of the state's proud and touchy aristocracy. Pemberton's chances of becoming popular there were never very good, but his fall into disfavor was spectacular.

First, he recommended abandoning and dismantling Fort Sumter, which he considered of no value to the defense of Charleston. Whether or not this judgment was sound militarily, a more foolish move politically would be hard to imagine. Pemberton had disregarded the tremendous symbolic importance of those few acres of masonry in Charleston harbor to both North and South. The South Carolinians were beside themselves, and their indignation reverberated all the way to Richmond, though Pemberton's reputation there remained intact. Pemberton then added to his troubles by alienating the powerful Rhett family. Pemberton's wife was seriously ill and was being attended by Dr. George Rhett. Upon meeting one of his old friends one day, an army doctor, Pemberton thoughtlessly asked him to come look at his wife and see what could be done for her. Rhett was offended and refused to have anything more to do with the case.[46]

Blunders like these were compounded by his naturally reserved and sometimes brusque manner and his poor choice of birthplace—a mistake southerners rarely forgave. Pemberton was a pariah in South Carolina, and there went up a prodigious cry for his removal—even from the governor himself, who characterized Pemberton in letters to Davis as totally incompetent and "confused and uncertain about everything."[47] There arose at the same time a clamor for a return to Charleston of the Hero of Sumter, South Carolina's darling, G. T. Beauregard.

Davis's confidence in Pemberton was undiminished, and he was disturbed enough by the outcry against Pemberton to undertake the fruitless task of persuading the governor of South Carolina to be reasonable.[48] Failing in this endeavor he had to begin looking for another post for Pemberton. Then, around the end of August 1862, Beauregard reported for duty and was assigned to the southern Atlantic coast region as Pemberton's superior, making Pemberton's position largely superfluous.[49] About a month later, as the need materialized for a general to look after the Mississippi River defenses Van Dorn had left behind, Pemberton was the obvious choice. He took over the command, making his headquarters in Jackson, Mississippi, around the beginning of October.[50] The first impression he made on Mississippians was generally good.[51] Newpapers spoke highly of him and even the president's brother Joseph was favorably impressed.[52]

Pemberton had barely arrived before Van Dorn met his defeat at Corinth. This setback created a curious command situation. It was obvious that Van

Dorn would not be advancing into West Tennessee, much less carving out a department for himself. This threw him back into what was now Pemberton's department. Yet Van Dorn outranked Pemberton. The whole situation was so anomalous that Pemberton felt he could no longer carry on according to his original orders and wrote to Richmond for new instructions.[53] Van Dorn, too, found the arrangement disturbing as well as embarrassing. Earlier on the very day that he had learned of Pemberton's assumption of command over Mississippi, he had issued an order of his own, taking charge of all troops in that state under a directive sent out from Richmond before the assignment of Pemberton, when it appeared that nothing else would bring cooperation between Van Dorn and Price. Thoroughly disgruntled, Van Dorn wrote to the secretary of war, complaining of the abrupt change and stating, "I hope this will be corrected."[54]

Though Van Dorn did not know it yet, the matter had already been corrected and not in a way he would like. As soon as Davis had learned of Van Dorn's defeat at Corinth, he had had Pemberton promoted to lieutenant general over the head of Van Dorn, who at that time was the senior major general in the army.[55] That way Pemberton would unambiguously outrank the Mississippi general, and the matter would be settled. Though Davis did not have as low an opinion of Van Dorn as many held after the battle of Corinth – the president's brother wrote that "when Van Dorn was made a general, it spoiled a good captain" – his confidence in Van Dorn as an independent commander was probably shaken.[56] He admitted that the Mississippi campaign had been a failure because "we were out-generaled."[57] Furthermore, Van Dorn had become odious in Mississippi, not only because of his defeat but also because of his scandalous private life and unpopular imposition of martial law.[58] Davis therefore decided he could not maintain Van Dorn in top command in Mississippi but could use him as a valuable subordinate to Pemberton.

With these reforms the more glaring organizational problems of the Perryville and Corinth campaigns had been corrected. Bragg would now command the cooperation of Kirby Smith, and in Mississippi command was unified under Pemberton. Theoretically, there even existed a sort of unified command structure for all of the western theater between the Appalachians and the Mississippi, since Bragg was still considered as commanding Pemberton and the Confederate forces in Mississippi, though some confusion remained about this. In reality Pemberton functioned as commander of an independent department, reporting directly to Richmond.[59] Davis, however, was not finished with his reorganization in the West. He was waiting to apply what he considered to be a better and more permanent solution – the appointment of one man to oversee everything from the mountains to the Mississippi – as soon as the man he had in mind for the job, Gen. Joseph E. Johnston, became available.

Joseph Eggleston Johnston was born in 1807 in Cherry Grove, Virginia. His mother was a niece of Patrick Henry, and his father fought in the Revolutionary War under the famed Light-horse Harry Lee, father of Robert E. Lee. In 1811 the family moved to Abingdon in southwestern Virginia. In 1825 Joseph's father, who served thirteen terms in the state assembly and two of them as speaker, secured for him an appointment to West Point. There he was a classmate and good friend of Robert E. Lee. He knew fellow cadet Jefferson Davis only casually, and though in later years the legend spread that Johnston and Davis had a falling-out as rivals for the affections of a "tavern keeper's daughter"—supposedly leading to a contest of fisticuffs from which Johnston emerged victorious—there is no factual foundation for this story.[60] Johnston, like his friend Lee, did not partake in the type of rowdy escapades that sometimes snared Cadet Davis. He was a good student and, upon graduation in 1829, ranked thirteenth in his class of forty-six.

Johnston served with distinction in the Seminole Wars, part of the time as an aide to Gen. Winfield Scott, and was slightly wounded in a skirmish with the Indians. In the Mexican War he again distinguished himself as lieutenant colonel of a regiment of light infantry, being wounded on two occasions and winning a brevet colonelcy. Johnston's propensity for drawing enemy fire elicited from Winfield Scott the quip that "Johnston is a great soldier, but he had an unfortunate knack of getting himself shot in nearly every engagement."

At the close of hostilities Johnston's regiment was mustered out of service, and he fell back to his permanent rank of captain in the topographical engineers.[61] In the years that followed, he displayed his extreme sensitivity about rank—something that would later cause problems for the Confederacy—by pestering the War Department with the claim that he should be considered a colonel because of his wartime brevet. In his response to these requests Secretary of War Davis showed the same impatience toward foolishness from officers that would later strain his relations with several generals, Johnston among them.[62] Still, Davis had respect for Johnston's ability as an officer, and when two new regiments were created in 1855, Johnston became lieutenant colonel of the new First Cavalry. In the years since the Mexican War, Johnston and Lee, who now held a corresponding position in the Second Cavalry, had drifted apart, and their relationship had become more formal. In fact, during the Civil War Johnston would occasionally express envy and criticism of his old friend.

In the summer of 1860 the position of quartermaster general became vacant. The search for another officer to fill that post ended with two finalists—Albert Sidney Johnston (no relation) and Joseph E. Johnston. Though this affair is not quite clear, it seems that Davis, a member of the Senate Military Affairs Committee, supported the claims of his friend A. S. Johnston. J. E. Johnston, however, also had connections, notably his cousin by marriage Secretary of War John B. Floyd (the same who later fled Fort Donelson); J. E. got the appointment and the promotion it entailed to the rank of brigadier general.[63] Whether Johnston knew of Davis's opposition is unclear, but there are indica-

Joseph Eggleston Johnston (National Archives)

tions that his feelings toward Davis during the closing months of peace were somewhat less than cordial.

When the crisis of union came, Johnston remained noncommittal and did not respond to Davis's offer of a Confederate brigadier general's commission. Finally, after the firing on Fort Sumter and the secession of Virginia, Johnston resigned his United States commission and offered his services to the South.[64] United States Secretary of War Simon Cameron later recalled that Johnston, upon communicating his resignation, said secession "was ruin in every sense of the word, but he must go."[65] From this statement it appears that Johnston never considered victory possible in the first place—a revelation that goes far in explaining his later actions and attitudes.

Johnston's wife had urged him not to go with the South—not because she favored the Union cause but because she feared, as she warned her husband, that Jefferson Davis "hates you, he has power, and he will ruin you."[66] Actually, this was far from the truth. The hostility between Davis and Johnston was mostly if not entirely on Johnston's part, and whatever ill will Davis may have harbored against Johnston he was able to set aside in making objective decisions on the general's merit. Though feelings of friendship often led Davis astray, his judgment was rarely warped by feelings of hostility.

In appearance Johnston was short and bald, and he was so sensitive about the latter that he wore a hat whenever possible, even at the dinner table.[67] A chief trait of his personality was his fear of failure. A friend reported that Johnston hated "to be beaten, even in a game of billiards."[68] Another associate noted that though Johnston was considered a fine shot, he rarely brought back game from his hunting excursions since he would not fire unless he was sure of a hit. The situation was never quite perfect, and he was afraid to risk his reputation as a marksman.[69]

At the outbreak of war Johnston was immediately appointed to a highly responsible command within the Confederate army. Johnston participated in the battle of Bull Run, and afterward his relations with the president, like Beauregard's, were strained by the controversy that arose over the question of whether the victory had been adequately exploited. There was also a matter of rank. In the summer of 1861 when Congress had created the rank of full general, Davis had appointed five men to this grade. Top-ranked was Adj. and Insp. Gen. Samuel Cooper, from whom Davis had expected much but who had turned out to be a cipher. Next came Albert Sidney Johnston, then Robert E. Lee, Joseph E. Johnston, and P. G. T. Beauregard. These rankings were in keeping with another law the Confederate Congress had passed, specifying that within a given grade, the relative rank of officers should be based on their previous relative rank in the United States Army. Cooper and Albert Sidney Johnston had both held the permanent rank of colonel, with Cooper being senior. Lee had been a lieutenant colonel and Beauregard a major. As quartermaster general, Joseph E. Johnston had held the staff rank of brigadier general, but there was a sharp separation at that time between staff rank and line rank. A staff officer could not command troops in his staff rank except by special assignment. For practical purposes, then, Johnston's rank was that of lieutenant colonel, and since Lee was senior to him and only Beauregard had occupied a lower rank, it was fitting that Joseph E. Johnston should have been made the fourth of the Confederacy's original five full generals.[70]

Johnston did not agree. As far as he was concerned, a promotion was a promotion, and he maintained that his rank as brigadier general in the United States Army fully entitled him to be the top general of the Confederacy. It was his right; in denying it to him, Jefferson Davis was stealing what was rightfully his. Furious, he wrote Davis a letter setting forth at some length his curious theory of public office as an item of private property. What the president—and Congress, by confirming the appointments—had done was "in violation of my rights as an officer, of the plighted faith of the Confederacy and of the Constitution and laws of the land." A grave matter indeed, and Johnston believed it "a duty as well as a right" for him to protest against it. He also stated, "I now and here declare my claim that, notwithstanding these nominations made by the President, and their confirmation by Congress, I still rightfully hold the rank of first general in the armies of the Southern Confederacy."[71] It was an extraordinary epistle.

Though Davis's reply was brusque and insulting, he at least avoided the sort of point-by-point lawyer's refutation into which he often slipped. Showing considerable restraint, he limited his reply to: "I have received and read your letter of the 12th instant. Its language is, as you say, unusual; its arguments and statements utterly one-sided, and its insinuations are as unfounded as they are unbecoming."[72] It was certainly not the kind of wise and conciliatory letter Lincoln would have sent in a similar situation, but at least it laid the matter to rest and allowed both the president and general to turn their attention to more important concerns.

However, more tension arose between Davis and Johnston regarding military operations under Johnston's command in Virginia. During the war Johnston was to gain for himself a reputation as the most skillful—and frequent—retreater on either side. At least in respect to how frequently he retreated, the reputation was well founded. He would neither initiate a battle nor stand and receive an enemy attack unless everything was perfect. Instead he would fall back. His retreat from Harpers Ferry, Virginia, in June 1861 had been the occasion of some of the first murmuring in Richmond against the Davis administration, which was held responsible by the public for the loss.[73] In the spring of 1862 Johnston had fallen back precipitately and, as Davis felt, unnecessarily, abandoning huge stockpiles of supplies. In the peninsula campaign later that year, Johnston had retreated again and again up the peninsula toward Richmond, sacrificing more vital supply depots and installations, until Federal troops had approached to within sight of Richmond without engaging in a single major battle.[74]

Davis had tried to find out from Johnston what course of action he had in mind, but on the subject of military plans Johnston was a veritable sphinx. He would share nothing with his commander in chief but vague generalities.[75] This was because he either did not have a plan or because he was afraid to reveal anything lest the plan should not work out and he should be thought to have failed. He dared not risk his reputation as a strategist. Despite this Davis maintained Johnston in command of the Army of Northern Virginia, the Confederacy's most prestigious army. Davis believed Johnston had deservedly won the confidence of his men and surmised that removing him would be bad for morale, especially in the midst of an important campaign.[76] Also, Davis still believed that Johnston was an intelligent and skillful officer who could be valuable to the Confederacy if he could only be made to fight.

As the retreating army reached the outskirts of Richmond, Davis jacked up the pressure on his weak-kneed general. "If you will not give battle, I will appoint someone to command who will." Under this threat to his proud position Johnston finally summoned up the nerve to fight.[77] The resulting engagement was inconclusive, and true to form, Johnston managed to get himself shot. Though the wound was not life-threatening, Johnston was laid up for several months. In the meantime, Robert E. Lee took over the Army of Northern Virginia and in a brilliant campaign drove the Union forces back down the peninsula and then shifted the scene of action all the way into Maryland. Obviously, when Johnston finally did recover, he would not be getting his old job back.

Davis's confidence in Johnston had been shaken somewhat by that general's apparent willingness to retreat right up to and through Richmond without a fight, but he still thought Johnston was skillful and needed only to be put in a position where he could overcome his skittishness in order to be effective.[78]. A month after Johnston had been wounded, the president wrote to Mrs. Davis, who had not yet returned to Richmond after being evacuated when the city seemed about to fall: "Genl. J. E. Johnston is steadily and rapidly improving. I wish he was able to take the field. Despite the critics who know military affairs by instinct, he is a good soldier . . . and could at this time render most valuable service."[79] Davis knew just where he wanted to place Johnston as soon as he became available, and even had he not known, there was no shortage of advice to the same effect. Generals, politicians, and others bombarded Davis with requests that Johnston be given overall command in the West.[80] Perhaps there, Davis may have reasoned, Johnston could use his skill as a strategist without needing the nerve to commit an individual army to battle. By November 12, 1862, Johnston had recovered from his wound and on that date reported for duty at the War Department in Richmond.[81] The man to whom he presented himself was Secretary of War George Wythe Randolph, who was just then in the middle of a major falling-out with President Davis.

In setting up the new organizational system in the West after Bragg's retreat from Kentucky, Davis had stressed the importance of cooperation among the three main Confederate armies there: Bragg's in Middle Tennessee, Pemberton's in Mississippi, and Holmes's in the trans-Mississippi department.[82] Davis concluded that the Confederate objectives should be retaking the cities of Nashville, Memphis, and Helena (on the Mississippi in Arkansas, below Memphis), and for this purpose, he pointed out in a letter to Holmes, "the concentrations of two or when practicable of all the columns in the attack upon one of the enemy's armies is so obviously desirable that it is needless even to state it."[83] The day before, Randolph had also written to Holmes, with Davis's approval, spelling out in more specific terms what Richmond expected of its trans-Mississippi commander. Randolph suggested that Holmes take Helena at once as a preliminary step to crossing into Tennessee for cooperation with Pemberton and Bragg.[84] Davis and Randolph were thus in complete agreement on western strategy and, in particular, on the course that ought to be followed by Holmes's army. Ironically, however, it was over this same issue that the president and secretary of war had their breach.

Randolph and Davis did not work well together, and in any case, Randolph was tired of the pressures and burdens of public life. Some sort of rupture between the two may, therefore, have been only a matter of time. The nature of the disagreement was determined in part by the numerous and vocal critics of the Davis administration, one of whose favorite refrains was that Randolph was a mere clerk who never made important decisions.[85] Actually, Davis saw the role of secretary of war as that of "constitutional advisor" to the president and had made a point of holding long and frequent conferences with Randolph about strategic options.[86] If the final decision always lay with Davis, such was fitting since he was, after all, commander in chief. Still, the taunts stung the proud and aristocratic Randolph and may have prompted him to take the action he did. On the other hand, he may simply have thought he was elaborating a policy already decided on by the president. Regardless, on October 27, a week after he and Davis had written their letters to Holmes stressing the importance of concentrating the three western armies, Randolph wrote Holmes another letter, this time without consulting Davis. He again mentioned the importance of cooperation with Pemberton and told Holmes that "when necessary" he was authorized to cross the Mississippi with as much of his force as he thought best and, by virtue of his rank, command "the combined operations on the eastern bank."[87] All of this was in complete agreement with what Davis had previously told Holmes; Randolph had merely spelled out what Davis had implied. Still, it was an important matter, and Randolph had not, as was customary, discussed it with the president in advance.

This fact stuck in Davis's craw when, on November 12, he learned of Randolph's letter. Davis was extremely sensitive about his presidential prerogative and his reputation as a strategist, and Randolph's action offended in both these regards. It suggested first that strategic decisions, or at least minor elaborations of strategic decisions, could be made in Richmond and passed on to generals without the president's knowledge. To Davis, that was intolerable. Randolph's action also insinuated that some elaboration of Davis's previous missive had been necessary. If so, why had the president not ordered it? Was Jefferson Davis an inferior strategist? That was again intolerable. Either way, the offending letter had to be repudiated.

Immediately upon learning what Randolph had done, Davis wrote out a stern and not especially honest note to the secretary of war. It must have astonished Randolph. "The co-operation designed by me," Davis asserted, "was in co-intelligent action on both sides of the river. . . . The withdrawal of the commander of the Trans-Mississippi Department for temporary duty elsewhere would have a disastrous effect, and was not contemplated by me. It was rather hoped that he would be able to retake Helena."[88] The assertion that Davis had not "contemplated" a transfer of forces across the Mississippi was not strictly true. Not only had Davis "contemplated" moving Holmes and his men temporarily to the east bank of the river, he had also personally written that general that such a course was "so obviously desirable that it is needless even to state it." As for taking Helena, Randolph intended Holmes to do so before crossing the river, and the president had to be aware of this. But Davis's pride had been touched, and it was to have far-reaching consequences.

The first outcome was the end of Randolph's tenure as secretary of war. Randolph was understandably irritated by Davis's self-serving rebuke. Since Davis had ordered him to countermand his instructions to Holmes and since he considered Davis's letter self-explanatory, he simply sent a copy of the letter to Holmes. This was not good enough for Davis: An official order should have been framed and sent though official channels. Davis penned another letter of reproof to Randolph.[89] By this time the secretary of war had had enough and promptly sent in his resignation, which Davis promptly accepted. As of November 15 the Confederacy was without a secretary of war.[90] One week later the office was filled by James A. Seddon. It was a miserable affair and certainly does not display Jefferson Davis to best advantage. On this one occasion during the war, he let his pride get the better of him to a serious extent.

Beyond the immediate consequences of this lapse were more significant long-range ones. Davis was now bound by his pride not to allow the trans-Mississippi forces to cross the river and join in a unified campaign. To do so would be to admit that Randolph had been right. The uncoupling of the Confederate defenses on either side of the Mississippi was now complete.

This was the mess into which Joseph E. Johnston unwittingly inserted himself when he reported for duty to Secretary of War Randolph on November 12, 1862, the date of Davis's first rebuke. Johnston had been notified informally that Davis intended to place him over the armies of Bragg and Pemberton. Completely ignorant of the present conflict between the president and the secretary of war, he was anxious to suggest to Randolph that it made more sense to bring Holmes's army across the Mississippi, unite it with Pemberton's, beat Grant, and then join Bragg to take care of Rosecrans. Johnston was still expounding this idea when Randolph stopped him and asked if he would like to hear something on the subject. Taking out his letter book, the secretary of war read Johnston the letter he had sent to Holmes recommending the same course as Johnston was describing. He then read the general the note he had just received from Davis, ordering that the instructions to Holmes be countermanded.[91]

Twelve days later, with Randolph gone and Seddon the new secretary of war, Johnston received his official orders to take command of Bragg's and Pemberton's departments.[92] He had been waiting for this and immediately sent to Davis, through Cooper, a letter setting forth the ideas he had explained to Randolph. This was a questionable undertaking in itself, since Johnston had just witnessed firsthand how strongly Davis felt on this subject and had no reason to believe Davis had changed his mind. Johnston further clouded the issue by arguing that it was impossible for troops to move back and forth quickly between Bragg's and Pemberton's armies.[93] However, this contention could be refuted simply by pointing to the rapid movement of Bragg's army from Tupelo to Chattanooga at the beginning of the Kentucky campaign. The impression given by the letter was that Johnston, upon being assigned to a new command, was not doing his best to carry out instructions but was instead finding fault with his superiors' orders. In fact, to a certain extent, this was precisely what Johnston was doing. Whenever he was given a new assignment, he complained constantly that he was not being properly supported by his superiors –with the consequent implication that failure was only to be expected and that any success that might be achieved was entirely the result of his own brilliance.

Davis ignored Johnston's letter. He had given the general a job, and he expected him to do it—not tell the president how he ought to do *his* job. However, if the Confederacy were to benefit from Johnston's skills, it meant avoiding unnecessary squabbles with him. Davis therefore refrained from writing the hostile reply that would no doubt have been his first impulse. He simply let the matter pass.

On December 4, 1862, Johnston arrived at Chattanooga and set up his headquarters there.[94] He was immediately faced with a difficult situation. Grant had launched a new offensive in Mississippi, and Pemberton was in serious trouble. Grant planned to march his own army overland from Memphis toward Jackson and then take Vicksburg in the rear. Meanwhile, another Federal force under Sherman would move down the river for a direct assault on Vicksburg. Pemberton, Grant reasoned, would not be able to meet both thrusts, and so, one or the other must succeed.[95] Even before he knew of Sherman's part in the plan, Pemberton decided he had not nearly enough troops to face Grant, who outnumbered him about two to one. Pemberton began retreating and calling for reinforcements.[96] Waiting for Johnston at Chattanooga was a dispatch from

Richmond describing Pemberton's plight and stating that though Holmes had been "peremptorily ordered" to send reinforcements to Pemberton (not, however, to cross the river with his whole force), it was feared his troops would not arrive in time. Perhaps, the president urged, Johnston ought to send some of Bragg's troops to Pemberton.[97]

Johnston's position had been created to handle exactly this type of situation. As theater commander he could, theoretically, decide where the real enemy threat lay and who could best spare the troops needed to meet it. In reality, however, Johnston was caught off-guard. He had had no occasion to familiarize himself with the western front, he had just arrived at Chattanooga, he had not visited either Bragg's or Pemberton's armies, and he had no idea where Pemberton's troops were or what their status was.[98] On top of this he was still predisposed to believe that troops from Bragg's army could not possibly reach Pemberton in time to help. He considered the rail route through Mobile too long and roundabout—notwithstanding Bragg's accomplishment that summer—and complained that the Tennessee River, infested as it was with Union gunboats, blocked a more direct route. Having convinced himself, in the absence of facts, that there was nothing he could do, Johnston did nothing, except to inform Richmond and Pemberton that Holmes had better hurry his men along.[99]

Actually, Holmes's men were not coming at all. The president's order that reinforcements be sent to Pemberton had not exactly been peremptory. Rather, like most Civil War orders, it had allowed Holmes to use his discretion if he thought the situation on his front, with which no distant commander in chief could be completely familiar, was too threatening. Holmes did, and he wrote to Richmond at great length, enumerating his excuses.[100] Davis was not convinced and reiterated his order.[101] Again Holmes refused, pleading that to send the reinforcements would be tantamount to abandoning Arkansas.[102] Davis still wished Holmes would send the troops but was reluctant to give a really peremptory order lest Holmes should be right and Arkansas really should be lost. Unfortunately, Davis's restraint was based on faulty logic, since if Vicksburg fell Arkansas would be lost anyway.

Against this setting Davis decided it might be helpful to visit the western theater personally, to see for himself what the situation was and, he hoped, to raise morale and promote recruitment.[103] This was no light matter, for Davis had been sick for some time, his weak health having yielded to the strain of his office. But if his health was weak, his will certainly was not, and it was this that drove him to undertake the journey. Those who encountered him along the way remarked on his sunken eyes and the manner in which he held his upper lip so tightly against his teeth that their shape could be made out through it. He left by train on December 10, taking only a single military aide and traveling incognito lest his departure be taken as an indication that Richmond was about to be evacuated (another huge Union army was just then advancing against Lee). Arriving in Chattanooga the next day, the president found Johnston under the weather from a flare-up of the wound he had received several months earlier in Virginia. Davis decided his discussion with Johnston could wait and traveled on to Bragg's headquarters at Murfreesboro.[104] There he stayed for two days and was very pleased with what he saw. He reviewed some of the troops and pronounced them "the best appearing troops he had seen, well appointed and well clad."[105] He was even more pleased with the spirit of the army. Clearly Polk's negative reports had been false. Officers and men were anxious for Rosecrans to come out from Nashville and confident they could beat him if he did. They doubted, however, that he had the nerve. Jubilantly Davis telegraphed Seddon back in Richmond, "Found the troops there in good condition and fine spirits. Enemy is kept close in to Nashville, and indicates only defensive purposes."[106]

All this prompted Davis to make a strategic decision he had no doubt been turning over in his mind awhile. He would order 10,000 men from Bragg's army to reinforce Pemberton in Mississippi.[107] If Johnston would not use his position to shift forces as Davis had intended, then Davis would do it for him. Bragg was opposed to the idea. He might be confident now, but if the president took a quarter of his infantry, it was hard to see how he could defeat Rosecrans. Besides, he had dispatched a cavalry force under Nathan Bedford Forrest to hit Grant's long supply line in Tennessee and felt this was all he could do. He also felt it would be enough to stop Grant.[108] Davis, however, had little faith that Forrest's cavalry raid would accomplish anything and insisted on the transfer of infantry. "Fight if you can," he told Bragg, "and fall back beyond the Tennessee" if necessary.[109] On returning to Chattanooga on the fourteenth, Davis ordered Johnston to transfer 9,000 men from Bragg's army to Pemberton's.[110] Johnston protested, but Davis specified exactly what units he wanted; since Davis was on the spot, Johnston had no choice but to obey.[111] A reinforced division under Gen. C. L Stevenson was promptly detached from Bragg's army and sent to Vicksburg by rail via Chattanooga and Mobile.[112]

On the sixteenth Davis continued his tour of inspection, leaving Chattanooga and arriving at Vicksburg on December 20.[113] There, Johnston, whom he had ordered to accompany him, continued his efforts to persuade Davis that troops should be brought over from the trans-Mississippi area to support Pemberton.[114] In this endeavor he was at least partially successful, and Davis made another attempt to wrest troops from Holmes. From Vicksburg he wrote Holmes a letter, but instead of ordering the recalcitrant general as he had ordered Johnston, Davis tried to persuade Holmes that it was safe to send some men.[115] Not surprisingly, Holmes continued to insist that he could spare no forces, and there the matter rested.[116] That Davis allowed Holmes to persist in this folly was another manifestation of the president's favoritism for his prewar friends. Friendship with Davis had helped Holmes win the appointment in the first place, and now it was allowing him to indulge in a serious strategic blunder simply because Davis would not give his friend a peremptory order. On Christmas Day the president left Vicksburg to return to Richmond.[117]

Meanwhile, Forrest's cavalry raid was having a great deal more success than Davis (or most others, for that matter) had thought possible. Forrest and his troops left Murfreesboro on December 11 and went rampaging through West Tennessee, destroying supply depots, cutting telegraph wires, tearing up some sixty miles of railroad track over which Grant's supplies were supposed to move, and leading their numerous pursuers on a fruitless chase before returning to Confederate lines in better condition than they had left.[118] Spectacular results were also achieved by another Confederate cavalry raid operating farther south, immediately to the rear of Grant's advancing army. This force was composed of almost all of Pemberton's available horsemen and was led by the dashing cavalier Earl Van Dorn. Van Dorn may have lacked what it took to be an effective army commander—certainly public opinion in Mississippi held to that view—but he was demonstrating his skill as a first-class cavalry leader.[119] On December 20 his force swept down on Holly Springs, Mississippi, Grant's advance base, and utterly destroyed the vast quantities of supplies accumulated there.[120]

The result was that Grant's army was without supplies, leaving him no choice but to retreat. With Grant out of the way Pemberton was able to concentrate all his forces at Vicksburg to meet Sherman's frontal attack. Because of the telegraph wires Forrest's men had cut, Sherman remained unaware of Grant's retreat and proceeded with his own attack, hurling his troops at the Confederate positions above Chickasaw Bayou, just north of Vicksburg, on December 29. In one of the most one-sided battles of the war, Sherman lost over 1,700 men while Confederate losses were negligible.[121] Pemberton had won an easy victory even before the arrival of Stevenson and the 9,000 men from Bragg's army.

The fall of 1862 was a time for reorganization and consolidation of the Confederacy's western defenses. Davis had been anxious to correct the problems that had led to the failure of the Perryville and Corinth campaigns. Realizing that he could not, from Richmond, direct military operations in the West and make certain that cooperation was achieved, he sought to accomplish this by appointing a senior general to oversee the entire western theater east of the Mississippi. It had been a mistake to draw the line at the river, and Davis had compounded it by his overreaction to Randolph's initiative. Still, as far as it went, the creation of the new unified command was a wise decision.

Davis's choice for commander of this huge area was not as prudent. Joseph E. Johnston may have been—as Davis and nearly everyone else, North or South, supposed—an intelligent and skillful officer, but he certainly lacked the qualities that make a great general and, in any case, considered Davis's new system unworkable.

For Johnston's two chief subordinates Davis chose to keep Bragg in Tennessee and appoint Pemberton in Mississippi. Retaining Bragg was sound, though Davis erred in not removing Leonidas Polk, the chief source of the backbiting and criticism that would eventually undermine Bragg's effectiveness. For the most part, Davis was blind to the effect Polk was having on other officers within the army; he could not believe his friend capable of such scheming.

Pemberton's appointment was a risky move. Though Davis had confidence in him, the South Carolinians, in whose state he had been stationed, despised him, partly for his tactlessness but also because they disliked his defensive arrangements. At best, Pemberton was an uncertain quantity in an extremely important position.

Davis's western trip was an act of almost heroic dedication, given his weakened physical condition, and though his efforts at morale boosting may well have succeeded, his attempt to set the region's strategic house in order was not particularly successful. It was probably a mistake not to give Holmes absolute, peremptory orders to reinforce Vicksburg. Like many of Davis's mistakes it sprang not from lack of dedication to the cause nor from any primary flaw in his strategic sense but from an inordinate deference to the opinions of a friend who was unworthy of Davis's staunch loyalty. Thus he allowed himself to be put off by Holmes's arguments that shifting troops to Mississippi would mean the loss of Arkansas. Even if this were true, it would not matter to the Confederacy what happened in Arkansas if Vicksburg fell. Davis probably saw this but remained reluctant to give Holmes an order he could not dodge. Also, Davis's pride may still have smarted from the affair with Randolph, involving as it did a closely related point. In any case, Davis did not force the issue with Holmes.

Instead, recognizing the importance of Vicksburg and discounting the effectiveness of cavalry in cutting Grant's supply line, he felt compelled to take a division from Bragg to reinforce Pemberton. Though understandable, it was a most unfortunate decision. Vicksburg seemed to be seriously threatened while Tennessee appeared to be in fine shape. Johnston was steadfastly refusing to exercise the authority Davis had given him. On the whole it was less surprising that Davis chose to exercise his own legitimate authority over Johnston than that he retained Johnston in command at all. Ordering the troop movement exemplified the sort of resolve that was required of a wartime president. Unfortunately, the president had finally brought himself to take decisive action in the wrong place at the wrong time. Few could have foreseen it—especially from Davis's angle of vision—but events in Mississippi soon demonstrated that the transfer had not been needed. Even more momentous events in Tennessee were about to prove that the division was very much needed in that state.

11

WINTER OF DISCONTENT

The Christmas season of 1862 was a cheerful one at Murfreesboro. The Army of Tennessee, as Bragg's army was coming to be called, was in high spirits, confident of victory whenever the enemy ventured out of his fortifications and happy to be spending this Christmas in the heart of Tennessee rather than several hundred miles farther south, as had seemed likely the previous spring. Highlight of the festivities, at least for the top brass, was the wedding of the local belle Martha "Mattie" Ready to the cavalry raider John Hunt Morgan.

Twenty-one-year-old Mattie Ready was the daughter of a prominent Murfreesboro lawyer. She had dark brown hair and gray eyes and seemed to be perfect in every respect. In school she had had perfect deportment, perfect posture, and perfect homework and was always amiable. She had had many offers from eligible bachelors but had turned them all down because she wanted to marry for love. In the dashing thirty-seven-year-old Morgan she had found it.[1] The story is told that while the Federals had occupied Murfreesboro the previous summer, Mattie had heard two Union officers roundly denouncing the rebel Morgan. Mattie did not know Morgan but spoke up so vigorously in his defense that one of the officers decided to take her name. "It's Mattie Ready," she had replied. "But by the grace of God one day I hope to call myself the wife of John Morgan." Morgan, it is said, heard of the incident, and things proceeded from there.[2]

Held on Sunday evening, December 14, the wedding was certainly in storybook style. Jefferson Davis had left the army to continue his journey that afternoon, but while in Murfreesboro he had personally signed and delivered Morgan's promotion to brigadier general. If the president could not be in attendance himself, the rest of the higher ranks were well represented. Leonidas Polk officiated, his bishop's robe draped over his general's uniform. Major General and former vice-president Breckinridge was an usher. Bragg, Hardee, Cheatham, and the entire headquarters staff were present. At the reception, music was provided by two regimental bands.[3]

After the dinner army surgeon D. W. Yandell entertained some of the guests in another room with his impersonations of high-ranking officers. Yandell's impersonations were known throughout the officer corps, and apparently they were pretty good. At the urging of his fellow officers, who were sitting around sipping wine and chatting, Yandell did first Polk and then Hardee, to the accompaniment of roars of laughter. Everyone knew, though, that he had one act that was better than all his others. "Do Bragg," they urged. Yandell gave in and went into his Bragg impersonation. Putting on an exaggeratedly stern face, he strode up and down, growling about lack of discipline and too much whiskey-drinking in the army—two of Bragg's pet peeves. Just then Bragg walked in. Yandell stopped and turned pale, but Bragg was as much in the spirit of the season and the occasion as anyone else. "Go on, doctor," he said. "Don't let me interrupt you. It is certainly entertaining and doubtless quite accurate."[4]

It was as pleasant a Christmas season as the Army of Tennessee would enjoy, but no sooner was the holiday past than the course of events abruptly brought back the ugly reality of the war. Secrecy in military operations was almost unknown in the Civil War, and the transfer of Stevenson's division from Bragg's army to Pemberton in Mississippi was no exception. A report of it even appeared in a Chattanooga newspaper.[5] Not surprisingly, Rosecrans was soon aware that his opponent's army had been weakened, and under considerable pressure from Washington to achieve some action on his front, he decided that now was as good a time as any to drive Bragg out of Middle Tennessee.[6] On the day after Christmas, Rosecrans's troops marched out of Nashville.[7] Bragg was quickly apprised of the advance and began collecting his troops and preparing to meet the Federals at Murfreesboro. Bad weather and harassing Confederate cavalry slowed the Federal march, and it took Rosecrans almost five days to cover the thirty miles from Nashville. By the evening of December 30, the day after Sherman had met his repulse at Vicksburg several hundred miles to the west, the two armies were drawn up within sight of each other and were sparring with their artillery.[8] The real contest, both sides knew, would come in the morning.

Bragg had positioned his army in front of Murfreesboro but close enough to the town to cover several of the important roads that converged there. This necessitated having the Confederate line straddle Stones River, a small stream flowing from southeast to northwest and passing within two miles or so of Murfreesboro.[9] That was not really much of a hazard, since the stream could be forded at almost any point.[10] Bragg's plan was to mass most of his troops on his left in order to strike Rosecrans's right and curl it back until the Confederates were astride the Nashville Pike in Rosecrans's rear, leaving the Union army cut off and well on its way to destruction.

Ironically, Rosecrans had decided on the very same tactic for his army: He would strike with his left at the Confederate right. He gave orders for the assault to begin the next morning as soon as the men had finished their breakfast, about 7:00 A.M. Bragg, who like Rosecrans knew nothing of his opponent's plans, had outgeneraled the northern commander on this point. His orders called for his troops to go in at daybreak.[11] If all went as planned, Bragg would beat Rosecrans to the punch. Unfortunately, Polk, for reasons best known to himself, had decided to rearrange the entire command system in his corps the night before the battle. The result was considerable confusion the next morning.[12] On top of that, the unit that was scheduled to open the Confederate attack—the division on the extreme left of Bragg's line—was commanded by John P. McCown. The blundering general had failed to get his troops into position as ordered, and so the attack was delayed while this situation was remedied.[13] On the opposite end of the long battle lines, Federal troops were already starting to ford Stones River in preparation for their assault.[14] Finally, shortly before seven o'clock, the Confederates crashed into the Federals' unsuspecting right flank.[15]

The Confederate line overlapped the Federal flank, surged around to the rear, and began rolling up the Union line, which, in expectation of the Federal offensive on the other end of the front, was weakly manned and totally unprepared. The Confederate juggernaut flattened everything in its path as Bragg's divisions went in, one after another, from left to right across the battlefield. Frantically, Rosecrans pulled troops from the left side of his line—all thoughts of attack now forgotten—and hastily shoved them into place to shore up his collapsing right flank, but the rampaging Confederates chewed up one Federal division after another.

Bragg's successful morning was not without its disappointments. McCown, whose bungling had delayed the assault in the first place, seemed bent on continuing in the same unfortunate vein. His division, which made up the outside edge of the huge right-wheel movement Bragg had ordered, went wandering off to the left of its designated line of advance, opening a large gap in the Confederate lines. In reserve behind McCown was the division of the Irish Confederate Pat Cleburne. Alert as always, Cleburne swung his unit into the gap without missing a beat.[16] His resourcefulness kept the Confederate drive from stalling at the very outset, but his division, which should have been saved for striking a decisive blow at the climactic moment of the battle, was now fully committed and would not be available to serve as Bragg's knockout punch. Blunders like McCown's could be costly.

Indeed, there was entirely too much blundering among Confederate officers on this morning, more than could be explained by Polk's ill-advised tinkering on the previous night. One Confederate soldier believed he knew the answer. "It was Christmas," he wrote. "John Barleycorn was general-in-chief. Our generals, and colonels, and captains had kissed John a little too often. They couldn't see straight. . . . They couldn't tell our men from the Yankees." Apparently there was a good deal of truth in this explanation.[17] Bragg had always done his best to suppress alcoholism in the army. Sometimes, though, it was a losing battle, and this seemed to be one of those times. A prime example of the problems high-ranking inebriates caused was the case of Maj. Gen. Benjamin Franklin Cheatham.

Cheatham had been with the Army of Tennessee since its inception and would remain with it until its demise, and whatever his faults, it could at least be said of him that as a division commander he was generally a hard fighter.

Born into a wealthy Tennessee family in 1820, Cheatham had the dubious distinction of being a descendant of the first man to bring slaves into the Tennessee Territory. When the Mexican War had broken out, young Cheatham had gone off as a captain in the First Tennessee. At Monterrey his regiment charged the main Mexican fort alongside Jefferson Davis's First Mississippi, and in later years it would be a source of enormous irritation to Cheatham that the Mississippi regiment would claim to have been the first into the fort. That honor belonged to Tennessee, Cheatham insisted, and Mississippi's claims were a "rascally, ungentlemanly, and unsoldierlike" attempt to "rob us of the honour and glory that we had won."[18]

After the Mexican War Cheatham joined the California gold rush, not to dig gold from the ground but to get it from those who did. Opening the Hotel de Mexico in Stockton, he prospered and decided to launch himself into California politics. He proved to be an effective if not overly fastidious politician and was soon presiding over a powerful political machine. Never one to shrink from whatever unsavory business he found necessary, Cheatham was not even above participating in a lynching—one that the sheriff, evidently a man of considerable courage, nearly prevented. As it was, after coolly walking the prisoner through an ill-tempered and obviously evil-intentioned mob toward the stoutly built jail, he found himself looking down the barrel of Cheatham's pistol. "Let the man go," growled Cheatham, who stood blocking the door of the jail, "or I'll shoot." The sheriff had no choice, and the unfortunate prisoner was soon hanged.[19]

Returning to Tennessee not long afterward, Cheatham became active in state politics and the Tennessee militia, in which he rose to the rank of brigadier general. With the outbreak of the Civil War he was commissioned to the same rank in the Provisional Army of Tennessee and then in the Confederate forces. While serving in the early battles on the western front, he made a name for himself as much by his vices off the field of battle as by his valor on it. His profanity was almost proverbial within the army, and though some of its members could be a fairly rough lot themselves, he could still impress a common soldier as "one of the wickedest men I ever heard speak."[20] An even more notable vice, however, was his heavy drinking, and there seems to be considerable evidence that this was his problem as he attempted to lead his division through the cedar brakes and limestone outcroppings that dotted the fields north of Murfreesboro on the wintry last day of 1863.[21]

First he was late in attacking, needing a prod from Bragg before he got moving.[22] Then he sent his brigades into action in a piecemeal and uncoordinated fashion.[23] Confusion reigned as his attack ground to a standstill. Not only was some of the momentum taken out of the Confederate offensive as a whole, but Cheatham's failure to advance allowed the Federals on his front to take Cleburne's advancing divison in flank.[24] Not that Cheatham's leadership lacked flamboyance. He galloped here and there exhorting the men in profane terms,

Benjamin Franklin Cheatham (Dahlgren Collection. Tennessee Historical Society holdings. Tennessee State Library and Archives.)

slashing the air with his sword, and personally heading his division's disjointed lunges.[25] He cut a curious figure, this short and portly general with dark skin and a big bushy moustache, riding furiously to and fro, his long wavy hair, which he liked to curl into ringlets over his ears, streaming behind him. After the battle someone reported he had fallen off his horse while waving his hat rather too vigorously in a gesture to encourage his men. After that, it was said, a staff member had to ride beside him and hold him on his horse. Whether this story was true or not, the fact remained that Cheatham was not a very effective division commander on this morning.[26]

Gradually some vestiges of order and coordination began returning to this sector; perhaps Cheatham was starting to sober up. The Confederate units on either side were able to assist, and the advance rolled forward.[27] By mid-morning the Confederate assault had folded the Union line back on itself until the battered right half of the line was at a right angle to the left. Rosecrans patched together one last defense in front of the Nashville Pike, his army's link with its base. If this line gave way, Rosecrans's situation would be desperate.

The attacking units on the Confederate left, however, were at the end of their tether. They pushed on the line along the Nashville Pike but no longer had the strength to break through it. The battle hung in the balance. If Bragg had had a fresh reserve division, he could have shattered the last Union defense and won a decisive victory; but the division that might have provided this reserve—Stevenson's—had been sent off to Mississippi on what proved to be a useless errand.[28] Even without a reserve Bragg was not ready to give up his hopes of crushing Rosecrans's army. He still had Breckinridge's division, the largest in his army and the only part of it still east of Stones River. That area had been quiet ever since the battle opened, and Breckinridge's men had seen no action at all that morning. Most of the Federal troops facing them had been drawn off to stem the tide of the Confederate assault. Now Bragg determined to put Breckinridge's division to use.[29]

There were a couple of ways this could be done. Breckinridge's troops could be brought around to the other end of the line and used to break the deadlock on the Nashville Pike, or they could be sent forward from their present position to push on the left side of the nearly doubled-over Federal army. Apparently, it was the latter course Bragg had in mind when at about 10:00 A.M. he sent an order to Breckinridge to advance with his division. To Bragg's surprise the former vice-president replied that he could not since he was about to be attacked.[30] This, of course, was nonsense. Attacking Breckinridge was the last thing the hard-pressed Rosecrans had in mind, but Breckinridge was confused by faulty intelligence reports.[31] When Bragg ordered him to drive off at once any Federals that might be threatening his position, Breckinridge prepared to comply. Meanwhile, Bragg learned that Breckinridge's information had been false and changed the order. Now Breckinridge was to send two brigades across the river to reinforce the rest of the army. Before he could obey,

Breckinridge received and accepted uncritically another piece of false intelligence, this one warning of a threat to his flank. He passed the information along to Bragg, who had no choice but to cancel his previous order and prepare to reinforce Breckinridge instead of drawing reinforcements from him. Within the hour Breckinridge informed Bragg he was "not certain" the enemy really was advancing on him as he had at first reported. By one o'clock it was obvious that there had been no threat to begin with. Bragg ordered Breckinridge to leave one brigade east of the river and bring the other four across to join the battle.[32]

By this time it was too late in the day to shift Breckinridge's brigades to the left end of the line on the Nashville Pike—if Bragg had ever intended that in the first place. Instead, the Confederate commander now determined to use them near the center of his line at the point where the Federal line angled back from its original position toward the turnpike.[33] At the apex of this angle was a little woodlot that was coming to be called the Round Forest. Here Union Gen. George H. Thomas, who was Rosecrans's senior corps commander and who held this part of the front, had assembled a large number of cannon with plenty of infantry support. Thomas was one of the best defensive commanders of the war, and the Confederates woud have their work cut out for them. Since the Round Forest lay in Polk's sector, he was to supervise the attack. His men had been hammering at it for hours by now but without success. Breckinridge's men presented the last chance to gain a decisive victory that day. Unfortunately, as Breckinridge's troops arrived two brigades at a time, Polk committed them to battle in even more piecemeal fashion, sending in now two brigades, now a brigade by itself, but making no concentrated assault.[34] The Confederate troops advanced bravely into the maelstrom of Union fire, which at times became so intense that southerners charging through the fields picked cotton from the open bolls to plug their ears against the roar of massed cannon.[35] The attacks were doomed to failure, and as nightfall brought the fighting to a close, the Federal position remained intact.

Still, Braxton Bragg and the Army of Tennessee had not done poorly at all. If their victory was not decisive, it was yet a victory. Four months later the Federal Army of the Potomac would retreat with its tail between its legs after being similarly handled by Robert E. Lee. That battle, Chancellorsville, would be rightly acclaimed as a brilliant southern victory. The first day at Murfreesboro was very nearly its precursor.

That night, several hundred miles away, Jefferson Davis, now on the more southerly return loop of his western tour, stood on the balcony of his hotel in Mobile, Alabama, and addressed a jubilant crowd on the subject of a recent string of Confederate successes in such diverse locations as Vicksburg, Mississippi, and Fredericksburg, Virginia. At the same time Union Gen. William Rosecrans and his corps commanders met in the farmhouse that served as Rosecrans's headquarters, behind Federal lines just north of Murfreesboro, Tennessee, for the purpose of deciding whether or not their army ought to retreat and, in so doing, augment the list of recent southern victories. Most of the generals were badly shaken. The Union army had suffered horrendous casualties, and its line of retreat was threatened. Nearly all the generals tended to think it might be wise to fall back. Only Thomas, who slept through most of the meeting, was unequivocally in favor of staying and fighting. Rosecrans seemed to be uncertain.[36] It is not quite clear how he finally made up his mind, but the decision he reached was to stay and fight.[37] The Federal army would not concede defeat by retreating.

The following day, New Year's Day, 1863, the two armies faced each other but did no serious fighting. Bragg's army, too, had taken tremendous punishment in the previous day's battle, and he was not anxious to resume his costly attacks now that the prospect of success was considerably diminished. He reported to Richmond that a great victory had been won and continued to hope that Rosecrans would realize this and withdraw.[38]

The last stage of the battle of Murfreesboro was fought on January 2. The Federals had seized a hill east of the river from which their cannon could enfilade Bragg's lines. They had to be removed, so Bragg ordered Breckinridge to storm the hill.[39] It was an attack the Federals were bound to expect, on a position that could be supported by artillery from other portions of the Union line. However, Bragg's alternative seemed to be to retreat, or at least to give up hope of going back on the offensive, and he desperately wanted to avoid that.[40] Having decided to make the attack, Bragg determined to do it quickly, without taking time to deliberate with his generals or wait till all the arrangements were perfect. Breckinridge's brigades had been sent back across the river after the first day's fighting, so his division was the obvious choice for the assault. Upon receiving his orders Breckinridge protested angrily. He had surveyed the enemy position and concluded that he knew more about it than Bragg. The commanding general, however, was in no mood to receive instruction from this somewhat unmilitary politician in uniform. "Sir, my information is different," he told the Kentucky general. "I have given the order to attack the enemy in your front and expect it to be obeyed." Angry with Bragg for forcing the attack, Breckinridge seemed to make a half-hearted effort.[41] To compound matters, among his brigade commanders was the infamous Pillow, temporarily replacing a general who had been wounded in the previous fighting. Rather than lead his brigade forward when the time came to advance, Pillow sent them forward while himself staying as far to the rear as possible and crouching behind a tree. Here Breckinridge found him. The Kentucky politician might have been an amateur general, but he was no coward. Such behavior he found shocking, and he ordered the cringing Pillow forward.[42] With such leadership the attack was probably doomed from the outset. Breckinridge never really got his division in hand. Some units did not advance at all. Others advanced in the wrong place, crossed the river (contrary to Bragg's instructions), and were slaughtered. In other areas the second wave of the Confederate assault crowded up so close to the first that it came under fire and, "returning it, took their friends in rear."[43] When the fiasco was finally over, 1,700 had fallen, and nothing had been accomplished.[44]

Bragg was now in a difficult position. He had done enough to win a victory— as most Civil War victories were counted—but his foe stubbornly refused to concede defeat by retreating, and his own army was in no condition to force the issue. He believed Rosecrans was receiving reinforcements, and though this was not true, the Confederate position was becoming increasingly precarious. The Federals would get more troops long before Bragg would, and there had been more of them to begin with. Fifteen minutes after midnight on the morning of January 3, Cheatham and another of Bragg's division commanders wrote Bragg a note urging that the army ought to retreat. Disaster, they warned, would be the result should Bragg remain in place. They took the note to their corps commander, Polk, who added a few lines of his own to the same effect and sent one of his aides to take it to Bragg. When the aide arrived at headquarters around 2:00 A.M., Bragg was asleep, but the aide awakened him and gave him the note in bed. Sitting up, Bragg read half the note, enough to see what it was getting at, and told the officer, "Say to the general we shall maintain our position at every hazard."[45]

Bragg hated the thought of retreating. It would transform his hard-earned victory to a defeat. Yet having suffered a third of his force in casualties (the Federals had lost more men, though a slightly lower percentage of their larger force), he could not afford to attack again. Nor could he expect to catch the Federals off-balance in such an attack. By morning, when the Federal army still remained in position and new information indicated it was even stronger than had been supposed, Bragg took a calmer view of the situation and, at the urging of all his senior generals, gave the order to retreat.[46] The army fell back about twenty miles to the vicinity of Tullahoma.[47] Rosecrans's army, equally devastated by the battle, made no attempt to follow.

News of Bragg's withdrawal, after his glowing reports of the success on December 31, came as quite a shock in Richmond and elsewhere. The Richmond authorities, receiving early reports of the retreat before the arrival of Bragg's explanatory telegram, greeted the news with disbelief.[48] When confirmed accounts of the withdrawal reached the public, the press, and the politicians, they were met with howls of rage. Those ill disposed toward Bragg, Davis, or both and those simply overcome by disappointment at what seemed to be another costly and mismanaged failure lashed themselves into a frenzy and heaped abuse on the hapless Bragg. Bragg had thrown away a victory, they claimed. His retreat from Murfreesboro had been cowardly. To make matters worse, staff officers of some of Bragg's generals were busily spreading the rumor that Bragg had fallen back from Murfreesboro against the advice of his generals and while the enemy was in full retreat.[49]

Bragg was no Albert Sidney Johnston and was not inclined to take the blame for the faults of others. He had endured all the unjust criticism he intended to take, and the invective was starting to get under his skin. He considered resigning and in a letter to a friend wrote, "With so little support, my aching head rebells against the heart, and cries for relief—still I shall die in the traces."[50] In an attempt to deflect some of the censure, Bragg took a highly unusual step. In a circular letter to each of his corps and division commanders he mentioned the abuse he was receiving and the erroneous reports concerning the withdrawal from Murfreesboro. Since the generals had advised him to retreat, he explained, he hoped they would say so in writing, in order to disprove the false rumors that were circulating. He urged them to be frank and, if they thought he had misunderstood them, to say so.

Had he left it at that, he would have been a great deal better off, but all the criticism was making him insecure and he needed some reassuring. "General Smith," he wrote, "has been called to Richmond, it is supposed, with a view to supersede me." (Actually, it was Holmes, not Bragg, whom Smith was to supersede.) Bragg wanted his generals to know that if what was being said about him was true, if he really had misunderstood them and retreated when he should not have, he would willingly step down. "I shall retire without regret," he continued, "if I find I have lost the good opinion of my generals, upon whom," he concluded in unwitting irony, "I have ever relied as upon a foundation of rock."[51] "Sand" would have been a more apt, if less flattering, metaphor. Bragg's sincere but ill-advised plea for reassurance from his generals provided an irresistible opening for his enemies.[52]

Unfortunately, at the time Bragg wrote the letter, six of his strongest backers among the generals were absent by reason of sickness or wounds.[53] Polk, though no Bragg supporter, was also absent on leave. The generals who were present, especially those in Hardee's corps who had been under that general's baleful influence, were hostile to Bragg, and they seized on the opportunity to agitate for Bragg's removal by choosing to interpret Bragg's circular as if it contained two points: one asking whether or not they had advised retreat from Murfreesboro, and the other asking whether or not Bragg ought to resign. It was a spurious interpretation, of course, but it was also a marvelous opportunity to blast their commander to his face without appearing guilty of insubordination. Most of them replied conceding that they had counseled retreat and assuring Bragg hypocritically that while they had the utmost regard for him personally, they felt the army had no confidence in him and he had better step down.[54]

Polk, on returning from his leave several weeks later, was anxious to reply to the circular but was handicapped by the fact that one of his division commanders had taken a more honest view of what Bragg was asking. That being the case, it would look bad if Polk responded to Bragg's "second" question without first making sure Bragg had intended a second question. Accordingly, he wrote Bragg a note asking how many questions the circular was supposed to contain and hinting broadly that he thought there were two and that he would relish the opportunity to answer both.[55] Bragg replied that there had been only one question, leading a much-chagrined Polk to write to Davis, spelling out—for at least the third time—exactly what his opinion of Braxton Bragg was.[56]

The difficult situation between Bragg and his subordinates had already come to the president's attention. Davis had not blamed Bragg after the retreat from Murfreesboro, probably remembering his own advice to that general when Stevenson's division was detached: "Fight if you can and fall back." Bragg had fought and fought well, and Davis recognized that the battle on December 31 had been in some aspects a victory and that Bragg had had no choice but to retreat. He had advised the general to find a strong position and dig in, and that was just what Bragg did.[57] "If I could furnish reinforcements to your glorious army which would enable them to crown the recent victory," the president wrote, "it would be done at once."[58] Still, Davis was disturbed to learn of Bragg's circular to his generals. The first description Davis heard of the note was apparently based on its interpretation by Bragg's enemies. Understandably, the president felt Bragg had come unhinged and immediately directed Johnston to go to Bragg's headquarters and see what needed to be done.[59] While assuring Johnston that "my confidence in General Bragg is unshaken," Davis wisely pointed out that if Bragg's men completely lost confidence in him, "a disaster may result which but for that cause would have been avoided." Davis was also concerned about the strange circular: "Why General Bragg should have selected that tribunal and have invited its judgements upon him, is to me unexplained." The president's letter of instruction to Johnston implied that if Johnston felt Bragg should be removed, Davis would comply, and it clearly stated that whether Bragg were removed or not, Johnston, as "General Commanding," would by his presence at Bragg's headquarters automatically assume direct supervision of the Army of Tennessee.[60]

Johnston arrived at Tullahoma around the end of January and was impressed by what he found. It was true that some of the generals were hostile to Bragg, particularly those whose failures at Murfreesboro Bragg had pointed out. Cheatham said "he would never go into battle under Bragg again."[61] McCown cursed the Confederacy as "a stinking cotton oligarchy . . . gotten up for the benefit of [Tennessee Governor] Isham G. Harris and Jeff Davis and their corrupt cliques." If Bragg were not removed, he muttered, he would go back to potato farming in Tennessee (probably the best thing he could have done for the Confederacy). Breckinridge pondered resigning his commission and challenging Bragg to a duel.[62] A few other generals such as Polk and Hardee were also disgruntled, but Johnston found that the rank and file were mostly in good spirits and showed no signs of a lack of confidence in their commander. He was also impressed with the condition of the army. Thanks to Bragg's administrative genius, it was well clothed, healthy, and well disciplined. Moreover, by early February, it numbered more than the total taken into battle on the last day of 1862, thanks to Bragg's efficiency in rounding up stragglers and enforcing the conscript act in Tennessee. Johnston fully approved of Bragg's conduct of the Murfreesboro campaign and recommended that Bragg be retained in command. If Davis should remove Bragg, Johnston concluded, the job should not go to anyone "in this army or engaged in this investigation"; that is, Johnston did not wish to take the helm for himself.[63]

This left Davis in a quandary, for while Johnston's faith in Bragg was growing, Davis's was declining. He feared that if the contempt of Bragg's generals filtered down to the ranks of the army, it would some day fail to fight under him the way it should. Davis had therefore determined to ease Bragg out of the command of the Army of Tennessee, and Johnston was Davis's chosen successor. The move seemed especially warranted since Johnston had for some time been grumbling to his friends that he would rather command an army than an entire theater. Indeed, Johnston had never really accepted his role as theater commander.

His complaining had started with his objections to the composition of his command even before receiving his official orders, and it had never stopped. The two armies under his control were, he believed, too far apart to support each other effectively. They had different objectives and different opponents, and thus there could be no meaningful cooperation between them. It followed that Johnston, as the supervisor of their cooperation, had nothing meaningful to do.[64] Convinced of this, he undertook no action on his own initiative except to gather up most of the cavalry in his department for use in large-scale raids.[65] His view of his job was accurate so long as the Federals maintained the initiative, and Joseph E. Johnston was not the man to wrest it from them.

A more fundamental cause of Johnston's dissatisfaction was his disappointed vanity. He had once commanded the Confederacy's most prestigious army, and he envied Lee the fame that general had won at the head of the force Johnston still thought was rightfully his. He desired the glory of army command rather than the responsibility of theater command. "I have already lost much time from service," he wrote, referring to the wound that had kept him out of action from late May to early November 1862, "and therefore can ill afford to be inactive at any time during the remainder of the war."[66] If he was going to rival Lee's fame he would have to do some impressive campaigning, and there was no time to lose.

Because of Johnston's expressed discontent with his present position and desire for army command, Davis considered him the natural choice to replace Bragg. This would be particularly convenient since Johnston's position meant he would need do nothing more than be in Tullahoma in order to have direct command of the army there. Then Bragg could be removed, or retained as a chief of staff. Johnston's refusal of Davis's subtle suggestion threw this plan into disarray.

Davis wrote a long letter to Johnston explaining the general's role as he saw it. Johnston was already in command in Tullahoma just by virtue of his presence there, Davis reminded him. Therefore, it could not possibly appear that Johnston was removing Bragg because he coveted the command of Bragg's army. Though Davis was glad to hear that the army was in such good condition, he felt that the bad attitude of the generals could not fail to trickle down and eventually infect the common soldiers. He also pointed out that Johnston's stipulations about the successor to Bragg left very few men from whom the president could choose.[67] Still Johnston refused to reconsider. Bragg, he insisted, should be maintained.[68]

Davis was not satisfied. Polk's constant urgings were probably beginning to have an effect on him, especially Polk's suggestion that Bragg be made some sort of inspector general in Richmond, where, as Polk saw it, he could do no harm but his feelings would be spared.[69] On March 9 Davis decided to take positive action. He had the secretary of war telegraph Johnston, "Order General Bragg to report to the War Department here for conference. Assume yourself direct charge of the army in Middle Tennessee."[70] Johnston replied that he would obey but, recognizing the order as a move to ease Bragg out of his position, urged against removing "that most meritorious officer."[71] Several days later, apparently unwilling to break the news to Bragg himself, Johnston requested the secretary of war to send a copy of the order to Bragg. This was promptly done, but three days later the reply came back from Johnston that Bragg could not go.[72] Bragg's wife, who was in nearby Winchester, Tennessee, was critically ill and not expected to live (actually, she survived the war and Bragg). It would be cruel to order Bragg away at this time. Besides, Johnston was expecting a Federal advance, and if it came, he would need Bragg.[73] By early April, Johnston himself was sick and unable to take the field, making Bragg's continued presence all the more necessary.[74] Davis did not press the issue. Bragg would remain in command of the Army of Tennessee.

The winter of 1862–63 had made a shambles of Davis's efforts of the preceding fall. He had tried to bring order and cooperation out of the confusion and cross-purposes of the Perryville and Corinth campaigns, but somehow the results had not been what he had intended. His attempt, during his visit to the West in December, to take charge personally by transferring Stevenson's division from Bragg to Pemberton may have cost the Confederacy a major victory.[75] The unnecessary troop movement had also aggravated Davis's personnel problems. The abuse that had been heaped on Bragg as a result of the failure at Murfreesboro had led that general to send his indiscreet circular to his subordinates. His enemies had made the most of it, and Davis had come to see that no matter how skillful or loyal a general might be, he could not be useful if his troops no longer trusted him. Such a loss of confidence, Davis feared, was only a matter of time for Bragg.

Davis could have avoided much of this trouble by removing Leonidas Polk, either before Perryville when Bragg had suggested it or after the battle when Polk had expressed his dissatisfaction. Even after Murfreesboro, Davis could and should have improved the army's morale and prevented further erosion of Bragg's position by relieving those generals who were especially vocal in their criticism (such as Polk) and Hardee, who was especially effective in undermining Bragg within the army. After the war one general went so far as to state, "It struck me that Bragg did not know whom to trust. He was not popular with his generals and hence I feared that zealous cooperation on their part was wanting. If he had caused even one or two of us to be shot, I firmly believe the balance would have done better."[76]

Davis seemed to be partially unaware of the mischief produced by Bragg's unfit subordinates. Bragg was reluctant to pursue the matter since he had already informed the president that these men were incompetent and had been given to understand that he would have to live with them. At the same time, when the various subordinates were loudly clamoring against Bragg, Davis could not sort out the facts from their slander. As the pressure of his position increased, Davis appeared uncertain and unable to cope. He made a growing number of bad decisions. One of them was his failure to enforce subordination to Bragg within the Army of Tennessee.

Instead, Davis chose to remove Bragg. His respect for Bragg's devotion to the cause led him to attempt to do so in a gentle manner. The result of this approach, however, was that Johnston was able to foil the move completely and bring about Bragg's retention. Johnston acted partly out of respect for Bragg's good qualities as a commander and partly out of sheer contrariness born of resentment for any higher authority. As a consequence, no action at all was taken to remedy the situation in the high command of the Army of Tennessee after Murfreesboro. It was the worst possible course, for it allowed the hostility and bitterness against Bragg to fester unchecked. Before the end of 1863 it was to bear bitter fruit.

Johnston himself was a major problem. His vanity and rancor against authority made him extremely difficult to work with, and his insistence that the position he held was useless became a self-fulfilling prophecy. Davis's attempts to explain what he expected from his western commander were for naught. Johnston stubbornly contended that cooperation was impossible and that there was nothing he could do. By mid-April 1863 the differences between Davis and Johnston had been rehashed at some length in their correspondence without any apparent progress being made toward an understanding with each other.[77] Though neither man knew it, they and the western defenses of the Confederacy were on the verge of their greatest test.

12

THE FALL OF VICKSBURG

Ulysses S. Grant hated retreating. Fortunately, it was not something he had to do very often. He had had no choice, though, when the Confederate cavalry leader Earl Van Dorn had destroyed his supply base at Holly Springs. Grant's men had fallen back from central Mississippi to West Tennessee, and the entire late-fall expedition against Vicksburg had to be given up as a failure. At least his troops had not gone hungry on their long retreat. In fact, they had eaten very well, thank you, at the expense of every Mississippi farm and plantation within fifteen miles of their line of march.[1] Grant, however, had other things on his mind just now. He did not give up easily, and he was not about to give up on Vicksburg. He would be back, and the next time there would be no cutting of supply lines. He would come straight down the river—an unbreakable supply line—and would stay at Vicksburg until it was his.

Jefferson Davis was at first unable to believe that the Federal offensive of December 1862 could have been so easily repulsed.[2] Finally realizing that the Union forces actually had pulled back, Davis was favorably impressed with Pemberton's handling of the affair.[3] In reality, Pemberton's task—holding a virtually impregnable position against an enemy who could advance from only one direction—had not been particularly difficult. That, however, was not apparent at the time. What was clear was that an unequivocal victory had been won. The Union forces had suffered heavy casualties, the Confederates almost none, and the Union army had retreated without accomplishing a thing.[4] Pemberton was mightily pleased with himself, even cocky, and boasted to his subordinates that he could have held Vicksburg against 100,000 men, which, given the handicaps under which the enemy had had to attack, was probably true.[5]

For several weeks all was quiet on the Vicksburg front. Then, about the end of January, Grant's army came down the river and began setting up camp a few miles above Vicksburg.[6] Davis was at once concerned and, as usual with a Mississippi River campaign, took an intense personal interest in the proceedings.[7] For the moment though, Pemberton had no battles to report to the anxious president.

Grant was not eager to provide a fresh example of what Sherman's troops had already demonstrated, to their dismay, in December: It was all but impossible to take Vicksburg by a frontal attack from the north along the bank of the river. In order to make any headway against the "Gibraltar of the West," the Federals would have to get in the rear of the town and cut if off from all supplies—no easy task. Perched as it was on its two-hundred-foot bluffs, the town of Vicksburg peered down on the Mississippi River to the west and on a maze of swamps and bayous to the north, east, and south. The first problem confronting any would-be attacker was how to get at the place from any angle that offered the slightest promise of a successful attack or siege. Grant, therefore, spent the rest of the winter on a series of operations aimed at getting around or behind Vicksburg.

The first project was a canal. Vicksburg was located on a bend of the river that extended eastward, creating a peninsula inside the bend on the western shore opposite the town. The object of the Federal canal was to cut across this neck of land so as to allow transports to descend the river past Vicksburg without running the Vicksburg batteries. Then Grant could proceed to take Vicksburg from behind. Work on the canal continued sporadically well into March, and though nothing ever came of it, the Confederates were at times very concerned that it might be successful.[8] Several times Davis anxiously inquired of Pemberton regarding the progress of the canal and what was being done to prevent its operation.[9] Just in case the canal did prove functional, Pemberton took some of his heavy guns and erected batteries at Warrenton and Grand Gulf, a few miles farther down the river. This he hoped would prevent Grant from landing in his rear or from continuing down the river and joining the Union forces that were now threatening Port Hudson.[10]

With the prospect of the canal's success in doubt, Grant undertook various other schemes for getting around Vicksburg. Most of them involved finding some way to traverse the largely interconnected tangle of lakes, streams, swamps, and bayous that covered the countryside around Vicksburg. If such a way could be found, it would provide the elusive, safe water-route past the Confederate fortress. Some of these endeavors led to the most improbable situations. In one operation, Union ironclad gunboats of several hundred tons each steamed through a landscape flooded by the late-winter rise of the river, knocking down full-grown trees and brushing their smokestacks against limbs and vines, while sailors stood on deck with brooms to sweep overboard the snakes, lizards, roaches, and other creatures that dropped from the dense foliage. All the while Pemberton did his best to make things more difficult for the Federals by sending detachments to snipe at the sailors and fell trees across the waterways to impede the boats' progress.[11] Despite the navy's persistence the expedition accomplished nothing. Another route which briefly showed more promise was closed off when a makeshift Confederate earthwork called Fort Pemberton proved impervious to the Union gunboats, cramped as they were in the confines of a watercourse better suited to canoes.[12]

Davis was actively interested in all of these operations, corresponding directly with Pemberton and others involved rather than channeling his communications through Cooper or the secretary of war as was his habit. He wanted to know about every aspect of Vicksburg's defense. How high was the river? Was it still rising? Could the Yazoo River be obstructed? Was Fort Pemberton still holding out? Pemberton wrote often and extensively to keep the president informed.[13]

Though Davis had had a few uneasy moments at the thought that the Federals might succeed with their canal or with one of their bizarre aquatic flanking movements, it appeared by April 1863 that Grant's new campaign would achieve no more than his previous attempt had. Pemberton, with a slight assist from the elements, had stopped Grant again. To a Mississippi politician who complained that Pemberton was unpopular, Davis responded with high praise for the Pennsylvania rebel, pointing out that Pemberton had "foiled . . . every attempt [of the enemy] to get possession of the Mississippi River."[14]

Indeed, there was evidence that Grant was conceding defeat and pulling his troops back up the river. Pemberton informed his superiors that intelligence reports indicated the Federals were making major preparations for a move upriver. He believed Grant's entire army was about to be transferred to Tennessee to join Rosecrans in a concerted attack that would crush Bragg.[15] Johnston and Davis agreed, and both warned Pemberton that if Grant really did move to reinforce Rosecrans, Pemberton was going to have to send some troops to help Bragg.[16] By April 11 Pemberton was convinced that Grant's forces were being withdrawn.[17] He informed Johnston that he could spare 8,000 men for Bragg and promised to send them on their way as quickly as possible.[18] Johnston approved and urged him to hurry.[19]

In reality, Pemberton had drastically misinterpreted the intelligence he was receiving. Part of this was the fault of his scouts, who had inadvertently sent him misleading information, and part the work of Grant, who was doing his utmost to confuse Pemberton.[20] Pemberton himself, however, seems to have been guilty of assuming his enemy would do what he hoped and expected him to do. Everyone knew that Yankees could not campaign in the Deep South during the summer; they would drop like flies in the sweltering heat. As spring came and it became apparent that another Union stratagem had failed, Pemberton reasoned, Grant would naturally retreat.

Retreating was the farthest thing from Grant's mind. The extensive preparation that Pemberton's scouts had observed was actually the build-up for an offensive rather than a retreat. Grant had never had much confidence in the various schemes for cutting a canal or bypassing Vicksburg. Instead, he had devised a bold and innovative plan, the execution of which awaited only the coming of spring. The very first element of the plan was extremely daring. On a dark night in April, Grant's empty transports, along with the gunboat fleet, would run the Vicksburg batteries. Sherman, with a portion of the army, would demonstrate around the old Chickasaw Bayou battlefield to keep Pemberton's attention away from Grant's real objective while Grant, with the rest of the army, marched down the west side of the river past Vicksburg. Then the transports would ferry the army across the river, and Grant would be where he had been trying to go all winter: on the east bank of the Mississippi in the rear of Vicksburg.

At this point, however, Grant's plan became even more daring. His retreat the previous December had taught him that the Mississippi countryside could amply supply a moving army. He therefore proposed to cut loose of his supply lines on the river and slash boldly toward Jackson, Mississippi, in the center of the state about forty miles or so east of Vicksburg.[21] From there he hoped to prevent any reinforcements from reaching Pemberton; then, advancing from the east, he could pin the Confederate forces against the river, transforming Vicksburg from a fortress into a trap.[22] Meanwhile, a Union cavalry force under Col. Benjamin H. Grierson, erstwhile music teacher, would go rampaging from one end of Mississippi to the other, spreading havoc and hopefully confusing Pemberton. It was a risky plan. If Pemberton moved quickly and energetically, it could easily be Grant's army that was trapped. Still, there seemed to be no other way to get at Vicksburg, and Grant was willing to gamble that his opponent would hesitate long enough to allow the plan to succeed.

Pemberton's first inkling that all was not as he had supposed came on April 16, 1863. Only the day before he had been confident that Grant was reinforcing Rosecrans, but now intelligence reports were conflicting. Pemberton nervously wired Johnston that he could not send as many troops as he had planned.[23] That night Pemberton received another indication that Grant was up to something. The officers of the Vicksburg garrison were celebrating their apparent victory over Grant by attending a festive ball with the citizens of the town. As couples waltzed around the floor to cheerful tunes, the music was suddenly drowned out by the roar of the big guns along the waterfront. The ball changed into pandemonium as muzzle flashes lit the sky outside the windows and the acrid smell of powder smoke seeped into the ballroom. Officers dashed off to join their units. Whatever it was, it was over quickly. The Vicksburg guns fell silent. A few minutes later the stillness of the night was again broken, this time by a distant rumbling and flashes on the southern horizon. The batteries at Warrenton, near the mouth of the old canal a few miles downriver, had gone into action. Soon they too ceased firing.

What had happened? All that seemed certain was that about half an hour before midnight an undetermined number of Union vessels had steamed past the Vicksburg batteries to the thunderous, if largely ineffective, accompaniment of every Confederate gun that could be brought to bear on the river. They had continued past Warrenton and were now somewhere in the long stretch of river between Vicksburg and Port Hudson. Some of them had been gunboats; Pemberton was sure of that because they had returned the fire of the batteries. There had probably been some transports, too, though Pemberton thought at least some of them had been destroyed by Confederate gunfire.[24] In any case, there was now a sizable Union fleet below Vicksburg, and Pemberton was more convinced than ever that he was in for another attack. He telegraphed Cooper and Johnston that the troops he had already dispatched to reinforce Bragg should be sent back, and he was readily given permission to recall them.[25]

He also wrote to Davis, warning that he was going to need more heavy guns if he was going to keep Federal boats' passing the batteries from becoming a regular occurrence.[26] Davis replied promptly, promising the extra guns and making various detailed suggestions on how to stop boats from running the batteries.[27] He also suggested that Pemberton see about cooperating with Kirby Smith, who had recently been appointed to command of the trans-Mississippi department.[28] This idea had already occurred to Pemberton. He had received reports that there was a large body of Federal troops moving down the west side of the river past Vicksburg and had contacted Kirby Smith to see what could be done about it.[29] Smith, who before leaving Richmond to take over his new command had been admonished at some length by the president that his primary efforts should "be directed to aiding in the defense of the Lower Mississippi, and keeping the great artery of the West effectually closed to northern occupation or trade," was about to demonstrate once again that he had a mind of his own when it came to following directions.[30] He was completely absorbed in stopping a trivial foray into Louisiana by the Union political general who was supposed to be besieging Port Hudson. Since the attacks on Port Hudson and Vicksburg had obviously been abandoned, Smith suggested, perhaps Pemberton should send some reinforcements to him.[31]

The simple fact was that for any cooperation to occur between the two sides of the river, Davis was going to have to issue peremptory orders and see that they were carried out.[32] Few generals situated comparably to Pemberton and Kirby Smith could have achieved substantial coordinated action on their own, and one Confederate campaign had already come to grief as a result of Smith's unwillingness to cooperate. Yet hundreds of miles away in Richmond, Davis, in poor health and distracted by other pressing matters both military and political, was in no position to enforce coordination. Pemberton could thus expect little help from the trans-Mississippi.

Meanwhile, the commander of the small force Pemberton had placed at Grand Gulf, a few miles down the river from Vicksburg, was reporting an ominous concentration of Federal gunboats in his sector of the river. It appeared the Federals might try to cross with some of their troops.[33] As if this were not enough trouble, a Union cavalry force was on the loose in Mississippi and seemed bent on spreading mayhem everywhere. Pemberton could do little to stop it since most of his cavalry had been appropriated by Johnston for his central cavalry force, which was now operating in Tennessee.[34] Frantically, Pemberton shuffled what cavalry he had around the state and for several days a full-scale chase was on. "All mounted men are actively engaged endeavoring to intercept the enemy," Pemberton informed Johnston.[35] Yet the Union cavalry eluded all of Pemberton's attempts. Johnston professed himself unable to spare any cavalry to help Pemberton and expressed doubt that Grant's plans to reinforce Rosecrans had even been called off.[36]

By this time Pemberton had good reason to think otherwise. On April 28 the commander at Grand Gulf reported that the Federals were obviously preparing to make a landing there and, later, that the gunboats were bombarding his position.[37] Pemberton thought this was just a decoy and was reluctant to send reinforcements, especially since the Federal force on the other side of Chickasaw Bayou seemed to be readying for an assault and Pemberton had already committed some of his infantry to chasing down that pestilent Federal cavalry.[38] Pemberton asked the Grand Gulf commander how few troops he could get by with.[39] The beleaguered officer replied that Pemberton had better send everything he could spare.[40] Then the telegraph wire went dead.[41]

This could mean one of two things. Either Colonel Grierson had finally cut the telegraph lines or else Grant's men had blasted their way across the river and driven the Confederates out of Grand Gulf. Pemberton was unsure which was the case, but the Grierson raid was driving him to distraction, and his attention stayed focused on it. Cavalry was becoming a fixation with him. Believing he could achieve nothing without it, he bombarded Johnston, Cooper, and Davis himself with his requests for more horsemen.[42] Davis, who was at the time so ill that he could receive no visitors, was also getting a stream of messages from the governor and various citizens of the state of Mississippi complaining that their state was left without cavalry protection, exposed to Yankee depredations.[43] The ailing president assured Pemberton and his other correspondents that he was doing what he could to round up some cavalry and renewed his urging that Pemberton cooperate with Kirby Smith.[44]

On the last day of April Pemberton's attention was finally drawn away from the Grierson raid by confirmed reports that the enemy had crossed the Mississippi River in force below Vicksburg.[45] By means of couriers, communications had been reestablished with the Grand Gulf force, which had been driven back from the river and was engaged in a desperate fight with an overwhelming force. Pemberton told its commander to hold on and promised to send every available man.[46] By May 1, however, the few thousand Confederates had been brushed aside, and the Union force had advanced into the interior.[47]

Once he became aware that the main Federal army had reached the east bank below Vicksburg, Pemberton had realized that he was in a completely different situation: He could now be cut off from the east.[48] What to do about this was another question, but Johnston answered that when he wrote Pemberton from Tullahoma advising him that if Grant had crossed the river the only option for Pemberton would be to unite all of his forces to defeat Grant in battle. If Grant were defeated, Pemberton would then be able to retake the places he had given up in drawing all his troops together.[49]

At first Pemberton did pursue this course. He ordered the bulk of his forces out of Jackson and Port Hudson, leaving barely enough behind to man the trenches. The rest he ordered to join his main body ten miles east of Vicksburg.[50] Immediately upon learning that the Federals were across the river, Pemberton had asked Davis for reinforcements.[51] Davis had promised that 5,000 men would be sent by Beauregard from Charleston.[52] With the promise of these troops and with his own men now somewhat more concentrated, Pemberton began to be in a more optimistic frame of mind. "We will be all right," he assured Davis.[53] The president was apprehensive, but he too felt Pemberton ought to be able to handle the situation. Grant was bound to have vulnerable supply lines, and that would be his undoing.[54]

Unfortunately, it was a telegram with further instructions from Davis that signaled Pemberton's undoing. Pemberton had informed Davis of his plans to pull the garrison out of Grand Gulf and Port Hudson in order to consolidate all his forces against Grant around Vicksburg and Jackson. This was what Johnston had advised, and this was Pemberton's best chance of stopping Grant. Sadly, Jefferson Davis did not agree.

The president had been sick off and on for weeks with bronchitis and neuralgia, brought on largely by overwork and anxiety; his doctors had begun to fear he would lose the sight in his one good eye.[55] Much of the time he was bedridden, and for several days at a stretch he was unable to speak.[56] Doggedly he continued to do his duty as he saw it, running the country from his sickroom. On May 4 he was able to venture out of the Confederate White House for the first time in weeks. Three days later, the day he replied to Pemberton's dispatch stating his plans, Davis was again prostrated by a recurring attack of his many illnesses and was unable to leave the house again for a week.[57] Nor was that all. Lee was meeting another and even more massive Federal advance in northern Virginia, and at the same time a Union cavalry raid had reached the outskirts of Richmond and thrown a considerable scare into the town before being driven off.

Under the circumstances Davis simply could not think clearly about the tactical situation in Mississippi. In his pain-fogged mind, he failed to grasp the purpose of Pemberton's proposed temporary evacuation of Port Hudson. Apparently all he could remember was the strategic concept that had been dictum for months: Both Vicksburg and Port Hudson must be held. Temporary evacuation became permanent abandonment in his mind. Pemberton must be ordered not to give up Port Hudson. Accordingly, on May 7 a dispatch went out for Pemberton, admonishing him that "to hold both Vicksburg and Port Hudson is necessary to a connection with the Trans-Mississippi." Instead, Davis suggested that Pemberton attempt to cut Grant's supply lines.[58]

Pemberton actually needed little encouragement in this direction. He was always insecure when his forces ventured out of the safe confines of fortifications. Boldness and daring made up no part of his nature. His original resolution to concentrate his forces against Grant had been out of character, probably brought on by a sudden realization of the urgency of the situation and sparked by Johnston's suggestion. If the president objected to such a plan, Pemberton was perfectly ready to keep his army cooped up in a few fortified posts. Immediately after receiving the president's telegram, he had ordered the whole garrison of Port Hudson to return to that post "and hold it to the last."[59] Conscientious and determined to do his duty, Pemberton conducted the rest of the campaign as if his army were chained to Vicksburg.

Pemberton positioned his main force on the railroad between Jackson and Vicksburg, about a quarter of the way from Vicksburg to the state capital. The place chosen was near to where the tracks crossed the Big Black River, a stream that flowed from northeast to southwest to empty into the Mississippi a few miles below Vicksburg.[60] Pemberton felt compelled by the president's instructions to keep a large number of troops covering every possible approach to Vicksburg, but with his remaining force he hoped to be able to prevent the enemy from moving on Jackson.[61] His difficulty was that he had only the vaguest idea as to the enemy's whereabouts, and the more uncertain he became, the more troops he tended to hold around Vicksburg–just in case the elusive Grant should suddenly crop up on his doorstep. Part of the problem was, once again, lack of cavalry, without which it was very hard for a general to obtain information. Pemberton had been deprived not only of his cavalry but also of his cavalry leader Earl Van Dorn by an order from Johnston back in January. Davis believed Van Dorn and his men should be returned by Johnston to Mississippi, but he hesitated to give such an order because, as ususal, he was unsure of Johnston's plans for them. Unwilling to risk creating confusion and bringing on a confrontation with the temperamental Johnston, Davis did nothing and Van Dorn remained in Tennessee.[62]

However, another general was sent to Vicksburg. Davis felt the situation demanded the presence of the theater commander, so when Johnston did not go of his own accord, Davis ordered him there.[63] Johnston complained that his health was not up to it but said he would go anyway.[64] Arriving in Jackson on the evening of May 13, Johnston discovered the Union forces had already positioned themselves between Pemberton and the small force at Jackson, "cutting off communication," or so Johnston claimed. He wired Richmond, "I am too late."[65]

This was a typical piece of pessimistic Johnston exaggeration. Certainly the situation was serious, but it was not as hopeless as Johnston made it sound. Somehow Johnston and Pemberton had to make contact and cooperate. Johnston knew this, and having established with Richmond that the task he was assigned was impossible and therefore no failure could be blamed on him, he promptly took steps to link up with Pemberton. Couriers could still circumvent the Federal forces, and Johnston sent Pemberton a note suggesting he attack the rear of the Federal forces that were threatening Jackson.[66]

Pemberton received the message the next morning, May 14. He replied immediately that he thought the move unwise but that he would "comply at once" with Johnston's order.[67] Pemberton then had second thoughts and called a council of war. Presenting his opinions to the generals, Pemberton explained that he was opposed to any move at all. The army must stay close to Vicksburg. The generals disagreed. The majority wanted to head straight for Jackson as Johnston had suggested. A small minority favored moving to the southeast to find and cut Grant's supply line. Pemberton felt that in the face of Johnston's order and the opinions of his generals he had to do something, but he was afraid to take the direct route for Jackson as specified by Johnston. Instead, he decided to follow the minority's advice. Leaving substantial forces at Vicksburg and on the Big Black, he took his remaining troops and went groping after Grant's nonexistent supply lines in an operation that was against the better judgment of his commanding general, himself, and most of his subordinate generals.[68]

While Pemberton hesitated and blundered about, Grant was wasting no time. Within hours of Pemberton's strange council of war, Grant's troops were marching into Jackson. Johnston and his small force, as yet unaware that Pemberton was planning to proceed southeast, retreated to the north, farther away from Pemberton's forces.[69] Grant kept moving so fast the Confederates had no chance to regain their balance. He was aided by the fact that the courier who had carried Johnston's first dispatch to Pemberton was a Union spy who had shown the message to the Union commander before continuing on his way. Thus, Grant had a fair idea of the general situation of his opponents' forces.[70]

On the morning of the sixteenth Pemberton received another dispatch from Johnston, informing him of the fall of Jackson and pointing out that it would now be dangerous for Pemberton to carry through with his plan for cutting Grant's supply lines, of which Johnston had in the meantime been informed by courier.[71] Accordingly, Pemberton swung back to the north–and straight into the path of Grant's advancing army coming west from Jackson. Pemberton made his stand on a piece of high ground known as Champion's Hill. His line ran north and south and faced east. The Federals struck first at the Confederate left, hoping to turn the flank of Pemberton's line. They were thwarted by the alertness of the brigade commander at that end of the line, Brig. Gen. Stephen D. Lee, who anticipated the movement and swung his troops back to meet the assault head-on. The Confederates gradually shifted their line to meet the Federal onslaught, swinging the left of their army back like a gate on a hinge to face north instead of east. For a time the situation stabilized as the two sides fought ferociously but inconclusively for possession of Champion's Hill, the key feature of the battlefield. Some plots of ground on the bloody hillside changed hands back and forth several times during the course of the day.

As the afternoon wore on, the Federal's pushed harder, and the Confederate

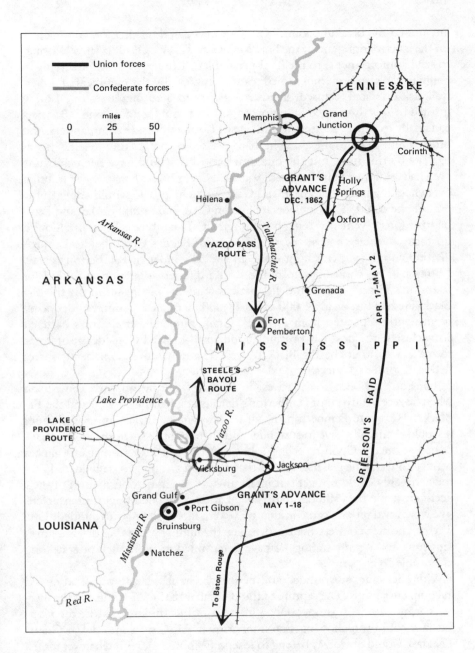

Map 12.1 *The Vicksburg Campaign, December 1862–May 1863*

line neared the breaking point.[72] Pemberton ordered his division commander on the inactive right end of the line, Maj. Gen. W. W. "Old Blizzards" Loring, to send reinforcements to the hard-pressed left. Loring, who while serving in Virginia had also been nicknamed "Scared Turkey" by the members of Stonewall Jackson's staff, refused. Pemberton sent repeated messages, but Loring insisted he was threatened on his own front and could send no one.[73] Pemberton finally rode over himself, found one of Loring's brigade commanders, and ordered him to go to the aid of his hard-pressed comrades on the left.[74] It was too late by this time, but the outcome probably would have been the same even had reinforcements been sent sooner.[75] Grant had the manpower to bring overwhelming pressure to bear, and Grant was a man who would apply all the pressure he could. The Confederate line on Champion's Hill broke, and Pemberton's forces went streaming back in retreat. The jubilant Federals followed up their advantage and seized the crossing of Baker's Creek before Loring's division could pass, cutting it off from the remainder of Pemberton's army. Loring had no choice but to pull out in a different direction and head for Johnston's force.[76] Pemberton fell back toward his old position on the Big Black. He had lost nearly 4,000 of his 23,000 men in casualties, besides being permanently separated from Loring.[77] Grant pursued Pemberton's battered army closely, the next day brushing aside a half-hearted Confederate attempt to make a stand at the Big Black River.[78] The remaining Confederate forces fled in disorder to Vicksburg.[79]

Johnston had been moving west in hopes of linking up with Pemberton when he received word of Pemberton's defeats at Champion's Hill and the Big Black.[80] He wrote Pemberton that if the army got bottled up in Vicksburg it would eventually have to surrender and therefore the town should be abandoned at once.[81] Upon receiving Johnston's order, Pemberton again called a council of war. The generals agreed that Vicksburg ought to be held and that they probably could not get out intact anyway. As if in confirmation of their decision, while they still debated Federal artillery opened fire on their defensive works and reports came in that they were rapidly being surrounded. One way or another couriers managed to get through the lines, and Pemberton sent Johnston a reply stating, "I have determined to hold Vicksburg as long as possible."[82]

With Vicksburg surrounded and besieged, Grant's daring plan had ended in complete success. The capture of the "Gibraltar of the West," and of Pemberton's army with it, was now only a matter of time—unless, that is, the Confederacy could somehow raise another army in Mississippi and defeat Grant. That task would obviously belong to Joseph E. Johnston, with whatever means Jefferson Davis would be able to give him.

Davis, ill and distracted with events in Virginia, did not fully comprehend what was going on. In fact, to his dying day, he never really understood what had happened in Mississippi during the first two weeks of May 1863. He had hoped that Grant's supply line could be cut, and writing nearly a decade after the end of the war, he still did not recognize that this had been impossible.[83] He believed Pemberton was right in allowing himself to be trapped in Vicksburg and depending on someone else to get him out.[84] Even after Johnston had notified him that Grant had Pemberton hemmed in at Vicksburg, Davis seemed confused as to the actual situation and continued to urge that Grant be prevented from reaching the river and reestablishing his communications— something for which it was already too late.[85] Finally, in a misplaced fit of state pride, Davis believed that Mississippians would rally in large numbers to drive out the invaders and actually counted on this as a source of reinforcements for Johnston.[86] In truth, Davis, like Pemberton, had been completely duped by Grant's brilliant campaign.

This fact did not bode well for Davis's supervision of Confederate efforts to raise the siege of Vicksburg, nor did the fact that the strained relationship between Davis and Johnston was now headed for outright feuding. Davis felt Johnston should have gone to Mississippi sooner, without awaiting orders from Richmond; and he believed that once in Mississippi, Johnston should have joined Pemberton directly, with or without the reinforcements that were supposed to be on the way.[87] Some of these criticisms were not altogether fair, but there was justice in his perception that Johnston was not energetic enough in his attempts to relieve Vicksburg.

Relieving Vicksburg was going to be a desperate endeavor. By the end of May, Grant had about 50,000 men around the beleaguered town and the prospect of large reinforcements within the near future.[88] Pemberton had about 31,000 in the Vicksburg trenches, and Johnston another 23,000 hovering to the east of Grant's forces.[89] The odds were long: Pemberton and Johnston would have to attack simultaneously from inside and outside Vicksburg, and the timing would be tricky now that every dispatch had to be laboriously smuggled through Union lines. Yet the odds were bound to get even longer, since the Confederacy would never be able to send troops to Johnston at the rate Grant was receiving reinforcements. Still Johnston did not make his move. Instead, he cabled Richmond to send him more men, at least 7,000 more; with 30,000 he might be able to accomplish something.[90] This sparked a completely useless exchange of dispatches between Johnston and Richmond regarding exactly how many troops Johnston had—Davis maintaining there had to be more men in Johnston's army than the general admitted. The president did, however, wisely point out that "we cannot hope for numerical equality and time will probably increase the disparity."[91] It was a warning that Johnston did not heed. He would not attack until everything was perfect. He had to have reinforcements.

There was one place where Davis could have pulled troops to send to Johnston. The Army of Northern Virginia was fresh from its brilliant victory at Chancellorsville. Secretary of War Seddon, who during this summer was Johnston's staunchest supporter on the cabinet, raised the idea of reinforcing John-ston with troops from Lee's army. While Davis was still bedridden, Seddon, no doubt with the consent of the president, telegraphed Lee on May 9 direct-ing that Pickett's division of Longstreet's corps be transferred to Mississippi to join Pemberton.[92] Longstreet, along with both Pickett's and Hood's divi-sions, had been detached on other duty during the recent battle of Chancel-lorsville.[93] If Lee could win such a spectacular victory without them, maybe one or both divisions could be spared for service elsewhere. Lee was of a dif-ferent mind. In a telegram and a letter sent to Seddon the next day—the day Stonewall Jackson died—Lee argued against sending a division from his army to Mississippi on the grounds that his army was already badly outnumbered, that the division would probably arrive too late to be of any help, and that troops traveling from Virginia to Mississippi in the summer would be subject to sickness due to the climate.[94] Lee also presented his case directly to the presi-dent, who was favorably impressed.[95]

The matter would not die, though. With the Confederacy's fortunes so high in Virginia and so low nearly everywhere else, the idea of drawing troops from Lee's army was bound to suggest itself to others, including one at least within that army itself. Lee's senior corps commander, Lt. Gen. James Longstreet, was already chafing to get out of the shadow of Lee and win more glory for himself. His plan called for both Pickett's and Hood's divisions, with himself in com-mand, to be sent to join Bragg for a grand offensive against Rosecrans, forestall-ing any possible drive by that general against Chattanooga and, he hoped, reliev-ing the pressure on Vicksburg.[96] This notion of concentrating Confederate strength for a great offensive in Middle Tennessee was extremely popular just then with a large and informal network of influential Confederates, both civilian and military, who were linked by kinship, by state or regional affiliations, or by political expediency.[97] Their urgings could not be lightly ignored.

On May 15, while Pemberton was searching Mississippi in vain for Grant's nonexistent supply line, Davis, Seddon, and Lee were meeting for a lengthy closed-door conference.[98] Only four days earlier Davis had been profoundly shocked by news of the death of Stonewall Jackson. "You must excuse me," he had told a man who came to speak with him on business. "I am staggering from a dreadful blow. I cannot think."[99] Now, on the day Jackson was buried out in the Shenandoah Valley, the president, still very weak from his lengthy bout with illness, sat down with his two chief advisors to decide what use the Confederacy should make of Lee's army. At first Davis was strongly inclined to agree with Seddon that Pickett's division, and possibly Hood's as well, should be sent to Johnston. He found it difficult, however, to resist Lee's arguments.[100] Davis always considered Lee his most valued military advisor. Later in the war he wrote the Virginia general, "I need your counsel."[101] Lee had a record of success with which it was hard to argue, and the polished Virginian could be very persuasive when he tried. Lee had an alternate plan he wanted the president to approve. Instead of reinforcing Mississippi, Lee argued, the Army of Northern Virginia should mount another offensive into Maryland and, perhaps, Pennsylvania. This might take some of the pressure off Vicksburg, Lee believed, but chiefly it seemed like the best way to keep the Federals in the East off-balance and out of Lee's beloved Virginia for most if not all of the coming summer.[102] It was against Davis's better judgment but reluctantly he gave in. Lee would move north with his entire army.[103]

Davis called a cabinet meeting for the next day and asked Lee to attend and explain his strategy. Lee did so with his usual persuasiveness, and that coupled with his almost legendary reputation was enough to win over every cabinet member but one. The one who disagreed was John H. Reagan of Texas, the energetic and efficient postmaster general. Since Reagan's home was in the trans-Mississippi, perhaps the importance of Vicksburg, and the connection with the trans-Mississippi that it guarded, were especially vivid to him. In any case, he was so agitated that he came by the Confederate White House very early the next morning (a Sunday) to ask Davis to call another cabinet meeting to reconsider the decision. The president agreed, but when the cabinet met later that day—while out in Mississippi Pemberton was being routed at Champion's Hill—the result was the same. The other members remained steadfastly in favor of Lee's plan.[104] Pickett's division would not, then, be riding the rails southwest toward Vicksburg but marching north toward a rendezvous with fame on a shell-torn hillside outside the Pennsylvania hamlet of Gettysburg.

Personal factors aside, Davis's decision to allow Lee to go North was a grave mistake. It would have required an overwhelming Confederate victory, possibly a series of victories, in Maryland or Pennsylvania to break Grant's grip on Vicksburg. On the other hand, a mere division from the Army of Northern Virginia would have increased Johnston's army by 25 percent. Yet Lee was by far the Confederacy's best general, and the Army of Northern Virginia its winning team. It is hard to fault Davis for betting on this combination rather than the vague and inscrutable Johnston. Lee was hesitant to mention this but had hinted at it. In arguing against sending Johnston a division, he had mentioned "the uncertainty of its employment" in the West.[105]

By late May it was clear that no more men would be going west. If Vicksburg were to be saved, Johnston would have to do it with what he had; and the longer he waited, the worse his chances would be. Still he delayed and called for more men, and so the month of June passed. Johnston wanted "such reinforcements as will give guarantee of success."[106] That was typical of Johnston. Davis and Seddon sought to know what Johnston's plans were, but the general declined to share this information with his superiors (possibly because he had no plans).[107] That too was vintage Johnston. By the middle of the month Grant had 77,000 men around Vicksburg, 34,000 of them in trenches facing toward Johnston in order to block any attempt to raise the siege.[108] Johnston still had substantially the same force he had had in late May. Every now and

then a letter from Pemberton found its way through the Federal lines, informing Johnston that the garrison might have food enough to take it through the
end of June, that the Union siege lines had been advanced to within twenty-
five yards of his works, then twenty-five feet.[109]

When informed that as theater commander he had the authority to draw
troops from Bragg's army, Johnston replied that to take enough men to do
any good would entail the loss of Middle Tennessee. Then he dodged responsibility by claiming that it was for Davis to decide which of the two, Middle
Tennessee or the Mississippi River, should be given up; they could not both
be held.[110] To make this position even more unpalatable to Davis, Johnston
shared his opinions with local civilian leaders, including the governor of Mississippi, and got them to write Davis letters to the same effect—with strong hints
that he should choose to hold the Mississippi.[111] Angrily Davis replied that
Johnston ought to know that everything within the power of the government
was being done to reinforce him and that to take the number of troops he
wanted from Bragg's army would mean not only the loss of Middle Tennessee
but the bisection of the Confederacy right through Georgia.[112]

As the month of June progressed, the Richmond authorities became increasingly desperate. New pleas went out to Kirby Smith to lend the aid of his
trans-Mississippi department. Smith was fairly willing now, but this time he
clashed with his chief subordinate, Gen. Richard Taylor. Taylor, son of former
United States president Zachary Taylor and brother-in-law to Davis, wanted
to move on New Orleans. He hoped this would cause the Federals to lift the
siege of Port Hudson, thus freeing its garrison to join Johnston in the relief
of Vicksburg. Kirby Smith had little faith in this elaborate scheme. He favored
an advance toward a point on the river opposite Vicksburg in order to sieze
and hold that much-sought-after mythical creature, Grant's overland supply
line, which, existing only in the minds of Confederate generals, could be
nearly ubiquitous. So time passed while Smith and Taylor ironed out their
differences—in Smith's favor—whereupon Taylor marched his troops to Milliken's
Bend opposite Vicksburg, temporarily drove off a construction battalion, and
accomplished nothing whatsoever of military significance. The trans-Mississippi's
efforts on behalf of Vicksburg had fizzled.[113]

Back in Richmond, Davis and Seddon were ready to try almost anything.
The president even toyed with the idea of going to Mississippi and taking command himself, but his health and the duties of his office would not permit
it.[114] In frustration he urged Johnston to undertake something at once, and
Secretary of War Seddon wrote Johnston that if he could do nothing else he
would have to make a desperate attack and that he, Seddon, was willing to
take the responsibility for it.[115] Still Johnston delayed. Perhaps he reasoned that
if the Confederacy had no chance of winning the war in the first place, there
was no point in risking his reputation in a desperate attempt to save Vicksburg.
Regardless, it finally took a suggestion from Pemberton for the surrender of

James A. Seddon (National Archives)

Vicksburg to goad him into any action at all. Pemberton proposed that Johnston approach Grant with a deal that would give Grant Vicksburg in exchange
for letting Pemberton's army march out with all its equipment.[116] Grant would
never have agreed to such a plan—he already considered Pemberton's men as
good as prisoners of war—but to Johnston the proposition suggested an appalling humiliation. Johnston made it clear that if there was to be any surrendering, Pemberton was going to have to do it himself.[117]

Johnston also decided to take steps to avoid the necessity of any surrender.
For some time he had believed that the most he could possibly accomplish
was saving Pemberton's army and abandoning Vicksburg.[118] Now he proposed
to do this by creating a diversion with his own army while Pemberton cut his
way out. He planned to begin the operation by July 7.[119] It never happened.
On July 4, as his troops were on their way to begin the feint, Johnston learned
that Vicksburg and its entire garrison had surrendered.[120] Five days later Port
Hudson followed suit, and the Confederacy was permanently split in two.[121]

Grant was still not through. With Vicksburg and Port Hudson disposed of,
he turned on Johnston, who had reoccupied Jackson after the Federals had
abandoned it in pursuit of Pemberton. By July 17 the capital of Mississippi
had fallen to Union forces for a second time.[122] Johnston retreated into the
pine woods of Mississippi and seemed content to watch as Grant completed
the conquest of the state.[123]

Davis, who was once again sick and theoretically confined to his room (though
his doctor had difficulty keeping him there) first got word of the surrender
of Vicksburg on the afternoon of July 6. Even then the news came not from
Johnston but from a low-ranking officer who was not quite clear about what
had happened. The War Department had to telegraph Johnston for confirmation. Davis was embittered against Johnston for the loss. When someone remarked that Vicksburg had apparently fallen from want of provisions, Davis
snapped, "Yes, from want of provisions inside, and a general outside who
wouldn't fight."[124] With Johnston again unwilling to fight while Grant ravaged
the state of Mississippi, Davis's patience with Johnston was exhausted. Irritated
at the general's constant refusal to share his plans, Davis telegraphed, "I have
to request such information in relation thereto as the government has a right
to expect from one of its commanding generals in the field."[125] Yet even this
harsh rebuke as well as subsequent insistent queries failed to elicit from Johnston any more than the nebulous explanation that he planned to stay where
he was until Grant forced him to retreat farther.[126] This was nowise satisfactory
to Davis, who complained to Lee, "I can only learn from him such vague purposes as were unfolded when he held his army before Richmond."[127]

Meanwhile, another squabble had sprung up between the president and his
chief western general. The Vicksburg campaign provided the occasion for this
disagreement as well, but in reality it was a culmination of Johnston's long
dissatisfaction with his position and the system of unified command in the

West. In short order it became a vent for both men's frustration with each other and with the turn events had taken.

The spark that set off this conflict was Seddon's telegram back in June, reminding Johnston that as theater commander he could draw troops from Bragg's army if he saw fit. Ever since his assignment to the western theater, Johnston had argued that one officer could not exercise such a command, mainly because he disliked it himself and wanted the glory of leading an army. Now, true to form, Johnston had replied to Seddon that it was impossible for him to know whether Bragg could spare any troops. Richmond would have to decide that.[128] He then added, "I have not considered myself commanding in Tennessee since assignment here, and should not have felt authorized to take troops from that department after having been informed by the Executive that no more could be spared."[129] Johnston had willfully misconstrued the instructions he had received, partly to acquire the wished-for command of a single army and partly out of resentment for the fact that he had had to obey orders from Davis—such as the order to send Stevenson's division to Mississippi in December 1862 or the order to take himself there in May 1863. He seemed to have the attitude that if Davis was going to give him orders, he would do only what he was specifically ordered and nothing more.[130]

Understandably, Johnston's announcement of his changed assignment came as a considerable surprise to the president.[131] Though in very poor health, Davis immediately wrote to Johnston without going through the secretary of war, assuring him that the order to go to Mississippi did not diminish his authority in Tennessee and asking when he (Davis) had ever written that no more troops could be spared from Tennessee.[132] This question put Johnston on the spot, so he ignored it. Davis repeated the question, somewhat more forcefully. He wanted to know the date of the letter or dispatch in which he had made the statement Johnston had alleged.[133] When the general finally replied, he explained lamely that when he said "Executive" he also meant the secretary of war; that the words "we have withheld nothing which it was practicable to give" were those he had interpreted as meaning no more troops could be spared from Tennessee; and that it was impossible for anyone to exercise the command Davis had assigned him.[134]

Johnston might as well have waved a red flag in front of a bull. Davis determined to set the record straight and sent to the War Department for copies of all the correspondence with Johnston during the Vicksburg campaign.[135] Then he sat down and wrote Johnston a dispatch seething with barely suppressed anger. In all the correspondence, he wrote, he could find no justification for Johnston's "strange error" in thinking himself no longer in command in Tennessee. As for the post being too big for one man, Davis notified Johnston that he was "engaged in correspondence with General Bragg on the subject of making such new arrangements as shall relieve you hereafter of the command of his department."[136]

Johnston replied stiffly, attempting to justify his interpretation of his orders and reiterating, "I considered my assignment to the immediate command in Mississippi as giving me a new position and limiting my authority to this department."[137] This missive was made even less welcome by the fact that it arrived on the same day as the news of "the disastrous termination of the siege of Vicksburg."[138] Davis, though so sick that on some days he could not get out of bed, resolved to set Johnston straight once and for all.[139] Again the War Department clerks trotted out the file on Johnston's correspondence.[140] In a week's time the president produced an exhaustive fifteen-page letter, rehearsing the entire history of Johnston's tenure in the western command and demolishing point by point Johnston's various justifications for his misconstruction of orders. The general's attitude was, Davis maintained, "extraordinary" and "a grave error."[141]

Johnston was somewhat chastened by this and, fearing that Davis might take formal action against him, wrote a more subdued response. In a long letter he again tried to show that he had had at least some reason to believe as he did and asked the president to reconsider his harsh interpretation of what Johnston was now characterizing as his "misapprehension."[142] Davis's reply was brief. Dismissing most of Johnston's arguments as irrelevant, he recognized with great satisfaction that Johnston had admitted he was wrong: "I now cheerfully accept your admission of your 'misapprehension.'"[143]

By this time it was September 1863, and yet another controversy had already arisen between Davis and Johnston, centering on the hapless Pemberton. Even before the surrender of Vicksburg, Pemberton's popularity had been on the decline.[144] This had been part of Davis's reason for ordering Johnston to go to Mississippi in person.[145] After the surrender—on July 4, of all days—Pemberton had a strong claim to the title of the most hated man in the South, certainly the most hated to wear a Confederate uniform. He was treacherous, the public stormed. He had sold Vicksburg; he had surrendered with abundant supplies on hand and against the advice of his generals.[146] "He had joined the South for the express purpose of betraying it, and this was clearly proven by the fact that he surrendered on the 4th of July, a day sacred to Yankees."[147] Pemberton did have a few friends who stuck up for him—one of them claimed he was only a "poor jerk."[148]

Davis, however, tended to hold a high opinion of Pemberton. Indeed, he came very close to believing that Pemberton had never made a wrong move during the entire Vicksburg campaign.[149] There were several reasons for this badly mistaken view. Davis had a tremendous devotion to the Confederate cause, and he respected those who shared his dedication. This partly explained his respect for Bragg, despite their prewar hostility. Pemberton had turned his back on a large fortune, as well as his mother and brothers, to go with the South.[150] Davis was impressed by this and thought highly of Pemberton because of it. A second reason for Davis's approval of Pemberton was that he and Pemberton had much in common. Both were doctrinaire state's-rights men; both prided themselves on their devotion to principle; both had been taking a great deal of criticism of late; and both had been utterly stupefied by Grant's brilliant Vicksburg campaign.

Davis was disturbed by the vilification of Pemberton by the general public and was therefore inclined to be especially outraged when he saw in a newspaper an unsigned letter, running to nearly six thousand words, blaming Pemberton for everything that had gone wrong in the Vicksburg campaign while defending Johnston on all counts. The writer had used information that could only have been available at Johnston's headquarters, and Davis determined to get to the bottom of the matter.[151] Another exchange of letters took place between Davis and Johnston, and it finally developed that the culprit had been a member of the general's staff.[152] Davis hinted strongly that the guilty party should be dismissed, but Johnston assured the president that the officer was contrite and maintained him on his staff.[153] There the affair ended, but with further hostility generated between Davis and Johnston.

By mid-August the ill feelings between the two men had been the subject of rumor throughout the Confederacy. One officer stationed in Mississippi, a mutual friend of Johnston and Joseph Davis, approached the president's brother to persuade him to use his "good offices" to smooth over what the officer assumed must be a misunderstanding.[154] Nothing ever came of this, and it is doubtful anything could have. The disagreement between Davis and Johnston was more than a misunderstanding. Davis believed Confederate victory possible, and though on rare occasions his pride interfered or his strategic sense was faulty, he was willing to take desperate measures to secure Confederate independence. Johnston may never have believed Confederate victory possible, and he almost certainly felt the cause was lost by late 1863. Therefore, he was not willing to attempt any reckless gambles to achieve an unlikely victory. Instead, as was his wont, he ventured only where success was certain, even if this would render ultimate defeat equally certain. Still, his reputation as a skillful general persisted, and despite all that had happened, the hope remained in Davis's mind that he could somehow be useful to the Confederacy.[155]

From the outset Davis had taken an active interest in the Vicksburg campaign. He had realized the importance of holding the Mississippi River and had done his best to supply adequate numbers of men, cannon, and provisions. Yet he had made four major mistakes that may have influenced the course of events. Two of them (his attempts to use Johnston and Pemberton) involved generals, and two (his failure to provide unity of command for the defenders of the east and west banks of the Mississippi and his approval of the Gettysburg campaign) involved strategy.

The decision to allow Lee to move north in the summer of 1863 was the least serious of these errors. Since the campaign ended in failure and, even if moderately successful, would probably not have saved Vicksburg, it must be regarded as a mistake. Yet hindsight also reveals that even with one or two or half a dozen divisions from the Army of Northern Virginia, Johnston would probably have found some excuse to delay until it was too late.

The failure to provide unified command for the east and west banks of the Mississippi was a more serious error. It meant that the trans-Mississippi forces, who could at least have made Grant's task more difficult, effectively took no part in the defense of the river. Making the Mississippi a dividing line between separate commands was a mistaken concept that Davis had advanced as early as January 1862. A year later his bias on the matter had been strengthened by Randolph's inadvertent blow to his pride. By the first half of 1863 the chance that he would change on this question was virtually nil, and by the last half of 1863 it was too late.

Davis's assignment of Pemberton to such an important command also reflects poorly on the president's military acumen. No prior acquaintance clouded his judgment of Pemberton, and though he respected the Pennsylvania Confederate for various reasons, there were others whom he respected but eased out of key positions when he felt they were not equal to the task. Very likely Davis's hostility to Johnston influenced him in Pemberton's favor. If Johnston was at fault, Davis may have reasoned, Pemberton must be blameless. The outcry against Pemberton would then be the efforts of Johnston's supporters, almost by definition the enemies of the president, to shift blame away from their idol. There was probably a grain of truth in this. In any case, Davis was unlikely to think harshly of Pemberton since Davis himself had been as befuddled by Grant's daring campaign as had the Pennsylvania Confederate. Under different circumstances—with Davis on the spot in Vicksburg, in reasonably good health, with nothing to occupy his attention but stopping Grant—the president might have fared vastly better than Pemberton had. As it was, most of Pemberton's mistakes had been Davis's as well.

Johnston's was a strange case. He may have had the intelligence and ability, but he seemed unwilling or unable to put them to work for the Confederacy. Davis had probably realized for some time that Johnston's attitude toward unified command made him the wrong man for the job, but he had no one else to whom he could give the task, and there was always the temptation of hoping that Johnston would somehow find himself and become an effective commander. Yet Davis's failure to take decisive action—either by removing Johnston or giving him peremptory orders to relieve Vicksburg—along with his failure to give the same sort of orders for the trans-Mississippi forces showed a dangerous indecisiveness.[156] Instead, Davis engaged in an extended and unprofitable argument to prove he had been right and Johnston wrong. Such was not the behavior of a man who felt himself in control of the situation.

The fall or Vicksburg had momentous consequences. It effectively ended

Pemberton's career as a general (though he was exchanged within weeks) and brought the tension between Davis and Johnston to open hostility, leading to the end of Johnston's command over Bragg and the Army of Tennessee. The Confederacy had lost what Davis would later call "the nailhead that held the South's two halves together."[157] With it had gone the trans-Mississippi with all its resources as well as a much-needed army of over 30,000 men. It was a tremendous blow to morale in the South and a corresponding lift in the North, especially the Northwest where control of the Mississippi Valley had always been a sensitive issue.[158] It freed Grant's army for use elsewhere and changed the states of Mississippi and Alabama into backwaters of the war; there was no point in the Federals occupying every hamlet and plantation. The focus of the war in the West would now turn exclusively to Tennessee.

13

THE LOSS OF TENNESSEE

All was not well in Tennessee. The sniping against Bragg by his officers that had prompted Davis to order Johnston to Tullahoma in January had not ended with that general's arrival and had continued after his departure. Also unabated was the public criticism of Bragg—fueled, Bragg reasonably surmised, by innuendoes from Polk and his coterie of malcontents. Polk might be able to assassinate a man's character without seeming to do so, but such subtlety was not a part of Bragg's personality. Again he was baited into taking the direct approach. This time the question at issue was Polk's disobedience of Bragg's orders during the Kentucky campaign. Bragg's Kentucky campaign was still a topic of public discussion, and Polk had but recently submitted his official report in which he had dodged responsibility for his disobedience by hiding behind advice his subordinates had given him at a council of war. Bragg decided to send a note to each of the generals involved, warning them that Polk was shifting responsibility to them and asking each one that "if consistent with your sense of duty, you will inform me to what extent you sustained the general in his acknowledged disobedience."[1]

The response was less than gratifying. Most of the generals refused to answer.[2] Buckner only admonished Bragg to be chivalrous and overlook the matter.[3] Hardee, immediately upon receiving Bragg's note, sent a copy of it to Polk, along with a note of his own assuring the bishop: "If you choose to rip up the Kentucky campaign you can tear Bragg into tatters."[4] In reply Polk sent a long, smug letter to Hardee, thanking him for "the prompt indication of what was brewing." He went on to say it did not surprise him; he had long thought there was as much to be feared from Bragg's headquarters as from Rosecrans's. Now Bragg would probably have him arrested and court-martialed. Polk continued that he was not worried, since he had not disobeyed orders. Bragg's dispatch had ordered him to attack with all his available force, and he had not had any force "available" for that attack. He concluded with the hope that Bragg had not "won his way into [Hardee's] confidence."[5]

Thus warned of what was afoot, Polk could take steps to see that nothing came of it. He promptly paid visits to each of the generals involved and demanded copies of their answers to Bragg's note.[6] When one officer's reply did not reflect as favorably on Polk as he felt was warranted, the bishop paid him another visit to "refresh" his memory, enabling him to write another note to Bragg correcting his previous statement.[7] Bragg did not pursue the matter further.

These intrigues occurred just as the Vicksburg campaign was heating up, with the opening of Grant's successful effort to get behind the Confederate fortress and trap Pemberton's army. Jefferson Davis's attention was riveted on the situation in Mississippi, and if he took note at all of the festering problems in the Army of Tennessee's high command, he apparently believed he could spare none of his energy to try to solve them.

The unpleasantness of the ongoing hostilities with Bragg did not prevent Polk and Hardee and the army's other generals from enjoying their winter and spring at Tullahoma. Hardee and Polk took turns scheduling gala social events for the local ladies, some of whom traveled from as far off as northern Alabama to attend. Hardee sent out staff officers to round up guests, and on one occasion there were upwards of five hundred women present. The events included reviews, tournaments, horse races, banquets, parties, serenades, and dances. When it was Polk's time to sponsor the fun, he scrupulously stipulated, "The horse-race I shall turn over to General Cheatham."[8]

Though the high command of the Army of Tennessee was in disarray and, for the most part, busy with their recreation, the rank and file enjoyed less luxury but seemed to be in better fighting trim.[9] A British officer visiting about this time noted, "The discipline in this army is the strictest in the Confederacy."[10] Nor was he the only one who was impressed. An aide whom Davis sent to Tullahoma to inspect the army found that everything Joesph E. Johnston had reported earlier in the year was true. The troops were "in a high state of efficiency, well clad and fed, and marked with every evidence of good discipline, high courage, and capacity for endurance." There had been a vast improvement in the condition of the army since the same aide had visited it a year earlier when it was under Beauregard's command. This the aide attributed to Bragg's administrative ability and concluded, "The army lacks no physical element of success."[11] The army was also increasing in numbers. So efficient was Bragg in administering the conscript act and rounding up stragglers that by late June 1863 the Army of Tennessee numbered over 43,000 men, more than it had had at Murfreesboro, despite having detached over 11,000 to assist Johnston in Mississipppi.[12]

It was with this force that Bragg was once again called upon to confront Rosecrans. The Federal general had been idle at Murfreesboro ever since the battle there the previous January. The authorities in Washington had urged him to advance in order to prevent Bragg from reinforcing Johnston, but when Rosecrans was in one of his balky moods, there was little that could move him. Finally, by late June, too late to have any effect on the Vicksburg campaign, the Union general considered himself ready. On June 24 his army headed south.[13] Though he had insisted on waiting till his supply arrangements were just so, Rosecrans was about to demonstrate just how good a general he could be when he got good and ready. In this endeavor he was aided by the fact that Bragg was unable to get top performance out of his cavalry.[14]

In April of that year, with the Vicksburg campaign in full swing several hundred miles away, it had appeared that at least one of Bragg's top cavalry officers
would be put out of commission by the direct action of another. Relations
had become increasingly strained between Forrest and Van Dorn. When the
latter reproached the former regarding some newspaper articles one of Forrest's
staff had written for a Chattanooga paper that glorified Forrest at Van Dorn's
expense, things came to a head in a stormy exchange at Van Dorn's headquarters. Van Dorn had been hit where it hurt—in his vanity—and now he
came down on Forrest pretty hard. One thing led to another, and soon Van
Dorn expressed his "belief in [Forrest's] treachery and falsehood" and suggested
they could settle it right there. With that he snatched his sword from where
it was hanging on the wall and jerked it out of the scabbard. Forrest jumped
to his feet and had half drawn his own sword when he stopped. Putting the
sword back he said, "General Van Dorn, you know I'm not afraid of you—but
I will not fight you." Their fighting, he continued, would be a bad example
to the men, and there was, after all, the cause to think about.[15]

Their fight never came off; instead, two weeks later Van Dorn was caught
for the last time by trouble of another sort. The Mississippi general had had
the "reputation of being [a] horrible rake," with his rumored indiscretions pro-
viding grist for the scandal mills of the entire Confederacy. Since being stationed in Middle Tennessee, Van Dorn had gotten into the habit of calling
on the young and pretty Mrs. George B. Peters in the absence of her much
older husband—or at least that was the story Peters gave after entering Van
Dorn's headquarters on May 7, approaching the general from behind, and blowing his brains out.[16] With the Vicksburg campaign approaching its climax and
Rosecrans preparing to advance on Bragg, the Confederacy would have to do
without the services of Earl Van Dorn.

Not long after this Forrest too was put out of action, if only temporarily.
In an artillery battery attached to Forrest's command was a Lt. A. Wills Gould.
Forrest had for some reason become dissatisfied with Gould's performance and
had ordered him transferred. Forrest had a way of arousing very strong feelings
in other people, and Gould was in any case a fiery young man. He stewed
over what he considered to be his grievance against Forrest until he was in a
very ugly frame of mind and then stormed off to talk to Forrest.

They met at the general's headquarters, where they stood and talked for some
time. Forrest, cool and apparently bored, idly twirled a small pocket knife,
and Gould, one hand shoved into the pocket of the linen duster he was wearing over his uniform, became increasingly heated. Finally, Forrest abruptly cut
off the conversation and turned to walk away. Gould drew out the pistol he
had been holding in his pocket, thrust it almost against Forrest's side, and
fired. Though seriously wounded, Forrest gripped Gould's pistol hand, opened
his penknife with his teeth, and stabbed the shocked lieutenant in the abdo-
men. Gould wrenched loose and fled. A doctor was hurriedly summoned and

Forrest's wound examined. When the doctor gravely stated that the wound might be fatal, Forrest cursed and said no man would kill him and live to tell of it. In a black rage he broke away from the doctor and dashed outside.

Spotting a pistol in the saddle holster on a horse hitched near the door, he seized it and set off in search of the man who had shot him. Forrest's headquarters was located on the public square of Columbia, Tennessee. The unfortunate lieutenant had run across the square, stumbled into a tailor shop, and collapsed. Two doctors had arrived and were examining the stab wound when the pistol-brandishing general stormed in the front door with unmistakably murderous intent. Gould staggered to his feet and out the back door into an alley. Forrest followed and fired at him but missed, wounding a bystander. The chase finally came to an end when Gould collapsed in the high weeds of an empty lot and bystanders persuaded Forrest that the young officer was dying. The general gradually calmed down and was soon urging the doctors to ignore him and treat Gould. It was no use. The lieutenant died several days later, after an emotional reconciliation with Forrest. The general himself was laid up for a week and a half, not taking to the saddle again until after Rosecrans's advance was already under way.[17]

A third Confederate cavalryman of fearsome reputation, John Hunt Morgan, was available to Bragg but ineffective. His past raids had thrown Union offensive movements off-balance before they were well started. Now, however, Morgan was not his old self. His marriage seemed to have taken all the fire out of him.[18] Anxious to recoup his fading reputation, he sought and received permission from Bragg to lead a foray behind enemy lines. Setting out on July 2—the Union advance was already well under way—with some 2,000 troopers, Morgan disregarded Bragg's instructions, crossed the Ohio River, and rode himself and his men right out of the campaign and, eventually, out of the war.

Then there was Bragg's chief of cavalry, Brig. Gen. Joseph "Fighting Joe" Wheeler. Relatively inexperienced in cavalry command and, at twenty-five, extremely young for the position he held, Wheeler was flamboyant and aggressive but not always very effective. In addition, neither Forrest nor Morgan had any use for the West Point-trained Wheeler. Thus with Van Dorn dead, Forrest laid up and, after his recovery, unable to get along with Wheeler, Morgan off on his wild goose chase, and Wheeler of questionable abilities to begin with, Bragg's cavalry was mostly unserviceable.[19] Without adequate cavalry reconnaissance, he was left in the dark about Rosecrans's sharp and skillful thrusts, when Rosecrans was dangerous enough to begin with.

Bragg's plan was for Hardee's corps to block the Federal army and fix it in place while Polk's corps, stationed a few miles to the west, would swing over and crush the Federal flank, ensuring a shattering Confederate victory. Such was not to be the case. Hardee and Polk, upon whose actions the success of the plan depended, did not understand their roles because their hostility to Bragg had resulted in an almost complete breakdown in communications.

Hardee had neglected to prepare entrenchments, and Polk was no more ready for the task that had been assigned to him.

Rosecrans opened the campaign by faking toward the Confederate left. Hardee was fooled and was pulled badly out of position, allowing Rosecrans to go around his right flank. Bragg, who was unable to get much information from his cavalry and on top of that was not well, was confused and saw little alternative to falling back on his prepared positions immediately around Tullahoma. Here he hoped to make a stand, but once again Rosecrans boldly feinted in one direction and then went the other way. Hardee and Polk lost their nerve and began pressing Bragg to retreat. Bragg held out for a while, but the lack of adequate scouting by the cavalry began to weigh heavily on him. The uncertainty coupled with his own debility finally broke his will, and he consented to retreat to the Elk River, another ten miles to the south. This was a weak position, and Bragg knew it. Thus he may not have been very surprised when Rosecrans again outflanked and forced him back, this time all the way to Chattanooga.[20] It was July 3; Lee was meeting his defeat in Pennsylvania; Vicksburg would surrender the next day; and the Confederacy had lost all of Middle Tennessee in a little over a week.

The campaign had been hard on both armies. They had traversed rough country during more than a week of almost incessant rains.[21] Bragg's army had suffered the added discouragement of being in retreat and had lost nearly 5,000 men, most of them stragglers.[22] Fortunately, Rosecrans decided his army needed a breather, and he paused to rest his troops and build up his supplies, giving Bragg six weeks' respite. The time was used to rest and refit, and at least some of the stragglers rejoined their regiments.[23]

Since the army had been healthy at the outset, there was the possibility it might regain its strength. The high command, on the other hand, only seemed to get worse. Early in the campaign, when Bragg had been little inclined to take orders from his subordinates, Hardee and Polk had flirted with the idea of mutiny. In a letter to Polk labeled "confidential," Hardee revealed that he had "been thinking seriously of the condition of affairs with this army." Bragg, he felt, was physically unfit to command the army. "What shall we do?" he asked suggestively. "What is best to be done to save this army and its honor?" Then he continued ominously, "I think we ought to counsel together. Where is Buckner? . . . When can we meet? I would like Buckner to be present." However, as the campaign progressed, Polk and Hardee were able to browbeat Bragg into conforming more or less with their advice, and mutiny became unnecessary.[24]

Even so, this failed to satisfy Polk. It irritated him immensely that his friend Jefferson Davis had still not sacked Bragg, after nearly a year's worth of advice to that effect from Polk. In an act of disloyalty that would have astonished the friend whose loyalty alone had made and kept him a general, Polk wrote to a fellow bishop outside the army, "The truth is, I am somewhat afraid of

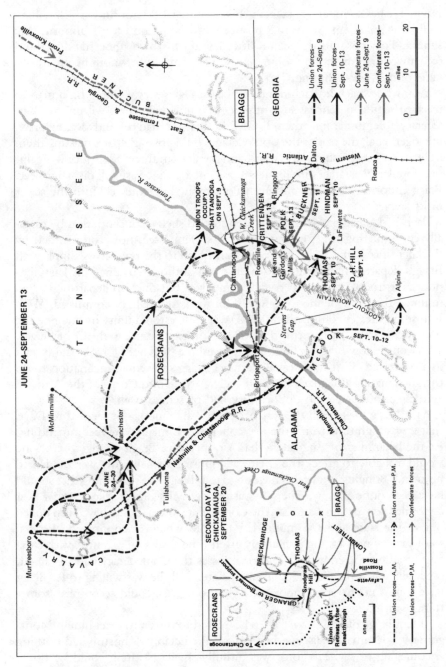

Map 13.1 Murfreesboro to Chickamauga, 1863

Davis. He has so much at stake on this issue that I do not find myself willing to risk his judgment. . . . He is proud, self-reliant, and I fear stubborn." He should, Polk continued, "lean a little less on his own understanding" and recognize that "there were some minds in the land from whom he might obtain counsel worth having."[25]

Meanwhile, back in Richmond, Jefferson Davis was working on a plan to reverse the tide in Tennessee. A number of influential people within the Confederacy, foremost among them P. G. T. Beauregard, had been advocating drawing together all the troops the Confederacy could possibly spare, massing them in Bragg's army, crushing Rosecrans, and going from there.[26] The idea was gaining popularity as affairs in Tennessee assumed an increasingly dismal aspect. Bragg endorsed the plan, and even Polk threw his "counsel" into the scales in its favor.[27]

Davis had already taken the first step toward such a concentration by formally consolidating the Department of East Tennessee, now commanded by Buckner since Kirby Smith had been transferred to the trans-Mississippi, with Bragg's department.[28] Bragg had been given authority to draw on East Tennessee for troops after the Perryville campaign, but the two departments had resumed their independence under Johnston's umbrella of command. With Johnston's theater command ended, Davis now restored unity by merging the only two western departments that still had any significance to the Confederacy. This would allow Bragg, if he chose, to combine Buckner's force with his own in a concerted effort to defeat Rosecrans. Bragg showed an inclination to do this, designating Buckner's force officially as the Third Corps of the Army of Tennessee, but as yet no opportunity had presented itself.[29]

With Bragg pushed all the way back into Chattanooga, it seemed to Davis that it was high time to try the mass offensive so many were recommending. At the beginning of August, he had Cooper wire Bragg asking whether he would feel able to attack the enemy if Johnston's small army were added to his own.[30] Bringing Johnston's men up to join Bragg was something that should have been done anyway. The war was over in Mississippi, at least so far as it concerned conventional armies. The Confederate forces should have been pulled out of the state and the militia left to hold whatever countryside Federal soldiers were not standing on at any given time. Davis, apparently, was reluctant to admit the enormous territorial losses the Confederacy had sustained, especially when they included his own state. Still, he was willing to let Bragg have Johnston's troops temporarily if he thought he could accomplish something with them.

At first Bragg did think so.[31] Then he invited Johnston to meet him in Montgomery, Alabama, to discuss the matter.[32] Predictably, Johnston had nothing encouraging to say. His force was pitifully small. Nothing could be done, especially nothing offensive. Bragg was in no frame of mind to overcome Johnston's bleak outlook. The criticism of the public and contempt of some of his generals had worn him down, and the retreat from Middle Tennessee had greatly depressed him.[33] Discouraged, he wired Davis, through Cooper, that "after examining all resources," he believed they were not adequate to justify such an attack.[34]

Adjutant and Inspector General Cooper was agitated enough about the plan and its prospects to step out of his accustomed role as the president's chief clerk. He suggested to Davis that Bragg be ordered to make the attack.[35] Davis declined to take such a measure. Revealing his understanding of the role of commander in chief, he explained that "however desirable a movement may be, it is never safe to do more than suggest it to a commanding general, and it would be unwise to order its execution by one who foretold failure."[36] For the most part Davis followed this rule throughout the war. The results obtained were dependent on how good the general was whom the president was allowing the exercise of discretion. With someone like Bragg such a system might work well. With the likes of Joseph E. Johnston it could be disastrous.

The plans for a concentrated offensive were, in any case, laid aside, but in Tennessee the pressure continued to mount. In mid-August a Union force under Gen. Ambrose Burnside moved from Kentucky against East Tennessee.[37] Buckner did not have sufficient troops to stop the advance and was compelled to fall back, finally joining Bragg at Chattanooga.[38] Early in September Burnside occupied Knoxville, severing the important direct rail link between Virginia and Chattanooga.[39] In the meantime Rosecrans had materialized in front of Chattanooga and seemed about to begin another offensive. By August 22 his artillery was shelling the town.[40] It appeared that Rosecrans and Burnside would unite to crush Bragg.[41]

Davis was concerned and telegraphed Bragg to see if there was some way he could stop Rosecrans's shelling and to urge him to hit either Rosecrans or Burnside before the two could make a junction. The president also set out to find some reinforcements for Bragg.[42] Johnston, it developed, could spare 9,000 men from his force in Mississippi, but Davis still feared this would not be enough.[43] It was of the utmost importance that Chattanooga, a vital rail and industrial center and the Confederacy's last foothold in Tennessee, be saved. Perplexed, the president summoned Lee to Richmond for nearly two weeks of conferences on what the Confederacy's next move ought to be.[44]

Davis felt sure of the need to reinforce Bragg, and Lee, gaining a better perspective on the war from the capital than he had had from the headquarters of an individual army, was not inclined to argue against such a move this time.[45] They agreed that two divisions of Lee's army under James Longstreet, his senior corps commander, should be sent to Bragg at once.[46] Davis thought Lee should personally take charge of the projected offensive in Tennessee. Lee said he would go if that was what the president wanted but believed that since he was unfamiliar with the situation in that state he would be more useful in Virginia. Davis acquiesced.[47] It was therefore Longstreet who would accompany the Virginia troops west, and Bragg who would command the coming campaign. Unfortunately, the loss of the railroad through East Tennessee meant that Longstreet's troops would have to take a circuitous detour on rickety railroads, down through the Atlantic coast states and then up through Atlanta to Chattanooga. The first division would not arrive until September 18, and by then much had changed on Bragg's front.[48]

In reality Rosecrans and Burnside were not planning to unite. Burnside was happy to stay in East Tennessee, and it looked as if Rosecrans could handle Bragg by himself. Once again Rosecrans made a flanking movement, turning Bragg's left flank this time.[49] Finally, Bragg determined to strike back. Davis had been advising him to attack either Rosecrans or Burnside.[50] Strengthened by reinforcements from Buckner and Johnston, Bragg now felt able to comply. Burnside was out of reach, so Bragg turned against Rosecrans. The required move to the southwest would mean giving up Chattanooga, but that could not be helped.[51]

Rosecrans's army was considerably spread out, and while Bragg pursued one part of it, other elements occupied Chattanooga on September 9.[52] Rosecrans believed Bragg's army was in headlong retreat and was greatly elated at the prospects before him. He was also greatly deceived. Bragg had worked hard to create this deception, sending carefully coached "deserters" into Federal lines with false information, but basically the Union commander had deceived himself.[53] Impressed with the cleverness that had enabled him to flank the Confederates out of one position after another, Rosecrans did not realize that the foe he was pursuing was not a beaten and disorganized rabble but a fully intact army with plenty of fight left in it. In order to round up all the Confederates before they could escape, he spread his three army corps even farther apart. By September 10 they were far out of supporting distance of each other—and Braxton Bragg and the Army of Tennessee were in perfect position to annihilate the center portion of Rosecrans's army.

Bragg had taken advantage of Rosecrans's misconception and skillfully maneuvered his army into position for the attack. It could hardly fail: Bragg outnumbered this fragment of Rosecrans's army nearly three to one and was about to fall on it from front, flank, and rear. With these Federals disposed of, Bragg would be well situated. Rosecrans would be left with two isolated fragments of an army, each smaller than the corps Bragg now faced, and Bragg would be right between them.[54] At last Bragg would have the decisive victory that had eluded him at Perryville and Murfreesboro. At this point, however, the high-command problems of the Army of Tennessee came home to roost.

The two columns that were to take the Federals in flank and rear were commanded respectively by Lt. Gen. D. H. Hill and Maj. Gen. T. C. Hindman. Hindman had achieved a fairly good record for himself in Arkansas but now seemed to have developed some peculiar ideas on the conduct of the army.[55] Hill, a North Carolinian and 1842 graduate of West Point where he had ranked

twenty-eighth out of fifty-six, had distinguished himself in the Mexican War
before resigning from the army to become a professor of mathematics. At the
outbreak of the Civil War he had become colonel of the First North Carolina
Volunteers and had risen in rank to command a division and then a corps in
Lee's army in Virginia. At times he could be an outstanding commander, but
overall he was less than satisfactory. He had a sharp tongue and a tendency
to criticize that had already created hard feelings in other commands.[56] He had
been sent to Bragg in July 1863 to replace Hardee, who had gone to serve
under Johnston in Mississippi.[57] Like Hindman, Hill entertained some strange
ideas about his role in Bragg's battle plan for September 10. The roads in front
of his position were obstructed, Hill complained to Bragg, and his best division commander, Cleburne, was sick. The assault simply could not be carried
out. Hindman agreed, and the two did nothing.[58]

Bragg, who had given orders for the attack, waited in vain to hear the roar
of battle. Growing impatient, he dismounted and paced back and forth. In
frustration he dug his spurs into the ground and smote the air with his fist—
still no firing.[59] He dispatched a note to Hindman and Hill telling them to
get on with it, but it was no use.[60] Finally, he rode off to Hill's headquarters
himself, but by then darkness had fallen and the moment was past. There was
no adequate explanation for what happened—or rather for what did not happen. Cleburne was not sick, and that would not have been a valid reason to
ignore orders anyway. Nor did the rest of Hill's and Hindman's excuses hold
water.[61] Apparently these two generals had caught the spirit of the high ranks
in the Army of Tennessee and believed that any orders given by Bragg were
bound to be disastrous and need not be obeyed. So the day passed with no
action, and what one of Bragg's officers described as an opportunity "which
comes to most generals only in their dreams" passed into the might-have-beens
of history.

All was not yet lost, though. The Federals still had not grasped the situation,
and Bragg had another opening the next day. Suppressing his anger, he issued
orders for the new attack. Again the plan was good; the prospects for success,
excellent. This time the flanking columns were commanded by Hindman and
Buckner. The outcome, unfortunately, was no different than on the previous
day. Hindman and Buckner met to discuss Bragg's plan, decided they did not
like it, and asked him to change it.[62] Bragg declined and told them to proceed
with the battle, whereupon the two generals refused Bragg's order and retreated to assume defensive positions.[63]

By this time the center corps of Rosecrans's army had been alerted and had
withdrawn to a safer position. Yet Bragg had one more chance to catch Rosecrans's army in its scattered deployment and beat it soundly. On September 13
the opportunity presented itself to crush the isolated left wing of the Federal
army. This time it was Polk who was ordered to attack. Polk thought the
enemy in front of him was too strong and informed Bragg that he was taking

Daniel Harvey Hill (National Archives)

up a good defensive position.[64] Bragg replied that he hoped Polk would not stay in his position unless he was under enemy attack. "We must force him to fight," Bragg explained with more patience than was to be expected under the circumstances, "at the earliest moment and before his combinations can be carried out." Bragg was certain that if Polk had access to all the information that he (Bragg) did, he too would see the need to strike at once. Just to reassure Polk, however, Bragg would take the risk of weakening his own right wing of the army to send Polk reinforcements, but he cautioned Polk against waiting for the arrival of the troops before attacking lest "another golden opportunity . . . be lost by the withdrawal of our game."[65] It was no use. Polk was not in the habit of obeying Bragg and thought he knew more than his commander anyway. Once again Polk disobeyed, with the same result as that after the disobedience of Hindman, Hill, and Buckner. The Federals discovered the danger they were in, withdrew, and another "golden opportunity" was lost.

By this time Rosecrans, realizing that his quarry had now turned on him, had taken steps to draw the dispersed portions of his army together. By September 19 both armies were massed a few miles south of Chattanooga near Chicamauga Creek.[66] Rosecrans had finally completed the concentration of his force. It had taken Bragg this long to get his balky army into position to attack, but now he was ready and determined to come to grips with his opponent. There was no longer any chance for an easy victory—Bragg's defiant subordinates had seen to that—but the first division of Longstreet's corps had arrived the previous day; and, Bragg would be going into this battle with a luxury very rare for Confederate commanders, a slight numerical superiority.[67]

Bragg's plan was simple. He would smash the Federal left, curl it back, push the Federal army into a mountain cul-de-sac known as McLemore's Cove, and seize the road that connected Rosecrans with his base at Chattanooga in the process. The battle opened early on the morning of September 19 and continued with unabated fury throughout the entire day. The struggle was most desperate on the Federal left, where both sides fed in division after division. At one point the Confederates actually got astride the vital road in Rosecrans's rear before being driven back by Federal reinforcements. When the day ended, Rosecrans had been battered and driven back nearly a mile in some places, but his left wing, under the redoubtable Thomas, still held the road to Chattanooga.[68]

That evening Longstreet arrived with the rest of his troops. The troops were a welcome addition, but Longstreet himself was a dubious asset. While many Civil War generals and one president had West Point records that were less than stellar, few could have been worse than that of James Longstreet, who graduated fifty-fourth among the fifty-six-man class of 1842. In the old army he had served creditably in the Mexican War, and in the Confederate army he had served in Virginia from Manassas to Gettysburg. On the Virginia front, the military genius of Lee had linked Longstreet with another military genius, Jackson, and Longstreet had become a fairly useful officer, known primarily

James Longstreet (National Archives)

for his stolid reliability. At Gettysburg, however, Longstreet demonstrated that he could be anything but reliable and more than a little childish when the plan chosen by his commander did not meet with his approval. The real trouble with Longstreet was that he believed the Confederacy had just three really first-rate generals: Joseph E. Johnston, Robert E. Lee, and, of course, James Longstreet. Of these three Lee probably rated the lowest, and Johnston was next. Lack of self-confidence was not a problem that plagued James Longstreet—a surprising circumstance since he arrived at Chickamauga fresh from the Gettysburg campaign, where he had come as close as anyone could to losing single-handedly what passed for the great battle of the war. After Gettysburg Lee had generously said, "It is all my fault," and on that point Longstreet was in complete agreement with his august commander.[69]

Now, however, Longstreet would be serving under a different commander. He arrived at Chickamauga station after nightfall and was angered that he was not met at the train depot with great fanfare and proper recognition as the emissary of the Army of Northern Virginia who had come to introduce the Army of Tennessee to the concept of victory.[70] Setting off for army headquarters in a surly mood, he arrived and reported to Braxton Bragg around 11:00 P.M. on the evening of the nineteenth, after a harrowing ride around the darkened battlefield during which the newcomer and his staff blundered into Union lines but successfully bluffed their way out.[71] Bragg was anxious to make use of the renowned general and so undertook the risky task of reorganizing the command structure of his army in the midst of a battle. Longstreet was to command the left wing of Bragg's army, and Polk the right. This had the bonus of reducing the responsibility of D. H. Hill, whose failure on the tenth Bragg had not forgotten. On the other hand it dangerously increased the responsibility of Polk.[72] The plan for the next morning called for Polk to attack the battered Federal left flank at dawn and for Longstreet to hit the other end of the line as soon as Polk's assault was well under way.[73]

Somehow, as was becoming normal in the Army of Tennessee, things did not quite work out as planned. Polk, as commander of the right wing, was responsible for seeing that his units were in position to open the assault at dawn, but his mishandling of this task started that very evening. Hill sent Breckinridge a dispatch telling him to move his division into position for the next day's fighting; Polk, who was then with Breckinridge, told him to ignore the order—there would be time for that later.[74] That night Polk issued orders to prepare for an attack the next morning but failed to see that they were carried out. Some of his officers got word of the attack; but Hill, whose troops were to lead the assault, was not even able to find Polk's headquarters, nor could Polk's couriers find Hill, and it seems that neither general made a very serious attempt to contact the other.[75] The reorganization may have added to the confusion, but regardless, the result was that Hill knew nothing of the planned attack.[76] Daybreak came and went. Bragg, listening at his headquarters for the roar of cannon on the right that would indicate the attack was under way, was perplexed by the silence. As more time passed and nothing happened, he dispatched a staff officer to Polk's headquarters to see what was causing the delay.[77] The staff officer found Polk an hour after sunrise, sitting on the porch of the farmhouse he was using as his headquarters three miles from the fighting front, placidly reading a newspaper, and waiting for his breakfast. Did he know why there was no firing on the right? He did not. When the staff officer reported this to Bragg, the normally temperate commander responded with what his aide euphemistically called "a terrible exclamation," jumped on his horse, and galloped off to find Polk himself. Arriving at the farmhouse, he found that Polk, having foreseen some such visitation, had just left to look into the matter. "Do tell General Bragg," he had said as he went out the door, "that my heart is overflowing with anxiety for the attack. Overflowing with anxiety, sir."[78] An incensed Bragg also set off for the front to try to get some action.

Meanwhile, Polk had given up on finding Hill and sent orders directly to Hill's division leaders to attack at once. The courier bearing the orders found Hill and his division commanders together around 7:00 A.M. Still no attack was forthcoming, since no preparation had been made; it would take time to get the units aligned properly for an assault.[79] Bragg himself arrived in Hill's sector around 7:30 A.M., where he found Hill complacently having breakfast rations issued to his troops. "No attack ought to be made," Hill thought, "till the men had taken their breakfast."[80] So Hill's men took their breakfast, and Rosecrans took the time to send more reinforcements to his threatened left flank and build entrenchments there, without which the Federal left might well have crumbled under the Confederate assault. By the time Hill felt he was ready, some four hours past the scheduled time, the Federals were ready, too.[81]

The attack finally went in around 10:00 A.M., and when it did, even the reinforced Federal left was barely able to stop the hard-driving Confederates.[82] Repeatedly the Union General Thomas, who commanded on this part of the battlefield, had to call for more men to shore up his sagging lines. Still, the Federal lines held, and it began to appear that Bragg's attack might lead to little more than another day of costly failure. Then the situation took a sudden change.

In response to Bragg's pressure on his left, Rosecrans had become somewhat confused and, in his concern to reinforce the threatened sector, had issued an ambiguous order to a division commander near the center of his line. The order seemed to indicate the division should be pulled out of the line and moved to the left. The division commander obeyed, leaving a great gaping hole in Rosecrans's line. Just then Longstreet launched his attack. His first division, commanded by the aggressive John B. Hood, happened to be aimed directly at the gap in the Union line. The result was devastating. The Confederates surged through the gap and began to roll up brigades and divisions. A third of the Federal army went to pieces. Rosecrans's headquarters were overrun, and the discomfited Union commander galloped up the road to Chattanooga amid the fleeing remnants of his army. Two of his corps commanders fled with him.[83]

The other corps commander was George H. Thomas, a notoriously stubborn fighter. He had held the Round Forest at Murfreesboro, and now, with the reinforced left section of Rosecrans's line and with such other units as could make their way to him out of the collapsing Federal right and center, he fell back a short distance and took up a position on a horseshoe-shaped ridge. Here he withstood attack after attack throughout the long afternoon, finally retreating in good order around sundown, still pressed by the victorious Confederates.[84]

With hindsight it appears that Bragg should have been more vigorous in pursuing the beaten Federals, but at the time there were any number of reasons not to. It was dark. The men were tired. Units were in disarray. A great victory had been won at great cost, and it hardly seemed worthwhile to risk mishap by reckless pursuit of an obviously beaten foe.[85] The next morning Bragg ordered Polk to press after the retreating Federals in the direction of Chattanooga.[86] Polk's cavalry reported that it looked as if the Federals had no intention of stopping at Chattanooga but were hastily preparing to continue northward.[87] Bragg was well content to let them go.

Rosecrans did not go, however. Instead, he began entrenching around Chattanooga while his mangled army mended. Bragg, having lost a third of his army at Chickamauga, was understandably skeptical of the wisdom of assaulting an entrenched Federal army, even one as badly mauled as his own. Lack of supplies and transportation precluded any attempt to go around Rosecrans's flank. Instead, Bragg took possession of the heights that overlooked Chattanooga from the south.[88]

The town of Chattanooga lay in a deep valley. To the southeast stretched the long barrier of Missionary Ridge. To the southwest rose Lookout Mountain. To the north was Waldens Ridge and more rugged country beyond. Through the valley meandered the Tennessee River. Rising in the mountains of East Tennessee, the Tennessee River flowed southwest, past Chattanooga and into Alabama before making a broad curve and flowing due north from the southern border of Tennessee to its mouth at Paducah on the Ohio. Only this last section of the Tennessee, from its mouth to northern Alabama, was accessible to Union gunboats, but barge and boat traffic moved on the river all the way to Chattanooga and beyond. The Tennessee Valley provided the chief supply line for Rosecrans's army in Chattanooga. Supplies were shipped down by rail from Nashville to Bridgeport, Alabama, on the Tennessee River about fifty miles below Chattanooga. From there they could be taken up the river by boat or could travel along the river's banks by road or rail.

Bragg positioned his forces so as to block this flow of supplies. His line began where Missionary Ridge approached the Tennessee River above (that is, to the northeast of) Chattanooga. The line ran along the crest of heavily wooded Missionary Ridge, continued across the valley between Missionary Ridge and Lookout Mountain, over a shoulder of Lookout Mountain, and finally down to the Tennessee River below Chattanooga. It was this latter part of the line, from the mountain on, that created problems for Rosecrans. Confederate artillery and snipers on Lookout Mountain made river, road, and railroad impassable for Union supplies. The only remaining route open to Rosecrans was a miserable wagon road over Waldens Ridge and through the rough country on the other side. The trickle of supplies that could be brought in this way was a mere fraction of the army's needs. The troops were gradually being reduced to a desperate state of hunger, and the army's animals fared even worse. Nor could Rosecrans easily extricate his army from this difficult position. In the presence of the enemy it would be nearly impossible to get everyone out over the same wretched road that was inadequate even to supply the army. In effect Bragg had Rosecrans under siege, and it looked like momentous results might yet come from the hard-fought victory at Chickamauga.[89]

Nevertheless, harmony still did not prevail in the high command of the Army of Tennessee. The hostility to Bragg had poisoned the higher-ranking officers and was beginning to contaminate the rest of the army. An officer from the Army of Northern Virginia, arriving with Longstreet late on the night of the first day's fighting at Chickamauga, had immediately noticed that "Bragg was the subject of hatred and contempt, and it was almost openly so expressed."[90] The next round between Bragg and his subordinates was set off by the commanding general's having the temerity to inquire why his orders had not been obeyed during the recent campaign. Two days after the battle of Chickamauga, Bragg had a note sent to Polk requesting an explanation for the long delay of the attack Bragg had ordered for daybreak on the second day of the battle.[91] The bishop did not deign to reply. Three days later another note was sent, reminding Polk that Bragg expected a report "without delay."[92] It still took Polk another three days to reply.[93] He had important business to attend to first.

The day after Bragg sent his second note to Polk, the bishop made arrangements to meet with Longstreet and Hill, the two lieutenant generals who had recently come to the Army of Tennessee and on whom Polk had not previously had much chance to exercise his charm. He was gratified to find their views entirely compatible with his own. Hill, who was sour and critical by nature, and Longstreet, who considered himself competent to criticize Robert E. Lee, had lost no time in getting into the spirit of things in the Army of Tennessee. The three concurred that Bragg had to go.[94] Polk, aware that the president had already had abundant opportunity to read his opinion of Bragg, wanted Longstreet to write to Davis. Longstreet felt that since Davis had not asked his opinion on military affairs for some time, it would be impertinent to write to him. He did, however, agree to write to Secretary of War Seddon and to Lee, asking them to use their influence with the president to bring about Bragg's downfall.[95] It was then decided that Polk would again presume on his friendship with Davis and write directly to the president for the removal of Bragg.[96]

Longstreet got his letter off that very day. To Seddon he wrote that Bragg had not made a single right move since Longstreet's arrival, except to order the attack at Chickamauga. Longstreet hoped Lee would be sent to replace

Bragg. This change, he assured the secretary of war, was the only ingredient necessary for the complete reconquest of Tennessee. He concluded by stating, "I desire to impress on your mind that there is no exaggeration in these statements," and urging Seddon to act quickly.[97] Longstreet knew Lee had already declined to take the western command and would probably do so again. Since Longstreet, second in rank only to Bragg within the Army of Tennessee, had not silenced the rumors that he was to supersede that unhappy general, it was obvious that he was angling to have the command himself.[98] In fact, this may have been his reason for urging the reinforcement of Bragg's army in the first place. Before he left Virginia, he had suggested to Lee that he (Longstreet) be given command of Bragg's army and Bragg be given command of Longstreet's corps in the Army of Northern Virginia.[99] Failing that, he was now out to steal Bragg's army by other means.

Polk wrote his letters the next day. For added insurance he wrote one to Lee as well as one to Davis.[100] To the president he covered most of the points Longstreet had touched on in his letter to the secretary of war, urging Bragg's replacement by Lee. He also had the nerve to state that Bragg had had "Genl. Rosecrans' army twice at his mercy, and has allowed it to escape both times."[101] Lee responded to Polk and Longstreet by modestly explaining that his health did not permit him to take the western command.[102] Davis made a more aggressive reply, but not before the situation in the Army of Tennessee had further deteriorated.

Two days after his meeting with Longstreet and Hill, Polk finally got around to replying to Bragg's request for an explanation of the delayed attack of September 20. Polk's explanation dumped all of the blame squarely on his fellow conspirator D. H. Hill.[103] Although this was about half true, Bragg was fed up with Polk's disobedience and Polk's attitude. The action Bragg took was probably based as much on Polk's previous acts of insubordination as it was on the case at hand. Four months earlier Bragg had perfectly summarized Polk's character in a letter to Davis: "Genl. Polk by education and habit is unfitted for executing the plans of others. He will convince himself his own are better and follow them without reflecting on the consequences."[104] Now, Bragg was determined to deal with this problem and felt he should have done so long ago.[105] Polk was relieved of his command and ordered to proceed to Atlanta—away from the army—to await orders.[106] The same day a similar order was issued concerning T. C. Hindman, whose disobedience had squandered opportunities on the tenth and eleventh of September.[107]

Polk did not take his removal lying down. He immediately sent notes to the other officers (including Hill) who had been involved in the September 20 attack, asking them to provide information with which he could justify himself at a court of inquiry.[108] To the secretary of war he wrote protesting Bragg's "arbitrary and unlawful order" and requesting a court of inquiry.[109] To Davis he erupted in another violent diatribe against Bragg, claiming that the delay in the attack had been inconsequential and, in any case, had not been his (Polk's) fault. Polk was becoming more and more aggrieved with Davis for not ridding him of Bragg, and this letter displays for the first time a certain stiffness toward the president.[110] Most of Polk's wrath, however, was directed at Bragg, toward whom he seethed with hatred. To his daughter Polk wrote, "I feel a lofty contempt for his puny effort to inflict injury upon a man who dry-nursed him for the whole period of his connection with him, and has kept him from ruining the cause of the country by the sacrifice of its armies."[111]

While Polk fumed in Atlanta, the strife continued within the Army of Tennessee. Unfortunately, the enmity had progressed so far by the time Bragg took concrete action against it that the punishment of Polk and Hindman, rather than serving as an example to the other officers and reminding them of their duty, only goaded them to further acts of insubordination. On October 4 another secret meeting was held by the dissidents, this one including most if not all of the anti-Bragg corps and division commanders. A petition to the president was drawn up, bitterly denouncing Bragg while making loud pretenses of respectfulness.[112] Just who wrote this extraordinary document is not clear. Longstreet, who undoubtedly played a leading role in the affair, denied authorship and said Hill wrote it.[113] Years later Hill admitted that he had gladly signed the petition but said Buckner wrote it.[114] Much of the evidence seems to point to Buckner. His name was apparently the first one placed on the petition, and Buckner had been mentioned as a possible replacement for Bragg, so he was not without a personal motive.[115]

Back in Richmond a much-dismayed Jefferson Davis observed with growing alarm the turmoil in the Confederacy's main western army. The case would obviously demand some action on his part, and the aspect that required the most immediate attention—or so Davis felt—was Bragg's removal of Polk. As a routine matter Bragg had notified the Adjutant and Inspector General's Office, headed by Cooper, of the action he had taken.[116] Cooper immediately realized that this was something the president would want to see and promptly sent the dispatch on to him. Davis returned it with a notation that Bragg could arrest an officer but could not merely relieve that officer of command without arresting him; and, if he did arrest him, Bragg would have to bring formal charges against the officer before a court-martial.[117] It was an absurd technicality. Davis was unhappy with Bragg's action, and true to his nature when angry or under pressure, he resorted to legalities and technicalities.

Cooper dutifully forwarded the substance of Davis's note to Bragg, but by the next day the president had collected his thoughts and sent Bragg a telegram himself.[118] It was "unfortunate," he said, that Bragg had not simply pointed out the problem to Polk "to prevent its recurrence" and then maintained accord in the army "by abstaining from further action." He concluded by stating, "It is now believed that the order in [Polk's] case should be countermanded."[119]

Bragg replied that "the case is flagrant and but a repetition of the past." If

Davis was going to restore Polk, then he had better do the same for Hindman. If this were done, Bragg hoped that Polk might be sent to Mississippi in exchange for Hardee, who would then take Polk's place in the Army of Tennessee.[120] Davis was still determined to convince Bragg to reinstate Polk voluntarily, and for that purpose he wrote Bragg a somewhat longer letter. He could understand, he said, Bragg's frustration that all had not gone as he had planned it, but removing Polk would only stir up strife. "Believing that he [Polk] possessed the confidence and affection of his corps, it seemed to be better that his influence in your favor should be preserved by a lenient course."[121] Obviously, Davis was completely out of touch with reality. He did at least recognize shortly after writing this letter that nothing was going to be solved in this manner. Therefore, at the urging of one of his aides who was with the Army of Tennessee and had some idea of the turmoil there, Davis decided to pay a personal visit to Bragg.[122]

Leaving Richmond on October 6 and stopping over in Atlanta for a briefing from his aide, the president arrived at Bragg's headquarters on the ninth.[123] While in Atlanta he had also talked to Polk and been completely convinced that Bragg's action against that general was unjustified.[124] The formal charges Bragg had filed would be dismissed and Polk restored.[125] At this Polk balked. He was looking forward to an official court of inquiry, which he was planning to turn into more of a trial of Bragg than of himself.[126] In any case he absolutely refused to serve under Bragg again. Though Davis would not agree to dismiss Bragg as Polk wanted, he did promise to have Polk transferred to Mississippi.[127]

Upon his arrival at Bragg's headquarters, Davis had a long conference with him. Bragg offered to resign if that would help the cause, but Davis had other ideas.[128] He was contemplating a bold strategy for restoring harmony to the Army of Tennessee. He may have had this plan in mind before leaving Richmond and may have discussed it with Seddon.[129] Davis would call a council at which he, Bragg, and the four senior generals of the army—Longstreet, Hill, Buckner, and Cheatham—would be present. Then he would ask each general to express his opinion of Bragg. Apparently Davis reasoned that the reported hostility to Bragg was greatly exaggerated and that even if some of the generals had been engaging in loose talk here and there, they would surely profess loyalty to Bragg in his presence and the president's.[130] The generals would then be on record as supporting Bragg and would feel compelled to live up to their statements. Bragg, in turn, would be reassured that his generals really did support him, and he could thus be more lenient with their mistakes.

The council was called, and the four generals assembled. Davis opened the meeting by initiating a roundtable discussion of the military situation and the army's plans and prospects for the future before bringing up the real purpose of the gathering. Turning to Longstreet, the senior of the four, he asked for his opinion of Bragg. Longstreet, not wishing to seem too eager, made a half-hearted attempt to dodge the question, but Davis insisted on a straight answer. He got one—no doubt much to his embarrassment and Bragg's mortification.[131] Jefferson Davis was nothing if not a stubborn man, and he now doggedly stuck to his plan as it proceeded to miscarry in the most horrifying fashion. Buckner was next in seniority, and he gave the same answer: Bragg had to go. Davis was genuinely surprised, for he had expected better from the normally chivalrous Kentuckian. "Why, General Buckner," he blurted, "General Bragg recommended you for promotion in this recent action." Buckner, who was no doubt thinking of promotion to the position Bragg now occupied, remained adamant. Davis, to his credit, found such ingratitude impossible to comprehend. Through what must have been an extraordinary exercise of will, the president managed to remain cool and amiable during the rest of the discussion as the two other corps commanders expressed similar opinions. Bragg sat quietly and said nothing throughout the ordeal. One observer later remarked that he seemed "a little confused."[132]

The meeting must have been excruciating for Davis (to say nothing of Bragg), for he was very reticent about it afterward. In a dispatch to Seddon several days later he said enigmatically, "The conversation was held, but was of little importance."[133] Several months later he denied that he had asked the generals for an expression of their opinion on Bragg, and in his lengthy two-volume memoirs, written after the war, he neglected to mention the episode altogether.[134]

Despite the open hostility of the generals to Bragg, Davis decided to maintain him in command of the Army of Tennessee. His reason was not so much confidence in Bragg as lack of anyone better to take his place. Beauregard would have been a disaster, and Davis was not yet desperate enough to try Joseph E. Johnston again. Lee was needed in Virginia. Hardee, off in Mississippi, was a lackluster sort, and Davis apparently had too much respect for military discipline to appoint someone like Polk, Longstreet, or Buckner, each of whom had strenuously agitated against Bragg. Davis was in an impossible situation. He had allowed Polk and his band of malcontents to undermine Bragg so completely that to support Bragg properly would now require sacking half the officer corps of the Army of Tennessee. The alternative was undermining discipline by granting a victory to insubordination, removing Bragg, and replacing him with someone who would very likely be inferior. Davis still tended to underrate the problems that could be caused by dissension among officers. "My recollections of my military life," he wrote a few weeks later, "do not enable me to regard as necessary that there should be kind personal relations between officers to secure their effective cooperation in all which is official."[135] Davis believed that others would try as hard as he did to overcome personal hostilities for the good of the cause. Thus it was natural that, of the two unsatisfactory options available to him, he chose to retain Bragg.

Bragg was not at all sure that he ought to be retained. In fact, he was determined to step down, and it was only with difficulty that Davis was able to persuade him not to. Bragg insisted that if he stayed, "he would never countenance disobedience of or non-compliance with orders from any officer, however high in position, regardless of consequences." Davis assured him of his support in this policy.[136] Thus encouraged, Bragg determined to rid himself of Hill.[137] In a way this had been the president's suggestion. In writing to Bragg to persuade him to let Polk off the hook, Davis had argued that it would not be fair to punish Polk while passing over Hill, who was generally acknowledged to have been more guilty in the incident.[138] Bragg had thought about it for a few days and decided the president was right. Davis granted Bragg's request for the general's removal, and Hill—unlike Polk—was left to languish at home the rest of the war without an assignment.[139] The cancer of discontentment, however, was not to be so easily excised.

Davis remained at Bragg's headquarters for several days, dealing with a number of issues. One of them was the question of what to do with John C. Pemberton, former defender of Vicksburg. Pemberton had accompanied Davis on his visit to the army, and the president, who still had complete faith in the Pennsylvanian, hoped a corps command could be found for him. Bragg was willing to be helpful, and no doubt any change would have been a welcome relief after the likes of Polk, Hill, and Longstreet; but discreet inquiry revealed that the army would mutiny if Pemberton were given any command.[140] Another matter was the army's future operations. Bragg proposed and Davis accepted a plan to get behind the Federal army and force its withdrawal, much as Bragg had done to Buell's army in this same region little over a year before.[141] Apparently no one had much faith in the chances of starving Rosecrans out of Chattanooga. In any case, the movement, which was to be started as soon as the army could be prepared, was postponed indefinitely because heavy rains had made the roads impassable.[142]

Then there was the matter of Forrest. The unorthodox cavalry leader had also run afoul of Bragg. Several weeks earlier he had proposed, both through channels and in a direct letter to Jefferson Davis, that he be allowed to take four hundred men behind enemy lines in northern Mississippi, West Tennessee, and western Kentucky. There he hoped to recruit a large force and operate against the enemy. The idea had appealed both to the president and to Bragg, but both men thought it would be unwise at the moment in view of the pending showdown with Rosecrans.[143] Forrest had stayed with the Army of Tennessee and fought well at Chickamauga, but after the battle problems had arisen. Bragg made certain changes within the Army of Tennessee's cavalry that were not to Forrest's liking, and he told Bragg as much in an apparently insubordinate letter. After a face-to-face meeting, Forrest thought Bragg had come over to his point of view, but when the cavalryman returned from a ten-day furlough, he found Bragg had made other unwelcome changes.

At this Forrest went into a towering rage. Taking a staff officer with him, he stormed off to army headquarters. Bragg, who had no idea that Forrest was on the warpath again, stood up, walked around his desk, and extended his hand in greeting. Forrest left him standing that way and launched into a furious tirade. "I have stood your meanness as long as I intend to," he roared. "You have played the part of a . . . scoundrel, and are a coward, and if you were any part of a man I would slap your jowls and force you to resent it. You may as well not issue any more orders to me, for I will not obey them. . . . and I say to you that if you ever again try to interfere with me or cross my path it will be at peril of your life." With that he turned on his heel and stalked out, his staff officer close behind.

Bragg decided to overlook the affair, not because he was a coward–that he certainly was not–but because he did not want Forrest's valuable services to be lost to the South as the result of the court-martial Forrest had coming to him. Besides, Bragg did not consider Forrest as a real army officer but as an effective and highly irregular guerrilla leader.[144]

Yet if the outburst could be overlooked, the general situation with respect to Forrest could not, especially since Forrest, after thinking about it a few more days, sent his resignation to Bragg for forwarding to Richmond. However, Davis was by this time at Bragg's headquarters, and since he was anxious that Forrest not be lost to the service, he took a personal interest in the dispute. Writing Forrest a gracious letter declining his resignation, Davis suggested they meet in Montgomery, Alabama, several days later to talk things over. This seemed to satisfy Forrest.[145]

On October 13 Davis prepared to leave.[146] Before returning to Richmond, he intended to visit Johnston's command in Mississippi to see if any more troops could be spared to reinforce Bragg.[147] The night before he was to depart the president was called upon to make a speech, and he did his best to garner support for Bragg. A newspaper described his speech as "complimenting Gen. Bragg in the highest terms." The president "said that notwithstanding the shafts of malice that had been hurled at [Bragg], he had bravely borne it all, and the bloody field of Chickamauga plainly stamps him as a military commander of this first order."[148] This was more or less true, but Bragg's enemies were probably beyond influencing.[149]

After visiting Mississippi Davis traveled back to Montgomery, Alabama, and there met with Forrest as arranged. The two then journeyed together to Atlanta. Before leaving Army of Tennessee headquarters, Davis had discussed with Bragg the advisability of Forrest's earlier proposal to operate behind Union lines in northern Mississippi and West Tennessee; at Davis's urging Bragg had given his tentative consent. Now after talking with Forrest, Davis wrote Bragg from Atlanta again advising that Forrest's request be granted. Acquiescing in the president's judgment, Bragg issued the necessary orders, and Forrest was on his way.[150]

The president's second trip to the West had failed to achieve harmony in the Army of Tennessee, and after his departure, the bickering went on. With Polk and Hill gone, the torch was taken up by Longstreet and Buckner. It was

Buckner who had the next serious squabble with Bragg. Bragg, with his gruff exterior, and Buckner, with his high regard for smoothness and style, were such a contrast in personalities that they were almost bound to clash. Besides, Buckner was not above jealousy and bitterness at not advancing in rank as rapidly as he had hoped, and these feelings he seemed to vent on Bragg.[151] The immediate occasion of their collision was a matter of military procedure that would not ordinarily have resulted in conflict. When Buckner had come south with most of his force to join Bragg at Chattanooga, a few regiments of his command had gone the other direction into southwestern Virginia and had since been incorporated into the Confederate forces operating there. Inexplicably, Buckner continued to act as if he commanded an independent department that included the troops in southwestern Virginia.[152] He sent officers to command them and orders for them to carry out.[153] Bragg instructed him to stop but to no avail. Finally Davis had to step in, and at last Buckner was induced to obey.[154] Bragg, however, was understandably reluctant to have such a man as a corps commander. Rearranging his army, he reduced Buckner to command of a division. The Kentuckian was furious and wrote a number of violently abusive letters to Bragg.[155] Bragg, attempting as he had promised Davis to show "forbearance but firmness," did not put the insubordinate letters on file but returned them to Buckner "for his reconsideration, and with a hope that he will calmly review his course and withdraw [them]."[156]

Further reorganization of the army's command system was aimed at breaking up cliques—within corps, divisions, and brigades—of officers who were feeding one another's animosity toward Bragg. This was especially true of units that included a high percentage of officers from Kentucky or Tennessee.[157] The Tennesseeans hated Bragg because of his disagreements with their native sons—the popular but incompetent McCown and the even more popular but somewhat irresponsible Cheatham. The Kentuckians had never forgiven Bragg for his frankness over Kentucky's failure to support the Confederate invasion in 1862. As final moves in reorganization, Breckinridge was elevated to corps command, and Hardee, in accordance with the agreement between Polk, Bragg, and Davis, was brought over from Mississippi to command Polk's old corps. How little Davis understood the true state of affairs among his generals is indicated by the fact that he expected Hardee to be a peacemaker and an influence for harmony and good discipline within the army.[158]

While the Army of Tennessee's generals continued skirmishing with their commander and its morale sank lower and lower, the northern army in Chattanooga was preparing to extricate itself from its difficult position. The Washington authorities had been very displeased with Rosecrans after his defeat at Chickamauga, and their displeasure mounted as he kept his army docilely in Chattanooga and allowed Bragg to besiege him. Lincoln noted that since the battle of Chickamauga Rosecrans had acted "confused and stunned like a duck hit on the head."[159] The unfortunate northern general was soon relieved of his command and replaced by George H. Thomas, "The Rock of Chickamauga." More important, U. S. Grant was given overall command of all Federal forces in the West. Grant determined to go to Chattanooga and supervise personally the operations there. Reinforcements were on the way as well. Sherman was to follow Grant as quickly as possible with a large portion of the army that had taken Vicksburg, and from Virginia two small corps of the Army of the Potomac were rushed west by rail. Altogether, over 37,000 Federal reinforcements would soon be arriving in Chattanooga.[160]

Grant's first task upon arriving in the besieged city was to open up a supply line for the nearly starving army. A plan had already been devised for this purpose, and this Grant quickly executed. Just below Chattanooga the Tennessee River turned to the south and flowed in that direction to the base of Lookout Mountain before making a sharp bend back to the north. It was this convolution of the river, known as Moccasin Bend, that brought the river with its attendant road and railroad within range of Confederate artillery and sharpshooters on Lookout Mountain. The Federal plan was to build a wagon road across the base of the narrow peninsula formed by Moccasin Bend, then attack and drive back the part of the Confederate line that extended past Lookout Mountain. The Confederate line there was anchored on the Tennessee River at Brown's Ferry, and if the Federals could control this place, they would reopen the Tennessee Valley as a supply route and the starving times would be over in Chattanooga. The plan was put into action on the night of October 26. A Union brigade floated down the river in boats and landed at Brown's Ferry, overwhelming the sparse Confederate defenders. Within hours a pontoon bridge was thrown across the river at that point, and Federal troops were crossing in force.

Longstreet commanded the Confederate troops in this sector, and his handling of the affair could hardly have been worse. Some explanation for this can be traced to the Georgian's dissatisfaction with Bragg—and with Davis for failing to give Longstreet command of the Army of Tennessee. Besides, he had been opposed to besieging Chattanooga from the start.[161] When James Longstreet was not getting his way, he tended to become obtuse almost to the point of deliberately sabotaging his commander's plans. However, Longstreet's miserable performance at Brown's Ferry also stemmed from an unbelievably petty game of power politics Longstreet was playing within his own corps.

When John B. Hood had been wounded during the battle of Gettysburg, command of his division had devolved upon senior brigade commander Evander McIvor Law. Though Law had done a fine job of leading the division through that battle, Longstreet later brought in a protégé of his, Brig. Gen. Micah Jenkins. Since Jenkins ranked Law, he would have de facto command of the division in the absence of Hood. It was largely for this reason that Hood's officers, who abhorred the incompetent Jenkins, talked Hood into returning to the division for the Chickamauga campaign (not that Hood needed much convincing).[162] With Hood once again wounded and apparently out of action more or less permanently, Jenkins again succeeded to temporary command. The question was who would get the promotion to major general and permanent command of the division. Not surprisingly, Longstreet's choice was Jenkins, but the officers of the division were unanimous for Law, who was in any case the better officer. When Davis had visited the army to try to clear up the larger problems involving Bragg and his generals, he had also talked to Longstreet about this situation, urging that he accept Law. Longstreet agreed at last that Law should have the promotion. Davis said nothing more about it, leaving Longstreet to handle the formal arrangements. Then with Davis gone, Longstreet defiantly gave the promotion to Jenkins. Through all of this Longstreet and Jenkins seem to have developed a resentment of Law, as if they and not he were the aggrieved parties. This small-minded feuding had a significant role in the fiasco that allowed the opening of the Union supply line.

The left wing of Longstreet's front was held by Jenkins's division, and the crucial sector in the valley beyond Lookout Mountain was assigned to Law. Jenkins gave Law only two regiments for this task. Law realized at once that a full division would be needed to hold this part of the line and so informed Longstreet, but the most the stubborn corps commander would do was have Jenkins send the other three regiments of Law's brigade. The next day, however, Jenkins ordered the three regiments back over the mountain; and Longstreet, despite repeated warnings from Law as well as notices from Bragg that the enemy seemed to be preparing a movement in that direction, let things stand that way. The result was that when the Federals launched their attack, all that stood in their way was a virtual token force. Law did what he could, but he was bound to fail. Apparently, that was what Longstreet and Jenkins had intended.[163]

To top off his mishandling of this incident, Longstreet completely neglected to inform Bragg of what had happened. Bragg, having heard firing during the night, dispatched a staff officer to the top of Lookout Mountain the next morning to see what was going on. This officer saw that Union troops had made a lodgment at Brown's Ferry and so reported to Bragg. Bragg was "incensed" and had good reason to be.[164] It was obvious that the Federals were attempting to open a supply line. If they did, Bragg's plan of starving the Union army in Chattanooga (he had given up on the idea of striking for the Union rear) would be ruined. It was crucial that the Federals at Brown's Ferry be thrown back across the river.

Bragg at once ordered Longstreet to counterattack and retake the position, but the day of October 27 passed with no action. At nightfall Bragg renewed his order, telling Longstreet he was free to use all of his own corps plus a division of another corps. About ten o'clock the next morning Bragg went up to Lookout Mountain himself to see why he heard no firing. There he met

Longstreet and to his surprise learned that no preparations had been made for an attack. Again Longstreet was ordered to attack. This time he requested yet another division to support him. Bragg granted his request, and then, inexplicably, Longstreet informed Bragg that he intended to use no more than a brigade for the actual assault. Bragg ordered him to use no less than a division, but when the attack was finally made before dawn on the morning of October 29, more than two days after the Federal landing, Longstreet employed only two small brigades, more or less as he had planned.[165] The explanation seems to have been Longstreet's continuing attempts to make Jenkins look good at Law's expense. He got Law out of the way by sending him with two brigades to take up a blocking position to prevent the Federals from bringing in more troops than were already present, while Jenkins, with the division's other two brigades, would make the actual attack. Thus Jenkins would win all the glory and the acceptance of the men of the division. As it turned out, there was no glory to be had. Neither force, Law's nor Jenkins's, was nearly large enough for the task Longstreet had assigned it.[166] The result was a disaster, and the last chance to close off the new Union supply line, dubbed by jubilant Federals the "Cracker Line," was gone.[167]

After the opening of the Cracker Line, Grant sat back to await the arrival of his reinforcements. For a time all was quiet around Chattanooga. Bragg had to decide what to do next, now that his siege of Chattanooga had been broken. The plan he adopted was one that had been proffered by Davis. A few days earlier the president had written to Bragg suggesting that if nothing much else was going on he might detach Longstreet's corps to chase Burnside out of East Tennessee. This would be doubly beneficial since it would put Longstreet in a position from which he could quickly rejoin Lee by way of southwestern Virginia.[168] This whole scheme had, in turn, been suggested to Davis by Lee, who was extremely concerned about the weakened condition of his army and anxious to have Longstreet's troops back.[169]

Bragg thought the idea was sound and immediately took steps to send Longstreet on his way.[170] In this his judgment was probably affected by his desire to be rid of the disobedient Longstreet, as well as by the fact that he simply did not know what else to do. The move was a foolish one, for it weakened Bragg's already outnumbered army just when Grant was almost ready to strike. Bragg compounded the mistake when, on November 22, he dispatched Buckner's division to reinforce Longstreet.[171] Longstreet had asked for help, and perhaps it was tempting to be rid of Buckner as well.

By November 13 all of Grant's reinforcements had arrived, and ten days later his long-awaited offensive was launched.[172] The first day's fighting was not particularly spectacular: The center of Grant's line under Thomas drove in Bragg's pickets in front of Missionary Ridge.[173] Grant's plan for the next day called for Thomas to threaten the Confederate center and for other Federal forces to assault Lookout Mountain; meanwhile, the main attack would be carried out by Sherman's men at the other end of the line against the Confederate right flank on the extreme northeastern end of Missionary Ridge.[174] However, events did not unfold as Grant had planned. On Sherman's front the Confederate position that had appeared the weakest actually turned out to be quite strong. In addition, the Confederates there were commanded by the best division commander in the Army of Tennessee, Pat Cleburne.

After being wounded at the battle of Richmond, Kentucky, in September of the previous year, Cleburne had returned to duty in time to be wounded again at the battle of Perryville. After another speedy recovery, he returned to his command in time to save the army's wagon trains, which a panicked Kirby Smith was considering destroying on the retreat from Kentucky. In December 1862 Cleburne had finally been promoted to major general; in fact Davis had brought the commission with him when he visited the army during that month.[175]

Unfortunately, Cleburne was under the influence of Hardee, his corps commander. As a result he became embroiled in the anti-Bragg feuding that followed the battle of Murfreesboro. When Bragg sent out his circular, Cleburne, conforming to the actions of Hardee and the other generals in his corps, responded by stating that Bragg had lost the confidence of the army and should resign.[176] Aside from the overall damage to the Confederacy of undermining Bragg, Cleburne's individual contribution made him appear contentious and insubordinate and hurt his chances of advancement. Though Davis might be slow to remove those (especially his prewar friend Polk) who were so viciously maligning Bragg, he would be equally slow to reward insubordination by promoting anyone who had played even a small role in the matter. One can hardly fault Davis for this basically sound policy, but holding to it in Cleburne's case certainly cost the South a great deal. The struggling Confederacy could ill afford to waste his genius in any other position than the highest he was capable of filling.

Cleburne gave another demonstration of that genius when Sherman and his Federals tried to drive him out of the rugged jumble of hills at the northeast end of Missionary Ridge. He was badly outnumbered, and Sherman's men were tough veterans who believed they could not be stopped. On this day, however, it seemed that no army in the world would be able to dislodge Cleburne. In desperate fighting that was sometimes hand-to-hand, Cleburne skillfully used every advantage of terrain and repulsed all of Sherman's furious assaults.[177]

At the other end of the line, however, the Federal diversionary attack on Lookout Mountain turned into a startling success. The Confederate position here was actually not as strong as it appeared, since the rocky peak of the mountain was of no tactical military value. The Confederate line ran along the shoulder of the mountain about half-way up. The position was but sparsely manned, and the Confederate division commander in charge of the defenses showed himself to be incapable. By nightfall the Federals were in possession of the mountain, and the beaten Confederates withdrew to join the forces on Missionary Ridge.[178]

The next day, November 25, Sherman renewed his attack on Cleburne with no more success than before. The Confederates simply could not be pushed back. To assist Sherman, Grant ordered the Union troops on Lookout Mountain to threaten the Confederate left on Missionary Ridge. When this still failed to cause Bragg to weaken his right flank, Grant, around two o'clock in the afternoon, instructed Thomas to advance and take the line of rifle pits at the base of Missionary Ridge.[179]

The sector of the Confederate line that included Missionary Ridge was held by the men of John C. Breckinridge's corps. Breckinridge, only recently elevated to corps command, had been acting strangely of late. At a council of war Bragg had called after the previous day's loss of Lookout Mountain, Breckinridge, contrary to the urgings of the other corps commanders, had argued vehemently that the army could and should hold its ground on Missionary Ridge. He was overflowing with bravado, but his arguments were irrational.[180] Irrational was also a good description of his behavior on the day of the battle. Early that afternoon he had sent off a courier with a verbal order. When the courier returned, Breckinridge asked him to repeat the order. Though the hapless soldier recited it word for word, Breckinridge flew into a rage. While those present watched in embarrassment, he called for another courier and reissued the order in a slightly different form.[181] Whatever the reason for Breckinridge's confused state of mind (Bragg would later report that the hard-drinking Kentucky politician had been inebriated throughout the battle[182]), his corps was very poorly disposed to receive an attack. Whether Breckinridge had made the arrangements himself or merely acquiesced in the mistakes of a subordinate, some inexplicable blunders had been made in plotting the defensive positions. In the first place, the main defense line was laid out along the geographical crest of the ridge (the highest point) rather than the military crest (a point on the forward brow of the ridge from which the entire slope was visible). This meant that attacking forces would be sheltered from the defenders' fire by the contour of the ridge itself for at least part of the trip up the slope. It also meant the attackers could pause to catch their breath just under the brow of the ridge before making the final rush at Confederate lines. Another strange disposition was that only two-thirds to three-fourths of the defenders were placed in the main line. The remainder, rather than being held in reserve, were located in a cordon of rifle pits at the base of the ridge out in front of the primary position.[183] It was these rifle pits that Grant ordered Thomas to take.

It took time to get the Federal army situated for the attack, but by 3:30 P.M. all was in readiness, and the troops advanced.[184] There were some 20,000 of them, more than Pickett had had in his famous charge at Gettysburg, and they created a formidable spectacle as their orderly ranks moved across nearly a mile of open ground, much of it under artillery fire from the crest of the ridge, to reach the Confederate rifle pits.[185] The defenders here at the bottom of the slope were hopelessly outnumbered. They were too many for a skirmish line but too few to stop an assault. The troops were not sure whether they were expected to fire a volley and fall back or make a determined stand. In the face of the overwhelming mass of Federal troops advancing on them, most of the Confederates stampeded and began clambering up the ridge as fast as they could go.[186]

Having possessed themselves of the line of rifle pits at the base of the ridge, Thomas's men had done all that their orders required. At this point, however, it developed that some of the units had ambiguous orders and their officers thought they were to continue on and storm the ridge. In other units officers quickly realized that the rifle pits were exposed to Confederate fire and that the men would actually be safer on their way up the slope than staying where they were. Other outfits simply plunged upward because their neighboring commands had done so. Watching the battle from the top of a knoll near the town, Grant realized a general assault was under way and angrily wanted to know who had ordered it. Thomas and the other officers standing nearby assured him they had not, and Grant muttered grimly that if the charge failed someone was going to pay.[187]

On top of the ridge Bragg, too, knew that an assault was in motion. He had visited Cleburne's position that morning and, satisfied with the state of affairs there, was now back on the central section of the ridge. Bragg watched the Union troops advance, confident that his line could stop them. At least for the section where Bragg was, that confidence proved justified, as the thin Confederate line held. Bragg was riding along the line congratulating the troops when he received word that the Federals had broken through and were on top of the ridge farther north. Reinforcements were quickly dispatched to plug the breach, but they were unable to stem the flood of Federal troops who were pouring up onto the ridge, fanning out to the left and right and taking the defenders in flank. The reinforcements were swept back along with the rest of the disintegrating line. It then developed that the Confederate line had also given way to the south of Bragg's position.[188] In fact, the Confederate line on top of Missionary Ridge had been pierced at half a dozen different points almost simultaneously, and presently it started going to pieces.[189] "A panic which I had never before witnessed," Bragg later wrote, "seemed to have seized upon officers and men, and each seemed to be struggling for his own personal safety, regardless of his duty or his character."[190]

Bragg's enemies had accused him of many things, most of them untrue, but few had ever suggested he lacked personal courage. Now, with his army going to pieces around him and the exultant foe in hot pursuit, he rode into the fleeing mob, calling on the men to rally around him. "Here's your commander!" he shouted. From among the fleeing rabble someone yelled back, "Here's your mule!"–the punch line of a favorite joke among Confederate soldiers.[191]

Not all the Confederate officers on the ridge took the same attitude Bragg did. As his troops broke for the rear, Breckinridge yelled, "Boys, get away the best you can."[192] Perhaps it was no use anyway. Intent on escape, the troops streamed down the back side of the ridge in a frenzied stampede.[193] Meanwhile, at the northeastern end of the ridge where Cleburne's men had held out stubbornly against Sherman's repeated attacks, the Irish general managed to position a couple of brigades across the ridge to prevent his division from being rolled up like the rest of the army. His men retreated in good order and, along with the few other units that had maintained their discipline, gradually fell back, fighting hard to cover the retreat until late into the night.[194]

The successful Union assault on Missionary Ridge had come as a shock to both victor and vanquished, as well it might have. After the war when it was suggested to Grant that Bragg had considered Missionary Ridge impregnable, he replied with a smile, "Well, it was impregnable."[195] Certainly, the climax of the battle of Chattanooga was one of the incidents of the Civil War that, by all the rules, simply should not have happened. It was true that Bragg's line had been thin–he lacked manpower partially as a result of sending Longstreet and Buckner to East Tennessee–but thinner lines had held weaker positions and inflicted fearful punishment on attackers at other times during the war. It was also true that the Confederate position was not well laid out and that the retreat of the men from the rifle pits at the base of the ridge caused confusion and sometimes blocked the fire of their comrades on the crest. Finally, the Federal attack was unusually determined and resolute. Yet somehow all this fails to explain why the Army of Tennessee disintegrated as it did. Given the advantage that was held by the tactical defensive throughout the Civil War, Bragg seems justified in stating later that "the position was one which ought to have been held by a line of skirmishers against any assaulting column." Bragg was not able to account for the failure.[196] Something more than mere tactical factors had been at work here, and the most probable explanation is that the army had become completely demoralized and had lost faith in its commander as a result of the bickering and backbiting by most of the army's generals against Bragg.[197] It had taken a long time, but distrust of Bragg had finally filtered down through the ranks to the private soldiers; the men, haunted by the fear that their lives might be sacrificed through a blunder of their commander– a blunder they had come to believe was very likely–were unable to face the test of battle.

From near the old Chickamauga battlefield where the first night's retreat had paused, Bragg sent a telegram notifying Richmond of the disaster.[198] Davis replied immediately that he hoped Bragg would be able to scrape up enough troops from rear areas to stop the Federals, but to no avail.[199] Bragg was forced to withdraw to Ringgold, Georgia, and then, on the third day after the battle, to Dalton, nearly thirty miles from Chattanooga.[200] The only reason he was able to stop there rather than retreat right on through Atlanta and beyond was that the Union army lacked horses, mules, and wagons and needed a thorough refitting that would take several months. Besides, Grant wanted to detach some of his troops to chase Longstreet out of East Tennessee, where that officer had been conducting an uninspired campaign that confined Burnside to the Knoxville fortifications but achieved little else.[201]

It was now Longstreet's turn to come in for some criticism; as his nickname was "Pete," his soldiers started calling him (behind his back) "Peter the Slow."[202] His efforts in East Tennessee had been hindered by his constant quibbling with and scheming against certain of his officers. He continued his vendetta against Evander McIvor Law, finally removing that officer from command. He also sacked and brought charges against two of his division commanders, ostensibly for failing to show enough confidence in Longstreet's highly questionable plans for the campaign. In at least one of these cases, however, that of Lafayette McLaws, the real reason seems to have been that McLaws refused to join Longstreet and the others in plotting against Bragg while Longstreet and his troops were still back in Chattanooga.[203] With a substantial portion of his energies diverted to his imagined personal enemies within Confederate ranks, Longstreet sleepwalked through the East Tennessee campaign, concluding it by getting a large number of his men slaughtered in the sort of useless head-on assault he so liked to condemn in his superiors. Now, with Bragg defeated and Grant sending a powerful force to aid Burnside, Longstreet had to fall back into extreme northeastern Tennessee, where he spent an unhappy winter before continuing through southwestern Virginia to rejoin Lee and the Army of Northern Virginia.

The debacle at Chattanooga fanned the flames of criticism against Bragg, and demands for his removal came from all quarters.[204] Bragg himself felt it was time that he step down, and four days after the battle, as soon as the situation had settled down somewhat, he requested to be relieved.[205] This time Davis immediately granted his request.[206] On December 2 Bragg officially turned over command of the Army of Tennessee to Hardee, the senior officer present, and left for a much-needed rest.[207] In a letter to Davis the day before stepping down, Bragg referred to the defeat at Missionary Ridge as "my shameful discomfiture" and took responsibility for the loss. "The disaster admits of no palliation," he wrote, "and is justly disparaging to me as a commander." Then, before passing on to other matters, he remarked trenchantly, "I fear we both erred in the conclusion for me to retain command here after the clamour raised against me."[208]

The events of the summer and fall of 1863 provide one of the gloomiest chapters in the story of Jefferson Davis's exercise of the role of commander in chief. Though he had tried hard and had made some moves that were necessary and proper, even these actions turned out to be too little, too late, while his mistakes were disastrous.

Davis had failed to take quick and decisive action to strengthen Bragg for a counterstrike once Rosecrans's maneuvering had forced Bragg back to Chattanooga. In part this was because much of Davis's attention was still focused on his squabble with Joseph E. Johnston over trivialities of the wretched Vicksburg campaign. The action Davis finally took, combining Bragg's and Buckner's departments and offering Bragg the troops under Johnston's command, was sound but did not go far enough. He should have transferred Buckner's and Johnston's forces to Bragg along with everything that could be spared from the rest of the Confederacy; put a man he could trust over the whole; and let it be known that he expected aggressive measures in the near future. However, Davis lacked the self-confidence to bring off such decisive action.

The president's decision to send troops from Lee's army to reinforce Bragg was commendable. It took a great deal for Davis to overcome his solicitude for the prestigious—and nearby—Virginia front. Unfortunately, it also took too long: two weeks of conference with Robert E. Lee, on whom Davis was coming to lean ever more heavily as disaster after disaster rocked the faltering Confederacy. By the time Davis resolved to send the reinforcements, the direct rail link between Richmond and Chattanooga had been broken, and the Confederacy's slim chance of holding the vitally strategic city of Chattanooga had given way to an even slimmer chance of retaking it. Once again the president's hesitation and uncertainty had proved costly.

The mistake by which Davis did the most harm to Bragg's chances for success in the Chickamauga campaign, however, had been made long before. By leaving both Polk and Bragg in the Army of Tennessee, Davis had allowed such demoralization to develop within the army's officer corps that three good opportunities were wasted before the armies actually met at Chickamauga and Bragg's conduct of the battle itself was handicapped. Davis, apparently unable to believe his friend Polk guilty of such duplicity, had no comprehension of the true state of affairs in the army. Yet even after the battle when the real situation was brought home to him in the most forceful manner by Bragg's disciplinary action against Polk and the subsequent miscarriage of Davis's personal effort to restore harmony, Davis still did not take concrete action to solve the problem. Solving the problem could mean only one thing. A year earlier cashiering Polk and a few others would have sufficed. By mid-1863 Bragg's usefulness had been destroyed. Though not primarily through any fault of his own, he had become a liability and should have been removed. He had sensed this and wanted to step down but had stayed at Davis's urging. The president had indeed erred.

Davis's suggestion that Bragg send Longstreet to East Tennessee while the armies were facing each other at Chattanooga was another mistake and a hard one to understand. Bragg was already badly outnumbered, and detaching troops and further lengthening the odds made little sense. Perhaps Davis simply felt uneasy at having the army sit idle while the foe took the initiative. It would have been in character for the Confederate president to believe that any action was preferable to waiting for the enemy to choose the time, place, and circumstances of battle. Such a view had much to recommend it, but in this case the action Davis suggested and Bragg carried out was worse than no action at all.

After the defeat at Chattanooga, Davis finally acquiesced in Bragg's request to step down. It was the right move, but it came too late to avert—if anything could have averted—a defeat that was at once recognized throughout the South as "one of the most disastrous of the war."[209]

14

TO ATLANTA AND BEYOND

The defeat at Chattanooga opened the door for a Federal advance on Atlanta, and though Grant was unable for the moment to follow up his victory, it was clear to every high-ranking Confederate what the objective of the Federal army in Chattanooga would be as soon as it got around to moving. That would probably be in the spring of 1864, though it could be earlier. Before that happened, Jefferson Davis would have to effect some important changes in the Confederacy's defenses.

The first step was removing Bragg, but Davis was loath to forego his services completely. Less than two months after granting Bragg's request to be relieved of command, Davis summoned him to Richmond for consultation.[1] Several weeks later an official order was issued assigning Bragg "to duty at the seat of government as commanding general."[2] This was the position Lee had held during the spring of 1862.[3] In practice it meant that Bragg would serve as chief of staff and top military advisor to the president. Re-creating this position and appointing Bragg to fill it was one of the best decisions Davis would make during the winter of 1863–64. The harassed and overworked president needed the help, and Bragg was just the man for the job. The move was not popular politically, but that did not seem to bother Davis. Indeed, one observer felt that the president enjoyed "a secret satisfaction in triumphing thus over popular sentiment, which is just at this time much averse to Gen Bragg."[4]

There remained the problem, however, of finding a new commander for the Army of Tennessee. Lt. Gen. William J. Hardee, senior corps commander since Polk's transfer to Mississippi and now acting army commander, was a possibility. He was unspectacular, to say the least, but he had not been accused of any monstrous blunders and his nickname in the army was "Old Reliable"–a sobriquet he usually lived up to as long as one did not rely on him to accomplish great things. His anti-Bragg activity was not realized in Richmond, or even by its victim.

The president's first intention was to appoint Hardee to permanent command of the army, but perversely Hardee wrote back stating he did not want the position.[5] Davis was not so easily put off, and he dispatched his military aide posthaste to Dalton to persuade Hardee to take the job after all.[6] It was no use. Hardee simply refused the promotion. His primary motivation was apparently a profound dread of responsibility.[7] As much as he enjoyed finding fault with Bragg, he lacked the nerve even to try bettering Bragg's record. Hardee had an added personal reason for not desiring army command. As long as he continued as head of the army, it would be impossible for him to go on leave—and leave was important to him just then because he needed to go to Alabama for his wedding.[8] While stationed in Mississippi, the forty-eight-year-old widower had met and courted the twenty-five-year-old Mary Foreman Lewis. The bride-to-be, it was said, "would have been a beauty but for her extreme thinness." She also happened to be the heiress of a wealthy planter. After declining command of the army, Hardee was eventually able to obtain leave to attend the wedding at the bride's home in Mobile. It was a gala affair with many guests, including numerous high-ranking officers resplendent in full dress uniform. Champagne flowed freely—perhaps a bit too freely, as one of the generals who spent the night was unable to find his trousers the next morning.[9] In any case, Hardee rejoined the army at Dalton in early February, very much a husband and a corps commander and nothing more.[10]

In the meantime, Davis had had to face the issue of finding a new commander for the Army of Tennessee with Hardee definitely out of the running. It had not been an easy decision. Davis had considered Beauregard, still commanding in a backwater of the war at Charleston.[11] Could he have been wrong in his previous assessment of the Creole? Others had also thought of Beauregard. Lee, writing from the headquarters of the Army of Northern Virginia, suggested Beauregard might be "suitable for the position." Lee confided that he had been considering "with some anxiety the condition of affairs in Georgia & Tennessee"; and he gave Davis some good advice by recommending that "every effort should be made to concentrate as large a force as possible under the best commander" in order to set things to rights in that part of the country. All the Confederacy's forces outside Virginia should be drawn on to reinforce the Army of Tennessee, since, as Lee astutely pointed out, if Georgia could not be held, neither could Virginia. The Union armies in the West were threatening Richmond just as directly as the Federals his own men were eyeing on the far side of the Rapidan.[12]

Davis pondered this for a day or two and then decided to take Lee's advice, insofar as it called for putting the Army of Tennessee "under the best commander." Who better than Lee himself? Davis had never been very enthused about Beauregard; if Lee was interested in Georgia, why not send him there? Accordingly, Davis got off a dispatch to Lee asking if the Virginia general felt he could go west.[13] This was not what Lee had had in mind, and he hastened to reply. "I can if desired," he wrote, but he expressed reservations about the "expediency" of such a move. He was not sure the Army of Northern Virginia could manage without him, and he doubted that he would "receive cordial cooperation" if he did go west.[14] Davis's response came back two days later. Lee was to report to the president in Richmond at once. Lee thought he was being transferred after all. "I am called to Richmond this morning by the President," he wrote in a brief note to a subordinate. "I presume the rest will follow. My heart and thoughts will always be with this army."

He assumed the transfer would be temporary, for he ended the note, "I expect to be back."[15]

If Davis's intention in ordering Lee to Richmond was to send him on to Georgia, he was not sure enough of his purpose to do so unless he could talk Lee into approving it. When the general reached the capital, he and Davis entered into a week of conferences along with members of the cabinet on the subject of who should command in Georgia. By about the middle of the week Lee had succeeded in persuading the president not to choose him. In his place Lee urged that Beauregard be sent, but by this time Davis had made up his mind that the temperamental Louisianan was not the answer. Sensing this, Lee shifted his support to Joseph E. Johnston.

Lee was not alone in backing Johnston. Secretary of War Seddon also urged that Johnston be given another chance. From Mississippi came a letter from Polk, who was now serving as Johnston's second in command, recommending that Johnston take Bragg's old job. The good bishop, who stood to succeed to top command in Mississippi should Johnston be sent to the Army of Tennessee, hastened to assure the president that no such selfish consideration inspired his advice.[16] Others sought Johnston's appointment out of motives that were less than public-spirited, including his growing faction of supporters in Congress.[17] These men were, in reality, not so much Johnston's friends as Davis's enemies, and they saw in Johnston a political weapon to use against the president. They believed Davis disliked Johnston and therefore wanted to force Davis to take him.

They were correct in their assessment of Davis's feeling for Johnston, but that enmity was certainly no secret by this time. A Richmond diarist noted, "The President detests Joe Johnston for all the trouble he has given him, and General Joe returns the compliment with compound interest. His hatred of Jeff Davis amounts to a religion. With him it colors all things."[18] Davis, for his part, was not likely to forget Johnston's failure in the Vicksburg campaign or his attempt to cast the blame for his inaction on Davis. Lest it did slip his mind, Johnston's allies in Congress provided plenty of reminders, as they busily circulated copies of one of Johnston's long and self-serving letters sent to Davis the previous summer.[19] Appointing Johnston would be a bitter pill to swallow, but Davis was dedicated to the Confederacy's success and would even bring himself to choose his old enemy if he thought it would further the cause. The problem was he was not at all sure it would. Johnston's ability as a general was a matter on which Davis entertained increasing doubts – doubts strengthened by Judah P. Benjamin, Confederate secretary of state and one of the president's most trusted advisors, who felt Johnston was overly timid and was prone to retreat in the presence of the enemy.[20] Still, Benjamin was alone among the president's top advisors in opposing Johnston, and Davis himself remained uncertain. Finally, after much hesitation and somewhat against his better judgment, Davis ordered Johnston to go to Dalton and take command of the Army of Tennessee.[21]

Johnston was surprised and delighted to learn of his new command. He had thought that he would never be given another important position. Upon arriving in Dalton, Johnston found waiting for him a letter from Davis. It was a surprisingly cordial letter, even friendly. In it Davis urged Johnston to "communicate fully and freely" and promised to cooperate and give all possible assistance. Considering Davis's personality and what had already passed between the two men, that letter must have represented a prodigious amount of self-discipline and dedication to the cause. However, Johnston was apparently not all that impressed with Davis's gesture, having worked himself into a state bordering on paranoia concerning the president.[22] Despite his pleasure at receiving the Army of Tennessee post, he believed Davis meant him no good. He judged this belief confirmed when he learned that Davis wanted him to undertake an offensive to regain the territory that had been lost the previous summer. Johnston immediately undertook to talk the president out of it. He would like to launch a drive, he wrote, "but difficulties appear to me in the way."[23] Of course, to Johnston difficulties would always appear in the way. The general's characteristic inability to think in terms of an offensive became yet another source of friction between him and the president. Back and forth between Richmond and Dalton went dispatch after dispatch on the subject of taking the offensive, with Davis constantly urging the necessity of action and Johnston arguing the impossibility of any move into Tennessee and suggesting that it might be necessary to fall back.[24]

The debate was interrupted in February by a Federal raid. Grant sent Sherman and 21,000 men to Vicksburg to strike straight across the state of Mississippi toward the town of Meridian, 150 miles to the east.[25] The Confederates had still been drawing a certain amount of supplies from the Mississippi countryside, and the Federal occupation troops were being harassed by guerrilla raids. Meridian was an important railroad center, supply depot, and base for Confederate guerrillas. Sherman's job was to eliminate it. Polk, who commanded the Confederate troops in this sector, was informed of Sherman's advance as early as January 23 but refused to believe it.[26] By early February he had made the transition from complacency to panic. Sherman was marching with 35,000 men, the frantic bishop telegraphed Johnston and Davis simultaneously.[27] Confusion reigned in the Confederate high command. Polk thought Sherman was headed for Mobile; Davis thought Montgomery a more likely target.[28] He also thought Johnston should reinforce Polk.[29] Johnston, naturally, was of an entirely different opinion. He claimed first that Polk's cavalry alone ought to suffice to stop Sherman and next that "to make sure of success" he would have to send Polk (who professed to have only 8,000 men himself) 24,000 reinforcements. Such a transfer, he maintained, would result in the loss of Atlanta and ought not to be tried.[30] Meanwhile, the congressional delegations of Mississippi and Alabama kept up an insistent clamor that something be undertaken to defend their constituents. "We consider it of the highest importance," they informed Davis, "to check the advance of the enemy upon Mobile & middle Alabama."[31] The president continued to nag and wheedle Johnston and, failing to persuade the reluctant general, finally ordered him to send most of an army corps.[32]

Sherman, meanwhile, had reached Meridian and was making a shambles of it. Polk had failed to get all the Confederate stores and supplies out of the town, and now Sherman's men destroyed everything they could lay hands on, including some two million bushels of corn plus arms and clothing, all of which Sherman estimated at a value of $50 million.[33] While Meridian burned, Johnston continued to fiddle around. He wanted to know if Beauregard could send some troops to replace the ones being sent to Polk.[34] The reply came back from Richmond: Inquiry would be made.[35] Then Johnston suggested that since Beauregard was sending troops to him and he to Polk, why not simplify matters and have Beauregard send troops to Polk and Johnston keep all his men?[36] In the meantime Beauregard had announced that he could spare no troops at all.[37] Davis telegraphed Johnston to send the troops from the Army of Tennessee and be quick about it: "Promptitude, I have to repeat, is essential."[38]

By this time Sherman had finished his work in Meridian and returned to Vicksburg, tearing up over a hundred miles of railroad on the way and leaving, in his own words, "a swath of desolation fifty miles broad across the State of Mississippi." To Halleck Sherman wrote, "Polk retreated across the Tombigbee and left me to smash things at pleasure, and I think it is well done." Besides, if the raid had accomplished nothing else, at least, as Sherman put it, "I scared the bishop out of his senses."[39] The bishop, who had by this time regained his composure and was congratulating himself on having won a great victory, telegraphed Davis that it was too late to do anything more. Davis, to his disgust, had to pass the news along to Johnston on the same day that he had ordered that general to hurry the transmission of reinforcements.[40] The whole brief campaign had, in many ways, been a rehearsal for the next summer's operations. From the Confederate point of view it was not at all auspicious.

While all this was happening and, indeed, before it started, important decisions were being made about the composition and personnel of the Army of Tennessee. One of Johnston's first concerns upon taking command was to carry out a major reorganization of the army. As Johnston found it, the Army of Tennessee, whose corps and even division structure had been juggled several times in the preceding months, consisted of two corps; but, after the transfer, demotion, or disgrace of so many officers in the preceding campaign, it had only one general of the proper rank to command a corps. Since Johnston felt the army could be maneuvered better if it were rearranged into three corps, he requested that two lieutenant generals be sent and recommended several officers for those positions.[41] His final choices seemed to be T. C. Hindman and Mansfield Lovell.[42] Perhaps not coincidentally, neither of Johnston's suggestions found favor in the president's eyes. Davis felt the two-corps organization was adequate for the Army of Tennessee at its present strength and refused to authorize the creation of a third. There was still one new corps commander to be found, but Johnston's choices were not to Davis's liking.

T. C. Hindman was not a professional—a point that weighed heavily with Davis—and his military record was checkered. He had shown some skill in his adopted state of Arkansas but had also shown himself to be headstrong to his superiors and tyrannical to his subordinates. Then he had led his army to defeat at Prairie Grove. Transferred to the Army of Tennessee, Hindman had performed very poorly during the early phases of the Chickamauga campaign, but in the battle itself he had revealed considerable dash and courage and been severely wounded. There was a chance he would have developed into an acceptable corps commander, but it would have been a long shot. In any event, his health seems to have been seriously impaired by his Chickamauga wound, and it is doubtful that he would have been equal to the task physically.

Mansfield Lovell was a different case. He was a northerner, and he had lost New Orleans (or at least that was the interpretation most southerners gave to the events by which the city had fallen into Yankee hands). These two facts made him execrable to the South. Davis may not have joined in the unreasoning vilification of Lovell, but he had to recognize that it existed. When Seddon pointed out that "it would be injudicious to place a corps under the command of Gen. Lovell" because "it would not give confidence to the army," Davis had to concur.[43] He also had to consider that the war had since passed Lovell by. Except for his brief and unhappy stint as a corps commander during Van Dorn's dismal Corinth campaign, the northerner had spent the war on the sidelines. Although he could be charged (fairly) with no serious errors, there were by this time other men whose experience and performance qualified them far more than Lovell to lead a corps in battle. This factor, along with his overwhelming unpopularity, made him an unlikely choice for the vacancy in the Army of Tennessee.

Even after eliminating these candidates, Davis still need not have looked far to find a good corps commander. There were already in the Army of Tennessee at least two men who would have made excellent choices. The best, by all odds, was Patrick Ronayne Cleburne. The Irish general's performance had been the only bright spot for the Confederacy on the dark day of Missionary Ridge. During the retreat Hardee had ordered Cleburne to take command of two other divisions besides his own and cover the army's withdrawal.[44] With this improvised corps Cleburne had been nothing short of brilliant during the hours following the disaster, in staving off an aggressive Federal pursuit. Bragg had noted this in his report of the battle and had commended Cleburne "to the special notice of the Government."[45]

"The Government" would have done well to take Bragg's advice. Cleburne was a dynamic battlefield leader, but the real basis of his success was his painstakingly thorough preparation of himself and his command. This winter was no exception. While the army was in winter quarters, Cleburne held daily classes for the further instruction of his brigade commanders on every aspect of warfare and saw to it that this instruction was passed down through the ranks all the way to the company officers.[46] By January 1864 Cleburne was unquestionably the best division commander in the Confederacy and the most promising prospect for corps command. Yet there is no indication that Davis so much as considered him for the position.

There were several factors that could possibly have counted against Cleburne in Davis's reckoning. First, Cleburne was foreign-born, one of only two foreign-born officers to reach the rank of major general in the Confederate army.[47] This probably did not count for much with Davis himself, who was more enlightened than most southerners, but it is possible that the president might have doubted the enthusiasm with which such a promotion would be received in the South. A more likely explanation for Cleburne's failure to advance beyond the rank of major general was the Irishman's lack of a West Point education and prewar professional military career. Such things were important to Davis, who had once written disparagingly of those who claimed to "know military affairs by instinct." Though he took some criticism for it—primarily from politicians disgruntled at not having secured high-ranking military positions for themselves—Davis's prejudice in favor of West Pointers (as his enemies called his preference for military professionals) served him well most of the time. Yet it was a costly mental habit if it prevented him from seeing Cleburne's merits.

Another possibility is that Davis was influenced against Cleburne as a result of a paper Cleburne presented to his fellow generals in the Army of Tennessee that winter. On the second evening of 1864 the generals at Dalton gathered at the house Johnston was using as his headquarters in order to hear some thoughts Cleburne had about the problems the Confederacy faced and a possible solution. None of them was prepared for the shockingly radical proposition Cleburne presented to them that night. The Irish-born general had never owned a slave and was relatively free of the cultural baggage most southerners dragged with them through life. Unhindered by such things, Cleburne's astute mind cut straight to the heart of the South's dilemma. Southern manpower was simply running out under the steady drain of a long and bloody war. There was just one logical solution. A new source of manpower must be tapped, and the only possible alternative involved a step that was literally unthinkable to a great many southerners: arming and ultimately freeing the slaves. The generals listened aghast as Cleburne explained his plan for making soldiers out of slaves and motivating them to fight for the South by the promise of freedom for themselves and their families.

Many of the officers were simply dumbfounded by Cleburne's suggestion. Most of the rest were beside themselves with rage. Johnston was not among those most incensed by the idea, but he knew a politically charged issue when he saw one. The proposal, he pointed out, was political, and therefore it would not be proper for him as a general to forward it to Richmond. Since it would have been equally improper for Cleburne to send it over his superior's head, the whole matter might have died right there had it not been for Maj. Gen. W. H. T. Walker.[48] Walker was not inclined to be in a good mood these days. He was the senior major general in the army, and he had been an acting corps commander during the Chickamauga campaign.[49] Now he was back to commanding a division, a situation not at all to his liking.[50] Cleburne's proposal sent him into a towering fury and perhaps awakened in him some hope of attracting the favorable notice of the Richmond authorities. Denouncing the plan as "incendiary" and well nigh treasonable, he demanded of Cleburne a copy of the paper to forward to Richmond. Cleburne was happy to provide him with one as he honestly believed the plan was necessary and was glad for the chance to lay it before the authorities even if it was by means of the unfavorably disposed Walker. Walker lost no time in sending the paper along with a few choice remarks of his own, and the whole mess landed in Jefferson Davis's lap.[51]

The advocacy of such a controversial idea could hardly have helped Cleburne's chances, whatever they were, for advancement.[52] Yet it was not the deciding factor against him, at least not for this promotion. Davis had apparently already made his decision about the present vacancy in the Army of Tennessee by the time he learned of Cleburne's suggestion. Additionally, Jefferson Davis was less likely to be outraged by such a concept than Walker had assumed. Davis had more vision than most southerners. A year later, at the urging of Robert E. Lee, he would push through Congress a version of the program Cleburne was now advocating. Yet Davis, as a southerner, could see what Cleburne did not seem to—that such a step would be controversial enough to tear the Confederacy apart. Therefore, it could be used only at the point of absolute desperation, when the alternative was obviously certain defeat. In the end Davis's own timing was off, and he waited too late to play this last card. It was a tricky business: too soon, and the Confederacy would fall apart amid furious dissension; too late, and nothing would be able to save the Confederacy. The ideal moment may never have existed when such a plan could have worked. In any case, Davis's instincts were probably sound in sensing that the country was not ready for so bold a step during the winter of 1864. He took no action against Cleburne but did ensure that word of the matter did not leak and thus stir up the general public or the common soldiers. Orders were sent to Johnston that all the officers with any knowledge of the plan be strictly enjoined to say nothing more about it. The orders were obeyed, and a shroud of silence descended over the issue.

In the final analysis, Cleburne's prospects may have been damaged less by this incident than by the role into which he had been drawn in the ugly world of Army of Tennessee politics.[53] Cleburne, through his friendship with Hardee, had been pulled into the anti-Bragg camp. He had not joined the scheming and intriguing, but Davis may well have come to associate him with more insubordinate and disruptive officers such as Longstreet, Buckner, and D. H. Hill, and the president seemed to take a dim view of such behavior. D. H. Hill had in effect been demoted from lieutenant general to major general. Buckner was reduced from corps to division command, and though promoted later in the war, he was shipped to the trans-Mississippi—not generally a vote of confidence from Jefferson Davis. Longstreet was Lee's "old warhorse," and Lee got him back; but he was not considered for further promotion. Polk seems to have escaped more or less unscathed, but that was to be expected. It may be that Davis believed promoting Cleburne would be interpreted as rewarding the sort of insubordination that had so weakened the Army of Tennessee. In any case, Davis did not choose Cleburne.

Nor did he choose Maj. Gen. A. P. Stewart. Like Cleburne, Stewart commanded a division in the Army of Tennessee, and also like the Irish Confederate, he would have made an excellent lieutenant general. Alexander Peter Stewart was born in Rogersville, Tennessee, in 1821 and graduated from West Point in 1842, twelfth out of a class of fifty-six. That put him sixteen places ahead of his classmate D. H. Hill, forty places ahead of his classmate Van Dorn, and forty-two places ahead of his roommate Longstreet. After serving briefly in the Third Artillery, he became an assistant professor of math at West Point, where he taught cadets George McClellan and Stonewall Jackson. In 1845 he resigned from the army to accept a professorship at Cumberland University in Lebanon, Tennessee. He taught there and at the University of Nashville until the war, turning down the chancellorship of Washington University in St. Louis as well as the presidency of Cumberland University itself because he wanted to remain, as he put it, "close to the students." His concern for the students led him to organize the country's first college chapter of the Young Men's Christian Association. Like many Tennesseans Stewart found himself pulled in two directions as the Civil War approached. He was strongly opposed to slavery, and though he believed a state had the right to secede, he felt such action would be unwise and inexpedient. He voted against the secession of Tennessee, but he acquiesced in it once it was fact and immediately offered his services to help defend his state.[54]

He was appointed a major and posted to Fort Pillow. Albert Sidney Johnston wanted him for the key command at Fort Donelson, but Richmond had other ideas. Transferred to Columbus, Stewart served ably at the battle of Belmont and a few days later was promoted to brigadier general at Johnston's recommendation. Thereafter he served with distinction at Shiloh, Perryville, Murfreesboro, Chickamauga, and Missionary Ridge. Throughout this roll call of the Army of Tennessee's battles and the routine camp life that came in between, Stewart had won for himself a reputation—not widespread but solid among those who knew him—as a fine administrator and a hard fighter. Like Stonewall Jackson, he was a devout Presbyterian—so devout, in fact, that before the war he had often been called upon to fill the pulpits of absent pastors. Even his battle reports reflected his deep Christianity. "In conclusion," he wrote near the end of his report on Chickamauga, "I desire to express my humble but most grateful acknowledgements to Almighty God for the signal success that has crowned our arms. . . . Let all the praise be ascribed to His holy name."[55] Along with Cleburne he was one of the Army of Tennessee's best division commanders.

Like Cleburne, he had been taken in by the anti-Bragg talk of his superiors and had expressed such opinions from time to time.[56] Yet his criticism of Bragg had been relatively restrained and unobtrusive, and as a result it may have gone completely unnoticed in Richmond. Unfortunately, though, the same also seems to be true of Stewart's considerable merits. As one story relates, when Davis visited the army after Chickamauga and toured the battlefield, he passed through the area fought over by Stewart's division and was impressed by the many evidences, still strewn about the grisly field, that it had been a desperate struggle and that the troops that had carried the position had accomplished something extraordinary. Yet rather than thinking of Stewart, Davis was taken with one of Stewart's brigade commanders, several of whose dead mounts he had seen on the ground, and shortly thereafter had him promoted to major general over the head of every other brigadier in the army.[57] Later in the war Stewart was finally promoted to corps command and was outstanding in that capacity, but for now Davis was unmindful of this valuable officer.

Thus either Cleburne or Stewart could have filled the vacancy within the Army of Tennessee. Cleburne was senior to Stewart by about seven months as a major general and would probably have been the better choice, but either man would have done credit to Davis in any position to which he might promote him.[58] These were realistic choices. There was one other name that would be mentioned in later years, if not in connection with this particular promotion then at least as one who was never given as high a position as he was qualified to fill. That was Nathan Bedford Forrest. After the war was over, Forrest would come to be seen as one of the South's most brilliant generals, and within his limited sphere, he may have been. Yet it is very unlikely that anyone in the Confederacy in January 1864, from president down to private and everyone in between including Forrest himself, considered the hard-riding, hard-fighting cavalry leader as a possibility for anything much different from what he was doing.

Long after the war, at Forrest's funeral, Davis would express regret that the high-ranking western generals such as Bragg and Joseph E. Johnston had not presented Forrest to him as anything more than a "bold and enterprising raider and rider." Davis "never knew how to measure" Forrest until, impressed by his exploits in 1864, he had gone back and reread Forrest's earlier reports and come to the conclusion that Forrest was actually a great general.[59] Although indulging in his bad habit of blaming others for his own failings, Davis here may have been less than fair to himself. Certainly Forrest could not have been a realistic candidate for the vacant corps command in the Army of Tennessee during the winter of 1864. He had never commanded anything but cavalry and had held the rank of major general just a little over a month.[60] Most of his operations had involved the unconventional raiding activity to which his reputation was confined. Understandably then, Davis did not choose—or even consider—Forrest. Indeed, the president had made up his mind well before Johnston suggested the need of one or two more lieutenant generals. Soon after the battle of Chickamauga, Davis had decided who would fill the next vacancy in that rank: John Bell Hood.[61]

Like Albert Sidney Johnston, Hood was a Kentucky native who had made Texas his adopted state. He was born in 1831, the son of a wealthy doctor and planter. Hood gained a reputation early in life as an unruly lad who was often involved in fistfights. At the age of eighteen he received from his uncle (who was a member of Congress) an appointment to the United States military academy.[62] Cadet Hood's performance at the academy was anything but inspiring. Upon graduation in 1853 he ranked forty-fifth of fifty-two in his class and lacked just four of the two hundred demerits that would have brought his expulsion.[63] Yet West Point left its mark on Hood, most significantly in the life-long admiration he developed for the man who was superintendent during his senior year there: Col. Robert E. Lee.

Hood's class standing determined that infantry would be his postgraduation assignment. And so Hood spent his first two years of active army life with the Fourth Infantry in California. Then, in 1855, Secretary of War Jefferson Davis began selecting officers for the crack new Second Cavalry. Davis appointed to the regiment those whom he considered to be the army's best, and not coincidentally, the Second Cavalry's roster of officers reads almost like a hall of fame of future Confederate generals. A billet in the Second was not something to which a young officer with a dismal West Point record and a humdrum army career could well aspire, but John Bell Hood could be resourceful and ambitious at times. He wrote to a boyhood friend asking that he use his influence on his behalf.[64] The friend happened to be John C. Breckinridge, not only a prominent Kentucky politician but also a close political ally of Jefferson Davis in the previous year's Kansas-Nebraska battle.[65] Whether through Breckinridge's intercession or for other reasons unknown, Hood got the appointment and spent the next few years as a lieutenant of cavalry, fighting Indians on the Texas frontier.[66] Hood adapted avidly to Albert Sidney Johnston's policy of carrying the fight to the hostile Indians, on one occasion boldly pursuing and attacking a band of warriors that outnumbered his own force three to one.[67] Then, as throughout his military career, Hood walked a fine line between audacity and foolhardiness. Hood's years with the Second Cavalry were also significant in that during them he developed an even deeper admiration and respect for Lee, the lieutenant colonel of the Second, who at times was almost like a father to the unsophisticated young lieutenant.[68]

John Bell Hood (Library of Congress)

With secession and the threat of war, Hood suffered none of the painful division of loyalties that made the decision of whether to follow state or nation so difficult for many Americans. Whereas his hero Lee chose the South only when his state left the Union, Hood was so disgusted at the failure of Kentucky to secede that he decided to make Texas his home and enlisted from there instead.[69] Given a chance to prove himself under fire, Hood turned out to be an excellent combat commander. Serving in Virginia first under Joseph E. Johnston and then under Lee, Hood rose rapidly in rank from lieutenant to brigadier general and gained fame as commander of the Army of Northern Virginia's Texas brigade. An aggressive, ferocious fighter, Hood came to be considered one of Lee's better brigade commanders and was soon promoted to major general. His conspicuous battlefield leadership was not without its price, though. At Gettysburg on July 2, 1863, he had received a wound that permanently disabled his left arm.[70]

Recuperating in Richmond, Hood launched an unfortunate campaign of his own, the object of which was Sally Buchanan Preston, "Buck" to her friends. A member of one of the first families of South Carolina, Buck was a sophisticated southern belle who was also an incurable flirt. She had, as Richmond diarist Mary Boykin Chesnut put it, "a knack of being 'fallen in love with' at sight, and never being 'fallen out of love with.'" Hood was smitten. Not exactly a prepossessing figure, Hood was described by a staff officer as "a tall, rawboned country-looking man" who "looked like a raw backwoodsman, dressed up in an ill-fitting uniform." He had a long face, a long tawny beard, a large nose, and eyes with the sad expression of a hound dog. Still, he was "the gallant Hood," one of the most celebrated division commanders in Lee's famous army. He first met Buck in March 1863, while his division was passing through Richmond, and Hood, the relentless fighter, later confessed he had "surrendered at first sight."[71]

Hood had not yet completed his recovery from his Gettysburg wound when Longstreet's corps, of which his division was a part, was ordered to join Bragg before the battle of Chickamauga. Hood need not have gone, but it was not in him to miss a fight. On his way south he stopped in Petersburg, Virginia, where Buck was staying at the time, and proposed to her. Buck did not like to be pressed for a decision and so was as equivocal as she could be. As Hood put it, she "half promised me to think of it. She would not say yes, but she did not say no, that is not exactly." The artless young general was not quite sure how to take this confusing answer and, deciding it might be best to take it as affirmative, left saying, "I am engaged to you." To which a horrified Buck Preston replied, "I am not engaged to you!"

With this send-off Hood continued on to join Bragg's army and fight at the battle of Chickamauga. There his division was the first to pour through the gap in Rosecrans's line, and there, while trying to form up his men for further exploitation of the breakthrough, Hood went down with a minié ball in his right leg. The bone was shattered beyond all hope of repair, and the limb had to be amputated halfway up the thigh.[72] For a time his life was despaired of, and in Richmond he was actually reported as dead.[73] Proving to be much tougher than anyone had suspected, Hood survived and several weeks later was brought back to Richmond for another and longer convalescence.

In the capital Hood's health improved rapidly. Soon he was getting about on crutches and sporting a cork leg bought for him by the men of his old Texas brigade, who had subscribed $3,100 for that purpose in a single day. Soon too his seesaw courtship of Buck Preston, which, he confided to Mrs. Chesnut, "was the hardest battle he had ever fought in his life," was in full swing again. After losing his leg at Chickamauga, Hood had thought all hope of marrying the South Carolina belle was gone, but once he got back to Richmond her behavior raised his hopes again. Those hopes were dashed on Christmas Eve, when Hood's campaign of the heart suffered a severe setback. "I was routed," said the dejected general. "She said there was 'no hope.'"

While this unhappy story was playing itself out, Hood developed a close friendship with Jefferson Davis and his family. Davis had already decided to promote Hood to lieutenant general in place of D. H. Hill, whose nomination Davis had withdrawn from Senate consideration after Hill's unsatisfactory performance in the Chickamauga campaign.[74] By early January Hood was able to ride a horse—strapped into the saddle because of his missing leg—and Davis invited the general to join him on rides around Richmond.[75] Before this the two had met only briefly, when Hood was a brigade commander during the peninsula campaign of 1862.[76] Now they grew to know each other well and developed a mutual respect. [77] Their friendship came to be the talk of Richmond, as they were often seen together at social events, and on one occasion Hood sat with the Davises in the president's pew at St. Paul's Episcopal Church. After the service the president was seen helping the maimed general down the front steps.

The fellowship extended to the president's family as well. During one of the stormy interludes of Hood's courting of Buck Preston, the general went for a chaperoned carriage ride with Davis's sister-in-law, the young and attractive Maggie Howell, who lived with the Davises in the Confederate White House.[78] In February he escorted the president's wife, Varina, to a dinner, at which he was to experience another dismal chapter in his romantic pursuit. Hood and Varina sat at a small table prepared for the first lady and lingered there talking after many of the other guests had gotten up and gone into other rooms. As they talked, they heard Buck's "clear, ringing, musical . . . voice from another room where," as Mrs. Davis described it, "she was flirting. . . .'Absurd!' Buck was saying. 'Engaged to that man! Never! For what do you take me?'" Trying to cheer Hood up, Varina mentioned that she had heard another general say that if he had been hit as often as Hood had been, "he would wince and dodge at every ball." The compliment to his courage brought no relief to the general's gloom. "Why wince," he said, "when you would thank God for a ball to go through your heart and be done with it all?" Describing the scene to a friend, Varina added, "This is high tragedy and not a farce, for there was the bitterness of death in his tone . . . and the silvery voice from the other room came, calm and clear, 'Absurd—oh, you foolish creatures—to fancy I would.'"

Hood was nothing if not persistent, and he determined to make one last bold advance in his winter campaign on Buck Preston. He and Buck went for a carriage ride, during which Hood held out his hand and demanded an answer to his long-standing question. Buck protested; Hood insisted. "Say yes or no. I will not be satisfied with less." He continued to hold out his hand, and reluctantly Buck gave him hers. Hood was ecstatic. "Now I will speak to your father. I want his consent to marry you at once." Buck was aghast. Hood remained enraptured for days, telling everyone he knew. To Mrs. Chesnut he said, "I am so proud. So grateful. The sun never shone on a happier man. Such a noble girl—a queen among women." Buck's parents, however, opposed the match, considering Hood a bumpkin.[79]

At this point, the events of the war and the progress of Hood's recovery mercifully ended his awkward romance with Buck Preston. It was now mid-February 1864, and Davis was ready to assign Hood to the new post he had in mind for him. Hood was ready, too. For over a month he had been making frequent rides around Richmond in the company of the president. While they had ridden, they had talked, and whatever else they may have discussed, the war was certainly one focus of conversation. Davis shared with Hood his intention of reinforcing Johnston's army for an offensive into Tennessee, his ideas for such an offensive, and his hopes of what it might accomplish. He also asked if Hood would like to command a corps in the venture. Hood's wounds had not taken any of the fight out of him, and he willingly agreed.[80] By the end of January the matter had been settled, and Hood was looking forward to his new command with fierce eagerness.[81]

The appointment of Hood as a corps commander had much to recommend it. He was widely regarded as one of the best brigade and division commanders in Lee's army. At Chickamauga he had, in effect, commanded a corps. After the death of Stonewall Jackson in May and the subsequent reorganization of the Army of Northern Virginia, Lee had considered Hood for command of the new Third Corps. Though another had been chosen, Lee had written that Hood was a "capital officer" who was "improving . . . and will make [a] good corps . . . [commander] if necessary." At one time or another, Jackson, Bragg, and Longstreet had all made similar statements. Besides, Hood was not involved in the various interrelated factions of the Army of Tennessee, and that army certainly needed no more factionalism.[82]

On the other hand there were some serious problems with placing Hood in a highly responsible active command. For one thing, Hood's record of service was not as solid as it might at first glance appear to be. He had done his best fighting as a brigade commander, and his flashy battlefield heroics coupled with his careless handling of administrative matters might have suggested that that was the peak level to which he was suited. At Gettysburg he had led a division but had been wounded before the fight was well under way. At Chickamauga, as acting corps commander, his success had resulted from the confusion in Federal ranks that had opened the gap through which his troops passed, more by accident than design.[83] Besides being relatively untested, Hood was young, three years younger than Cleburne and a decade younger than Stewart. Nor had Hood, at thirty-three, demonstrated a mental and emotional stability beyond his years that might have justified vesting him with such heavy responsibility.

Still, Hood's relative youth might have been counterbalanced by a corresponding strength had he been in better physical condition than the other men who could have been named for the job. That Hood could claim no such advantage involved what was probably his greatest shortcoming. With one leg missing and one arm useless, he would always be impaired in moving about the battlefield to control and direct his troops. He might tire more quickly, and if so his judgment might often be clouded by fatigue as well as pain from his old wounds.[84]

Thus while Davis could undoubtedly have done worse than Hood in his selection of a corps commander for the Army of Tennessee, he probably could have done better too. All of this was more important that it seemed. The men who held the rank of lieutenant general now would be those from whom Davis could select, if necessary, a new full general five or six months into the future. Conversely, capable officers who were not promoted now would in future months lack the experience and the demonstrated ability to fill a higher position if needed.

Johnston meanwhile was anxious to have his new corps commander and, having been informed that this would be Hood, telegraphed Richmond in mid-February that "Lieutenant-General Hood is much wanted here."[85] Hood left Richmond near the end of the month and assumed his duties with the Army of Tennessee on the twenty-ninth (this being a leap year). A week later he wrote the president that the army was in good condition and fine spirits and that he hoped it would receive enough reinforcements to allow it to take the offensive. Hood himself seemed to be feeling fit during these days. Buoyed up by the excitement of a new command and the prospect of a glorious campaign, he was riding as much as twenty miles a day with no apparent difficulty. One soldier "was surprised to find how well [Hood] looked on horseback, though his cork leg is very perceptible & hangs very stiffly, a man follows immediately in his rear with his crutch." An officer also noticed Hood's cork leg but added, "He wears a boot and spur on it as he does the other." The soldiers started referring to him as "Old Pegleg."[86]

With Hood's arrival in Dalton, Davis once again stepped up his efforts to persuade Joseph E. Johnston to take the offensive. Hood had come to Georgia, as far as he and the president were concerned, to join in a grand forward movement, and now his presence with the army only emphasized in Davis's mind the continuing lack of aggressive action. On top of that, Hood, whether by previous agreement with Davis or merely through an instinct for self-promotion, had begun sending a stream of letters to the president representing that the army was in top shape "and eager for the fray."[87] Davis said nothing to Johnston of the fact that his new corps commander was going behind his back, but figured that if Hood was present with the army and thought it prepared to undertake an offensive, then such must be the case.[88] He became more determined than ever to goad Johnston into action.

Along with his reports that the army was capable of advancing, Hood had also included a plan for the campaign, calling for combining the forces of Polk, Johnston, and Longstreet and maneuvering around to the enemy's rear.[89] In offering such suggestions he was not alone. Indeed, nearly every Confederate commander in the West seemed to have something to say on the subject. Johnston, to be sure, had nothing aggressive in mind, but if by way of preparing for an offensive the government wanted to send him "large additions to the number of troops, a great quantity of field transportation, subsistence stores and forage, a bridge equipage, and fresh artillery horses," that would be fine with him.[90] Polk proposed that some of Johnston's men be sent to him for a foray into Tennessee, to begin as soon as Grant's and Sherman's combined forces fell on Johnston's army.[91] Longstreet, not to be outdone, had an idea that called for the government somehow to procure enough horses and mules to mount his entire command, which at this time was languishing in the far northeastern corner of Tennessee. Then the whole force was to hoof it across Tennessee and Kentucky in an enormous raid.[92] A few days later he produced an even more fantastic plan, in which Lee was to join him in East Tennessee while Johnston's army swung up into Virginia to cover Richmond in a gigantic game of military musical chairs.[93]

In Richmond, President Davis fortunately had better counsels than these. After months of frustration in dealing with Johnston and weeks of fruitless urgings that he undertake something, Davis was ready to take some positive steps. In consultation with Lee and Bragg, Davis devised an offensive. This in itself was a departure from Davis's normal practice of allowing generals fairly broad latitude, but with Johnston the president felt it was necessary.[94] Davis anticipated that at worst the plan would, as Lee put it, allow the Confederates to "take the initiative and fall on [the enemy] unexpectedly" so as to "derange their plans and embarrass them the whole summer."[95] At best Lee hoped it might "open the country . . . to the Ohio."[96] The plan called for both Longstreet and Johnston to be reinforced by troops from Charleston and Mississippi; then they would each slip around the Federal forces confronting them, link up between Chattanooga and Knoxville, and move toward Nashville, cutting Grant's supply lines and forcing him to retreat.[97]

Longstreet and Johnston immediately opposed the plan, warning that it would end in disaster.[98] Davis and Bragg then followed the usual method of trying to coax Johnston into compliance. One of Johnston's chief objections was that he was short of supplies, so in mid-March Bragg telegraphed Johnston asking simply if he had enough supplies to accommodate some reinforcements.[99] Johnston quickly declared that supplies were no problem—send the troops at once.[100] To this Bragg replied by referring Johnston to the proposal for offensive operations and stating, "Should you adopt suggestions, all possible means will be promptly given."[101] An irritated Johnston then reverted to claiming he lacked adequate supplies and therefore could not make the movement.[102]

Realizing that Richmond craved some action from him, Johnston submitted a counterproposal. His plan called for the concentration of all the forces the Confederacy could spare with his army. While the main part of the army remained south of Chattanooga, a part of it would sidle around to the east and cut the flow of supplies up the Tennessee Valley from Chattanooga to Knoxville. Knoxville would thus be unsupplied, and the Federal army at Chattanooga would have to come out and fight to drive the Confederates away—or at least so Johnston reasoned. If the Confederates should be defeated, they would have a convenient line of retreat, something Johnston valued very highly. Besides, Johnston thought Grant would probably take the initiative and strike before a Confederate offensive could be prepared. Therefore, it would be best to send the reinforcements right away and not think too seriously about an attack.[103]

This was not at all what Davis and Bragg had envisioned. It was one thing to weaken Confederate defenses in other areas to strengthen Johnston if an offensive into Tennessee would give the Confederacy the initiative and draw attention away from the enfeebled points. It was another thing to weaken these areas in order to provide Johnston with a huge army that would sit idle until the Federals were accommodating enough to attack it and thus make it easier for Johnston to win laurels. Davis and Bragg suspected with good reason that amassing such a comfortably enormous army was exactly what Johnston had in mind. The general was accordingly informed that he could have the reinforcements when he undertook the president's proposed campaign and not before.[104]

Throughout the rest of March and the first three weeks of April the argument continued, Davis and Bragg trying to persuade Johnston to accept their plan and the general remaining obstinate.[105] As one of Bragg's correspondents in the Army of Tennessee put it, Johnston "desires the troops to be sent here, and it be left to him as to what use should be made of them."[106] Johnston himself expressed it differently. To a friend in the Confederate Senate he wrote,

"I learn that it is given out that it has been proposed to me to take the offensive with a large army & that I refused. Don't believe any such story."[107] Whatever Johnston's allies may have believed, the story's ending was beyond dispute: No offensive took place. Davis and Bragg finally gave in. By April 22 the concentration of Union forces in preparation for the spring offensive had progressed to the point that Davis and Bragg felt the plan they had recommended six weeks earlier would no longer be practical.

Instead, they decided to let Johnston go ahead with his own plan. For this purpose a small division (about 4,000 men) was to be transferred from Polk to Johnston.[108] When the order was sent to Polk, however, Davis made the mistake of adding a proviso that the division was to be sent if it was "not essential for immediate operations."[109] This was the only loophole Polk needed. The division, he hastened to inform Richmond, could not be spared.[110] There were further delays while attempts were made to find reinforcements for Johnston elsewhere.[111] Bragg, who knew Polk's ways much better than the bishop's West Point comrade Jefferson Davis, urged the president to give peremptory orders for the transfer of the division, but that Davis could not bring himself to do.[112] Nothing was undertaken, and the Army of Tennessee was still in its camps around Dalton when, on May 4, 1864, the Union launched its end-the-war offensive, with simultaneous thrusts aimed at Richmond and Atlanta.

Grant had assumed command of all Federal armies and was himself supervising the offensive in Virginia. Sherman would lead the advance toward Atlanta. In these two generals and the system they established, the Confederacy would be facing something ominously novel. No longer would Federal commanders behave like a balky team, no two pulling at once. There would be no repetition of Rosecrans's performance of the early summer of 1863, when he idled at Murfreesboro while Bragg detached troops to aid Johnston in Mississippi. Henceforth unrelenting pressure would be maintained on all fronts until the Confederacy collapsed. And collapse it would unless northern war-weariness forced Grant and Sherman to halt before their work was complete.

This was the Confederacy's remaining hope. The North would be holding elections in the fall of 1864. If the South could make the summer military campaigns costly for the North and if both northern offensives could be stopped—that is, if Richmond and Atlanta could be held—there was a fairly good chance that the North might elect a president and Congress that would seek peace even at the price of dismemberment of the Union and southern independence. There was much at stake, therefore, in the Atlanta campaign, even beyond the enormous military and industrial importance of the city itself.

On both fighting fronts, Virginia and Georgia, the North would have a numerical advantage of about ten-to-six. In Virginia Lee and his Army of Northern Virginia had faced these odds before and could be counted on to stop Grant if it was humanly possible. The Georgia front excited the most uncertainty. Would the Army of Tennessee fight or run away as it had at Missionary Ridge? More significant, would Joseph E. Johnston summon the nerve to commit an army to battle? Davis had reason to feel anxious as reports of the enemy advances began to reach Richmond.

One of Davis's first reactions to the news that Sherman was on the move was to yield to Bragg's urging that peremptory orders be given to Polk to reinforce Johnston. Accordingly, an order was issued. Unlike the previous order it told Polk to take the 4,000-man division, along with "any other available force" he had, and report to Johnston at once.[113] The words "available force" were, to Polk's way of thinking, a loophole big enough to drive a battery of artillery through. Indeed, this loophole proved large enough to admit the passage of an extra 10,000 men. Polk's desire to have the most men possible under his command meant that, though he had no troops "available" to send, he had a great many to bring along. In fact, he brought along nearly the entire Confederate force in Mississippi, some 14,000 men.[114] Ironically, it was the right move strategically but was not what Davis had intended. How Bragg viewed the absent defense of Mississippi is unclear, but he was not disposed to be patient with Polk's self-willed twisting of orders. The result was an exchange of harsh letters between Polk and Bragg.[115]

The arrival of Polk's troops was fortunate for Johnston, since he had just been completely deceived by one of Sherman's feints and was in trouble. The intervention of Polk's men allowed the Army of Tennessee to squirm out of the trap and fall back some ten miles to the town of Resaca, on the north bank of the Oostanaula River.[116] The news that Dalton—and Johnston's supposedly impregnable position on Rocky Face Ridge just outside of town—had been abandoned more or less without a fight was unwelcome in Richmond, but Davis expected Johnston to turn and fight somewhere north of the Oostanaula.[117] Johnston did, briefly, in a line of defensive works he had had prepared in advance north of Resaca. Under these advantageous circumstances the army gave a fairly good account of itself in one day's inconclusive fighting, but then Johnston became uneasy about his flanks and put his troops in retreat across the Oostanaula.[118]

This time the withdrawal did not stop until it reached Cassville, another twenty-five miles to the rear and just short of another important river line, the Etowah. Once again Davis was disappointed but anticipated that Johnston would finally engage in a decisive battle somehwere north of the river.[119] Decisive battle was, in fact, exactly what Johnston had in mind. Sherman was making another one of his wide-swinging flanking maneuvers, and Johnston saw the chance to catch one wing of the Federal army by itself, crush it, and then turn on the remainder. By way of preparation he issued a grandiose "I lead you into battle" address to the "Soldiers of the Army of Tennessee," to be read in every regiment on the morning of the attack.[120] It was, but that was about the only thing that went as planned for the Confederacy in this miserable affair.

Polk and Hood were to have the task of annihilating the isolated Federal segment while Hardee entertained the rest of Sherman's army. Unfortunately, Hood was in the process of discovering that leading a corps effectively was a different proposition from commanding a brigade or division. With his typical carelessness about details, he had neglected to carry out an adequate recon-naissance on his exposed flank. As a result he was thrown into a state of con-sternation when a Union force of undetermined origin and size suddenly ap-peared on his flank and rear just as he was advancing to open the attack. Though the troops in question were part of a small fragment of Sherman's army that had taken a wrong turn someplace farther north and was fumbling its way back to it division, Hood knew none of this and accordingly panicked. He hurriedly pulled his troops back to what was supposed to have been the jumping-off point for the attack and set them to digging entrenchments as rapidly as possible to meet this devilish Yankee flanking maneuver.[121]

Johnston was shocked by Hood's report of what he had seen. "It can't be," he said, but on second thought, he was inclined to have doubts. Not surpris-ingly in a person of Johnston's nature, the doubts rapidly won the upper hand, and orders went out to Polk and Hood cancelling the assault. Johnston still thought the army might be able to hold its ground north of the Etowah. The position he held at Cassville was, he would remark in later years, "the best I saw occupied during the war."[122] Hood and Polk, however, were of a dif-ferent mind altogether. They considered the position indefensible, and after conferring with each other, they decided to have a talk with Johnston. They gathered evidence to support their case and met with Johnston over dinner that evening. Hood and Polk apparently favored attacking but opposed waiting in their present position to receive an attack.[123] Johnston felt it was too late to resume the offensive.[124] If the position could not be defended, then they would have to retreat. Johnston, who never needed much persuading in that direction anyway, quickly conceded. The decision was made, and the meeting broke up before Hardee, who opposed retreat, could arrive to protest.[125] The Army of Tennessee once again turned southward, crossing the Etowah River and continuing some four miles beyond to take up a position at Allatoona.[126] Now the constant retreating began to tell on the army's morale. "I could not restrain my tears," wrote one staff officer, "when I found we could not strike."[127] But on top of the failure to attack, the retreat across the Etowah began to look like a rout before it was over.[128] The troops were discouraged and could not understand why they were forced to fall back again and again.[129] Cleburne real-ized the effect this was having. He could not see why, he confided to Hardee during the retreat, "after the order read to the troops, General Johnston should have changed his plan."[130] Yet somehow Johnston did not comprehend the effect his actions were having on the army or, if he did, was more concerned about other things.

And so the campaign went, one retreat after another. As the Army of Ten-nessee fell back mile after mile and the distance between Atlanta and the fighting front steadily decreased, Davis became increasingly apprehensive. His dispatches to Johnston began to reflect his dissatisfaction with the progress of the campaign and his expectation that some aggressive action should be undertaken to halt Sherman's relentless advance.[131] Johnston, however, continued to insist that he had no choice but to retreat.[132] Twice Davis had presumed that Johnston would bring on a decisive battle rather than surrender an important river barrier, and twice Johnston had failed. First the Oostanaula and then the Etowah had been left behind. There was no telling where—if anyplace—Johnston would halt the retreat, and each mile the army fell back not only brought the Federals closer to Atlanta but also uncovered vital centers of production in Alabama and western Georgia.[133] How many more chances could Davis afford to give Johnston? Replacing an army commander in the midst of a crucial campaign was serious business. Yet in Virginia, in Mississippi, and now in Georgia, Johnston had furnished ample evidence that he simply did not have the inner strength necessary to lead an army. The longer Davis waited to remove Johnston, the more difficult it would be for his successor to salvage the situation.

But who would this successor be? That in itself was perhaps the most vexing problem of all. Lee was busy with the Army of Northern Virginia, Bragg had been discredited, and Beauregard would very likely be no better than Johnston. Longstreet was an obvious failure and by this time was out of action with a wound received in Virginia. Hardee had let it be known the preceding winter that he was not interested in the position, and Davis can be given credit for not making Polk an army commander. That left Hood, who had been steadily sending Davis letters, outside of proper channels, deploring the army's constant retreating.[134] This general, at least, could be counted on to fight. Yet Davis vacillated. Years later he stated that at this point, as when Johnston had remained inactive during the siege of Vicksburg, he had considered going down and taking the general's place himself but had decided against that option since he feared the Confederacy's vice-president, the unstable Alexander Stephens, could not be trusted to run the country in his absence.[135] In the end he did nothing—besides urging Johnston to turn and fight—and the retreat went on.

Johnston, for his part, had an idea for solving the Confederacy's dilemma. It did not, to be sure, involve any fighting to speak of by his own army; nevertheless, it had much to recommend it. The remedy for the situation would be to send Forrest and his cavalry, now stationed in Mississippi, on a raid against Sherman's long and presumably vulnerable supply lines. It was a good idea, and Johnston was not the only one to think of it. For weeks now Forrest had been champing at the bit to get at the railroad that carried Sherman's supplies down from Nashville. Even before the Federal offensive had gotten under way, he had written to Polk (then his department commander), Johnston, and even directly to Davis, urging that he be turned loose in Middle Tennessee to "break up [Sherman's] plans."[136] He was confident he could do this and was still anxious to try. Another who was also giving serious consideration to the possibilities of such a raid was Sherman himself. To guard against such an event, Sherman built scores of blockhouses along the railroad, each garrisoned with enough troops to fight off cavalry raiders and situated so as to protect key bridges, trestles, and tunnels. He also had special repair crews and plenty of materials on hand so that any breaks in the railroad could be quickly restored.[137] Yet Forrest's cavalrymen fought with the toughness and tenacity of infantry, and the blockhouses might not be enough to hold them off. As for quick repairs, when Forrest's men wrecked a railroad, unlike most Civil War cavalry, they did a thorough job of it.[138] It might not be so easy to get it back into operation again. To evade such imponderables as these, Sherman hoped to keep Forrest entertained by various minor expeditions into Mississippi.

For the Confederates, sending Forrest against Sherman's supply lines was an inviting prospect. Politicians and generals such as Hardee, Polk, and finally even Robert E. Lee joined Johnston in urging the president to order such a step.[139] That it was not done was primarily the fault of the rapidly degenerating Confederate departmental system. Mississippi, where Forrest was stationed, was part of another military department separate from that commanded by Johnston in northern Georgia. Davis had established the system early in the war as a way of organizing the defense of the Confederacy's territory and making the best use of the means available. Through most of the war the system had functioned tolerably well under Davis's leadership, but now it was increasingly divorced from reality and becoming an absolute hindrance. The incident with Forrest was a prime example.

Forrest's brigade was a part of Gen. Stephen D. Lee's Department of Mississippi and Eastern Louisiana. Johnston pressured Lee to use Forrest to stop Sherman's drive into Georgia, and Lee agreed. Davis's permission was sought and received, and Forrest was given orders to prepare to raid Middle Tennessee and cut Sherman's supply lines. Then, however, Lee received word of an expedition into Mississippi by Federal troops operating out of Memphis. He immediately cancelled Forrest's orders and utilized that general's hard-riding, hard-fighting troopers for the defense of his department. This may have made sense for S. D. Lee, whose whole responsibility was Mississippi and eastern Louisiana, but it was sheer folly for the Confederacy, for whom Mississippi had become a backwater and Georgia the scene of a life-and-death struggle. The man whose responsibility it was to ensure that such departmental misallocation of resources did not happen was Jefferson Davis. He was the only competent military man in a position to weigh and compare the competing needs of the various departments. Unfortunately, he chose not to issue a peremptory order that Forrest be turned loose on Sherman's supply lines. Instead, as so many other times during the war, he chose to let the department commander make the final decision and take the responsibility.[140] In this case that meant Forrest would stay in Mississippi, and Sherman's supply lines would remain unmolested—exactly what Sherman intended in authorizing the expedition in the first place.[141]

The Confederate retreat continued. Though there were no major battles, there were numerous small ones and almost constant skirmishing as the two armies probed at each other in the rough and heavily wooded country of northern Georgia. Johnston prided himself on sparing his army through these constant retreats, but his men actually suffered over 10,000 casualties during the month of May. While the Federals' losses were slightly higher, Johnston's losses represented a larger percentage of his force.[142] In June the story was much the same.

Even generals were not immune to the slow attrition of this grinding campaign. On June 14 Johnston and some of the other top officers of the Army of Tennessee had gone to the summit of a large hill to survey the terrain in front. The hill, known as Pine Top, gave an impressive view of the surrounding country, while simultaneously making the viewer an impressive target. Cleburne had been up there the day before. Cautioned by the troops holding that part of the line that the Yankee artillery had the range, he had no sooner appeared above the parapet than a shell whistled by in uncomfortable proximity. The next shot was even closer. Under these circumstances it took very little time for Cleburne to satisfy his curiosity. "Let's get out of this," he said to his aide. "I have seldom known one to go where he had no business but that he got hurt."[143]

Now the brains of the Army of Tennessee, having received a similar warning about the dangers of the site, were about to prove Cleburne's commonsense remark. The clump of officers on the exposed hilltop presented a tempting target and, predictably, drew Federal artillery fire. On the impact of the first shell the officers made an undignified scramble for cover. Except, that is, for Polk, who walked off slowly, apparently unmindful of the danger. He was struck by the third shell and killed instantly.[144] Davis, who to the end had never recognized that his friend had been a detriment to the military, ranked Polk's death as a catastrophe comparable to the deaths of Albert Sidney Johnston and Stonewall Jackson.[145] To take over command of Polk's corps Davis promoted A. P. Stewart.[146] It was a wise choice, unquestionably one of the best Davis could have made, but it should have come months earlier.

By July 5 Johnston had fallen back to a line of heavy entrenchments just north of the Chattahoochee River, the last natural barrier north of Atlanta.[147] Davis's patience was wearing thin. Pointedly, he telegraphed Johnston that every available man had been sent and that the Federal advance had to be stopped.[148] Johnston replied that he had had no option but to retreat and asked again that Forrest be turned loose on Sherman's supply lines.[149] Davis had already rejected the idea of compelling Lee to send Forrest and was not inclined to change his mind now. To him Johnston's constant clamoring for this solution smacked of the general's perpetual unwillingness to perform the task he had been assigned with the troops the government could afford to give him. Johnston had cavalry; let him send his own horsemen to hit the Yankee supply lines. In fact, for some time Fighting Joe Wheeler had been begging Johnston to allow him to make the raid in Sherman's rear, but Johnston had consistently refused. He felt the army's own cavalry was needed for reconnaissance and screening against Sherman and could not be spared for such a foray. In any case at the rate Johnston was retreating, Atlanta would fall before Forrest or any other Confederate could reach Sherman's supply lines.[150]

Here was Davis's dilemma. Johnston was running out of room to retreat—at least without relinquishing Atlanta—and yet the reluctant general gave no assurance that the backward progress would be stayed. To be sure, Johnston made the same hollow declarations that had marked the army's southward trek all the way from Dalton, but Davis was learning how to weight such pronouncements. If he required a further demonstration of their value, Johnston provided one when on July 9 Sherman flanked him again and got troops across the Chattahoochee upstream from Johnston's position. A congressional delegation was then visiting Johnston, trying to warn him that if he continued to do nothing he was apt to be removed from his command. One of the congressmen mentioned that people in Richmond were quoting the president as saying that "if he were in your place he could whip Sherman now."

"Yes," spat Johnston contemptuously, "I know Mr. Davis thinks he can do a great many things other men would hesitate to attempt. For instance, he tried to do what God failed to do. He tried to make a soldier of Braxton Bragg, and you know the result. It couldn't be done."

At this promising juncture in the conversation, word was brought in of Sherman's crossing of the Chattahoochee. To the surprise of the politicians, Johnston boldly announced that the time had arrived to destroy Sherman's army. They left the general's headquarters well satisfied that Johnston had finally found his resolve, but in the days that followed there was no battle. Johnston meekly pulled back south of the Chattahoochee.[151] Clearly, whatever assurances Johnston might give the Richmond authorities that he was seeking an opportunity for battle were not to be confused with indications that such battle was imminent.

It had already been a difficult summer for Jefferson Davis. First, there was his deteriorating health. Besides his other ailments, his dyspepsia (possibly an ulcer) seemed to grow worse as the pressures increased. Combined with the emotional stress of being too sensitive not to take offense at the vicious criticism of politicians and press yet too disciplined to vent his feelings, these factors brought Davis to a condition in which, by early 1864, he showed little interest in food of any sort. He would remain in his office, working through and beyond mealtimes. To remedy this situation, Varina began preparing the most tempting lunch possible, bringing it to his office on a tray, and staying to see that he ate it. On the last day of April, while Jefferson and Varina chat-

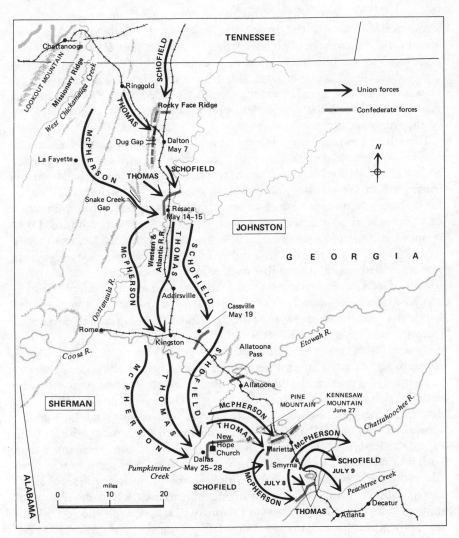

Map 14.1 The Campaign for Atlanta, May–July 1864

ted over his lunch, a servant interrupted with word that their young son Joseph had fallen from a second-story balcony to the pavement below. His parents rushed to the scene, but the boy died as they reached him. Jefferson Davis was prostrate with grief.[152]

Less than a week later the Federal offensives in Virginia and Georgia were under way. The Virginia front aroused anxiety as Grant hammered at Lee's dwindling army. So far Lee had succeeded in keeping Grant out of Richmond, but casualties had been high, among them the South's ideal cavalier, J. E. B.

Stuart, killed at a fight near Richmond—so close, in fact, that there had been a considerable scare that the city would be taken by the raiding Federals before Stuart turned them back in his last battle. The deadly grapple of the two main armies in Virginia had drifted southward until they came to a stop at Petersburg in late June. There they remained, deadlocked, and the Confederate capital was in effect besieged. Within the city, Davis—tired, sick, overworked, and worn down with sorrows public and private—had to face the added anxiety of the enemy at the gates.

Then there was the matter of Georgia and Johnston's insufferable retreating. Unlike Lee, who had made Grant pay a fearsome price for every mile gained, Johnston had showed little inclination to defend the region that had been entrusted to him. Now, with Johnston having given away nearly the entire distance from Dalton to Atlanta, numerous strong defensive positions in the mountains, and the third and last major river barrier to Sherman's advance, Davis confronted a nightmarish possibility. There were signs that Johnston really would give up Atlanta without a fight. In apparent preparation for further retreat, he had recommended that the Federal prisoners being held at Andersonville, Georgia, well to the south of Atlanta, be moved at once.[153] If such was Johnston's intention, he had to be removed immediately. On the other hand, Davis was painfully aware of the dangers of changing commanders with the army in such a desperate situation.[154]

By now many within the Confederacy were impatient at the president's failure to act. Though the enemies of the administration had chosen Johnston as their rallying point and could be counted on to attack Davis viciously if he removed the general, there was also a growing outcry for the president to do just that. Since late June rumor in Richmond had had it that Johnston's removal was imminent.[155] Delegations of prominent Georgians arrived in the capital to plead that Johnston be relieved before he gave away their entire state by bits and pieces. However, when the president pressed them as to whom they would appoint to take his place, they seemed as much at a loss as he.[156] Davis's cabinet members joined in urging him to sack Johnston. Even Seddon, who had once been Johnston's staunchest supporter in the administration, now threw his vote toward removal.[157] Still, against the advice of his entire cabinet, Davis hesitated.

Hoping to find some help with this difficult decision, Davis ordered Bragg to Atlanta to investigate.[158] By the time Bragg arrived on Wednesday, July 13, Johnston had retreated without a fight into the fortifications around Atlanta itself.[159] Accordingly, Bragg's first reports from Atlanta confirmed the president's worst fears.[160] "The indications," Bragg wrote, "seem to favor an entire evacuation of this place."[161] Supplies and machinery were being removed from the town, and most of the population had already left. Even without taking Atlanta, the Federals, situated as they now were, could cut off the flow of foodstuffs from Mississippi and Alabama that fed Lee's army in Virginia.[162] All in all, there was nothing encouraging to report.[163] Davis had not yet come to a final decision on Johnston's future, but he had already begun to cast about for a replacement. Since the situation was critical and the fight for Atlanta, if there was to be one, could come at any time, Johnston's replacement would have to be someone already with the army. That meant one of the army's three corps commanders. Since Stewart had only been promoted to corps command after Polk's death a month earlier, he was not really in the running. Nor was Cleburne, still a major general commanding a single division. Davis's previous decisions had narrowed his present options to two men: William J. Hardee and John B. Hood.

Davis was willing to consider both men, and since Hood had served under Lee for a year and a half, it was natural that Davis should turn to Lee for advice on Hood's abilities. In a dispatch to Lee on July 12 Davis stated bluntly, "General Johnston has failed, and there are strong indications that he will abandon Atlanta. . . . It seems necessary to relieve him at once. Who should succeed him? What think you of Hood for the position?"[164] Lee replied the same day, cautioning against changing commanders at such a time and stating that while he knew Hood to be a good fighter, he was not so sure Hood had the qualities necessary for army command. Hood was "very industrious on the battlefield, careless off," Lee warned, "and I have had no opportunity of judging of his action when the whole responsibility rested upon him." He concluded by hinting that Hardee had had more experience in handling an army.[165]

This seems to have been the president's first inclination as well, despite Hardee's rejection of army command the previous summer. Apparently Bragg had carried with him to Atlanta an order from Davis directing Hardee to take command of the army. There is evidence that before his departure Bragg and the president had discussed the matter at length and had decided that once in Atlanta, Bragg should deliver the order if he thought the circumstances called for it or if he received positive orders from Davis.[166]

Choosing Hardee would be the cautious course, but would it save Atlanta? Hood would fight, but could he handle the army? Hood had been a lieutenant in the Second Cavalry, but Hardee had been a major in the same regiment, and Hardee was still senior to Hood in Confederate rank as well. On the other hand, Hardee had proved to be an uninspired and uninspiring general while Hood had racked up an impressive war record with Lee's Army of Northern Virginia. Additionally, Davis now knew Hood well, admired him, and apparently liked the way he thought. Yet with the army in a desperate position and the fate of Atlanta in the balance, the president had leaned toward experience and had had the order drawn up for Hardee.

That he still wavered rather than have the order delivered at once was due to the influence of Braxton Bragg, who greatly preferred Hood. Hardee's contempt for his former commander was long-standing, and Bragg was apparently beginning to realize how instrumental Hardee had been in turning other officers against him. Besides, Bragg, who unlike Davis had had firsthand experience with Hardee's generalship, harbored some well-founded doubts about his abilities. It was therefore on the basis of Bragg's impression once he reached Atlanta that Davis would make the final decision: Johnston, Hardee, or Hood.

At least one of the candidates did not believe in leaving matters to chance. Hood had long been angling for the job of army commander and now saw his opportunity. Shortly after Bragg arrived in Atlanta, Hood handed him a letter, one-sided to the point of not being entirely truthful, which expressed his views on the campaign. He had always been in favor of fighting, the letter claimed, but Johnston had insisted on retreat and had been sustained and encouraged in that policy by Hardee. What was needed now, Hood maintained, was vigorous aggressive action, and the strong implication was that he was the man to provide it.[167] Though this echoed the theme of the many letters he had been sending to Richmond throughout the campaign, the truth was that Hood, more often than Hardee, had counseled Johnston to retreat. Hood was letting his ambition get the better of his honesty. He was behaving like a man who had something to prove. Maybe it was the useless arm and the missing leg. Very likely it had something to do with Buck Preston. It seems Hood had been writing her for some two weeks that Johnston would be removed and he would be given command of the Army of Tennessee.[168] In any case, the ambitious general held extensive conversations with Bragg, and while the content of these talks is unknown, it is a fair supposition that they followed the same lines as Hood's misleading letters. Bragg was impressed.

Meanwhile, back in Richmond, Davis continued to agonize over the decision that only he could make. He had Lee's telegram now, gently advising that Hardee might make a better choice or that it might be better to leave Johnston in place. Davis had enormous respect for Lee both as a man and as a general. Yet Lee was not in Atlanta, nor had he commanded Hardee since the latter was a major and he a lieutenant colonel of cavalry in earlier days of peace. Such considerations increased the weight of Bragg's opinion. Uncertain but still leaning toward Hardee, Davis telegraphed Bragg on July 14 to say that the general should use his own discretion as to when and whether, but that if Johnston had to go and Hardee seemed to be the man to replace him, Bragg should "adopt advice and execute as proposed."[169]

Bragg's answer shot back in a telegram the next day: "I am decidedly opposed, as it would perpetuate the past and present policy [of retreat] which he had advised and now sustains." The substance of his opinion had been heavily influenced by Hood's shading of the truth. As a result Bragg concluded that a decision to place Hardee in command would carry with it all of the unfortunate side effects of making a change at this time without altering the army's previous disastrous policies. Furthermore, Bragg rightly doubted the extent of the army's confidence in Hardee. As for Hood, Bragg reported to Davis in glowing terms that "if any change is made Lieutenant-General Hood would give unlimited satisfaction."[170]

The president carefully weighed the facts and the options—and hesitated. He decided to give Johnston another chance. On July 16 Davis telegraphed Johnston, referring to the critical situation around Atlanta and stating, "I wish to hear from you as to the present situation and your plan of operations so specifically as will enable me to anticipate events."[171] If Johnston would spell out a clear plan of action for throwing back the threatening Federal army, Davis would give him an opportunity to carry it out.

The general's reply came back the same day. He was so badly outnumbered, he claimed, that all he could do was wait and react to the enemy's movements— what he had in fact done all the way from Dalton to Atlanta. Then he added the clincher: He was planning to pull his army out of the Atlanta fortifications and commit the defense of the city to the Georgia militia so that the Army of Tennessee's "movements may be freer and wider."[172] To Davis this looked like abandoning Atlanta, and that is probably what it amounted to. The small force of half-trained Georgia militia available would not have lasted long in the face of Sherman's battle-hardened veterans. Later, a high-ranking Confederate officer estimated the Federals would have had Atlanta within twenty-four hours of the time Johnston's veterans filed out of the trenches.[173]

This confirmed Davis's worst fears that Johnston would retreat right past Atlanta without a fight. There could be no more postponing the decision. Since Hardee (so Davis was told) would be no improvement, an order was sent out the next day relieving Johnston and placing Hood in command of the Army of Tennessee.[174]

Hood was junior to Hardee, but this was remedied by giving the new commander a temporary promotion to full general. Davis thought, rather naively as it turned out, that because Hardee had previously declined command of the army he would not now object to Hood's being promoted over him.[175] Hood's old corps was commanded initially by Cheatham, but Hood perceived the need for a better corps commander and three days later wrote to Davis requesting one. Of the several possibilities Hood suggested, Davis quickly chose Stephen D. Lee, currently in charge in Mississippi. Lee, then, would take Hood's place as corps commander.[176] Cleburne had again been passed over.

Whatever Hood had done or said to get the job, he had it now and that was that. At first, he was not so sure he liked the idea, at least under the present conditions. Perhaps he thought that Davis would not change commanders with the army backed up against Atlanta but was looking for someone to replace Johnston should that officer allow the city to fall. As it was, Hood would be stepping into a desperate situation. The day after being informed of his new position, he telegraphed Richmond that though he had officially assumed command, he felt it was "dangerous to change commanders at this time" and hoped that no change would be made "until the fate of Atlanta is decided."[177] Later in the day he joined with Hardee and Stewart in sending another dispatch to the same effect.[178] Leaving Johnston to decide the "fate of Atlanta" was exactly what Davis had wished to avoid, and regardless, the deed was done. Reversing his action now and reinstating Johnston would only make a bad situation worse. Davis so informed the three generals and exhorted them to "sacrifice . . . every personal consideration" for the good of the cause.[179]

Hood was still uneasy and, feeling unequal to the job suddenly dumped in his lap, begged Johnston to stay on and advise him in the defense of Atlanta. Johnston was reluctant but finally agreed, stipulating that he would ride into Atlanta first and then return to Hood's headquarters. That night, however, without another word to Hood, Johnston left for Macon, Georgia, no doubt hoping and confidently expecting that Hood would promptly suffer an annihilating defeat.[180]

Many a Civil War general, confronted with the awesome responsibility of command, would become paralyzed by caution and indecision—not John B. Hood. Having assumed command on July 17, he had the army in action by the twentieth. Sherman actually had left him little choice. The Federal general had his army spread out in another of the turning movements that had pushed Johnston all the way from Dalton. Hood could attack or, as Johnston had always done, fall back. Falling back now would mean the loss of Atlanta, and under the circumstances Hood could hardly have made a different choice than he did.

Sherman's plan called for one part of his army to swing wide to the east of Atlanta while the other part threatened the city from the north. It was this latter part that Hood decided to hit, hoping to catch it in the act of crossing Peachtree Creek, just north of Atlanta. Somehow the command system of the Army of Tennessee again proved to be extraordinarily stiff-jointed and slow-moving. S. D. Lee had not yet arrived from Mississippi, so Cheatham was still leading Hood's olds corps. Either through inexperience or for other reasons peculiar to himself, Cheatham was late in getting his troops into position and in fact never really did get them in quite the right place. Hardee, who was consumed with envy at having been passed over for command of the army, sulked, delayed, and generally told Hood as little as he could of what was happening at the front. Hood should have supervised matters more closely, but he was trying to follow the example of Robert E. Lee in giving broad, discretionary orders.[181] Sometimes that system of command failed to work even for Lee, and it certainly did not work for Hood. By the time the attack began in earnest, the Federals, under Thomas, had completed their crossing of the creek and were entrenched and waiting. The result was predictable. The Confederates gave Thomas a few bad hours but in the end suffered 5,000 casualties without making a dent in Union lines.[182]

Hood was not discouraged in the least and decided that if this part of Sherman's army was strong, the other part (the flanking force) ought rightly to be weak.[183] Therefore, immediately after the setback on Peachtree Creek, he put into action a plan to flank the flankers. It was, Hood felt, just what his hero Lee would have done, and in reality, it was not a bad plan at all. On the morning of July 22 the armies again collided east of Atlanta. Despite another miserable performance by Hardee, Hood's attack was nearly successful. Indeed, had the Federals not unwittingly, in the course of a routine maneuver for other purposes, formed their troops in the best possible position to receive the onslaught before it began, there might have been no stopping Hood's men.[184] As it was, the Federals were staggered by the force of the blow. At times parts of the Union line were under fire from front and rear simultaneously. The Union commander of this part of the northern army was Gen. James McPherson, Sherman's most trusted lieutenant. Back at West Point McPherson had been a classmate of Hood and had finished first in the class in which Hood had ranked forty-fifth. Sometimes McPherson had helped the unstudious Hood with his lessons. Now they were on opposite sides in a hard-fought battle. Early in the fight a bullet from one of Hood's men found McPherson, and he fell mortally wounded.[185] Yet when the day was over, the Federals had held on and escaped destruction—though by the thinnest of margins—and Hood's army had lost another 10,000 men.[186] Though both armies were momentarily stunned by the force of the blows they had exchanged, they quickly recovered—Sherman swinging his flanking force back around to the west of Atlanta and Hood moving to stop him. On July 28 Hood struck savagely at the Federals near a country meetinghouse called Ezra Church.

The plan for the destruction of the Union flanking force called for S. D. Lee's corps to entrench in front of the Union force and hold it in place while Stewart's corps took it in flank and routed it. Although the plan had much to commend it, it never got off the ground. When Lee moved to take up the position Hood had assigned to his corps, he discovered it was already occupied by entrenched Federals.[187] Lee had come to the Army of Tennessee fresh from an extremely costly and far from satisfactory affair at Tupelo, Mississippi. At that engagement Lee, who had evidently forgotten how his entrenched troops had been able to inflict severe punishment on Sherman at Chickasaw Bayou a year and a half before, had flung his men in headlong attack against Union breastworks. The result was a casualty list that ran to 40 percent of his total force and ten times the number suffered by the enemy.[188] Lee apparently brought these straight-ahead tendencies with him to his new assignment, without also bringing the experience requisite to a corps commander. The result was an uncharacteristic lapse, for Lee was on the whole a competent officer.

Finding the enemy in his assigned position, Lee neither informed Hood nor waited for Stewart's flanking force to get into position. Without pausing even to arrange a coordinated attack with his whole corps, he immediately threw forward whatever unit came first to hand. The result was a piecemeal attack that only shook the enemy when a concerted effort might have dislodged him. For all that, it was a savagely hard-fought battle. Stewart heard the firing, knew something had gone wrong, and marched toward the sound of the guns. Soon his men were joining Lee's in the attack.[189]

The fight continued all day, yet not once did Hood ride to the front to see what was going on or find out why the battle had deviated from his plan.[190] Perhaps riding did not come so easily after all to the one-legged general. Or perhaps Hood, who had undoubtedly had his finest moments as a brigade commander, never really got the knack of handling an army.[191] Instead, Hood sent Hardee to the scene of the fighting "to look after matters," though why he should have expected good results from this after Hardee's performance in the previous week's fight is not clear.[192] In any case, the battle was another failure for the Confederates and a costly one. Five thousand of Hood's men became casualties, and General Stewart received a wound that put him out of action for two weeks while Cheatham filled in for him.[193] It could have been worse, for only the poor condition of the local roads kept Sherman from skirting the flank of Lee's and Stewart's poorly positioned forces.[194]

The battle of Ezra Church, coming as it did on top of Peachtree Creek and the battle of Atlanta (as the two previous clashes were called), left both armies badly shaken. Hood's army was by now terribly depleted. It had lost some 20,000 men in nine days. Sherman's losses could not have been much more than half that, and Sherman could better afford them.[195] Still, the grim northern general had been shocked by the force of Hood's blows and, apparently more than he liked to admit, disturbed at how close some of them had come to succeeding. He had gained a new respect for Hood, and from now on, he would maneuver cautiously, waiting for an opening and being careful not to present one to Hood.[196] Hood, with his bloodied army, could do little better. Nor were the armies and their commanders the only ones who were shaken. Back in Richmond Davis was appalled as the casualty reports came in for the three battles around Atlanta. He urged Hood to avoid further frontal assaults of the nature that had brought such heavy losses—something Hood for the moment was inclined to forego anyway.[197] He could only stay inside the Atlanta fortifications and try to hold the town as long as possible without getting his army trapped. Trapping Hood's army was precisely Sherman's intent, and throughout the month of August the Union general gradually extended his forces to the southwest, stretching out to cut the railroad that was Atlanta's lifeline while Hood's army licked its wounds inside the city's defenses.

Hood had his own ideas about cutting rail lines. He sought and received permission from Davis to send Wheeler with most of the Army of Tennessee's cavalry on a raid to break up the railroad in Sherman's rear. Wheeler set out on August 10.[198] Hood had high hopes for the undertaking, and early reports from Wheeler seemed to confirm these. In reality—and unknown to Hood—Wheeler was riding himself right out of the campaign. First he did some halfhearted railroad wrecking south of Dalton. Tearing up a railroad thoroughly was hard work that could not be done from horseback. Accordingly Wheeler's men, like most Civil War cavalrymen, showed little interest in it. Having done a slapdash job of track wrecking—hardly even a nuisance for Sherman's fast-working repair crews—Wheeler next decided to disobey his instructions and ride all the way up into East Tennessee beyond Knoxville. Finally crossing the Tennessee River, he reentered Confederate territory in northern Alabama by way of Nashville, where he was supposed to have gone in the first place. "Fighting Joe" Wheeler might lack a sense of strategy and the discipline to make his men demolish railroads, but he always lived up to his nickname. Throughout his long jaunt across the state of Tennessee, he fought just about every Federal force he fell in with, whether there was any good reason to or not. By the time he reached Alabama in early September, his cavalry was pretty well used up.[199]

Others, however, among the Confederates had hit upon the idea of hitting Sherman's supply lines. When Hood took over the Army of Tennessee and S. D. Lee succeeded him as corps commander, Lee's Mississippi department fell to Richard Taylor. One of Taylor's first actions as a new department commander was to inform his brother-in-law, the president, that he was sending the dreaded Forrest against Sherman's supply lines. As he had with S. D. Lee, Davis readily agreed; sending Forrest was fine if that was what the Mississippi department commander wanted. By mid-September Forrest was on his way to Middle Tennessee. Forrest was a much different cavalryman than Joe Wheeler, and given the right chance he might do some real damage. Certainly Sherman had feared just such a raid as Forrest was now launching, but by the time the raid got started the situation in Georgia had changed so drastically that Forrest was able to accomplish little in Middle Tennessee.[200]

On August 30 Sherman had won the position he sought astride Hood's railroad lifeline at Jonesboro, southwest of Atlanta. Hood would have to give battle again to restore his communications or else give up the city. True to form, Hood chose to fight it out, but for the moment at least, there seemed to be very little spark left in the Army of Tennessee. Hood ordered Hardee to take his own corps, commanded for the occasion by Cleburne, as well as that of S. D. Lee, march to Jonesboro, and drive the Federals out of their threatening position. Whether because of his continued hostility toward Hood or because he simply could do no better, Hardee badly mishandled the movement. So slow were his preparations that the Federals had ample time to entrench, making the whole operation highly problematical. Then Lee, young and inexperienced, again went off half-cocked. Hearing heavy skirmish firing, he attacked prematurely. The result was another poorly coordinated, piecemeal assault that, unlike the one at Ezra Church, was not carried out with much vigor by troops that may have begun to suspect that their generals did not know what they were about.[201] Only about 1,500 casualties were suffered before the attack was given up.[202] Afterwards, even Lee had to admit that "the attack was a feeble one and a failure."[203]

It was all over then. Hood had no choice but to pull his battered army out of Atlanta and retreat southward. On September 2 Federal troops occupied the city.[204] The fall of Atlanta was perhaps the last great turning point of the war. If eventual Confederate military collapse had been a certainty before Atlanta, immediate collapse was a certainty after it. At best, the Confederacy might eke out a few more months' meager existence, but the end could not be even a year away. The Confederacy's already inadequate industrial and transportation system had been struck a fatal blow by the loss of Atlanta, and a Union army had penetrated the interior of the South and had more strategic possibilities open to it than the Confederates could hope to counter.

Most important, the capture of Atlanta had raised northern morale to the point that Lincoln's reelection was assured. During the long summer, as Union casualty lists had lengthened and Grant and Sherman had stalled before Richmond and Atlanta, northern war-weariness had reached a peak. It had appeared for a time that Lincoln would be defeated by a "peace" candidate, and at one point, Lincoln thought so himself.[205] After Atlanta all this was changed. Other factors, of course, played a role: There was Farragut's victory at Mobile Bay and Sheridan's at Winchester; and it can never be known whether Lincoln might not have won the election even without any of these victories. Yet the fall of Atlanta, more than any other event, had helped to guarantee that the northern electorate would once again choose Lincoln and, in so doing, choose to continue the war to its ultimate conclusion.

Jefferson Davis did not recognize this, and it probably would not have moved him if he had. There was no quitting in the man. For the third time in the war Davis traveled to the western theater, this time to try to alleviate a hopeless situation. Hood had suggested a visit, and since some action clearly was needed, the president went.[206]

The trip had several purposes, and one of them was dealing with the perennial squabbles among the Army of Tennessee's high command. The problem centered now on Hardee. The plodding corps commander was furious with Davis for appointing Hood to command of the army and, very likely, angry with himself for having refused that same post eight months earlier. During the fighting around Atlanta, Hardee had retaliated by being uncooperative and thus had incurred the enmity of Hood. This sentiment he returned with compound interest. The result was that for weeks both officers had been begging to have Hardee transferred out of the Army of Tennessee. Davis, who had mastered his bitterness against Joseph E. Johnston in order to make one final attempt to use that officer for the good of the Confederacy, could not understand generals who lacked the self-discipline to suppress their personal feelings and work together for the good of the cause. Naturally, therefore, he had consistently refused the transfer requests and urged Hood and Hardee to cooperate. It was no use, though, and finally resolving the matter was one of Davis's reasons for making his visit.[207]

A more fundamental if low-key problem was apparent dissatisfaction with Hood among a number of the army's generals.[208] Davis himself seems to have been not altogether easy about the uncertain qualities of Hood's aggressive brand of generalship. The trip to Georgia would give the president his first opportunity for face-to-face discussions with the Kentucky-born Texan since the latter had come into command of the army. It would also give Davis a chance to consider firsthand how to bring harmony into the army's upper ranks.

Then there was the matter of morale, both in and out of the army. If the fall of Atlanta had been a tremendous boost to northern spirits, it could only have had an opposite effect in the South. The common people, especially in Georgia, might soon conclude that the war was over and that it was time to throw in the towel. The president hoped to squelch that attitude, while also raising morale in the army. The soldiers understood little more than that under Johnston there had been relatively few casualties and Atlanta had not fallen, whereas under Hood the reverse had occurred. However, looming above all these motivations for Davis's trip to Georgia was the need to discuss strategy with Hood and arrive at a plan to remedy the desperate situation in the West. Hood had written to Richmond with an interesting suggestion on the future operations of the Army of Tennessee, and it had triggered in the president's mind some ideas that he was anxious to talk over with the general.

Davis reached Hood's headquarters in Palmetto, Georgia, on September 25. At the station he was met by an honor guard composed of Tennessee troops. It was raining, and the bedraggled soldiers standing in the oozing red Georgia clay must have looked a forlorn sight. Davis decided to go straight into his morale-raising activities and addressed extemporaneous remarks to the dripping soldiers. "Be of good cheer," he concluded his brief address, "for within a short while your faces will be turned homeward and your feet pressing the soil of Tennessee." This brought a roar of cheers and rebel yells from the Tennesseeans, but amid the cheers were cries of "Johnston! Give us Johnston!"[209] Obviously, the president had his work cut out for him.

The business of Davis's visit proceeded during the next few days as he met with various generals of the Army of Tennessee. Hardee was adamant about not serving under Hood. When questioned about whom he would recommend, Hardee responded that Johnston would make a good commander, but Davis would hear none of that. Hardee then changed his tack and named Beauregard. The Creole general would, he assured the president, "be very acceptable to the army."[210] Other generals offered similar advice.[211]

Though Davis would not consider Johnston, he was ready to give Beauregard another try, and he had needed no suggestions from Hardee or the other generals to reach that point. Before leaving Richmond, Davis had consulted

Lee about the "availability and willingness" of Beauregard for assignment to the West. Beauregard was at that time serving under Lee with the forces around Richmond. As far as Lee was concerned, Beauregard, whose presence was at best awkward, was eminently available. And Beauregard was always more than willing to get out from under whatever authority he could.[212] This information Davis kept in mind as he considered who, if anyone, should replace Hood.

Hood himself was somewhat chastened by his loss of Atlanta and the disapproval of his subordinate generals. He offered to resign, but Davis had other ideas.[213] Hood would be retained, and Hardee transferred to command at Charleston. Hardee's place as corps commander would be assumed by Cheatham.[214] For Beauregard Davis was considering a role that tied in closely with the Army of Tennessee's new strategy. Before Davis had left Richmond, Hood had sent a dispatch outlining his thoughts about the army's next move. He proposed to put his forces in a position to threaten Sherman's railroad supply line between Atlanta and Dalton. A few cavalry raids along the railroad could be ignored, but not a whole army. Sherman would either have to go after Hood and drive him off—actually recrossing some of the ground over which he had pursued Johnston toward Atlanta—or else head south to open up a supply line on the Gulf or Atlantic coasts. If Sherman chose the latter course, Hood proposed to follow and do what damage he could.[215]

Davis had been impressed with the idea and was even more so after discussing it with Hood. He not only approved the plan but also suggested a refinement. If Sherman did try to drive Hood off his communications, as it was expected he would, Hood should fall back on Gadsden, Alabama, whence he could draw supplies by rail from the southwest. His own supply lines would thus be secure while, in that position, he remained a continual threat to Sherman's.[216] Whatever happened, Hood was to follow Sherman wherever he went, north or south.[217]

To facilitate execution, Davis thought it best to have some coordination between Hood's army and the troops in Mississippi under Richard Taylor. The two Confederate forces would be brought much closer together by the new strategy, and they could now be reasonably confident of not finding Sherman between them. Forrest, a part of Taylor's command, was believed to be at this very moment raising havoc in Middle Tennessee, just north of Hood's proposed new area of operations. Perhaps even more could be accomplished by reestablishing the unified command that Joseph E. Johnston had held but failed to exercise nearly two years before. It was for this post that Davis had Beauregard in mind. He first wanted to talk with the Creole general in person, though, and so he held off on issuing the order for him to take command.

Taking leave of Hood and the Army of Tennessee on the twenty-seventh, Davis began working to achieve his other goal in making the trip, that is, raising civilian morale and exhorting the populace to rally to Hood's standard.[218] By this time government records showed that there were over 100,000 men absent without leave from the Confederacy's various armies. If but a fraction of these men would come to the colors, Davis hoped to convince them, all would yet be well.[219] His first stop was Macon, Georgia, where he made a powerful speech. "Our cause is not lost," he proclaimed earnestly. "Sherman cannot keep up his long line of communication; and retreat sooner or later he must. And when that day comes, the fate that befell the army of the French Empire in its retreat from Moscow will be reenacted."[220] From Macon he continued to Montgomery, scene of his first inauguration more than three and a half years ago. Then it was on to Augusta and finally Columbia, South Carolina.

While in Augusta Davis met personally with Beauregard, who had come down from Virginia for that purpose, and finalized his decision to appoint that general to command both Hood's and Taylor's departments.[221] It was a wise move in several respects. Many people had been calling for the appointment of Beauregard to a more important position.[222] The president's action would not only still this clamor but also take some of the wind out of the sails of the political opposition and help to accomplish some of the morale raising Davis aimed at by dusting off the old "Hero of Manassas" to save the South in its hour of peril. At best Beauregard's contribution might be smooth coordination between Hood and Taylor and sound advice for Hood as a young and inexperienced general.[223] At worst Beauregard, not having direct command of an army, would not make things any worse than they already were.

Overall, Davis's efforts to lift Confederate spirits seemed to be successful.[224] However, in trying to convince the populace that prospects for victory were still good, he let his enthusiasm lead him to commit some rather severe breaches of military secrecy. In his speech at Columbia, Davis proclaimed, "His [Hood's] eye is now fixed upon a point far beyond that where he was assailed by the enemy."[225] Perhaps Davis believed the next move was so obvious that it would be plain to any intelligent observer on either side of the battle lines. That would have been characteristic of Jefferson Davis. Or the president may simply have decided that raising morale was so desperately necessary as to justify the loss of the advantage of strategic surprise. Sherman, who read the text of Davis's speech with great interest when it appeared in the newspapers a few days later, was inclined to a different explanation. "The taking of Atlanta," Sherman wrote, "broke upon Jeff. Davis so suddenly as to disturb the equilibrium of his usually well-balanced temper, so that . . . he let out some thoughts which otherwise he would have kept to himself."[226] Whatever the reason for Davis's indiscretion, it was apparently of some use to Sherman. He had been contemplating a deeper drive into Georgia, but taking heed of Davis's warning, he turned back to meet the new threat to his communications.

Still, even had Davis known this, he could have returned to the Confederacy's capital well pleased with what he had achieved on his third wartime visit to the western front. He had succeeded in shoring up civilian morale and perhaps the army's morale as well. If deserters were not flocking back, at least the armies of the Confederacy had not completely evaporated amid mass desertions. The new strategy he had worked out with Hood was excellent, and the appointment of Beauregard would at least deprive the administration's enemies of political ammunition and might even do some good. It remained now to see how the president's dispositions and plans would be put into operation.

The beginning was highly auspicious, despite Sherman's foreknowledge. Hood carried out the plan to perfection. Swinging west and then north, he took up a position astride Sherman's supply lines in north Georgia. The Union general, as expected, moved to destroy this menace, but Hood slipped out of Sherman's grasp and renewed his threat to the Federal lifeline at another point. For the next six weeks the two armies maneuvered around northwestern Georgia, with Sherman constantly trying to come to grips with the elusive Confederate and Hood wisely declining to accept battle while maintaining his threat to Sherman's supplies. So far the Davis-Hood strategy had been eminently successful. Not only was Sherman unable to exploit the capture of Atlanta, he was now traversing the same ground he had fought over months before. Sherman was aware of this and found it intensely frustrating. Finally, when Hood tried to lure him all the way into northern Alabama, Sherman completely lost his patience. He would let the pestilent Hood go where he wanted. "If he will go to the Ohio River I will give him rations," Sherman fumed. "Let him go north. My business is down South." This last was a reference to what Sherman planned to do instead of chasing Hood. By the established rules of warfare, it was pure folly, but Sherman was audacious enough to try it. First, he divided his army, sending Thomas and 30,000 men to deal with whatever Hood might try to do next. With his remaining 60,000 men Sherman moved back to Atlanta, cut loose of his supply line, tore up the railroad in his rear, and struck out for the coast, three hundred miles away through enemy territory. His army would live off the land, and so it would have to keep moving and stay spread out to forage. This would be impossible in the presence of a Confederate army, but the Confederates had no army to oppose Sherman. "I can make this march," the Union general assured his superiors, "and make Georgia howl."[227]

Hood, meanwhile, had come up with a plan of his own, and it was not so very much different from what Sherman had said he would be glad to have the Confederate attempt. Hood felt it would be folly to pursue Sherman, who already had a headstart and would certainly leave no foodstuffs in his wake for the Army of Tennessee to subsist on.[228] Instead, Hood proposed to move north, beat Thomas, seize Nashville, and proceed from there. Sherman, Hood believed, would be forced to follow him, and with the Confederate recruits that would come in from Tennessee and Kentucky, Hood would be a match for him.[229] The plan skirted about the far edges of reality, but under the circumstances it might have been as good as anything else he could have done—provided he moved very fast and made no mistakes.[230]

On October 20 Hood presented his idea to Beauregard at Gadsden, Alabama. The Creole general had cooked up a few unrealistic plans in his day, but he was shocked at what Hood had in mind. It was completely contrary to the strategy that Davis and Hood had worked out at Palmetto in September and on which Davis had briefed Beauregard a few days later at Augusta. According to that scheme Hood was to follow Sherman if he went south. Now Hood was proposing to go the opposite direction. Still, Beauregard, unwilling to take the responsibility of rejecting the plan, reluctantly gave his consent but stipulated that Hood send Wheeler and the Army of Tennessee's cavalry to harass Sherman's march. In Wheeler's place Hood would receive Forrest and his cavalry. Above all, Beauregard stressed, Hood must move quickly.[231]

Within the next few days, both Hood and Beauregard wrote to inform the Richmond authorities of the change in strategy. Hood seemed as glad to part company with Sherman as the latter had been to see the last of him. "Should he move . . . south from Atlanta," Hood wrote Davis, "I think it would be the best thing that could happen for our general good." Gleefully he added, "Beauregard *agrees with me* as to my plan of operation."[232]

With some reservations Davis approved the movement, though against Bragg's advice.[233] The president urged on Hood the importance of defeating the Federals before their army could be reunited or reinforced. If indeed a large part of the Federal forces in Georgia was moving south, then, he told Hood, "You may first beat him in detail and subsequently without serious obstruction or danger to the country in your rear advance to the Ohio River."[234] This did not sound exactly like Hood's strategy, but Hood must have figured it was close enough. Eagerly he prepared to carry out his grand offensive.

Everything depended on how fast Hood could move his army. In Tennessee, Thomas was busily trying to make an army out of various occupation and garrison troops which he was hurriedly gathering around the nucleus of men he had brought from Georgia. If Hood could strike quickly, he might hit Thomas before the Federal general was ready to receive him.[235] Davis had urged rapid movement and so had Beauregard, but somehow it never happened. Some of the reasons for this were beyond Hood's control: Heavy rains, muddy roads, and high water in the Tennessee River delayed Hood's movement.[236] Yet there also seemed to be something wrong with the general and his army. Hood had inherited a poor administrative system from Johnston but had shown little interest in improving it. When Hood's chief of staff was removed for his failure to get large stocks of supplies out of Atlanta before it fell, the system deteriorated further. One officer remarked that the army's command system was so poor that it was impossible to know whether Hood's orders had even reached the corps commanders.[237] As for supplies, Hood had never been much interested in the logistical side of warfare. Beauregard finally had to take care of such details, of which, he noted, "General Hood was disposed to be oblivious."[238]

To make matters worse, Hood had begun to resent Beauregard, perhaps because of Beauregard's insistence on reminding him of military reality. It was an ironic turn of events indeed that made the imaginative Creole the proponent of realism against the fantasies of his subordinate, but Hood was behaving less and less rationally. All summer he had behaved like a man ridden by an obsession. Perhaps it was the maiming at Chickamauga the year before. Perhaps it was the repeated humiliations at the hands of Buck Preston and the desire to prove to her and her parents that he was worthy of her, even with only one leg and a crippled arm. Or maybe it was ordinary ambition run amuck in a man who had suddenly become aware of having risen very far very fast. It had first shown up in his somewhat dishonest promotion of himself and simultaneous undermining of Johnston and Hardee during the retreat to Atlanta. Then as the failures had mounted – the result of his questionable execution of his often brilliant planning – he had become embittered against his generals, who he believed were incompetent, and even the common soldiers, who he convinced himself were cowards. Now, consumed by the need to succeed, he began to ignore unpleasant facts that might stand in the way and to resent Beauregard for calling them to his attention.

To avoid this nuisance, Hood simply avoided all contact with Beauregard. He left his superior uninformed about nearly everything, including the army's frequent changes of headquarters. As a consequence Beauregard often had to go looking for the army he was supposed to oversee. This pattern reached such ridiculous extremes that when Beauregard showed up at Tuscumbia, Alabama, where the army was preparing to cross the Tennessee River, Hood moved his headquarters across the river to Florence. This campaign would be run Hood's way without pestering from anyone.

By the time Hood cleared the Tennessee River and moved north, it was November 21.[239] Various problems in finding a suitable river crossing had forced Hood to swing west all the way to Tuscumbia, a less-than-ideal starting point for his drive into Tennessee. By the time the last of Hood's troops marched away from the river, Sherman was already four days south of the smoldering remains of Atlanta, bound for the sea and determined to "make Georgia howl" along the way. Around Nashville Thomas's preparations were nearing completion. Time was running out for the Army of Tennessee, but in the ranks the men felt a strange excitement. Marching north on roads that were alternately muddy bogs or frozen ruts, buffeted by raging storms of snow and sleet, they were nevertheless eager to return to the region they had defended for so long. One soldier wrote, "The ground is frozen hard and a sharp cold wind is blowing but as my face is toward Tennessee, I heed none of these things."[240]

Hood knew the many delays at Tuscumbia had helped Thomas but still felt the movement had good prospects for success.[241] At first it looked as if he might be right. Thomas had posted General Schofield with 28,000 men in southern Tennessee to delay Hood's march while final preparations for his

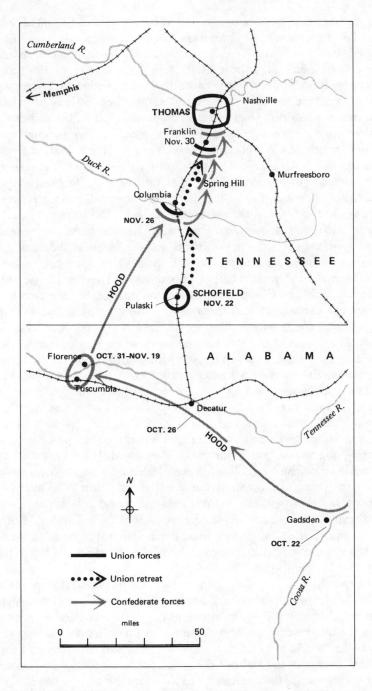

Map 14.2 *Hood's Tennessee Campaign, October–November 1864*

reception were made in Nashville. Hood hoped to beat Schofield, his former West Point roommate, to Columbia, Tennessee, where the road to Nashville crossed the Duck River. If he did, he would be between Schofield and whatever Federal forces might be in Nashville and, at least theoretically, in an excellent position to destroy one or both Federal fragments.

After the first few days of sleet and snow, the weather turned fair. The troops marched north in high spirits through the balmy Indian summer, cheered by the distinctly prosouthern inhabitants of this, Tennessee's richest plantation district. South of Columbia the road passed a church that had once been Leonidas Polk's when he had lived in Tennessee. St. John's Episcopal was built in the English gothic style and looked as if it had been lifted out of the British Isles and set down in Middle Tennessee. Its stone walls and steep-sloping roof were cloaked in ivy, and the graves in the churchyard were interspersed with flowers and shrubs somehow still green and fresh in late November. Pat Cleburne reigned up in front of the church to take in this idyllic scene. Cleburne was still a division commander and still the best the army had or would ever have. Of the army's present corps commanders, Stewart and Lee had been his juniors in rank, and Cheatham was much his inferior. So were they all for that matter; but Cleburne, for whatever reason, had been passed by. Perhaps it did not weigh all too heavily on him, for he had found other reasons to be happy in this fourth year of the war. Last February when Hardee had finally gotten leave to go to Mobile and wed his rich young bride, Cleburne had gone along as best man. There the shy bachelor-general met twenty-four-year-old Susan Tarleton, "a young maiden of rare accomplishments and intelligence" and the maid of honor to Hardee's bride. It was apparently love at first sight. Cleburne visited Mobile again that winter, and by early March the couple was engaged.[242] Thereafter they had written faithfully, and perhaps the end of another year's campaigning would bring another wedding in Mobile.

Very likely Cleburne thought of Sue Tarleton as he sat on his horse surveying the peaceful churchyard and quiet, stately church—so like the one he had known as a boy back in County Cork—but if he did, he kept such thoughts to himself. The thoughts he voiced were ones of the uncertainties of war and the beauty of the scene before him. After sitting quietly for a time, he remarked to a staff officer that it would be "almost worth dying for, to be buried in such a beautiful spot."[243]

The march went on, and though Hood found Schofield waiting for him on the north bank of the Duck River at Columbia, he still had high hopes of getting between the Union force and Nashville. "The enemy must give me fight," he told his chaplain next morning, "or I'll be in Nashville before tomorrow night."[244] His plan called for Lee with most of his corps and the army's artillery to remain in front of Columbia and distract Schofield while the rest of the army swung three miles east to ford the river and strike out for a point between Schofield and Nashville. This time Hood decided to supervise things in person and rode along with the flanking column. The maneuver worked as Hood had planned, and by the afternoon of that day, November 29, Hood had his troops in place near Spring Hill, ten miles behind Schofield's line and in perfect position to cut off the Federal army and destroy it.[245]

It was not to be. For one last time the command system of the Army of Tennessee malfunctioned. The Federal escape route at Spring Hill was held by a single division. In the fading light of a November late afternoon, Cleburne had hit them hard and driven them back to within yards of the vital turnpike. The Federals knew what the stakes were and were fighting desperately, but another attack ought to dislodge them. Another attack was just what the Irish Confederate had in mind, but orders arrived from Cheatham to delay the assault until another Confederate division could come up. The division was slow arriving and then slow getting into position. Confusion mounted, and finally the whole affair just fizzled out. Well after dark, Hood, who had been straightening out some minor confusion at the rear of the column, arrived on the field. There was still plenty of time to seize the pike and cut off Schofield's retreat, even in the dark. Hood was nearly exhausted, having been strapped into the saddle all day long, and the stump of his leg was paining him. He later said he gave the order for the attack to be renewed, and perhaps he did. In any case he turned in very shortly after arriving on the field, leaving others to see that his orders, if he actually gave any, were carried out. They were not, of course, and may not even have been delivered.[246] Hood blamed Cheatham for the failure. Cheatham, who may have been in his cups again, blamed Hood. In any case, Hood failed to see that his orders were carried out. The result was one of the most inexplicable episodes of the war: The entire Federal force marched out of the Confederate trap, passing within gunshot along the entire length of Hood's line, for the most part unmolested by the Confederates.[247]

The next morning, when Hood woke up and realized what had happened, something in him seemed to snap. The failure was unbearable, so Hood convinced himself that he had not failed. His generals—Cheatham, Cleburne, and the others—had let him down. They were incompetent and probably cowardly, too. The soldiers, cowardly and afraid to charge an entrenched enemy, had also failed him. And Hood had their penance ready: They would catch the Federals and smash them, regardless of casualties. No more fancy flanking maneuvers—from now on, his men were going to go right down the enemy's throat.[248]

At once he sent his army marching up the road after the enemy in the direction of Nashville. Schofield, who had since been informed by Thomas that all was in readiness and that he could fall back to Nashville at any time, did not have a very big headstart. When he came to the Harpeth River at Franklin, Tennessee, and found no bridges there, he deployed his force in a defensive perimeter around the town while work details built temporary bridges.[249] Leading elements of Hood's army arrived in front of the Federal entrenchments late that afternoon, and Hood ordered an immediate frontal assault even though most of his artillery and one of his three corps were not up yet.[250] Several of his generals protested, but Hood was adamant. At four o'clock that afternoon, therefore, the Army of Tennessee advanced. For a few brief minutes there under the slanting rays of the late-afternoon sun on that balmy, Indian-summer day, the picture-book war thousands of boys had enlisted to see three autumns ago came to life one last time. Twenty thousand men were lined up and marched should-to-shoulder across two miles of open fields and up a gentle slope toward the Federal works. Battle flags fluttered in the autumn breeze, and as the Confederate bands struck up "Dixie" and "The Bonnie Blue Flag" a chorus of rebel yells rose from the solid, steady gray ranks. From the other side of the field the Federals watched in awe. "It was worth a year of one's lifetime," one of them later wrote, "to witness the marshalling and advance of the rebel line of battle." For some of the Federals and a great many of the Confederates it was going to cost all their years, for this pageant was deadly serious.

As the Confederates came within range, the picture-book war came to an abrupt end and the ugly reality returned. The Federals, some of them with repeating rifles, opened a murderous fire. Even some of the Union soldiers were astonished at the hurricane of firing they had unleashed. It was "the most terrific I ever heard," one of them related afterward, "not a rattling fire, but one unceasing volley."[251] Among the men in tattered gray and butternut out in the open the slaughter was horrendous, yet a handful of determined survivors actually forced their way into the Federal lines in places, and fierce hand-to-hand fighting erupted. Driven back, the Confederates charged again and again. Federal officers in some sectors reported "that their lines received as many as thirteen distinct attacks."[252] In some places Confederates held the ditch in front of the Federal works, and the opposing forces shot, stabbed, and clubbed each other viciously across the parapet. "Blood actually ran in the ditch and in places saturated our clothing where we were lying down," one of the Confederate survivors wrote.[253] The fighting continued on into the night, but no sooner had it stopped than Hood, who had stayed in the rear and failed to call off the hopeless slaughter, began making plans to renew the assault in the morning.[254] Mercifully, that turned out to be unnecessary. Schofield was perfectly happy to continue the march to Nashville that Hood's arrival the previous afternoon had interrupted. The next morning the Federal works were empty, and the Confederates were left to bury their dead and tend their wounded.

It was an enormous task. Over 1,700 southerners were dead and something like 4,500 others wounded. The gruesome scene of slaughter made a deep impression on those whose misfortune it was to draw duty on the burial details. "I have seen many battlefields," an Alabamian wrote, but "none to equal this. The ground in front of the works . . . is covered with dead bodies and the ditch in front is filled with them." Indeed, in some parts of the ditch the dead were piled seven-deep.[255] In a sector where some of the hottest fighting had taken place and where the Confederates had made their deepest penetration, a burial party found, a few yards in front of the Union works, the body of Pat Cleburne. The Irishman was buried in the serene churchyard of St. John's Episcopal.

Nor was he the only general Hood lost that day. Five others were killed, five wounded, and one captured. Fifty-five regimental commanders fell, and the high casualty rates left two brigades under the command of captains. About 25,000 men remained in the ranks, but many of the bravest had fallen. Hood's army was wrecked.[256]

With the Union forces now concentrated and firmly ensconced in Nashville, Hood, unable to think of anything better to do, took his mangled army and followed. Lacking enough men to encircle and besiege Nashville, Hood at least did not fling his troops to certain slaughter against the city's formidable defenses. Instead, he had them entrench just south of town and wait—for nothing in particular. In a vain attempt to cover all the various roads leading south out of the Tennessee capital, he spread them out over hill and dale in an atrocious defensive position. They were not inconveniencing Thomas in the least, and that general took all the time he needed making his final preparations for the disposal of Hood's army. He had some 55,000 men; Hood, less than half that number. As if the odds were not already long enough, Hood, who did not seem to realize how badly he was outnumbered, detached Forrest with 6,500 men on the unnecessary errand of taking the town of Murfreesboro, some fifteen miles to the southeast.[257]

While Hood waited, Sherman and his men continued to blaze their sixty-mile-wide "thoroughfare for freedom" through the heart of the Confederacy from Atlanta to the sea. As Sherman's men approached the coast, Thomas, who had been under considerable pressure from Grant to finish off Hood's army, at last felt ready. On December 15 he dealt Hood a crushing blow. In the first day's fighting Hood was driven back, and his left was hard-pressed. Pulling back some two miles to a stronger defensive position that night, Hood weakened his right wing to reinforce the battered left. When Thomas unleashed another overwhelming onslaught the next morning, the right and center of Hood's line collapsed.[258] S. D. Lee's corps, which had been on the left, maintained a semblance of order and did its best to cover the retreat, but it was a dismal rout despite all Lee and his men could do. In these last two days of fighting and the retreat that followed, the Army of Tennessee virtually ceased to exist.[259] As its shattered fragments drifted southward, the war in the West was over.

The final disastrous year of the war in the West reveals Jefferson Davis perhaps more clearly than the years that had gone before: He was a brave, determined, hard-working, and intelligent man, trying desperately, but never quite succeeding, to fill a role that was simply too big for him. Davis had devoted considerable attention to the West, but the decisions he made had failed to achieve the results he sought.

Davis's appointment of Bragg to perform the duties of chief of staff in Richmond was wise, but the president reduced the benefit that might have accrued from such an arrangement by failing, at times, to heed Bragg's generally excellent advice. The selection of Joseph E. Johnston to replace Bragg as Army of Tennessee commander was less fortunate. Though experienced, Johnston lacked the nerve to risk battle and probably lacked faith that Confederate victory was possible. He regarded his reputation as a great general too valuable to be gambled on the outcome of a battle unless victory was certain. This unwillingness to take risks led him to retreat in the face of Sherman's skillful maneuvering all the way from Dalton to Atlanta, and Johnston was probably within a few days of abandoning Atlanta—without a fight—when Davis relieved him.

Yet in December 1863 Davis had little choice but to recall Johnston. Of the Confederacy's full generals—those with appropriate rank to command a major field army—the selection was lean. Cooper had never been competent to command more than a desk. Albert Sidney Johnston was dead. Robert E. Lee was needed in Virginia. Joseph E. Johnston and P. G. T. Beauregard had each demonstrated their inadequacy, and Davis had allowed Polk and his cronies to destroy the effectiveness of Bragg as an army commander. All of the Confederacy's surviving lieutenant generals had revealed themselves as either incompetent to command anything larger than a corps, or insubordinate, or both. Hardee, a lieutenant general who was considered a viable candidate, declined the job. Under the circumstances Johnston seemed like the best of a bad lot. However, this dilemma itself was largely the result of Davis's failure over the previous three years to select good generals, promote good generals, and remove bad ones. A related error was choosing Hood rather than Stewart or, better, Cleburne to fill the vacancy of corps commander in the Army of Tennessee. Hood had much to recommend him, but he had physical problems and was at best an indifferent organizer. As it turned out, he was also of questionable emotional stability. Cleburne would have been more satisfactory in every respect and might have proved to be a superior army commander after Johnston's failure.

The offensive plan that Davis devised with the help of Lee and Bragg may have been a good one, but it is uncertain whether, by the winter of 1863–64, the Confederacy's resources were adequate to carry it off successfully. Certainly some form of offensive, so long as it did not involve costly frontal attacks, would have been helpful in throwing the Federals off-balance. As it was, Sherman took the initiative at the outset and chose the time and place of every action until the removal of Johnston.

Davis failed to act decisively by ordering Johnston to undertake some sort of offensive and ordering Polk to reinforce Johnston. This showed not only Davis's lack of self-confidence and unwillingness to take the responsibility of issuing orders, but also, in the case of the troops in Mississippi, his tendency to allow his forces to become scattered. Apparently the lesson of the importance of concentration learned during and after the Shiloh campaign either was not learned well enough or was too soon forgotten. The maintaining of effective units in Mississippi, where they could not possibly affect the outcome of the war, hampered the Confederate side throughout the Atlanta campaign. Most significant in this aspect was Davis's refusal to send Forrest against Sherman's supply lines. Had Davis taken the advice of Johnston and others and sent Forrest, the campaign could conceivably have taken a much different course.

The removal of Joseph E. Johnston was a decision over which the president agonized. No commander in chief was more reluctant to remove failed generals than Jefferson Davis. Yet Davis knew the vital importance of holding Atlanta. Could he have foreseen that Johnston would give up mountainous northern Georgia and retreat to the gates of Atlanta without a major battle, Davis probably would have removed him much earlier. Not knowing this, the president hoped from day to day that a few more miles to the rear Johnston would find a place to stand and fight. Not until it became apparent that Johnston would never fight did Davis take the drastic step of removal. In retrospect it seems likely that Johnston should have been removed after retreating across the Oostanaula and Etowah rivers without a fight.[260] Once he had passed the Chattahoochee, it may already have been too late to save Atlanta.[261] Davis's hesitation was understandable, but the Confederacy needed a commander in chief who could more quickly assess the man and the situation.[262]

The selection of Hood, like that of Johnston, was dictated by availability, and that in turn had been at least partially determined by Davis's earlier decisions. Of the two possible choices for the post, Hood, with all his faults, was probably the better.[263] He was a hard fighter; and if he spent manpower as if there were no tomorrow, it must be admitted that if he was not victorious, the Confederacy would, indeed, have no tomorrow. Taking over command with the army already backed up against Atlanta, he was able to stave off the city's fall for over a month when Johnston would have lost it within days.[264] After the loss of Atlanta, the campaign he waged in northern Georgia with the president's advice was well conceived, well executed, and probably about the best thing he could have undertaken. It was also notably thrifty of casualties.

Only in the Nashville campaign did Hood's weaknesses as a commander become obvious. With the war all but lost, Hood's judgment apparently gave out. His plan for a raid into Tennessee was of questionable wisdom to begin with, as it allowed Sherman to rampage across Georgia while promising uncertain results in Tennessee. The unavoidable delays at the outset of the campaign doomed it, although Hood, through excellent maneuvering, nearly gained a brilliant victory at Spring Hill. His own failure as well as that of the Army of Tennessee's command system in allowing this near-victory to slip away seemed to push Hood over the edge. In sheer frustration the next day he ordered thousands of men to their deaths—needlessly. From there it was all downhill.

Davis had had strong reservations about Hood's undertaking and doubted that much good could come to the Confederacy by it unless Hood's army was able to cross the Ohio River and carry the war to the northern states.[265] As usual, though, Davis never made his misgivings operative through clear-cut orders that would have called Hood back to face Sherman. By this time, however, it was not likely to have much influence on the final outcome of the war. In that connection, it can be said in defense of Davis that the situation may have been desperate enough to justify the desperate campaign Hood proposed and Davis allowed.

Davis's performance during the final year of significant operations in the western theater constitutes neither the best nor the worst chapter of his service as wartime president. It contained neither the mistakes and omissions that had caused Bragg's downfall nor the brilliance of ruthless concentration of forces and steadfast support of a good general that had brought victory within reach at Shiloh. Instead, the year's efforts presented a composite picture of Davis's wartime service. Davis was revealed as a dedicated and determined man, highly competent within certain limits, but dwarfed—somewhat intimidated—by the magnitude of the task he faced.

15

THE COMMANDER IN CHIEF

At the outbreak of the Civil War, few men in America seemed to be better prepared for the role of commander in chief than Jefferson Davis. He could boast a West Point education and regular army experience. He had commanded both regulars and volunteers, the latter in combat. He had held both administrative and political positions within the government. Indeed, had one laid out an ideal program of preparation for a wartime president, it could hardly have been different from the career of Jefferson Davis prior to 1861.

By contrast Abraham Lincoln had no military training and hardly any military experience. Nor had he served in any administrative post prior to the presidency. Yet Lincoln brought with him to the office certain abilities that enabled him to become an effective commander in chief. First, Lincoln was a fast learner, quickly grasping new concepts and new ways of doing things. He could not only grow into a job but also grow with the job as its demands changed or became greater. Second, Lincoln had an ability to withstand tremendous pressure and fatigue and yet maintain his good judgment; an ability to get along with people; and an extraordinary ability to cut to the heart of whatever problem was under consideration. Finally, Lincoln had the self-confidence, the nerve, or whatever it was he needed to take decisive action. Whether ordering troop movements or removing incompetent generals, Lincoln did not hesitate to act and take the responsibility.

It was in areas such as these that Davis's abilities, though considerable, did not quite measure up to the monumental task he faced. The Confederate president brought with him to the position of commander in chief a number of preexisting friendships with military men—good, bad, and indifferent. Unfortunately, he tended to rely on these friendships a little too heavily, sometimes failing to exercise the good judgment and decisive leadership his role demanded. His preparation was excellent, his determination and diligence exemplary. Yet if he lacked the final measure of greatness that would have propelled him into the ranks of history's most renowned figures, it was probably that he could not see the faults of his friends and that he lacked adequate ability to handle pressure and—most important—take decisive action.

In considering Davis's record as commander in chief, one can divide the war into four chronological periods: (1) a period of fairly adequate and sometimes excellent performance, lasting until the battle of Shiloh; (2) a time of the war's increasing demands and Davis's increasing difficulty in meeting them, continuing until the president left on his first visit to the western front in December 1862; (3) a time of frustration and growing inadequacy, through the battle of Missionary Ridge; and (4) a period of brave but unavailing perseverance during which Davis, in the face of fantastic odds, showed both the determination that had carried him and the Confederacy so far as well as the shortcomings that nevertheless prevented him from reaching the goal he so earnestly desired.

The initial phase of the war was, understandably, a period of experimentation and groping through an unfamiliar situation. Davis therefore cannot be faulted too severely for such unfortunate experiments as the appointment of Twiggs to the New Orleans command. Twiggs was, if nothing else, at least experienced. Nor did Davis during this early period make any shockingly bad decisions. All in all he did much right and a few things wrong. Still, the mistakes, understandable as they may have been, were also costly for the South and hinted at the shortcomings in Davis that would ultimately keep him from his goal.

Besides Twiggs, another unfortunate experiment—and one that displayed Davis's tendency to overrate his friends—was the appointment of Samuel Cooper to the post of adjutant and inspector general, the highest-ranking officer in the army. The idea for such a position, a sort of commanding general or chief of staff, was excellent. Here Davis showed rare insight and possibly some lessons he learned as secretary of war about the workings of the War Department. Certainly Davis needed such an assistant to ease some of his crushing load of work. However, because of Cooper's inadequacy and Davis's reluctance to replace him, that aid was not available except during the relatively brief periods that Lee and Bragg served in Richmond late in the war. Had Davis had the help of a competent officer in this position, he might have avoided some of his later mistakes.

Davis again allowed himself to be blinded by personal feelings in appointing Leonidas Polk. There was some justification for this in Polk's popularity and knowledge of the region—some, but not enough. The appointment very quickly redounded to the detriment of the Confederacy when Polk seized Columbus, Kentucky, alienating undecided sentiment in that state and destroying whatever chance the Confederacy might have had of gaining Kentucky's allegiance. Davis's real mistake here, though, was that even after Polk's willful and unauthorized action, producing as it did such disastrous results, Davis failed to retire the bishop-general. Experiments were necessary, and it could be argued that in the unique circumstances of the Confederacy, such a bizarre experiment as making a major general out of an Episcopal bishop of Polk's questionable military qualifications was justified. Yet when an experiment fails that spectacularly, there can hardly be any excuse for not terminating it.

Third, immediately after news of Polk's invasion of Kentucky, Davis failed to act quickly and decisively to salvage the situation. Many prominent Kentuckians and Tennesseeans, in positions to know the temper of the state of Kentucky, felt that if Davis would disclaim the move and order a withdrawal, all was not yet lost. Whether or not they were right cannot be known with certainty. In any case Davis did nothing. Even sending reinforcements to Polk to drive Grant out of Paducah and occupy other key points in the state would have been preferable to allowing the Confederacy to drift aimlessly for several days with its Kentucky policy being determined haphazardly by a local commander on the basis of what he deemed to be local military necessity. In Davis's defense it can be said that he was ill at this time, but it can also be said that the Confederate president's frail health and habit of working and worrying himself sick were among his major shortcomings as a commander in chief. For whatever reason, Davis did not act as energetically and decisively as the situation demanded.

A fourth error during this period was the president's tendency to overestimate the importance of the Virginia theater and his corresponding neglect of the needs of the West. One factor in this was the president's almost touchingly exaggerated and unrealistic reliance on his old friend Albert Sidney Johnston. With Johnston in charge in the West, Davis considered it one less thing to worry about. Certainly there were plenty of other cares elsewhere. The demands of the eastern front were great and tended, by their very proximity to the capital, to elbow their way into top priority. The East was important, but Davis would have done better to concern himself more with the West. As it was, he allotted a sadly inadequate share of the South's already inadequate resources in men and material to the western front. Although Johnston's genius enabled him to cover the front for several months with the meager forces Davis gave him, the president did not correct the situation until it had resulted in disaster.

Aside from these failed experiments and early missteps, this first phase of Davis's command also saw what—at least militarily speaking—might be called Davis's finest hour. He rose to a difficult situation and seemed to improve in the face of adversity after the staggering defeats at Forts Henry and Donelson. For several reasons Davis was able to cope with this first great crisis in the West better than with those that followed. First, he had not previously been fully engaged in the western conflict and therefore had a reserve of mental and emotional strength with which to meet the shock of disaster. Because his involvement had been relatively small, he could easily respond by stepping up his efforts in that area. Second, the loss of the forts occurred early in the war as a relatively isolated disaster rather than as part of the catalogue of defeats that filled the later stages of the conflict. Hence the stress did not cripple Davis as did that of later setbacks. Finally, at the time of the loss of the forts, Davis still had Albert Sidney Johnston to lean on.

Thus enabled to meet the war's first great disaster, Davis responded by playing an active and valuable role in the ensuing Shiloh campaign. The president gave Johnston sound strategic advice in recommending that the western commander combine his forces and destroy one of the segments of the Federal army before it could unite. This was the offensive-defensive strategy Davis had chosen, working just as it was intended. The president also gave encouragement and support at a time when the fainthearted were clamoring for Johnston's removal. Davis never wavered in his loyalty to his general, nor did he again leave Johnston without the means of success. He realized by now that it would be necessary to concentrate the Confederacy's forces in large armies rather than small garrisons and to supply adequate forces for the West. This he accomplished by pulling troops out of several quiet coastal sectors, notably Pensacola, from which he took not only troops but also the able Braxton Bragg, whose talents the Confederacy needed in more active fields. Davis worked hard to scrape up the troops and get them concentrated in northeastern Mississippi in time for the showdown. Although it may be argued that he was not ruthless enough in concentrating his forces, since substantial numbers of troops were still left in areas where the war was not going to be decided, Davis's role in the Shiloh campaign was significant in bringing together the ingredients for a near-victory. It would be hard to imagine such results with someone less able than Jefferson Davis in the Confederate White House.

The battle of Shiloh marks the end of the first and most successful phase of Davis's exercise of the role of commander in chief and the beginning of a second phase that revealed certain ways in which he was unequal to his task. At Shiloh the culmination of Davis's best efforts in the West had failed to achieve the decisive victory he had sought. Thereafter the demands of the western theater would increase, while Davis's capacity remained constant or actually declined because of sickness, stress, and fatigue. The slight failings of earlier months, barely noticeable among the understandable fumblings of a man thrust into a situation nearly unprecedented in his country's history, now grew more glaring. Yet the most important change wrought by Shiloh in the western situation was the loss of Albert Sidney Johnston. Johnston was a man in whom Davis reposed enormous confidence and who came astonishingly close to justifying that confidence. With Johnston removed from the scene, Davis's interaction with his generals would become vastly more complex and problematical.

This immediately became apparent as Beauregard succeeded Johnston to command of the western army. Prostrated by nerves and not up to the responsibility of leading an army, Beauregard also neglected to keep Davis adequately informed. Though he believed Beauregard was inadequate, the president nevertheless seemed to lack the resolve to remove him promptly and authoritatively. Instead, he waited until the general had virtually removed himself by going on an unauthorized sick leave.

Other incidents during this period also increasingly revealed Davis's shortcomings. During Bragg's Perryville campaign, Davis again hesitated and failed to take decisive action to ensure vitally needed cooperation between Bragg and Kirby Smith. By the time the president did move to unify command in the

West, the best opportunity was past. The man Davis chose for overall command, Joseph E. Johnston, was uncooperative, and Davis was not forceful enough to secure his cooperation. It was probably the president's insecurity that led him to react savagely to Randolph's suggestion that Holmes cross the Mississippi–though Davis himself had at least hinted at just such a movement by the trans-Mississippi forces. The president's overreaction ended permanently any hope of meaningful collaboration between the armies on either side of the Mississippi. Finally, Davis's favoritism toward his old friends by now had taken on alarming proportions, especially in the case of Polk, who was allowed to remain in the Army of Tennessee where he continued to undermine Bragg's authority. Bragg was Davis's general. As commander in chief of the army, it was Davis's responsibility to enforce proper subordination to the generals he appointed. Only someone with extraordinary self-assurance and firmness could have enforced discipline on the fractious personalities of the Confederate high command. Davis's loyalty to Polk made the situation almost impossible. He equivocated, and the disastrous state of affairs in the Army of Tennessee deteriorated. Meanwhile, his blindness to Polk's faults not only kept Polk in a position to do damage but also prevented more able officers such as Cleburne from advancing as quickly as they might have.

Davis's visit to the western front in December 1862 marked the advent of the third and most unfortunate phase of his exercise of the role of commander in chief. Whatever else it may have been, it was not a time of neglect of the West on the part of Jefferson Davis. Between December 1862 and November 1863, Davis made two trips to the western front and had troops sent there from Virginia. Yet partly as a result of Davis's wrong decisions, late decisions, and nondecisions, the year was calamitous for the Confederacy in the West.

Davis made two serious errors during his 1862 tour of inspection. Once again the president allowed overreliance on personal ties to cloud his judgment, this time causing him to permit trans-Mississippi commander Theophilus Holmes, an old friend, to refuse to send troops to aid Pemberton. Instead, he arrived at the right decision in the wrong place and at the wrong time, ordering troops from Bragg rather than Holmes and doing it so late that the reinforcements did not arrive until the danger in Mississippi was past. It was one of the few occasions in the war when Joseph Johnston was right and Davis wrong, although it can again be offered in the president's defense that he was in poor health. In any case he made an unfortunate choice in a tough situation, and the result may have been to deprive Bragg's army of a good chance of victory at Murfreesboro.

After the battle of Murfreesboro, Davis incomprehensibly neglected to straighten out the mess in the officer corps of the Army of Tennessee. His partiality to an old friend enabled Polk to go on conniving against Bragg, and his hesitance, lack of nerve, and reluctance to take responsibility–in removing Bragg or making Johnston remove him–combined to create the worst possible climate, one that would sap the army's morale and lead eventually to disaster. It would not have been easy to set things to rights in the Army of Tennessee, but it was something that needed to be done.

The crisis in Tennessee was succeeded by one in Mississippi, the fateful Vicksburg campaign. Here can be seen the toll on Davis of sickness, exhaustion, prolonged worry, and the distractions of the conflict in Virginia. Though Davis's will never bent under the greatest pressure, he did not possess the great reserves of mental and physical stamina necessary to bear up under the load he never tried to shirk. He became more indecisive. His strategic judgment deteriorated, and he lost some of his mental flexibility. Thus he was unable to grasp new concepts such as Grant's bold turning movement against Vicksburg. Twenty years later Davis still did not understand that Grant had had no supply lines for the Confederates to cut or that Pemberton, in allowing himself to be bottled up in Vicksburg, had made the worst possible move. Once the siege had begun and time was of the utmost importance, Davis should have acted quickly and decisively by forcing garrison commanders such as Beauregard to send every available man for Vicksburg's relief. Most important, he should have either gotten action from Johnston or gotten rid of him. Before the curtain finally—mercifully—descends on the dismal events of the Vicksburg campaign, one is treated to the unflattering spectacle of a commander in chief poring over War Department files for ammunition in a petty argument with his chief western general as to whether or not that general had misunderstood his orders. These are not the actions of a man who is confidently in command. Stress and fatigue not surprisingly tended to bring out Davis's weaknesses. His almost compulsive drive to prove himself right and his subordinate wrong— and to demonstrate this to his subordinate with extensive documentation— displays the president's insecurity at its worst.

The final months of this phase of Davis's career saw the ruinous Chickamauga and Chattanooga campaigns. Though Davis finally did authorize a major concentration of forces—including the transfer of troops from the otherwise untouchable Army of Northern Virginia—to reverse the tide in the West, he hesitated too long and was not ruthless enough. Consequently, the redeployment was not as big or as early as needed to achieve the results he had hoped for it. If he had acted sooner and sent more troops, the campaign might have produced more than the hollow victory at Chickamauga. More likely, however, any efforts in the West were vain as long as the wretched situation in the Army of Tennessee's high command remained unchanged. Here too the fault ultimately has to rest with Davis. As commander in chief it was his duty to secure harmony and subordination among his generals. This he simply had not done. Jefferson Davis had a difficult set of generals to work with, and it had not taken very much on his part to create the mess that now existed—only a little uncertainty and vacillation and some misplaced loyalty to a friend. The army had become virtually unmanageable. To his credit Davis at least realized that something needed to be done and traveled to Chattanooga to face the problem himself. By this time it would have taken a veritable genius of human relations to gain cordial cooperation or at least a ruthless iron-fisted taskmaster to gain any sort of cooperation at all. Unfortunately for the Confederacy, Davis did not quite fit either of these descriptions. The dissension and consequent low morale he left behind him when he continued on his journey resulted within a few weeks in the disgraceful defeat at Missionary Ridge.

With the Army of Tennessee routed at Missionary Ridge and driven out of the state whose name it bore, the Confederacy's position in the West was nearly hopeless. Davis was left to face the last year of western operations without enough troops or able generals and with very little chance of winning the war. If Davis's finest hour militarily had been the Shiloh campaign, this last year and a half of the war was his finest hour as a leader of men. Confronted with enormous odds, in poor physical condition, vilified by many within the country he was trying to lead, Davis, by his own determination and unflinching courage, may well have prolonged the war for six months or more beyond the point at which it would have ended had almost anyone else been the Confederate president. During the last eighteen months of the Confederacy's existence, Davis's military performance was about as good as could be expected. He made no drastic errors, and especially toward the end, he made some tough decisions under daunting circumstances. Still, the shortcomings that he had already displayed continued to mar his otherwise impressive leadership and prevented him from achieving all that was possible even at this late stage of the war.

Left with little choice but to remove Bragg, Davis could find no one better than Joseph E. Johnston to replace him. Perhaps if younger men had been advanced more quickly, some young but experienced and proven corps commander would have been available to fill the post. But Davis understandably had stuck with tried (if not always proven) generals in most positions. And then there was Polk to be sustained, as well as other old friends of whom the president could not bring himself to think ill. It was in some ways the safest course, but it led to Davis's options narrowing impossibly by the final stages of the war. Thus Davis turned back to Johnston, a general who had been tried twice before with less than satisfactory results.

Through the winter months of 1864, while the North prepared for its end-the-war offensive, the Confederate president was reduced to arguing with Johnston over whether or not the Confederacy should take the initiative and knock the northern forces off-balance. A more resolute and self-reliant commander might have compelled the action he felt the situation required, but Davis hesitated to take such a bold step. During these months Davis also tended to revert to his old habit of allowing Confederate forces to become dispersed. The departmental system that had been a useful tool in earlier days was now unresponsive and clumsy in Davis's hands. This problem was particularly evident in his maintaining troops in Mississippi, where they could have minimal impact.

The appointment of Hood to a corps command within the Army of Tennessee was not necessarily a bad move, but it was definitely not the best—or even the second best—decision Davis could have made. Hood had much to commend him, but he also had serious flaws. If nothing else, his injuries alone should have dictated that the proper place for him was in an honored retirement. Cleburne or Stewart would have each been preferable to Hood. Had Davis made a better choice at this point, he would have had a better option open to him when, a few months later, it became necessary to replace Johnston. The fact that an inadequate general like Johnston was chosen because there was no one else should have led Davis to prevent such an occurrence from happening again.

The situation in the high command of the Army of Tennessee on the eve of the disastrous 1864 campaign was almost a preprogrammed failure. The general commanding had already shown on several occasions that he lacked the moral courage to send his army into battle and would always retreat if faced with even a halfway resolute enemy. He did not possess the confidence of the president who had appointed him, and he was in the habit of being so uncommunicative that the president could rarely determine what he was doing or why. To remedy this, the president prompted, or at least allowed, his subordinate Hood to send letters outside of channels, informing on and undermining the commanding general. Here was the ludicrous spectacle of a government spying on one of its own generals. This did nothing to create confidence or improve morale within the army's high command. Each of the decisions that had caused this state of affairs had seemed reasonable under the circumstances, almost unavoidable, but the combined result was a situation ripe for disaster.

When the Union offensive started, the difficulty of Davis's position became acute. Johnston quickly began to display his preference for retreating over risking battle. If he would not fight to hold Atlanta, he had to be removed. Every day he remained in command would make it that much more difficult for a successor to salvage the situation. Yet changing commanders was dangerous at such a juncture, and who could succeed Johnston anyway? Such considerations kept Davis from acting until Johnston had allowed the Federals to reach the gates of Atlanta. A more sure-handed judge of men might have responded much sooner, say, after Johnston's disappointing retreat from Cassville across the Etowah River. That probably would have been better. Instead, Davis hesitated. Had Johnston fought and won a battle during that time, the president's course would have been vindicated. But Johnston had already given ample evidence that he was not the sort of general who fought battles. Instead, Davis's hesitation to do what became an unavoidable necessity cost the South territory that could have made the defense of Atlanta more viable while also protecting the vital munitions-productions centers of Alabama and western Georgia.

When Davis finally did remove Johnston, his choice of Hood was the best decision possible under the circumstances. Others should have been in Hood's place, who would have now made far better army commanders. (It is interesting, for example, to speculate what Cleburne would have done had he taken over the Army of Tennessee just south of the Etowah.) Yet a division commander, as Cleburne still was, or a recently promoted corps commander, such as Stewart, could hardly be considered for the job. Of the acceptable candidates for command of the Army of Tennessee in mid-July 1864, Hood was still the best available. Hardee, with his fear of responsibility, might have proved to be another Joseph E. Johnston and in any case was not particularly skillful. Hood at least would fight and, in the subsequent battles around Atlanta, showed surprising tactical skill.

With the army backed up against the city as it was, Hood's efforts were unavailing. Atlanta was finally lost. With it went the last realistic hope of demoralizing the North into abandoning the fight. With stubborn determination Davis likewise refused to give up, and for a time he persuaded enough of the southern people to keep fighting, too. Together with Hood he worked out a bold strategy with which to operate against Sherman in north Georgia. The plan enjoyed a fair degree of success and might have had even more had Hood stuck with it and followed Sherman south.

Still, it is impossible to know what would have happened had a different course been followed. It may be that Hood's invasion of Tennessee was as promising as anything else the southerners could have attempted at that point. Davis had misgivings about Hood's undertaking, but true to form, he allowed Hood and Beauregard to be the final judges of whether or not to go through with it. In the event, the strategy may have been sound, but Hood's tactics, his careless style of command, and the continued failures of many of the Army of Tennessee's other generals proved to be disastrous. Hood's unsuitability to command an army was finally demonstrated beyond all doubt. Once again seemingly small misjudgments and slight hesitations on the part of Jefferson Davis had led to a major catastrophe for the South.

Assessing Jefferson Davis as a commander in chief is a complex task. The simple labels of "success" or "failure" will not do for him. Nor do the words "greatness" or "mediocrity" fit the facts of his case. The true measure of this unusual man is far more complicated and much more difficult to package neatly. He had tremendous strengths. He undertook an enormous task. He made many good decisions at times when a mistake would have been fatal to his cause. Few could have done as well, and very few could have done better. In the end he fell short, not because the task was impossible, but because he was wanting in only a few small qualities that separate the great victors of history from the great vanquished. Thus Jefferson Davis was a man of great abilities and great determination who stood head and shoulders above most of his contemporaries in the South; yet, though he came very close, he proved to be lacking the final measure of greatness that might have brought him success and the South its independence.

The myth that the South could not have won its independence regardless of anything Davis might have done or not done is a tenacious one. Admittedly, the margin of error allowed Davis may well have been smaller than that enjoyed by his northern counterpart. Yet so often during the course of the war, so much was decided by so small a margin—the result, at least indirectly, of a decision by Davis—that it is impossible to conclude otherwise than that the South not only could have won its independence but actually came extremely close to doing so. Had Kentucky neutrality not been violated, had Davis allocated more of the South's forces to the West, had the work on Forts Henry and Donelson been pressed more energetically, had Beauregard not been sent west, had Kirby Smith been made to cooperate with Bragg during the Kentucky campaign—the list could go on at length. Although it is impossible to know exactly what would have happened had different decisions been made in each of these situations, it seems safe to conclude that the war would have been very different and that the outcome might very well have been different, too. This is not to say that Davis alone bears the responsibility for the South's defeat. If every southerner—or even all of the South's generals—had performed as well as Davis did, it is difficult to imagine how the South could have lost. The point is simply this: There have been persons who possessed the qualities necessary to lead such a cause to victory. Lincoln was probably one of them, but Davis was not.

What then were these qualities? That is, where did Davis fall short? One of the first characteristics that comes to mind is Davis's inordinate loyalty to and dependence on his friends. If extreme loyalty to one's friends is a fault, it is surely an admirable fault; in some ways Davis is more likable for having had it. Nor is it surprising for a man to depend on his friends to a certain extent. But Davis carried reliance on his friends far beyond the point at which he should have realized they were becoming destructive both to himself and, more important, to the cause he was duty-bound to uphold. Polk is the most obvious case on this score, and undoubtedly Davis's stubborn support for the incompetent and headstrong bishop-general did incalculable damage to the Confederacy's fortunes in the West. Yet the same tendency of Davis's was displayed to a lesser extent in his dealings with Cooper, Holmes, and possibly even Hood. Even Albert Sidney Johnston, who was deserving of loyal support, suffered from the president's undue trust: Davis seemed to think Johnston could defend the West without adequate numbers of men and arms. Beyond what was normal or understandable dependence, Davis clung to his friends the way a drowning man would cling to a life preserver.

Another of Davis's failings was his need to be recognized as always being right. He was rarely willing to admit a mistake, and then only in a way that implied that others were actually responsible for the error (because they had supplied him with false information, faulty advice, and the like). While it is not an especially endearing trait, it is not the sort of fault that one would immediately suspect of having hindered him in his efforts to win the war. Nevertheless, such seems to have been the case. This sort of pride is often least acceptable to those who most clearly harbor it themselves. In both generals and politicians, Davis was surrounded by very proud men. His determination in all disagreements, past or present, trivial or significant, to prove himself right and others wrong made him many enemies. Such internal opposition complicated his task in dealing with his generals by increasing the likelihood that disgruntled politicians would back some failed general, such as Joseph E. Johnston or Beauregard, and attempt to use that general as a political bludgeon with which to attack Davis. Of course, they might have done the same thing anyway, but Davis's unfortunate propensity provided easy openings. The need to prove himself right also drove Davis into his squabble with Secretary of War George W. Randolph, with the result that for the crucial first half of 1863, Davis's pride would not permit him to enforce effective cooperation across the Mississippi. Finally, his pride led him to waste a great deal of time and energy—and no doubt mental strain as well—in pointless arguments such as the one he carried on with Johnston during and after the Vicksburg campaign. This bickering accomplished nothing and distracted the president from other more worthy considerations.

At least some of Davis's other failings, whether a prickly temper or a particular strategic misjudgment, can be ascribed to his frequent and severe health problems during the time he was serving as Confederate president. Yet these health problems themselves were partly the result of another of Davis's shortcomings: a tendency to overwork and overworry. Although it is true that Davis had certain physical weaknesses that made his health susceptible to breakdown under stress (which might in itself be counted an additional, although purely physical, shortcoming), it is also true that Davis lived nearly a quarter of a century after the war ended, mostly enjoying better health than he had while serving as Confederate president. Clearly, Davis's propensity to overwork himself and to worry intensely and constantly was a major factor in the breakdown of his health. Ironically, the poor health thus created reduced his capacity for work and for making sound decisions in the face of the strategic problems about which he worried so much.

It may also have aggravated what was almost certainly his most serious fault. The Confederate president found it almost impossibly difficult not to be hesitant and indecisive. He hesitated to compel cooperation between generals when only he was in a position to see the need for such cooperation. He hesitated to force generals to act on his better strategic judgment. He hesitated to remove and to lay on the shelf once and for all generals who had proved themselves failures or, as in the case of Bragg, who had been rendered no longer useful. He hesitated to effect proper subordination among his generals by drastic and forceful action. He hesitated to concentrate the Confederacy's armies, to take risks, to make decisions, to promote younger officers and retire older and less effective ones. Such vacillation on the part of Davis can be seen somewhere in most of the Confederacy's great failures during the war. True, the decisions he faced were extremely complex, the stakes were high, and the temptation to waffle or do nothing, extreme. But part of that measure of greatness Davis lacked was the ability to make excruciatingly difficult decisions quickly, surely, and correctly.

What was at the heart of Jefferson Davis's shortcomings? Considering such a question may indeed tread the borders of the realm of speculation, but it seems as good an explanation as any to propose that all of Davis's major failings were the result of a basic insecurity. Davis did not have the confidence in himself, in God, in Providence, or whatever, that might have enabled him to overcome each of these shortcomings. Taken together with his many and considerable strengths both of character and intelligence, Davis's shortcomings are few and small. They loom large only insofar as they prevented him from achieving the level of greatness necessary to complete the enormous task he almost carried the distance. Far from mediocrity, Jefferson Davis was a man of remarkable talents who fell short only by the narrowest of margins. Perhaps that, after all, is as good an epitaph as any for the Old South: It produced some great men who, in the end, were not quite great enough.

NOTES

PREFACE

1. Cass Canfield, *The Iron Will of Jefferson Davis* (New York: Harcourt Brace Jovanovich, 1978); Elisabeth Cutting, *Jefferson Davis, Political Soldier* (New York: Dodd, Mead, 1930); William E. Dodd, *Jefferson Davis* (Philadelphia: George W. Jacobs, 1907); Clement Eaton, *Jefferson Davis* (New York: Free Press, 1977); Hamilton J. Eckenrode, *Jefferson Davis: President of the South* (New York: Macmillan, 1930); Herman Frey, *Jefferson Davis* (Nashville, Tenn.: Frey Enterprises, 1978); Eric Langhein, *Jefferson Davis, Patriot* (New York: Vantage Press, 1962); Robert McElroy, *Jefferson Davis, The Unreal and the Real* (New York: Harper & Brothers, 1937); Hudson Strode, *Jefferson Davis, American Patriot, 1808–1861* (New York: Harcourt Brace, 1955); Hudson Strode, *Jefferson Davis, Confederate President* (New York: Harcourt Brace, 1959); Hudson Strode, *Jefferson Davis: Tragic Hero* (New York: Harcourt Brace, 1964); Allen Tate, *Jefferson Davis: His Rise and Fall* (New York: Minton, Balch, 1929); Irving Werstein, *Abraham Lincoln versus Jefferson Davis* (New York: Thomas Y. Crowell, 1959); Robert W. Winston, *High Stakes and Hair Trigger: The Life of Jefferson Davis* (New York: Holt, 1930).

2. T. Harry Williams, *P. G. T. Beauregard: Napoleon in Gray* (Baton Rouge: Louisiana State University Press, 1955); Don C. Seitz, *Braxton Bragg: General of the Confederacy* (Columbia, S.C.: The State Company, 1924); Grady McWhiney, *Braxton Bragg and Confederate Defeat* (New York: Columbia University Press, 1969); William C. Davis, *Breckinridge: Statesman, Soldier, Symbol* (Baton Rouge: Louisiana State University Press, 1974); Frank H. Heck, *Proud Kentuckian: John C. Breckinridge, 1821–1875* (Lexington: University Press of Kentucky, 1976); Arndt M. Stickles, *Simon Bolivar Buckner: Borderland Knight* (Chapel Hill: University of North Carolina Press, 1940); Irving A. Buck, *Cleburne and His Command* (Jackson, Tenn.: McCowat-Mercer, 1959); Howell Purdue and Elizabeth Purdue, *Pat Cleburne, Confederate General* (Tuscaloosa, Ala.: Portals Press, 1973); Robert Selph Henry, *"First with the Most" Forrest* (Indianapolis: Bobbs-Merrill, 1944); Nathaniel C. Hughes, *General William J. Hardee: Old Reliable* (Baton Rouge: Louisiana State University Press, 1965); Richard M. McMurry, *John Bell Hood and the War for Southern Independence* (Lexington: University Press of Kentucky, 1982); Charles M. Cummings, *Yankee Quaker, Confederate General: The Curious Career of General Bushrod Rust Johnson* (Cranbury, N.J.: Fairleigh Dickinson University Press, 1971); Charles P. Roland, *Albert Sidney Johnston: Soldier of Three Republics* (Austin: University of Texas Press, 1964); Gilbert E. Govan and James W. Livingood, *A Different Valor: The Story of General Joseph E. Johnston, C.S.A.* (Indianapolis: Bobbs-Merrill, 1956); Herman Hattaway, *General Stephen D. Lee* (Jackson: University Press of Mississippi, 1976); James A. Ramage, *Rebel Raider: The Life of General John Hunt Morgan* (Lexington: University Press of Kentucky, 1986); John C. Pemberton, *Pemberton: Defender of Vicksburg* (Chapel Hill: University of North Carolina Press, 1942); Joseph H. Parks, *General Leonidas Polk, C.S.A., The Fighting Bishop* (Baton Rouge: Louisiana State University Press, 1960); Albert E. Castel, *General Sterling Price and the Civil War in the West* (Baton Rouge: Loui-

siana State University Press, 1968); Robert E. Shalhope, *Sterling Price: Portrait of a Southerner* (Columbia: University of Missouri Press, 1971); Joseph H. Parks, *General Edmund Kirby Smith, C.S.A.* (Baton Rouge: Louisiana State University Press, 1954); Marshall Wingfield, *General A. P. Stewart: His Life and Letters* (Memphis: West Tennessee Historical Society, 1954); Robert G. Hartje, *Van Dorn: The Life and Times of a Confederate General* (Nashville, Tenn.: Vanderbilt University Press, 1967); Ezra Warner, *Generals in Gray* (Baton Rouge: Louisiana State University Press, 1959).

3. Stanley Horn, *The Army of Tennessee* (Indianapolis: Bobbs-Merrill, 1941); Thomas Lawrence Connelly, *Army of the Heartland: The Army of Tennessee, 1861–1862* (Baton Rouge: Louisiana State University Press, 1967); Thomas Lawrence Connelly, *Autumn of Glory: The Army of Tennessee 1862–1865* (Baton Rouge: Louisiana State University Press, 1971).

4. Archer Jones, *Confederate Strategy from Shiloh to Vicksburg* (Baton Rouge: Louisiana State University Press, 1961); Thomas Lawrence Connelly and Archer Jones, *The Politics of Command: Factions and Ideas in Confederate Strategy* (Baton Rouge: Louisiana State University Press, 1973).

CHAPTER 1. THE MAN AND THE HOUR

1. Montgomery's imposing Union Station, which now serves primarily as a restaurant, was not built until the 1890s.

2. Hudson Strode, *Jefferson Davis, American Patriot, 1808–1861* (New York: Harcourt Brace, 1955), 406–7; Eric Langhein, *Jefferson Davis, Patriot* (New York: Vantage Press, 1962), 49; Allen Tate, *Jefferson Davis: His Rise and Fall* (New York: Minton, Balch, 1929), 83–84; Jefferson Davis, *The Rise and Fall of the Confederate Government*, 2 vols. (New York: D. Appleton, 1881), 1:230, 231.

3. William E. Dodd, *Jefferson Davis* (Philadelphia: George W. Jacobs, 1907), 223; Frank E. Vandiver, *Their Tattered Flags* (New York: Harper & Row, 1970), 22–23; Strode, *Jefferson Davis, American Patriot*, 406–7; Cass Canfield, *The Iron Will of Jefferson Davis* (New York: Harcourt Brace Jovanovich, 1978), 54; William C. Davis, *Deep Waters of the Proud* (Garden City, N.Y.: Doubleday, 1982), 82–83.

4. Haskell M. Monroe and James T. McIntosh, eds., *The Papers of Jefferson Davis* (Baton Rouge: Louisiana State University Press, 1971), 1:liii, lxvii–lxviii.

5. Dodd, *Jefferson Davis*, 17; Strode, *Jefferson Davis, American Patriot*, 3; Herman Frey, *Jefferson Davis* (Nashville, Tenn.: Frey Enterprises, 1978), 9. The Davis cabin had four rooms and was said to be the first in the area to have glass windows.

6. Monroe and McIntosh, *The Papers of Jefferson Davis*, 1:liii, lxvii–lxviii.

7. Ibid., lxix–lxxi, 3–4.

8. Dodd, *Jefferson Davis*, 19.

9. Monroe and McIntosh, *The Papers of Jefferson Davis*, 1:lxix–lxxi, 3–4.

10. Ibid., lxxi–lxxiv.

11. Ibid., lxxvi–lxxviii; Clement Eaton, *Jefferson Davis* (New York: Free Press, 1977), 2–11.

12. Dodd, *Jefferson Davis*, 20–22.

13. Eaton, *Jefferson Davis*, 241; Dodd, *Jefferson Davis*, 22.

14. William Catton and Bruce Catton, *Two Roads to Sumter* (New York: McGraw-Hill, 1963), 30; Charles P. Roland, *Albert Sidney Johnston: Soldier of Three Republics* (Austin: University of Texas Press, 1964), 6–52.

15. Monroe and McIntosh, *The Papers of Jefferson Davis*, 1:11.

16. Ibid., lxviii, lxxviii–lxxx.

17. Ibid., 10.

18. Ibid., lxxviii–lxxx.

19. Ibid., 14–16.

20. Ibid., 17.

21. Ibid., 14, 27.

22. Eaton, *Jefferson Davis,* 12–15; Strode, *Jefferson Davis, American Patriot,* 42; Frey, *Jefferson Davis,* 29.

23. Monroe and McIntosh, *The Papers of Jefferson Davis,* 1:55–80, 17–101; Eaton, *Jefferson Davis,* 12–15.

24. Robert W. Winston, *High Stakes and Hair Trigger: The Life of Jefferson Davis* (New York: Holt, 1930), 12–13; Strode, *Jefferson Davis, American Patriot,* 42; Frey, *Jefferson Davis,* 29.

25. Frey, *Jefferson Davis,* 30; Canfield, *The Iron Will of Jefferson Davis,* 9; Strode, *Jefferson Davis, American Patriot,* 47.

26. Canfield, *The Iron Will of Jefferson Davis,* 9.

27. Dodd, *Jefferson Davis,* 25; Eaton, *Jefferson Davis,* 12–15.

28. Eaton, *Jefferson Davis,* 12–15.

29. Monroe and McIntosh, *The Papers of Jefferson Davis,* 1:liii–lxv.

30. Ibid., lxxxiv.

31. Dodd, *Jefferson Davis,* 25.

32. Ibid., 28–31.

33. Monroe and McIntosh, *The Papers of Jefferson Davis,* 1:117.

34. Eaton, *Jefferson Davis,* 15–17; Monroe and McIntosh, *The Papers of Jefferson Davis,* 1:246–48; Strode, *Jefferson Davis, American Patriot,* 70–71.

35. Dodd, *Jefferson Davis,* 30.

36. Varina Howell Davis, *Jefferson Davis, Ex-President of the Confederate States of America. A Memoir by His Wife,* 2 vols. (New York: 1890), 1:81; Dodd, *Jefferson Davis,* 33–34.

37. Monroe and McIntosh, *The Papers of Jefferson Davis,* 1:lxix.

38. L. J. Lasswell, ed., "Jefferson Davis Ponders His Future, 1829," *Journal of Southern History* 41 (November 1975): 516–22.

39. Eaton, *Jefferson Davis,* 18–19.

40. Monroe and McIntosh, *The Papers of Jefferson Davis,* 1:409–10; Eaton, *Jefferson Davis,* 21–23.

41. Eaton, *Jefferson Davis,* 21–23.

42. Ibid., 23, 47–51.

43. Dunbar Rowland, ed., *Jefferson Davis, Constitutionalist, His Letters, Papers and Speeches,* 10 vols. (Jackson: Mississippi Department of Archives and History, 1923), 1:46.

44. Strode, *Jefferson Davis, American Patriot,* 157. The rifles used by Davis's regiment were designed at the United States armory at Harpers Ferry in 1841 and were manufactured under contract by Eli Whitney. James Alan Treadwell, "Jefferson Davis as Secretary of War: A Reappraisal" (Master's thesis, Rice University, 1985), 56.

45. Eaton, *Jefferson Davis,* 60; Dodd, *Jefferson Davis,* 79–80.

46. Bernard DeVoto, *The Year of Decision: 1846* (Boston: Little, Brown, 1943), 285–86; Eaton, *Jefferson Davis,* 62; Dodd, *Jefferson Davis,* 84; Joseph H. Parks, *General Edmund Kirby Smith, C.S.A.* (Baton Rouge: Louisiana State University Press, 1954), 56.

47. Roland, *Albert Sidney Johnston,* 138; Strode, *Jefferson Davis, American Patriot,* 169.

48. DeVoto, *The Year of Decision,* 471; Eaton, *Jefferson Davis,* 62–65; Dodd, *Jefferson Davis,* 88–89; Winston, *High Stakes and Hair Trigger,* 49; Strode, *Jefferson Davis, American Patriot,* 180–81.

49. Dodd, *Jefferson Davis,* 89.

50. Strode, *Jefferson Davis, American Patriot,* 186.

51. Eaton, *Jefferson Davis*, 62–65; DeVoto, *The Year of Decision*, 471.

52. James T. McIntosh, Lynda L. Crist, and Mary S. Dix, eds., *The Papers of Jefferson Davis* (Baton Rouge: Louisiana State University Press, 1981), 3:149.

53. W. A. Evans, "Jefferson Davis, His Diseases and His Doctors," *The Mississippi Doctor* (June 1942):3–4; Canfield, *The Iron Will of Jefferson Davis*, 32–33; Winston, *High Stakes and Hair Trigger*, 51.

54. Eaton, *Jefferson Davis*, 64–65.

55. Milo Milton Quaife, ed., *The Diary of James K. Polk*, 4 vols. (Chicago: McClung, 1910), 3:29.

56. Monroe and McIntosh, *The Papers of Jefferson Davis*, 1:liii–lxv.

57. Dodd, *Jefferson Davis*, 127–28.

58. Ibid., 128.

59. Monroe and McIntosh, *The Papers of Jefferson Davis*, 1:liii–lxv; Dodd, *Jefferson Davis*, 133–34; Treadwell, "Jefferson Davis as Secretary of War," 69–84.

60. Monroe and McIntosh, *The Papers of Jefferson Davis*, 1:liii–lxv.

61. Frey, *Jefferson Davis*, 51.

62. Dodd, *Jefferson Davis*, 181–82.

63. Rowland, *Jefferson Davis, Constitutionalist*, 4:564–65; Winston, *High Stakes and Hair Trigger*, 158–59.

64. Jefferson Davis, *The Rise and Fall of the Confederate Government*, 1:237; Dodd, *Jefferson Davis*, 220.

65. Canfield, *The Iron Will of Jefferson Davis*, 53.

66. Davis to Howell Cobb, March 1, 1861, L. S. Ruder Collection, Beauvoir Jefferson Davis Shrine, photocopy, Jefferson Davis Association, Rice University (henceforth JDA); Dodd, *Jefferson Davis*, 234–35.

67. Strode, *Jefferson Davis, American Patriot*, 48; Winston, *High Stakes and Hair Trigger*, 26.

68. Hudson Strode, *Jefferson Davis, Confederate President* (New York: Harcourt Brace, 1959), 3.

69. Ibid., 74.

70. W. A. Evans, "Jefferson Davis," 7; Strode, *Jefferson Davis, Confederate President*, 12; Eli N. Evans, *Judah P. Benjamin: The Jewish Confederate* (New York: Free Press, 1988), 151; James McPherson, *Battle Cry of Freedom: The Civil War Era* (New York: Oxford University Press, 1988), 429.

CHAPTER 2.
ORGANIZING THE WESTERN THEATER

1. Frank E. Vandiver, *The Making of a President: Jefferson Davis, 1861* (Richmond: Virginia Civil War Commission, 1962), 6.

2. Hudson Strode, *Jefferson Davis, American Patriot, 1808–1861* (New York: Harcourt Brace, 1955), 415.

3. Hudson Strode, *Jefferson Davis, Confederate President* (New York: Harcourt Brace, 1959), 12.

4. Clement Eaton, *Jefferson Davis* (New York: Free Press, 1977), 132–34.

5. Strode, *Jefferson Davis, Confederate President*, xv; James McPherson, *Battle Cry of Freedom: The Civil War Era* (New York: Oxford University Press, 1988), 337; Timothy H. Donovan, Jr., Roy K. Flint, Arthur V. Grant, Jr., and Gerald P. Stodler, *The American Civil War*, West Point Military History Series (Wayne, N.J.: Avery Publishing Group, 1987), 12.

6. Rowena Reed, *Combined Operations in the Civil War* (Annapolis, Md.: Naval

Institute Press, 1978), throughout. Reed argues that after the removal of McClellan from overall command in the spring of 1862, the northern leadership lacked the strategic vision to see the potential of combined operations. This situation was exacerbated by the baneful influence of general in chief and later chief of staff Henry W. Halleck, with his thoroughly "Jominian" and "continental" mindset.

7. Frank E. Vandiver, "Jefferson Davis and Confederate Strategy," in *The American Tragedy: The Civil War in Retrotspect,* Avery O. Craven and Frank E. Vandiver, eds. (Hampden-Sydney, Va.: Hampden-Sydney College, 1959), 20.

8. Rembert W. Patrick, *Jefferson Davis and His Cabinet* (Baton Rouge: Louisiana State University Press, 1944), 104–14; Richard D. Goff, *Confederate Supply* (Durham, N.C.: Duke University Press, 1969), 8.

9. Patrick, *Jefferson Davis and His Cabinet,* 104–14.

10. Dunbar Rowland, ed., *Jefferson Davis, Constitutionalist, His Letters, Papers and Speeches,* 10 vols. (Jackson: Mississippi Department of Archives and History, 1923), 5:371–72, 374.

11. Patrick, *Jefferson Davis and His Cabinet,* 114.

12. Davis endorsement on Maj. J. B. Moore to Cooper, July 26, 1864, Papers received by the Confederate Adjutant and Inspector General's Office, National Archives, microfilm M-474, roll 129, frame 685, JDA.

13. Ezra Warner, *Generals in Gray* (Baton Rouge: Louisiana State University Press, 1959), 62–63.

14. Jefferson Davis, *The Rise and Fall of the Confederate Government,* 2 vols. (New York: D. Appleton, 1881), 1:308; Ellsworth Eliot, Jr., *West Point in the Confederacy* (New York: G. A. Baker, 1941), 318.

15. Davis to James A. Seddon, July 26, 1864, Papers received by the Confederate Adjutant and Inspector General's Office, National Archives, microfilm M-474, roll 139, frame 716, JDA.

16. Bruce Catton, *The Coming Fury* (Garden City, N.Y.: Doubleday, 1961), 228–29.

17. Grady McWhiney, *Braxton Bragg and Confederate Defeat* (New York: Columbia University Press, 1969), 56, 57.

18. James T. McIntosh, Lynda L. Crist, and Mary S. Dix, eds., *The Papers of Jefferson Davis* (Baton Rouge: Louisiana State University Press, 1981), 3:437, 293–94.

19. Shelby Foote, *The Civil War,* 3 vols. (New York: Random House, 1958), 1:295.

20. Catton, *The Coming Fury,* 228–30, 236, 238.

21. United States War Department, *The War of the Rebellion: A Compilation of the Official Records of the Union and Confederate Armies,* 128 vols. (Washington, D.C.: Government Printing Office, 1880–1901), 3:690 (hereafter O.R.: except as otherwise noted, all volumes cited are from Series 1).

22. Rowland, *Jefferson Davis, Constitutionalist,* 5:136–37; O.R., 53:744.

23. Thomas O. Moore to Davis, September 7, 1861, JDA.

24. Rowland, *Jefferson Davis, Constitutionalist,* 5:136–37.

25. Twiggs to Davis, October 10, 1861, by permission of the Houghton Library (Dearborn Collection), Harvard University, photocopy, JDA.

26. Rowland, *Jefferson Davis, Constitutionalist,* 5:136–37; Bruce Catton, *Terrible Swift Sword* (Garden City, N.Y.: Doubleday, 1963), 238.

27. Clement Eaton, *The Mind of the Old South* (Baton Rouge: Louisiana State University Press, 1967), 209.

28. Haskell M. Monroe and James T. McIntosh, eds., *The Papers of Jefferson Davis* (Baton Rouge: Louisiana State University Press, 1971), 1:lxxx.

29. Eaton, *The Mind of the Old South,* 209–12.

30. Joseph H. Parks, *General Leonidas Polk, C.S.A., The Fighting Bishop* (Baton Rouge: Louisiana State University Press, 1960), 33.

31. Eaton, *The Mind of the Old South,* 209–12; Parks, *General Leonidas Polk,* 34–110.

32. McWhiney, *Braxton Bragg and Confederate Defeat,* 214n; Parks, *General Leonidas Polk,* 113.

33. Eaton, *The Mind of the Old South,* 212; Parks, *General Leonidas Polk,* 111–13.

34. Eaton, *The Mind of the Old South,* 213–15; Parks, *General Leonidas Polk,* 125.

35. Parks, *General Leonidas Polk,* 127.

36. Ibid., 153–57.

37. Ibid., 158–59.

38. Ibid., 154–55.

39. Herman Hattaway and Archer Jones, *How the North Won: A Military History of the Civil War* (Urbana: University of Illinois Press, 1983), 164.

40. McWhiney, *Braxton Bragg and Confederate Defeat,* 214n.

41. Isham G. Harris to Davis, July 2, 1861, by permission of the Houghton Library (Dearborn Collection), Harvard University, photocopy, JDA.

42. Thomas Lawrence Connelly, *Army of the Heartland: The Army of Tennessee, 1861–1862* (Baton Rouge: Louisiana State University Press, 1967), 47.

43. Stanley Horn, *The Army of Tennessee* (Indianapolis: Bobbs-Merrill, 1941), 48; McIntosh, Crist, and Dix, *The Papers of Jefferson Davis,* 3:91n.

44. Milo Milton Quaife, ed., *The Diary of James K. Polk* (Chicago: McClung, 1910), 4:5–9, 22.

45. Connelly, *Army of the Heartland,* 47.

46. Arndt M. Stickles, *Simon Bolivar Buckner: Borderland Knight* (Chapel Hill: University of North Carolina Press, 1940), 134.

47. John D. Martin to Davis, July 1, 1861, Manuscript Department, Perkins Library, Duke University, photocopy, JDA; O.R., 4:364; vol. 52, pt. 2, 119–20.

48. Lynda Lasswell Crist and Mary Seaton Dix, eds., *The Papers of Jefferson Davis* (Baton Rouge: Louisiana State University Press, 1985), 5:476.

49. McIntosh, Crist, and Dix, *The Papers of Jefferson Davis,* 3:172–73.

50. Papers of the Confederate Secretary of War, National Archives, microfilm, JDA.

51. Leonidas Polk to Davis, May 14, 1861, in Walter R. Benjamin, *The Collector* (dealer's catalog, 1932).

52. Parks, *General Leonidas Polk,* 165–66.

53. John B. Jones, *A Rebel War Clerk's Diary,* ed. Earl Schenck Miers (New York: Sagamore Press, 1958), 28.

54. Parks, *General Leonidas Polk,* 166–67.

55. O.R., vol. 52, pt. 2, 115.

56. Davis to Polk, February 7, 1862, National Archives, photocopy, JDA.

57. T. Harry Williams, *Lincoln and His Generals* (New York: Vintage Books, 1952), 260.

CHAPTER 3. KENTUCKY

1. O.R., 4:362.

2. Ibid., 365–66; vol. 52, pt. 2, 128–29.

3. Ibid., vol. 52, pt. 2, 117.

4. John D. Martin to Davis, July 1, 1861, Manuscript Department, Perkins Library, Duke University, photocopy, JDA; O.R., 4:364; vol. 52, pt. 2, 119–20.

5. O.R., vol. 52, pt. 2, 118.

6. Stanley Horn, *The Army of Tennessee* (Indianapolis: Bobbs-Merrill, 1941), 49.

7. O.R., 3:317.

8. Thomas Lawrence Connelly, *Army of the Heartland: The Army of Tennessee, 1861–1862* (Baton Rouge: Louisiana State University Press, 1967), 49.

9. Joseph H. Parks, *General Leonidas Polk, C.S.A., The Fighting Bishop* (Baton Rouge: Louisiana State University Press, 1960), 177–78.

10. Ibid., 203.

11. Bruce Catton, *The Coming Fury* (Garden City, N.Y.: Doubleday, 1961), 369–83; Bruce Catton, *Terrible Swift Sword* (Garden City, N.Y.: Doubleday, 1963), 10–21.

12. Catton, *Terrible Swift Sword*, 33–35; James McPherson, *Battle Cry of Freedom: The Civil War Era* (New York: Oxford University Press, 1988), 356–57.

13. Jefferson Davis, *The Rise and Fall of the Confederate Government*, 2 vols. (New York: D. Appleton, 1881), 1:386.

14. O.R., 4:376.

15. Ibid., vol. 52, pt. 2, 128–29.

16. L. P. Walker to Davis, September 2, 1861, Manuscript Department, Perkins Library, Duke University, photocopy, JDA; Davis to Polk, September 2, 1861, Leonidas Polk Papers, Southern Historical Collection, Library of the University of North Carolina at Chapel Hill, photocopy, JDA; O.R., vol. 52, pt. 2, 133–34.

17. O.R., 4:376.

18. Connelly, *Army of the Heartland*, 20–45.

19. O.R., vol. 52, pt. 2, 100–101.

20. Connelly, *Army of the Heartland*, 40.

21. Ibid., 51.

22. O.R., 4:378, 396–97.

23. Ibid., 396–97.

24. Ibid., 3:466–67.

25. Ibid., 141–42.

26. Ibid., 4:399.

27. Ibid., 181.

28. Ibid., 179.

29. Ibid., 180.

30. Ibid., 3:149–50.

31. Ibid., 4:191.

32. Davis to Polk, September 2, 1861, Leonidas Polk Papers, Southern Historical Collection, Library of the University of North Carolina at Chapel Hill, photocopy, JDA.

33. Jones, *A Rebel War Clerk's Diary*, 21.

34. Mary Boykin Chesnut (Ben Ames Williams, ed.), *A Diary from Dixie* (Boston: Houghton Miflin, 1905), 84.

35. Jones, *A Rebel War Clerk's Diary*, 41.

36. Ibid., 41; Davis to Polk, September 2, 1861, Leonidas Polk Papers, Southern Historical Collection, Library of the University of North Carolina at Chapel Hill, photocopy, JDA.

37. I. G. Harris to Davis, September 4, 1861, I. G. Harris Papers, Tennessee State Library and Archives, photocopy, JDA; O.R., IV, 180.

38. Endorsement by Jefferson Davis, September 5, 1861, on telegram from Isham G. Harris to Davis of September 4, 1861, National Archives, RG109, "Documents in the Official Records," microfilm, JDA. This important endorsement, which appears in Davis's own handwriting, seems to have been overlooked by previous scholars of Davis and the Civil War. Its complete text reads: "Secty of War–Telegraph promptly to Genl Polk to withdraw troops from Ky–& explain movement[.] Ans–Gov. Harris

inform him of action & that movement was unauthorized–[over] Ask Gov. Harris to communicate to Gov. Magoffin."

39. Walker sent a total of three telegrams in carrying out these orders. One went to Harris (O.R., v. 4, 189), and the other two to Polk. Of these, one appears in O.R., v. 4, 181, and asks a reason for the movement. The other, that ordering the "prompt withdrawal" of Polk's troops, seems to be presented in O.R., v. 4, 180, but with the date September 4, 1861. It is probable that this date is incorrect and that the dispatch, like the other two, was sent on the fifth, although very likely before the other telegram from Walker to Polk. There are several reasons for believing it was sent on the fifth rather than the fourth: (1) The Davis endorsement on Harris's September 4 telegram, known to have been received in Richmond on the fifth, seems to indicate that Polk's action was previously unknown there; (2) the wording of Walker's telegram seems to be a response to the information contained in Harris's, particularly in that the troops involved are referred to as belonging to Pillow's command; (3) Walker's telegram fits perfectly the description of what Davis, in his endorsement, ordered him to send, and no other dispatch fitting this description has been found; (4) it is unlikely that news of Polk's action could have reached Richmond by any means in time for Walker to send such a dispatch on the fourth, nor is there any indication as to what source could have provided such prompt intelligence.

40. O.R., IV, 180.

41. O.R., IV, 180.

42. O.R., IV, 181.

43. Jefferson Davis to Leonidas Polk, September 5, 1861, Polk Papers, Library of Congress. The text of this brief telegram contains two small but significant differences from that contained in O.R., v. 4, 181. It reads: "Your Telegram Recd[.] The necessity must justify the action." The telegram in question is Polk's dispatch to Davis of September 4, 1861 (O.R., v. 4, 181). The *Official Records'* version of Davis's telegram reads simply, "The necessity justifies the action." Since the O.R. version of these nearly identical dispatches is shorter and also probably incorrectly dated September 4, it would appear to be in fact merely a truncated and erroneous version of the same telegram. This shorter wording, much more favorable to Polk's course of action, was contained in a group of recopied dispatches that Polk sent to the Confederate War Department in mid-September 1861. Taken over with the rest of the War Department files at the end of the war, these were more or less uncritically printed in the *Official Records*, v. 4, 179–184.

44. Jones, *A Rebel War Clerk's Diary,* 46.

45. Rembert W. Patrick, *Jefferson Davis and His Cabinet* (Baton Rouge: Louisiana State University Press, 1944), 117, 162–69.

46. Jones, *A Rebel War Clerk's Diary,* 40.

47. Eli Evans (*Judah P. Benjamin: The Jewish Confederate* [New York: Free Press, 1988], throughout) depicts Benjamin as brilliant, influential, and virtually Davis's alter ego throughout the war. At the other extreme William C. Davis (*Deep Waters of the Proud* [Garden City, N.Y.: Doubleday, 1982], 205) calls Benjamin "manifestly unqualified" to be secretary of war, says he was an almost unmitigated failure, and claims the Confederacy had no chance of success while he held that post. The truth probably lies somewhere between these two extremes.

48. O.R., 4:185.

49. Ibid., 402.

50. Arndt M. Stickles, *Simon Bolivar Buckner: Borderland Knight* (Chapel Hill: University of North Carolina Press, 1940), 1–50.

51. Catton, *Terrible Swift Sword,* 34–35.

52. Horn, *The Army of Tennessee*, 437n; Stickles, *Simon Bolivar Buckner*, 86–87.

53. Stickles, *Simon Bolivar Buckner*, 88–89, 94.

54. O.R., 4:189–90.

55. Ibid., 190.

56. Ibid., 188.

57. Horn, *The Army of Tennessee*, 54.

58. Dunbar Rowland, ed., *Jefferson Davis, Constitutionalist, His Letters, Papers and Speeches*, 10 vols. (Jackson: Mississippi Department of Archives and History, 1923), 8:232.

CHAPTER 4. THE COMING
OF ALBERT SIDNEY JOHNSTON

1. Hudson Strode, *Jefferson Davis, American Patriot, 1808–1861* (New York: Harcourt Brace, 1955), 45–46.

2. Charles P. Roland, *Albert Sidney Johnston: Soldier of Three Republics* (Austin: University of Texas Press, 1964), 6–131.

3. James T. McIntosh, Lynda L. Crist, and Mary S. Dix, eds., *The Papers of Jefferson Davis* (Baton Rouge: Louisiana State University Press, 1981), 3:457.

4. Roland, *Albert Sidney Johnston*, 6–131.

5. Richard Taylor, *Destruction and Reconstruction*, ed. Charles P. Roland (Waltham, Mass.: Blaisdell, 1968; originally published 1879), 232.

6. Roland, *Albert Sidney Johnston*, 132–36.

7. McIntosh, Crist, and Dix, *The Papers of Jefferson Davis*, 3:104, 402, 109n.

8. Richard M. McMurry, *John Bell Hood and the War for Southern Independence* (Lexington: University Press of Kentucky, 1982), 17.

9. Roland, *Albert Sidney Johnston*, 140–250.

10. Bruce Catton, *The Coming Fury* (Garden City, N.Y.: Doubleday, 1961), 431.

11. Jefferson Davis, *The Rise and Fall of the Confederate Government*, 2 vols. (New York: D. Appleton, 1881), 1:309.

12. Roland, *Albert Sidney Johnston*, 251–59.

13. Clifford Dowdey and Louis H. Manarin, eds., *The Wartime Papers of R. E. Lee* (New York: Bramhall House, 1961), 53–54.

14. O.R., vol. 50, pt. 1, 566.

15. Roland, *Albert Sidney Johnston*, 251–59.

16. Dunbar Rowland, ed., *Jefferson Davis, Constitutionalist, His Letters, Papers and Speeches*, 10 vols. (Jackson: Mississippi Department of Archives and History, 1923), 8:232, 9:206, 270, 292. Thomas Lawrence Connelly (*Army of the Heartland: The Army of Tennessee, 1861–1862* [Baton Rouge: Louisiana State University Press, 1967], 60–61) argues, essentially from the same facts recounted here, that Johnston's career prior to 1861 was undistinguished and gave no basis for the belief, widely held in both North and South, that he would be a good general.

17. Dowdey and Manarin, *The Wartime Papers of R. E. Lee*, 69–70.

18. Stanley Horn, *The Army of Tennessee* (Indianapolis: Bobbs-Merrill, 1941), 54.

19. O.R., 3:687–88.

20. Roland, *Albert Sidney Johnston*, 260.

21. O.R., 4:189–90, 192–93.

22. Jefferson Davis, *The Rise and Fall of the Confederate Government*, 2:67.

23. Ibid., 1:309.

24. O.R., 4:405.

25. Ibid., 6:788–89.

26. Ibid., 4:189.
27. Bruce Catton, *Terrible Swift Sword* (Garden City, N.Y.: Doubleday, 1963), 38.
28. O.R., vol. 52, pt. 2, 145.
29. Ibid., 4:190.
30. Ibid., 193–94.
31. Ibid.
32. Ibid., 4:193.
33. Roland, *Albert Sidney Johnston*, 261, 265–66.
34. O.R., 4:191.
35. Roland, *Albert Sidney Johnston*, 265–66.
36. Jefferson Davis, *The Rise and Fall of the Confederate Government*, 1:407; O.R., 3:530.
37. Horn, *The Army of Tennessee*, 55–56.
38. O.R., 4:193–94.
39. Horn, *The Army of Tennessee*, 58–59.
40. O.R., 4:430.
41. Horn, *The Army of Tennessee*, 58; Jefferson Davis, *The Rise and Fall of the Confederate Government*, 1:408.
42. Jefferson Davis, *The Rise and Fall of the Confederate Government*, 1:408.
43. Connelly, *Army of the Heartland*, 33–35.
44. Ibid., 25–45.
45. Jefferson Davis, *The Rise and Fall of the Confederate Government*, 2:69.
46. O.R., 4:416.
47. Ibid., 417, 430.
48. Horn, *The Army of Tennessee*, 60; Roland, *Albert Sidney Johnston*, 277.
49. Roland, *Albert Sidney Johnston*, 271–72.
50. O.R., 4:531.
51. Lloyd Lewis, *Sherman: Fighting Prophet* (New York: Harcourt Brace, 1932), 182–207.
52. O.R., 4:444–45. Connelly (*Army of the Heartland*, 65) argues that during this period "the defense of Bowling Green became an obsession with Johnston. He toiled over the routine matters of army management there as if he were merely a district commander."
53. O.R., 4:491.
54. Horn, *The Army of Tennessee*, 76–77; O.R., 7:710–11.
55. Connelly, *Army of the Heartland*, 79–80.
56. O.R., 7:710–11.
57. O.R., 4:481.
58. Horn, *The Army of Tennessee*, 76; William Eric Jamborsky, "Confederate Leadership and Defeat in the West," *Lincoln Herald* (Summer 1984): 57; Marshall Wingfield, *General A. P. Stewart: His Life and Letters* (Memphis: West Tennessee Historical Society, 1954), 42–45.
59. O.R., 4:491–92.
60. O.R., 7:779, 813, 817–18; vol. 52, pt. 2, 239, 245–46.
61. Horn, *The Army of Tennessee*, 77; Joseph H. Parks, *General Leonidas Polk, C.S.A., The Fighting Bishop* (Baton Rouge: Louisiana State University Press, 1960), 188; Connelly, *Army of the Heartland*, 80–85; Benjamin Franklin Cooling, *Forts Henry and Donelson: The Key to the Confederate Heartland* (Knoxville: University of Tennessee Press, 1987), 58–59; O.R., 7:699–700, 710–11.
62. O.R., 4:491.
63. Ibid., 513.

64. Ibid., 513–14.

65. Ibid., 517.

66. Polk to Davis, November 6, 1861, by permission of the Houghton Library, (Dearborn Collection), Harvard University, photocopy, JDA. Parks (*General Leonidas Polk,* 189) maintains that "there does not appear to have been any connection between Johnston's order for the transfer of Pillow's division and Polk's" resignation.

67. O.R., 4:539.

68. Ibid., 22:406.

69. Ibid., 3:311.

70. Ibid., 4:539, 543.

71. Parks, *General Leonidas Polk,* 195.

72. Horn, *The Army of Tennessee,* 438n.

73. Wingfield, *General A. P. Stewart,* 47–49.

74. Parks, *General Leonidas Polk,* 190–94.

75. O.R., vol. 52, pt. 2, 206.

76. Ibid., 3:739; 7:705.

77. Parks, *General Leonidas Polk,* 197.

78. Ibid., 200.

79. O.R., 3:739; 4:550–51, 553.

80. Thomas Lawrence Connelly and Archer Jones (*The Politics of Command: Factions and Ideas in Confederate Strategy* [Baton Rouge: Louisiana State University Press, 1973], 94) assert that "Davis's vision in establishing such a broad command probably has been overrated." They feel it was the result not of Davis's insight but of his failure to grasp the Federal threat to Tennessee. This is very possible since with an increasing awareness of the magnitude of the threat in the West, Davis showed an increasing tendency to fragment the command structure there.

81. Connelly (*Army of the Heartland,* 62–63) argues that Johnston was a poor commander who presided over a "weak command structure" and was sometimes manipulated by his generals, especially Polk. He also asserts that Johnston "had no over-all departmental strategy" and failed to achieve any "coordinated defensive effort between his district commanders."

CHAPTER 5. THE GATEWAY TO EAST TENNESSEE

1. Bruce Catton, *Terrible Swift Sword* (Garden City, N.Y.: Doubleday, 1963), 54–55.

2. Harris to Davis, July 13, 1861, Isham G. Harris Papers, Tennessee State Library and Archives, photocopy, JDA.

3. O.R., 4:365–66.

4. Ibid., vol. 51, pt. 2, 180; John B. Jones, *A Rebel War Clerk's Diary,* ed. Earl Schenck Miers (New York: Sagamore Press, 1958), 41.

5. O.R., 4:374.

6. Ibid., 375.

7. Thomas Lawrence Connelly, *Army of the Heartland: The Army of Tennessee, 1861–1862* (Baton Rouge: Louisiana State University Press, 1967), 88–89.

8. O.R., 4:516–17.

9. Ibid., 527.

10. Ibid., vol. 52, pt. 2, 219.

11. Lynda Lasswell Crist, Mary Seaton Dix, and Richard E. Beringer, eds., *The Papers of Jefferson Davis* (Baton Rouge: Louisiana State University Press, 1983), 4:9n.

12. Ellsworth Eliot, Jr., *West Point in the Confederacy* (New York: G. A. Baker, 1941), 320.

13. Crist, Dix, and Beringer, *The Papers of Jefferson Davis,* 4:9n.

14. Haskell M. Monroe and James T. McIntosh, eds., *The Papers of Jefferson Davis* (Baton Rouge: Louisiana State University Press, 1971), 1:446; James T. McIntosh, Lynda L. Crist, and Mary S. Dix, eds., *The Papers of Jefferson Davis* (Baton Rouge: Louisiana State University Press, 1981), 3:123.

15. McIntosh, Crist, and Dix, *The Papers of Jefferson Davis,* 3:123, 165.

16. Ibid., 262.

17. Crist, Dix, and Beringer, *The Papers of Jefferson Davis,* 4:8, 9n, 312; McIntosh, Crist, and Dix, *The Papers of Jefferson Davis,* 3:431; Lynda Lasswell Crist and Mary Seaton Dix, eds., *The Papers of Jefferson Davis* (Baton Rouge: Louisiana State University Press, 1985), 5:280, 477; Davis to James A. Stewart, January 9, 1857, Library of Congress, photocopy, JDA.

18. Dunbar Rowland, ed., *Jefferson Davis, Constitutionalist, His Letters, Papers and Speeches,* 10 vols. (Jackson: Mississippi Department of Archives and History, 1923), 5:151–52.

19. Ibid.; O.R., 7:740.

20. O.R., vol. 52, pt. 2, 219.

21. Connelly, *Army of the Heartland,* 96. Connelly thinks Zollicoffer would have fared better had he been left to himself and allowed to carry the fight to the enemy in December 1861. This was prevented by Davis's placing him under the command of Crittenden. Both Davis and Crittenden, Connelly considers, were ignorant concerning the state of affairs in Zollicoffer's sector.

22. O.R., 7:706.

23. Ibid., 763.

24. Rowland, *Jefferson Davis, Constitutionalist,* 5:151–52; O.R., vol. 52, pt. 2, 219.

25. O.R., 7:745.

26. Ibid., 763.

27. Ibid., 764.

28. Ibid., 690, 697, 715.

29. Ibid., 697.

30. Ibid., 715.

31. Ibid., 686.

32. Connelly, *Army of the Heartland,* 87.

33. O.R., 7:734.

34. Ibid., 725.

35. Ibid., 753.

36. Ibid., 773; William Eric Jamborsky, "Confederate Leadership and Defeat in the West," *Lincoln Herald* (Summer 1984): 55.

37. T. Harry Williams, *Lincoln and His Generals* (New York: Vintage Books, 1952), 252.

38. O.R., 7:10–12, 725, 753, 763.

39. Ibid., 753.

40. Ibid., 780, 786.

41. Ibid., 783–84.

42. Stanley Horn, *The Army of Tennessee* (Indianapolis: Bobbs-Merrill, 1941), 68; O.R., 7:838–39.

43. O.R., 7:104. Connelly (*Army of the Heartland,* 97) believes Zollicoffer would have had a better chance if allowed to stay in his entrenchments on the north bank of the Cumberland rather than being ordered to attack, against his better judgment, by Crittenden.

44. R. M. Kelley, "Holding Kentucky for the Union," *Battles and Leaders of the Civil*

War, ed. Robert Underwood Johnson and Clarence Buell, 4 vols. (New York: Yoselof, 1956), 1:389; Shelby Foote, *The Civil War,* 3 vols. (New York: Random House, 1958), 1:179; Jamborsky, "Confederate Leadership and Defeat in the West," 55.

45. Catton, *Terrible Swift Sword,* 131–32.

46. Horn, *The Army of Tennessee,* 69–70.

47. O.R., 7:855.

48. Ibid., 849–50; vol. 52, pt. 2, 256–57.

49. Ibid., 7:850.

50. Ibid., 862–63.

51. Ibid., 855.

52. Ibid., 872.

53. Ibid., vol. 10, pt. 2, 379.

54. Crittenden to Davis, November 12, 1862, Papers received by the Confederate Adjutant and Inspector General's Office, National Archives, microfilm M-474, roll 13, frame 495–501, JDA.

55. Jefferson Davis, *The Rise and Fall of the Confederate Government,* 2 vols. (New York: D. Appleton, 1881), 2:19–22.

56. Rowland, *Jefferson Davis, Constitutionalist,* 5:184.

57. Ibid., 216–19.

58. O.R., 7:844–45; 130–31.

CHAPTER 6. COLLAPSE

1. Thomas Lawrence Connelly (*Army of the Heartland: The Army of Tennessee, 1861–1862* [Baton Rouge: Louisiana State University Press, 1967], 65) argues that Johnston became obsessed with the defense of Bowling Green and largely ignored the Tennessee and Cumberland river defenses.

2. O.R., 7:831.

3. Ibid., 835, 839.

4. Joseph H. Parks, *General Leonidas Polk, C.S.A., The Fighting Bishop* (Baton Rouge: Louisiana State University Press, 1960), 206.

5. O.R., 7:839.

6. Ibid., 833, 835.

7. Shelby Foote, *The Civil War,* 3 vols. (New York: Random House, 1958), 1:181; Benjamin Franklin Cooling, *Forts Henry and Donelson: The Key to the Confederate Heartland* (Knoxville: University of Tennessee Press, 1987), 85.

8. O.R., 7:840–41, 859–69.

9. T. Harry Williams, *P. G. T. Beauregard: Napoleon in Gray* (Baton Rouge: Louisiana State University Press, 1955), 2–42.

10. Lynda Lasswell Crist and Mary Seaton Dix, eds., *The Papers of Jefferson Davis* (Baton Rouge: Louisiana State University Press, 1985), 5:286.

11. Williams, *P. G. T. Beauregard,* 42–50.

12. Mary Boykin Chesnut, *A Diary from Dixie,* ed. Ben Ames Williams (Boston: Houghton Mifflin, 1905), 31, 33; John B. Jones, *A Rebel War Clerk's Diary,* ed. Earl Schenck Miers (New York: Sagamore Press, 1958), 28, 35.

13. Beauregard to Davis, February 10, 1861, Beauregard Papers, Manuscript Department, Perkins Library, Duke University, photocopy, JDA.

14. Jefferson Davis to F. W. Pickens, March 1, 1861, The Rosenbach Museum and Library, Philadelphia, AMs 356/26, photocopy, JDA.

15. Douglas Southall Freeman states that Beauregard and Davis were "old friends"

and that "Davis as United States Secretary of War had known Beauregard well." *Lee's Lieutenants: A Study in Command* (New York: Charles Scribner's Sons, 1942), 1:4. It seems unlikely that Davis and Beauregard were ever close personal associates.

16. Davis to Howell Cobb, March 1, 1861, L. S. Ruder Collection, Beauvoir Jefferson Davis Shrine, photocopy, JDA.

17. Richard D. Goff, *Confederate Supply* (Durham, N.C.: Duke University Press, 1969), throughout; Goff presents Northrop as being less incompetent than many have claimed.

18. Williams, *P. G. T. Beauregard*, 96–105.

19. O.R., 2:508.

20. Chesnut, *A Diary from Dixie*, 67–68, 83–84.

21. O.R., 2:508.

22. Ibid.

23. Bruce Catton, *Terrible Swift Sword* (Garden City, N.Y.: Doubleday, 1963), 70.

24. Jones, *A Rebel War Clerk's Diary*, 53.

25. Herman Hattaway and Archer Jones, *How the North Won: A Military History of the Civil War* (Urbana: University of Illinois Press, 1983), 155.

26. Williams, *P. G. T. Beauregard*, 63–65.

27. Davis to Polk, February 7, 1862, National Archives, photocopy, JDA.

28. Williams, *P. G. T. Beauregard*, 113–14.

29. Connelly (*Army of the Heartland*, 129) argues that beginning at this point Johnston allowed Beauregard to usurp from him almost complete control of the army.

30. Williams, *P. G. T. Beauregard*, 51–53.

31. Davis to Polk, February 7, 1862, National Archives, photocopy, JDA.

32. Parks, *General Leonidas Polk*, 208–9.

33. Catton, *Terrible Swift Sword*, 141; Cooling, *Forts Henry and Donelson*, 78–79.

34. Stanley Horn, *The Army of Tennessee* (Indianapolis: Bobbs-Merrill, 1941), 80–83; Cooling, *Forts Henry and Donelson*, 101–6.

35. O.R., 7:867.

36. Ibid., 861–62.

37. Ibid., 130–31.

38. Goff, *Confederate Supply*, 31–37.

39. Catton, *Terrible Swift Sword*, 145; Timothy H. Donovan, Jr., Roy K. Flint, Arthur V. Grant, Jr., and Gerald P. Stodler, *The American Civil War*, West Point Military History Series (Wayne, N.J.: Avery Publishing Group, 1987), 32–34.

40. O.R., 7:880.

41. Charles P. Roland, *Albert Sidney Johnston: Solider of Three Republics* (Austin: University of Texas Press, 1964), 295.

42. Connelly (*Army of the Heartland*, 109–10) argues that Johnston expected an overland move against Fort Donelson by Buell's forces rather than a move up the river by Grant's.

43. O.R., 7:779, 792, 796.

44. Catton, *Terrible Swift Sword*, 45–48; Bruce Catton, *The Coming Fury* (Garden City, N.Y.: Doubleday, 1961), 417–18.

45. Catton, *The Coming Fury*, 173–74, 176.

46. Connelly (*Army of the Heartland*, 112) argues that Johnston "abdicated command responsibility for Donelson" and "was losing command of himself and of the Army" when he assigned Floyd to command Fort Donelson, though why this should be true in this case, any more than in any other case in which a department commander delegates the defense of a particular point to a subordinate, is unclear to say the least.

It is true, however, that Johnston, like Lee, tended to trust his subordinates too much and allow them too much discretion.

47. O.R., 7:861–62.

48. Ibid., 6:823–24; 7:862–63, 867–69.

49. Ibid., 7:878–79; vol. 52, pt. 2, 272.

50. Ibid., 7:865, 869; vol. 52, pt. 2, 272.

51. Ibid., vol. 52, pt. 2, 274.

52. Catton, *Terrible Swift Sword*, 146–47.

53. O.R., vol. 52, pt. 2, 274; 7:880, 255.

54. Catton, *Terrible Swift Sword*, 147–48.

55. Foote, *The Civil War*, 1:207.

56. O.R., 7:255.

57. Ibid.; Cooling, *Forts Henry and Donelson*, 180.

58. Horn, *The Army of Tennessee*, 93.

59. O.R., 7:314–16.

60. Arndt M. Stickles, *Simon Bolivar Buckner: Borderland Knight* (Chapel Hill: University of North Carolina Press, 1940), 144.

61. O.R., 7:296–97.

62. Ibid., 278–85.

63. Cooling, *Forts Henry and Donelson*, 132; Stickles, *Simon Bolivar Buckner*, 18, 40–41. During the occupation of Mexico City at the conclusion of the Mexican War, Pillow, along with two other officers, was active in a feud against United States commanding general Winfield Scott. Scott ordered the three fractious officers arrested and court-martialed, but Pres. James K. Polk, Pillow's former law partner, let them off. Buckner was a great admirer of Winfield Scott. When a decade later Buckner visited Tennessee and found that in the Senate campaign then taking place, Pillow, who was one of the candidates, had become so carried away in bragging about his Mexican War exploits that he had begun criticizing Scott, Buckner was outraged. Pillow lost the election, and after it was over Buckner had three separate articles published anonymously in the newspapers denouncing Pillow and his claims in terms of sarcasm and ridicule. In case Pillow could not figure out who had written the articles, Buckner wrote him a letter informing him. For a time speculation was rife that the two would fight a duel, but Pillow contented himself with the safer expedient of replying with more newspaper articles.

64. O.R., 7:297–99.

65. Ibid., 299–300.

66. Ibid., 296–97.

67. Foote, *The Civil War*, 1:212.

68. Horn, *The Army of Tennessee*, 96–98.

69. O.R., 7:258–61.

70. Jones, *A Rebel War Clerk's Diary*, 68; Hudson Strode, *Jefferson Davis, Confederate President* (New York: Harcourt Brace, 1959), 197; James McPherson, *Battle Cry of Freedom: The Civil War Era* (New York: Oxford University Press, 1988), 405.

71. Jefferson Davis, *The Rise and Fall of the Confederate Government*, 2 vols. (New York: D. Appleton, 1881), 2:48–49; Chesnut, *A Diary from Dixie*, 198–99; Dunbar Rowland, ed., *Jefferson Davis, Constitutionalist, His Letters, Papers and Speeches*, 10 vols. (Jackson: Mississippi Department of Archives and History, 1923), 5:215–16.

72. Rowland, *Jefferson Davis, Constitutionalist*, 5:214.

73. Catton, *Terrible Swift Sword*, 208–12.

CHAPTER 7. SHILOH

1. O.R., 7:878.
2. Ibid., 887–88.
3. Thomas Lawrence Connelly (*Army of the Heartland: The Army of Tennessee, 1861–1862* [Baton Rouge: Louisiana State University Press, 1967], 138–42) argues that after the fall of Nashville, Johnston gradually lost his control of the army and himself came under the influence of Beauregard even to the extent of meekly accepting orders from that general. Connelly feels that it was Johnston's intention to operate out of Stevenson, Alabama, drawing his supplies from Chattanooga, before Beauregard persuaded him to shift to West Tennessee. This interpretation of the relative roles of Johnston and Beauregard differs sharply with Charles P. Roland's account in *Albert Sidney Johnston: Soldier of Three Republics* (Austin: University of Texas Press, 1964), as well as Grady McWhiney's in *Braxton Bragg and Confederate Defeat* (Columbia, S.C.: The State Company, 1924). It is undoubtedly true that Beauregard, upon first agreeing to go to the West and at certain times thereafter, desired command of all the western armies, schemed to get it, and even acted as if he already had it by making various organizational changes without Johnston's permission; and, that Johnston, as was his wont, delegated to Beauregard large, indeed excessive, authority in organizational and planning matters. However, it also seems clear that the barrage of messages Beauregard sent to Johnston during this period begging the latter to come to his aid were not part of a design to manipulate Johnston out of his control of the army—an endeavor under other circumstances by no means beyond the shifty Creole general—but rather the result of Beauregard's very genuine and sincere panic and state of virtual nervous collapse.
4. Roland, *Albert Sidney Johnston*, 305.
5. O.R., 7:679.
6. Ibid., 666.
7. Ibid., 905.
8. Ibid., 911.
9. Ibid., 917.
10. O.R., vol. 10, pt. 2, 310.
11. Ibid., 42, 310; pt. 1, 29.
12. Ibid., pt. 2, 42.
13. Ibid., 361.
14. Ibid., 7:437.
15. Jefferson Davis to Joseph Davis, February 21, 1862, printed in Washington (D.C.) *Daily Morning Chronicle*, May 13, 1864.
16. Allen Tate, *Jefferson Davis: His Rise and Fall* (New York: Minton, Balch, 1929), 125; Irving Werstein, *Abraham Lincoln versus Jefferson Davis* (New York: Thomas Y. Crowell, 1959), 186–87; Hamilton J. Eckenrode, *Jefferson Davis: President of the South* (New York: Macmillan, 1930), 169–70.
17. James McPherson, *Battle Cry of Freedom: The Civil War Era* (New York: Oxford University Press, 1988), 403.
18. William E. Dodd, *Jefferson Davis* (Philadelphia: George W. Jacobs, 1907), 265.
19. A. Wright to Davis, February 24, 1862; A. B. Bacon to Davis, February 25, 1862, Perkins Library, Duke University, photocopies, JDA; Robertson Topp et al. to Davis, February 24, 1862, Pritchard von David Collection, University of Texas at Austin, photocopy, JDA: Roland, *Albert Sidney Johnston*, 300; Connelly, *Army of the Heartland*, 138; Hudson Strode, *Jefferson Davis, Confederate President* (New York: Harcourt Brace, 1959), 199.

20. Dunbar Rowland, ed., *Jefferson Davis, Constitutionalist, His Letters, Papers and Speeches,* 10 vols. (Jackson: Mississippi Department of Archives and History, 1923), 5:46.

21. Shelby Foote, *The Civil War,* 3 vols. (New York: Random House, 1958), 2:643.

22. Davis to A. S. Johnston, March 26, 1862, National Archives, photocopy, JDA.

23. Rowland, *Jefferson Davis, Constitutionalist,* 5:213, 215–16; Davis to A. S. Johnston, March 26, 1862, National Archives, photocopy, JDA.

24. Rowland, *Jefferson Davis, Constitutionalist,* 5:227.

25. Jefferson Davis to Joseph Davis, February 21, 1862, printed in Washington (D.C.) *Daily Morning Chornicle,* May 13, 1864.

26. Herman Hattaway and Archer Jones, *How the North Won: A Military History of the Civil War* (Urbana: University of Illinois Press, 1983), 218–19.

27. Rowena Reed, *Combined Operations in the Civil War* (Annapolis, Md.: Naval Institute Press, 1978), 55–56.

28. McWhiney, *Braxton Bragg and Confederate Defeat,* 1–119.

29. James. T. McIntosh, Lynda L. Crist, and Mary S. Dix, eds., *The Papers of Jefferson Davis* (Baton Rouge: Louisiana State University Press, 1981), 3:143–49n.

30. McWhiney, *Braxton Bragg and Confederate Defeat,* 136–92.

31. O.R., 6:788–89.

32. Ibid., 797–98.

33. McWhiney, *Braxton Bragg and Confederate Defeat,* 197–98.

34. O.R., 6:826–27, 894, 834–35.

35. Rowland, *Jefferson Davis, Constitutionalist,* 5:216–19.

36. O.R., 6:834; McWhiney, *Braxton Bragg and Confederate Defeat,* 204–5.

37. McWhiney, *Braxton Bragg and Confederate Defeat,* 202–3.

38. T. Harry Williams, *P. G. T. Beauregard: Napoleon in Gray* (Baton Rouge: Louisiana State University Press, 1955), 118.

39. O.R., 7:912.

40. Ibid., 895–96.

41. Ibid., vol. 10, pt. 2, 297.

42. McWhiney, *Braxton Bragg and Confederate Defeat,* 205.

43. O.R., vol. 10, pt. 2, 327, 302.

44. Ibid., 370–71.

45. Roland, *Albert Sidney Johnston,* 303–4; Bruce Catton, *Terrible Swift Sword* (Garden City, N.Y.: Doubleday, 1963), 204.

46. Carl von Clausewitz, *On War,* ed. Anatol Rapoport (New York: Penguin, 1968), 164.

47. Catton, *Terrible Swift Sword,* 213.

48. Roland, *Albert Sidney Johnston,* 319.

49. O.R., vol. 10, pt. 2, 390–91.

50. Catton, *Terrible Swift Sword,* 215–16.

51. McWhiney, *Braxton Bragg and Confederate Defeat,* 226–27; Williams, *P. G. T. Beauregard,* 132; Wiley Sword, *Shiloh—Bloody April* (Dayton, Ohio: Press of Morningside, 1983), 106–8. Joseph H. Parks (*General Leonidas Polk, C.S.A., The Fighting Bishop* [Baton Rouge: Louisiana State University Press, 1960], 230) claims Bragg and Polk wanted to stay and fight and only Beauregard favored retreat. As pertains to Bragg this contradicts both McWhiney and Sword (cited here) and is probably incorrect. William C. Davis (*Deep Waters of the Proud* [Garden City, N.Y.: Doubleday, 1982], 119) says Breckinridge also wanted to stay and fight but was sick and spent the conference lying down on a nearby blanket.

52. Rowland, *Jefferson Davis, Constitutionlist,* 5:227.

53. Ibid., 213, 215–16; Jefferson Davis to Joseph Davis, February 21, 1862, Washington (D.C.) *Daily Morning Chronicle,* May 13, 1864.

54. Catton, *Terrible Swift Sword,* 216; Sword, *Shiloh,* 108.

55. Roland, *Albert Sidney Johnston,* 325.

56. O.R., vol. 10, pt. 2, 387.

57. McWhiney, *Braxton Bragg and Confederate Defeat,* 221, 223–24.

58. Parks, *General Leonidas Polk,* 223–24, 231; James Lee McDonough, *Shiloh – In Hell before Night* (Knoxville: University of Tennessee Press, 1977), 73–75.

59. McWhiney, *Braxton Bragg and Confederate Defeat,* 217, 221, 223–24.

60. Parks, *General Leonidas Polk,* 231.

61. O.R., vol. 10, pt. 2, 93–94.

62. Ibid., pt. 1, 89.

63. Williams, *P. G. T. Beauregard,* 134.

64. Catton, *Terrible Swift Sword,* 219.

65. Roland, *Albert Sidney Johnston,* 332; Sword, *Shiloh,* 222.

66. Roland, *Albert Sidney Johnston,* 335.

67. Sword, *Shiloh,* 222, 224.

68. O.R., vol. 10, pt. 1, 405–12.

69. Roland, *Albert Sidney Johnston,* 336.

70. Stanley Horn, *The Army of Tennessee* (Indianapolis: Bobbs-Merrill, 1941), 134. Sword (*Shiloh,* 443–40) gives an extensive discussion of the nature of Johnston's wound.

71. O.R., vol. 52, pt. 2, 275.

72. Horn, *The Army of Tennessee,* 134.

73. Ibid., 134–35; Catton, *Terrible Swift Sword,* 223; Sword, *Shiloh,* 244–45, 276, 279–80.

74. O.R., vol. 10, pt. 1, 566–72; Sword, *Shiloh,* 244–45, 276, 279–80.

75. Catton, *Terrible Swift Sword,* 233.

76. O.R., vol. 10, pt. 1, 463–70.

77. Ibid., 384–92.

78. Parks, *General Leonidas Polk,* 235.

79. O.R., vol. 10, pt. 1, 405–12. Confederate chances for victory and the wisdom of Beauregard's order calling off the attack on the evening of the first day at Shiloh have been the subject of much dispute. Many scholars (among them, Connelly, *Army of the Heartland,* 171; Parks, *General Leonidas Polk,* 235; Catton, *Terrible Swift Sword,* 224; McDonough, *Shiloh,* 168–78; Davis, *Deep Waters of the Proud,* 122, and *Breckinridge: Statesman, Soldier, Symbol* [Baton Rouge: Louisiana State University Press, 1974], 310–11; Foote, *The Civil War,* 1:341–42; McPherson, *Battle Cry of Freedom,* 410; and Horn, *The Army of Tennessee,* 137) have attempted to argue to a greater or lesser degree that Confederate victory was impossible on April 6 and that Beauregard's order calling off the attack that evening was justified. Others (Sword, *Shiloh,* 365–66; Nathaniel C. Hughes, *General William J. Hardee: Old Reliable* [Baton Rouge: Louisiana State University Press, 1965], 109; and Strode, *Jefferson Davis, Confederate President,* 233–35) tend to take the opposite view, and Grady McWhiney in *Braxton Bragg and Confederate Defeat* (243–45) and especially in "General Beauregard's 'Complete Victory' at Shiloh: An Interpretation" (*Journal of Southern History,* 49 [August 1983]: 421–34) presents an extremely strong case that truly complete Confederate victory was very much possible during the late daylight hours of April 6 had not Beauregard foolishly stopped the fighting. Of course it is difficult if not impossible to say what *would* have happened had different decisions been made in any historical situation. The point, however, is that due to Beauregard's order the matter was never put to the test; and considering the price the Confederates had paid to get where they were and the slim likelihood they

would ever be in such a situation again, a final attack, whatever the odds, was a gamble the Confederates could not afford *not* to make. They should at least have tried.

80. McWhiney, *Braxton Bragg and Confederate Defeat,* 243-45.

81. O.R., vol. 10, pt. 1, 405-12, 463-70, 566-72.

82. Connelly, *Army of the Heartland,* 171.

83. O.R., vol. 10, pt. 1, 384-92.

84. Ibid., 384.

85. Davis to Van Dorn, April 7, 1862, Pierpont Morgan Library, New York, and William Preston to Davis, April 7, 1862, Mason Barret Collection of A. S. and W. P. Johnston Papers, Tulane University Library, both photocopies, JDA.

86. Davis to Congress, April 8, 1862, The Museum of the Confederacy, Richmond, Virginia, photocopy, JDA.

87. O.R., vol. 10, pt. 2, 546; Davis to Van Dorn, April 7, 1862, Pierpont Morgan Library, New York, and Davis to Congress, April 8, 1862, The Museum of the Confederacy, Richmond, Virginia, both photocopies, JDA.

88. McDonough, *Shiloh,* 9-11.

89. O.R., vol. 10, pt. 2, p. 403.

90. Ibid., 451, 463, 482-84, 487, 502-3, 505-6, 508-9, 517, 532-33, 535, 538, 540; pt. 1, 777-79.

91. Ibid., pt. 2, 544-47.

92. Ibid., pt. 1, 762.

93. Mary Boykin Chesnut, *A Diary from Dixie,* ed. Ben Ames Williams (Boston: Houghton Mifflin, 1905), 224.

94. O.R., vol. 10, pt. 2, 407; Rowland, *Jefferson Davis, Constitutionalist,* 5:231.

95. Clifford Dowdey and Louis H. Manarin, eds. *The Wartime Papers of R. E. Lee* (New York: Bramhall House, 1961), 145; O.R., vol. 52, pt. 2, 232.

96. O.R., vol. 10, pt. 2, 407; vol. 52, pt. 2, 300; Rowland, *Jefferson Davis, Constitutionalist,* 5:230-31.

97. O.R., vol. 10, pt. 2, 529-30.

98. Ibid., 546.

99. Ibid., vol. 17, pt. 2, 594-95.

100. Strode, *Jefferson Davis, Confederate President,* 266.

101. Rowland, *Jefferson Davis, Constitutionalist,* 5:279-80.

102. Ibid., 274.

103. O.R., 53:247; Connelly, *Army of the Heartland,* 180.

104. Jefferson Davis to Varina Davis, June 13, 1862, The Museum of the Confederacy photocopy, JDA.

105. O.R., vol. 17, pt. 2, 599, 601.

106. Connelly (*Army of the Heartland,* 181) believes Davis may have deliberately allowed Beauregard to leave his post without permission in order to have an excuse to remove him.

107. Rowland, *Jefferson Davis, Constitutionalist,* 5:279, 283; O.R., vol. 17, pt. 2, 599, 612; Bragg to Davis, June 19, 1862, Manuscript Department, Perkins Library, Duke University; Davis to Bragg, June 19, 1862, The Museum of the Confederacy; Davis to Gov. J. J. Pettus, June 19, 1862, Mississippi Department of Archives and History—all photocopies, JDA.

108. Rowland, *Jefferson Davis, Constitutionalist,* 5:283; Connelly (*Army of the Heartland,* 182) states that in replacing Beauregard with Bragg, Davis was substituting an "old friend" for an "old enemy" and continues: "Now Davis's prestige would be challenged in any dispute over Bragg's generalship. A censure of Bragg would be a censure of Davis as well." Clearly, however, Bragg was anything but an "old friend" of Davis,

and the president's regard for that general sprang not from personal factors but from a professional military assessment and a respect for Bragg's wholehearted devotion to the cause. Davis's ego was not engaged in the matter of Braxton Bragg, at this point, any more than in the selection of any other general.

109. Foote, *The Civil War*, 2:391.

110. Werstein, *Abraham Lincoln versus Jefferson Davis*, 182–83.

111. McPherson, *Battle Cry of Freedom*, 428.

112. Jefferson Davis to Varina Davis, June 21, 1862, Jefferson Davis Collection, Eleanor S. Brockenbrough Library, The Museum of the Confederacy, Richmond, Virginia, photocopy, JDA.

CHAPTER 8. THE GIBRALTAR OF THE WEST

1. Samuel Carter III, *The Final Fortress: The Campaign for Vicksburg, 1862–1863* (New York: St. Martin's, 1980), 12.

2. Stanley Horn, *The Army of Tennessee* (Indianapolis: Bobbs-Merrill, 1941), 111, 144–45, 153.

3. O.R., vol. 10, pt. 2, 579.

4. Carter, *The Final Fortress*, 51–52.

5. Thomas O. Moore to Davis, September 6, 1861, JDA; Dunbar Rowland, ed., *Jefferson Davis, Constitutionalist, His Letters, Papers and Speeches*, 10 vols. (Jackson: Mississippi Department of Archives and History, 1923), 5:138–41.

6. John B. Jones, *A Rebel War Clerk's Diary*, ed. Earl Schenck Miers (New York: Sagamore Press, 1958), 66.

7. O.R., 6:877, 883.

8. Ibid., 883.

9. Ibid., 876–77.

10. Ibid., 510–11.

11. Rowland, *Jefferson Davis, Constitutionalist*, 5:232–33.

12. United States Naval War Records Office, *Official Records of the Union and Confederate Navies in the War of the Rebellion*, 30 vols. (Washington, D.C.: Government Printing Office, 1894–1922) (hereafter O.R.N.), ser. 2, 1:640.

13. Mary Boykin Chesnut, *A Diary from Dixie*, ed. Ben Ames Williams (Boston: Houghton Mifflin, 1905), 234.

14. O.R., 53:802; Rowland, *Jefferson Davis, Constitutionalist*, 5:232–33.

15. O.R., 6:510–11, 883–84.

16. Ibid., 15:6–12; vol. 10, pt. 2, 430–31.

17. Ibid., 15:741–42.

18. Ibid., 742, 746; vol. 10, pt. 2, 547.

19. Ibid., 15:6–12.

20. Ibid., 769.

21. Ibid., 6:641–43.

22. Ibid., 53:803.

23. Ibid., 6:657–58.

24. J. J. Pettus to Jefferson Davis, June 19, 1862, by permission of the Houghton Library (Dearborn Collection), Harvard University; Joseph Davis to Jefferson Davis, June 18 and 22, 1862, Jefferson Davis Papers, Transylvania University Library—all photocopies, JDA.

25. O.R., 6:656–57. Some scholars have argued that Davis "actively and deliberately tried to burden Lovell permanently with responsibility for the Confederate loss

of New Orleans." Daniel E. Sutherland, "Mansfield Lovell's Quest for Justice: Another Look at the Fall of New Orleans," *Louisiana History* (1983): 233–59; Charles L. Dufour, *The Night the War Was Lost* (Garden City, N.Y.: Doubleday, 1960), and "The Night the War Was Lost: The Fall of New Orleans: Causes, Consequences, Culpability," *Louisiana History* 2 (1961): 157–74. It seems more likely that Davis, at this relatively early stage of the war, possessed the flexibility and political perception to see that the continuance of Lovell in an independent command would have been a grave political mistake. Lovell later served as a corps commander under Van Dorn in Mississippi. This is the kind of arrangement Davis later sought for another discredited northern general, John C. Pemberton. Davis's more active role in defending Pemberton is probably attributable to the president's admiration for what he considered to be that general's heroism and to Davis's progressive loss of flexibility and political perception as the war continued and its pressures on him increased.

26. Robert J. Hartje, *Van Dorn: The Life and Times of a Confederate General* (Nashville, Tenn.: Vanderbilt University Press, 1967), 6–15.

27. Bruce Catton, *Terrible Swift Sword* (Garden City, N.Y.: Doubleday, 1963), 207.

28. James T. McIntosh, Lynda L. Crist, and Mary S. Dix, eds., *The Papers of Jefferson Davis* (Baton Rouge: Louisiana State University Press, 1981), 3:441.

29. Jefferson Davis, *The Rise and Fall of the Confederate Government*, 2 vols. (New York: D. Appleton, 1881), 2:388.

30. Joseph H. Parks, *General Edmund Kirby Smith, C.S.A.* (Baton Rouge: Louisiana State University Press, 1954), 96–98.

31. Hartje, *Van Dorn*, 15–77.

32. Catton, *Terrible Swift Sword*, 207.

33. Ezra Warner, *Generals in Gray* (Baton Rouge: Louisiana State University Press, 1959), 200–201; Hartje, *Van Dorn*, 100–104.

34. Shelby Foote, *The Civil War*, 3 vols. (New York: Random House, 1958), 1:278.

35. Hartje, *Van Dorn*, 157.

36. Foote, *The Civil War*, 1:286–91; James McPherson, *Battle Cry of Freedom: The Civil War Era* (New York: Oxford University Press, 1988), 405; William C. Davis, *Stand in the Day of Battle* (Garden City, N.Y.: Doubleday, 1983), 247–48.

37. O.R., 8:789–90.

38. Hartje, *Van Dorn*, 175.

39. O.R., vol. 17, pt. 2, 613.

40. O.R., vol. 10, pt. 2, 544.

41. Ibid., vol. 17, pt. 2, 627.

42. Van Dorn to Davis, July 12 and 14, 1862, The Samuel Richey Collection of the Southern Confederacy, Miami University Libraries, Oxford, Ohio, photocopies, JDA; Rowland, *Jefferson Davis, Constitutionalist*, 5:294.

43. Van Dorn to Davis, June 22, 1862, The Samuel Richey Collection of the Southern Confederacy, Miami University Libraries, photocopy, JDA; O.R., vol. 52, pt. 2, 324; 15:767, 14.

44. O.R., vol. 52, pt. 2, 324.

45. Ibid., 15:767; Rowland, *Jefferson Davis, Constitutionalist*, 5:294.

46. Van Dorn to Davis, July 14, 1862, The Samuel Richey Collection of the Southern Confederacy, Miami University Libraries, photocopy, JDA.

47. Van Dorn to Davis, July 15, 1862, The Samuel Richey Collection of the Southern Confederacy, Miami University Libraries, photocopy, JDA.

48. Van Dorn to Davis, July 16 and 22, 1862, The Samuel Richey Collection of the Southern Confederacy, Miami University Libraries, photocopy, JDA.

49. Van Dorn to Davis, July 24, 1862, The Samuel Richey Collection of the Southern Confederacy, Miami University Libraries, photocopy, JDA.

50. O.R., 15:6–12.

51. Ibid., 778–79.

52. Lawrence Lee Hewitt, *Port Hudson, Confederate Bastion on the Mississippi* (Baton Rouge: Louisiana State University Press, 1987), 2.

53. Van Dorn to Davis, July 15 and 16, 1862, The Samuel Richey Collection of the Southern Confederacy, Miami University Libraries, photocopy, JDA.

54. O.R., 15:776–77.

55. Ibid., 785–86.

56. William Catton and Bruce Catton, *Two Roads to Sumter* (New York: McGraw-Hill, 1963), 13; Haskell M. Monroe and James T. McIntosh, eds., *The Papers of Jefferson Davis* (Baton Rouge: Louisiana State University Press, 1971), 1:23–24; William C. Davis, *Breckinridge: Statesman, Soldier, Symbol* (Baton Rouge: Louisiana State University Press, 1974), 3–13, 273.

57. Davis, *Breckinridge*, 20–38, 44–57, 293.

58. Lynda Lasswell Crist and Mary Seaton Dix, eds., *The Papers of Jefferson Davis* (Baton Rouge: Louisiana State University Press, 1985), 5:67–68; Davis, *Breckinridge*, 95–109, 118–19.

59. Horn, *The Army of Tennessee*, 55, 437n; William C. Davis, *Deep Waters of the Proud* (Garden City, N.Y.: Doubleday, 1982), 109; Davis, *Breckinridge*, 294–95.

60. Davis, *Breckinridge*, 315; Davis, *Deep Waters of the Proud*, 217.

61. Thomas Lawrence Connelly, *Autumn of Glory: The Army of Tennessee, 1862–1865* (Baton Rouge: Louisiana State University Press, 1971), 30.

62. Davis, *Breckinridge*, 299.

63. O.R., 15:1124; vol. 52, pt. 2, 334.

64. Ibid., 15:14; Jones, *A Rebel War Clerk's Diary*, 92; Jefferson Davis, *The Rise and Fall of the Confederate Government*, 2:243–44.

65. Van Dorn to Davis, August 11, 1862, The Samuel Richey Collection of the Southern Confederacy, Miami University Libraries, photocopy, JDA.

66. Ibid.

67. O.R., vol. 17, pt. 2, 675; 15:797.

68. Ibid., 53:823.

69. Ibid., 15:795; Hewitt, *Port Hudson*, 15.

70. Ellsworth Eliot, Jr., *West Point in the Confederacy* (New York: G. A. Baker, 1941), xx–xxviii.

71. Foote, *The Civil War*, 2:46.

72. William C. Davis, *Battle at Bull Run: A History of the First Major Campaign of the Civil War* (Garden City, N.Y.: Doubleday, 1977), 245–46.

73. Douglas Southall Freeman, *Lee's Lieutenants: A Study in Command* (New York: Charles Scribner's Sons, 1942), 1:145, 274, 582–83.

74. Ibid., 584.

75. Herman Hattaway and Archer Jones, *How the North Won: A Military History of the Civil War* (Urbana: University of Illinois Press, 1983), 212.

76. Warner, *Generals in Gray*, 137–38; Howell Purdue and Elizabeth Purdue, *Pat Cleburne, Confederate General* (Tuscaloosa, Ala.: Portals Press, 1973), 27; Foote, *The Civil War*, 2:46.

77. Parks, *General Edmund Kirby Smith*, 254.

78. McPherson, *Battle Cry of Freedom*, 668; Foote, *The Civil War*, 2:46; Davis, *Stand in the Day of Battle*, 248–49.

79. Foote, *The Civil War*, 2:46; McPherson, *Battle Cry of Freedom*, 668; Glenn

Tucker, *Chickamauga: Bloody Battle in the West* (Indianapolis: Bobbs-Merrill, 1961), 68–69.

80. O.R., vol. 52, pt. 2, 320.

81. Ibid., 596.

82. Davis, *Stand in the Day of Battle,* 170.

83. Timothy H. Donovan, Jr., Roy K. Flint, Arthur V. Grant, Jr., and Gerald P. Stodler, *The American Civil War,* West Point Military History Series (Wayne, N.J.: Avery Publishing Group, 1987), 102.

CHAPTER 9. BRAGG MOVES NORTH

1. Bruce Catton, *Terrible Swift Sword* (Garden City, N.Y.: Doubleday, 1963), 362.

2. O.R., 7:862–63.

3. Arndt M. Stickles, *Simon Bolivar Buckner: Borderland Knight* (Chapel Hill: University of North Carolina Press, 1940), 232.

4. O.R., 7:879.

5. Ibid., 908.

6. Joseph H. Parks, *General Edmund Kirby Smith, C.S.A.* (Baton Rouge: Louisiana State University Press, 1954), 12–121.

7. Douglas Southall Freeman, *Lee's Lieutenants: A Study in Command* (New York: Charles Scribner's Sons, 1942), 1:41; William C. Davis, *Battle at Bull Run: A History of the First Major Campaign of the Civil War* (Garden City, N.Y.: Doubleday, 1977), 133.

8. Thomas Lawrence Connelly, *Army of the Heartland: The Army of Tennessee, 1861–1862* (Baton Rouge: Louisiana State University Press, 1967), 192–93; Davis, *Battle at Bull Run,* 224–25.

9. Freeman, *Lee's Lieutenants,* 1:71; Davis, *Battle at Bull Run,* 226. Connelly (*Army of the Heartland,* 192–93) says Smith's wound was in the neck; W. C. Davis says it was in the chest. Joseph H. Parks (*General Edmund Kirby Smith,* 137–38) quotes Kirby Smith saying, "The ball . . . entered just back of the collarbone on the right shoulder, passing under the muscles of the shoulder blade and the muscles of the spine, missing the artery and the spine and leaving at the left shoulder," which left "a painful and troublesome flesh wound twelve inches in length."

10. Connelly, *Army of the Heartland,* 192–93; Parks, *General Edmund Kirby Smith,* 136–37. Jefferson Davis actually conferred this honor on Smith's second in command when, upon reaching the field of battle that evening, he said, "General Elzy, you are the Blücher of the day!" The public seemed to associate the concept more with Smith than Elzy. Shelby Foote, *The Civil War,* 3 vols. (New York: Random House, 1958), 1:83.

11. Connelly, *Army of the Heartland,* 192–93.

12. Parks, *General Edmund Kirby Smith,* 139–56.

13. O.R., vol. 10, pt. 2, 536, 554.

14. Ibid., 554, 596; pt. 1, 921; vol. 16, pt. 2, 684–85.

15. Ibid., vol. 10, pt. 2, 571.

16. Ibid., 483, 491.

17. Ibid., 481, 483, 584.

18. Ibid., 483, 584.

19. Ibid., vol. 16, pt. 2, 679.

20. Ibid.

21. Ibid., vol. 10, pt. 2, 596.

22. Ibid., vol. 16, pt. 2, 679–81.

23. Ibid., 701–2, 707–9, 711, 720.

24. Ibid., 53:246.

25. Dunbar Rowland, ed., *Jefferson Davis, Constitutionalist, His Letters, Papers and Speeches,* 10 vols. (Jackson: Mississippi Department of Archives and History, 1923), 5:284–85.

26. O.R., vol. 16, pt. 2, 701–2.

27. Ibid.

28. Ibid., vol. 52, pt. 2, 324–25.

29. Ibid., vol. 16, pt. 2, 701–2.

30. Ibid., 726–27; vol. 17, pt. 2, 626, 630.

31. Grady McWhiney, *Braxton Bragg and Confederate Defeat* (New York: Columbia University Press, 1969), 262–71; Ellsworth Eliot, Jr., *West Point in the Confederacy* (New York: G. A. Baker, 1941), 384. Parks (*General Edmund Kirby Smith,* 198) suggests that McCown was sent because his seniority as a division commander made it more or less obligatory that if anyone were sent, it would be McCown.

32. Connelly, *Army of the Heartlnad,* 192; Parks, *General Edmund Kirby Smith,* 198.

33. O.R., vol. 16, pt. 2, 726–27; vol. 17, pt. 2, 626, 630.

34. Ibid., vol. 17, pt. 2, 652.

35. Ibid., vol. 16, pt. 2, 726–27.

36. Ibid., 721–22.

37. Ibid., vol. 10, pt. 2, 780–86.

38. Ibid., vol. 17, pt. 2, 652.

39. Ibid., vol. 16, pt. 2, 731.

40. Ibid., vol. 17, pt. 2, 626.

41. Ibid., 644–46.

42. Ibid., 652.

43. Robert Selph Henry, *"First with the Most" Forrest* (Indianapolis: Bobbs-Merrill, 1944), 13–81.

44. Catton, *Terrible Swift Sword,* 355.

45. B. A. Botkin, ed., *A Civil War Treasury of Tales, Legends, and Folklore* (New York: Promontory Press, 1960), 185.

46. Connelly, *Army of the Heartland,* 194–95.

47. James A. Ramage, *Rebel Raider: The Life of General John Hunt Morgan* (Lexington: University Press of Kentucky, 1986), 20–83.

48. Ibid., 104–12; James McPherson, *Battle Cry of Freedom: The Civil War Era* (New York: Oxford University Press, 1988), 513–14.

49. O.R., vol. 16, pt. 1, 763, 766–70.

50. In fact, much of Morgan's information was, at best, badly exaggerated. Gary Donaldson, "'Into Africa': Kirby Smith and Braxton Bragg's Invasion of Kentucky," *Filson Club History Quarterly* 61 (October 1987): 450. Ramage (*Rebel Raider,* 102, 126, 132) points out that Morgan mistook interest in himself for support for the southern cause. This exaggeration of Confederate feeling in Kentucky was a "disservice" to the Confederacy and to Bragg and gave "the offensive a basic weakness to begin with; it was an unrealistic dream launched under a false premise."

51. McWhiney, *Braxton Bragg and Confederate Defeat,* 268.

52. O.R., vol. 17, pt. 2, 656, 897; vol. 52, pt. 2, 330–32.

53. Robert G. Hartje (*Van Dorn: The Life and Times of a Confederate General* [Nashville, Tenn.: Vanderbilt University Press, 1967], 209) suggests that Bragg may have done this deliberately because he did not trust Van Dorn with the entire command. This, however, seems unlikely since Bragg, who had a great appreciation of military professionalism, distrusted Price more than he possibly could Van Dorn. Bragg may also have doubted his authority to place Price under Van Dorn and give the latter officer respon-

sibility for a northward movement, since the orders placing Van Dorn at Vicksburg had come from Richmond. Bragg recommended that Price be placed under Van Dorn for the purpose of a northward movement as soon as Van Dorn's troops were no longer needed for the defense of Vicksburg; Albert E. Castel, *General Sterling Price and the Civil War in the West* (Baton Rouge: Louisiana State University Press, 1968), 93, 98–99.

54. O.R., vol. 17, pt. 2, 627–28, 667–68.

55. Ibid., 654–55, 658.

56. Ibid., 627–28, 654–55, 673.

57. Donaldson, "'Into Africa,'" 447.

58. Thomas Lawrence Connelly and Archer Jones, *The Politics of Command: Factions and Ideas in Confederate Strategy* (Baton Rouge: Louisiana State University Press, 1973), 106.

59. O.R., vol. 16, pt. 2, 745–46.

60. Ibid., 734–35.

61. Ibid., 741.

62. Ibid., 745–46, 751.

63. Rowland, *Jefferson Davis, Constitutionalist,* 5:313.

64. Davis to Kirby Smith, July 28, 1862, E. Kirby Smith Papers, Southern Historical Collection, Library of University of North Carolina at Chapel Hill, photocopy, JDA.

65. O. R., vol. 16, pt. 2, 751.

66. Ibid., 752–53.

67. Donaldson, "'Into Africa,'" 451.

68. O.R., vol. 16, pt. 2, 741–42; vol. 17, pt. 2, 675–76.

69. Ibid., vol. 16, pt. 2, 748.

70. Connelly, *Army of the Heartland,* 195.

71. O.R., vol. 16, pt. 2, 752–53.

72. Donaldson, "'Into Africa,'" 453.

73. O.R., vol. 16, pt. 2, 748–49.

74. Ibid., 751.

75. Ibid., 752–53.

76. Ibid., vol. 52, pt. 2, 340; Kirby Smith to Davis, August 13, 1862, by permission of the Houghton Library (Dearborn Collection), Harvard University, photocopy, JDA.

77. O.R., vol. 16, pt. 2, 755.

78. Ibid., 766–67.

79. Donaldson, "'Into Africa,'" 464.

80. O.R., vol. 16, pt. 2, 775.

81. McWhiney, *Braxton Bragg and Confederate Defeat,* 270–71.

82. O.R., vol. 16, pt. 2, 768–69, 775–76.

83. Ibid., 782–83.

84. Ibid., 897; vol. 17, pt. 2, 683, 685.

85. Ibid., vol. 16, pt. 2, 799–800, 811, 996.

86. Ibid., 782–83.

87. Catton, *Terrible Swift Sword,* 390–91.

88. O.R., vol. 17, pt. 2, 697.

89. Ibid., vol. 16, pt. 2, 782.

90. Ibid., vol. 17, pt. 2, 690, 694.

91. Ibid., vol. 16, pt. 2, 782.

92. Ibid., 799–800.

93. Ibid., 815.

94. Ibid., 799–800.

95. Ibid., 811.

96. Foote, *The Civil War,* 1:650–51.

97. Irving A. Buck, *Cleburne and His Command* (Jackson, Tenn.: McCowat-Mercer, 1959), 72–77.

98. Thomas Robson Hay, "Pat Cleburne, Stonewall Jackson of the West," in Buck, *Cleburne and His Command,* 20; Howell Purdue and Elizabeth Purdue, *Pat Cleburne, Confederate General* (Tuscaloosa, Ala.: Portals Press, 1973), 22.

99. Purdue and Purdue, *Pat Cleburne,* 20, 31–32.

100. Hay, "Pat Cleburne," 20–21.

101. Buck, *Cleburne and His Command,* 87.

102. Ibid., 104–5.

103. Ibid., 78, 80; Purdue and Purdue, *Pat Cleburne,* 113.

104. Buck, *Cleburne and His Command,* 80.

105. Foote, *The Civil War,* 1:753; Buck, *Cleburne and His Command,* 104–8.

106. O.R., vol. 16, pt. 2, 815.

107. Stanley Horn, *The Army of Tennessee* (Indianapolis: Bobbs-Merrill, 1941), 168.

108. O.R., vol. 16, pt. 2, 837.

109. Connelly, *Army of the Heartland,* 233; McWhiney, *Braxton Bragg and Confederate Defeat,* 286–92.

110. Herman Hattaway and Archer Jones, *How the North Won: A Military History of the Civil War* (Urbana: University of Illinois Press, 1983), 252–54.

111. Davis to Bragg, September 4, 1862, Buell Papers, Woodson Research Center, Rice University.

112. O.R., vol. 16, pt. 2, 847, 852–54, 859–61, 865, 873.

113. Ibid., 859.

114. Ibid., 866.

115. Ibid., 775–78.

116. Catton, *Terrible Swift Sword,* 390; Donaldson, "'Into Africa,'" 458.

117. O.R., vol. 16, pt. 2, 845–46.

118. Donaldson, "'Into Africa,'" 459.

119. O.R., vol. 16, pt. 2, 876.

120. Richard Hawes to Davis, September 2, 1862, Margaret I. King Library, University of Kentucky, photocopy, JDA.

121. Castel, *General Sterling Price and the Civil War in the West,* 3–15; Robert E. Shalhope, *Sterling Price: Portrait of a Southerner* (Columbia: University of Missouri Press, 1971), 4–75.

122. Castel, *General Sterling Price and the Civil War in the West,* 90–91; Shalhope, *Sterling Price,* 213.

123. Castel, *General Sterling Price and the Civil War in the West,* 90–91; Shalhope, *Sterling Price,* 213. In fact, Magruder had no sooner set out for the trans-Mississippi than he was recalled and replaced by Theophilus Holmes, as discussed above. This was seen by Price and his supporters as a further indication of Davis's hostility to them.

124. O.R., vol. 17, pt. 2, 663–66.

125. Van Dorn to Davis, August 11, 1862, The Samuel Richey Collection of the Southern Confederacy, Miami University Libraries, photocopy, JDA; O.R., vol. 17, pt. 2, 663–64, 675; 15:797; 53:823.

126. O.R., vol. 17, pt. 2, 662, 667, 675–77, 682, 685, 697; vol. 16, pt. 2, 782–83.

127. Ibid., 53:823; vol. 17, pt. 2, 691–92, 897; 15:804.

128. Ibid., vol. 17, pt. 2, 665.

129. Ibid., 687, 690, 693.

130. Ibid., 691–92, 696.

131. Castel, *General Sterling Price and the Civil War in the West,* 106.

132. O.R., vol. 17, pt. 2, 690, 693, 695–96, 698.

133. Ibid., 703.

134. Castel, *General Sterling Price and the Civil War in the West,* 101–3. Castell says that "although relations between Price and Van Dorn remained officially harmonious, true respect and trust did not exist."

135. Hattaway and Jones, *How the North Won,* 251–52.

136. Castel, *General Sterling Price and the Civil War in the West,* 101–3.

137. O.R., vol. 17, pt. 2, 707, 709–10.

138. Van Dorn to Davis, September 9, 1862, The Samuel Richey Collection of the Southern Confederacy, Miami University Libraries, photocopy, JDA; O.R., vol. 17, pt. 2, 698, 701, 710.

139. O.R., vol. 17, pt. 2, 703–4.

140. Ibid., 714.

141. Van Dorn to Davis, August 11 and September 9, 1862, The Samuel Richey Collection of the Southern Confederacy, Miami University Libraries, photocopies, JDA; O.R., 53:823; vol. 17, pt. 2, 698, 701.

142. Anonymous to Davis, September 19, 1862, Manuscript Department, Perkins Library, Duke University; J. J. Pettus to Davis, September 28, 1862, Pritchard von David Collection, University of Texas at Austin; J. J. Pettus to Davis, September 29, 1862, Mississippi Department of Archives and History–all photocopies, JDA.

143. O.R., vol. 17, pt. 2, 707.

144. Ibid., 698–99.

145. Ibid., 700.

146. Ibid., 715.

147. Hartje, *Van Dorn,* 215–19.

148. Ibid., 234–35.

149. O.R., vol. 17, pt. 1, 376–82; William S. Rosecrans, "The Battle of Corinth," *Battles and Leaders of the Civil War,* ed. Robert Underwood Johnson and Clarence Clough Buell, 4 vols. (New York: Yoselof, 1956), 2:737–57.

150. O.R., vol. 16, pt. 2, 896–97.

151. Ibid.

152. Connelly (*Army of the Heartland,* 247) states, "The plan was bold and smacked of Lee and Jackson at Second Manassas. But it was unrealistic." If so, this was because of the marked difference between Leonidas Polk and Stonewall Jackson. McWhiney (*Braxton Bragg and Confederate Defeat,* 303–6) believes the plan would have been eminently successful had Polk followed orders.

153. O.R., vol. 16, pt. 1, 1099–1100. Polk's biographer, while admitting that "Polk's decision that he had no troops 'available' for such a move might have been an unjustified play on words," nevertheless maintains it was a wise course (Joseph H. Parks, *General Leonidas Polk, C.S.A., The Fighting Bishop* [Baton Rouge: Louisiana State University Press, 1960], 265).

154. McWhiney, *Braxton Bragg and Confederate Defeat,* 303–11.

155. O.R., vol. 16, pt. 2, 904–5, 912.

156. Ibid., pt. 1, 1099.

157. Ibid., vol. 15, pt. 2, 920–21; pt. 1, 1095; McWhiney, *Braxton Bragg and Confederate Defeat,* 307–11.

158. Connelly, *Army of the Heartland,* 253.

159. O.R., vol. 16, pt. 1, 1096.

160. Connelly, *Army of the Heartland,* 256.

161. Parks, *General Leonidas Polk,* 273.

162. O.R., vol. 16, pt. 1, 1087–88.

163. Hattaway and Jones, *How the North Won,* 258–60.

164. Ibid., 259.

165. Parks, *General Leonidas Polk,* 271–72.

166. Hattaway and Jones, *How the North Won,* 260; O.R., vol. 16, pt. 2, 943, 949.

167. O.R., vol. 16, pt. 2, 951–52.

168. Ibid., 959.

169. Kirby Smith to Davis, October 20, 1862, by permission of the Houghton Library (Dearborn Collection), Harvard University, photocopy, JDA.

170. Papers of Confederate Secretary of War, National Archives, microfilm, JDA.

171. Donaldson, "'Into Africa,'" 464.

172. McWhiney, *Braxton Bragg and Confederate Defeat,* 329–33.

CHAPTER 10. UNIFIED COMMAND

1. William Williams, et al. (several citizens of Murfreesboro) to Davis, October 24, 1862, Manuscript Department, Perkins Library, Duke University, photocopy, JDA; John B. Jones, *A Rebel War Clerk's Diary,* ed. Earl Schenck Miers (New York: Sagamore Press, 1958), 110.

2. Thomas Lawrence Connelly and Archer Jones, *The Politics of Command: Factions and Ideas in Confederate Strategy* (Baton Rouge: Louisiana State University Press, 1973), 60.

3. Dunbar Rowland, ed., *Jefferson Davis, Constitutionalist, His Letters, Papers and Speeches,* 10 vols. (Jackson: Mississippi Department of Archives and History, 1923), 5:13.

4. Grady McWhiney, *Braxton Bragg and Confederate Defeat* (New York: Columbia University Press, 1969), 323–24.

5. Kirby Smith to Davis, October 20, 1862, by permission of the Houghton Library, Harvard University, photocopy, JDA.

6. Thomas Lawrence Connelly, *Autumn of Glory: The Army of Tennessee, 1862–1865* (Baton Rouge: Louisiana State University Press, 1971), 20–21.

7. McWhiney, *Braxton Bragg and Confederate Defeat,* 328–29.

8. Nathaniel C. Hughes, *General William L. Hardee: Old Reliable* (Baton Rouge: Louisiana State University Press, 1965), 3–44. Hughes asserts that Hardee worked closely with Davis in the creation of the new tactics manual. However, James Alan Treadwell ("Jefferson Davis as Secretary of War: A Reappraisal" [Master's thesis, Rice University, 1985], 69–71) demonstrates that Davis had only minimal involvement with the project and may not even have known of it until after its completion.

9. William C. Davis, *Deep Waters of the Proud* (Garden City, N.Y.: Doubleday, 1982), 118.

10. Hughes, *General William J. Hardee,* 43–85.

11. Ibid., 118.

12. O.R., vol. 17, pt. 2, 627–28, 667–68.

13. Connelly, *Autumn of Glory,* 20–21, 90.

14. Davis to Bragg, October 17, 1862, L. S. Ruder Collection, Beauvoir Jefferson Davis Shrine, photocopy, JDA.

15. O.R., vol. 16, pt. 2, 970.

16. Ibid., vol. 52, pt. 2, 382.

17. Ibid., vol. 16, pt. 2, 976.

18. Ibid., 976–78.

19. McWhiney, *Braxton Bragg and Confederate Defeat,* 326.

20. Davis to Kirby Smith, October 29, 1862, Edmund Kirby Smith Papers, Southern Historical Collection, Library of the University of North Carolina at Chapel Hill, photocopy, JDA.

21. O.R., 13:906–7; Jones, *a Rebel War Clerk's Diary,* 111; Rowland, *Jefferson Davis, Constitutionalist,* 5:356–57.

22. Davis to Kirby Smith, October 29, 1862, Edmund Kirby Smith Papers, Southern Historical Collection, Library of the University of North Carolina at Chapel Hill, photocopy, JDA.

23. Ibid.

24. Kirby Smith to Davis, November 1, 1862, Davis Papers, War Department Collection of Confederate Records, National Archives, photocopy, JDA.

25. Joseph H. Parks, *General Edmund Kirby Smith, C.S.A.* (Baton Rouge: Louisiana State University Press, 1954), 248.

26. McWhiney, *Braxton Bragg and Confederate Defeat,* 326–28.

27. Parks, *General Edmund Kirby Smith,* 245.

28. O.R., vol. 20, pt. 2, 386–88.

29. McWhiney, *Braxton Bragg and Confederate Defeat,* 328.

30. Ibid.

31. O.R., vol. 52, pt. 2, 369; vol. 16, pt. 2, 858, 888, 997; Jones, *A Rebel War Clerk's Diary,* 103–4.

32. O.R., vol. 16, pt. 2, 1000.

33. Ibid, 945, 1002.

34. Ibid., vol. 20, pt. 2, 386–87, 492–93.

35. Ibid., 385.

36. Ibid., 384–85.

37. Ibid., 421–23; vol. 17, pt. 1, 591–92.

38. Ibid., vol. 20, pt. 2, 403.

39. J. J. Pettus to Davis, September 28, 1862, Pritchard von David Collection, University of Texas at Austin; J. J. Pettus to Davis, September 29, 1862, Mississippi Department of Archives and History, photocopies, JDA.

40. Davis to Pettus, September 30, 1862, Mississippi Department of Archives and History, photocopy, JDA; O.R., vol. 17, pt. 2, 716–18.

41. John C. Pemberton, *Pemberton: Defender of Vicksburg* (Chapel Hill: University of North Carolina Press, 1942), 7–12.

42. McWhiney, *Braxton Bragg and Confederate Defeat,* 12, 23.

43. Ellsworth Eliot, Jr., *West Point in the Confederacy* (New York: G. A. Baker, 1941), xx–xxiii.

44. Pemberton, *Pemberton,* 7–32; Eliot, *West Point in the Confederacy,* 116.

45. Richard Taylor, *Destruction and Reconstruction,* ed. Charles P. Roland (Waltham, Mass.: Blaisdell, 1968; originally published 1879), 111–12.

46. Pemberton, *Pemberton,* 7–32.

47. O.R., 53:246–47; Herman Hattaway and Archer Jones, *How the North Won: A Military History of the Civil War* (Urbana: University of Illinois Press, 1983), 212.

48. Rowland, *Jefferson Davis, Constitutionalist,* 5:311, 319.

49. Pemberton, *Pemberton,* 34.

50. O.R., vol. 17, pt. 2, 718.

51. E. Barksdale to Davis, November 11, 1862, Hargrett Rare Book and Manuscript Library, University of Georgia Libraries, photocopy, JDA.

52. Pemberton, *Pemberton,* 43–48; Joseph Davis to Jefferson Davis, October 29 and November 11, 1862, Jefferson Davis Papers, Thomas Library, Transylvania University, photocopy, JDA.

53. O.R., vol. 17, pt. 2, 724.

54. Ibid., 726–27.

55. Ibid., 724, 726–28; Robert G. Hartje, *Van Dorn: The Life and Times of a Confederate General* (Nashville, Tenn.: Vanderbilt University Press, 1967), 243.

56. Joseph Davis to Jefferson Davis, October 7, 1862, Jefferson Davis Papers, Thomas Library, Transylvania University, photocopy, JDA; Jefferson Davis, *The Rise and Fall of the Confederate Government*, 2 vols. (New York: D. Appleton, 1881), 2:388, 389; Hartje, *Van Dorn*, 241.

57. Hudson Strode, *Jefferson Davis, Confederate President* (New York: Harcourt Brace, 1959), 317.

58. Taylor, *Destruction and Reconstruction*, 112.

59. O.R., vol. 17, pt. 2, 752–53, 716–18.

60. Gilbert E. Govan and James W. Livingood, *A Different Valor: The Story of General Joseph E. Johnston, C.S.A.* (Indianapolis: Bobbs-Merrill, 1956), 12–22; Cass Canfield, *The Iron Will of Jefferson Davis* (New York: Harcourt Brace Jovanovich, 1978), 9; Burton J. Hendrick, *Statesmen of the Lost Cause: Jefferson Davis and His Cabinet* (Boston: Little, Brown and Company, 1939), 19. Shelby Foote (*The Civil War*, 3 vols. [New York: Random House, 1958], 1:125) identifies the girl as Benny Haven's daughter. The story apparently originated in a letter from James Augustus Bethune to W. L. Fleming, June 12, 1908. Hudson Strode (*Jefferson Davis, American Patriot, 1808–1861* [New York: Harcourt Brace, 1964], 38) and Irving Werstein (*Abraham Lincoln versus Jefferson Davis* [New York: Thomas Y. Crowell, 1959], 179–80) point out the story's lack of factual basis.

61. Govan and Livingood, *A Different Valor*, 12–22.

62. Lynda Lasswell Crist and Mary Seaton Dix, eds., *The Papers of Jefferson Davis* (Baton Rouge: Louisiana State University Press, 1985), 5:440.

63. Connelly and Jones, *The Politics of Command*, 56–57.

64. Govan and Livingood, *A Different Valor*, 21–28.

65. Bruce Catton, *The Coming Fury* (Garden City, N.Y.: Doubleday, 1961), 432.

66. Govan and Livingood, *A Different Valor*, 28.

67. Hattaway and Jones, *How the North Won*, 30–31; Clement Eaton, *A History of the Southern Confederacy* (New York: Macmillan, 1954), 112.

68. Govan and Livingood, *A Different Valor*, 30–31.

69. Clement Eaton, *Jefferson Davis* (New York: Free Press, 1977), 157.

70. Taylor, *Destruction and Reconstruction*, 19–20. Richard M. McMurry contends that "Davis's ranking of the generals was inconsistent and unfair." He asserts that Cooper was given the highest rank because he held a staff rank of brigadier general. "'The *Enemy* at Richmond': Joseph E. Johnston and the Confederate Government," *Civil War History* 27 (March 1981):6.

71. O.R., vol. 52, pt. 2, 605–8.

72. Ibid., 511.

73. Jones, *A Rebel War Clerk's Diary*, 27.

74. Richard D. Goff, *Confederate Supply* (Durham, N.C.: Duke University Press, 1969), 55–56.

75. Jefferson Davis, *The Rise and Fall of the Confederate Government*, 2:101–2.

76. Ibid., 88.

77. Hamilton J. Eckenrode, *Jefferson Davis: President of the South* (New York: Macmillan, 1930), 177–78.

78. Strode, *Jefferson Davis, Confederate President*, 337.

79. Jefferson Davis to Varina Davis, June 23, 1862, Confederate Museum, photocopy, JDA.

80. O.R., vol. 17, pt. 2, 727; Govan and Livingood, *A Different Valor,* 162.

81. Joseph E. Johnston, *Narrative of Military Operations Directed during the Late War between the States* (New York: Appleton, 1874), 147.

82. Davis to Bragg, October 17, 1862, L. S. Ruder Collection, Beauvoir Jefferson Davis Shrine, photocopy, JDA; O.R., vol. 16, pt. 2, 970.

83. Rowland, *Jefferson Davis, Constitutionalist,* 5:356–57.

84. O.R., 13:889–900.

85. Rembert W. Patrick, *Jefferson Davis and His Cabinet* (Baton Rouge: Louisiana State University Press, 1944), 127–29.

86. Rowland, *Jefferson Davis, Constitutionalist,* 5:374, 371–72.

87. O.R., 13:906–7.

88. Ibid., 914–15. Strode (*Jefferson Davis, Confederate President,* 332) says Davis intended Holmes's troops to cross the river, not, as Randolph ordered, Holmes himself.

89. Rowland, *Jefferson Davis, Constitutionalist,* 5:371.

90. Randolph to Davis, November 15, 1862, Randolph Family Papers, Edgehill Randolph Collection, University of Virginia, photocopy, JDA; Rowland, *Jefferson Davis, Constitutionalist,* 5:374.

91. Patrick, *Jefferson Davis and His Cabinet,* 132.

92. O.R., vol. 17, pt. 2, 757–58.

93. Ibid., 758. Connelly (*Autumn of Glory,* 36–37, 93–98) argues that Johnston's command was unworkable for just this reason – the difficulty of shifting troops between Bragg and Pemberton. He goes on to state: "There seemed good cause for Johnston's belief that the government deliberately gave him a nominal command with little power, but with heavy responsibilities." On the other hand, James McPherson (*Battle Cry of Freedom: The Civil War Era* [New York: Oxford University Press, 1988], 576) maintains that while the desire to silence critics by putting Johnston in some important position may have been part of Davis's motivation, the president really did want Johnston to exercise genuine authority in coordinating the western armies. The position was not nominal.

94. O.R., vol. 20, pt. 2, 439.

95. Foote, *The Civil War,* 2:63; Catton, *This Hallowed Ground* (New York: Doubleday, 1956), 246; Catton, *Never Call Retreat* (New York: Doubleday, 1965), 28; Timothy H. Donovan, Jr., Roy K. Flint, Arthur V. Grant, Jr., and Gerald P. Stodler, *The American Civil War,* West Point Military History Series (Wayne, N.J.: Avery Publishing Group, 1987), 72; McPherson, *Battle Cry of Freedom,* 579. Rowena Reed (*Combined Operations in the Civil War* [Annapolis, Md.: Naval Institute Press, 1978], 234, 237–39) argues that the purpose of Sherman's move was merely to open an alternate line of supply for Grant by moving up the Yazoo. "No direct assault on Vicksburg or its water defenses was intended or prepared for" (234). According to Reed, Sherman's assault took place only because the expedition could not move up the Yazoo unless the mines and obstructions in it were cleared, and this could not be done unless the Confederate batteries commanding it could be silenced. Since the gunboats could not do this, it remained for the infantry to take the batteries by assault.

96. O.R., vol. 17, pt. 2, 772.

97. Ibid., 777.

98. Ibid., 780–81.

99. Ibid., vol. 20, pt. 2, 441, 447.

100. Ibid., vol. 17, pt. 2, 783–84; Rowland, *Jefferson Davis, Constitutionalist,* 5:384.

101. O.R., vol. 17, pt. 2, 786.

102. Ibid., 793.

103. Rowland, *Jefferson Davis, Constitutionalist,* 5:384.

104. Ibid., 294–95; Johnston, *Narrative of Military Operations*, 151; Connelly, *Autumn of Glory*, 40; Foote, *The Civil War*, 2:4–7; Dodd, *Jefferson Davis*, 294; Donovan et al., *The American Civil War*, 576–77.

105. Joseph H. Parks, *General Leonidas Polk, C.S.A, The Fighting Bishop* (Baton Rouge: Louisiana State University Press, 1960), 282.

106. Foote, *The Civil War*, 2:8.

107. Connelly, *Autumn of Glory*, 42.

108. O.R., vol. 17, pt. 2, 781; vol. 20, pt. 2, 492–93.

109. Foote, *The Civil War*, 2:9.

110. O.R., vol. 20, pt. 2, 492–93.

111. Johnston, *Narrative of Military Operations*, 151–52; O.R., vol. 20, pt. 2, 449–50.

112. O.R., vol. 17, pt. 2, 800.

113. Ibid., 21:1062; vol. 17, pt. 2, 800; Johnston, *Narrative of Military Operations*, 152.

114. O.R., vol. 17, pt. 2, 800–801.

115. Rowland, *Jefferson Davis, Constitutionalist*, 5:387–88.

116. Holmes to Davis, December 29, 1862, Perkins Library, Duke University, photocopy, JDA.

117. Johnston, *Narrative of Military Operations*, 153.

118. Catton, *Never Call Retreat*, 32–33.

119. Hartje, *Van Dorn*, 269.

120. O.R., vol. 17, pt. 1, 503; pt. 2, 811–12.

121. Ibid., pt. 1, 625; Herman Hattaway, *General Stephen D. Lee* (Jackson: University Press of Mississippi, 1976), 68.

CHAPTER 11. WINTER OF DISCONTENT

1. James A. Ramage, *Rebel Raider: The Life of General John Hunt Morgan* (Lexington: University Press of Kentucky, 1986), 57–58, 134.

2. The story is oft repeated (by, for example, Shelby Foote, *The Civil War*, 3 vols. [New York: Random House, 1958], 2:83–84; Bruce Catton, *Never Call Retreat* [New York: Doubleday, 1965], 2–3; James Lee McDonough, *Stones River—Bloody Winter in Tennessee* [Knoxville: University of Tennessee Press, 1980], 46) but not by Morgan's most recent biographer, Ramage.

3. Joseph H. Parks, *General Leonidas Polk, C.S.A., The Fighting Bishop* (Baton Rouge: Louisiana State University Press, 1960), 282; William C. Davis, *Breckinridge: Statesman, Soldier, Symbol* (Baton Rouge: Louisiana State University Press, 1974), 331.

4. Ramage, *Rebel Raider*, 134–35.

5. O.R., vol. 20, pt. 2, 479.

6. Stanley Horn, *The Army of Tennessee* (Indianapolis: Bobbs-Merrill, 1941), 196; Catton, *Never Call Retreat*, 35; Foote, *The Civil War*, 2:81.

7. O.R., vol. 20, pt. 1, 663.

8. Ibid., 661, 663–67; pt. 2, 463, 468; vol. 52, pt. 2, 401.

9. Some scholars criticize Bragg's choice of position at Murfreesboro. McDonough, *Stones River*, 73–75; Thomas Lawrence Connelly, *Autumn of Glory: The Army of Tennessee, 1862–1865* (Baton Rouge: Louisiana State University Press, 1971), 47.

10. Foote, *The Civil War*, 2:83.

11. Horn, *The Army of Tennessee*, 200.

12. McDonough, *Stones River*, 97–100.

13. O.R., vol. 20, pt. 1, 663–72, 771–79.

14. Catton, *Never Call Retreat*, 39.

15. O.R., vol. 20, pt. 1, 663–72.

16. Foote, *The Civil War,* 2:87; Christopher Losson, "Major General Benjamin Franklin Cheatham and the Battle of Stone's River," *Tennessee Historical Quarterly* (Fall 1982):280; Irving A. Buck, *Cleburne and His Command* (Jackson, Tenn.: McCowat-Mercer, 1958), 119–20.

17. McDonough, *Stones River,* 104.

18. Timothy D. Johnson, "Benjamin Franklin Cheatham: The Early Years," *Tennessee Historical Quarterly* (Fall 1983):266–75.

19. Johnson, "Benjamin Franklin Cheatham," 275–78.

20. Losson, "Major General Benjamin Franklin Cheatham," 279; Johnson, "Benjamin Franklin Cheatham," 278–80.

21. Losson, "Major General Benjamin Franklin Cheatham," 286; McDonough, *Stones River,* 227; Herman Hattaway and Archer Jones, *How the North Won: A Military History of the Civil War* (Urbana: University of Illinois Press, 1983), 320–21; Connelly, *Autumn of Glory,* 84–85.

22. O.R., vol. 20, pt. 1, 663–72.

23. Losson, "Major General Benjamin Franklin Cheatham," 281–82; Connelly, *Autumn of Glory,* 55.

24. McDonough, *Stones River,* 97–100.

25. Ibid., 106; Losson, "Major General Benjamin Franklin Cheatham," 282–83; Foote, *The Civil War,* 2:88.

26. Losson, "Major General Benjamin Franklin Cheatham," 286; Connelly, *Autumn of Glory,* 84–85.

27. Losson, "Major General Benjamin Franklin Cheatham," 282–83.

28. Catton, *Never Call Retreat,* 34–45. Connelly (*Autumn of Glory,* 56–60) argues that Bragg would not have won the battle even with Stevenson's division present. Connelly presumes essentially that Bragg could have won the battle with the troops he had but did not; therefore, he would not have done so even with 33 percent more infantry. McDonough (*Stones River,* 146, 220) tends to take a similar view, although with some reservations.

29. O.R., vol. 20, pt. 1, 663–72.

30. Ibid., 789; Connelly, *Autumn of Glory,* 53. Connelly, who is extremely critical of Bragg throughout, argues that Bragg should have sent this order earlier.

31. Bragg to Davis, December 1, 1863, William P. Palmer Collection of Braxton Bragg Papers, photocopy, JDA; William C. Davis, *Stand in the Day of Battle* (Garden City, N.Y.: Doubleday, 1983), 9–11; Davis, *Breckinridge,* 356.

32. O.R., vol. 20, pt. 1, 789–90; Foote, *The Civil War,* 2:93; Davis, *Breckinridge,* 336–48; McDonough, *Stones River,* 36; Connelly, *Autumn of Glory,* 53.

33. O.R., vol. 20, pt. 1, 663–72; McDonough, *Stones River,* 148.

34. Grady McWhiney, *Braxton Bragg and Confederate Defeat* (New York: Columbia University Press, 1969), 347–64; Foote, *The Civil War,* 2:93; McDonough, *Stones River,* 149; Connelly, *Autumn of Glory,* 60.

35. Catton, *Never Call Retreat,* 41.

36. Foote, *The Civil War,* 2:94–95.

37. McDonough, *Stones River,* 161–62; Horn, *The Army of Tennessee,* 206; Foote, *The Civil War,* 2:94–95.

38. O.R., vol. 20, pt. 1, 662; vol. 52, pt. 2, 402.

39. Foote, *The Civil War,* 2:97.

40. McDonough, *Stones River,* 179–97.

41. Connelly, *Autumn of Glory,* 64–65; Davis, *Breckinridge,* 341–43, and *Stand in the Day of Battle,* 12.

42. Davis, *Stand in the Day of Battle*, 13.

43. O.R., vol. 20, pt. 1, 663–72; McDonough, *Stones River*, 193; Connelly, *Autumn of Glory*, 64–65; Davis, *Breckinridge*, 343–46.

44. Horn, *The Army of Tennessee*, 208.

45. O.R., vol. 20, pt. 1, 700.

46. Ibid., 662.

47. Ibid., pt. 2, 492.

48. Ibid., 484.

49. Ibid., pt. 1, 699; Connelly, *Autumn of Glory*, 74; Davis, *Breckinridge*, 350.

50. McWhiney, *Braxton Bragg and Confederate Defeat*, 376.

51. O.R., vol. 20, pt. 1, 699.

52. Bragg had originally considered sending a circular which asked the opinion of his generals as to whether he had lost the confidence of the army and should resign, but his staff talked him into sending one that inquired only whether the generals had counseled retreat. Connelly, *Autumn of Glory*, 74–75.

53. McWhiney, *Braxton Bragg and Confederate Defeat*, 376–78.

54. O.R., vol. 20, pt. 1, 682–84.

55. Ibid., 701, 698–99.

56. Ibid., 702.

57. Ibid., 698–99.

58. Dunbar Rowland, ed., *Jefferson Davis, Constitutionalist, His Letters, Papers and Speeches*, 10 vols. (Jackson: Mississippi Department of Archives and History, 1923), 5:418.

59. Ibid., 420.

60. Ibid., 420–21.

61. Johnston to Davis, February 3, 1863, Joseph E. Johnston Papers, E. G. Swem Library, College of William and Mary, photocopy, JDA.

62. McWhiney, *Braxton Bragg and Confederate Defeat*, 375; Davis, *Breckinridge*, 331–33.

63. Johnston to Davis, February 3 and 12, 1863, Joseph E. Johnston Papers, E. G. Swem Library, College of William and Mary, photocopy, JDA.

64. Johnston to Davis, January 10, 1863, Joseph E. Johnston Papers, E. G. Swem Library, College of William and Mary, photocopy, JDA.

65. O.R., vol. 17, pt. 2, 813, 816–17, 822; vol. 20, pt. 2, 476.

66. Johnston to Davis, January 10, 1863, Joseph E. Johnston Papers, E. G. Swem Library, College of William and Mary, photocopy, JDA.

67. Rowland, *Jefferson Davis, Constitutionalist*, 5:433–35.

68. Johnston to Davis, March 2, 1863, James Schoff Civil War Collection, Clements Library, University of Michigan, photocopy, JDA.

69. O.R., vol. 20, pt. 1, 698–99.

70. Ibid., vol. 23, pt. 2, 674.

71. Ibid., 684–85.

72. Ibid., 698.

73. Ibid., 708.

74. Ibid., 745–46.

75. McDonough, *Stones River*, 220.

76. McWhiney, *Braxton Bragg and Confederate Defeat*, 362.

77. Rowland, *Jefferson Davis, Constitutionalist*, 5:448, 452, 468–69; O.R., vol. 23, pt. 2, 713, 726–27, 741, 745–46.

CHAPTER 12. THE FALL OF VICKSBURG

1. Shelby Foote, *The Civil War,* 3 vols. (New York: Random House, 1958), 2:72.

2. Dunbar Rowland, ed., *Jefferson Davis, Constitutionalist, His Letters, Papers and Speeches,* 10 vols. (Jackson: Mississippi Department of Archives and History, 1923), 5:383–84.

3. Ibid., 464–65.

4. O.R., vol. 17, pt. 1, 625, 669; Pemberton to Davis, January 5, 1863, "Autograph Letters, Manuscripts, and Historical Documents," (catalogue issued by Thomas F. Madigan, Inc., of New York, 1937), 59; photocopy, JDA.

5. O.R., vol. 24, pt. 3, 597.

6. Ibid., 599–600.

7. Rowland, *Jefferson Davis, Constitutionalist,* 5:424–27.

8. O.R., vol. 24, pt. 3, 599–600, 603; Foote, *The Civil War,* 2:192–200.

9. Rowland, *Jefferson Davis, Constitutionalist,* 5:427, 433, 444.

10. O.R., vol. 24, pt. 3, 657, 668–69; 15:1009–10; Timothy H. Donovan, Jr., Roy K. Flint, Arthur V. Grant, Jr., and Gerald P. Stodler, *The American Civil War,* West Point Military History Series (Wayne, N.J.: Avery Publishing Group, 1987), 98–99.

11. Earl Schenck Miers, *The Web of Victory: Grant at Vicksburg* (New York: Alfred A. Knopf, 1955), 115–24; Samuel Carter III, *The Final Fortress: The Campaign for Vicksburg, 1862–1863* (New York: St. Martin's, 1980), 135–49; Foote, *The Civil War,* 2:206–11; Herman Hattaway, *General Stephen D. Lee* (Jackson: University Press of Mississippi, 1976), 80–82.

12. O.R., 15:1009–10; vol. 24, pt. 3, 663, 665–66; Miers, *The Web of Victory,* 110–15; Foote, *The Civil War,* 2:201–3.

13. Rowland, *Jefferson Davis, Constitutionalist,* 5:427, 433, 444; O.R., vol. 24, pt. 3, 631–32, 657, 663, 665–66, 669–70.

14. Rowland, *Jefferson Davis, Constitutionalist,* 5:464–65.

15. O.R., vol. 24, pt. 3, 712, 714, 717, 719, 733.

16. Ibid., 714; vol. 23, pt. 2, 741; Rowland, *Jefferson Davis, Constitutionalist,* 5:469.

17. O.R., vol. 24, pt. 3, 733.

18. Ibid., 738.

19. Ibid.

20. Hattaway, *General Stephen D. Lee,* 83.

21. James McPherson, *Battle Cry of Freedom: The Civil War Era* (New York: Oxford University Press, 1988), 629.

22. Rowena Reed (*Combined Operations in the Civil War* [Annapolis, Md.: Naval Institute Press, 1978], 239–40) argues that Grant's Vicksburg campaign, far from being clever and resourceful, was "the unenviable result of impulsiveness and lack of administrative skill."

23. O.R., vol. 24, pt. 3, 745, 747.

24. Ibid., 751; Foote, *The Civil War,* 2:328–29; McPherson, *Battle Cry of Freedom,* 626; Hattaway, *General Stephen D. Lee,* 83–84.

25. O.R., vol. 24, pt. 3, 751, 753, 766, 767.

26. Ibid., 760.

27. Rowland, *Jefferson Davis, Constitutionalist,* 5:475–76.

28. Ibid.

29. O.R., 15:1045.

30. Joseph H. Parks, *General Edmund Kirby Smith, C.S.A.* (Baton Rouge: Louisiana State University Press, 1954), 255–56.

31. O.R., 15:1047.

32. Donovan et al., *The American Civil War,* 102.

33. O.R., 15:1047; vol. 24, pt. 3, 769.

34. O.R., vol. 24, pt. 3, 769, 773; Robert G. Hartje, *Van Dorn: The Life and Times of a Confederate General* (Nashville, Tenn.: Vanderbilt University Press, 1967), 273; Foote, *The Civil War,* 2:176–77, 345; Donovan et al., *The American Civil War,* 94, 170; Hattaway, *General Stephen D. Lee,* 79.

35. O.R., vol. 24, pt. 3, 782, 786, 789, 791, 798.

36. Ibid., 791.

37. Ibid., 797, 801–2.

38. Ibid., 797, 801; McPherson, *Battle Cry of Freedom,* 628; Foote, *The Civil War,* 2:338.

39. O.R., vol. 24, pt. 3, 797.

40. Ibid.

41. Ibid., 801.

42. Ibid., 797, 801–2.

43. James S. Phelan to Davis, April 25, 1863, and James H. Rives to Davis, March 31, 1863, Papers of the Confederate War Department, National Archives, microfilm, JDA.

44. O.R., vol. 24, pt. 3, 801; Rowland, *Jefferson Davis, Constitutionalist,* 5:479.

45. Pemberton to Davis, April 30, 1863, in G. A. Baker catalogue 34, 1939, New York Public Library, photocopy, JDA.

46. O.R., vol. 24, pt. 3, 807–8.

47. Ibid., 808.

48. Ibid., 807.

49. Ibid., 808, 815.

50. Ibid., 820; 15:1071.

51. Ibid., vol. 24, pt. 3, 807.

52. Ibid., 807, 815, 827.

53. Ibid., 821.

54. Jefferson Davis to Joseph Davis, May 7, 1863, Lise Mitchel Papers, Tulane University, photocopy, JDA; Donovan et al., *The American Civil War,* 108; Foote, *The Civil War,* 2:355; Lawrence Lee Hewitt, *Port Hudson, Confederate Bastion on the Mississippi* (Baton Rouge: Louisiana State University Press, 1987), 124.

55. Hudson Strode, *Jefferson Davis, Confederate President* (New York: Harcourt Brace, 1959), 385–94.

56. Eli Evans, *Judah P. Benjamin: The Jewish Confederate* (New York: Free Press, 1988), 227–29.

57. Hamilton J. Eckenrode, *Jefferson Davis: President of the South* (New York: Macmillan, 1930), 221.

58. Rowland, *Jefferson Davis, Constitutionalist,* 5:482.

59. O.R., 15:1080.

60. Ibid., vol. 24, pt. 3, 846.

61. Ibid., 858.

62. Strode, *Jefferson Davis, Confederate President,* 376.

63. O.R., vol. 24, pt. 1, 215.

64. Ibid.

65. Ibid.

66. Ibid., pt. 3, 870.

67. Ibid., 877.

68. Ibid., pt. 1, 217–18; Donovan et al., *The American Civil War,* 112; Foote, *The Civil War,* 2:361–62.

69. O.R., vol. 24, pt. 3, 877–78.

70. Carter, *The Final Fortress*, 195–96; Miers, *The Web of Victory*, 173; Foote, *The Civil War*, 2:369–70, 424.

71. O.R., vol. 24, pt. 3, 882.

72. Hattaway, *General Stephen D. Lee*, 86–87.

73. Foote, *The Civil War*, 2:374.

74. Donovan et al., *The American Civil War*, 114.

75. Foote, *The Civil War*, 2:374.

76. Hattaway, *General Stephen D. Lee*, 87.

77. Carter, *The Final Fortress*, 198–200; Miers, *The Web of Victory*, 178–95; O.R., vol. 24, pt. 1, 217–18.

78. O.R., vol. 24, pt. 3, 889–90; Donovan et al., *The American Civil War*, 115.

79. Carter, *The Final Fortress*, 204–7; Miers, *The Web of Victory*, 198.

80. O.R., vol. 24, pt. 1, 216, 220–23.

81. Ibid., pt. 3, 888.

82. Ibid., 889–90.

83. Jefferson Davis, *The Rise and Fall of the Confederate Government*, 2 vols. (New York: D. Appleton, 1881), 2:411.

84. Ibid.

85. O.R., vol. 15, pt. 1, 216–17; Rowland, *Jefferson Davis, Constitutionalist*, 5:489–90.

86. Rowland, *Jefferson Davis, Constitutionalist*, 5:489–90, 505.

87. Jefferson Davis, *The Rise and Fall of the Confederate Government*, 2:404–5.

88. Carter, *The Final Fortress*, 239.

89. O.R., vol. 24, pt. 1, 220–23.

90. Ibid., 194, 220–23.

91. Rowland, *Jefferson Davis, Constitutionalist*, 5:499–500; O.R., vol. 24, pt. 1, 194–95, 223–24.

92. Clifford Dowdey and Louis H. Manarin, eds., *The Wartime Papers of R. E. Lee* (New York: Bramhall House, 1961), 482.

93. Foote, *The Civil War*, 2:261.

94. Dowdey and Manarin, *The Wartime Papers of R. E. Lee*, 482.

95. Eckenrode, *Jefferson Davis*, 221.

96. Foote, *The Civil War*, 2:436.

97. Thomas Lawrence Connelly and Archer Jones, *The Politics of Command: Factions and Ideas in Confederate Strategy* (Baton Rouge: Louisiana State University Press, 1973), 132.

98. Eckenrode, *Jefferson Davis*, 221.

99. Strode, *Jefferson Davis, Confederate President*, 399.

100. Ibid., 404.

101. Dowdey and Manarin, *The Wartime Papers of R. E. Lee*, 637.

102. Ibid., 528; Foote, *The Civil War*, 2:249.

103. McPherson, *Battle Cry of Freedom*, 646; Eckenrode, *Jefferson Davis*, 221; William E. Dodd, *Jefferson Davis* (Philadelphia: George W. Jacobs, 1907), 307.

104. Foote, *The Civil War*, 2:430–33; Eckenrode, *Jefferson Davis*, 224–25. Eckenrode's account contains a number of errors.

105. Dowdey and Manarin, *The Wartime Papers of R. E. Lee*, 482.

106. Johnston to Davis, June 3, 1863, Joseph E. Johnston Papers, E. G. Swem Library, College of William and Mary, photocopy, JDA.

107. O.R., vol. 24, pt. 1, 223–24.

108. Carter, *The Final Fortress*, 239.

109. O.R., vol. 24, pt. 3, 953, 963, 967.

110. Ibid., pt. 1, 226; pt. 3, 969.

111. Ibid., vol. 52, pt. 2, 209, 493–94; Pettus to Davis, June 18, 1863, E. G. Swem Library, College of William and Mary, photocopy, JDA.

112. Rowland, *Jefferson Davis, Constitutionalist*, 5:513, 519, 527–28.

113. Parks, *General Edmund Kirby Smith*, 269–72; Foote, *The Civil War*, 2:394, 405–6.

114. Strode, *Jefferson Davis, Confederate President*, 418–19.

115. Davis to Johnston, June 15, 1863, Joseph E. Johnston Papers, E. G. Swem Library, College of William and Mary, photocopy, JDA; O.R., vol. 24, pt. 1, 227–28.

116. O.R., vol. 24, pt. 3, 974.

117. Ibid., 980.

118. Johnston to Pemberton, May 29, 1863, Joseph E. Johnston Papers, E. G. Swem Library, College of William and Mary, photocopy, JDA; O.R., vol. 24, pt. 3, 963, 966.

119. O.R., vol. 24, pt. 3, 987.

120. Ibid., pt. 1, 199.

121. Ibid., 201; vol. 52, pt. 2, 507.

122. Ibid., vol. 24, pt. 1, 208.

123. Rowland, *Jefferson Davis, Constitutionalist*, 5:578–80.

124. Strode, *Jefferson Davis, Confederate President*, 443–45.

125. Rowland, *Jefferson Davis, Constitutionalist*, 5:540.

126. O.R., vol. 24, pt. 1, 208.

127. Rowland, *Jefferson Davis, Constitutionalist*, 5:573–74.

128. O.R., vol. 24, pt. 1, 226.

129. Ibid., 209.

130. Ibid., 196, 198.

131. Rowland, *Jefferson Davis, Constitutionalist*, 5:556–63.

132. Ibid., 520.

133. Ibid., 522.

134. O.R., vol. 24, pt. 1, 196–97.

135. John B. Jones, *A Rebel War Clerk's Diary*, ed. Earl Schenck Miers (New York: Sagamore Press, 1958), 230.

136. Rowland, *Jefferson Davis, Constitutionalist*, 5:534–35.

137. O.R., vol. 24, pt. 1, 198.

138. Rowland, *Jefferson Davis, Constitutionalist*, 5:540.

139. Jones, *A Rebel War Clerk's Diary*, 237.

140. Ibid., 238.

141. O.R., vol. 24, pt. 1, 202–7.

142. Ibid., 209–13.

143. Davis to Johnston, September 7, 1863, Henry E. Huntington Library and Art Gallery, San Marino, California, JO 86, photocopy, JDA.

144. Rowland, *Jefferson Davis, Constitutionalist*, 5:464–65; O.R., vol. 52, pt. 2, 468–69.

145. Rowland, *Jefferson Davis, Constitutionalist*, 5:556–63.

146. Jones, *A Rebel War Clerk's Diary*, 248–49.

147. Richard Taylor, *Destruction and Reconstruction*, ed. Charles P. Roland (Waltham, Mass.: Blaisdell, 1968; originally published 1879), 112.

148. Herman Hattaway and Archer Jones, *How the North Won: A Military History of the Civil War* (Urbana: University of Illinois Press, 1983), 375.

149. Rowland, *Jefferson Davis, Constitutionalist*, 5:542; Jefferson Davis, *Rise and Fall of the Confederate Government*, 2:404–11.

150. Rowland, *Jefferson Davis, Constitutionalist*, 5:464–65.

151. Ibid., 582–83; Strode, *Jefferson Davis, Confederate President*, 462–63.

152. O.R., vol. 24, pt. 3, 1070; Johnston to Davis, August 13, 1863, Joseph E.

Johnston Papers, E. G. Swem Library, College of William and Mary, photocopy, JDA.

153. Rowland, *Jefferson Davis, Constitutionalist*, 6:1; Johnston to Davis, September 8, 1863, Joseph E. Johnston Papers, E. G. Swem Library, College of William and Mary, photocopy, JDA.

154. O.R., vol. 30, pt. 4, 490–91.

155. Richard McMurry ("'The *Enemy* at Richmond': Joseph E. Johnston and the Confederate Government," *Civil War History* 27 [March 1981]: 31) attributes the entire Davis-Johnston controversy to the pride of both men. "The two men suffered from a *hubris* that made it impossible for them to communicate or for either to overlook what he considered to be an insult from the other. Neither could admit error or ask forgiveness." This is undoubtedly very close to the truth but may do some injustice to Davis by overlooking the several occasions on which he swallowed his pride in order to appoint Johnston to some important command. Certainly Davis was a proud man, but just as certainly he never equaled the self-serving pride of Joseph E. Johnston. Besides, there was a basic difference between the two men in the extent of the risks they were willing to take for the cause of the Confederacy.

156. McMurry ("'The *Enemy* at Richmond,'" 10–11) points out that "Davis has often been accused of meddling too much in military affairs. In many ways the reverse criticism is more appropriate." Davis failed to enforce cooperation among his generals, and his failure to order troops from the trans-Mississippi to aid Pemberton is one example.

157. Foote, *The Civil War*, 2:346.

158. McPherson, *Battle Cry of Freedom*, 637–38; William C. Davis, *Stand in the Day of Battle* (Garden City, N.Y.: Doubleday, 1983), 195; Hewitt, *Port Hudson*, xi, 4; Eckenrode, *Jefferson Davis*, 234. Thomas Lawrence Connelly ("Vicksburg: Strategic Point or Propaganda Device?" *Military Affairs* 34 [April 1970]:49–53) argues that the fall of Vicksburg was less important in real material terms than has been often represented but that its main significance was its propaganda value. He states that even before the fall of Vicksburg little actually crossed the river, and moreover, the South had poor means of transporting further what did cross. He also states that Confederate strategy did not take advantage of the ability to shift troops across the Mississippi before Vicksburg fell, and even after it fell the river was not completely sealed. Although these points deserve consideration and undoubtedly it would be possible to overestimate the material importance of Vicksburg, neither should it be underrated. Some things did get across the river before Vicksburg fell, and if the South's transportation system was less than ideal, things did move from one part of the Confederacy to another. The Confederacy did not shift troops across the river as much as it should have before Vicksburg fell, but it did shift Hardee's force from Arkansas to Kentucky in 1861 and Van Dorn's army from Arkansas to Mississippi the following year. After Vicksburg fell, scattered individuals and even occasional small shipments might make it across the river, but no organized military force could cross. This was amply demonstrated when Kirby Smith looked into the possibility of crossing during 1864. So effectively was the river sealed at that time by Union gunboats that Gen. John A. Wharton, commanding Smith's cavalry, was prompted to remark that "a bird, if dressed in Confederate gray, would find it difficult to fly across the river" (quoted in Parks, *General Edmund Kirby Smith*, 427). Connelly is correct, however, in pointing out the tremendous significance of Vicksburg to morale in both North and South.

CHAPTER 13. THE LOSS OF TENNESSEE

1. O.R., vol. 16, pt. 1, 1097–98.
2. Ibid., 1101, 1105–7.
3. Ibid., 1105–7.
4. Ibid., 1097–98.
5. Ibid., 1101–3.
6. Ibid., 1104–7.
7. Ibid., 1104.
8. Nathaniel C. Hughes, *General William J. Hardee: Old Reliable* (Baton Rouge: Louisiana State University Press, 1965), 151; Joseph H. Parks, *General Leonidas Polk, C.S.A., The Fighting Bishop* (Baton Rouge: Louisiana State University Press, 1960), 303–4.
9. Shelby Foote, *The Civil War,* 3 vols. (New York: Random House, 1958), 2:175.
10. Ibid., 670.
11. O.R., vol. 23, pt. 2, 757–61.
12. Ibid., pt. 1, 585; pt. 2, 848.
13. Ibid., pt. 1, 403.
14. Thomas Lawrence Connelly, *Autumn of Glory: The Army of Tennessee, 1862–1865* (Baton Rouge: Louisiana State University Press, 1971), 112–28.
15. Robert Selph Henry, *"First with the Most" Forrest* (Indianapolis: Bobbs-Merrill, 1944), 142–44.
16. Robert G. Hartje, *Van Dorn: The Life and Times of a Confederate General* (Nashville, Tenn.: Vanderbilt University Press, 1967), 308–17.
17. Henry, *"First with the Most,"* 160–64.
18. James A. Ramage, *Rebel Raider: The Life of General John Hunt Morgan* (Lexington: University Press of Kentucky, 1986), 146–67.
19. Connelly, *Autumn of Glory,* 26–28, 123–29.
20. O.R., vol. 23, pt. 1, 583–84; pt. 2, 891–92; Timothy H. Donovan, Jr., Roy K. Flint, Arthur V. Grant, Jr., and Gerald P. Stodler, *The American Civil War,* West Point Military History Series (Wayne, N.J.: Avery Publishing Group, 1987), 171–73; Foote, *The Civil War,* 2:669.
21. O.R., vol. 23, pt. 1, 403.
22. Ibid., 585–86.
23. Ibid., pt. 2, 937–38, 941, 948.
24. Parks, *General Leonidas Polk,* 315.
25. Ibid., 321.
26. Herman Hattaway and Archer Jones, *How the North Won: A Military History of the Civil War* (Urbana: University of Illinois Press, 1983), 442.
27. O.R., vol. 23, pt. 2, 920, 932–33.
28. Ibid., vol. 24, pt. 1, 235.
29. Ibid., vol. 23, pt. 2, 954.
30. Ibid., 948.
31. Ibid.
32. Ibid., 950.
33. John B. Jones, *A Rebel War Clerk's Diary,* ed. Earl Schenck Miers (New York: Sagamore Press, 1958), 252; Stanley Horn, *The Army of Tennessee* (Indianapolis: Bobbs-Merrill, 1941), 237.
34. O.R., vol. 23, pt. 2, 952.
35. Jones, *A Rebel War Clerk's Diary,* 260–61.
36. O.R., vol. 23, pt. 2, 953.

37. Ibid., vol. 30, pt. 4, 526.

38. Ibid.; pt. 2, 21.

39. Ibid., pt. 4, 621.

40. Ibid., 531.

41. Ibid., 566.

42. Duncan Rowland, ed., *Jefferson Davis, Constitutionalist, His Letters, Papers and Speeches*, 10 vols. (Jackson: Mississippi Department of Archives and History, 1923), 5:597.

43. Johnston to Davis, August 22, 1863, Joseph E. Johnston Papers, E. G. Swem Library, College of William and Mary, photocopy, JDA; O.R., vol. 30, pt. 4, 540.

44. James Longstreet, *From Manassas to Appomattox* (Bloomington: Indiana University Press, 1960), 434-35.

45. Hattaway and Jones, *How the North Won*, 443.

46. Longstreet, *From Manassas to Appomattox*, 435-36. Some scholars believe that the importance of this move has been greatly exaggerated. They point to the relatively small number of troops (five thousand) that arrived in time to take part in the battle of Chickamauga and assert that the real reason for sending them was not beating Rosecrans and protecting Georgia but rather guarding East Tennessee and thereby the western approach to Virginia. Connelly, *Autumn of Glory*, 152; Thomas Lawrence Connelly and Archer Jones, *The Politics of Command: Factions and Ideas in Confederate Strategy* (Baton Rouge: Louisiana State University Press, 1973), 44-45.

47. Clifford Dowdey and Louis H. Manarin, eds., *The Wartime Papers of R. E. Lee* (New York: Bramhall House, 1961), 596; Rowland, *Jefferson Davis, Constitutionalist*, 5:26.

48. Longstreet, *From Manassas to Appomattox*, 436-37.

49. O.R., vol. 30, pt. 4, 583-84.

50. Ibid., vol. 52, pt. 2, 521.

51. Ibid., vol. 30, pt. 2, 21-22.

52. Ibid., 22.

53. Ibid., 26-37.

54. Bruce Catton, *Never Call Retreat* (New York: Doubleday, 1965), 232.

55. Ibid.

56. Douglas Southall Freeman, *Lee's Lieutenants: A Study in Command* (New York: Charles Scribner's Sons, 1942), 1:19-22; Ellsworth Eliot, Jr., *West Point in the Confederacy* (New York: G. A. Baker, 1941), xx-xxviii.

57. O.R., vol. 23, pt. 2, 909; vol. 24, pt. 3, 1028.

58. Ibid., vol. 30, pt. 2, 26-37.

59. Glenn Tucker, *Chickamauga: Bloody Battle in the West* (Indianapolis: Bobbs-Merrill, 1961), 67-68.

60. O.R., vol. 30, pt. 4, 634.

61. Tucker, *Chickamauga*, 67-69.

62. Catton, *Never Call Retreat*, 233.

63. O.R., vol. 30, pt. 4, 636.

64. Ibid., 26-37.

65. Ibid., 49.

66. Horn, *The Army of Tennessee*, 273.

67. Catton, *Never Call Retreat*, 231.

68. Horn, *The Army of Tennessee*, 257-58.

69. Longstreet, *From Manassas to Appomattox*, 399-409.

70. Connelly, *Autumn of Glory*, 211.

71. Longstreet, *From Manassas to Appomattox*, 438.

72. Tucker, *Chickamauga*, 214, 221. Tucker believes, with good reason, that "Bragg . . . erred in giving Polk command of the right wing." He thinks Bragg should

have relegated Polk to the position of second in command of the army or else supervised him more closely.

73. O.R., vol. 30, pt. 2, 26–37.

74. William C. Davis, *Stand in the Day of Battle* (Garden City, N.Y.: Doubleday, 1983), 285.

75. Parks, *General Leonidas Polk,* 336–37; Davis, *Stand in the Day of Battle,* 286.

76. O.R., vol. 30, pt. 2, 64.

77. Ibid., 56.

78. Foote, *The Civil War,* 2:729–30.

79. O.R., vol. 30, pt. 2, 64.

80. Ibid.

81. Catton, *Never Call Retreat,* 237.

82. O.R., vol. 30, pt. 2, 56.

83. Horn, *The Army of Tennessee,* 263–64.

84. Catton, *Never Call Retreat,* 238.

85. O.R., vol. 30, pt. 2, 26–37.

86. Ibid., 53.

87. Horn, *The Army of Tennessee,* 276–77.

88. O.R., vol. 30, pt. 2, 26–37.

89. Catton, *Never Call Retreat,* 244–45.

90. Horn, *The Army of Tennessee,* 259.

91. O.R., vol. 30, pt. 2, 54.

92. Ibid.

93. Ibid., 47.

94. Ibid., 67–68.

95. Longstreet, *From Manassas to Appomattox,* 464.

96. O.R., vol. 30, pt. 2, 67–68.

97. Ibid., pt. 4, 705–6.

98. James Lee McDonough, *Chattanooga—A Death Grip on the Confederacy* (Knoxville: University of Tennessee Press, 1984), 29–30.

99. Connelly, *Autumn of Glory,* 51; Donovan et al., *The American Civil War,* 178.

100. O.R., vol. 30, pt. 2, 69.

101. Polk to Davis, September 27, 1863, by permission of the Houghton Library (Dearborn Collection), Harvard University, photocopy, JDA.

102. O.R., vol. 30, pt. 2, 69.

103. Ibid., 47.

104. Bragg to Davis, May 21, 1863, William P. Palmer Collection of Bragg Papers, The Western Reserve Historical Society, Cleveland, Ohio, photocopy, JDA.

105. O.R., vol. 52, pt. 2, 534.

106. Ibid., vol. 30, pt. 2, 56.

107. Ibid., 55.

108. Ibid., 56–57.

109. Ibid., 68–69.

110. Ibid., 67–68.

111. McDonough, *Chattanooga,* 29.

112. O.R., vol. 30, pt. 2, 65–66.

113. Longstreet, *From Manassas to Appomattox,* 465.

114. Horn, *The Army of Tennessee,* 286.

115. McDonough, *Chattanooga,* 30; Arndt M. Stickles, *Simon Bolivar Buckner: Borderland Knight* (Chapel Hill: University of North Carolina Press, 1940), 234–38; Connelly, *Autumn of Glory,* 239–40.

116. O.R., vol. 30, pt. 2, 55.
117. Ibid.
118. Ibid.
119. Ibid., vol. 52, pt. 2, 533.
120. Ibid., 534.
121. Ibid., 535.
122. Ibid., 535, 538.
123. Ibid., 535, 540; 51:772; Longstreet, *From Manassas to Appomattox*, 465; Jones, *A Rebel War Clerk's Diary*, 289.
124. McDonough, *Chattanooga*, 35.
125. O.R., vol. 30, pt. 2, 54, 56.
126. Ibid., 67–68.
127. McDonough, *Chattanooga*, 35; Rowland, *Jefferson Davis, Constitutionalist*, 5:62–63.
128. Hudson Strode, *Jefferson Davis, Confederate President* (New York: Harcourt Brace, 1959), 479.
129. O.R., vol. 30, pt. 4, 751.
130. Connelly (*Autumn of Glory*, 241) says Davis "evidently believed that Bragg's charges against his generals were more the product of his nervous temper than reality" and that Davis believed he could reconcile the differences between Bragg and his generals.
131. Longstreet, *From Manassas to Appomattox*, 465–66. Accounts favorable to Davis (Strode, *Jefferson Davis, Confederate President*, 480) tend to state that Longstreet volunteered his criticism of Bragg without prompting from Davis. This seems doubtful. The president must at least have raised the issue. Connelly, *Autumn of Glory*, 245.
132. Stickles, *Simon Bolivar Buckner*, 236.
133. O.R., vol. 30, pt. 4, 751.
134. Horn, *The Army of Tennessee*, 288; Jefferson Davis, *The Rise and Fall of the Confederate Government*, 2 vols. (New York: D. Appleton, 1881), 2:433–36.
135. Jefferson Davis to Braxton Bragg, October 29, 1863, The Rosenbach Museum and Library, Philadelphia, AMs 530/7, photocopy, JDA.
136. O.R., vol. 30, pt. 4, 745–46.
137. Ibid., pt. 2, 148.
138. Ibid., vol. 52, pt. 2, 535.
139. Ibid., vol. 30, pt. 2, 148–49.
140. John C. Pemberton, *Pemberton: Defender of Vicksburg* (Chapel Hill: University of North Carolina Press, 1942), 258–59; O.R., vol. 30, pt. 4, 742–43.
141. O.R., vol. 30, pt. 4, 745–46, 761.
142. Ibid., vol. 52, pt. 2, 545, 548.
143. Henry, *"First with the Most,"* 169–72.
144. Foote, *The Civil War*, 2:813.
145. Connelly, *Autumn of Glory*, 240–41; Henry, *"First with the Most,"* 198–200.
146. O.R., vol. 30, pt. 4, 742–43.
147. Ibid., 745–46, 751.
148. Newspaper clipping, October 13, 1863, Leonidas Polk Papers, Southern Historical Collection, Library of the University of North Carolina at Chapel Hill, photocopy, JDA.
149. McDonough, *Chattanooga*, 37.
150. Henry, *"First with the Most,"* 200–201.
151. O.R., vol. 52, pt. 2, 546.
152. Ibid., 548.
153. Stickles, *Simon Bolivar Buckner*, 232, 237–38.

154. Rowland, *Jefferson Davis, Constitutionalist,* 5:64, 68–69.
155. McDonough, *Chattanooga,* 39.
156. O.R., vol. 52, pt. 2, 557.
157. Connelly, *Autumn of Glory,* 250–51.
158. Ibid., 246.
159. T. Harry Williams, *Lincoln and His Generals* (New York: Vintage Books, 1952), 285.
160. Catton, *Never Call Retreat,* 243–44.
161. Tucker, *Chickamauga,* 379.
162. Richard M. McMurry, *John Bell Hood and the War for Southern Independence* (Lexington: University Press of Kentucky, 1982), 76.
163. Guy R. Swanson and Timothy D. Johnson, "Conflict in East Tennessee: Generals Law, Jenkins, and Longstreet," *Civil War History* 31 (June 1985):101–10.
164. McDonough, *Chattanooga,* 85.
165. O.R., vol. 52, pt. 2, 556; Swanson and Johnson, "Conflict in East Tennessee," 105.
166. Swanson and Johnson, "Conflict in East Tennessee," 104–6.
167. Catton, *Never Call Retreat,* 248.
168. Davis to Bragg, October 29, 1863, Philip H. and A. S. W. Rosenbach, The Rosenbach Museum and Library, Philadelphia, photocopy, JDA.
169. O.R., vol. 29, pt. 2, 742; Dowdey and Manarin, *The Wartime Papers of R. E. Lee,* 604–5.
170. O.R., vol. 52, pt. 2, 557.
171. McDonough, *Chattanooga,* 110, 124; Connelly, *Autumn of Glory,* 267.
172. Bruce Catton, *Grant Takes Command* (Boston: Little, Brown, 1968), 63, 70.
173. O.R., vol. 31, pt. 2, 673.
174. Catton, *Grant Takes Command,* 70–71.
175. Irving A. Buck, *Cleburne and His Command* (Jackson, Tenn.: McCowat-Mercer, 1959), 110–18.
176. O.R., vol. 20, pt. 1, 682–84.
177. McDonough, *Chattanooga,* 117–28.
178. Ibid., 129–42.
179. Catton, *Grant Takes Command,* 77–79.
180. Connelly, *Autumn of Glory,* 273.
181. William C. Davis, *Breckinridge: Statesman, Soldier, Symbol* (Baton Rouge: Louisiana State University Press, 1974), 389.
182. Bragg to Davis, November 30 and December 1, 1863, William P. Palmer Collection of Braxton Bragg Papers, Western Reserve Historical Society, Cleveland, Ohio, photocopy, JDA. Breckinridge's biographer William C. Davis (*Breckinridge,* 395–99) argues that Breckinridge was not drunk.
183. McDonough, *Chattanooga,* 227–28.
184. O.R., vol. 24, pt. 2, 664–67.
185. Catton, *Grant Takes Command,* 80–81; O.R., vol. 31, pt. 2, 664–67.
186. McDonough, *Chattanooga,* 186–87.
187. Catton, *Grant Takes Command,* 81–85.
188. O.R., vol. 31, pt. 2, 664–67.
189. McDonough, *Chattanooga,* 194.
190. O.R., vol. 31, pt. 2, 664–67.
191. Horn, *The Army of Tennessee,* 301.
192. Davis, *Breckinridge,* 390. There is some reason to suspect Breckinridge may have been drunk at Missionary Ridge. His fondness for alcohol, especially bourbon, was

well known. His friends had once congratulated him on an election victory by sending him some eighteen gallons of whiskey. During the war his wife kept him supplied by sending him an occasional bottle of his favorite beverage. There may, of course, have been other sources. Breckinridge's whereabouts for the two hours that followed the battle of Missionary Ridge are unknown, and his biographer admits he may have "just wandered." Bragg later recounted that Breckinridge had showed up at army headquarters that night and "soon sank down on the floor, *dead drunk,* and was so in the morning." Bragg ordered the commander of the rear guard "if necessary, to put him in a wagon and haul him off" when the army continued its retreat but under no circumstances to leave the drunken general or permit him to give an order. When the army reached Dalton, Georgia, Bragg relieved Breckinridge of his command. He said Breckinridge "acknowledged the justice of it, but said it was the deepest mortification of his life." William C. Davis argues against the veracity of Bragg's account and asserts that Breckinridge was not drunk. In any case, Breckinridge died in 1875, at the age of 54, of complications arising out of cirrhosis of the liver. Davis, *Breckinridge,* 58, 391–95, and *Stand in the Day of Battle,* 297; Frank H. Heck, *Proud Kentuckian: John C. Breckinridge, 1821–1875* (Lexington: University Press of Kentucky, 1976), 159; Foote, *The Civil War,* 3:992–94.

193. O.R., vol. 31, pt. 2, 664–67.

194. McDonough, *Chattanooga,* 206–19.

195. Foote, *The Civil War,* 2:859.

196. O.R., vol. 31, pt. 2, 664–67.

197. Connelly, *Autumn of Glory,* 235.

198. O.R., vol. 31, pt. 2, 679.

199. Rowland, *Jefferson Davis, Constitutionalist,* 6:90.

200. O.R., vol. 31, pt. 2, 681–82.

201. Catton, *Grant Takes Command,* 87–88.

202. Mary Boykin Chesnut, *A Diary from Dixie,* ed. Ben Ames Williams (Boston: Houghton Mifflin, 1905), 327.

203. Connelly, *Autumn of Glory,* 295–96.

204. Thomas Hill Watts to Davis, November 27, 1863, by permission of the Houghton Library (Dearborn Collection), Harvard University, photocopy, JDA; Jones, *A Rebel War Clerk's Diary,* 312–13.

205. O.R., vol. 31, pt. 2, 682.

206. Ibid.

207. Bragg to Davis, December 1, 1863, and Bragg to Cooper, December 1, 1863, William P. Palmer Collection of Braxton Bragg Papers, Western Reserve Historical Society, Cleveland, Ohio, photocopy, JDA.

208. Bragg to Davis, December 1, 1863, William P. Palmer Collection of Braxton Bragg Papers, Western Reserve Historical Society, Cleveland, Ohio, photocopy, JDA.

209. O.R., vol. 52, pt. 2, 566–67.

CHAPTER 14. TO ATLANTA AND BEYOND

1. Dunbar Rowland, ed., *Jefferson Davis, Constitutionalist, His Letters, Papers and Speeches,* 10 vols. (Jackson: Mississippi Department of Archives and History, 1923), 5:164.

2. W. P. Johnston to Cooper, February 23, 1864, Papers received by the Confederate Adjutant and Inspector General's Office, National Archives, microfilm, JDA, M-474, roll 93, frame 658–659.

3. John B. Jones, *A Rebel War Clerk's Diary,* ed. Earl Schenck Miers (New York: Sagamore Press, 1958), 341.

4. Ibid.

5. O.R., vol. 38, pt. 5, 988; Rowland, *Jefferson Davis, Constitutionalist*, 6:132, 305, 334–35; Mary Boykin Chesnut, *A Diary from Dixie*, ed. Ben Ames Williams (Boston: Houghton Mifflin, 1905), 328.

6. Hudson Strode, *Jefferson Davis, Confederate President* (New York: Harcourt Brace, 1959), 502–3.

7. Nathaniel C. Hughes, *General William J. Hardee: Old Reliable* (Baton Rouge: Louisiana State University Press, 1965), 184.

8. Ibid., 186.

9. Thomas Robson Hay, "Pat Cleburne, Stonewall Jackson of the West," in Irving A. Buck, *Cleburne and His Command* (Jackson, Tenn.: McCowat-Mercer, 1959), 50–51.

10. Hughes, *General William J. Hardee*, 189.

11. Thomas Lawrence Connelly, *Autumn of Glory: The Army of Tennessee, 1862–1865* (Baton Rouge: Louisiana State University Press, 1971), 282.

12. Clifford Dowdey and Louis H. Manarin, eds., *The Wartime Papers of R. E. Lee* (New York: Bramhall House, 1961), 641–42.

13. Rowland, *Jefferson Davis, Constitutionalist*, 6:93.

14. Dowdey and Manarin, *The Wartime Papers of R. E. Lee*, 642.

15. Connelly, *Autumn of Glory*, 282–83; Dowdey and Manarin, *The Wartime Papers of R. E. Lee*, 642.

16. Polk to Davis, December 8, 1863, Manuscript Department, Perkins Library, Duke University, photocopy, JDA.

17. Connelly, *Autumn of Glory*, 282–83.

18. Chesnut, *A Diary from Dixie*, 317.

19. Connelly, *Autumn of Glory*, 243.

20. Shelby Foote, *The Civil War*, 3 vols. (New York: Random House, 1958), 2:886–87.

21. O.R., vol. 31, pt. 3, 835–36; Strode, *Jefferson Davis, Confederate President*, 510.

22. Richard McMurry, "'The *Enemy* at Richmond': Joseph H. Johnston and the Confederate Government," *Civil War History* 27 (March 1981): 18–20.

23. Foote, *The Civil War*, 2:892. McMurry ("'The *Enemy* at Richmond,'" 27, and "The Atlanta Campaign of 1864: A New Look," *Civil War History* 22 [March 1976]:12) believes Johnston was correct in this assessment.

24. Rowland, *Jefferson Davis, Constitutionalist*, 6:135–37; O.R., vol. 32, pt. 2, 510–11, 559–60.

25. Herman Hattaway and Archer Jones, *How the North Won: A Military History of the Civil War* (Urbana: University of Illinois Press, 1983), 509.

26. Lloyd Lewis, *Sherman: Fighting Prophet* (New York: Harcourt, Brace, 1932), 332–33.

27. O.R., vol. 32, pt. 2, 716.

28. Ibid.; Rowland, *Jefferson Davis, Constitutionalist*, 6:175–76.

29. O.R., vol. 32, pt. 2, 716.

30. Ibid., 716–17, 729, 751–52.

31. Papers of the Confederate Secretary of War, National Archives, microfilm, JDA.

32. Rowland, *Jefferson Davis, Constitutionalist*, 6:177–78.

33. Lewis, *Sherman: Fighting Prophet*, 333.

34. O.R., vol. 32, pt. 2, 763.

35. Rowland, *Jefferson Davis, Constitutionalist*, 6:182.

36. O.R., vol. 32, pt. 2, 775.

37. Ibid., 772–73.

38. Ibid., vol. 52, pt. 2, 627.

39. Lewis, *Sherman: Fighting Prophet,* 333; Foote, *The Civil War,* 2:934.

40. O.R., vol. 52, pt. 2, 627; Joseph H. Parks, *General Leonidas Polk, C.S.A., The Fighting Bishop* (Baton Rouge: Louisiana State University Press, 1960), 362–63.

41. O.R., vol. 31, pt. 3, 882.

42. Jones, *A Rebel Clerk's Diary,* 330–31.

43. Ibid.

44. Buck, *Cleburne and His Command,* 171.

45. O.R., vol. 31, pt. 2, 664.

46. Buck, *Cleburne and His Command,* 187.

47. Ezra Warner, *Generals in Gray* (Baton Rouge: Louisiana State University Press, 1959), 53–54.

48. Buck, *Cleburne and His Command,* 187–200.

49. Foote, *The Civil War,* 2:690.

50. Connelly, *Autumn of Glory,* 320.

51. Buck, *Cleburne and His Command,* 187–200.

52. Bell Irvin Wiley in foreword to Buck, *Cleburne and His Command,* 8.

53. Richard M. McMurry, *John Bell Hood and the War for Southern Independence* (Lexington: University Press of Kentucky, 1982), 138.

54. Marshall Wingfield, *General A. P. Stewart: His Life and Letters* (Memphis: West Tennessee Historical Society, 1954), 9–95, 152–61.

55. Glenn Tucker, *Chickamauga: Bloody Battle in the West* (Indianapolis: Bobbs-Merrill, 1961), 216.

56. Connelly, *Autumn of Glory,* 251.

57. Tucker, *Chickamauga,* 181.

58. Cleburne's commission as major general was dated December 13, 1862. Stewart's was dated June 6, 1863. Howell Purdue and Elizabeth Purdue, *Pat Cleburne, Confederate General* (Tuscaloosa, Ala.: Portals Press, 1973), 115; Warner, *Generals in Gray,* 53–54.

59. Foote, *The Civil War,* 2:1052–53.

60. McMurry, "'The *Enemy* at Richmond,'" 21.

61. Henry, *"First with the Most,"* 209.

62. McMurry, *John Bell Hood,* 1–9.

63. John B. Hood, *Advance and Retreat: Personal Experiences in the United States and Confederate States Armies* (Bloomington: Indiana University Press, 1959), 5–8.

64. McMurry, *John Bell Hood,* 10–15.

65. William C. Davis, *Breckinridge: Statesman, Soldier, Symbol* (Baton Rouge: Louisiana State University Press, 1974), 118–19.

66. McMurry, *John Bell Hood,* 14–15.

67. Ibid., 17, 23.

68. Hood, *Advance and Retreat,* 5–8.

69. McMurry, *John Bell Hood,* 21, 24.

70. Hattaway and Jones, *How the North Won,* 607.

71. McMurry, *John Bell Hood,* 33, 69.

72. Ibid., 76–77.

73. Chestnut, *A Diary from Dixie,* 299.

74. McMurry, *John Bell Hood,* 83–86.

75. Hood, *Advance and Retreat,* 67; Chesnut, *A Diary from Dixie,* 367.

76. McMurry, *John Bell Hood,* 40.

77. Hood, *Advance and Retreat,* 67.

78. McMurry, *John Bell Hood,* 83–87.

79. Ibid., 89–91.

80. Hood, *Advance and Retreat,* 67.

81. Chesnut, *A Diary from Dixie*, 367.
82. McMurry, *John Bell Hood*, 71, 88–89.
83. Ibid., 77.
84. Some scholars believe Hood's judgment may have been clouded by more than pain. He may have been taking a derivative of laudanum as a painkiller. Richard M. McMurry, *The Road past Kennesaw: The Atlanta Campaign of 1864* (Washington, D.C.: National Park Service, 1972), 42.
85. O.R., vol. 32, pt. 2, 763.
86. McMurry, *John Bell Hood*, 91–115.
87. Jones, *A Rebel War Clerk's Diary*, 350–51.
88. Connelly, *Autumn of Glory*, 323.
89. Jones, *A Rebel War Clerk's Diary*, 350–51.
90. O.R., vol. 32, pt. 2, 808–9.
91. Ibid., 813–14.
92. Hattaway and Jones, *How the North Won*, 483.
93. Connelly, *Autumn of Glory*, 297.
94. Thomas Lawrence Connelly and Archer Jones, *The Politics of Command: Factions and Ideas in Confederate Strategy* (Baton Rouge: Louisiana State University Press, 1973), 147.
95. O.R., vol. 32, pt. 2, 667.
96. Hattaway and Jones, *How the North Won*, 484.
97. Ibid.
98. O.R., vol. 52, pt. 2, 634, 642–44.
99. Ibid., 642.
100. Ibid.
101. Ibid.
102. Ibid., 642–44. The viability of the plan, devised in cooperation with Lee and Bragg and urged on Johnston by the president, is open to dispute. Thomas L. Connelly and Archer Jones (Connelly, *Autumn of Glory*, 299–300; Connelly and Jones, *Politics of Command*, 41–42, 148) have concluded that the plan was "impractical," "unrealistic," and "not . . . workable." This is, or course, possible, although it can never really be known since the plan was never given a fair chance by Johnston. Certainly some credit must be given to the considerable strategic abilities of Lee, Bragg, and even Davis himself. In any case, Johnston's continual moaning that he could undertake no significant offensive—the Richmond plan or any other—due to lack of supplies seems hollow at best. Richard Goff (*Confederate Supply* [Durham, N.C.: Duke University Press, 1969] 209) points out that Johnston's ostensible supply problems "appear to be a rationalization rather than a legitimate justification for remaining on the defensive" and attributes this not only to Johnston's incurable pessimism but also to a "too-rigid adherence to traditional military concepts of effective supply." Goff concludes: "What a Lee, a Jackson, or a Forrest might have done with the western armies is, and has been, an enticing matter of speculation." Yet speculation it must remain, since the Army of Tennessee was not in the hands of a Lee, a Jackson, a Forrest, or even a Cleburne, men who sometimes succeeded in doing what seemed impossible, but rather in the hands of Joseph E. Johnston, who just as often succeeded in making what others might have done seem impossible.
103. O.R., vol. 52, pt. 2, 642–44.
104. Ibid., 644.
105. Hood, *Advance and Retreat*, 94; O.R., vol. 52, pt. 2, 657; Rowland, *Jefferson Davis, Constitutionalist*, 6:227–30.

106. Hood, *Advance and Retreat*, 94.

107. Foote, *The Civil War*, 3:118.

108. O.R., vol. 38, pt. 3, 625; Jefferson Davis, *The Rise and Fall of the Confederate Government*, 2 vols. (New York: D. Appleton, 1881), 2:549–50.

109. O.R., vol. 38, pt. 3, 625, 627 (see especially Davis's endorsement on Bragg's note of April 22).

110. Ibid., 627.

111. Ibid., vol. 52, pt. 2, 663.

112. Ibid., vol. 38, pt. 3, 625; vol. 52, pt. 2, 663.

113. Ibid., vol. 39, pt. 4, 661.

114. Ibid., 669.

115. Ibid., 733, 735, 737, 740.

116. McMurry, *John Bell Hood*, 101–2; Foote, *The Civil War*, 3:324–30.

117. Connelly, *Autumn of Glory*, 406.

118. O.R., vol. 38, pt. 4, 716; Foote, *The Civil War*, 3:332–34.

119. Rowland, *Jefferson Davis, Constitutionalist*, 6:255; Connelly, *Autumn of Glory*, 406.

120. Foote, *The Civil War*, 3:340–41.

121. McMurry, *John Bell Hood*, 107–8, 167.

122. Foote, *The Civil War*, 3:342.

123. McMurry, *John Bell Hood*, 108–9; Connelly, *Autumn of Glory*, 352. Connelly believes Hood and Polk did not really want to attack. McMurry (*The Road past Kennesaw*, 16) takes the opposite view.

124. O.R., vol. 38, pt. 4, 728, 736.

125. Connelly, *Autumn of Glory*, 352; Foote, *The Civil War*, 3:342–43.

126. Foote, *The Civil War*, 3:343.

127. Ibid.

128. Connelly, *Autumn of Glory*, 372.

129. McMurry, *The Road past Kennesaw*, 16.

130. Buck, *Cleburne and His Command*, 215–16.

131. Rowland, *Jefferson Davis, Constitutionalist*, 6:255; O.R., vol. 52, pt. 2, 671–72.

132. O.R., vol. 38, pt. 4, 736.

133. Connelly, *Autumn of Glory*, 369–70.

134. In these letters Hood tended to gloss over–to put it mildly–the less than glorious role he had played in the campaign. Davis, who carefully refrained from mentioning this highly irregular and unsolicited correspondence to Johnston, did not know this. Bruce Catton, *Never Call Retreat* (Garden City, N.Y.: Doubleday, 1965), 304; Connelly, *Autumn of Glory*, 323; McMurry, *John Bell Hood*, 89.

135. Strode, *Jefferson Davis, Confederate President*, 418–19.

136. Foote, *The Civil War*, 3:112–13.

137. Connelly, *Autumn of Glory*, 435–37.

138. Henry, *"First with the Most,"* 112.

139. O.R., vol. 52, pt. 2, 672–73; vol. 38, pt. 4, 774; Henry, *"First with the Most,"* 347.

140. O.R., vol. 52, pt. 2, 672–73, 678; Herman Hattaway, *General Stephen D. Lee* (Jackson: University Press of Mississippi, 1976), 113–14; Foote, *The Civil War*, 3:338–40, 365; Connelly and Jones, *The Politics of Command*, 87, 152–53, 159, 172, 183. Connelly and Jones point out the deterioration of Davis's use of the departmental system but also feel that S. D. Lee was at fault for becoming "possessive and overcautious" within his department and missing opportunities to strike Federal supply lines.

141. Hattaway and Jones, *How the North Won*, 594. McMurry ("The Atlanta Cam-

paign of 1864," 13) thinks it "doubtful that the Confederate cavalry in Mississippi could have disrupted Sherman's railroad long enough to have affected Federal operations in Georgia."

142. Hattaway and Jones, *How the North Won*, 625–26n.

143. Buck, *Cleburne and His Command*, 223.

144. Joseph E. Johnston, *Narrative of Military Operations Directed during the Late War between the States* (New York: Appleton, 1874), 337; O.R., vol. 38, pt. 4, 775; Foote, *The Civil War*, 3:355–56.

145. Jefferson Davis, *The Rise and Fall of the Confederate Government*, 2:554–55.

146. O.R., vol. 38, pt. 4, 787; McMurry, *The Road past Kennesaw*, 23.

147. O.R., vol. 38, pt. 5, 865.

148. Rowland, *Jefferson Davis, Constitutionalist*, 6:283.

149. O.R., vol. 38, pt. 5, 868–69.

150. Connelly, *Autumn of Glory*, 368, 410.

151. Foote, *The Civil War*, 3:413–14.

152. Robert W. Winston, *High Stakes and Hair Trigger: The Life of Jefferson Davis* (New York: Holt, 1930), 231; Hamilton J. Eckenrode, *Jefferson Davis: President of the South* (New York: Macmillan, 1930), 290.

153. O.R., vol. 52, pt. 2, 692.

154. Jefferson Davis, *The Rise and Fall of the Confederate Government*, 2:556–61.

155. Connelly, *Autumn of Glory*, 363.

156. William E. Dodd, *Jefferson Davis* (Philadelphia: George W. Jacobs, 1907), 332.

157. Foote, *The Civil War*, 3:416; Jefferson Davis, *The Rise and Fall of the Confederate Government*, 2:556–61.

158. Rowland, *Jefferson Davis, Constitutionalist*, 6:286.

159. O.R., vol. 38, pt. 5, 873.

160. Connelly, *Autumn of Glory*, 411–14. Connelly asserts that Bragg was angling to get his old command back. This seems unlikely.

161. O.R., vol. 38, pt. 5, 878.

162. Don C. Seitz, *Braxton Bragg: General of the Confederacy* (Columbia, S.C.: The State Company, 1924), 448–50; O.R., vol. 38, pt. 5, 881.

163. O.R., vol. 38, pt. 5, 878.

164. Ibid., vol. 52, pt. 2, 692.

165. Dowdey and Manarin, *The Wartime Papers of R. E. Lee*, 821–22.

166. McMurry, *John Bell Hood*, 119.

167. O.R., vol. 38, pt. 5, 879–80; McMurry, *John Bell Hood*, 118–19.

168. Connelly, *Autumn of Glory*, 321–22, 417. Connelly says Hood was "at best . . . a chronic liar."

169. McMurry, *John Bell Hood*, 119. This is the reading usually given to this rather enigmatic telegram. Davis was attempting to prevent telegraph operators and others into whose hands the message might fall from being privy to the decision-making process of the Confederate high command.

170. O.R., vol. 38, pt. 5, 881; vol. 52, pt. 2, 707.

171. Rowland, *Jefferson Davis, Constitutionalist*, 6:295.

172. O.R., vol. 38, pt. 5, 883.

173. G. W. Smith to J. B. Hood, January 23, 1874, in Hood, *Advance and Retreat*, 147.

174. O.R., vol. 38, pt. 5, 885.

175. Rowland, *Jefferson Davis, Constitutionalist*, 6:334–35. Connelly (*Autumn of Glory*, 419) argues that Davis knew Hood's appointment would anger Hardee.

176. O.R., vol. 38, pt. 5, 892; Hattaway, *General Stephen D. Lee*, 126.

177. O.R., vol. 38, pt. 5, 888–89.

178. Ibid., vol. 52, pt. 2, 708–9.

179. Rowland, *Jefferson Davis, Constitutionalist,* 6:295–96.

180. Hood, *Advance and Retreat,* 128.

181. McMurry, *John Bell Hood,* 128–30; Connelly, *Autumn of Glory,* 441; Hughes, *General William J. Hardee,* 225.

182. Catton, *Never Call Retreat,* 364–65; Foote, *The Civil War,* 3:474–75.

183. O.R., vol. 38, pt. 5, 894.

184. McMurry, *John Bell Hood,* 132; Hughes, *General William J. Hardee,* 228; Foote, *The Civil War,* 3:484; Connelly, *Autumn of Glory,* 450.

185. McMurry, *John Bell Hood,* 132–33.

186. Stanley Horn, *The Army of Tennessee* (Indianapolis: Bobbs-Merrill, 1941), 355–59.

187. McMurry, *John Bell Hood,* 133.

188. Hattaway, *General Stephen D. Lee,* 123–24.

189. McMurry, *John Bell Hood,* 133–34; Hattaway, *General Stephen D. Lee,* 128.

190. Hattaway, *General Stephen D. Lee,* 128.

191. McMurry (*John Bell Hood,* 84) says that Hood's wounds probably "produced no major changes and that his behavior after 1863" was consistent with his earlier behavior. He does, however, point out (p. 151) that Hood's physical disabilities may provide part of the explanation for the large gap between what he ordered and what the army did.

192. Connelly, *Autumn of Glory,* 455.

193. Catton, *Never Call Retreat,* 367; Hattaway, *General Stephen D. Lee,* 128; McMurry, *John Bell Hood,* 138.

194. McMurry, *John Bell Hood,* 133–34.

195. Catton, *Never Call Retreat,* 363–68.

196. McMurry, *John Bell Hood,* 134.

197. Connelly, *Autumn of Glory,* 433.

198. Foote, *The Civil War,* 3:519–20.

199. Connelly, *Autumn of Glory,* 435.

200. Foote, *The Civil War,* 3:596–601.

201. Hattaway, *General Stephen D. Lee,* 130–31; McMurray, *John Bell Hood,* 148.

202. O.R., vol. 38, pt. 5, 1016.

203. Hattaway, *General Stephen D. Lee,* 131.

204. Catton, *Never Call Retreat,* 367–68.

205. Ibid., 363.

206. O.R., vol. 38, pt. 5, 1023; Chesnut, *A Diary from Dixie,* 435–36.

207. Hughes, *General William J. Hardee,* 244–47.

208. Connelly, *Autumn of Glory,* 423; Foote, *The Civil War,* 3:606.

209. Foote, *The Civil War,* 3:604–5.

210. Hughes, *General William J. Hardee,* 248.

211. Connelly, *Autumn of Glory,* 472.

212. William J. Cooper, "A Reassessment of Jefferson Davis as a War Leader: The Case from Atlanta to Nashville," *Journal of Southern History* 36 (1970): 198; O.R., vol. 38, pt. 2, 846.

213. Connelly, *Autumn of Glory,* 472.

214. Foote, *The Civil War,* 3:605–6.

215. Hood, *Advance and Retreat,* 252–53.

216. Hattaway and Jones, *How the North Won,* 632–34; Foote, *The Civil War,* 3:607.

217. Foote, *The Civil War,* 3:607.

218. McMurry, *John Bell Hood,* 157.

219. Catton, *Never Call Retreat,* 378.

220. Dodd, *Jefferson Davis*, 334.

221. Rowland, *Jefferson Davis, Constitutionalist*, 6:348.

222. Jones, *A Rebel War Clerk's Diary*, 431.

223. Cooper, "A Reassessment of Jefferson Davis as War Leader," 200–201. McMurry (*John Bell Hood*, 158) states that "Davis did not give Beauregard any real authority. Rather, he was merely to advise his subordinates. Davis's action seems intended more to silence his critics . . . than to provide a real change in the western command structure." Connelly, (*Autumn of Glory*, 472) also takes this view. It seems more accurate, however, to conclude that Beauregard could probably have had more authority had he been willing to take more responsibility. That was contrary to the Creole's inclinations, and Davis knew it.

224. Cooper, "A Reassessment of Jefferson Davis as War Leader," 199.

225. Hattaway and Jones, *How the North Won*, 631–32.

226. Ibid., 634.

227. Foote, *The Civil War*, 3:613–15.

228. Hood, *Advance and Retreat*, 278–80.

229. Catton, *Never Call Retreat*, 388.

230. Hattaway, *General Stephen D. Lee*, 132.

231. Cooper, "A Reassessment of Jefferson Davis as War Leader," 202–3; Foote, *The Civil War*, 3:616–17; Connelly, *Autumn of Glory*, 485; Hood, *Advance and Retreat*, 273.

232. Hood, *Advance and Retreat*, 273.

233. O.R., vol. 52, pt. 2, 748.

234. Rowland, *Jefferson Davis, Constitutionalist*, 6:398–99.

235. Catton, *Never Call Retreat*, 389; Hattaway, *General Stephen D. Lee*, 132.

236. Hood, *Advance and Retreat*, 274; O.R., vol. 45, pt. 1, 1215, 1225.

237. McMurry, *John Bell Hood*, 153.

238. Ibid., 163.

239. Hood, *Advance and Retreat*, 274; O.R., vol. 45, pt. 1, 1215, 1225.

240. McMurry, *John Bell Hood*, 169–70.

241. Hood, *Advance and Retreat*, 278.

242. Purdue and Purdue, *Pat Cleburne*, 167–68; Buck, *Cleburne and His Command*, 51.

243. Buck, *Cleburne and His Command*, 280; Foote, *The Civil War*, 3:663.

244. Foote, *The Civil War*, 3:657.

245. Catton, *Never Call Retreat*, 389–90. Connelly (*Autumn of Glory*, 490–92, 501–2) and McMurry (*John Bell Hood*, 169) argue that Hood had no plan when he moved north from the Tennessee River except possibly to take Nashville by getting there ahead of Schofield. He was not, they argue, trying to cut off Schofield.

246. Hattaway, *General Stephen D. Lee*, 134; Foote, *The Civil War*, 3:658–61.

247. Hattaway and Jones, *How the North Won*, 646–47; McMurry, *John Bell Hood*, 173–74. McMurry argues that the importance of Spring Hill has been exaggerated because Hood was not trying to destroy Schofield but to beat him to Nashville and because even had Hood's orders been obeyed, Schofield could still have gone around him.

248. Connelly, *Autumn of Glory*, 504.

249. Catton, *Never Call Retreat*, 390; Foote, *The Civil War*, 3:664.

250. Hattaway, *General Stephen D. Lee*, 136–37.

251. McMurry, *John Bell Hood*, 175.

252. Horn, *The Army of Tennessee*, 399–402.

253. McMurry, *John Bell Hood*, 176.

254. Connelly, *Autumn of Glory*, 505.

255. McMurry, *John Bell Hood*, 176.

256. Ibid.

257. Connelly, *Autumn of Glory*, 507–8.

258. McMurry, *John Bell Hood*, 179.

259. Catton, *Never Call Retreat*, 391–95; Hattaway, *General Stephen D. Lee*, 146.

260. Connelly (*Autumn of Glory*, 406) says Davis could have removed Johnston at this point had he been seeking an occasion to do so.

261. Bell Irvin Wiley in foreword to McMurry, *The Road past Kennesaw*, i.

262. McMurry (*John Bell Hood*, 122) believes the removal of Johnston was a wise move, but Connelly (*Autumn of Glory*, 421) characterizes it as a costly error.

263. Hughes, *General William J. Hardee*, 217; McMurry, *John Bell Hood*, 122–23.

264. Cooper, "A Reassessment of Jefferson Davis as War Leader," 197.

265. Rowland, *Jefferson Davis, Constitutionalist*, 6:413.

BIBLIOGRAPHIC ESSAY

Primary source material on the Civil War is abundant. The standby of every Civil War writer, including this one, is the series *War of the Rebellion: A Compilation of the Official Records of the Union and Confederate Armies* (abbreviated as O.R. in the Notes). With over one hundred volumes published between 1880 and 1901, this series was particularly useful in providing the battle and campaign reports of Bragg, Beauregard, the Johnstons, and their subordinate generals, among others, as well as correspondence among the generals or between various generals and Davis.

Also of great importance was the primary source material found in the holdings of the Jefferson Davis Association (JDA), Rice University, Houston, Texas. These include literally thousands of letters and telegrams to or from Davis. A small fraction of the most important of these will eventually be published in some five volumes of the war years alone; six volumes have been already published, which follow Davis's life through the end of his tenure as United States secretary of war. I had the privilege of using the unedited holdings for the wartime years, most of them photocopy or microfilm facsimilies of actual manuscripts. Especially useful among these, besides correspondence between Davis and his generals, was the correspondence between Davis and his wife, his brother Joseph, and various Confederate politicians. Another source of Davis papers was the ten-volume *Jefferson Davis, Constitutionalist, His Letters, Papers and Speeches* (Jackson: Mississippi Department of Archives and History, 1923), edited by Dunbar Rowland.

Other primary sources used in this work included diaries (John B. Jones, *A Rebel War Clerk's Diary,* ed. Earl Schenck Miers [New York: Sagamore Press, 1958], and Mary Boykin Chesnut, *A Diary from Dixie,* ed. Ben Ames Williams [Boston: Houghton Mifflin, 1905]); personal memoirs (Jefferson Davis's two-volume *The Rise and Fall of the Confederate Government* [New York: D. Appleton, 1881] and Varina Howell Davis's *Jefferson Davis, Ex-President of the Confederate States of America. A Memoir by His Wife* [New York: 1890]); Joseph E. Johnston's *Narrative of Military Operations Directed during the Late War between the States* (New York: Appleton, 1874); Richard Taylor's *Destruction and Reconstruction,* ed. Charles P. Roland (Waltham, Mass.: Blaisdell, 1968; originally published 1879); John B. Hood's *Advance and Retreat: Personal Experiences in the United States and Confederate States Armies* (Bloomington: Indiana University Press, 1959); and James Longstreet's *From Manassas to Appomattox* (Bloomington: Indiana University Press, 1960).

Extensive use has also been made of secondary sources, although not, for the most part, of Davis biographies, most of which are of very disappointing quality. Several works stand out among the available ones. William E. Dodd's excellent work (*Jefferson Davis* [Philadelphia: George W. Jacobs, 1907]) may still be the best available, a sad commentary on the overall state of Davis scholarship considering that it was published in 1907. Robert W. Winston's *High Stakes and Hair Trigger: The Life of Jefferson Davis* (New York: Holt, 1930) is at least a refreshing break from the pro-Davis bias that pervades most Davis biographies but is weak on the war years. Hudson Strode's three-volume work (*Jefferson Davis, American Patriot, 1808–1861, Jefferson Davis, Confederate President,* and *Jefferson Davis, Tragic Hero*—all published by Harcourt Brace, in 1955, 1959, and 1964, respectively) devotes a fair amount of attention to the war and to Davis's conduct thereof but tends to be among the worst of the hymns of praise to the Confederate president. Clement Eaton's *Jefferson Davis* (New York: Free Press, 1977) is the best of the more recent works, although many scholars still find it unsatisfactory.

Biographies of individual generals have proved far more useful, and several are worthy of mention. Grady McWhiney's *Braxton Bragg and Confederate Defeat* (New York: Columbia University Press, 1969) corrects many of the more outrageous denunciations of Bragg but unfortunately carries Bragg's story only as far as Murfreesboro. T. Harry Williams's biography of Beauregard (*P. G. T. Beauregard: Napoleon in Gray* [Baton Rouge: Louisiana State University Press, 1955]); Richard M. McMurry's *John Bell Hood and the War for Southern Independence* (Lexington: University Press of Kentucky, 1982); and Charles P. Roland's *Albert Sidney Johnston: Soldier of Three Republics* (Austin: University of Texas Press, 1964) are also excellent and were very useful in this study. Nathaniel C. Hughes's *General William L. Hardee: Old Reliable* (Baton Rouge: Louisiana State University Press, 1965) is sound and free of much of the bias often found in biographies. Excellent works also exist on generals who occupied the second tier of positions in the West. Notable here are Robert J. Hartje's *Van Dorn: The Life and Times of a Confederate General* (Nashville, Tenn.: Vanderbilt University Press, 1967); Herman Hattaway's *General Stephen D. Lee* (Jackson: University Press of Mississippi, 1976); studies of Sterling Price by Robert E. Shalhope (*Sterling Price: Portrait of a Southerner* [Columbia: University of Missouri Press, 1971]) and Albert E. Castel (*General Sterling Price and the Civil War in the West* [Baton Rouge: Louisiana State University Press, 1968]); and James A. Ramage's *Rebel Raider: The Life of General John Hunt Morgan* (Lexington: University Press of Kentucky, 1986).

Among other works, Thomas L. Connelly's *Army of the Heartland: The Army of Tennessee, 1861–1862* (Baton Rouge: Louisiana State University Press, 1967) and *Autumn of Glory: The Army of Tennessee, 1862–1865* (Baton Rouge: Louisiana State University Press, 1971) are useful studies of the Army of Tennessee. James McDonough has written a series of valuable works on that army's battles, including Shiloh, Murfreesboro, and Chattanooga, the last of which this writer found especially helpful (*Chattanooga— A Death Grip on the Confederacy* [Knoxville: University of Tennessee Press, 1984] and *Stones River—Bloody Winter in Tennessee* [Knoxville: University of Tennessee Press, 1980]). Wiley Sword's *Shiloh—Bloody April* (Dayton, Ohio: Press of Morningside: 1983) was also of use, as well as Glenn Tucker's *Chickamauga: Bloody Battle in the West* (Indianapolis: Bobbs-Merrill, 1961), which provided some interesting insights on Braxton Bragg. *The Politics of Command: Factions and Ideas in Confederate Strategy* (Baton Rouge: Louisiana State University Press, 1973), on which Connelly collaborated with Archer Jones, deals with political factors and personal relationships behind Confederate strategy. Eli Evans's *Judah P. Benjamin: The Jewish Confederate* (New York: Free Press, 1988) provided information on Davis's physical condition, among other things.

Certain general works on the war were also of use. Chief among these was Bruce Catton's excellent trilogy, *The Coming Fury, Terrible Swift Sword*, and *Never Call Retreat*, (all published by Doubleday—1961, 1963, and 1965, respectively). Shelby Foote's three-volume history (*The Civil War* [New York: Random House, 1958]) is also good and vastly more detailed. It was particularly useful in this study because of its distinctly southern orientation. Also worthy of note are James McPherson, *Battle Cry of Freedom: The Civil War Era* (New York: Oxford University Press, 1988), and Timothy H. Donovan, Jr., Roy K. Flint, Arthur V. Grant, Jr., and Gerald P. Stodler, *The American Civil War*, West Point Military History Series (Wayne, N.J.: Avery Publishing Group, 1987).

INDEX